American
Jewish
Year Book

American

Jewish

Year Book 1986

VOLUME 86

Prepared by THE AMERICAN JEWISH COMMITTEE

Editors

MILTON HIMMELFARB

DAVID SINGER

Assistant Editor

RUTH R. SELDIN

THE AMERICAN JEWISH COMMITTEE

NEW YORK

THE JEWISH PUBLICATION SOCIETY OF AMERICA

PHILADELPHIA

ISBN 0-8276-0269-3

Library of Congress Catalogue Number: 99-4040

PRINTED IN THE UNITED STATES OF AMERICA
BY THE HADDON CRAFTSMEN, INC., SCRANTON, PA.

Preface

The present volume features an article commemorating the founding, 100 years ago, of the Jewish Theological Seminary of America: "A Century of Conservative Judaism in the United States," by Abraham J. Karp.

Articles focusing on Jewish life in the United States include "Los Angeles Jewry: A Demographic Portrait," by Bruce A. Phillips, "California Jews: Data from the Field Polls," by Alan M. Fisher and Curtis K. Tanaka, and "Attitudes of American Jews Toward Israel: Trends Over Time," by Eytan Gilboa.

Other articles on Jewish life in the United States are Murray Friedman's "Intergroup Relations" and George E. Gruen's "The United States, Israel, and the Middle East." Alvin Chenkin provides revised estimates for the U.S. Jewish population.

Jewish life around the world is reported on in a series of articles about Israel, Canada, Great Britain, France, West Germany, East Germany, and the Soviet Union. New estimates for the world Jewish population are given.

Carefully compiled directories of national Jewish organizations, periodicals, and federations and welfare funds, as well as religious calendars and obituary notices, round out the 1986 AMERICAN JEWISH YEAR BOOK.

We are very grateful to our colleagues Michele Anish and Robert Rosenbaum for their proofreading efforts and to Diane Hodges for compiling the index. We also acknowledge the aid of Cyma M. Horowitz, director of the Blaustein Library, Lotte Zajac, and all our other co-workers in Information and Research Services.

THE EDITORS

Contributors

ALVIN CHENKIN: research consultant (retired), Council of Jewish Federations, New York.

SERGIO DELLAPERGOLA: senior lecturer, Jewish demography, Institute of Contemporary Jewry, Hebrew University, Jerusalem.

ALAN M. FISHER: associate professor, political science, California State University, Dominguez Hills.

MURRAY FRIEDMAN: director, Middle Atlantic region, AJC, Philadelphia.

EYTAN GILBOA: lecturer, international relations, Hebrew University, Jerusalem.

ZVI GITELMAN: professor, political science, University of Michigan.

GEORGE E. GRUEN: director, Israel and Middle East affairs, AJC, New York.

ABRAHAM J. KARP: Philip S. Bernstein Professor of Jewish Studies, University of Rochester.

LIONEL E. KOCHAN: Bearsted Reader in Jewish History, University of Warwick, Oxford.

MIRIAM KOCHAN: journalist, translator, Oxford.

ARNOLD MANDEL: novelist, reporter, literary critic, Paris.

RALPH MANDEL: journalist, translator, Jerusalem.

BRUCE A. PHILLIPS: associate professor, Jewish communal studies, Hebrew Union College–Jewish Institute of Religion, Los Angeles.

FRIEDO SACHSER: reporter, editor, Düsseldorf.

U. O. SCHMELZ: associate professor, Jewish demography, Institute of Contemporary Jewry, Hebrew University, Jerusalem.

CURTIS K. TANAKA: lecturer, psychology, California State University, Dominguez Hills.

HAROLD M. WALLER: associate professor, political science, McGill University, Montreal.

Table of Contents

Special
Articles

A Century of Conservative Judaism in the United States

by ABRAHAM J. KARP

CONSERVATIVE JUDAISM, THE movement in American Jewish religious life that has attracted the largest number of adherents, celebrates this year the 100th anniversary of the founding of its mother institution, the Jewish Theological Seminary of America. The movement is a product of both the ideological ferment in nineteenth-century Jewish life and the sociological realities of twentieth-century America. The former brought about the coalition of acculturated Orthodox and moderate Reform rabbis and laymen that founded the Seminary in 1886; the latter influenced the distinctive mission and program of the Conservative synagogue.

For half of its first century, Conservative Judaism thought of itself as the historically authentic expression of traditional Judaism, believing that it alone could stay the corrosive influences of Reform that the insulated, isolating form of Orthodoxy transplanted from Eastern Europe could neither confront nor defeat. The mother institution, the Seminary—conservative as institutions are wont to be—felt comfortable and secure in its self-proclaimed status as guardian of authentic traditionalism. At the same time, its children, the rabbis it ordained, increasingly proclaimed the Judaism they espoused to be a distinct movement within the American Jewish religious community. Seeking to blend Orthodoxy's devotion to tradition with the open-mindedness of Reform, adherents of Conservative Judaism proclaimed themselves—in the words of Louis Finkelstein—"the only group in [American] Israel with a modern mind and a Jewish heart, prophetic passion and western science."[1]

Although the post-World War II era saw the ascendancy of Conservative Judaism as the preferred religious affiliation of over 40 percent of American Jewry, its history has been marked by a constant groping for an ideology that would adequately define and effectively direct the movement. Having its historic origin as a protest against both the excesses of Reform and the insularity of Orthodoxy, Conservative Judaism has suffered from the same malady as other protest movements: strong in negation, imprecise in affirmation. Holding a centrist position, it has operated as a coalition movement

---

[1]"The Things That Unite Us," *Proceedings of the Rabbinical Assembly*, 1927, p. 53.

3

in which agreement is reached through consensus. This posture has made it vulnerable to accusations from both the right (Orthodoxy) and the left (Reform) that it is a movement lacking in conviction, a halfway house for timid Reformers and compromising Orthodox. The centrist position has, however, permitted Conservative Judaism to claim to be the authentic voice and path of the golden mean, espousing faith tempered by reason, reason uplifted by faith, and a reasonableness that surrenders neither heart nor mind.

In his presidential address to the United Synagogue of America in 1918, Professor Louis Ginzberg said, "Nothing is easier, but nothing is more dangerous than definitions; I shall attempt a description."[2] Writing to Rabbi Herman H. Rubenovitz in 1939, Professor Robert Gordis asserted that "the activity of Conservative rabbis and Conservative congregations [rather than the written word] is a far better index to what Conservatism is."[3] Based on these observations, this study focuses in the main on the activities of Conservative rabbis and congregations. At the same time, following Solomon Schechter's admonition that "a life without guiding principles and thoughts is a life not worth living," attention is given to the continuous quest for an ideology, and its formulation in different eras.

BEGINNINGS

Roots: European

The twofold experience of enlightenment and emancipation that permitted Jews to enter the modern world provided them with opportunities, but also confronted them with the challenge to justify their continued corporate existence in a world that welcomed their assimilation. One response was that of Reform Judaism, which posited a God-given mission as mandate for survival, and which viewed Jewish historic experience as a mandate to alter traditional beliefs and forms in conformity to the most progressive demands of the larger world the Jew was now entering. Declared Samuel Hirsch, rabbi in Germany and America and Reform's philosopher: "The need of the time is the highest law of Judaism. . . . The Jews of the present day must, before all else, participate in the work of the age with all their powers; for their work is the object of Jewish history. Yes, it is the be-all and end-all of Judaism."[4] While German Reform leader Abraham Geiger advocated evolutionary change in the Judaism fashioned by the rabbis, Samuel

---

[2]Louis Ginzberg, *The United Synagogue of America* (New York, 1918), p. 6.
[3]Herman H. and Mignon L. Rubenovitz, *The Waking Heart* (Cambridge, 1967), p. 156.
[4]David Philipson, *The Reform Movement in Judaism* (1931), pp. 351–352.

Holdheim demanded radical reform of biblical Judaism itself. The emphasis of both, however, was on change.

Samson Raphael Hirsch, the founder of neo-Orthodoxy, articulated the response of those who rose to defend tradition against the onslaught of change. Jewish law, biblical and rabbinic, is eternal and unchangeable, he argued. The revealed word and will of the eternal God is manifested to His people Israel in the Torah—the written and oral law—"an eternal code set up for all ages by the God of eternity."[5] Reform's allegiance was to the world and its needs; neo-Orthodoxy's, to God and His demands. Samuel Hirsch urged the Jew to alter the tradition as service to the world would require of him; Samson Raphael Hirsch demanded that the Jew direct his life in steadfast loyalty to the total demands of the tradition.

Hewing a middle path between these two positions was Zacharias Frankel, the learned rabbi of Dresden, later head of the Jewish Theological Seminary at Breslau. Though he instituted moderate reforms, such as the abolition of the recitation of the *piyyutim,* he insisted that only changes that were not in conflict with the spirit of "positive-historical Judaism" should be permitted in the ritual.[6]

What was the "positive-historical Judaism" advocated by Frankel, or, more important to our discussion, how was this concept understood by the architects of Conservative Judaism? Louis Ginzberg, who, as the leading figure on the faculty of the Seminary, had a significant influence on the shaping of Conservative Judaism, wrote:

The best illustration of his conception of Judaism is the instance which induced Frankel to leave the Frankfort Conference [of Reform rabbis in 1845], on which occasion he, for the first time, made use of the expression "positive-historic" Judaism. The matter at hand was a discussion of the question of whether and to what extent the Hebrew language should be retained in the Synagogue; and when the majority decided that Hebrew must be kept there only out of consideration for the old generation, Frankel took his departure. . . . The underlying principle at stake was this: *does the essence of Judaism lie exclusively in the Jewish religion, that is, ethical monotheism, or is Judaism the historical product of the Jewish mind and spirit?* The Hebrew language is of course not a religious factor, and even from the strictest standpoint of the *Shulhan Aruk,* it would be difficult to adduce any fundamental objection to the use of any other language of prayer. Still it is true that in the long development of the synagogue service the Hebrew tongue became . . . the language of the Jewish spirit, and [therefore] an essential component of our devotional sentiment. . . . The recollection that it was the Hebrew language in which the Revelation was given, in which the Prophets expressed their high ideals, in which generations of our fathers breathed forth their sufferings and joys, makes this language a holy one for us.[7]

---

[5]Cited in Mordecai M. Kaplan, *Judaism as a Civilization* (New York, 1934), p. 534.
[6]*Encyclopedia Judaica,* Vol. 7 (Jerusalem, 1972), p. 80.
[7]Louis Ginzberg, *Students, Scholars, Saints* (Philadelphia, 1928), pp. 203–204.

Ginzberg saw in Frankel's views the origins of the Conservative definition of Judaism as "the historical product of the Jewish mind and spirit." Central to Judaism, then, is the Jewish people itself, possessors of that mind and spirit. In the unfolding development of Judaism, Frankel maintained, norms must obtain as to what may be altered and who may determine what needs to be changed. In the words of Ginzberg, "That which the whole community has adopted and recognized may not be repealed . . . [and] only those who recognized the Law as specifically Jewish, could have the right to decide what portions of it had incorporated themselves into the national consciousness."[8]

More recently, Ismar Schorsch has argued that the term positive-historical Judaism

> immediately suggests the opposite of "negative," and, often enough in his writing Frankel condemned the program of radical Reform for being utterly negative. . . . But the word "positive" also carried a well-established technical connotation, implying either law in general or posited law as opposed to natural law. . . .

> By choosing the adjective "positive" to describe his conception of Judaism, Frankel defiantly reasserted its fundamental legal character and rejected any effort to dilute it.[9]

At the heart of Judaism is a legal system. Among those who adhere to this concept of Judaism, however, there are those who place the emphasis on the historical integrity of the tradition and those who stress its evolutionary character.

Frankel's concept of positive-historical Judaism was adopted and adapted by students and disciples who came to America: graduates of the Jewish Theological Seminary at Breslau, such as Alexander Kohut and Frederic de Sola Mendes; Benjamin Szold, who spent his formative years at Breslau; and men like Marcus Jastrow, Aaron Wise, and Aaron Bettelheim who chose to be identified with the historical school. Frankel's followers practiced a moderate form of Reform Judaism and cooperated with Reform colleagues and institutions, until these veered off to radical Reform. Then the moderates turned for religious camaraderie and joint enterprise to acculturated Orthodox colleagues. Together they founded the Seminary and thus laid the foundation for Conservative Judaism.

Roots: American

By the middle of the nineteenth century, American Jews already had the option of identifying with either of two religious tendencies, traditionalist or

---

[8]Ibid., p. 209.
[9]Ismar Schorsch, "Zacharias Frankel and the European Origins of Conservative Judaism," *Judaism,* Summer 1981, pp. 345–346.

Reform, whose spokesmen were, respectively, Isaac Leeser and Isaac Mayer Wise. Leeser, a German immigrant who served Sephardi congregations in Philadelphia, had the faith that traditional Judaism could flourish in the New World if American Jewry willed it and matched will with enterprise. Through his publication *The Occident* he advocated loyalty to Torah and *mitzvot*. At the same time, through the introduction of the English sermon, a supplementary Jewish school system, popular religious literature in the vernacular, and the like, he sought to make traditional Jewish living compatible with social and cultural integration into the larger society.

Wise, an energetic and optimistic religious leader from Bohemia who was to become the architect of Reform Judaism in America, believed that Judaism would in time become the religion of all enlightened modern people. First, however, it had to be modernized and democratized, or, as he advocated, "Americanized." He became the exponent of a moderate, pragmatic Reform Judaism, responsive to the pressures and practical necessities of living in an integrated society in the modern age. Thus, while Leeser issued the traditional prayer book with his own English translation, the only change being the incorporation of "A Prayer for a Republican Government," Wise published *Minhag America,* an abridged liturgy that eliminated all references to the restoration of sacrifices, the coming of the messiah, and the return to Zion.

Reform and traditionalist elements joined together at a conference in Cleveland in 1855, but the conference led not to unity but to further subdivision, a rift between the moderate, practical Reform of the West and the radical, ideological Reform of the East that was to divide that movement for three decades.

As early as 1866, Jonas Bondi—rabbi, publisher, and editor—noted that there had developed in American Jewish religious life a "golden middleway" which was termed "orthodox" by the left and "heterodox or reformer" by the right and was apparently making such progress that it "is hated on both sides."[10] He identified this movement with "positive historical Judaism . . . [which] contains all the ideas of the development of Judaism.[11] Sigmund Hecht described the distinctive religious pattern of this third group as he saw it operating on the American scene in 1882:

> Conservatism seeks to reconcile the differences of opinion, to harmonize the written Law (Torah) and the oral law (tradition) with the claims of this advanced age; to maintain venerable institutions, although purified and rendered more attractive, and to impart more sanctity and devotion to the divine service, not by discarding the traditional mode entirely, but by retaining it in the main and only removing those features that are antagonistic to its purpose.[12]

---

[10]*Hebrew Leader,* Vol. 8, June 29, 1866, p. 4.
[11]Ibid., Vol. 9, Feb. 8, 1867, p. 4.
[12]Sigmund Hecht, *Epitome of Post-Biblical History* (Cincinnati, 1882), p. 113.

Because the three religious tendencies—they could not yet be called movements—that existed in the late 1860s and 1870s were still in the formative stage, the definition of each was far from clear.[13] Simon Wolf, for example, after worshiping in Philadelphia's Rodef Shalom during the high holy days of 1869, was surprised to learn that its rabbi, Dr. Marcus Jastrow, was called Orthodox. "To say that the Reverend Jastrow is Orthodox were doing him a great injustice," Wolf noted, "for a minister who is in favor of a temple, an organ, pews . . . cannot be considered as reflecting the ideas of the past."[14]

Wolf would have agreed fully with the unanimous designation of Jastrow's Philadelphia colleague Reverend Sabato Morais, of K.K. Mikveh Israel, as Orthodox. Yet in the early 1870s Morais put forth this seemingly radical plan for the ritual and liturgy of the American synagogue:

> The demand is for a simpler prayer-book. . . . Expurge, then, what relates to the ordinances followed by the ancients in the performances of sacrificial rites; strike out what belongs to Mishnic and Talmudic lore . . . avoid, as far as practical, the reiterating of supplication, confession or sacred song . . . compare philologically long-established rituals . . . select what is more chaste in style, more exalting in ideas . . . then endeavor to fill up a portion of the space made empty by the expurgatory process with compositions suited to our existing wants, the printed and unedited writings of our philosophers and poets can supply a vast deal, the learning of our modern Rabbis may also be of service. . . .[15]

The religious radicalization of Reform and the growing insularity of Orthodoxy brought men with centrist tendencies closer together. Those from the right carried a commitment to Jewish law and its ritual and the synagogal mode of westernized traditional Jews—decorum, the sermon, and the use of the vernacular; those from the left contributed an ideology expressive of the positive-historical Judaism of Frankel.

The founding of the Jewish Theological Seminary came in response to the religiously radical platform adopted by the conference of Reform rabbis meeting in Pittsburgh in November 1885, and in reaction to the rapid retreat from the tradition by the Union of American Hebrew Congregations, established in 1873 as a synagogal union for *all* congregations, and its Hebrew Union College, whose purpose was to provide rabbis for *all* American synagogues. The UAHC had its roots in a moderate Reform outlook which held that a line should be drawn beyond which Reform should not venture,[16] but it was a line that dissolved fairly quickly.

---

[13]W.M. Rosenblatt, in "The Jews, What They Are Coming To," *Galaxie,* Jan. 1872, p. 47, consigned "Dr. Wise, Dr. Huebsch and Dr. Mielziner" to the Conservatives.

[14]*Jewish Times,* Vol. 1, Oct. 22, 1869, p. 5.

[15]Cited in Moshe Davis, *The Emergence of Conservative Judaism* (New York, 1963), pp. 163–165.

[16]*Proceedings of the Union of American Hebrew Congregations,* 1879, pp. i, ii.

Any adherence to the dietary laws fell in the summer of 1883 at the banquet celebrating the eighth annual meeting of the council of the UAHC and the first graduating class of the Hebrew Union College. No less than four varieties of forbidden shellfish were served, causing two rabbis to leave the banquet. But the other 198 diners remained. Wise, president of the college, refused to take responsibility for the menu, but did not dissociate himself from those responsible, attacking instead the critics with jeering references to "kitchen Judaism."

Two years later, Alexander Kohut, newly arrived to the pulpit of New York's Ahavath Chesed, raised the alarm against the kind of Reform he found in America:

> A reform which seeks to progress without the Mosaic rabbinical tradition, such a reform is a deformity: is a skeleton of Judaism without flesh and sinew, without spirit and heart. . . . Only a Judaism true to itself and its past, only a Judaism which does not disown the character of its worthy antiquity, but is receptive of the ideas of the present, and accepts the good and the beautiful from whatever source it may come; only such a Judaism can command respect and recognition.[17]

Kohut's lecture was translated into English and published in the *American Hebrew.* Kaufmann Kohler, rabbi of Temple Beth El in New York, who had inherited from his father-in-law, David Einhorn, the mantle of spokesman for radical Reform, was quick to respond:

> There is a novelty offered to our New York Jews in the appearance of a new rabbi of renown who, with laudable courage and independence, gives free utterance to his rigid conservatism, boldly challenging Reformed Judaism by the open declaration, that he who disowns the statutes and ordinances of Mosaico-Rabbinical Judaism on principle has forfeited the name Jew.[18]

The controversy continued, the antagonists mounting vigorous attacks which, unlike other rabbinic confrontations, never descended to personal invective. The issue was joined: positive-historical Judaism, which the Breslau-ordained Kohut professed, or radical Reform, which Kohler advocated —which would become the Judaism of the American Jew?

It was more the conviction that the UAHC (despite its protestations) had become a Reform organization, and that the Hebrew Union College would produce rabbis espousing radical Reform, than the Pittsburgh conference itself, that caused the coalescing of forces which founded the Seminary. A number of leading rabbis and laymen were eager to set a new course. A half century later, H. Pereira Mendes, minister of New York's Shearith Israel, America's oldest congregation, recalled:

---

[17] Alexander Kohut, *The Ethics of the Fathers* (New York, 1885), pp. 12–13.
[18] Kaufmann Kohler, *Backwards or Forwards?* (New York, 1885), p. 7.

Calm and thoughtful conservative and Orthodox Rabbis . . . Doctors Alexander Kohut, Aaron Wise, Henry S. Jacobs, F. de Sola Mendes, Moses Maisner, Bernard Drachman of New York met for consultation. . . . Doctors Sabato Morais and Marcus Jastrow in Philadelphia were not idle; and further afield . . . Rabbis [Aaron] Bettelheim, [Henry] Schneeberger, [Shepsel] Schaffer (Baltimore), etc. proclaimed their sympathies. Prominent laymen gathered about them, Doctors Cyrus Adler, Aaron and Harry Friedenwald, S. Solis Cohen . . . the Honorables Mayer Sulzberger . . . Adolphus Solomon, Joseph Blumenthal. . . . Their numbers grew.

One day, Dr. Morais called on me, to propose changing our action of meetings, debates, press-communications, accusations, recriminations . . . with no tangible results, into something that would advance the cause so dear to us both, the preservation of Historical and Traditional Judaism, by establishing a Jewish Institute of Learning, by educating, training and inspiring teachers, Rabbis who would stand la Tora v'lat'udah, "for the Torah and the Testimony."[19]

Half the rabbis mentioned by Mendes—Morais, Drachman, Maisner, Schneeberger, Schaffer, and Mendes himself—were proponents of traditional (Orthodox) Judaism; the rest were identified with the moderately Reform historical school. The leader of the former group was Morais, who, though hazzan-minister of an Orthodox congregation, had for many years been participating with Reform colleagues in communal and religious activities and communal enterprises. The spokesman for the latter group was Alexander Kohut.

The "Institute of Learning" proposed by Morais was created at a meeting held at Shearith Israel on January 31, 1886. Its aim was to train rabbis and teachers "in sympathy with the spirit of conservative Judaism." Morais was named president of the faculty.[20]

The Seminary

The founders of the new institution described it as a

seminary where the Bible shall be impartially taught and rabbinical literature faithfully expounded, and more especially where youths, desirous of entering the ministry, may be thoroughly grounded in Jewish knowledge and inspired by the precept and the example of their instructors with the love of the Hebrew language, and a spirit of fidelity and devotion to the Jewish law.[21]

Morais took active charge of the day-to-day affairs of the school, but it was Alexander Kohut who determined the fundamental character of the Seminary. When, for example, the question of the name of the new institution arose, Morais suggested that it be called "The Orthodox Seminary,"

---

[19]H. Pereira Mendes, "The Beginnings of the Seminary," in Cyrus Adler (ed.), The Jewish Theological Seminary of America (New York, 1939), pp. 36–38.

[20]American Hebrew, Vol. 25, Feb. 5, 1886, pp. 200–201. Cited in Davis, op. cit., pp. 237–238.

[21]From the preamble of the constitution of the Jewish Theological Seminary Association, adopted at its founding convention, May 9, 1886.

but Kohut influenced him to call it "The Jewish Theological Seminary." It was Kohut who expressed the purpose of the Seminary at its inaugural exercises:

> In the new Seminary a different spirit will prevail, different impulses will pervade its teachings and animate its teachers. This spirit will be that of *Conservative Judaism*, the conserving Jewish impulse which will create in the pupils of the Seminary the tendency to recognize the dual nature of Judaism and the Law; which unites theory and practice . . . acknowledges the necessity of observing the Law as well as studying it.[22]

The newly founded school held its first session on Monday, January 3, 1887, in the vestry room of the Shearith Israel Congregation. "Ten pupils were enrolled in the [preparatory] class," Joseph Blumenthal, president of the Jewish Theological Seminary Association, reported to its first biennial convention, "and the tuition was for a time imparted by various members of the Advisory Board."[23] Of the ten students in the preparatory class, four had been born in New York, three in Hungary, and three in Russia. The four New Yorkers and two of the students from Hungary were attending the City College of New York; the others, recent arrivals, were enrolled in public schools. Their average age was 15. There were also four students in a junior class—aged 17, 19, 25, and 27—who had recently arrived from Russia. Of the total enrollment of 14 students, only one continued on until ordination—Joseph Herman Hertz, who eventually rose to the position of chief rabbi of the British Empire.

The delegates also heard President Sabato Morais's vision of the Seminary's mission:

> Our Seminary has created itself a church militant, to fight skepticism arrayed against the history and traditions that have rendered Israel deathless. . . .

> Well-meaning, but unwise orthodoxy, tells us that by keeping altogether aloof from "Reformer" . . . we will guard our children from the effects of teaching subversive to Holy Writ. . . . Isolation is an impossibility. It would be inadvisable if it were possible. . . .

> [The Seminary] is the laboratory in which we try to mould the minds of men who will mightily battle for the religion. By the moral force of our disciples, synagogues will be stripped of meretricious garments. . . . Pulpits now converted into a nursery for the propagation of heresies, will become strongholds of the written and oral law.[24]

Who the Seminary's constituency would be was not clear. Both Sabato Morais and H. Pereira Mendes looked for support to the East European

---

[22]*American Hebrew,* Vol. 29, Jan. 7, 1887, p. 137. Cited in Davis, op. cit., p. 239.
[23]*Proceedings of the First Biennial Convention of the Jewish Theological Seminary Association, held in New York on Sunday, March 11, 1888* (New York, 1888), p. 6.
[24]Ibid., pp. 19–20.

immigrant community in New York. When that community chose instead to channel its funds and energies to the importation of a "chief rabbi," Jacob Joseph of Vilna, both men expressed public disapproval. "I am familiar with the manner in which the Hebrews in the place whence he comes are educated," Morais told a reporter of the *New York Herald*. "He does not possess the knowledge nor the literary attainments which a rabbi should possess."[25] Mendes argued that only graduates of an American seminary, speaking the language of the land, would be able to appeal to the younger generation. "Do not give way to false hopes," he warned New York's Lower East Side Jewry, "[since] those who come after you will be Americans, full-blooded Americans like your brethren uptown."[26] The pleas fell on deaf ears. With few exceptions, East European immigrant Jewry ignored the new seminary, though the student body was drawn from that community.

During the first 15 years of the Seminary's existence, 1886–1900, a period in which more than half a million Jews arrived from Eastern Europe, the Seminary benefited little from this influx. The immigrants came, transplanted their *shtiblach,* and appointed cantors and traditionally ordained rabbis, who eked out a living largely through *kashrut* supervision. The Seminary and the rabbis it produced or was about to produce—leaders of the East European religious community inveighed—would expose Judaism and the faithful Jews to influences that would destroy both. The group that would later become the Seminary's natural constituency—acculturated East European immigrants and their children—had not yet come into being.

The composition of the Seminary's Advisory Board of Ministers and the "congregations entitled to representation" reflected the coalitional nature of the constituency that founded the new institution. Five of the rabbis on the board—Sabato Morais (president of the faculty), H. Pereira Mendes, Bernard Drachman, Henry W. Schneeberger, and Abraham P. Mendes—were traditionalists who comfortably termed themselves Orthodox; the others—Alexander Kohut, Marcus Jastrow, Henry S. Jacobs, Frederic de Sola Mendes, and Aaron Wise—had broken with traditional Judaism and considered themselves adherents of historical Judaism at the border of Reform (which side of the border is open to dispute).[27]

---

[25]*New York Herald,* July 21, 1888. Cited in Abraham J. Karp, "New York Chooses a Chief Rabbi," in *Publications of the American Jewish Historical Society,* Vol. 44, No. 3 (March 1955), p. 153.

[26]*American Israelite,* Mar. 30, 1888. Cited in Karp, ibid.

[27]On the ideological orientation and identification of the rabbinic founders of the Jewish Theological Seminary, see Davis, op. cit.; Charles S. Liebman, "Orthodoxy in Nineteenth Century America," *Tradition,* Vol. 6, No. 2 (Spring-Summer 1968), pp. 132–140; and Abraham J. Karp, "The Origins of Conservative Judaism," *Conservative Judaism,* Vol. 14, No. 4 (Summer 1965), pp. 3–48. See also the opening section of Jeffrey S. Gurock's "Resisters and Accommodators," in Jacob R. Marcus and Abraham J. Peck (eds.), *The American Rabbinate* (Hoboken, N.J., 1985).

Not one member of the Advisory Board of Ministers was succeeded by a graduate of the Seminary. The reason lies in the character of the congregations they led, which ranged all the way from the Sephardi Shearith Israel and the Ashkenazi Zichron Ephraim of New York, officially Orthodox and formally traditional, to Ahavath Chesed, Rodef Sholom, and Shaarey Tefila of New York, then and now in the Reform camp. (Of the founding congregations, only B'nai Jeshurun of New York and Chizuk Amuno of Baltimore have always been and are today Conservative congregations.)

Loyalty to the Seminary or what it stood for was virtually nonexistent. Marcus Jastrow, rabbi of Philadelphia's Rodef Shalom, decried his congregation's decision to engage a Reform rabbi in the "Farewell Sermon Delivered on the Occasion of His Retirement" in 1892: "I did forewarn you; I told you that it was impossible for a congregation to be conservative with a minister of radical convictions . . . but you would not listen to my voice, and now the king that has been chosen will soon be among you."[28] The congregation had rejoined the UAHC, and the new "king" came from the religiously radicalized Hebrew Union College. The death of Alexander Kohut in 1894 took from the Seminary's ranks the only leader who could marshal support from what remained of its leftist constituency.

The lack of desirable pulpits for its graduates was only one of the obstacles facing the fledgling institution. It is actually surprising that the Seminary survived into the twentieth century, lacking as it did the ingredients that gave Hebrew Union College, for example, life and strength: a natural constituency, an ideology that served the felt needs of that constituency, and a charismatic, energetic leader.

The German-Jewish immigrant community had established its synagogues in the middle of the nineteenth century as sanctuaries of faith and portals to America. In the last decades of the century, the Hebrew Union College was needed to provide English-speaking rabbis for the second generation of German Jews, who had rapidly Americanized and were well along in a total emancipatory process. The Pittsburgh Platform, with its expression of broad religious universalism, sanctioned national, cultural, and religious assimilation. Isaac Mayer Wise, who intuited the felt needs of that community, had the imagination, skills, and energy to fashion institutions to meet them. In the space of a quarter of a century he succeeded in enlisting almost every major congregation in America in the Union of American Hebrew Congregations, which then provided ready pulpits for graduates of his Hebrew Union College.

To his credit, H. Pereira Mendes continued his leadership after the death of Sabato Morais in 1897, but at best it was a holding action. In an attempt

---

[28]Marcus Jastrow, *The Warning Voice* (Philadelphia, 1892), p. 8.

to organize support in the Orthodox community, in 1898 he established the Union of Orthodox Jewish Congregations. The organizational meeting was called by the Seminary; it met at Shearith Israel and in attendance were lay leaders and teachers of the Seminary. Dr. Mendes was elected president, but within two years the new body was dominated by East European immigrants whose loyalty was to Yeshivah Etz Chaim (from which Yeshiva University eventually emerged), not the Seminary.

As early as 1890 Morais had recognized the need for a younger, more charismatic leader. Dr. Solomon Solis-Cohen of Philadelphia recalled that "in the year 1890, I had the privilege of bearing a message from Sabato Morais and his colleagues of the Jewish Theological Seminary . . . asking Schechter to consider the possibility of joining the teaching staff of that institution."[29] For a dozen years thereafter, sporadic attempts were made to bring to America Solomon Schechter, Reader in Rabbinics at Cambridge University, author of scholarly works written in elegant English, a man of great energy and unmistakable charisma. A product of Rumanian and Galician yeshivahs, he had continued his studies in Vienna and Berlin, adding Western scientific order and method to the knowledge he had amassed in the East. His subsequent "discovery" of the Cairo *genizah* brought him international fame. In the early nineties, Dr. Cyrus Adler and Judge Mayer Sulzberger visited him in England. They came away impressed with the man and convinced that America should be his field of activity. Together with fellow Philadelphian Solomon Solis-Cohen they corresponded with Schechter and in 1895 brought him for a series of lectures to the newly established Gratz College. America had its appeal for Schechter, as he wrote to Sulzberger in 1898: "In your country I can hope to 'make school' and leave students . . . useful to the cause of Judaism. . . ."[30]

THE SCHECHTER ERA (1902–1915)

In the first years of the new century a group of American Jewish leaders joined forces to bring Solomon Schechter to these shores. Philadelphia provided the intellectual leadership and persuasive powers of Cyrus Adler, Mayer Sulzberger, and Solomon Solis-Cohen, while New York contributed the philanthropic generosity of Jacob H. Schiff, the Lewisohns, and the Guggenheims.

---

[29]*Students' Annual, Jewish Theological Seminary of America, Schechter Memorial* (New York, 1916), p. 61.

[30]See Abraham J. Karp, "Solomon Schechter Comes to America," *American Jewish Historical Quarterly*, Vol. 53, No. 1 (Sept. 1963), pp. 44–62.

The Seminary

Cyrus Adler described how Schechter came to be the head of a reorganized and newly endowed Jewish Theological Seminary, which officially came into being on April 14, 1902:

> In 1901, I . . . was invited to a man's party at the house of Mr. [Isidor] Straus. . . . I said that the Jewish community of New York was allowing its only institution of higher Jewish learning to perish, and I told them something of the precarious situation of the Seminary. Mr. Schiff, who was a man of quick decisions, said to the men standing around, "Dr. Adler is right," and a few weeks later I received a letter from him asking me when I was coming to New York next time, so that he might invite a few men to meet with us. . . . Within a few months an Endowment Fund of over one-half million dollars had been secured . . . which rendered it possible to invite Doctor Solomon Schechter . . . to come to America, as head of the Seminary.[31]

The moneyed elite exacted certain conditions in helping to revive the Seminary: Solomon Schechter was to serve as president of the faculty; Cyrus Adler was to function as chief executive; Louis Marshall would become chairman of the executive committee; and the elected board of the Jewish Theological Seminary Association would be replaced by a new, essentially self-perpetuating board. In order to demonstrate continuity with the previous administration, the second article of the bylaws of the old Seminary Association was incorporated into the new one, pledging the Seminary's continued adherence to "historical Judaism, as ordained in the Law of Moses, and expounded by the prophets and sages of Israel in Biblical and Talmudical writings."

Despite such an assurance, a new type of seminary was, in fact, coming into being, reflecting the personality and religious views of the new faculty president. Morais, Mendes, and Drachman, the chief administrators of the "old" seminary, had designated themselves as Orthodox. Schechter, though pious and observant, was a proponent—if not altogether an adherent—of the positive-historical school. This had already been noted by Rabbi Morris Joseph in his review of Schechter's *Studies in Judaism,* published in 1896. The review dwelled at length on the introduction, in which the author presented the positive-historical position, which, the reviewer wrote, was "formulated by men who were at once liberal in their opinions and conservative in practice." Although Schechter wrote with obvious approval of this religious stance, Joseph lamented, "Mr. Schechter is more content to expound the theory of the historic school than adopt it."[32]

---

[31]Adler, op. cit., pp. 9–10.
[32]*The Jewish Chronicle* (London), May 15, 1896, pp. 22–23.

What promise did Solis-Cohen, Sulzberger, and Adler see in Schechter's coming to America? The first saw in him the leader needed to give direction to American Jews, who were "striving vaguely, not knowing what they want, but knowing that they want something. . . ." Sulzberger thought the time propitious for laying the foundations for a cultured American Jewry. "He who has scholarship, talent and enthusiasm may be more appreciated for the first time in our history than he who leads a party." Adler saw Schechter as the one man whose stature could enlist the support of Schiff and his friends for the Seminary—the one institution, Adler believed, that could eventually turn the tide against Reform.

Schiff, the Lewisohns, the Guggenheims, and their group were motivated by concern about the children of the East European immigrants. Poverty moved many of the immigrants to espouse political radicalism. Social flux, the breakdown of the family unit, and bewildering differences in social patterns sometimes led to aberrant behavior. These uptown Jews saw in the Seminary-ordained rabbis and their teachings a force capable of bringing moderation, stability, and order into the community, one that could ease the Americanization of the East European immigrants and their children. Inherent in the enterprise was the confidence that such rabbis would wield great influence on the new generation, would indeed play a determinant role in the shaping of American Jewry.

Schechter brought with him the requisite background to fashion a school that would train such a rabbinate. A devotee of *Jüdische Wissenschaft* and the positive-historical school, he had learned as a resident in England the need for standards in congregational affairs and dignity in worship. Schechter gathered about himself a faculty which, through its scholarly activities, succeeded in laying a strong intellectual foundation for the movement, while creating a major center for higher Jewish learning. Louis Ginzberg charted new paths in rabbinic scholarship, employing a critical method that made use of the disciplines of sociology, economics, and comparative religion, demonstrating how "Judaism remained alive by reinterpreting its ideas and practices." Alexander Marx's contributions were in the fields of history and bibliography. The Seminary library that he fashioned became the center for the scientific study of Judaism in the United States. Israel Friedlaender was a biblical scholar, religious thinker, and communal leader who advocated the cultural creativity and spiritual Zionism that became hallmarks of Conservative Judaism. Israel Davidson laid open the rich treasures of medieval Jewish literature. No man had greater impact on Jewish religious thinking in America than Mordecai M. Kaplan, a Seminary graduate, to whom Schechter entrusted the directorship of the Teachers Institute in 1909.

The course of study that was adopted reflected Schechter's pledge to draw up a curriculum that would include in it almost every branch of Jewish literature: "The Bible; Talmud of Babylon and Jerusalem; Jewish History and the History of Jewish Literature; Theology and Catechism; Homiletics, including a proper training in Elocution and Pastoral work; and Hazanuth . . . optional with the students of the Senior Class."[33] The requirements for ordination called for the successful completion of four years of postgraduate studies. The admission requirements, in addition to "the Degree of Bachelor of Arts . . . from a university or college of good standing," included knowledge of the Hebrew language, the ability to translate and interpret at sight any portion of the Pentateuch, stated selections from the books of Judges, Isaiah, the Psalms, and Daniel, most of *Seder Moed* of the Mishnah, and the first 13 pages of *Gemara Berakhot,* as well as a knowledge of the prayer book and Jewish history.

Schechter sought to produce a learned rabbinate committed to the disciplines of Judaism but also open to its multifaceted ideological composition. As he told the students:

> You must not think that our intention is to convert this school of learning into a drill ground where young men will be forced into a certain groove of thinking, or, rather not thinking; and after being equipped with a few devotional texts, and supplied with certain catchwords, will be let loose upon an unsuspecting public to proclaim their own virtues and the unfallibility of their masters. . . . I would consider my work . . . a complete failure if this institution would not in the future produce such extremes as on the one side a roving mystic who would denounce me as a sober Philistine; on the other side, an advanced critic, who would rail at me as a narrow-minded fanatic, while a third devotee of strict orthodoxy would raise protest against any critical views I may entertain.[34]

Schechter's expectation that the Seminary would produce religious diversity was fulfilled in his own lifetime. Mordecai M. Kaplan and Jacob Kohn were among the first of the "advanced critics," while C.E. Hillel Kauvar and Herman Abramowitz called themselves Orthodox.

The Rabbis

During the incumbency of Solomon Schechter as president of the Seminary—1902–1915—the Conservative rabbinate developed a character of its own and began to play an influential role in the religious life of American Jewry. In 1901, when the Alumni Association of the Jewish Theological Seminary was organized, 15 graduates and former students were considered eligible for membership.[35] By 1916 the Alumni Association's membership had grown to 61 rabbis occupying pulpits or engaged in related activities. Conservative rabbis could be found in New York, Boston, Syracuse,

---

[33]Solomon Schechter, *Seminary Addresses* (Cincinnati, 1915), p. 20.
[34]Ibid., p. 22.
[35]*American Hebrew,* Apr. 11, 1902, pp. 635–636.

Rochester, Buffalo, Toledo, Columbus, Detroit, Chicago, Minneapolis, Sioux City, Denver, Spokane, Dallas, Kansas City, Montgomery, Louisville, Greensboro, Pittsburgh, Altoona, Baltimore, and Newark.

What did a newly ordained Seminary rabbi face? The experiences of two young rabbis illustrate the nature of synagogue life in that period. Paul Chertoff became rabbi of Congregation Beth Israel, Rochester, New York, an Orthodox synagogue that had separate seating of men and women, fully traditional Sabbath and weekday services, a cantor facing the ark, and an all-male choir. In contrast, his contemporary and colleague Herman H. Rubenovitz introduced the use of the organ and a mixed choir to his Conservative congregation, Mishkan Tefila, Boston.

Rubenovitz described what he found when he arrived in Boston in 1910:

> Assimilation was rampant, and its leading exponent was . . . the Rabbi of Reform Temple Israel, the wealthiest and most socially prominent Jewish congregation in New England. Hebrew had been practically eliminated from its service . . . the traditional Sabbath had been made secondary to the Sunday service. Even intermarriage between Jew and gentile was openly advocated. But what was even more menacing to the future of Judaism hereabouts, was the fact that by far the greater part of the Sunday morning Congregation which Rabbi Charles Fleischer addressed,[36] was made up of the sons and daughters of Orthodox Jewish parents. The Orthodox . . . synagogue worship . . . was, with few exceptions, utterly devoid of decorum, and its spiritual quality all too often lost in noise and confusion . . . and alienated the youth. When . . . these young people purchased seats for the High Holidays, they saw little of the interior of the synagogue, but instead mostly congregated on the sidewalk outside. . . . Religious instruction of the boys —the girls were completely neglected—was conducted in dark and dingy vestries, or by itinerant *rebbes*. . . teaching the Bar Mitzvah chant and the Kaddish prayer. Little congregations sprang up like mushrooms. . . . Every other day the community was rocked by some new scandal connected with the administration of *Kashrut.*[37]

The natural constituency for the Conservative rabbi was the sons and daughters of the East European immigrant community, some of whom Rubenovitz saw either filling the pews at the Sunday services of the Reform temple or socializing in front of the Orthodox synagogues on the holiest days, but with the majority turning away from all religious mooring. Rubenovitz reminisced:

> Wherever I went I appealed to the younger generation to accept a new synthesis of tradition and modern spirit; to provide well-housed and properly graded Hebrew schools; to participate actively in the upbuilding of Zion; to create a comprehensive program of adult education.[38]

---

[36]For the radical nature of Rabbi Fleischer's religious views, see Arthur Mann, *Growth and Achievement: Temple Israel* (Cambridge, 1954), pp. 63–83.

[37]Rubenovitz and Rubenovitz, op. cit., pp. 27–28.

[38]Ibid., p. 30.

Rabbi Rubenovitz remained at Mishkan Tefila for the remainder of his life and saw it become the leading Conservative congregation in New England. More typical of the challenges facing a Seminary graduate in the early years of the twentieth century was the tenure of Rabbi Paul Chertoff at Congregation Beth Israel, Rochester.[39] Founded in 1874 as an Orthodox synagogue for Rochester's growing community of East European immigrants, the congregation was forced by its younger, more acculturated members to engage Seminary-ordained Nathan Blechman in 1906 as "preacher and teacher." The title "rabbi" was reserved by the congregation for the communal Orthodox rabbi. In 1911, Seminary-ordained Paul Chertoff was elected to serve as preacher, "to deliver lectures and teach in daily school at a salary of $1,200, for one year trial by a vote of 35–16." During his tenure, Rabbi Chertoff instituted a broad program of education through the congregational school and youth clubs. His Hebrew school and Sunday school ledger lists 30 students in the weekday Hebrew school and 30 in the religious (i.e., Sunday) school. The rabbi was principal of the school and taught the most advanced classes, "Hebrew translation and writing, Abbreviated *Humash* and Jewish Biblical History and Religion."

The congregation was in constant financial difficulties. In addition, it was split by the issue of *rov* vs. preacher, which was but an indication of a more deeply rooted division between adherence to Orthodoxy and a growing tendency toward Conservative Judaism among younger members. Rabbi Chertoff encouraged the latter, a group of whom left in 1915 to organize a Conservative congregation, Beth El; he himself departed a year later.

The Conservative rabbi in the first decades of the century perceived himself as standing in confrontation with Orthodoxy, whether he was a liberal like Rabbi Rubenovitz—in conflict with members of his congregation opposed to his program of changes in synagogue ritual—or a traditionalist like Rabbi Chertoff—chafing at the denial of rabbinic status by the Orthodox communal *rov* and his followers. Schechter saw things differently. To him the real confrontation was with Reform, which, he charged, asserted that "the destruction of the Law is its fulfillment." He feared that the Conservative rabbi would be tempted to emulate his visibly successful Reform colleague.

Schechter felt strongly about the importance of continued study for the rabbi. "It is hardly necessary to remark," he noted wryly in his inaugural address in 1902, "that the Jewish ministry and Jewish scholarship are not irreconcilable." Six years later, having observed that in the American rabbinate scholarship and success were not synonymous, he urged his graduating students to "engage in some scientific work, publishing occasionally a

---

[39]See Abraham J. Karp, "From Hevra to Congregation: The Americanization of the Beth Israel Synagogue, Rochester, N.Y., 1874–1912," typescript.

learned article."[40] Believing the study of the Torah to be a transforming sacrament without which the rabbi would become a mere technician, Schechter urged rabbis to become exemplars of an enlightened piety based on learning.

The United Synagogue of America

As demonstrated by Rabbi Chertoff's experience in Rochester, early graduates of the Seminary often served congregations that did not accord them full rabbinic status (whether in title or in fact) and that were almost always in financial straits as well as in ideological conflict. Clearly, what was needed, a growing number of rabbis felt, was a national organization of like-minded congregations that would recognize the rabbinic status of Seminary ordination, help strengthen the individual congregations through programmatic aid, and help fashion the ideological stance of Conservative Judaism.

In the fall of 1909, Rabbi Rubenovitz suggested to Rabbi Charles I. Hoffman, president of the Alumni Association of the Jewish Theological Seminary, that the graduates of the Seminary take the lead "in the establishment of a union of conservative forces in America." At its annual meeting, the association voted unanimously to sponsor the launching of "a Union of Conservative Congregations." Some of the purposes of such a union would be

> to print an inexpensive prayerbook; to prevent the isolated man [i.e., rabbi] and the isolated synagogue from being swallowed up; to see that our views are fairly represented in the Jewish press; to have a regular traveling representation; to have a Sabbath observance department.[41]

The leaders of the Alumni Association urged that the organization be a union of *Conservative* congregations, but the more traditionally oriented rabbis and the leaders of the Seminary insisted that it be directed, as Cyrus Adler expressed it, to "the 1600 congregations remaining outside the fold of Reform." Schechter argued that, traditionalist and liberal forces having joined to found the Seminary, the same should obtain in establishing the union of congregations.

A "union for promoting traditional Judaism" had long been a dream of Schechter. As co-workers in his endeavor he sought out those lay leaders of the Seminary who were traditional Jews, chief among them Cyrus Adler, to whom he wrote, in the summer of 1909, that such an organization was of signal importance to the American Jewish community. Nearly four years

---

[40]Schechter, op. cit., p. 131.
[41]Rubenovitz and Rubenovitz, op. cit., p. 46.

later, Schechter and the converts to the cause among his friends, together with the disciples in the rabbinate whom he had trained and inspired, were ready to bring their dream to fruition.[42]

On Sunday, February 23, 1913, Schechter welcomed delegates of 22 congregations in Baltimore, Boston, Detroit, Montreal, New York, Norfolk, Philadelphia, Rochester, and Denver as well as some "thirty rabbis, the faculties of the Seminary, Dropsie College and Gratz College and a number of prominent laymen" to the large assembly hall of the Seminary and invited them to join "the United Synagogue of America, which is entering upon its existence this day, [upon which] depends the continuance and the survival of traditional Judaism in this country."[43]

The meeting began in an auspicious way when the Seminary's first graduate, the Rev. Dr. Joseph H. Hertz, who had just been elected chief rabbi of the British Empire, was called upon to say a prayer. The afternoon session was devoted to discussing the platform of the newborn organization. As formulated in the preamble of the proposed constitution, it read:

RECOGNIZING the need of an organized movement for advancing the cause of Judaism in America and maintaining Jewish tradition in its historical continuity, we hereby establish the United Synagogue of America, with the following ends in view:

TO ASSERT and establish loyalty to the Torah and its historical exposition,

TO FURTHER the observance of the Sabbath and the Dietary Laws,

TO PRESERVE in the service the reference to Israel's past and the hopes for Israel's restoration,

TO MAINTAIN the traditional character of the liturgy, with Hebrew as the language of prayer,

TO FOSTER Jewish religious life in the home, as expressed in traditional observances,

TO ENCOURAGE the establishment of Jewish religious schools, in the curricula of which the study of the Hebrew language and literature shall be given a prominent place, both as the key to true understanding of Judaism, and as a bond of holding together the scattered communities of Israel throughout the world.[44]

How the platform would be understood and applied would depend on the nature of the congregations which this "union" was meant to serve. Dr.

---

[42]See Herbert Rosenblum, "The Founding of the United Synagogue of America, 1913," Ph.D. dissertation, Brandeis University, 1970; Abraham J. Karp, *A History of the United Synagogue of America, 1913–1963* (New York, 1964).

[43]*The United Synagogue of America Report* (New York, 1913), p. 14.

[44]Ibid., p. 9.

Judah L. Magnes, who had left the pulpit of the country's leading Reform congregation to enter the ranks of Conservatism, brought the matter to the floor. Speaking as a "layman" who was neither Orthodox nor Reform, he expressed a desire to see the new organization make itself the representative of a new third trend. "The sense of the meeting," the *American Hebrew* reported, "was evidently against this suggestion, and the principle was laid down that the new movement should combine the tendencies common to both Orthodox and so-called Conservative congregations." Schechter underscored this sentiment in his keynote address: "This United Synagogue has not been called into life with any purpose of creating a new division." He envisioned the United Synagogue as an organization broad enough to encompass congregations called Orthodox, as well as "such congregations as have not accepted the Union Prayer-book nor performed their religious devotions with uncovered heads."[45]

Schechter's words heartened the traditionalist rabbis, who could continue to call themselves Orthodox. The rabbis of liberal orientation, though unhappy with Schechter's stance, accepted it as a necessary compromise for the time. In practical terms, Schechter's position virtually guaranteed that the ferment within the congregations would continue, with the rabbis pulling and being pulled either to the right or to the left. At the conclusion of the founding session, Schechter was elected to the presidency of the United Synagogue, and a board of 21 members was chosen to work with him.

At the second annual meeting of the United Synagogue, presided over by Dr. Cyrus Adler, Schechter's chosen successor, Mordecai M. Kaplan, head of the Seminary's Teachers Institute, presented a report of the Committee on Education. A total of 4,481 students (2,385 boys, 2,096 girls) were enrolled in the religious schools of the 24 congregations affiliated with the United Synagogue. The congregations, Kaplan pointed out,

> have to maintain a double system of schooling in order to meet the wishes of the two classes of members that are usually to be found in every congregation, namely, those whose slogan is "more Judaism," and those who ask for "less Judaism." Most congregations, therefore, maintain both a Sunday School and a Hebrew School.[46]

The textbooks were "beneath criticism," Kaplan asserted, and the teacher situation was not better. Some teachers possessed "no qualifications beyond the ability to read beforehand the lesson in some elementary textbook used by the children." Only one-third of the children attended more than once a week, and there was no uniform curriculum, no grading system, and hardly any advanced classes. He challenged the United Synagogue to help

---

[45]Schechter, op. cit., p. 20.
[46]*The United Synagogue of America Report of the Second Annual Meeting* (New York, 1914), p. 34.

"create a demand for more Jewish education" and urge its extension to those below and above the school age through kindergartens, junior congregations, and uniform standards for bar mitzvah and confirmation practices and children's services.[47]

The Sabbath Observance Committee devoted itself to "furthering legislation on the observance of the Sabbath, in issuing calendars, and in bringing to the attention of the people the need of a great Sabbath observance." The Committee on Propaganda sent visiting speakers and organizers to congregations needing guidance and direction. The Committee on Religious Observance concerned itself with finding work for "men and women who desire to observe the Sabbath . . . with work among university students . . . the publication of a book of sermons . . . and efforts . . . to secure the observance of Jewish law by Jewish institutions."[48]

The fourth annual convention, meeting on July 9–10, 1916, mourned the loss of its "founder, master and beloved friend," Dr. Solomon Schechter, who, three years before the founding of the United Synagogue, had written of the proposed organization: "This will be the greatest bequest which I shall leave to American Israel."[49]

Schechter's Legacy

Schechter's bequest was greater, however, than the synagogal union he had established. It was a religious movement emanating out of a theological seminary that in a dozen years had developed into one of the primary centers of *Jüdische Wissenschaft;* a growing body of congregations and rabbis hewing out a new path in American Judaism; and an emerging ideology, as yet unarticulated, but sharply focused.

When Schechter arrived in America, as Cyrus Adler noted, "he saw a vision of creating a theological center which would be all things to all men, reconciling all parties and appealing to all sections of the community." It did not take him long, however, to recognize that the radical nature of Reform and the insular stance of Orthodoxy would permit, at best, only competitive cooperation. He was convinced that neither could secure the future of a living Judaism in America. Radical Reform's "attempt to dispense with the sacred language and to emphasize the universal elements at the expense of the ceremonial law and its national aspects," he was certain, "must result in disaster." Orthodoxy was a reservoir of piety and learning but stagnant, and therefore, as Schechter observed, "subject to a process of constant attrition which must become dangerous if the tide of immigration

---

[47]Ibid., pp. 32–40.
[48]Ibid., pp. 32–46; 23–27.
[49]*The United Synagogue of America Fourth Annual Report* (New York, 1916), p. 15.

should be stopped for a few years." The tide did come to an end less than a decade after Schechter's death. By that time, the children of the immigrants who had arrived found that the institutions that Schechter had fashioned and the disciples he had trained and inspired presented to them a Judaism that better served their spiritual needs as Jews and as Americans than Reform or Orthodoxy.

It was Schechter, also, who pointed to the symbiotic relationship of Zionism and Judaism in America. According to Samuel Halperin, "It was Schechter . . . who won for the tiny Zionist following in America [in the early years of the twentieth century] its first great accretion of strength—the Conservative Movement in Judaism . . . despite the threats and imprecations of the Seminary's Reform-dominated Board of Directors. . . ."[50] In "Zionism: A Statement," published in the *American Hebrew* in 1906 and circulated as a pamphlet by the Federation of American Zionists, Schechter proclaimed:

> Zionism declares to the world that Judaism means to preserve its life by *not* losing its life. It shall be a true and healthy life . . . not only for the remnant gathered within the borders of the Holy Land, but also for those who shall, by choice or necessity, prefer what now constitutes the Galuth. . . .
>
> The activity of Zionism must not be judged by what it has accomplished *in* Zion and Jerusalem . . . but by what it has thus far achieved *for* Zion and Jerusalem, through awakening of the national Jewish consciousness. . . . Zionism . . . is the Declaration of Jewish Independence from all kinds of Slavery, whether material or spiritual. . . . Whilst constantly winning souls for the present . . . it is at the same time preparing for us the future, which will be a Jewish future.[51]

Schechter, Conservative Judaism's foremost personality, did not formulate an ideology for the movement. Rather he determined its parameters, suggested its agenda, and set its tone.

The leading ideologist of Conservative Judaism in the Schechter era and its most active Zionist spokesman was Israel Friedlaender.[52] As a disciple of both Ahad Ha'am and Simon Dubnow, he labored for Jewish national and cultural rebirth in Palestine and for a vital Jewish community in America, emphasizing the religious component. In 1907, in a lecture he called "The Problem of Judaism in America," Friedlaender presented an ideological base and visionary goal for Conservative Judaism:

> Judaism represents the inner characteristics of the Jewish people as manifested in its culture, in its mode of living and in its intellectual productivity. . . .

---

[50]Samuel Halperin, *The Political World of American Zionism* (Detroit, 1961), p. 102.
[51]*American Hebrew,* Dec. 28, 1906, pp. 191–194.
[52]See Baila Round Shargel, *Practical Dreamer: Israel Friedlaender and the Shaping of American Judaism* (New York, 1985).

It was the fatal mistake of the Jews of emancipation, . . . that, in order to facilitate their fight for political equality they introduced Judaism not as a culture, as the full expression of the inner life of the Jewish people, but as a creed, as a summary of a few abstract articles of faith, similar in its character to the religion of the surrounding nations. . . .

If Judaism is to be preserved amidst the new condition . . . it must break the narrow frame of a creed and resume its original function as a culture, as the expression of the Jewish spirit and the whole life of the Jews. . . .

It will have to take in and digest the elements of other cultures . . . while it will endeavor to preserve all those features of Jewish practice which give shape and vigor to Judaism. . . . It will give full scope to our religious genius. . . . It will develop our literature, create or preserve Jewish art in all its functions, stimulate and further Jewish scholarship. . . .

The only place where such a Judaism has a chance of realization is America. For America . . . is fast becoming the center of the Jewish people of the Diaspora. . . . The American Jews are fully alive to the future of their country as a center of Jewish culture.

A full and successful participation in all phases of American life is reconcilable with a deep attachment to Judaism in all its aspects. . . . In the great palace of American civilization we shall occupy our own corner, which we will decorate and beautify to the best of our taste and ability. . . .[53]

THE ADLER ERA (1915-1940)

Cyrus Adler's appointment as head of the Seminary, following the death of Solomon Schechter in November 1915, was a temporary measure, since he was neither a rabbi nor a distinguished Jewish scholar. It was war-time, Adler explained, and the board was reluctant to appoint anyone but a native-born American. The logical candidates seemed to be Israel Friedlaender, who had acted in Schechter's stead during his sabbatical in 1911, and Louis Ginzberg, the senior member of the faculty. The board, however, was not enthusiastic about either man: Friedlaender was a communal activist and Zionist spokesman, given to a liberal view of traditional Judaism; Ginzberg's administrative ability was questioned. Still, both men positioned themselves to strengthen their candidacies. Ginzberg accepted the presidency of the United Synagogue when Adler resigned in 1917 and assumed the chairmanship of its Committee on the Interpretation of Jewish Law. For a decade he was, in effect, the movement's chief rabbi. Friedlaender published *Past and Present* in 1919, putting forward a vision of a vibrant Jewish community in America, with scholarship, verve, and

---

[53]Israel Friedlaender, *Past and Present* (Cincinnati, 1919), pp. 159–184.

imagination. Eventually, however, both men came to realize that their strivings were in vain. Ginzberg returned to his scholarly work; Friedlaender to communal activity, which led to a martyr's death while he was on a mission of mercy to fellow Jews in the war-devastated Ukraine.

In 1924, after eight years as acting president, Adler was awarded the full title. Born in Van Buren, Arkansas, and raised in Philadelphia, he had been the recipient of the first doctorate in Semitics granted by an American university. During a long and distinguished career of service to the Jewish community, he served as president of Dropsie College, the American Jewish Historical Society, and the American Jewish Committee, and as editor of the *American Jewish Year Book,* 1899–1905, and the *Jewish Quarterly Review,* 1916–1940. A proven administrator, a man of prudence and discretion, a devout Jew who moved in the highest circles of both the Jewish philanthropic and American intellectual establishments, Adler gave the Seminary able, devoted, and effective leadership until his death in 1940. With the help of the Schiff family, Louis Marshall, and other friends, budgets were met and the buildings that house the Seminary to the present day (save the new library building dedicated in 1984) were erected. The quarter century of the Adler administration saw the emergence of the Conservative synagogue as a distinctive institution and the maturation of the Conservative rabbinate, as it sharpened and refined the tools of its vocation.

Congregations and Schools

Schechter had charged the Conservative rabbinate "to organize new congregations and to raise the old ones from the sloth of indifference and the vice of strife into which they have fallen." The generation of rabbis that issued from what was now called "Schechter's Seminary" set itself to this task.[54] The post-World War I American scene saw a turning away from the ideology of the melting pot to that of cultural pluralism. Within the American rabbinate, Conservative rabbis became the most fervent adherents of the new ideology, taking their cue in this regard from Mordecai M. Kaplan.

Kaplan viewed with alarm the condition of the synagogue as he found it in his day. Noting that it owed its existence "more to the momentum of the past, than to any new forces created in this country," he warned that only the concentration of "all possible material and moral resources" might save the synagogue from "impending doom."[55] He proposed the creation of

---

[54]This designation, or simply "Schechter's," was the popular name for the Jewish Theological Seminary in the East European Jewish community until World War II:

[55]*The Jewish Community Register of New York City, 1917–1918* (New York, 1918), pp. 121–122.

a new type of synagogue, a Jewish center whose purpose would be to afford its users "pleasures of a social, intellectual and spiritual character."[56] According to Kaplan, such a synagogue-center, a *bet am* ("house of the people"), would include

> Jewish elementary school facilities; recreational facilities such as gymnasia, showers, bowling alleys, pool tables, and game rooms; adult study and art groups; communal activities; religious services and festival pageants and plays; [and] informal meetings of friends and associates.[57]

This was precisely the kind of synagogue that Schechter had warned against,[58] but precisely the kind of synagogue that might win the second-generation Jew to Conservative Judaism. A synagogue so conceived and so fashioned had great appeal to a generation of American Jews, the children of the East European immigrants, who were desirous of maintaining a Jewish identity while intent on integrating fully into the American scene. Reform temples, Marshall Sklare has written, "hesitated to expand their activities and to gain too many new adherents. . . . They were suspicious of too much non-religious activity on synagogue premises, which would be an expression of racial consciousness." Moreover, they did not want to attract and serve "the unaffiliated," who were of a lower socioeconomic class.[59] For its part, the Orthodox *shul* viewed expansion as change, and therefore resisted it, since any change was seen as fraught with peril to the faith. The "synagogue center" was solely the creation of the emerging Conservative movement.

How did such a synagogue come into being? In some instances it was established by seceding members of an Orthodox synagogue; more often it resulted from the transformation of an existing Orthodox synagogue. Thus, for example, in 1915 a group of young members of the Orthodox Beth Israel synagogue in Rochester, New York, left to form a new congregation that would better answer their needs. They issued a call: "Recognizing that it is our duty as Jews to bear witness to the truths of our Faith in our days and generation as our Fathers did in theirs . . . we hereby constitute ourselves a Jewish congregation for the purpose of conserving Judaism." Their new synagogue, which they later named Beth El, provided the following: family pews for men and women; prayers in Hebrew and English,

---

[56]*American Hebrew*, Mar. 22, 1918.

[57]Kaplan, op. cit., p. 428.

[58]In his last public address at the commencement exercises of the Seminary, June 6, 1915, Schechter had warned against "the Institutional Synagogue [i.e., a synagogue center] in which the worship of God must become in the end subordinated to the material service of man and his amusements" (*Seminary Addresses*, p. 252).

[59]Marshall Sklare, *Conservative Judaism* (Glencoe, Ill., 1955; new augm. ed., New York, 1972), p. 131.

conducted by a rabbi, cantor and Jewish choir; head covering and tallith; congregational singing and music with organ; daily services, with special services on Friday evening, Saturday morning, and holidays; and daily and Sunday school.[60]

Within a year the group purchased and adapted for synagogue use the Park Avenue Baptist Church and by 1922 could boast of having the largest Jewish congregational school—270 pupils. In the 1920s and 1930s Beth El's sisterhood, men's club, junior congregation, Boy Scout troop, youth clubs, and athletic teams made it the "established coequal" of Reform Temple B'rith Kodesh, long the city's largest, wealthiest, and most prestigious congregation.[61]

Rabbi Ralph Simon described the first steps in transforming the Orthodox Rodef Sholom synagogue in Johnstown, Pennsylvania, into a Conservative congregation in the 1930s:

> This congregation was a traditional Orthodox synagogue which was founded by East European immigrants about the year 1885. I was the first Seminary rabbi to serve them. . . . The decision to invite a Conservative rabbi came as a result of the insistence of a younger group who correctly believed that the next generation would join the Reform temple unless the synagogue was modernized. The older generation was suspicious of innovations. . . . The rabbi had to walk a narrow line in order to remain on good terms with the elders as well as to satisfy the rebellious young people. . . . Very few changes [were made] in the Sabbath and holidays Synagogue service. It was only in Friday evening late service that changes could be made, since the leaders of the older group did not attend and did not recognize it as an authentic service. The major changes were sermons in English, insistence on decorum and interpretation of the liturgy. One activity which won the elders over to a trust in the new rabbi was the formation of a Talmud study group.
>
> The major area of change was in the cultural and social program. All the activities envisioned in the synagogue-center program of Dr. Kaplan were introduced. Adult education classes were organized. A good Hebrew school was conducted. There was an active Men's Club, Sisterhood and Youth Group. There were frequent programs of music, a new choir, dramatic presentations and guest speakers.
>
> The unique aspect of the new Conservative rabbi was his multifaceted role. He was the preacher, pastor, teacher, executive and communal figure. . . . One activity of the rabbi was received with great approval by practically the entire Jewish community. He began to appear before church and civic groups who welcomed an erudite Jewish spokesman. As the rabbi became popular with the non-Jewish community, his popularity increased with the Jewish community.[62]

---

[60]Minute Book of Temple Beth El, Rochester, N.Y. (Beth El archives), unpaged.

[61]Stuart E. Rosenberg, *The Jewish Community of Rochester, 1843–1925* (New York, 1954), p. 179.

[62]Cited in Abraham J. Karp, "The Conservative Rabbi," in Marcus and Peck (eds.), op. cit., p. 126.

Traditionalist Conservative rabbi Israel H. Levinthal, whose Brooklyn Jewish Center offered the entire gamut of synagogue-center activities, was aware of the accusation that "Synagogue Centers have tended to detract from the centrality of religion in Jewish life."[63] In 1926 Levinthal wrote in defense of the institution:

> If the Synagogue as a Beth Hatefilah has lost its hold upon the masses, some institution would have to be created that could and would attract the people so that the group consciousness of the Jew might be maintained. The name center seems to work this magic with thousands who would not be attracted to the place if we simply called it Synagogue or Temple. . . .

> The Center is a seven-day synagogue. From early morning to late at night its doors should be open. It is true that many will come for other purposes than to meet God. But let them come.[64]

Few congregations, of course, could afford a full program of religious, cultural, social, and athletic activities—"a *shul* with a pool," as Rabbi Joel Blau described the new type of institution. Most contented themselves with interpreting "synagogue-center" to mean that it aimed to serve the religious and cultural needs of the majority of its congregants, fulfilling a threefold function as *bet ha-tefillah* (house of worship), *bet ha-midrash* (house of study), and *bet ha-knesset* (house of assembly).

At the heart of each congregation, old or new, were the services of worship—daily, Sabbaths, and holidays. Conservative innovations included the incorporation of English into the traditional service, insistence on decorum during prayers, and the introduction of the late Friday-night service. The following account by a "successful professional man who had the usual Orthodox upbringing" demonstrates the magnitude of change represented by the Conservative synagogue:

> The biggest shock of all to me was the temple services on New Years and Yom Kippur. . . . I was born and bred in an orthodox shul with the accompanying multitudinous prayers, jams of people and children all joined together in a cacophonous symphony of loud and sometimes raucous appeals to the Almighty. Here it was so different. A large group of Jews, men and women, sitting quietly together for hours at a stretch, subdued prayers, no mass movements, no rustling and bustling, no weeping and wailing, no crying children, just the music of the choir and cantor being the only loud sounds heard. Truly it was a revelation to me. I looked around the congregation and saw a large number of younger people sitting intently and reverently reading their *Machzors* [holiday prayer books]. They supplied you with a talis and yarmelke [skullcap] at the door. No carrying packages. The Machzor was clear, concise and arranged in order so as to be easily followed when the rabbi announced the page numbers. I soon immersed myself

---

[63] Abraham J. Feldman, "The Changing Functions of the Synagogue," in *Reform Judaism, Essays by Hebrew Union College Alumni* (Cincinnati, 1949), p. 212.
[64] *United Synagogue Recorder,* Vol. 6, No. 4, Oct. 1926.

in the prayers and responsive readings. I listened to the sermons and understood what it was all about. . . . It is so different for me. Like another world.[65]

The late Friday-night service was an innovation that evoked mixed responses. Rabbi Louis M. Levitsky explained the rationale for the practice and shared his misgivings about it in the *United Synagogue Recorder*, in 1927:

> The late Friday night services are an attempt to satisfy what we have been hoping are the spiritual needs for public worship for the vast preponderant majority of our men and women who because of economic pressure cannot be with us on Shabbos morning. Were it not for these late Friday night services by far most of the members of our congregations would not be found in the synagogue between Yom Kippur and Rosh Hashonah. With the further weakening of the Shabbos atmosphere at home, it becomes all the more necessary to bring into the lives of our men and women a little of the Shabbos spirit. This we hope to accomplish by the late Friday services.

> But the problems that we face are several and serious. We must face a congregation tired from a day's business and anticipating the Saturday business for which they prepare most of the week. To this physical weariness and preoccupied mind is added the drowsiness that follows a heavy meal. Add to this the very small initial interest in religious worship and we can readily see where the weather (either good or bad), and now the radio, have become obstacles to people attending Friday night services. But if the speaker is one whose name is familiar or the topic promises to be thrilling, they may succeed in overcoming these difficulties. For after all, most of our people come to the late Friday night services to listen to the address and hardly to worship. The older people have worshipped at sunset, and among the rest we find many who cannot follow interestingly, or not at all, the Hebrew of our services. We must therefore make the worship part of these services interesting by means of elaborate choirs, and thus make a concert out of the service. I believe that few of us delude ourselves with believing that any of these or all combined give the worshipper a sense of reverence.

Rabbi Levitsky urged that the pulpit not be used, as it too often was, for "book reviews, dramatic criticisms and political orations," but rather for the "instruction of the congregation . . . to teach Jewish history, Jewish theology, or Jewish ethics," arguing that "once the congregation will feel that the rabbi utilizes his time in the pulpit toward real spiritual ends and constructive teaching they will in time be infected with the spirit."[66]

In the emerging Conservative synagogue, great emphasis was placed on the youth element—the congregational school and clubs. A 1938 report on the Beth El religious school in Rochester, New York, prepared by Dr. Ben Rosen, indicated the problems facing the Conservative congregational school of that period. The Beth El school had a Sunday department and a weekday department. Of the 275 pupils, 144 attended one day a week for

[65]Sklare, op. cit., p. 112.
[66]*United Synagogue Recorder*, Vol. 7, No. 4, Oct. 1927, p. 11.

two hours, 76 twice a week for one hour each, 42 three times a week for a total of five and a half hours, and 13 four times a week. Only 20 percent of the pupils, then, received more than two hours of instruction per week. Rosen found that the curriculum "was not well formulated . . . nor strictly adhered to; nor in terms of the purposes of a school of this type . . . sufficiently rich in content or broad enough in scope. . . . The educational achievement . . . falls below the standard of better congregational schools of this size in other communities." Compared with the total Jewish school population in Rochester, Beth El's students attended fewer hours but for a longer span of years. Almost one-third of the former received instruction five times a week, but only 9 percent were in the high-school department; at Beth El, where less than 5 percent attended four days a week, 35 percent were students in the older preconfirmation and confirmation classes (meeting two hours a week).[67]

Since it was generally recognized that the hours per week and the number of years spent in the classroom were inadequate, supplementary education through club activities was offered by almost all Conservative congregations. The program at New York's B'nai Jeshurun Synagogue in 1923 was as follows:

> There are six such Junior Clubs, the Z'eire Yisroel of boys between 10–12, B'nai Am Chai of boys between 12–14, the Girl Scout Troop of girls between 10–12, the Emmunoh Club of girls between 12–14, the Beta Alpha and the B'nai Jeshurun Juniors. The existence of these clubs has been a wonderful asset for the Religious School, because of the splendid group spirit which they have created. . . .

> Center Clubs have also been organized for a group of adolescents between the ages of 14–17. There is a group of "Scrolls and Quills," consisting of boys between the ages of 14–16. There is an Alumni Association consisting of boys and girls of the ages from 15–18, who were formally [sic] members of the Religious School, and from whom come some of the leaders of the younger groups.[68]

The United Synagogue

The fifth annual convention, held on July 1–2, 1917, marked the coming of age of the United Synagogue. Delegates heard that a Kosher Directory listing 300 eating places in 107 cities had been prepared; that textbooks were in the offing; that regional units had been established and were functioning; that 26 congregations had affiliated during the year; and that Rabbi Samuel M. Cohen had been appointed full-time supervising director. Particularly significant was the establishment of a "a standing Committee of the United

---

[67]Mimeo and typescript, June 22, 1938. In possession of the author.
[68]*United Synagogue Recorder*, Vol. 3, No. 2, Apr. 1923.

Synagogue to be known as the Committee on the Interpretation of Jewish Law."[69] This was in response to Dr. Adler's call a year earlier to reverse the "semi-anarchy" which had developed because of the "absolute independence and autonomy of every congregation" by appointing "some sort of Rabbinical authority, which fully basing itself upon the Jewish law and tradition, can interpret at least for the people of the congregations whom we have brought together in union."[70]

The committee's creation marked a step forward in the transformation of the United Synagogue from an association of "non-Reform" congregations to the representative body of a self-consciously emerging movement within American Jewry. The Committee on the Interpretation of Jewish Law, consisting of "five members learned in the Law" and chaired by Professor Louis Ginzberg, issued *responsa* written by the chairman, covering a broad range of issues. Among them were: May a synagogue sell its old building for commercial purposes to use the money for the building of a new one? May a part of the lower floor of a synagogue be set aside as a social center, and be used for prayers as well? A vexing issue which rent many congregations was that of mixed seating.

Question: Would family pews be a departure from traditional Judaism?
Answer: The earliest reference to separating the sexes in the houses of worship is found among the Jews Therapeutae of which Philo tells us that the women were separated from the men by a wall three to four cubits in height so that they might listen to the service without infringing the rules of modesty becoming to women. As we otherwise do not lead the life of these Jewish "monks and nuns" there does not seem to be any valid reason why we should attempt to imitate their synagogue regulations. . . . In Talmudic times the sexes were separated in the synagogue . . . not by a partition, only that the men had their places on one side and the women on the other. . . . The women's gallery is, comparatively speaking, a modern invention. Taking into consideration the conditions of today, I do not see any reason for insisting on continuing the women's gallery, but the separation of the sexes is a Jewish custom well established for about 2,000 years and must not be taken lightly.[71]

When the convention turned to consider the plight of Jewry abroad, an issue developed that was vigorously debated before culminating in a historic decision. The Resolutions Committee proposed that the United Synagogue join with the Zionists throughout the world in voicing the claim "for a Jewish homeland in Palestine." Despite the opposition of a determined minority led by Cyrus Adler himself, a rephrased resolution was adopted which affirmed Dr. Friedlaender's assertion that "unless Zionism is realized, there is no hope for Judaism here or elsewhere" and that Conservative

---

[69]Cited in Karp, *History of the United Synagogue,* p. 25.
[70]*The United Synagogue of America Fourth Annual Report* (New York, 1916), p. 17.
[71]Karp, op. cit., p. 45.

Judaism could not possibly fulfill its highest function "unless Zionism is realized." The resolution read:

> WHEREAS, the present world crisis opens a new vista for the realization of the ever-cherished hope of the Jewish people for the rehabilitation of the land of our forefathers,
>
> BE IT RESOLVED, that the United Synagogue of America reaffirms its faith in the fulfillment of our ancient Zionist hope in the early restoration of Palestine as the Jewish homeland as the means for the consummation of the religious ideas of Judaism.[72]

What gave added importance to this resolution was the fact that organized Reform Jewry was zealously anti-Zionist.

From the inception of the United Synagogue, its annual conventions brought together Seminary faculty, rabbis, and laymen. The first three presidents—Schechter, Adler, and Ginzberg—were members of the faculty; the next two—Elias L. Solomon and Herman Abramowitz—were rabbis. It was only in 1927, with the election of S. Herbert Golden, that the tradition of lay presidents began.

Golden's election reflected the growing assertiveness of the organization's lay leadership. A reporter commenting on the 1926 convention stated that the rabbis "did too much of the speaking," though outnumbered ten to one. Two years later, the newly elected lay president stated diplomatically but firmly what the division of responsibilities would henceforth be: "By drafting the *baalebatim* into the administrative tasks of the organization, we can leave the rabbis free to devote themselves to the religious and educational phases of our program."[73]

The Rabbinical Assembly

An alumni association of the Jewish Theological Seminary had been organized in 1901. In 1918 it took a more appropriately descriptive name —the Rabbinical Assembly of the Jewish Theological Seminary. In 1933, in recognition of the growing number of non-Seminary graduates on its roster, and in order to establish a position of independence and parity in the triad of Conservative Judaism with the Seminary and the United Synagogue, it changed the designation from "of the Jewish Theological Seminary" to "of America."

As the Rabbinical Assembly grew, reaching 158 members in 1922, its annual convention came to serve a number of important functions. It was the forum where the central concerns of the movement could be voiced and

---

[72]Ibid., p. 29.
[73]Ibid., p. 59.

ideological differences debated. It also offered rabbis an opportunity to air professional problems and frustrations. Rabbis complained, for example, that most of their time and energy had to be given to the management of struggling synagogues, rather than to intellectual activity. At the same time, however, they recognized the necessity of the administrative function. They had to create new synagogues or strengthen frail, struggling ones by filling their membership rolls, establishing their schools, initiating their activities, and securing their budgets. They also had to build new buildings and then worry lest the leaders of the congregation decide that a new building needed a new rabbi.

Jacob Kraft described his duties as rabbi of Beth Shalom Congregation, Wilmington, Delaware, in the 1930s:

> This rabbi acted as a *kol bo* [all-purpose functionary], taking charge of the services, preaching weekly, explaining Torah portion on Sabbath morning. He supervised the school, taught, took care of assemblies, visited the sick several times a week, the hospitals, visited the home during shivah period and conducted services, taught some converts of Judaism (about 3 or so during the 30's) etc., etc.[74]

What kept rabbinic morale alive was the conviction that what they were doing was of crucial importance to the future of Judaism in America, that they were engaged in creating something new, and that even "managing" a synagogue called for a high order of creativity. They were also strengthened by two of their teachers at the Seminary, Mordecai M. Kaplan, who, as one rabbi phrased it, "opened a new world to me," and Louis Ginzberg, whose towering scholarship validated their traditionalist tendencies. Ginzberg provided solid roots, Kaplan gave them wings.

Schechter's expectation that the Seminary training would make for an ideologically diverse Conservative rabbinate was prophetic. Such was the diversity that at the 1927 annual meeting of the Rabbinical Assembly, vice-president Louis Finkelstein felt impelled to present a paper on "The Things That Unite Us."[75] Still, while conservatives and liberals might disagree on the content of the tradition and the dynamics making for change, they were united in the view that, as Rabbi Norman Salit put it, "Orthodoxy has our yesterday, and Reform our to-day, [but] Conservatism has our to-morrow."[76] Finkelstein was even bolder in asserting this point:

> We are the only group in Israel who have a modern mind and a Jewish heart, prophetic passion and western science. . . . And it is because we are alone in combining the two elements that can make a rational religion, that we may rest convinced that, given due sacrifice and willingness on our part, the Judaism of

---

[74]Cited in Karp, "The Conservative Rabbi," in Marcus and Peck (eds.), op. cit., p. 126.
[75]*Proceedings of the Rabbinical Assembly* (hereafter *PRA*), 1927, p. 42ff.
[76]Ibid., p. 18.

the next generation will be saved by us. Certainly it can be saved by no other group. We have before us both the highest of challenges and the greatest of opportunities.[77]

At the 1928 conference, president Max Drob was proud to announce as "the greatest accomplishment of the year" the organization of a committee on Jewish law to replace the United Synagogue committee which, for its ten-year tenure, had been dominated by Louis Ginzberg. The R.A. committee, reflecting the diversity within the movement, consisted of four members representing the liberal tendency—Mordecai Kaplan, Jacob Kohn, Herman Rubenovitz, and Solomon Goldman; four representing the conservative tendency—Max Drob, Louis M. Epstein, Louis Finkelstein, and Julius H. Greenstone; and two others—Harry S. Davidowitz and Morris Levine—chosen by the eight. A unanimous opinion would become authoritative; lacking unanimity, "the opinions of the minority as well as the majority" were to be submitted to the questioner. Chairman Drob hailed the creation of the law committee as the first step toward the organization of an American "Beth Din Hagadol . . . which will study the problems arising in our new environment, and solve them in the spirit of our Torah. . . . The time is not too far distant when all ritual and domestic problems will be brought to us for solution."[78]

The question of how contemporary problems were to be addressed and solved and the ideological underpinning of the procedure to be pursued were considered in the three major papers presented at the 1929 R.A. conference. Max Drob, calling his address "A Reaffirmation of Traditional Judaism," spoke as follows: "As to the content of Judaism, there is really no difference between the Traditional Judaism as it was taught at the Seminary and Orthodox Judaism. We believe in the divine revelation and the duty to practice the Laws of Judaism as promulgated in the Torah, as interpreted by the Talmud and as codified by the Sages of Israel. . . ." Referring, no doubt, to Mordecai Kaplan's God concept, he asserted, "I certainly shall not accept the mandate to create a God pleasing to certain elements. My God cannot be made to order." And to the colleague who ten years earlier had pleaded, "If the young must dance, let them dance in the Synagogue; if they must play, let them play in the Synagogue; if they must swim, let them swim in the Synagogue," his response was that they *have* danced, played, and swum in the synagogue, "but they still have to pray in the Synagogue. . . . It is about time that we and not the laymen's committee on Ritual decide whether the prayers are to be retained or not." Emphasizing his uncompromising loyalty to the received tradition, Drob climaxed his exhortation by citing Cyrus Adler's

[77]Ibid., p. 53.
[78]*PRA*, 1928, pp. 21–22.

words, "What has been preserved for four thousand years, was not saved that I should overthrow it."[79]

Drob's successor to the presidency of the Rabbinical Assembly, Louis Finkelstein, titled his presidential address "Traditional Law and Modern Life." In it he argued that the religious "restrictions which bore easily on our ancestors of the ghettos, can be observed by us only with great difficulty. . . . It is impossible to expect the mass [of American Jews] to give the greater part of the holiday to Synagogue and prayer and at the same time to maintain that they are enjoying the festival." He asked: "Have we, rabbis, any authority to deal with the problem of Jewish custom and Law so as to bring our observance more in conformity with the ideals of Judaism than it is under the general practice today?" The solution, he argued, was to be found in legislation through reinterpretation:

> The position that has been held before us by all the great scholars of our people . . . is that recognized authorities may take it upon themselves to accept, for the purposes of interpreting the law, the lenient principles established by ancient scholars rather than the more severe opinions that may accidentally have crept into general practice. We shall, where facts warrant it, seek to take advantage of such leniencies as the law permits and such adjustments as it warrants. . . .

> Once more, after many years, a group of rabbis are prepared to deal with the problems of Jewish Law and life not merely from a technical and repressive attitude, but from one of worldly wisdom and mature understanding.[80]

Eugene Kohn, speaking for the religious liberals in the Rabbinical Assembly, questioned whether "judicial interpretation is a sufficient method for the adjustment of Law to life."

> When man had the conception of the Law as a perfect and sufficient rule of life, the search for a hidden meaning of the Law that would reconcile it with their vital interests was an honest search for something that they believed to exist. . . . It is unwarranted aspersion on the honesty of our forefathers to assume that they deliberately created legal fictions in order to circumvent a law. From our modern point of view, however, which regards law as a human institution . . . a search for something that we do not believe to exist and the devising of a legal fiction . . . ceases to be honest interpretation and becomes legislative amendment masquerading as interpretation. . . .

> Dr. Finkelstein being impressed with the danger of spiritual anarchy . . . has chosen to preserve the formal method of Orthodoxy even while discarding the naive theology by which alone that method can find legitimate moral sanction.

Admitting that the attitude advocated by him and his colleagues, disciples of Mordecai M. Kaplan, would be considered dangerous by more traditionally minded colleagues, Kohn argued that "the crisis which confronts

---

[79]*PRA,* 1929, pp. 43–50. The address was also published in the Oct. 1929 issue of the *Jewish Forum,* an Orthodox periodical.

[80]Ibid., pp. 18–30.

Judaism at the present time is an unprecedented one and reliance on the precedents of the past will not suffice for the present emergency . . . in which life itself has put Judaism in a position where it must live dangerously or die." He urged acceptance of the viewpoint of Dr. Kaplan's disciples:

At the present time the Torah functions in our life not in any strict sense as Law, but rather as lore, as a nexus of inherited habits and attitudes that we honor because of their inherent value and because of their emotional associations, but that we do not either in theory or practice accept as an infallible guide in all the situations of life and that we cannot by any means impose on our fellow Jews. Under such conditions, it seems impossible to escape from the necessity and responsibility of exercising a large measure of individual judgment and allowing a large measure of individual liberty in applying the principles of our Torah. . . .

We conceive of God's guidance being exercised in other ways than by juridic interpretation of the received Torah and do not shudder with fear at the thought that the Jewish Nation may have to assume a consciously creative share in the development of the Torah by which its conduct is to be guided.[81]

By the time that the Rabbinical Assembly met for its 40th annual convention in June 1940, its membership had grown to 282, which represented an increase of about 40 percent during the preceding decade. The Committee on Jewish Law reported deliberating on a broad range of issues: the use of an organ at Sabbath and festival services; consumption of cooked vegetables and broiled fish in nonkosher restaurants; autopsies; civil marriage; birth control; whether a physician may act as a *mohel*; and the question of relief for the *agunah* (a women whose husband has disappeared or abandoned her without having granted her a Jewish divorce), a problem that had been troubling the assembly since the first years of its existence.

The convention theme, the state of the rabbinate, afforded an opportunity for serious self-examination. Rabbi Morris Adler of Congregation Shaare Zedek in Detroit reminded his colleagues:

. . . whereas in our day of specialization every profession has contracted the area of its intensive study and operation, the office of the rabbi has, on the contrary, assumed new and multiple duties. . . . He is, or is expected to be, at once scholar, teacher, priest, pastor, preacher, administrator, communal-leader, social worker and ambassador of good-will. To him come many and diverse appeals for assistance, for counsel . . . leadership. . . . In the brief span of a fortnight a rabbi, to give a concrete example, has been approached on behalf of the Yiddish Scientific institute, the Zionist organization, the publication of a Biblical encyclopedia, a B'nai B'rith project, the Federation of Polish Jews and the Agudath Israel. Nor is the appeal exclusively for financial aid. The rabbi is urged to take part in the leadership of these numerous causes.

Adler argued that the rabbi could not remain aloof from "the multitudinous manifestations of Jewish life in the community" nor "from the social and

---

[81]Ibid., pp. 31–39.

cultural movements of American society. . . . In the desire to preserve the character and strength of the synagogue [the rabbi] must seek to guide, to channel and inform with something of his spirit, the streams of Jewish life that course outside of the synagogue."[82]

Given the reality of the expanding responsibilities of rabbis, Mordecai Kaplan proposed a division of labor:

> It will not be possible for the rabbi, whose official duties bind him to the synagogue, to keep up with the growing needs of Jewish life. . . . The principle of division of labor would have to be applied to the function of the rabbi. Some rabbis would serve congregations, others would specialize in educational work, and still others in the various types of communal endeavor. . . . It will be necessary for men with a rabbinic training and outlook to serve in administrative capacities in every phase of Jewish activity. . . . When Jewish institutions come to prefer as administrators those who have had an intensive Jewish training, the entire trend of Jewish life will be transformed from one of decline to one of ascent.[83]

The Quest for an Ideology

Cyrus Adler saw the Seminary as an institution

> for the teaching and promotion of Jewish learning . . . to create a learned Rabbinate who will use this learning to a religious purpose—the promotion and practice of Traditional Judaism. . . . The Seminary has not modified its prayerbook, it has not changed the calendar, it has not altered the dietary laws . . . and although some of its founders and some of its graduates have, without protest from the Seminary, attempted changes in the ritual, the Seminary itself has never adopted or approved of any of these changes.

While Adler accepted Schechter's view that "the Seminary must always shelter men of different types of mind," he expressed the hope that what had happened to Schechter would happen to those who came forth from the school: "At one time in his life, [Schechter] was accounted a Liberal, [but] as the years passed [he] became more conservative."[84]

While some Seminary graduates may indeed have become more conservative, with the passage of time the greater number became more liberal. This tendency was due only in part to the cultural climate of twentieth-century America and the demands of congregants. By far the greatest influence on Seminary students and graduates in terms of their liberalization was the teachings of Mordecai M. Kaplan. During his one-year tenure (1932–1933) as president of the Rabbinical Assembly, Kaplan delivered an address to his colleagues on the subject of "The Place of Dogma in Judaism," in which he urged them to reorient their thinking from the past to the present and future:

---

[82]*PRA*, 1940, pp. 89–92.
[83]Ibid., pp. 288, 289.
[84]*United Synagogue Recorder*, Vol. 3, No. 4, Oct. 1923.

If we want to render the Jewish religion articulate and communicable, nothing could be so pointless as to state the beliefs we hold concerning the Jewish civilization of the past. . . . [They cannot] serve as a definition of what the Jews really mean to do with their Judaism. That can only be set forth in terms of "wants" on which all Jews can unite. . . . The affirmations of Judaism would no longer have to be assent to facts, the truths of which are often challenged by reason. . . . Rather they would set forth what [they] expect of [their] civilization, if it is to inspire [them] to perpetuate it, to enrich it, and to make it a source of blessing to mankind.[85]

Samuel Rosenblatt, among the most traditionalist of Conservative rabbis, maintained that "Judaism may be a civilization as Professor Kaplan describes it," but that "belief in God and his Torah . . . is the center of gravity which cannot be disturbed without danger to the entire structure." Asserting that the lack of a "clearly formulated creed" was the cause of Judaism's weakness at present, he exhorted his colleagues to clarify their views, "the dogmas we subscribe to." He concluded: "There are few thinkers as eminently fitted to this task as Professor Kaplan."[86]

Kaplan did define his views in his magnum opus, *Judaism as a Civilization*, published in 1934, but they were hardly to Rabbi Rosenblatt's liking. A work that exerted singular influence on Conservative rabbis and laymen, it came in for wide-ranging criticism as well. In analyzing "The Current Versions of Judaism" in the volume, Kaplan gave no place of its own to Conservative Judaism, discussing it only as "the right wing of Reformism" and again as "the left wing of Neo-Orthodoxy." He completely ignored the considerable body of Conservative literature fashioned by his colleagues—papers delivered at United Synagogue and Rabbinical Assembly conventions, articles in periodicals, discussions and correspondence in which he himself had participated. The views of Israel Friedlaender received but fleeting notice; those of Louis Ginzberg, Louis Finkelstein, Jacob Kohn, Eugene Kohn, Israel Levinthal, and Louis Epstein, none at all!

Rabbi Max Arzt, who identified himself as "a disciple of Dr. Kaplan," hailed the volume as a "courageous, comprehensive analysis of the complex problems facing Jews and Judaism in our day," expressing the belief "that no creative reconstruction of Jewish life will come unless we reckon with the basic issues so splendidly formulated and analyzed therein." Still, Arzt criticized Kaplan's ambivalence toward religion and its place in Jewish civilization, warning that "Judaism becomes an empty shell" without the religious dimension. Arzt was also critical of Kaplan's demoting "the mitzvot to the primitive status of folkways," an act whose effect was to "destroy their main sanction and purpose as forms of group expression dedicated to God and uniting Israel with its God." Arzt went on to summarize the dominant centrist position in Conservative Judaism as he saw it:

---

[85]*PRA*, 1930–1932, pp. 305–306.
[86]Ibid., pp. 309–310.

Dr. Kaplan says that revision of the entire system of Jewish custom is imperative.
. . . What we need is not an official revision but rather some agreement as to what
forms of observance we should emphasize. . . . Conservative Judaism aims to do
just this thing. It does not announce its negations. It proclaims its affirmations.
It stresses Sabbath observance, the dietary laws, the retention of Hebrew in prayer
and in Jewish education, and the restoration of Palestine. There is so much in our
law that is vital, soul-stirring and full of aesthetic possibilities that we should not
be concerned about the inevitable obsolescence of a few mitzvot. . . .

Judaism is essentially Halachic in its nature and development. . . . Judaism will
always demand of the individual to exert all efforts to order his life according to
the Torah rather than order the Torah to fit exactly into his personal desires and
tastes. Therefore, I differ with Dr. Kaplan who would eliminate the concept of
Law from Mitzvot. Such a suggestion would violate the criteria which he himself
suggests. It would destroy Judaism's continuity, its individuality and its organic
character.[87]

The most representative and comprehensive formulations of Conservative Judaism in its period of early maturation (1920–1945) were provided
by two young Seminary-trained rabbis: Louis Finkelstein, who went on to
become the head of the movement during the period of its greatest growth
(1940–1972), and Robert Gordis, who became Conservative Judaism's most
articulate ideologist. In 1927 Finkelstein focused on those elements which
he saw as common to all Conservative Jews:

1. *The Concept of God*   We are a unit in our understanding of the ultimate basis
of all religious life and insist that only in our faith, which is frankly based on our
emotions and intuition, but which we seek to formulate with proper recognition
of the scientific facts which have been established, is there room for the conception
of God that can remain living and effective in our children's minds.

2. *Our Attitude Toward the Torah*   Judaism is a developing religion, which has
undergone an historical and definable change through the periods of the prophets
and the rabbis; this change was not one of deterioration and ossification but of
growth, self-expression, and foliation. . . . Because we regard the Torah as pro-
phetically inspired . . . the legalism of the rabbis as the finest and highest expression of human ethics, we accept the written and oral Law as binding and
authoritative. . . . But we are entirely unwilling to cajole or intimidate our
following or our children into being loyal to the Torah through threats and the
fear of punishment.

---

[87]Max Arzt, "Dr. Kaplan's Philosophy," *PRA*, 1939, pp. 195–219. For an appreciation of
the "enduring impact" of *Judaism as a Civilization*, see Myer S. Kripke's article in *Conservative
Judaism*, Mar./Apr. 1981, pp. 17–23. "[It] was certainly *a* (if not *the*) highwater mark in
American Jewish self-study. . . . [Its] critique of Reform was one of the reasons . . . a major
one, for the drastic change in Reform in the last 40 years or so. . . . Conservative Judaism
particularly bears the imprint of his teaching, his thought, his progressivism, his bold encounter with the realities of Jewish life at every significant point, ritual, ideology, instruction and
organization. But Conservative Judaism did not become Reconstructionist. Where he had
most earnestly hoped to succeed, his central theological ideas were held at intellectual arm's
length, even though his influence was readily acknowledged." For a critique of Kaplan's
theology by his most gifted disciple, Milton Steinberg, see *PRA*, 1949, pp. 379–380.

We are drawn to the Torah [by] love for its ceremonies, its commandments, its rules, and its spirit. We delight in its study, and find in it comfort and consolation, discipline and guidance.

3. *Our Attitude Toward Change in Ceremonial*   If the shifting of values and the introduction of new devices will actually bring Jews back to God, to the Torah, and to the Synagogue, they will doubtless be accepted. . . . As to the proposed innovations and new interpretations, there is none of us so bigoted as to refuse to cooperate with those who are attempting them, provided always that the ultimate purpose of change is to strengthen the attachment of Israel to the whole of the Torah, and that it does not defeat its own end by striking at the fundamentals of Judaism.

4. *Our Attitudes Toward Israel*   Israel is a great and ancient people; it has done great things and there is no reason for doubting its ability to create further. We love it as our people. We recognize that it has weaknesses . . . our loyalty to it does not depend on our belief in its singular excellence. We decry any attempt to establish loyalty to it on such basis. . . .

5. *Our Attitude Toward Palestine*   We want to see Palestine, . . . for which we have an intuitional, unreasoning and mystic love . . . rebuilt as the spiritual center of Israel. . . . We want Eretz Israel established as a Jewish community; if possible as an autonomous one.

6. *Our Attitude Toward the Hebrew Language*   We are entirely sympathetic to the establishment of Hebrew as the language of conversation, Jewish literature and learning. . . . We find ourselves in opposition to those who have permitted the excision of Hebrew from their prayerbook, and have dropped it as a subject for instruction in their schools. A Hebrewless Judaism we conceive to be an impossibility.

7. *The Seminary*   Through it we have become not only comrades in arms, but also brothers. . . . Within our ranks there is wide difference of opinion . . . [which should not] justify any separation in our ranks, in view of our substantial unity of outlook and the difficulty in serving our cause even when we are together. . . . We are all of us "Seminary Men."[88]

Fourteen years later, Robert Gordis presented his formulation of Judaism as "A Program for American Judaism," a chapter in his book *The Jew Faces a New World.*[89] Conceding that Conservative Judaism's critics were not altogether unjust in calling it a watered-down Orthodoxy or a timid Reform, because it lacked a platform, Gordis attributed this lack to the

---

[88]*PRA*, 1927, pp. 42–53.

[89]Robert Gordis, *The Jew Faces a New World* (New York, 1941), pp. 195–214. The chapter served as the basis for Gordis's widely read *Conservative Judaism: An American Philosophy,* published for the National Academy of Adult Jewish Studies of the Jewish Theological Seminary by Behrman House in 1945. In the foreword, Gordis stated: "For a variety of reasons, [Conservative] scholars and leaders have until recently been loath to elaborate its philosophy. . . . Even this modest attempt to present a survey of Conservative Judaism has been a difficult and challenging task, with few sources and virtually no precedents to guide the writer."

American character of the movement, which was "pragmatic rather than theoretical." He then went on to point to a number of thinkers who had shaped his own understanding of Conservative Judaism: Zacharias Frankel, Solomon Schechter, Ahad Ha'am (Asher Ginzberg), Israel Friedlaender, Louis Ginzberg, and Mordecai M. Kaplan. The influence of Kaplan is clearly discernible in many of Gordis's formulations, particularly in his definition of Judaism as the evolving religious civilization of the Jewish people:

> The evolving character of Judaism: Judaism has never been static; it has always adapted itself to new thought and new conditions. . . .
>
> Judaism is the culture or civilization of the Jewish People. It is not merely a religion, in the sense of a few articles of belief or a handful of practices, as Reform teaches, or a longer list of beliefs and practices, as maintained by orthodoxy. It is a complete culture or civilization, possessing all the varied attributes of language and literature, art, music, customs and law, institutions and history. . . .
>
> Since it is the civilization of the Jewish people, Judaism must have a locale, one corner of the world where it can grow and flourish. . . . Therefore, Palestine, as the center of the Jewish people, must be the living center of Judaism, and the more strongly and firmly Jewish life is established in the Homeland, the richer Jewish life will everywhere be. . . .
>
> Judaism has many aspects, but religion is primary. The recognition of God in the world and the drive for ethical perfection are the two great Jewish contributions to the world—two that are really one. . . .
>
> Jewish nationalism and religion are the body and soul of a living organism.
>
> Jewish nationalism without religion is in danger of becoming . . . destructive and brutal. . . . Jewish religion without nationalism is a disembodied ghost, without vitality and staying power. . . . Judaism as the evolving religious civilization of the Jewish people—therein lies the distinctive attitude of Conservative Judaism that makes it . . . the most vital and promising tendency for the future, if it adheres to its program with intelligence.[90]

THE FINKELSTEIN ERA (1940-1972)

Following Cyrus Adler's death in 1940, the man chosen to succeed him was Louis Finkelstein, a professor of Talmud and theology who had become Adler's assistant in 1934 and provost of the Seminary three years later. Finkelstein was born in Cincinnati and grew up in Brooklyn, the son of a respected Orthodox rabbi who provided him with his early talmudic education. Finkelstein went on to earn a B.A. from the College of the City of New

---

[90]Ibid.

York and a Ph.D. from Columbia University, as well as ordination from the Seminary. A charismatic personality, Finkelstein made the Seminary the fountainhead of Conservative Judaism, while he himself became the acknowledged leader of the Conservative movement. The years of his stewardship saw Conservative Judaism emerge as the largest Jewish religious grouping on the American scene, with its influence extending into the community at large.

The factors leading to the growth of the Conservative movement were closely linked to social forces that were at work in American life in the years following World War II. The postwar phenomenon of suburbanization greatly affected Jews, drawing them in large numbers to new communities. The need to establish roots and secure status, combined with the elevated prestige of religion in general, produced a climate conducive to the establishment of new synagogues.

The Conservative synagogue, which by the late 1930s had become a "synagogue-center" offering religious, cultural, and social programming for the entire family, was ideally suited to meet the needs of Jews in the rapidly growing suburban communities. The Conservative mode of worship was one that returning Jewish servicemen had experienced in the armed forces, and Conservatism's broad ideological framework made it appealing to young families coming from a variety of religious backgrounds. In addition, as the Jewish religious movement that had had the longest and strongest identification with Zionism,[91] Conservative Judaism benefited from American Jewry's identification with the new State of Israel.

Congregations and Schools

In March 1949, 365 congregations were affiliated with the United Synagogue; by 1954 that number had reached 492—serving a total of more than 200,000 Jewish families. The 600 affiliated sisterhoods had a membership of some 160,000. The Rabbinical Assembly saw its membership grow from 282 in 1940 to 600 strong in 1954.

At the center of most suburban synagogues stood the congregational school. As the result of an aggressive program carried out by the Commission on Jewish Education of the United Synagogue, directed by Abraham E. Millgram, the complexion of Conservative Jewish education changed dramatically in the course of a decade. Curricula were planned, tested, evaluated, and published. A steady flow of publications included textbooks in Hebrew and in English that reflected modern pedagogical methods as

---

[91]See Abraham J. Karp, "Reactions to Zionism and the State of Israel in the American Jewish Religious Community," *Journal of Jewish Sociology,* Vol. 8, No. 2 (Dec. 1966), pp. 150–174.

well as a Conservative religious orientation; preschool materials; parent-education guides; audiovisual aids; and school-administration manuals. With the cooperation of the Teachers Institute of the Seminary, which had been educating teachers for religious schools since 1906, a teacher-training program for nursery schools was established. Sunday school education was eliminated (save for the first two grades), replaced by the congregational or Hebrew school meeting two or more afternoons as well as Sunday.

The highly successful United Synagogue Youth movement (USY) first developed in the Midwest, as did Camp Ramah, which was established by the Chicago Council of the United Synagogue. In describing the camp, Rabbi Ralph Simon, chairman of the camp's Program and Operations Committee, said: "Creative self-expression will be the goal of the camp program, and the religious approach of Conservative Judaism will pervade the spirit of the camp." The official language of the camp was Hebrew, and the program included classes in Bible and Hebrew literature as well as athletics and the arts; services were conducted daily and on the Sabbath.

The first Conservative Jewish day school, offering Judaic as well as secular studies, opened in 1950 in Rockaway Park, New York, organized by Rabbi Robert Gordis. This was the beginning of a nationwide effort to provide a more intensive Jewish education than could be offered in the congregational supplementary schools, an effort that produced the network of Solomon Schechter Day Schools.

There were important developments in the area of liturgy during this period. In 1946, the Joint Prayer Book Commission of the Rabbinical Assembly and the United Synagogue published the *Sabbath and Festival Prayer Book,* edited by Rabbi Morris Silverman. Robert Gordis, chairman of the commission, identified the three fundamental principles that had guided the work of editing and compilation: continuity with tradition; relevance to the needs and ideals of the present generation; and intellectual integrity. In conformity with the first principle, the prayer book followed traditional liturgy. The second principle found expression in the modern translation and the expansion of the liturgy to include responsive readings and hymns culled from various sources, both ancient and modern. In obedience to the last principle, a number of minor changes were made, such as reference to sacrifices as a past rather than a future obligation, and switching from a negative to a positive formulation in the preliminary blessings —from "thou hast not made me a woman . . . slave . . . gentile" to "thou hast made me in thy image . . . free . . . an Israelite."

The Rabbis

The 1950s and 1960s were the golden age of the American rabbinate. Religion was esteemed as a significant force in American life, and the synagogue was universally recognized as the preeminent institution of the Jewish community. Rabbis, therefore, were accorded wide respect and were able to exert influence far beyond their congregations.

The American rabbi became an extraordinarily busy man, and particularly so the Conservative rabbi. While the Orthodox rabbi preached on Saturday morning, and the Reform rabbi on Friday evening, the Conservative rabbi preached at the two major services. The Orthodox rabbi dealt with *b'nai mitzvah* and the Reform rabbi with confirmands, but the Conservative rabbi dealt with both. The Conservative rabbi needed to work hard to retain his status in the institutions serving the most parochial Jewish interests, e.g., the *vaad hakashrut,* where the credibility of his Orthodox colleague was not in question, even as he struggled for acceptance as a significant participant in interfaith activities, in which his Reform colleague had long been the recognized spokesman for the Jewish community.

Here is how one Conservative rabbi serving a large congregation in the Northeast described his activities in 1964:

Preacher   Two sermons weekly at the late Friday evening and the Sabbath morning services, as well as at all holiday services.

Teacher   Mondays: Men's Club Downtown Study Group, at noon. Subject: "The Living Talmud."

Tuesdays: Confirmation class and post-Confirmation class. Subjects: "Conservative Judaism"; "History of Religions."

Wednesdays: Three six-week semesters of Adult Education Institute, two courses each session. Subjects: "The Legacy of Solomon Schechter—Conservative Judaism"; "The Wisdom Literature of the Bible."

Saturdays: Talmud study group, the tractate Berakhot. Monthly young-marrieds discussion group. Biweekly Sabbath-afternoon LTF study group.

Sundays: Jewish current events discussion groups at post-minyan breakfasts.

Administrator   The congregation dedicated its new synagogue building in June 1962 after four years of planning, fund raising, and building, in all of which the rabbi participated.

Attended meetings of congregational board, Ritual Committee, School Committee, Adult Education Committee. Conducted weekly staff meetings. Wrote weekly column for congregational bulletin.

Ecclesiastical functionary   Officiated at forty-two weddings and thirty-nine funerals, all in the congregational family. Premarital interviews; attendance at wedding receptions; visited with bereaved families before funeral; officiated at one or more services at mourners' home, conducting a study session. Attended daily morning services on Sunday, Monday, and Thursday mornings. Officiated at unveilings, *Brit Milah,* and *mezuzah* ceremonies in new homes.

Jewish community activities   On boards of Jewish Community Federation, Jewish Family Service, Israel Bonds, Day School, *Vaad Hakashrut.*

Community activities   Member, Mayor's Advisory Board; Committee on Religion and Race; boards of Association for the United Nations, Friends of the Public Library.

Weekly radio program, *From a Rabbi's Study.*

National activities   Member Executive Council, Rabbinical Assembly; Editorial Board, *Conservative Judaism*; Rabbinic Cabinet, Jewish Theological Seminary; Executive Council, American Jewish Historical Society; Publications Committee, Jewish Publication Society.

Pastor   Congregants felt free to call upon the rabbi for counseling at all hours.[92]

While the postwar period was one of dynamism and growth for Conservative Judaism, there were problems as well. Rabbi Max Gelb of White Plains, New York, for example, saw his congregation grow fourfold within a short period of time. "I have had to adjust myself to a new congregation . . . every few years," he told colleagues at the 1949 Rabbinical Assembly convention. More disturbing to him than increased numbers, however, was the impact of the suburban milieu: "The pull of the Christian environment is very powerful. Every Christmas presents a crisis in our school. There are scores of homes in which children experience a Christmas tree and parents argue with the rabbi whether it is a national or religious holiday."[93]

The task of winning over members to religious observance and genuine commitment called for unceasing effort, as the experience of Rabbi Reuben J. Magil of Temple Beth El in Harrisburg, Pennsylvania, testifies. His congregation held services on a daily basis—morning and evening—conducted Hebrew and Sunday schools, and had the usual gamut of congregational activities, but creative efforts were required to maintain it all. Thus, even though breakfast was served after the morning service to help assure a daily *minyan,* members still had to be drafted by the brotherhood's *minyan* committee. The Saturday-morning service had an abridged *musaf* and the junior congregation was brought in to participate. Simhat Torah was revived by the introduction of a consecration service for children beginning their Hebrew studies. To assure a respectable attendance at the Megillah reading, a "sort of supper and carnival, the Annual Family Party," was inaugurated. Finally, to attract increased attendance, the Hebrew school graduation was moved from Sunday to the final Friday-evening sermon service.[94]

---

[92]See Karp, "The Conservative Rabbi," in Marcus and Peck (eds.), op. cit., pp. 148–149. The rabbi was Abraham J. Karp, Temple Beth El, Rochester, N.Y.
[93]*PRA,* 1949, pp. 178–180.
[94]Ibid., pp. 169–173.

A source of deep frustration to many Conservative rabbis was the relative disinterest of synagogue members in worship, unless it was linked to social activity, such as a bar mitzvah. A 1950 survey conducted by the United Synagogue was very revealing in its documentation of members' attitudes.[95] Some 60 percent of the respondents considered the Friday-night prayers to be the "main Sabbath service." Nonetheless, the survey noted, attendance at Friday-night services "is at an appalling disproportion with congregational membership." As for Saturday-morning services, only 17 percent of respondents attended "quite regularly or often," while 77 percent attended "never or once in a while."

Another problem area in many Conservative synagogues was the absence of dignity in congregational demeanor and in relations with rabbis. This problem had existed since the earliest immigrant days, but the postwar move to suburbia and the proliferation of congregations made it all the more acute. Well-meaning men and women, new to congregational leadership, were often unaware of their responsibility for the maintenance of congregational dignity. At its 1952 convention, the United Synagogue asked its affiliated congregations to adopt a "Proposed Guide to Standards for Congregational Life." Among the standards adopted were those pertaining to rabbinic authority, Sabbath observance, *kashrut,* rites and ceremonies, dignity in fund raising, and relationships with other congregations and the community.

The Seminary and the Movement

Throughout this period, Louis Finkelstein was the undisputed central figure of the Conservative movement. While his views (which, like Schechter's, became even more traditional) were often challenged, none could gainsay his scholarship, his administrative skills, and his contributions toward developing an ideology for Conservative Judaism. Finkelstein's appointment to national commissions by Presidents Eisenhower and Kennedy and appearance on the cover of *Time* magazine helped to make him the most widely known and respected Jewish religious leader in America.

Chancellor (his title after 1951) Finkelstein believed not only that Conservative Judaism was the authentic expression of traditional Judaism and that "the Judaism of the next generation will be saved by us," he was also convinced that Judaism had a vital message for all of America. It was in that light that he launched the Conference on Science, Philosophy and Religion in order to give Judaism a platform in the academic world, and

---

[95]*Report on the Findings of the National Survey on Synagogue Attendance, Children's Jewish Education, Adult Jewish Education, and Youth Work in Conservative Congregations Undertaken by the United Synagogue of America,* 1950.

the Institute for Religious and Social Studies, to provide an ecumenical setting in which Judaism could join with the other great faiths in helping to establish the moral climate of America. The "Eternal Light" programs on radio and "Frontiers of Faith" programs on television depicted the riches of the Jewish tradition to a broad general audience. The prestige that accrued to the Seminary from the success of these programs gave strength to the movement as a whole and status to its associated congregations.

Finkelstein attracted gifted co-workers, chief among them Rabbis Simon Greenberg, Max Arzt, and Moshe Davis. Greenberg came to the Seminary from Philadelphia, where he had fashioned Congregation Har Zion as the model Conservative synagogue, noted especially for its educational system. As provost and vice-chancellor, his most notable contribution was the geographic expansion of the Seminary: the founding of the University of Judaism in Los Angeles, and the American Student Center and the Schocken Institute for Jewish Research in Jerusalem. Moshe Davis, the first American student to receive a doctorate from the Hebrew University, was chosen, on his ordination from the Seminary, to strengthen and expand its program of education. As dean of the Teachers Institute and provost, he created and expanded programs for disseminating Hebrew language and culture, including the flourishing Camp Ramah network and special programs in Israel. The Jewish Museum became an important component of New York's cultural life and, through traveling exhibits, extended its program nationwide. Max Arzt left his flourishing congregation in Scranton, Pennsylvania, to build the financial base for the Seminary's and the movement's expansion. The joint campaign that he launched was Seminary-centered and reached out to the Conservative constituency through the congregations. Arzt succeeded not only in establishing a sound fund-raising vehicle, but also in developing a cadre of Conservative lay leaders who were devoted to the Seminary as the heart of Conservative Judaism.

Finkelstein focused on rebuilding the faculty. To the Schechter-chosen senior professors—Louis Ginzberg, Alexander Marx, Mordecai M. Kaplan —he added H.L. Ginsberg, Robert Gordis, Boaz Cohen, and Hillel Bavli. Finkelstein brought Saul Lieberman from Jerusalem, Shalom Spiegel from the Jewish Institute of Religion, and Abraham Joshua Heschel from Hebrew Union College.

In addition to the Rabbinical School, the Teachers Institute, and the College of Jewish Studies, the Seminary expanded its mandate to include the Cantors Institute, the College of Jewish Music, and a graduate school offering master's and doctoral programs in all areas of Jewish studies. Offshoots of the professional schools were the Educators Assembly, which brought high professional standards to the field of Jewish education, and the Cantors Assembly, which transformed the American cantor from a pulpit-riveted leader of prayer to a clergyman engaged in the educational, cultural, and pastoral activities of the congregation.

Within the organizational structure of the movement itself a struggle for parity was waged between the Seminary, the United Synagogue, and the Rabbinical Assembly. The posture of the Seminary administration and faculty was staunchly traditionalist (Kaplan always excepted), with the more liberal members yielding to the authority of the chancellor and the rector, Saul Lieberman, who succeeded Louis Ginzberg as head of the Talmud faculty. The course of study emphasized rabbinics, and the Rabbinical School remained central to the institution.

The explosive growth of the United Synagogue in the postwar years, under the imaginative leadership of Rabbi Albert I. Gordon, was welcomed and aided by the Seminary. But when Gordon accorded a central role to lay leaders in a projected formulation of an ideology for Conservative Judaism, his attempt was frustrated by the Seminary administration. Finkelstein argued that ideological formulation should be the exclusive concern of rabbis and scholars who had adequate training in the Judaic sources. When similar confrontations led to Gordon's resignation, Simon Greenberg assumed his post, while also retaining his position in the Seminary administration.

Similarly, in 1952, when the Rabbinical Assembly began to pursue vigorously a solution to the problem of the *agunah* that the traditionalists on the Seminary faculty considered a departure from strict *halakhic* process, Finkelstein insisted that the Seminary be given a partnership role in the endeavor. The resultant Joint Law Conference succeeded in removing decision making in this matter from the rabbinic group. It was only when the conference was dissolved in 1968 that the Rabbinical Assembly adopted what it considered an adequate solution to the problem.

In a movement that had from its inception accepted and permitted diversity, and was committed to both tradition and change, the Seminary's self-chosen role was that of upholder of the tradition and restraining influence on those impatient for change. Perhaps the greatest contribution of the Seminary in the Finkelstein years was to demand spiritual content and *halakhic* discipline of a movement growing at so rapid a pace that sociological needs threatened to overwhelm theological imperatives. And perhaps its gravest mistake was doing this in so imperious a manner as to inhibit the evolutionary expansion of *halakhic* parameters in the 1940s, 1950s, and 1960s.

Within the Rabbinical Assembly itself, the question of *halakhic* development continued to engender controversy, with the mainline Conservative rabbis refusing to go beyond interpretation and the progressives urging "legislation." The disciples of Mordecai M. Kaplan proclaimed ever more aggressively their belief that Judaism had entered a post-*halakhic* age in which standards rather than laws obtained. The renaming of the Committee on Jewish Law as the Committee on Jewish Law and Standards in 1948 had been a symbolic accommodation to this view, though to the frustration of the Reconstructionists, no substantial changes had ensued. The controversy came to a head at the 1958 Rabbinical Assembly convention, at which Rabbis Jack Cohen, Jacob Agus, and Isaac Klein presented papers on "Theoretical Evolution of Jewish Law,"[96] from left, centrist, and rightist positions respectively. Rabbi Cohen recommended that the Rabbinical Assembly "declare publicly that ritual can no longer be a matter of law" and that synagogue members be "encouraged to participate in an effort to develop standards for the entire community." Rabbi Klein reacted strongly: "Rabbi Cohen's paper is a philosophy of *halachah* to do away with *halachah*. . . . We have no common platform." For his part, Rabbi Agus attempted to mesh both viewpoints—*halakhah* and standards—into an integrated whole. The issues were highlighted but remained unresolved.

The first full-scale study of Conservative Judaism, published by sociologist Marshall Sklare in 1955, identified sources of strength, as well as shortcomings, in the movement. Sklare's probing analysis, which viewed social and economic factors as more significant determinants of behavior than theology or ideology, caused discomfort to many Conservative leaders, who were all too aware of the unresolved tensions within the movement. Sklare's basic argument was as follows:

> (1) Conservatism represents a common pattern of acculturation—a kind of social adjustment—which has been arrived at by lay people. It is seen by them as a "halfway house" between Reform and Orthodoxy. It possesses no ideological system in the usual sense of the term. (2) The lack of ideology does not constitute a serious problem for most laymen, but it has harassed many rabbis. (3) There has been a somewhat greater interest in recent years in ideological problems. This is traceable to the operation of social forces, and to organizational trends in the Jewish community. (4) The resistances and obstacles to ideological clarification are formidable. (5) The rabbis have been very hesitant about officially sanctioning any departures from Jewish tradition. . . .

> Although a few attempts have been made by the rabbis to develop a distinctive Conservative ideology and to obtain consensus, such endeavors have met with only very limited success. They have hardly been able to describe what is actually in existence in the Conservative movement, or to relate present realities to theoretical principles. The functionaries have not succeeded in spreading the few ideas which they have evolved among the laity. The concepts which they have presented are largely improvised. They express the needs and training of the religious specialists rather than of the mass of Conservative Jewry. The "ideology" has not

[96]*PRA*, 1958, pp. 81–117.

as yet reached the stage of justifying—with any degree of sophistication—various institutional imperatives, although this is its present aim.[97]

Sklare paid tribute to Conservative Jewry for having made a "notable contribution to survivalism and . . . providing a significant institutional framework for a possible revivified Judaism." "Perhaps," he concluded, "Conservatism will not rest upon this accomplishment but will come to play a new and as yet unforeseeable role in the Jewish life of the future."[98]

THE COHEN ERA (1972-1985)

Upon his retirement, Louis Finkelstein was succeeded as chancellor by Gerson D. Cohen, a Seminary graduate and professor of history at the Seminary and at Columbia University. Important changes were taking place at the Seminary and in the movement at the time of Cohen's accession. A new faculty, the majority American-born, Seminary-educated, was replacing the European-trained giants. For rabbis this spelled the end of a special attitude of reverence for teachers who were "masters" and its replacement by one of simple respect for colleagues who were also scholars.

A new kind of student was entering the Rabbinical School. In earlier days the great majority had come from Orthodox backgrounds, while in the post-World War II era an increasing number came from Conservative homes, products of Camp Ramah and day schools—not an insignificant number of them sons of Conservative rabbis. The late 1960s brought a new group. Of the 30 students in the class of 1969, only four had attended a day school through high school, and only one had attended a yeshivah while in college. A member of the class described them as "virtually unfamiliar with the intensity of Jewish tradition, its complex web of law and custom, its texts . . . until [they] reached the Seminary."[99]

Tradition and Change

In the classic expression of the Conservative commitment, "tradition and change," the old administration had given nearly all emphasis to tradition. Under Chancellor Cohen, change was elevated to a position of parity, and the liberal elements in the faculty felt free to express their views. The primary focus of this new posture was the role of women in Judaism, especially their participation in public worship and ritual. On

---

[97]Sklare, op. cit., pp. 229, 241.
[98]Ibid., pp. 250, 252.
[99]Martin N. Levin, "2001: Blueprint for the Rabbinate in the Twenty-First Century," *PRA*, 1979, pp. 115–116.

the congregational level, pressure for equal participation of women was growing, and the issue was being vigorously debated throughout the movement. A 1955 ruling of the Rabbinical Assembly already made it possible for women to be called to the Torah for *aliyot*. Supporters of women's equality were further strengthened when the Rabbinical Assembly law committee issued a ruling *(takkanah)* in 1973 allowing women to be counted to a *minyan*.

It was not surprising, therefore, when the 1973 United Synagogue convention adopted a resolution urging admission of women to the Rabbinical School of the Seminary. Four years later the Rabbinical Assembly convention called on Chancellor Cohen to appoint a committee to study the matter. He did so, establishing the Commission for the Study of the Ordination of Women as Rabbis, with himself as chairman and 14 commission members drawn from the faculty, rabbinate, and laity representing the gamut of views in the Conservative movement. Regional meetings at which opinions were aired and testimony taken disclosed wide-ranging support for the admission of women to the Rabbinical School. The commission's report, issued in 1979, argued that there were no *halakhic* barriers to women's ordination. The vote of 11–3 in favor of ordination was an appeal to the faculty to follow suit, for it was the faculty's legal prerogative to make the decision.[100]

Cohen assumed personal leadership in the struggle to win approval from a faculty that was so bitterly divided on the issue it took four years for the crucial vote to take place. On October 24, 1983, with some of the traditionalists absenting themselves, the faculty voted 34 to 8, with one abstention, to admit women into the rabbinical program of study. In May 1985 Amy Eilberg became the first woman to receive ordination from the Seminary; a month later, at its annual convention, the Rabbinical Assembly accepted her to membership.

Calling the faculty decision "one of our proudest achievements," Cohen spelled out its significance in a letter to colleagues.

> It is important because this faculty had the courage to confront directly what had become to many a challenge to the relevance of *halakhah* in the contemporary world. . . . Perhaps, most important, this decision provides a paradigm for the way *halakhah* evolves within Conservative Judaism. The method is not new—countless examples can be found in the deliberations over the years of our Committee on Jewish Law and Standards—but it took an issue on which public opinion was so strong, and so divided, to familiarize our laity with the procedure, and with the flexibility within limits which it permits our movement. Most

---

[100]For more on women's ordination see *Conservative Judaism*, Summer 1979, pp. 62–80; *PRA*, 1979, pp. 217–251; Robert Gordis, "The Ordination of Women," *Midstream*, Aug.-Sept. 1980. The most comprehensive presentation of the issues is in "Women as Rabbis—A Many-Sided Examination of All Aspects," *Judaism*, Winter 1984, pp. 6–90.

important, it enabled the Seminary to assert its authority as a leading force in determining the direction of Conservative Judaism.[101]

A group of rabbis and laymen of a traditionalist bent, who regarded the ordination decision as a deviation from *halakhah* in both substance and process, organized themselves as the Union for Traditional Conservative Judaism. But the great majority of rabbis and lay people accepted Cohen's assertion:

> Our decision to ordain women is a prime example of the evolution of *halakhah*. Without controverting Jewish law, we have adapted it to the religious and ethical norms of a new generation. . . . I believe deeply that . . . we behaved as our ancestors did on occasion when they found new forms of response for new challenges.[102]

Robert Gordis evaluated the decision and its consequences this way:

> If history is any guide at all, it is clear that this move, important as it is, will prove neither as world-shaking as its proponents believe, nor as catastrophic as its opponents maintain. . . .

> However welcome this accession of new strength and idealism may be, [the ordination of women] will not drastically transform the character and function of the rabbinate. . . .

> One important by-product of women's ordination will be the beginning of the end of the psychological reign of terror exerted by contemporary Orthodoxy over some rabbis and laymen in the Conservative movement. . . . By this act Conservative Judaism will have demonstrated that the Jewish tradition is truly viable and as sensitive to human needs and aspirations in the present as it has been in the past.[103]

In 1979 the Seminary had published the *Guide to Jewish Religious Practice* of Rabbi Isaac Klein, the leading traditional scholar in the movement. The book grew out of a course on "Laws and Standards for Religious Observance" that Louis Finkelstein had invited Rabbi Klein to conduct, beginning in 1959. The volume, which Chancellor Cohen described in his foreword "as written in the authentic spirit of the Conservative Movement," was intended, its author stated, as a "guide for those congregations that are affiliated with the United Synagogue and the World Council of Synagogues, as well as for individuals in accord with their principles." In spirit and form, the *Guide to Jewish Religious Practice* followed the classic codes of the Jewish legal tradition. However, as the author noted, "in preparing this work I insisted on the authority of

---

[101]Gerson D. Cohen, typed letter, Aug. 26, 1985, pp. 1, 4.

[102]Ibid., p. 3.

[103]Robert Gordis, "The Ordination of Women—A History of the Question," *Judaism*, Winter 1984, p. 12.

our Conservative Scholars and on the validity of the practices of our Conservative Congregations."

Cohen continued the Seminary tradition of devotion to Jewish scholarship and commitment to excellence. Under his leadership a new library building was completed, thus making the Seminary's rich resource of books and manuscripts more easily available to students and scholars. Among graduates of the Seminary who did not enter the pulpit rabbinate were young scholars who joined the faculties of leading universities in the United States and Israel. In 1985 members of the Seminary faculty received significant honors: David Weiss-Halivni, professor of Talmud, was awarded the Bialik Prize (the Israeli equivalent of the Pulitzer Prize) for his completed four volumes of a ten-volume series, *Sources and Traditions*; David Roskies received a Guggenheim Fellowship; and Ivan G. Marcus was appointed chairman of the History of Judaism section of the American Academy of Religion.

The United Synagogue

In the immediate post-World War II era, the United Synagogue had played a central role in the expansion of Conservative Judaism, helping to establish new congregations in suburbia, and providing them with guidance in administration, programming, and education. Its joint Commission on Jewish Education, working with the Rabbinical Assembly, had developed curricula, published textbooks, and made the afternoon Hebrew school the central educational institution of the movement. By the 1970s, however, the excitement had spent itself. What remained were mundane realities—retaining congregational loyalties (and dues) and trying to meet growing demands for service with a limited budget. Attracting lay leadership of a high calibre became increasingly difficult, and weakened morale was not helped by the realization that the United Synagogue had been relegated to the status of the least influential component of the triad of Conservative Judaism. Although it continued to participate with the Rabbinical Assembly and the Seminary in addressing the challenges that faced the movement, it remained essentially a synagogue service agency.

Functioning as an effective service agency was a challenge of no small proportion, however. By 1985 a total of 830 congregations, most with men's clubs, sisterhoods, and youth organizations affiliated with the national movement, were being served through 20 regional offices. The number of synagogues in the Sunbelt states was on the rise—65 in California, 48 in Florida—many of them young congregations in new areas, asking for extra guidance and service. The Solomon Schechter Day School Association had 65 affiliates, and United Synagogue Youth claimed the largest membership of any Jewish youth organization in the country.

A mere listing of the United Synagogue's departments and services demonstrates the range of its concerns: Programs; Synagogue Administration; Regions; Education; Israel Affairs and Aliyah; Youth Activities; Community Relations and Public Policy; the Joint Commission on Social Action; Tour Service; Book Service; Committee on Congregational Standards; and *The United Synagogue Review.*

Perhaps the greatest challenge facing the United Synagogue in the eighties was deciding how to respond to the demographic and social changes that were taking place in the Jewish community and in American society at large. Individual congregations were attempting to solve problems posed by growing numbers of divorced and single persons and single-parent families, the mobility of a salaried professional class, and the high rate of intermarriage. The national organization was beginning to coordinate and disseminate the programs and approaches created in the field and to provide guidance in these areas.

The Rabbinical Assembly

Between 1955 and 1985 membership in the Rabbinical Assembly increased threefold—from some 400 to well over 1,200. In that period more than 600 Orthodox and Reform rabbis applied for membership, while fewer than 10 left for other rabbinic associations. In 1980 the Rabbinical Assembly counted 94 members in Israel, 29 in Canada, 11 in Latin America, and 7 in Europe.

New problems and challenges faced the rabbi of the 1970s and 1980s. Congregations grown large in the 1960s were seeking ways to humanize and personalize religious experience. The *havurah,* a product of the Jewish student counterculture movement of the 1960s, was seized upon by a large number of synagogues as one hopeful approach. Rabbi Harold M. Schulweis, who pioneered the use of *havurot* in Congregation Valley Beth Shalom, Encino, California, addressed his colleagues about the matter at the 1973 Rabbinical Assembly convention.

We are challenged to decentralize the synagogue and deprofessionalize Jewish living so that the individual Jew is brought back into the circle of shared Jewish experience. . . . In our congregation, a *havurah* is comprised of a *minyan* of families who have agreed to meet together at least once a month to learn together, to celebrate together and hopefully to form some surrogate for the eroded extended family. . . .

Cerebration must not eclipse celebration. . . . I know what it means for children to see ten Jewish males with hammers and saws helping to build a sukkah . . . the *havurot* plan their own Sedarim . . . they wrestle with the Haggadah and the decision to add and delete . . . The *havurah* offers the synagogue member a community small enough to enable personal relationships to develop. It enables families to express their Jewishness. . . . Hopefully the synagogue itself will gradually be transformed into . . . a Jewish assembly [of] *havurot*. . . . My grandfather came to the synagogue because he was a Jew. His grandchildren come to the synagogue to become Jewish.[104]

Changing times and perceptions called for a new—or at least revivified —approach to liturgy as well. An ambitious publishing program was undertaken, with Jules Harlow, the Rabbinical Assembly's staff liturgist, as editor. The *Mahzor for Rosh Hashanah and Yom Kippur,* published in 1972, hewed to the tradition, but widened the parameters to include modern readings and poems that touched more immediately on the contemporary historical experience of the Jewish people and the existential needs of the modern Jew. A similar eclecticism informed the contents of *Siddur Sim Shalom,* a prayer book for Shabbat, festivals, and weekdays, published in 1985, some four decades after the first Conservative prayer book appeared.[105] Also made available was a Haggadah with modern commentaries and liturgies for *S'lihot,* Tisha B'av, and Purim.

The 75th-anniversary year of the Rabbinical Assembly—1975—was designated as a time for professional self-appraisal. Rabbi Wolfe Kelman, who had served for almost a quarter of a century as the organization's chief executive officer, urged an end to the unwarranted self-flagellation that had characterized such undertakings in the past. He was particularly perplexed, he told his colleagues at their annual convention, by the "internal and external chorus of anxiety and despair" that had accompanied the phenomenal growth of the Conservative movement. About Conservative rabbis, he asserted: "No other group of committed Jewish professionals in recent Jewish history has been more successful in achieving those goals to which it has been unequivocally committed. . . ."[106]

Not everyone shared Kelman's optimistic assessment. When Marshall Sklare took a second look at Conservative Judaism, some 20 years after his original research, he found that the ". . . group's progress in the 1950s and 1960s was so rapid that Conservatism overtook Orthodoxy and Reform and went on to achieve primacy on the American Jewish religious scene." However, noted Sklare, with all its apparent success, "the morale of the Conservative movement is on the decline . . . leaders are less satisfied with their movement . . . less sanguine about its future." Discontent and doubt, he said, were expressed particularly by the rabbis, who "have a special sensitivity to its problems."[107]

---

[104]Harold M. Schulweis, "Restructuring the Synagogue," *Conservative Judaism,* Vol. 27, No. 4, Summer 1973, pp. 13–23.

[105]*The Festival Prayer Book,* edited by Prof. Alexander Marx, was published by the United Synagogue in 1927, but it was a classically traditional *mahzor.*

[106]*PRA,* 1975, pp. 14–16.

[107]Marshall Sklare, "Recent Developments in Conservative Judaism," *Midstream,* Vol. 18, No. 1, Jan. 1972, pp. 3–19.

Already in 1965, in his presidential address to the Rabbinical Assembly, Rabbi Max Routtenberg had confessed:

During the past decades we have grown, we have prospered, we have become a powerful religious establishment. I am, however, haunted by the fear that somewhere along the way we have become lost; our direction is not clear, and the many promises we made to ourselves and to our people have not been fulfilled. We are in danger of not having anything significant to say to our congregants, to the best of our youth, to all those seeking a dynamic adventurous faith that can elicit sacrifice and that can transform lives.[108]

One cause for the crisis of morale in the Conservative rabbinate, Sklare suggested, was its misreading of the future of Orthodoxy in America. Routtenberg disclosed that he and his friends studying in yeshivah had "decided to make the break and become Conservative," because they despaired that Orthodoxy could hold the next generation of Jews to Judaism. "We loved the Jewish people and its heritage," and seeing "both threatened, we set out to save them" through Conservative Judaism, the wave of the future. But the unanticipated resurgence of Orthodoxy brought into question the old justification for turning to Conservatism—to secure Judaism's future.

Another cause for the crisis in morale was what Sklare described as "Conservatism's defeat on the ritual front, which can be demonstrated in almost every area of Jewish observance." A study published in 1970,[109] for example, disclosed that in Har Zion Congregation, Philadelphia, long regarded as the model Conservative synagogue, only 52 percent of members lit Sabbath candles, only 41 percent purchased kosher meat, and only 33 percent kept separate dishes for meat and dairy foods. A 1979 study of Conservative Jews[110] found that while 29 percent kept kosher homes, only 7 percent claimed to be "totally kosher." Sixty-five percent attended synagogue less than once a month and only 32 percent recited *kiddush* on Sabbath eve. There was little confidence among Conservative rabbis that the erosion of observance among Conservative Jews was reversible. They remembered the campaign for the revitalization of the Sabbath in the early 1950s with embarrassment. Hopes had been high; special rabbinic dispensation had been granted to drive to synagogue; an imaginative and far-reaching campaign was launched with great enthusiasm. Still, the measurable results were nil.

There was no lack of reasons adduced for the failure to elicit sacrifice, transform lives, and win widespread adherence to Torah and *mitzvot*. Some blamed the movement—and themselves.

Rabbi Gilbert Rosenthal stated:

---

[108]*PRA*, 1965, p. 23.

[109]Samuel Z. Klausner and David P. Varady, *Synagogues Without Ghettos* (Philadelphia, 1970).

[110]Charles S. Liebman and Saul Shapiro, "A Survey of the Conservative Movement and Some of Its Religious Attitudes," mimeo, 1979.

Despite our movement's official espousal of mitzvot . . . the pattern of personal observance among the bulk of our congregants is barely distinguishable from that of their Reform neighbors. . . . We have missed the boat in not making demands on our people . . . we have followed the outmoded and naive view of Schechter . . . that we must make a virtue of nonpartisanship. . . . He who seeks to be all things to all men, ends up being nothing to too many.

Rabbi Jordan Ofseyer added:

Many of our people . . . have become Conservative for reasons of compromise rather than conviction. Can we reasonably expect them to evince excitement or enthusiasm? . . . Should we expect anything but a decline in the level of observance when congregants are not asked to make any . . . commitment to mitzvot?[111]

Some blamed the Seminary for failing to prepare rabbis in a realistic manner. Sklare observed that the Seminary's curriculum, "centered about the study of the Jewish legalistic system," was appropriate for the training of rabbis who would be serving congregations made up of observant Jews, but was not relevant to the actual situation in most Conservative congregations. Moreover, Sklare noted, the emphasis on *halakhah* in rabbinic training apotheosized a rabbinate of authority. How then could a rabbi respect himself when he functioned in a world in which, as Sklare put it, "the sanction of a rabbi is no longer required for the correct practice of Judaism"?[112]

The Direction of the Movement

For the first third of its existence, Conservative Judaism was seen by many rabbis and laymen as synonymous with a modernized Orthodoxy. In the second third, it became a distinct movement, but one that still shared the "same neighborhood" with Orthodoxy, sociologically and ideologically. In the last three decades, however, there has been a clear move away from Orthodoxy and toward a rapprochement with Reform. This is due more to changes that have taken place within Orthodoxy and Reform than to changes within Conservatism itself. Two examples will illustrate.

In the early years of the State of Israel an approach was made to the Orthodox Hapoel Hamizrachi by some members of the Rabbinical Assembly who felt that a socially progressive Orthodox religious movement would make an ideal partner in the enterprise of nation building. Nothing resulted from the overture except the knowledge that cooperation with Orthodoxy, even its liberal branches, was not possible. For the past quarter of a century, in matters pertaining to the State of Israel cooperation has been with Reform Judaism, which has become enthusiastically Zionist in its outlook.

---

[111]"Morale and Commitment," *Conservative Judaism,* Fall 1972, pp. 12–26.
[112]Sklare, *Conservative Judaism,* pp. 177–178.

For four decades Conservative Jewish scholars labored on the problem of the *agunah*. In the 1930s Rabbi Louis Epstein, a *halakhic* authority, attempted to cooperate with the Orthodox rabbinate on this matter, but to no avail. In the early 1950s there was talk of a joint *bet din* with the Orthodox Rabbinical Council of America. Professor Saul Lieberman and Rabbi Joseph B. Soloveitchik, it was reported, were in consultation. As soon as word of possible joint action reached the Orthodox establishment, however, all talks ceased.

While the commitment of Conservative Judaism to *halakhah* remained constant, the utilization of the *halakhic* process itself became more adventurous. The new boldness was most dramatically expressed in the area of religious enfranchisement of women. While liberal rulings in this area caused dismay in some quarters, they were seized upon eagerly by substantial segments of the rabbinate and the laity. The rapid acceptance of change was documented in a 1983 survey of congregations that compared current practices with those in 1975: *aliyot* for women equally with men—(1975) 29.3 percent, (1983) 59.4 percent; *aliyot* for women regularly or on some occasion—(1975) 49.8 percent, (1983) 76.7 percent; women included in *minyan*—(1975) 37.1 percent, (1983) 59 percent.[113]

The view that the liberal rulings on women signaled a definite shift in thinking about the parameters of the *halakhic* process was expressed by Seymour Siegel, professor of theology and ethics at the Seminary, chairman of the Committee on Jewish Law and Standards, and the movement's most widely respected ideologist on *halakhic* matters. Siegel, who in 1977 had asserted that "the observance of Jewish law had been the main aim of the Conservative movement since its very beginning,"[114] expressed a modified view in 1985: "When Jewish law makes us insensitive, less human and more prone to withhold human rights from our fellow men, then it has lost its primacy in Jewish life. . . . *Halacha* is a means, not an end in itself. The means should be judged by the ends." Relating this specifically to the emergence of the women's movement, Siegel said:

> Try as one would, I am convinced that strict adherence to the demands of *halacha* would not permit the important changes in synagogue life which the past period has brought about. I am not bothered by that now. For it is clear in my mind, at least, that if strict halachic conformance frustrates our highest and best human instinct, then the halachic considerations should be secondary and yield to ethics and *menshlichkeit*. . . . It is not the exact halachic norms that should be primary but the goals of the Law, indeed of Judaism, which are to follow the *derekh*

---

[113]*Rabbinical Assembly News,* Feb. 1984, pp. 1, 8. The survey was conducted by Rabbi Stephen C. Lerner and Dr. Anne L. Lerner.

[114]Seymour Siegel, "The Meaning of Jewish Law in Conservative Judaism: An Overview and Summary," in Seymour Siegel (ed.), *Conservative Judaism and Jewish Law* (New York, 1977), p. xiii.

Hashem (the way of the Lord), *laasot tzedakah umishpat* (to do righteousness and justice).[115]

A friendly critic, Orthodox scholar Michael Wyschogrod, in surveying the American Jewish religious scene in 1985, wrote:

> While for a long time Conservative Judaism has been taking liberties with *halacha* that I could not approve, one still had the feeling that the movement was anchored in loyalty to Torah. In spite of everything it was not difficult to distinguish it from Reform Judaism. This is becoming far less the case.[116]

He expressed the fear that if Conservative Judaism continued in the direction it was moving, "the fusion of the two movements cannot be too far in the future," and warned that "the absorption of Conservative Judaism by Reform . . . can only lead to tragic results." As if to confirm Wyschogrod's fear, Rabbi Alexander M. Schindler, president of Reform's Union of American Hebrew Congregations, claimed that Conservative Judaism was following Reform's lead: "It usually takes them about 10 years—like on the woman's issue," he stated, referring to Conservative Judaism's decision to ordain women rabbis, which Reform had been doing since 1972.[117]

For his part, Gerson Cohen was well aware that expansion of the *halakhic* parameters was fraught with danger as well as promise. In a message to members of Ometz, the organization of Conservative university students, he stressed the importance of "developing *halakhah* within the movement," in a manner that reflects "our approach to *halakhah*, which differs from the traditional approach of the Orthodox." At the same time, he called for "a renewal of *halakhic* observance . . . and for the generation of renewed *halakhah*." It was essential, he emphasized, "to establish limits to pluralism. Just as liberty must not give way to license, pluralism does not mean that everything is acceptable."[118] Whether Conservative Judaism was ready to be led in such a direction was the chief question confronting it as it entered its second century.

Dr. Cohen announced his retirement in 1985. In discussing the future of Conservative Judaism, he urged fellow Conservatives to view their movement "as the dynamic and developing phenomenon which it is," instead of allowing themselves to be defined "by what we are not."

In comparison with its sister movements, Conservative Judaism has proven to be remarkably cohesive and consistent. The extremes in beliefs and life-style in Conservative Judaism are much closer than the extremes in Orthodoxy; Conservative rabbis and congregations of the 1920s and 1980s are much more similar in ideology and practice than their counterparts in

---

[115]Seymour Siegel, "After Fifteen Years—My Mind," *Sh'ma,* 15/300, Nov. 1, 1985, p. 155.
[116]Michael Wyschogrod, "After Fifteen Years—My World," *Sh'ma,* ibid., p. 153.
[117]*New York Times,* July 2, 1985, section A, p. 11.
[118]*Ometz Shaliach,* Vol. 1, No. 1, Winter 1984, p. 1.

the Reform movement. Solomon Schechter would be more comfortable in a Conservative synagogue today than his contemporaries Dr. Kaufmann Kohler in a Reform temple or Rabbi David Willowsky in an Orthodox synagogue affiliated with the Union of Orthodox Jewish Congregations.

In the matter of continuity and change, the "center has held." The changes over the past century have been pronounced, but the continuity more so. The continuing quest for an ideology and the persistent enterprise of making the tension between tradition and change a vitalizing force characterize Conservative Judaism today as they did a century ago and in all the years between.

As Conservative Judaism enters its second century, the mood within the movement is one of concern and apprehension—concern about its vitality as it confronts the buoyant elan of Orthodoxy; apprehension about its long-range viability as it reads demographic projections that Reform will soon overtake Conservatism as American Jewry's "movement of choice."

Stocktaking marked by concern and apprehension has been a "constant" in the movement's centennial experience. In 1927, Rabbi Israel Goldstein asked, "As Orthodoxy becomes more de-Ghettoized and Reform more conservatized, what is left for the Conservative Jew to do?"[119] A quarter of a century later, Rabbi Theodore Friedman confronted this question: "Is Conservatism, viewed in historical perspective, merely a stopover for Jews on the way from Orthodoxy to Reform?"[120]

Historically speaking, it needs to be noted that these disturbing questions were posed when Conservative Judaism was beginning to experience its two periods of greatest growth—in numbers, creativity, and influence. How Conservative Judaism will respond to the questions before it today, in its centennial year, we must leave to a future historian to record.

---

[119]*PRA*, 1927, p. 35.

[120]Theodore Friedman, "Jewish Tradition in Twentieth Century America—The Conservative Approach," *Judaism*, Fall 1954, p. 320.

Review
of
the
Year

UNITED STATES
OTHER COUNTRIES

Civic and Political

Intergroup Relations

IN NO PRESIDENTIAL ELECTION in recent U.S. history—not even that of John F. Kennedy in 1960—did religion play as central and decisive a role as it did in 1984. At issue this time, however, was not a candidate's personal creed. Rather, what emerged as a dominant theme was an increasingly assertive form of Christianity, one that threatened to upset the consensus on church-state separation and that caused Jews considerable uneasiness. For Jews, an additional cause of concern was the candidacy of black minister and civil-rights activist Jesse Jackson for the Democratic presidential nomination. During a stormy campaign, charges and countercharges of antisemitism and racism threatened to bring Jews and blacks into explosive confrontation.

Jesse Jackson

Jewish groups were guarded, initially, in their response to Jackson, who had earlier embraced the Arab cause and had made definite anti-Jewish statements. The concern was to preserve the black-Jewish alliance, which had shown clear signs of strain in recent years. Early in the year, the Jewish Defense League engaged in a number of inflammatory actions against Jackson, for which it was chastised by other Jewish groups. Jackson, recognizing that the wider Jewish community, not just the JDL, viewed him with suspicion, offered to meet with Jews willing to sit down with him. At one such meeting he declared his support for the existence of Israel as a Jewish state, at the same time calling on it to work out differences with its Arab neighbors on the basis of fairness to all sides. Jackson's difficulties, however, began in earnest when it became public on January 30 that the Arab League had made a previously undisclosed donation of $100,000 to PUSH for Excellence, Inc., the organization he took leave of in order to seek the presidency.

Jackson's problems were compounded by an episode that occurred in February. A black reporter for the *Washington Post,* at the end of a lengthy story on Jackson and the Jews, disclosed a private conversation in which Jackson had referred to Jews as "Hymies" and to New York as "Hymietown." Busily engaged at the time in the early New Hampshire primary, Jackson at first claimed "no recollection" of having used the words and insisted that the charge was "not accurate." On February 26, however, he acknowledged that the episode had in fact taken place. "It was not done in the spirit of meanness," he assured a crowd in a synagogue, admitting, however, that "it was wrong." While the "Hymie" incident inflamed Jackson's detractors, it caused his supporters to close ranks. One of them, Louis Farrakhan, head of a Muslim group and a close adviser—a man whom Jackson used to warm up black audiences prior to his platform appearances—declared that Jackson had received death threats and that Jewish groups were whipping up tensions. "If you harm Jesse Jackson," he warned, "in the name of Allah, that will be the last one you harm."

Initial reaction to the "Hymie" episode from Jewish organizations was cautious, leading Nathan Perlmutter, head of the Anti-Defamation League of B'nai B'rith, to note that in the past, anti-Jewish remarks by political leaders had evoked much heavier criticism. Howard Friedman, president of the American Jewish Committee, while urging the candidate to reexamine his statements on Jews, Israel, and the Holocaust, welcomed Jackson's plea to renew the dialogue between blacks and Jews. "If we have been timid in forcefully repudiating Jackson's inimical views," Rabbi Alexander Schindler, president of the Union of American Hebrew Congregations, declared, it was "lest we fan the flames of a black-Jewish confrontation on the American scene." That Jackson's remarks had, nonetheless, clearly hurt him was shown by an NBC poll early in March. Among whites questioned, 57 percent felt that Jackson's words raised questions about his character. By a margin of 44 to 37 percent, however, blacks—whose registration during the primaries jumped by nearly two million—disagreed with this assessment.

Reverberations from this incident had barely died down when Jackson was again embroiled in controversy with Jews, this time over remarks by Farrakhan. The *Chicago Tribune* reported a March 11 radio broadcast in which Farrakhan declared that Hitler was a "great man," a statement that elicited wide criticism (except from Jackson), including that of the black mayor of Newark, who took the opportunity to condemn the "Hymie" remark as well. Late in June, Farrakhan referred to Judaism in a broadcast as a "gutter religion" and described Israel and its supporters as "engaged in a criminal conspiracy." These remarks provoked even greater public criticism, including attacks from the NAACP and Urban League, as well as from representatives of church bodies. Attempting to distance himself somewhat from Farrakhan, Jackson labeled Farrakhan's remarks "reprehensible and morally indefensible." However, he refused to repudiate him directly.

Throughout the campaign, Jackson alternated between seeking reconciliation with Jews and offending many with his views on Middle East issues. On March 4, for example, he called for renewing the black-Jewish alliance, but coupled this with an appeal for a Palestinian "sovereign nation" alongside Israel. On May 26 he denounced Israel for allegedly selling military hardware to South Africa, which, he charged, was being used "to shoot down and oppress black people."

As the campaign progressed, Jewish civic and religious bodies became increasingly open in their public criticism of Jackson. At the same time, they continued efforts to preserve the black-Jewish alliance—in the words of the Orthodox Rabbinical Council of America—"despite traumas of the moment." Early in May, American Jewish Committee president Howard Friedman warned that Jews were worried about Jackson, seeing him as not sufficiently "anti-antisemitic." On May 31, Anti-Defamation League national director Perlmutter delivered the harshest personal attack yet made by a major Jewish leader, declaring that Jackson's statements "render the self-portrait of an anti-Semite." And on the eve of the Democratic National Convention, in mid-July, following a meeting in Chicago at which Jackson was escorted to the speaker's platform by a national spokesman for Farrakhan, the president of the American Jewish Congress, Theodore Mann, declared that unless Jackson disassociated himself from Farrakhan, the relationship would remain a problem for Democrats, a sentiment echoed by other Jewish groups.

The Democratic Convention

For the Democratic party, which in 1980 had seen the Jewish vote for Ronald Reagan climb to 39 percent, Jackson's candidacy and the public controversy that swirled around him posed a serious problem. On the one hand, since blacks were the single most loyal group in the diverse and often conflicted Democratic coalition, the party sought to bring even larger numbers of blacks to the polls. At the same time, the leadership did not want to alienate other traditional elements of their electoral base, particularly Jews. For the most part, the candidates for the Democratic nomination avoided coming into direct collision with Jackson during the primaries. On June 26, however, the Democratic front-runner, former vice-president Walter Mondale, clearly responding to appeals by Jews and others, declared Farrakhan's remarks to be "venomous, bigoted and obscene," and called on Jackson to repudiate the Muslim leader.

Despite pressure on the Democrats to adopt a resolution denouncing antisemitism, the Jackson forces (perceiving this as an attack on their candidate) prevented the Democratic convention from passing such a resolution. (The Republicans easily passed a similar resolution at their convention a month later.) Jackson supporters also slightly weakened the party's previous opposition to racial quotas in affirmative action programs. Seeking to put greater distance between Jackson and the party, the platform committee overwhelmingly defeated proposals by the Jackson forces favoring the establishment of a Palestinian state and opposing movement of the American embassy to Jerusalem. During the convention, Jackson delivered a graceful and conciliatory speech admitting mistakes he had made during the primaries and noting that Jews and blacks "are bound by shared blood and shared sacrifices." Mondale, who won the nomination, kept his distance from Jackson during the ensuing campaign. For Jews, Jackson receded in importance as other issues came to the fore.

Black-Jewish Relations

The Jackson campaign for the Democratic nomination was not the only source of friction between blacks and Jews. Early in the year, Mayor Edward Koch of New York City, who had been engaged for some time in battles with black leaders, published a best-selling and controversial political memoir, *Mayor*, in which he reiterated an earlier attack on "poverty pimps" and his belief that blacks are "basically anti-Semitic." During the election campaign, he said he was dissatisfied with Jackson's repudiation of Farrakhan and then went on to suggest that the black candidate had received campaign funds from Libya. Koch further angered blacks by defending the use of an examination for police sergeants, despite the high failure rate of black and Hispanic officers on the test, and by refusing to create a city holiday in 1985 to mark Rev. Martin Luther King, Jr.'s birthday. Responding to various actions of the mayor, the black-owned *Amsterdam News* acknowledged on June 30 that Farrakhan's remarks were "intemperate and obscure," but wanted to know "who will repudiate and denounce Edward I. Koch?" In an end-of-the-year editorial on the controversies surrounding Koch, the *New York Times* declared that the challenge facing black-Jewish relations in New York was how to get through 1985 without making things worse.

Survey research data made public during the year revealed how complex black-Jewish relations had become. On June 1 Louis Harris reported the results of an April survey which found "that on political and social matters, Jews and blacks are far closer than generally believed—on their underlying attitudes, including perceived discrimination against both blacks and Jews." He noted, too, the prevalence of the feeling that "we either hang together or separately." However, an equally respected public-opinion expert, William Schneider, reported in the *National Journal* on May 5 that rising black consciousness was leading to increased resentment of Jews and greater hostility toward Israel. He noted that earlier Harris materials showed younger blacks as more antisemitic and anti-Israel than older blacks. Some of this feeling was being played out on college campuses, such as Temple University in Philadelphia, Wesleyan in Connecticut, and San Diego State in California, as well as at primarily black institutions, where student groups extended invitations to Farrakhan to speak and welcomed him enthusiastically. At the University of Pennsylvania an acrimonious debate between black and Jewish students broke out in the letters-to-the-editor columns of the *Daily Pennsylvanian*. At issue was the campaign behavior of Jackson and Farrakhan and the nature of the traditional alliance between blacks and Jews. The alliance was depicted by black student leaders as having little importance, past or present, a position reflecting a revisionist view of the alliance's origins and history that was developing among elements of the black intelligentsia. In an essay in a newly published book, *Jews in Black Perspectives*, and in an article in the *Journal of American History*, David Levering Lewis argued at length that the relationship was an apparent rather than a real "soul fellowship" and that it had been only "minimally beneficial to Afro-Americans."

Controversies and conflicts notwithstanding, there were ample indications that the traditional supportive relationship between the two groups was not entirely dead. In March, 12 black congressmen signed a letter to President Reagan opposing arms sales to Jordan unless that country joined in peace talks with Israel, and in July, the same number cosponsored a bill to move the U.S. embassy from Tel Aviv to Jerusalem. In turn, Jewish members teamed up with black colleagues to add a series of provisions to the House version of the Export Administration Act which would substantially limit U.S. economic relations with South Africa, because of the latter's apartheid policies. Two of the leading critics of apartheid on Capitol Hill were, in fact, Jewish congressmen, Stephen Solarz of New York and Howard Wolpe of Michigan.

In Berkeley, California, blacks helped to defeat a ballot initiative calling for cuts in U.S. aid to Israel equal to Israeli expenditures for West Bank settlements. The proposition was voted down by a two-to-one margin, with blacks voting heavily on the side of the majority. By year's end both the American Jewish Committee and the Anti-Defamation League concluded in separate analyses that in spite of the stresses of the election, black-Jewish relations had not unraveled.

Throughout the year efforts continued both to reappraise the black-Jewish relationship and to open up dialogue between the two groups. In December a number of Jews and Jewish organizations joined the growing protest movement against apartheid in South Africa. Leaders of the Anti-Defamation League demonstrated at the United Nations, and on Christmas day some 250–300 Jewish protesters (representing the Union of American Hebrew Congregations, the Jewish Labor Committee, the New Jewish Agenda, and the American Jewish Committee) relieved Christian colleagues picketing near the South African embassy.

Arab-Americans

The election provided an opportunity for Arab-Americans to flex their political muscle, particularly as Jackson actively reached out to them. The candidate named James Zogby, executive director of the Arab Anti-Discrimination Committee, to his campaign staff, and addressed Arab groups in several cities during the campaign. Early in November the *New York Times* reported that Arab-Americans had raised some $300,000 for Jackson.

The National Association of Arab Americans continued its sponsorship of radio spot announcements in such cities as Washington, D.C., and New York, in which they charged that American aid to Israel took money away from needed social services.

Religion in the Campaign

During the election, the various religious groups were targeted by politicians for special attention. The two leading candidates for the Democratic nomination,

Walter Mondale and Sen. Gary Hart (D., Colo.), vied with each other about the strength of their respective positions on Israel. Each backed an effort under way in Congress to press the government to move the U.S. embassy from Tel Aviv to Jerusalem. The candidates' attempts to outdo each other became so shamelessly pandering that the American Jewish Committee was led to protest publicly, in March, that Jews cared about a broad range of issues, not only Israel.

It was Republican leadership, however, beginning with President Reagan, that introduced religion, specifically Christian triumphalism, into the campaign. In a speech before a group of religious broadcasters in the spring, the president declared, "God so loved the world He gave His only begotten Son that whosoever believeth in Him would not perish but have everlasting life." At a prayer breakfast in Dallas a day after the GOP convention, he charged that those who opposed such expressions of religion as voluntary prayer in the public schools were "intolerant of religion."

These statements aroused strong criticism from Jewish leaders. Following the Dallas address, Rabbi Mordecai Waxman, president of the Synagogue Council of America, declared that "religion is and should be a private commitment," while American Jewish Committee president Friedman reminded President Reagan that the Founding Fathers had written the separation of church and state into the Constitution. Jewish groups and others were angered, also, by a letter from Sen. Paul Laxalt (R., Nev.), the GOP campaign chairman, to 45,000 Protestant pastors, just before the Republican convention, addressing them as "Dear Christian Leaders" and urging them "to register church members." Delegates to the convention found copies of the New Testament in their kits (they were later removed), and among the resolutions adopted was one endorsing prayer in the schools. Although Jews welcomed the platform's explicit attack on antisemitism, eight leading Jewish groups urged Republican leaders "to reject the current divisive assault on the First Amendment's separation of church and state."

Faced with mounting criticism, the president went before a B'nai B'rith convention early in September and sought to calm Jewish fears. He wrote, also, to the chairman of the Anti-Defamation League indicating his opposition "to organized formal prayer at prescribed times in public schools." Jewish concern, however, was not assuaged. At the B'nai B'rith convention, Mondale accused the president of encouraging "an extreme fringe of fundamentalist Christian leaders to impose their faith on the nation." In September and early October, the National Jewish Community Relations Advisory Council convened eight regional consultations for the purpose of mobilizing the Jewish community to defend the separation principle. In October, the heads of the Orthodox, Conservative, and Reform rabbinic bodies issued a joint statement endorsing Mondale and urging their colleagues to support the Democratic presidential ticket.

Although the National Conference of Catholic Bishops issued a statement in March which carefully refrained from any expression that could be interpreted as support for a particular candidate, a number of leading prelates, including

Archbishop John J. O'Connor of New York and John Cardinal Krol of Philadelphia, made statements during the campaign suggesting that a candidate's stand on abortion should be a key issue. Their statements were understood to be directed against the Mondale-Ferraro ticket, since both the president personally and the Republican platform were on record as opposing abortion, while Mondale and his running mate, liberal Catholic Geraldine Ferraro, supported freedom of choice. So inflammatory was the insertion of the abortion issue into the campaign that on October 13 the administrative board of the National Conference felt constrained to announce that the bishops had no intention of creating a "voting bloc" and denied that the church was involved in single-issue politics.

The Christian Right

The election year provided an opportunity, also, for the Christian Right to seek greater support for its agenda. In the course of the year, this element succeeded not only in gaining control of the 14-million-member Southern Baptist Convention, the largest Protestant denomination, but also persuaded that body to reverse previous positions and take a stand against abortion and for school prayer. Christian activists also developed a massive voter-registration drive in an effort to register "true Christian" voters by November. "Born-again Christians," who had accounted for some two-thirds of the Reagan margin of victory in 1980, according to pollster Louis Harris, were a prime target of the activists.

The major and ultimately most successful goal, however, was the Republican convention and its party platform. Christian Right leaders Jerry Falwell, James Robison, and W.A. Criswell delivered benedictions at various points in the proceedings. They and others in the newly formed American Coalition for Traditional Values (ACTV), which brought together the various factions on the Right, helped steer the party platform in the desired direction on abortion, school prayer, women's rights, pornography, homosexuality, and nuclear freeze, despite some token resistance by key White House staff. The ACTV leaders were joined as primary architects of policy by a group of House Republicans organized in what they called the Conservative Opportunity Society. The adoption of the Republican platform prompted Falwell to declare, "If they had allowed us to write it, we'd have difficulty improving on the content."

Despite the seeming unity, however, there were important divisions between the political and the Christian Right. The latter had refused to go along with an earlier drive led by Richard Viguerie, Howard Phillips, and Paul Weyrich to break away from the Republican party and form a conservative "populist" party modeled on the old Progressive party of Wisconsin senator Robert LaFollette. The ministers' position reflected a desire to be viewed as legitimate religious leaders rather than as secular political operatives. Among the various right-wing groups backing the president, however, none wanted to run the risk of upsetting the reelection strategy, this despite dissatisfaction with the president's men, if not with Reagan himself. The

White House staff, it was believed, had promised more than they had delivered in trying to achieve conservative goals. Impatient right-wing Christians began pressing, therefore, for an even broader campaign on social issues to be launched once the president was reelected.

The Election and Its Aftermath

According to exit polls conducted by the *New York Times*-CBS News, *Washington Post*-ABC News, and NBC News, the Reagan-Bush ticket received 32, 31, or 35 percent of the Jewish vote. The conservative National Jewish Coalition, however, asserting that professional polls failed to factor in large concentrations of Jews to the extent required, claimed that 40 percent or more supported Reagan. An extensive analysis by the Jewish Community Relations Council of New York concluded that Reagan won some 38 percent of the Jewish vote in that city. The fact remained that apart from blacks and Hispanics, Jews were the only major grouping to maintain support for the Democratic party ticket, leading Earl Raab to write in a postelection analysis for the American Jewish Congress, "Jews still do not belong to the same social network as the middle and upper class white Protestants who form the Republican Party." Most analysts found that concern about Christianization and about groups like the Moral Majority weighed more heavily with Jews than fear of Jesse Jackson. To the majority of Jews it seemed clear that the Democratic party still provided a more congenial climate than did the Republican.

The voting patterns of other groups were also noteworthy. "Born-again" white Christians, who first came to public attention when Jimmy Carter ran for president in 1976, this time preferred the Republican candidate by a margin of 81 to 19 percent. According to the *New York Times*-CBS News poll, the Republican 8.5-million-vote margin among this group was slightly larger than the combined Democratic margin among Jews and blacks. White Catholics—formerly linked with Jews in the old Democratic coalition—divided 58 to 41 percent for President Reagan. Only 8 percent of Catholics polled, however, checked abortion as one of the two key issues of the campaign, while 18 percent of born-again Christians judged it of major importance.

After the election there were indications that leaders of the Christian Right felt jilted by the Jewish vote. "Sometimes I think that fundamentalist Christians are almost always supporting Israel, and our sharpest critics are liberal Democratic Jews," Dr. Ron Godwin, a vice-president of the Moral Majority, noted after the election. "But our commitment to supporting Israel and the Jewish community is unilateral," he added. The Christian Right itself found critics in evangelical Protestant circles, among them leading evangelical theologian Carl F.H. Henry and the influential magazine *Christianity Today*. In an editorial, the latter warned against repeating the mistakes of the twenties, referring to campaigns on behalf of Prohibition and the teaching of evolution, both of which had led to public humiliation.

There was recognition, also, among Republican strategists that the GOP had lost ground when it permitted Christian fundamentalism to figure so prominently. One such strategist argued that "just as the Falwell connection hurt with Jews, it also hindered Republican progress with young people and was not much help with Catholics." Sen. Robert Dole (R., Kan.) drew back from the GOP religious thrust, declaring that Republicans were "near the edge of the fine line in identifying with religious groups." And the *U.S. Catholic* called the performance of a small circle of bishops on the abortion issue "at best embarrassing and at worst unfair."

In the organization of the new Congress in January 1985, a swing to the middle of the political spectrum developed quickly. In five leadership contests the Republicans picked centrists, including Robert Dole as Senate majority leader and Robert Michel of Illinois as head of the group in the House. Indeed, as the new year got under way, House Republican leaders released a series of recommendations that were silent on school prayer and abortion and far more pragmatic overall than the controversial party platform adopted in Dallas.

The number of Jews in Congress held steady at 30, their proportion being considerably greater than that of Jews in the general population. There were eight Jewish senators, three of them from Minnesota, Nebraska, and Nevada—areas which did not have a significant Jewish presence.

Amid the furor surrounding the intrusion of religion into the election campaign, a few voices attempted a rational analysis of an appropriate role for religion in politics. In *The Naked Public Square,* Richard John Neuhaus argued for political discourse that welcomes moral and religious debate, instead of prohibiting it, so long as all play by the rules of a democratic society. Echoing the ideas of a Jesuit analyst, the late John Courtney Murray, he warned that when religion is banned from public life, leaving the public square "to the ambitious state and the isolated individual," a form of totalitarianism can result. Charles Krauthammer argued in the *New Republic* that the battle between sectarianism and secularism wrongly framed the issue. He offered in its place Robert Bellah's concept of a noncoercive and inclusive "civil religion" as an American reality that had inspired Abraham Lincoln and Martin Luther King.

The election aftermath included discussion of its long-range effects on Jews. Veteran political scientist Seymour Martin Lipset, writing in the *Washington Post,* and Rabbi Arthur Hertzberg, writing in the *New York Review of Books,* argued that recent predictions of Jews moving politically to the right had been exaggerated. The view that Jews continued their traditional liberal attachment was reinforced by the 1984 National Survey of American Jews, which was issued by the American Jewish Committee after the election. In the survey, self-defined liberals outnumbered conservatives by more than three to two, with "middle of the road" Jews about as numerous as liberals. Nevertheless, in the elections of 1972, 1976, 1980, and 1984 between 32 and 40 percent of Jews had chosen to pull the Republican lever, a substantial increase over the past. This new voting pattern, as well as the growing prominence of a cadre of neoconservative Jewish thinkers and writers who had received widespread attention, suggested that a longer-term conservative trend was indeed in the making among Jews.

Church and State

Early in the year the Senate took up a constitutional amendment intended to reverse the 22-year-old Supreme Court decision banning officially sponsored prayer in the schools. Although the measure, which had the support of President Reagan, was rejected by the Senate in March, the vote—56 in favor to 44 opposed—was only 11 short of the two-thirds necessary for passage. Some saw the move to push through an amendment calling for vocal prayer as politically motivated, since the president had earlier opposed a silent-prayer alternative which was beaten overwhelmingly.

The issue of silent prayer was very much alive on the state level, since nearly half the legislatures had already enacted measures calling for a moment of silence for public-school prayer or meditation. In April the Supreme Court agreed to rule on the constitutionality of "moment of silence" laws. At the same time, the Court affirmed an Alabama appellate court's decision that struck down a state law authorizing teachers to lead students in a state-composed prayer.

Following the school-prayer-amendment defeat, advocates of religion in the schools shifted their efforts to proposed "equal access" legislation. This threatened to withdraw federal money from school districts which would not permit high-school student religious groups to meet on school premises for prayer and religious discussion during noninstructional periods, in the manner of language clubs and marching bands. The measure was opposed by the American Jewish Committee, the American Jewish Congress, and the Anti-Defamation League, as well as by the National Education Association and the United Federation of Teachers. Supporting the measure, however, were such liberal church bodies as the National Council of Churches—which had opposed the school-prayer amendment—as well as several constitutional scholars who argued that at issue was the "free exercise of religion." The American Civil Liberties Union adopted a neutral posture on the grounds that the law would protect secular free speech as well as religious rights. Initially defeated in the House in May, the bill was approved by the Senate in June (by a margin of 88 to 11 in an amendment to an education bill), passed by the House in July, and signed into law by the president. Whether "equal access" would stand up to constitutional challenge was uncertain, since four federal appeals and state appellate courts in New York and California had barred various types of religious activities by student groups, citing the First Amendment's prohibition of the "establishment of religion."

In March the Supreme Court ruled in a 5-4 decision in a Pawtucket, Rhode Island, case that a city may include a Nativity scene as part of an official Christmas display without violating the constitutionally required separation of church and state. The ruling permitted, for the first time, the display of a symbol that is explicitly and exclusively Christian. While the decision did not automatically sanction all official Christmas displays—the justices based their decision on the fact that the Pawtucket crèche was part of a larger Christmas display of seasonal symbols —it drew sharp attacks from Jewish, Islamic, and some Christian groups. A number of Roman Catholic bishops and fundamentalist Christians, however, praised the decision.

Supporters of strict separation of church and state began to voice increased concern not only over specific legislative moves to bolster religion but also over the Supreme Court's apparent change in emphasis. There appeared to be movement away from the concept of a "wall of separation" that had guided previous High Court decisions and toward a greater spirit of accommodation. Instead of asking how religion and government can best be kept apart, the Court seemed more interested in determining what government can or must do to remove obstacles to voluntary religious observance.

Quotas and Discrimination

In June the Supreme Court ruled 6 to 3 in a case involving Memphis fire fighters that a court may not order an employer to protect the jobs of recently hired black employees at the expense of whites who have more seniority. Later in the year, William Bradford Reynolds, chief of the Justice Department's civil rights division, basing himself on the decision, declared that "the era of the racial quota has run its course."

In the fall, the City Council of New York passed, and Mayor Koch signed into law, a bill making it unlawful for private clubs with more than 400 members to discriminate on the basis of race, creed, color, national origin, or sex.

In a judgment labeled by the American Jewish Congress the largest ever handed down in the United States in an anti-Jewish discrimination case, a federal judge awarded two Jewish faculty members at Baylor College of Medicine in Houston $394,514 as compensation for the college's refusal to assign them to Saudi Arabia, based on its agreement with King Faisal Hospital.

Extremism

The Anti-Defamation League reported that Ku Klux Klan membership had dropped about 35 percent in the previous two years but warned that frustration growing out of the Klan's decline could lead to individual acts of terrorism. Part of the reason for the decline was a crackdown by federal prosecutors. In May a federal grand jury in Alabama indicted nine Klansmen on civil-rights charges resulting from a bloody melee with black demonstrators five years earlier in Decatur, Alabama. In July convicted murderer Joseph Paul Franklin was found guilty of bombing a synagogue in 1977, after confessing that he blew up "the synagogue of satan."

In June Denver radio talk-show host Alan Berg, an outspoken critic of right-wing extremist groups, was murdered in front of his home. The gun that was used in the killing was recovered by federal agents in October when they raided the Sandpoint, Idaho, home of Gary Yarbrough, a neo-Nazi leader. Yarbrough was taken into custody by Portland, Oregon, police following a shoot-out in November. In December more than 100 FBI agents converged on Whidbey Island, Washington, where they arrested four other neo-Nazis, but another one—the leader of the group, Robert J. Matthews—refused to surrender. His charred body was recovered the next morning from the ruins of their hideout.

Holocaust-Related Issues

The Justice Department's office of special investigations was continuing its hunt for Nazi war criminals who had slipped into the United States after World War II, but with limited success. The deportation of Archbishop Valerian D. Trifa, head of the Rumanian Orthodox Church in America—who was accused of persecuting Jews in his native Rumania during World War II—brought to three the number of people forced to leave the country since the office's opening five years earlier.

In November, in response to public protests, the California Library Association revoked a decision to open its statewide convention to a display of materials and an address by a "revisionist" historian who claimed that the Holocaust either never occurred or was highly exaggerated. After first supporting the invitation on the basis of free-speech rights, the ACLU backed off, explaining that the real issue was a contractual agreement, not freedom of expression.

In September the Senate Foreign Relations Committee voted for the fifth time since 1950 to recommend ratification of the 35-year-old genocide treaty already ratified by most major nations. Although earlier in the month President Reagan had announced his support and urged the Senate to act, it had failed to do so by the end of the year.

MURRAY FRIEDMAN

The United States, Israel, and the Middle East

FOR THE MIDDLE EAST, 1984 was primarily a year of anticipation and transition. Since a presidential election was being held in the United States, the prevailing feeling was that no major new American peace effort would be launched until after the November elections. Some observers in the Arab world hoped—and some in Israel feared—that if President Ronald Reagan won a second term, he would press forward more vigorously to implement his Middle East peace initiative of September 1982, which had been shelved after it aroused strong opposition from the Begin government in Israel as well as from radical Arab and Palestinian groups. Meanwhile, continuing Israeli and American preoccupation with the deteriorating situation in Lebanon was a prime reason for keeping the Reagan initiative on the back burner.

Lebanese Situation Deteriorates

The year opened to growing domestic criticism of American involvement in the peacekeeping operation in Beirut. It was clear that the original mission of the U.S. Marines—to help keep the peace while President Amin Gemayel pulled together the warring Lebanese factions in order to forge a stable central government—was not going to be achieved. With a presidential campaign approaching, President Reagan's political advisers worried that continuing military embroilment in Lebanon would benefit the Democratic opposition.

The key player in the Lebanese drama, President Hafez al-Assad of Syria, was doing everything possible to undermine the American position and bring about an early American withdrawal from the area. Increasingly tense American-Syrian relations had escalated from mutual recriminations to the point of direct armed confrontation on December 4, 1983, when the Syrians shot down two U.S. Navy jets, killing one flier and capturing the second, Lt. Robert O. Goodman, a bombardier-navigator. Explaining the flight over Syria, President Reagan said that the United States did not seek an escalation of conflict with Syria but had acted in self-defense against positions that had been shelling American forces.

A call by Syrian foreign minister Abdel Halim Khaddam for action against American "aggression" was followed by an announcement that Damascus would not release Goodman until the "war" had ended and U.S. troops had pulled out of Lebanon. U.S. warships shelled Syrian-controlled positions on December 13, following renewed attacks on American reconnaissance planes, and American officials announced the adoption of an "instant retaliation" policy. It was becoming clear that although President Reagan had declared Goodman's release to be a high priority, Syrian demands for an end to American overflights were viewed as too high a price to pay for the flier's release. U.S. special envoy Donald H. Rumsfeld, who conferred with Syrian officials in December on the broader Lebanese situation, was specifically enjoined by the White House from discussing the Goodman case, so as to avoid any hint of U.S. willingness to make political concessions to obtain the airman's release.

Jesse Jackson's "Pilgrimage" to Damascus

At this point President Assad found a willing partner in Rev. Jesse L. Jackson, the black minister and announced candidate for the Democratic presidential nomination, who was an outspoken critic of U.S. involvement in Lebanon. When Jackson announced that he would seek President Reagan's approval to make a personal appeal to Assad in behalf of Lieutenant Goodman, who also happened to be black, Jackson was shunned by the White House. Reagan aides subsequently claimed that this was not a political move to block Jackson but was intended to make clear to the Syrians that the U.S. government would not make any concessions to obtain Goodman's release. Nevertheless, Jackson departed on December 29 on a self-proclaimed "pilgrimage" to Damascus. At a meeting with President Assad on January 2, 1984, Jackson informed the Syrian leader of a growing consensus in the United States for the withdrawal of the U.S. Marines from Lebanon and suggested that Goodman's release could speed that process.

The following day Assad released the American prisoner to Jackson. Since he did not wish a continuing confrontation that could lead to broader conflict with the United States, Assad, by responding to Jackson's "humanitarian" appeal, could remove the irritant represented by Goodman without appearing to yield to pressure from the United States. For their part, American officials emphasized that the Reagan administration had not given in to Syrian demands. To underscore this point, the day following Goodman's release U.S. F-14 reconnaissance planes resumed their flights over Syrian positions, this time with no hostile reaction from the Syrians.

President Reagan promptly sought to gain both political and diplomatic advantage from the successful Jackson mission, telephoning congratulations to the Democratic presidential aspirant and to Goodman, and inviting both of them to a welcome-home ceremony at the White House. While presidential spokesman Larry Speakes had said that the administration viewed Goodman's release as a "humanitarian," not a diplomatic, gesture, Reagan sent a letter expressing "appreciation" to President Assad, in which he said, "This is an opportune moment to put all the issues on the table," and invited Syria to work with the United States to try to resolve the Lebanese problem. Reagan quickly dispatched presidential envoy Rumsfeld back to Syria, and the diplomat held what was described as a "fruitful" three-hour meeting with Assad on January 13.

Mounting Congressional Pressure for U.S. Withdrawal

As members of Congress returned to Washington at the start of the new year, they gave voice to a rising chorus of discontent—joined in by leaders of both parties—

over the lack of success of President Reagan's policy in Lebanon. For example, after a meeting of Democrats on January 3, Rep. Thomas P. O'Neill, Jr., the Speaker of the House, urged the president to make a new push for a diplomatic solution in Lebanon. He warned that "these initiatives must meet with some success quickly" because the present vulnerable position of the marines "is absolutely unacceptable," and "patience in Congress with Administration policies in Lebanon is wearing very thin." The Democratic criticism was echoed by Sen. Charles H. Percy, Illinois Republican and chairman of the Foreign Relations Committee, who told a press briefing on the same day that public support for the marine mission had "dropped considerably" in recent months, and that it would be "highly desirable" to replace American forces with other foreign troops.

It was noteworthy that many of those who were voicing impatience had the previous fall supported a congressional resolution authorizing the president to keep American troops in Beirut for 18 months—through the spring of 1985. On January 5, Washington sources revealed that the Lebanese government had asked for some American marines to be shifted to the region south of Beirut, to help the Lebanese army extend its authority, a request that was unlikely to be approved in view of the changing congressional mood. On the same day, in Damascus, Foreign Minister Khaddam told visiting senator John Tower (R., Tex.) that the withdrawal of U.S. and Israeli troops would help bring peace to the Lebanese and permit the Syrians to withdraw their forces.

The Reagan administration was deeply disturbed by congressional criticism. In testimony before the Senate Foreign Relations Committee on January 11, Deputy Secretary of State Kenneth W. Dam pointed to the congressional resolution authorizing the marine mission as proof that the president and Congress, "working together, could formulate and maintain a coherent and consistent long-term policy." He warned that "if our determination is now seen as flagging, . . . if the Congress were to curtail the period of its authorization for our Marines, then Syria would be encouraged to believe that it can win the game by digging in. Syria might conclude that we are finished in Lebanon and on the way out." Pointing to "the Iranian threat and to the concerns in the region about state terrorism," Secretary Dam added that administration representatives visiting the Middle East had been told by "the leaders of Israel and our most important moderate Arab friends that an American failure of nerve in Lebanon would be a disaster for all the forces of moderation in the region."

Democratic Candidates Press for Marine Withdrawal

With domestic pressure continuing to mount for an early withdrawal of the marines, U.S. policy in Lebanon was emerging as a major election-year issue. The Democratic contenders all voiced their opposition to remaining in Lebanon. Former vice-president Walter Mondale, in a statement issued on December 31, 1983, declared that although he had earlier supported American participation in the international peacekeeping effort, he had now become convinced that "it is time to withdraw the U.S. Marines from Lebanon." He accused Reagan of "not taking charge" and said that the administration's Lebanon policy had proven a failure. The United States, he said, should press the Lebanese government to work harder for national reconciliation. He also urged that the Lebanese army and UNIFIL (United Nations Interim Force in Lebanon) take charge of security in Beirut and that other neutral countries provide peacekeeping forces. The United States, he continued, while maintaining naval power off the shores of Lebanon, should "increase the diplomatic pressure on Syria to withdraw; and firm up our political and strategic relationship with Israel." Accusing the Reagan administration of repeatedly "backing away" from strategic cooperation with Israel, he added that as president, "I would make it meaningful and permanent."

The other Democratic contenders expressed similar criticisms of the administration's Lebanon policy in interviews with the *New York Times*. Sen. Alan Cranston (D.,Calif.) said that he would not have put the marines into Beirut without consulting Congress beforehand, adding that "the wisest course is to extricate ourselves as quickly as we can for the safety of the men as we withdraw them." Sen. John Glenn (D.,Ohio) pointed out that his Marine Corps training had taught him the importance of defining a mission precisely and then assigning adequate equipment and forces to accomplish it. The administration, he said, had failed to do that in Lebanon, and, he added, "the worst danger of all is to see this confrontation escalating just between the United States and Syria."

Sen. Ernest F. Hollings (D.,S.C.), who had opposed the marine deployment to Beirut from the start, said the troops lacked a credible "mission, there is no peace to keep, [and] we cannot forcefeed the Lebanese Government with 1,600 marines." Sen. Gary Hart (D.,Colo.), pointing out that the United States lacked either the military or the strategic capability to pacify and reconstruct Lebanon, urged the United States to concentrate on playing a diplomatic role. UN forces should replace the marines, he added, who "should have been gotten out a year ago." Asked about the Syrian role and whether the United States should negotiate with the Syrians and consider their interests, Hart responded: "They see Lebanon as a client-state of theirs" and exert "a dominant influence" there. As for the United States, he went on, "we may or may not [*sic*] be able to accept that. But they do have legitimate concerns about their security and their own borders and those concerns ought to be heard and ought to be satisfied. We ought to be dealing much more openly with them and urging the Gemayel government to do the same."

Former governor Reubin Askew of Florida and former senator George McGovern of South Dakota were among those who expressed doubts about the effectiveness of the marine mission and called for its termination. McGovern had harsh words to say about broader U.S. policy as well. In his view, the United States should have been more critical both of the Israeli invasion of Lebanon and of Israel's "aggressive settlement policy on the West Bank." Instead of easing the terms of aid to Israel, he asserted, the United States should have imposed "tougher requirements on Israel as a means of making clear to them that we're very serious about the necessity of concessions on the West Bank." He also said that the Reagan administration had been "insensitive" to Syria's legitimate aspirations by "hailing this new strategic arrangement with Israel at precisely the moment when we probably should have been somewhat more reluctant to go into that kind of arrangement."

The candidate who was most critical of the Reagan administration's policy of support for Israel was Jesse Jackson, who directly attributed the problems faced by the American marines in Lebanon, and the threat to American interests in the Middle East more generally, to the American identification with Israeli policies. "When the President, in a negotiation with Mr. Shamir, did not link that negotiation with a commitment [by Israel to change its policy] on Golan Heights, West Bank occupation, expanded settlements, and the offensive use of American weapons in the invasion and occupation of Lebanon," Jackson stated, the president "made America a party to the occupation and to the invasion." Because America had in effect "helped to finance that invasion and occupation," this "robbed America of any innocence or any moral authority. It took away from America the role of a neutral peacekeeping force and therefore made our boys the object of the hostility, more so than against the other nations that were there." Jackson went on to stress that "we have an obligation to support Israel's right to exist for [sic] security, not to support her right to occupy and expand." He concluded that the United States should take the initiative to be the first "to get out of Lebanon and to prevail upon Israel to go back with a guarantee of keeping Israel's borders and boundaries secure and then use our diplomatic leverage to get Syria to go back to Syria."

Reagan Rebukes Critics of Lebanon Policy

In an interview with the *Wall Street Journal* on February 2, President Reagan asserted that withdrawal of U.S. troops from Lebanon at this point would "mean the end of Lebanon," the end of overall Middle East peace propects, and a "pretty disastrous result" for American foreign policy around the world. In a specific criticism of House Speaker O'Neill, who was planning the following week to push for a vote on a nonbinding Democratic-sponsored resolution calling for immediate withdrawal of U.S. forces, Reagan declared: "He may be ready to surrender, but I'm not." The president insisted that "great progress" had been made in strengthening the Lebanese central government and asserted that America's European partners in the peacekeeping force "feel as strongly as we do" about staying in Lebanon. "Syria is bent on territorial conquest," Reagan said, and only the presence of the multinational force had prevented it from seizing even more. Questioned as to what had been done to carry out his pledge to retaliate against the terrorists who had attacked the marine compound in Beirut in October 1983, killing 241 American servicemen, Reagan hinted that U.S.-Israeli strategic cooperation was effective in fighting against terrorism. He indicated that the United States had been planning to act against pro-Iranian terrorists based in Baalbek, whom the United States accused of the Beirut attack. But "someone else . . . took that target out before we could get to it," he added with a smile.

While President Reagan was talking tough in public about sticking it out in Lebanon and giving optimistic estimates on the viability of the Lebanese central government, the situation on the ground was rapidly deteriorating. On February 4 Prime Minister Shafiq al-Wazzan submitted his resignation to President Gemayel, and the following day the entire cabinet resigned. Secretary of State George Shultz blamed "direct threats" by Syria on the Muslims in the cabinet for the resignations. At the same time, in renewed heavy fighting, Druze and Shi'ite militiamen took over control of most of West Beirut. On February 6 President Reagan ordered air and naval attacks against antigovernment forces around Beirut, an act described by administration officials as a warning to Syria and its Lebanese allies.

U.S. Forces Withdraw from Beirut

That it was an empty warning became evident the following day, February 7, when President Reagan made the announcement that President Assad had been waiting for. Although euphemistically termed a "request" by the president to the secretary of defense "to present me with a plan for the redeployment of the Marines from Beirut to their ships offshore," the American withdrawal from Beirut was accomplished before the end of the month. The swiftness with which a decision was made to carry out what was widely regarded as a fundamental reversal of policy evoked a storm of questions and criticism. On February 12, in an ABC-TV interview, Under Secretary of State for Political Affairs Lawrence S. Eagleburger refused to respond when asked whether the president had not already decided to pull U.S. forces out of Lebanon when he made his scathing attack on "Tip" O'Neill and other Democratic critics, or when he had reiterated in a radio program that he was "not going to cut and run" in Lebanon. Eagleburger insisted, as had Secretary of Defense Caspar Weinberger, earlier on the same program, that transferring the American forces to warships off the shore of Lebanon still constituted a "presence in Lebanon." He expressed the hope that the Syrians would come to recognize that "Syria's longer-term interests require some sort of accommodation."

The British, Italian, and French were in no mood to try by themselves to fill the vacuum left by the Americans. Vice-President Bush said on February 15 that the United States was "very interested" in a French proposal to have a UN peacekeeping force dispatched to replace American and European troops. However, when the French formally introduced the proposal in the UN Security Council on February 29, it was vetoed by the Soviet Union. The French, British, and Italian forces were withdrawn from Lebanon soon after.

Syria Replaces U.S. as Key Influence in Lebanon

With his Western protectors gone, President Gemayel had to rely increasingly on the Syrians for political survival. The Syrians—who were generally believed to have been behind the assassination of Gemayel's brother Bashir, shortly after his election as president in September 1982—were now content to have Amin Gemayel continue as nominal president, so long as he did not attempt to challenge Syrian hegemony. In March Lebanon announced its abrogation of the May 17, 1983, accord with Israel that had been arduously negotiated by Secretary Shultz. On April 26 Gemayel appointed to the premiership Rashid Karami, a Sunni Muslim leader who was known as a close supporter of Syria and whose appointment symbolized the extent to which Damascus had replaced Washington as the major influence on the policies of the faltering Lebanese government. However, given the failure of the Lebanese national reconciliation talks held in Geneva in March, Syria's entry into the faction-ridden morass of Lebanese politics had all the makings of a Pyrrhic victory. While Assad could prevent the Lebanese government from pursuing foreign policies that Damascus opposed, it was something else to put the Lebanese humpty-dumpty back together again.

Lebanon Fades as American Campaign Issue

Although the Democratic hopefuls continued on occasion to point to Lebanon when they wished to indicate the Reagan administration's foreign-policy shortcomings, once American servicemen were no longer at risk, the issue quickly faded from American television coverage and public consciousness. Remarkably, unlike the controversial Vietnam war, which played a major role in Lyndon Johnson's decision not to seek a second term, or the Iranian hostage crisis, which contributed to Jimmy Carter's image of weakness and eventual reelection defeat, the Lebanon debacle caused Ronald Reagan no significant loss in personal standing as a leader with the American public.

Although administration officials continued throughout the year to assert that the United States was committed, in Secretary Shultz's words, to "the emergence of a more stable and sovereign Lebanon," there was no invoking of the domino theory, i.e., that if Lebanon were to fall, all American interests in the Middle East would suffer. On the contrary, the official tone became more restrained, and the issue was defined, not as a focus for competition between the superpowers, but essentially as an internal Lebanese dispute. The new U.S. approach to Lebanon was expressed by Assistant Secretary of State Richard W. Murphy in testimony before the Subcommittee on Europe and the Middle East of the House Foreign Affairs Committee on July 25: "We will be supportive of every effort which advances the goals of restoring unity and national reconciliation and the withdrawal of foreign forces. In the final analysis, however," he emphasized, the Lebanese "themselves must take the primary responsibility in dealing with their own problems."

The Reagan administration, having failed to get the Syrians to behave by use of the stick, now tried the carrot. In contrast to earlier administration statements, which characterized Syria as a major cause of the Lebanese problem, Assistant Secretary for Near Eastern Affairs Murphy, who had gained experience in dealing with President Assad while serving as U.S. ambassador in Damascus, now told the House members that "we believe that Syria has been one of the helpful players" in recent positive-looking developments. He stressed that "Lebanon needs peaceful, cooperative relations with both Syria and Israel," and added that the United States would "continue to encourage Lebanon to deal directly with Israel" on the issue of Israeli withdrawal and security arrangements along the border.

Some committee members were taken aback by Murphy's favorable comments about Syria. Republican representative Ed Zschau of California asked how Syria could be described as "a helpful player" after it had so long been depicted as "the troublemaker in the region." Murphy responded that "times change," adding that after the Syrians had succeeded in their objective of "blowing up" the Lebanese-Israeli agreement of May 17, 1983, the Syrians "showed themselves ready to move in the direction of helping to restore stability in Lebanon." The Syrians had apparently reached a policy decision that "a stable Lebanon and a stable Beirut" were necessary for greater stability in the region. Rep. Larry Smith (D.,Fla.), a strong supporter of Israel, said he was "distressed" by the choice of the word "helpful." "It's a relative term," he continued, offering a homespun analogy: "If someone throws you down a well a hundred feet . . . and then they haul you up 50 feet and you can see the light at the top of the well, you feel a lot better and you call them helpful, but you never would have been down there in the first place if they hadn't thrown you down there."

U.S. Vetoes Lebanese UN Resolution Critical of Israel

Lebanese acceptance of Syrian direction did not make life easier for the United States. On August 29 the Security Council met at the request of Lebanon on a complaint that Israel had tightened security provisions for travelers entering Israeli-held territory. Rashid Fakhoury, Lebanon's chief delegate at the United Nations, appealed to the council to put into effect previous resolutions calling for Israeli withdrawal. He also appealed, specifically, for Israel to immediately "lift its siege" of southern Lebanon, where, he charged, the civilian population was living in a "continual state of terror" because of the "excesses of Israeli occupation." Israel's chief delegate, Ambassador Yehuda Z. Blum, said that the new security provisions were necessary to stop the infiltration of terrorists and weapons. He insisted that "there was not the slightest justification" for calling the council into session, adding that it reflected the combined effect of Syrian pressure and domestic rivalries within Lebanon, where fighting had once again flared up in the north and central regions. On September 6 the United States vetoed a Security Council resolution calling on Israel to "immediately lift all restrictions and obstacles" recently imposed on Lebanese civilians traveling through Israeli-occupied southern Lebanon. U.S. delegate Warren Clark explained that the United States had opposed the resolution because it was "unbalanced" and took "a selective, myopic look at only one part of the problem."

Bombing of U.S. Embassy Revives Domestic Debate

The UN vote prompted a renewed threat, on September 8, by a caller identifying himself with the Islamic Jihad, "to destroy a vital American interest in the Middle East" in retaliation for the veto. True to the warning, on September 20 an explosives-filled van blew up in front of the U.S. embassy annex in East Beirut, killing 23 persons. This tragic incident once again made the Reagan administration a target of media criticism. On ABC-TV on September 30, Secretary of State Shultz was grilled by reporters eager to determine who was going to accept responsibility. Shultz responded that "the responsibility is with people who, through the use of terrorism," are trying to undermine "our quest for peace and stability in the Middle East and other parts of the world." He called the American ambassador in Beirut, Reginald Bartholomew, "a hero" who was nearly killed three times and who together with his staff was doing everything possible to improve security "in a risky environment." Shultz's apparent denial of administration culpability led one reporter to remind him that, following the 1979 Iranian hostage crisis, Ronald Reagan had not hesitated to criticize President Carter's role in the tragedy. The real issue, Shultz's questioner demanded, was "why, after the first Embassy bombing by truck [in April 1983] and the second bombing of our Marines by a truck [in October 1983], there weren't adequate security devices to keep a third Embassy from being bombed by a truck?" Shultz responded that an investigation was being conducted, but insisted that American embassies are "on the front lines" and that the latest incident was only a symptom of a much broader problem. "The problem," he emphasized, "is getting hold of this issue of terrorism, and we are working on it. Don't mistake that." (Secretary Shultz did in fact take the lead in the Reagan administration in pressing for more vigorous and concerted action against international terrorism. See below.)

The strain placed on U.S.-Lebanon relations by the latest bombing was evident during a visit to Washington by Premier Rashid Karami some two weeks after the tragic incident. After rejecting the U.S. suggestion that he engage in direct negotiations with Israel, Karami asked the United States to take part in arranging an Israeli withdrawal. At a meeting with Karami on October 2, Secretary of State Shultz turned down the Lebanese appeal, saying that "much more flexibility" and "quite a change in mood" on all sides would be required before the United States would consider such an effort. Shultz reportedly raised the issue of terrorist attacks against American installations in a "direct and forceful" fashion and stressed that "terrorism will not change U.S. policies and should not change the policies of other governments."

Reagan Administration Pursues Antiterrorist Campaign

On October 19 President Reagan signed into law the 1984 Act to Combat International Terrorism. The new law authorized payment of rewards for information concerning terrorist acts and authorized the spending of $356 million on what Reagan described as "urgently needed security enhancements for U.S. missions abroad." After thanking Congress for responding "swiftly" to his request, the president said the new law was an important step in the administration's "multiyear effort," in cooperation with our allies, to counter "the insidious threat terrorism poses to those who cherish freedom and democracy." Citing statistics to the effect that "since the first of September, there have been 41 separate terrorist attacks by no fewer than 14 terrorist groups against the citizens and property of 21 nations," Reagan concluded by asserting that "this nation bears global responsibilities that demand that we maintain a worldwide presence and not succumb in [sic] these cowardly attempts at intimidation."

By acting forcefully to enhance embassy security, the president did much to defuse the terrorism problem of its potential as a Democratic campaign issue. Moreover, whatever advantage Walter Mondale may have had on this issue was effectively neutralized by the Republican strategy of referring to him as part of "the Carter-Mondale administration," thereby saddling him with the negative image of Carter's impotence in the Iranian hostage crisis.

Shultz Calls for Tougher Antiterrorism Strategy

On October 25 Secretary of State Shultz delivered a major address on "Terrorism and the Modern World" at the Park Avenue Synagogue, a leading Conservative congregation in New York. Calling on the democratic nations of the world to recognize that terrorism was directed "against our most basic values and often our fundamental strategic interests," Secretary Shultz went on to examine various aspects of his subject in depth. He began by tracing documented links among terrorist groups and the key role played by the Soviet Union in supporting these groups. He then went on to discuss the need to combat moral confusion as to what constituted terrorism. Firmly rejecting the "insidious claim that one man's terrorist is another man's freedom fighter," he quoted the "powerful rebuttal to this kind of moral relativism" given by the late senator Henry Jackson: "Freedom fighters or revolutionaries don't blow up buses containing non-combatants; terrorist murderers do. Freedom fighters don't set out to capture and slaughter school children; terrorist murderers do. Freedom fighters don't assassinate innocent businessmen, or hijack and hold hostage innocent men, women and children; terrorist murderers do."

Referring to the Beirut bombing, Shultz again firmly rejected the counsel of those who would have the United States change its policy of support for Israel. He noted that "one of the great tragedies of the Middle East . . . is that the many moderates on the Arab side—who are ready to live in peace with Israel—are threatened by the radicals and their terrorist henchmen and are thus stymied in their own efforts for peace."

Shultz went on to praise Israel for helping to "raise international awareness of the global scope of the terrorist threat" and also for its practical contributions, which included winning battles against terrorism "in actions across its borders, in other continents, and in the land of Israel itself." Noting that much of Israel's success in fighting terrorism was due to "broad public support for Israel's antiterrorist policies," Shultz concluded, "the rest of us would do well to follow Israel's example." He criticized the usual American response after each terrorist incident of "self-condemnation and dismay, accompanied by calls for a change in our policies or our principles, or calls for withdrawal and retreat." Such responses, he warned, only encourage terrorists to "commit more acts of barbarism" in the hope that American resolve will weaken.

The heart of Shultz's address was the delineation of a strategy for moving beyond passive defense to active measures of "prevention, preemption, and retaliation." According to Shultz, the key elements in a successful strategy for combating terrorism would include (1) strengthening our intelligence capabilities, "particularly our human intelligence," (2) a capability to use force, and (3) a public willingness to use military force. He emphasized repeatedly that the public must understand before the fact the risks involved in combating terrorism with overt power, including "potential loss of life of some of our fighting men and the loss of life of some innocent people." In Shultz's view, fighting in the "gray areas" of international terrorism called for swift action, even in the absence of "the kind of evidence that can stand up in an American court of law." He warned, "We cannot allow ourselves to become the Hamlet of nations, worrying endlessly over whether and how to respond." He then appealed for greater international cooperation in the fight against terrorism, noting that at their summit meeting in London in June the leaders of the industrial democracies had agreed to redouble their efforts. It was time for them to band together to fight terrorism, as they had successfully done in an earlier era to eradicate piracy, he concluded.

Split in Reagan Administration on Antiterrorism Tactics

When Vice-President Bush was asked by a broadcaster in Cincinnati the following morning for comment on Shultz's statement about potential civilian loss of life, he responded, "I don't agree with that." Bush stressed the need to "pinpoint the source of attack," adding, "We are not going to go out and bomb innocent civilians." Bush may have been seeking to follow the line taken by President Reagan, who had said —in the televised foreign-policy debate with Walter Mondale the previous Sunday (October 21)—"In dealing with terrorists, yes, we want to retaliate, but only if we can put our finger on the people responsible and not endanger the lives of innocent civilians."

After the Shultz speech, Reagan declined to comment on the apparent differences between his secretary of state and vice-president. He did say of Shultz's remarks that "I don't think it was a statement of policy." Secretary Shultz, he explained, was only listing the factors that had to be considered, and "you couldn't rule out the possibility of innocent people being killed." Within 30 minutes of Reagan's remarks, however, White House spokesman Larry Speakes called reporters to issue a clarification: "Shultz's speech was administration policy from top to bottom." All Shultz was saying, according to Speakes, was that "in isolated cases, innocent civilians may be killed in a retaliatory strike. I emphasize may be, not will be." Further clarification was provided by an unnamed White House official who told reporters that the Shultz speech did not reflect any new policy decision.

Washington insiders reported that Shultz's candid public remarks in New York reflected his growing frustration over the reluctance of others in the administration, including Secretary of Defense Weinberger and the covert branch of the Central Intelligence Agency, to endorse specific military action against terrorists unless specific conditions were met: there was proof of the identity of the guilty parties; there was assurance of easy success; and civilian casualties could be avoided. The Shultz speech had been reviewed and endorsed by Robert C. McFarlane, the White House national security adviser, like Shultz a former Marine Corps officer. Both men had been arguing for some time for a firmer use of military power against terrorists in Lebanon and also for more direct U.S. strategic cooperation with Israel than had been considered advisable by the Pentagon. Shultz's address, therefore, was part of the continuing broader dispute within the administration as to the wisdom of committing American military force in Lebanon and the Middle East more generally.

Bush's Remarks Trouble Israel's Friends

Despite efforts by the White House staff to smooth over the differences within the administration, it was well known that Bush's views of Middle East issues were generally closer to those of the Pentagon and the CIA than to those of the secretary of state.

Bush was also known as being more critical of Israeli involvement in Lebanon than others in the administration. In a luncheon meeting with reporters at the National Press Club in Washington in July, Bush had intimated that the United States had greater concern for human life than did Israel. The United States, he emphasized, would like to be "as surgical as possible" and was "reluctant to take an action that might prove our ability to retaliate, but in the process might wipe out many innocent people." When his remarks aroused criticism among supporters of Israel, Bush's press secretary, Martin Fitzwater, issued a clarification. The vice-president, he said, "didn't mean to comment on the validity of Israel's policy of retaliation, which is in different areas and different circumstances."

Bush aroused consternation once again within the American Jewish community and in Israel with remarks made during a campaign debate with Democratic vice-presidential candidate Geraldine Ferraro on October 12. In discussing the administration's failure to stop terrorist attacks in the Middle East, Bush observed: "And the answer then really lies in the Middle East and . . . is a solution to the Palestine question, the follow-on to Camp David under the umbrella of the Reagan September

1982 initiative." Although he conceded that such a step would only "reduce terror, it won't eliminate it," he appeared to be supporting the Arabists' view that Israel was responsible for the terrorist response of the Palestinians, and that satisfying Palestinian demands would remove the major cause of international terrorism. Some observers also noted that the man who was "only a heartbeat away" from the presidency had referred to "the Palestine question" and not the "Arab-Israel dispute," the former a term used after 1948 primarily by Arabs who did not wish to acknowledge the reality of Israel.

Realizing the potential harm caused the Reagan election campaign by some of his controversial remarks, Bush met with senior White House and State Department officials and inserted a last-minute section on terrorism into a previously scheduled speech to the Zionist Organization of America. Speaking on October 27, he declared: "Let me assure you of one thing, the United States under this administration will never—never—let terrorism or fear of terrorism determine its foreign policy." To rectify the impression left by his remarks during the debate with Mrs. Ferraro, Bush emphasized: "Terrorism is not only or even predominantly a Palestinian phenomenon. It is truly international. Many local groups have broad and, often, common international connections, and couldn't operate as they do without those connections." It was high time, Bush concluded, "that we recognize this and join with our allies in a truly international drive against this insidious international terrorism."

U.S. Proceeds Cautiously on Middle East Peace

As a result of its sobering experience in Lebanon, the administration seemed to lose its appetite for bold new moves in the Middle East; the administration also showed little inclination to pressure Israel to accept an imposed peace plan. On the contrary, as Assistant Secretary of State for Near Eastern Affairs Richard Murphy reiterated in his testimony before the House Foreign Affairs Committee on January 26, 1984: "Our strategy toward the peace process is to encourage all parties to assist in creating the conditions necessary for Jordan to enter talks with Israel." The United States, he said, hoped that Yasir Arafat, chairman of the Palestine Liberation Organization's executive committee, "will now understand that the only way to tangible gains for the Palestinians is through direct negotiations between Jordan and Israel and that violent struggle is doomed as a way to achieve Palestinian goals."

The lack of progress in the on-again, off-again talks between King Hussein of Jordan and Arafat contributed to the sentiment in Washington that the Arab-Israeli dispute might well benefit from a period of benign neglect on the part of the United States. The prevailing view, expressed informally by Reagan administration officials, was that "the ball is now in the Arab court." In other words, the United States would await more concrete signs from the states of the region of their readiness to advance the peace process before Washington would once again commit its own power and prestige.

Egypt Reenters Arab Mainstream

Not that the United States had given up on the search for a more comprehensive Arab-Israeli peace. Indeed, Washington sought to encourage any potentially hopeful signs. One such development was Egypt's return to the mainstream of the Arab and Islamic worlds. The first official Saudi visitor to Cairo in seven years arrived at the beginning of January, and later that month the Islamic Conference Organization (ICO), at its meeting in Casablanca, formally invited Egypt to resume its membership. Radical members failed in their attempt to set as a condition Egypt's renunciation of the 1979 peace treaty with Israel; Egypt emphasized that in joining the ICO it would continue to honor its prior diplomatic commitments. The rapprochement between King Hussein of Jordan and President Hosni Mubarak of Egypt, including the restoration of full diplomatic relations between Amman and Cairo, in September, and exchanges of visits to each other's capital, marked further progress in Egypt's efforts to overcome the ostracism that had been imposed by the Arab League following Egypt's signing of the peace treaty with Israel.

Joint discussions held by Mubarak and Hussein with President Reagan at the White House on February 14, in Reagan's words, "reaffirmed that Egypt and Jordan will remain leaders in efforts to bring peace and security to the Middle East." Recent events in the area "make it even more urgent to keep the broader peace process moving," President Reagan declared, adding that "the tragic events in Lebanon show that the occupation of territory by outside forces does not lead to peace but rather to continued turmoil." He therefore wished to "reaffirm my commitment and that of our government to the principles I set forth in September of 1982, and in particular to the principle that the Arab-Israeli conflict must be resolved through negotiations involving an exchange of territory for peace."

Mubarak Champions Palestinian Cause

President Mubarak was even more pointed in his remarks, stating that "coexistence and the mutual recognition between the Palestinians and the Israelis" had to be based on recognition of justice and rights, including, "first and foremost, the right of the Palestinian people's self-determination. . . ." Turning to President Reagan, President Mubarak continued, "The Palestinian people are entitled to your support and understanding. There is no substitute for a direct dialogue with them through their chosen representative, the PLO." Such a dialogue, he contended, "would immensely serve the cause of peace to which we are both committed." Alluding to divisions within the organization and to Syria's backing of the more radical anti-Arafat elements, Mubarak went on to assert that "Arafat is a responsible leader who has demonstrated tremendous courage under the most difficult circumstances." Consequently, the Egyptian leader asserted, "a dialogue with him would reassure the Palestinian people and rekindle their hope for a better future."

Mubarak surely did not expect the United States—especially during an election year—to reverse its long-standing policy of not recognizing or negotiating with the

PLO until that organization recognized Israel and accepted UN Security Council Resolutions 242 and 338. In all likelihood, the Egyptian leader was trying to buttress the position of those State Department officials who contended that the United States might informally explore the PLO's readiness to modify its anti-Israel position, without formally violating the terms of the American commitment made to Israel by Secretary of State Henry Kissinger in 1975 and reaffirmed by all subsequent U.S. administrations. Moreover, the Reagan administration had reacted favorably, despite the criticism of American Jews, to Mubarak's meeting with Arafat in Cairo the previous December. It seemed clear, too, that Mubarak was seeking to reassert Egypt's role as the primary champion of the Palestinian cause, especially now that Syria's cynical manipulation of the Palestinians for its own purposes had been revealed in the fighting in Tripoli at the end of 1983. (In that northern port city, Syrian troops had openly aided Lebanese forces besieging Arafat's men.) The final and possibly most important reason for Mubarak's statement was his realization that no real progress could be achieved unless Jordan was directly involved. Since King Hussein still felt the need of some authoritative Palestinian support, Egypt encouraged dialogue both between Jordan and the PLO and the PLO and the United States.

Egypt played a crucial role in the behind-the-scenes diplomatic maneuvering that led to the Palestine National Council's meeting in Amman in November 1984 and that culminated in an agreement between Hussein and Arafat in February 1985. While many differences between the PLO and the Hashemite kingdom remained to be ironed out, the assumption of an active role in the peace process by King Hussein in 1984 represented a significant change. For a long time Jordan had hesitated to take any peace initiative on its own, arguing that the Arab League decision at Rabat in 1974, which declared the PLO to be "the sole legitimate representative of the Palestinian people," had effectively deprived Jordan of a negotiating role. However, the PLO's debacle in Lebanon, the widening splits within the organization, and the disarray within the Arab League—most notably Syria's support for non-Arab Iran in the continuing war against Iraq—all contributed to eroding the importance of the league and its decisions.

Iraq Reduces Radical Rhetoric and Resumes Ties with U.S.

King Hussein knew that he could move closer to Egypt without arousing opposition from neighboring Iraq, because one consequence of the debilitating Iran-Iraq war had been to cool Baghdad's ardor to serve as leader of the anti-Israel campaign. The regime of Saddam Hussein could no longer afford to denounce pro-Western Arab states such as Egypt, Jordan, and Saudi Arabia, whose military, financial, and logistical help it eagerly sought. Iraq's newly acquired pragmatism was also reflected in a lessening of its anti-American rhetoric and the resumption, in November, of diplomatic relations with the United States, relations which Iraq had broken in June 1967 because of alleged American support for Israel during the Six Day War. In fact, during his visit to Washington in November, Foreign Minister Tariq Aziz told questioners that Iraq would no longer oppose efforts by Israel's Arab neighbors and the Palestinians to make peace with her. He singled out the leaders of Iran, Libya, and Syria as the only ones in the region who still harbored unrealistic ambitions directed against their neighbors and who did not share in what he characterized as the general shift to a more realistic stand on foreign-policy questions in general and the Arab-Israeli dispute in particular.

Decline in Strength of Arab Anti-Israel Pressure

Another factor in King Hussein's decision to assert a more active and direct role in West Bank affairs was a growing realization that time was no longer on his side. In the early years following the 1967 war, Hussein had assumed that the weight of Arab oil influence would lead the United States to pressure Israel to relinquish the occupied territories—territories lost by Jordan after Hussein ignored Israel's warning to stay out of the war. While the power of Arab petrodollars had increased after the 1973 war, subsequent developments made reliance on outside pressure less and less feasible. Chief among these were the removal of Egypt from the conflict, after the signing of the Egyptian-Israeli peace treaty in 1979; deteriorating relations between Syria and Jordan; Iraq's preoccupation with Iran; and the more recent global oil glut that reduced OPEC's power. Yet another factor that helped to convince the king that unless he took active measures to reverse the process the West Bank might soon be irrevocably lost was the stepped-up Israeli settlement program that followed the Likud's assumption of power in 1977, coupled with the Reagan administration's assertion that the settlements were not "illegal" under international law—as the Carter administration had claimed they were.

Impact of Israeli Elections on Peace Prospects

The prospect of a clear-cut Labor victory in the July parliamentary elections in Israel was awaited with scarcely concealed eagerness in Washington as well as Amman. For one thing, Shimon Peres had given qualified support to the Reagan initiative when it was first presented. For another, the Labor party's traditional position of seeking compromise with Jordan over the disposition of the West Bank (Judea and Samaria) seemed to offer greater chance of eventual agreement than did the Likud's refusal to see any part of these territories ever revert to foreign sovereignty. This did not mean that it would be easy to reach agreement, however. Even the Labor party position—which envisioned permanent Israeli control over West Bank areas considered vital to Israel's security and maintenance of Israeli sovereignty over an undivided Jerusalem—was significantly different from Hussein's vision of peace, which called for Israeli withdrawal to the pre-June 1967 armistice lines, with only minor modifications.

In the event, the Israeli election results proved indecisive. Almost two months of intensive bargaining and compromise between the nearly evenly balanced Labor (44

Knesset seats) and Likud (41 seats) blocs preceded the formation, on September 13, of an unprecedented form of national unity government. (See "Israel" article in this volume for details.) The agreement was that for the first half of the government's four-year term, Labor's Peres would serve as prime minister and the Likud's Yitzhak Shamir would be foreign minister as well as alternative prime minister. At the end of two years their roles would be reversed. Yitzhak Rabin, the former Labor prime minister, was to be minister of defense; Yitzhak Modai, energy minister under the previous Likud government, would become minister of finance.

The basic policy guidelines of the national unity government affirmed agreement on the necessity to "expedite the withdrawal of the Israel Defense Forces from Lebanon in a short time." On the broader Arab-Israeli conflict, the coalition agreement tried to finesse the partners' differing approaches. It declared the government's willingness to "continue the peace process in keeping with the framework for peace in the Middle East that was agreed upon at Camp David, and to resume negotiations to give full autonomy to the Arab residents in Judea, Samaria, and Gaza." At the same time, Labor managed to get approval for a formulation stating that the new government would "call on Jordan to enter into peace negotiations," without specifically insisting that the negotiations be based on the Camp David accords, in recognition of the fact that Jordan still regarded the Camp David framework as inadequate. On the controversial issue of settlements, a cabinet majority would be required for approval of new ones, in effect giving Labor a veto over settlements it regarded as contrary to Labor's Allon plan, which opposed settlements with no security function in densely populated Arab areas. Both major parties agreed "not [to] negotiate with the PLO," and not to apply "sovereignty, Israeli or other . . . to Judea, Samaria, and the Gaza District." "In the event of a disagreement over the territorial issue," the parties stipulated, new elections would be held. This meant that the national unity government could neither annex the territories, as advocated by Likud and some of its ultranationalist allies on the right, nor cede any West Bank territory to Jordan, as advocated by Labor and some of its supporters on the left.

Peres Makes Peace Overture to Hussein

While some Middle East observers concluded that this formula meant stalemate, Prime Minister Peres interpreted his mandate as permitting him to pursue negotiations actively. It was only once an agreement had been concluded with Jordan that he would have to bring it to the people for approval. Analysts of the Israeli political scene pointed out that such a development would not only help to fulfill Israel's deep desire for peace but would also enhance Peres's personal standing. Moreover, if an accord was reached before the end of his two-year tenure, the required new elections would provide Peres with a legitimate reason not to turn the premiership over to Shamir. Accordingly, Peres used his first speech to the new Knesset, on September 16, to call upon Jordan to enter direct negotiations with Israel. Peres declared: "From this podium, and at this special moment, I call on King Hussein to come to the negotiating table in order to attain a genuine peace." He made it clear that he was not demanding any prior commitment by Jordan to the Camp David accords or any other specific formula when he went on to state, "We are prepared to discuss with Jordan every proposal from its side on the assumption that it will be open to proposals coming from our side."

Alluding to the undisguised hostility that both Israel and Jordan faced from radical regimes and anti-Western Islamic fundamentalist elements, Peres noted that the two countries shared some basic interests. "Jordan has many enemies and Israel also has many enemies, and the enmity between the two of us can be settled by the courageous path of permanent dialogue. . . . Let the Jordan be the river that irrigates the farmers' fields, not a rift of endless quarrels and threats."

Although not widely known, perhaps, there was already a considerable amount of tacit cooperation between Jordan and Israel. This included measures to prevent the infiltration of PLO terrorists, to enable West Bank students to take Jordanian matriculation exams for admission to Jordanian and other Arab universities, and to keep open the bridges across the Jordan for the transit of people and goods to and from the West Bank. The threats to such cooperation were also real, however. Following Hussein's resumption of diplomatic relations with Egypt in September, the Syrians warned the king that he risked assassination for this action and for contemplating peace negotiations with Israel. The government-run Syrian radio quoted Vice-President Zohair Masharka as telling a rally in Damascus on October 1: "Jordanian leaders should expect their fate will not be different from that of the late Anwar Sadat," the Egyptian president who was killed by Muslim extremists in Cairo in 1981.

Hussein Rejects Israeli Peace Bid

Hussein's response to Peres was unusually tough and negative. In a speech opening the fall session of the Jordanian parliament, on October 1, the king rejected Prime Minister Peres's call for negotiations as "nothing more than an exercise in subterfuge and deception" designed to buy time for Israel to carry out its "expansionist" aims. If Israel really wanted peace, he said, it could show its good faith by affirming support of the UN resolutions, which Hussein interpreted as requiring total Israeli withdrawal. The Arabs wanted peace, he asserted, but would "never concede one speck of dust on the West Bank, the Gaza Strip, or the Golan Heights."

The specific reference to the Golan Heights, which Israel had captured from Syria in 1967, was presumably designed to reassure Damascus that Hussein was not about to follow Egypt's example and conclude a separate peace with Israel. So was Hussein's expression of support for solving the Arab-Israeli dispute through an international peace conference that would include participation of the Soviet Union and the PLO, as well as Syria and Lebanon, instead of through bilateral talks with Jordan, as proposed by Israel. The recurrent Soviet proposal for reconvening the international conference that had been cosponsored by the United States and the Soviet Union in Geneva in 1973 had most recently been reiterated in a statement by Tass, the official Soviet news agency, on July 29, which said that the Soviet government was concerned "over the remaining explosive situation in the Middle East." As expected, both the Reagan administration in Washington and the Israeli government in Jerusalem reiterated their opposition to the proposal from Moscow, the chief arms supplier and political backer of Syria and other anti-American states. A senior Israeli official also cited Moscow's breaking-off of diplomatic relations with Israel as an obstacle, noting that "a country that has no relations with a side in the conflict has lost its main role in a peace process."

Hussein Accuses U.S. of Encouraging Israeli "Intransigence"

In the same speech to parliament, Hussein gave vent to his anger at the United States for its "procrastination and hesitancy" in supporting Arab peace efforts and for pursuing policies in the Middle East that "provided Israel with further cause for intransigence." Hussein, who was planning a trip to Moscow, also threatened that Jordan would no longer rely primarily on U.S. arms "in light of the negative American stand with regard to the legitimate provision of Jordan with defensive weapons." Hussein was still piqued over the decision of the Reagan administration the previous March to cancel its planned sale of 1,613 Stinger surface-to-air missiles to Jordan and 1,200 to Saudi Arabia, after the proposed sales encountered strong congressional opposition. Sens. Bob Kasten (R.,Wis.) and Bob Packwood (R.,Ore.) had collected 55 signatures on a senatorial letter of opposition to the president, while Rep. Lawrence J. Smith (D.,Fla.) mounted a similar campaign in the House. Hussein himself had contributed to the defeat by making harshly critical comments about American Middle East policy to the *New York Times* (March 14) and on CBS-TV's "Face the Nation" (March 18). In his interview with Judith Miller of the *Times,* the king had ruled out participation in American-sponsored peace talks with Israel, charging that American credibility in the region had suffered and that "the United States is not free to move except within the limits of what AIPAC [the American Israel Public Affairs Committee], the Zionists, and the State of Israel determine for it."

Reagan Defends Arms for Jordan in UJA Speech

There was an ironic element in the king's timing on this matter, for the previous day, March 13, President Reagan had gone out of his way to make a case for the Jordanian arms sale in a speech before the Young Leadership Conference of the United Jewish Appeal. In the section of his speech explaining that the U.S. objective was to "go on promoting peace between Israel and its Arab neighbors," the president noted that "Syria is trying to lead a radical effort to dominate the region through terrorism and intimidation aimed, in particular, at America's friends." He pointed out that "one such friend we continue to urge to negotiate with Israel is King Hussein of Jordan." And precisely because Jordan was crucial to the peace process, he continued, "Jordan, like Israel, is confronted by Syria and faces military threats and terrorist attacks." Therefore, President Reagan concluded, "since the security of Jordan is crucial to the security of the entire region, it is in America's strategic interest, and I believe it is in Israel's strategic interest, for us to help meet Jordan's legitimate needs for defense against the growing power of Syria and Iran." (The reference to Iran was an allusion to the recently revealed administration plan to provide $220 million in equipment for a mobile Jordanian strike force intended to help its Arab friends along the Persian Gulf resist Khomeini-inspired insurrections.) President Reagan asserted that "such assistance to Jordan does not threaten Israel, but enhances the prospects for Mideast peace by reducing the dangers of the radical threat."

Reagan's call for military aid to Jordan was met with silence and scattered hisses by the ardently pro-Israel Jewish audience. The UJA group had earlier warmly applauded the president when he protested the persecution of Jews in the Soviet Union, pledged that the United States would provide more aid in the form of grants to Israel—"to ensure that Israel will maintain its qualitative military edge"—and denounced the "so-called anti-Zionism" of the Iranian and Libyan representatives at the United Nations as "just another mask for vicious anti-Semitism." President Reagan received a standing ovation from the audience after he bluntly warned: "If Israel is ever forced to walk out of the UN, the United States and Israel will walk out together." He was again applauded when he reaffirmed the "long-standing American commitment" that the United States "will neither recognize nor negotiate with the PLO" so long as it "refuses to recognize Israel's right to exist and accept Security Council Resolutions 242 and 338."

American political observers generally regarded it as a sign of political courage on the part of the president to choose the Jewish leadership group as the forum in which to present the case for arms to Jordan. In meetings with Prime Minister Shamir in November 1983, Reagan had argued that improving ties with Jordan was consistent with the expanded strategic cooperation between the United States and Israel. "Having said it privately to Shamir, the president thought it was important to do it publicly at a time these matters are before Congress," said White House deputy press secretary Robert Sims. Thus Reagan's speech to the UJA was a calculated part of the administration's campaign to persuade American Jews and other supporters of Israel that Jordan and Israel faced a common enemy in Syria.

In the Middle East, however, the president's speech was interpreted quite differently. King Hussein and some other Arabs regarded it as demeaning and offensive that the president of the world's leading superpower should plead for Jewish support, thereby appearing to give the supporters of Israel veto power over U.S. Middle East policy.

Reagan Reiterates Middle East Peace Plan

Choosing to regard Hussein's critical remarks to the U.S. media in March as only a temporary irritant, President Reagan continued to propound the main lines of his

Middle East policy, while at the same time strengthening strategic cooperation with Israel. Speaking before the international convention of B'nai B'rith in Washington on September 6, Reagan said that America's Middle East peace efforts "still stand on the foundation of the Camp David accords" and the "fair and balanced positions" he had outlined in the September 1, 1982, Reagan initiative. His plan, he recalled, included "firm opposition" to an independent West Bank–Gaza Palestinian Arab state, and incorporated the key issues that the negotiating parties would have to resolve. Since his audience knew that the Israeli government at the time did not accept the Reagan plan, the president indicated that the United States would go along with whatever Israel and Jordan agreed to in negotiations. In any case, the president once again pledged that "we will never attempt to impose a solution on Israel."

Israel Responds with Conflicting Voices

When the president formally reiterated U.S. support for the Reagan initiative in his speech to the UN General Assembly in October, Foreign Minister Yitzhak Shamir, who was representing Israel at the UN session in New York, quickly announced that the national unity government "rejected" the Reagan plan. This set off the first serious foreign-policy squabble within the ideologically divided government. Prime Minister Peres, who was about to embark on his first official visit to President Reagan, was eager to start off on the right foot, unencumbered by his predecessor's baggage. Back in Jerusalem, cabinet secretary Yossi Beilin, a close confidant of the prime minister, tried to soften the negative impact of Shamir's remark. Since the Reagan plan had not yet been on the cabinet's agenda, Beilin explained, the government could not be expected to have taken a position on a question it had not yet discussed. Following heated transatlantic phone calls between Shamir and Peres, a compromise formula was agreed upon, one that represented at least a temporary victory for Shamir. It stated that, having not yet undertaken its own examination of the Reagan plan, the new government remained bound by its predecessor's rejection of it. Moreover, to assure that Peres did not go off on his own to make far-reaching concessions, Shamir insisted that he accompany Peres to the forthcoming meetings in Washington.

Although Reagan's landslide reelection victory on November 6 meant the continuation of the Reagan plan as official U.S. policy, differences over the plan caused no qvert friction between the United States and Israel for the remainder of 1984. The new Reagan administration focused its attention on domestic economic matters and on preparing the groundwork for new arms negotiations with the Soviet Union. In Israel, the new government was still preoccupied with working out an arrangement for withdrawal of its forces from Lebanon that would not jeopardize Israel's security and with trying to devise emergency measures to cope with the country's steadily worsening economic crisis. On the Arab side there were as yet no buyers for the Reagan plan.

Palestine National Council Meets in Amman

After months of delay and in the face of Syrian threats, Arafat finally accepted Hussein's invitation to convene the Palestine National Council (PNC), the PLO's "parliament in exile," in Amman, Jordan, on November 22. After only narrowly achieving a quorum—because of the boycott by anti-Arafat elements in the PLO —the PNC voted to oust its speaker, Khalid Fahoum, who had tried to block the session. Fahoum declared that any resolutions adopted in Amman would be "illegal" and "will not be carried out by most groups of the Palestinian resistance." Arafat faced opposition from two sources: the Syrian-backed "National Alliance," including Abu Musa's rebels from Fatah, as-Saiqa, the Popular Front for the Liberation of Palestine–General Command, and the Popular Struggle Front; and from the more Marxist "Democratic Alliance," consisting of the Popular Front for the Liberation of Palestine, the Democratic Front for the Liberation of Palestine, and the Palestine Liberation Front. Nevertheless, neutral sources estimated that Arafat still retained the support of most of his original backers in al-Fatah, by far the largest PLO component, as well as the sympathy of the overwhelming majority of the Palestinians on the West Bank.

The PNC meeting was remarkable in several respects. It highlighted the reconciliation between Arafat and King Hussein, who had forcefully expelled the PLO in September 1970 after that organization tried to overthrow him. Moreover, the proceedings of the PNC were televised throughout the Arab world and were viewed with fascination by many Arabs in the West Bank as well as in Israel. In his address to the opening session of the PNC, King Hussein bluntly called upon the PLO to abandon the fruitless path of armed struggle and to join him instead in seeking a negotiated solution on the basis of Security Council Resolution 242. The king also repeated his call for an international conference under UN sponsorship, which, he said, should include all the parties to the Middle East conflict—including the PLO "on an equal footing"—as well as the permanent members of the Security Council. (The PNC did not respond directly to Hussein's appeal, but it was endorsed by President Mubarak of Egypt at the conclusion of a visit to Cairo by Hussein on December 3.)

The fact that the meeting was held at all was considered a victory for Arafat. After dramatically tendering his resignation, Arafat accepted reelection as chairman of the PLO. Also significant was the election of two former West Bank mayors to the PLO's executive committee, giving practical expression to Hussein's efforts to bring about a PLO–West Bank reconciliation under his aegis. The significance of this event was not lost upon the Syrians, who intensified their campaign of encouraging the assassination of Jordanian officials both at home and abroad. When Fahd Kawasmeh of Hebron, one of the two West Bankers elected to the PLO executive committee, was shot to death in Amman on December 29, Arafat blamed Syria for the assassination.

Middle East Issues in U.S. Presidential Campaign

Attention in the early months of the U.S. presidential campaign, before the conventions, focused on the controversial candidacy of black minister and civil-rights activist Jesse Jackson for the Democratic nomination. While other Democratic presidential aspirants sought to outdo one another in uncritical expressions of support for Israel, Jackson increasingly became an embarrassment to the Democrats among Jewish voters. During the campaign there was widespread reproduction of a photo of Jackson being embraced by PLO leader Yasir Arafat during a visit by Jackson to the Middle East in 1979. At the start of the 1984 campaign, Jackson reiterated his view that "the Palestinian question remains at the heart of the Middle East agony," and that "the no-talk policy toward the PLO has . . . deprived the American President of the ability to reduce Israel's enemies." Citing America's dual interests—"protecting Israel's right to exist in security within internationally recognized boundaries" and achieving "Palestinian justice, or self-determination, or a homeland for the Palestinian people"—he called on the United States to use "its strength to get the PLO and others to recognize Israel . . . and Israeli leaders to move toward a mutual recognition policy. . . ."

Most Jewish voters regarded Jackson's pro-Palestinian policies as harmful to Israel. Opponents also dug up a July 1980 speech to the "American Federation of Ramallah, Palestine" in which the Reverend Jackson had declared: "Zionism is rooted in race, it's a political philosophy. Judaism is religion and faith; it's a religion. We have the real obligation to separate Zionism from Judaism. . . . Zionism is a kind of poisonous weed that is choking Judaism." Fears concerning Jackson's true sentiments regarding Israel and Jews were heightened by pejorative epithets that he applied to New York Jews during the 1984 campaign and by his failure to reject the support of Louis Farrakhan, leader of a Black Muslim splinter group, who repeatedly made blatant antisemitic and anti-Israel comments. It was not until the end of June that Jackson explicitly criticized these views, without, however, denouncing Farrakhan personally.

Although Walter Mondale made it clear he did not share Jackson's approach to the PLO and other Israel-related issues, his seeming hesitation to denounce Jackson —so as not to alienate potential black voters—as well as the failure of the Democratic party convention to adopt an explicit condemnation of antisemitism, raised questions among some Jewish voters about Mondale's own capacity—once he won the nomination—to lead the Democratic party.

Democrats Adopt Pro-Israel Platform Plank

The efforts of Jesse Jackson's delegates on the Democratic platform committee to have their candidate's Middle East views incorporated in the platform were beaten back by the united action of the supporters of Mondale and Sen. Gary Hart.

The platform adopted by the party's convention in San Francisco at the end of June was specific in its support for Israel and opposition to "any consideration of negotiations with the PLO, unless the PLO abandons terrorism, recognizes the state of Israel, and adheres to UN Resolutions 242 and 338." Asserting that "Israel is strategically important to the United States, and we must enter into meaningful strategic cooperation," the Democrats also opposed the Reagan administration's "sales of highly advanced weaponry to avowed enemies of Israel, such as AWACS aircraft and Stinger missiles to Saudi Arabia." While helping to meet "the legitimate defensive needs of states aligned with our nation," the platform plank continued, "we must ensure Israel's military edge over any combination of Middle East confrontation states."

With regard to the search for a broader Arab-Israeli peace, the Democratic party condemned "this Administration's failure to maintain a high-level Special Negotiator for the Middle East," and urged speedy resumption of the Camp David peace process. After applauding the example of Israel and Egypt in taking "bold steps for peace," the Democrats asked the government to "press for negotiations among Israel, Jordan, Saudi Arabia, and other Arab nations." The explicit mention of Saudi Arabia, which has no common border with Israel, and the omission of Syria, which does, struck observers as curious. The choice may have reflected awareness that anti-American Syria was unlikely to respond favorably to American overtures. At the same time, the wording seemed to imply that the Saudis' desire for direct control over the AWACS planes scheduled to be transferred to them the following year could be used to win their support for American peace efforts. (Information provided by American-manned AWACS planes had already enabled Saudi pilots to repel an attack by Iranian jets before they could reach Saudi oil installations. The shooting down of one—and according to some reports two—Iranian planes managed to deter the Iranians from again intruding into Saudi airspace.)

The platform reemphasized the "fundamental principle that the prerequisite for a lasting peace in the Middle East remains an Israel with secure and defensible borders, strong beyond a shadow of a doubt, that the basis for peace is the unequivocal recognition of Israel's right to exist by all other states, and that there should be a resolution of the Palestinian issue."

Republicans Support Expanded U.S.-Israel Ties

The Middle East platform plank adopted by the Republican party at its convention in Dallas in mid-August differed little in substance from that of the Democrats, though it naturally sought to defend the record of the Reagan administration and to portray it as successful. The platform contended that President Reagan's Middle East policy "has been flexible enough to adapt to changing circumstances, yet consistent and credible so that all nations recognize our determination to protect our vital interests." It argued that "the President's skillful crisis management throughout the Iran-Iraq War has kept that conflict from damaging our vital interests" and that his peace efforts "have won strong bipartisan support and international applause." Regarding Lebanon, which had earlier in the year consumed so much of the Reagan administration's efforts, the platform simply noted that "Lebanon is still in turmoil, despite our best efforts to foster stability in that unhappy country." The Republicans warned that "with the Syrian leadership increasingly subject to Soviet influence, and the Palestine Liberation Organization and its homicidal subsidiaries taking up residence in Syria, the peace of the entire region is again at stake." The Republicans also reaffirmed their opposition to recognizing or negotiating with the PLO "so long as that organization continues to promote terrorism, rejects Israel's right to exist and refuses to accept U.N. Resolutions 242 and 338."

In the Republican view, partnership with Israel was the core of America's strategy of countering Soviet expansion in the Middle East. According to the platform, "Israel's strength, coupled with United States assistance, is the main obstacle to Soviet domination of the region. The sovereignty, security, and integrity of the state of Israel is a moral imperative. We pledge to maintain Israel's qualitative military edge over its adversaries." In an implicit rejoinder to Mondale's call for greater strategic cooperation with Israel, the Republican platform continued, "Under President Reagan, we have moved beyond mere words to extensive political, military and diplomatic cooperation. U.S.-Israeli strategic planning groups are coordinating our joint defense efforts, and we are directly supporting projects to augment Israel's defense industrial base. We support the legislation pending for an Israeli-U.S. free trade area."

Declaring that "our determination to participate actively in the peace process begun at Camp David" had won support for the Reagan administration "from moderate Arab states," the platform pledged "continued support to Egypt and other moderate regimes against Soviet and Libyan subversion" and called on them to assist American efforts for settlement of the region's "destructive disputes." (It had come as something of a shock to the Reagan administration when a few days earlier King Hassan of Morocco, one of the leading pro-Western Arab moderates, suddenly announced a union with the radical, Soviet-armed, anti-American Libya of Colonel Qaddafi. It later emerged that Hassan had managed to obtain a commitment from Qaddafi to stop aiding the Polisario rebels who were fighting Morocco for control of the Western Sahara. What Qaddafi obtained in return was not clear, although some suggested it was simply a measure of respectability. Qaddafi had earlier in the year been accused by President Mubarak of Egypt of laying mines in the Gulf of Suez, as well as of interfering in the Sudan, Chad, and other neighboring countries.)

Democrats Make Issue of U.S. Embassy in Israel

The one Israel-related issue on which there was a clear difference between the Reagan administration and the Democratic opposition was the location of the U.S. embassy in Israel. This was seized upon by the media and assumed exaggerated importance in the campaign. The American embassy had remained in Tel Aviv since

1948, despite the fact that Israel began moving its governmental headquarters to Jerusalem in 1949 and established its capital there. Both Democratic and Republican platforms agreed that "Jerusalem should remain forever undivided with free access to the holy places for people of all faiths." On the question of the city's status as Israel's capital, or on the location of the American embassy, the Republicans were silent. The Democrats, however, went on to assert in their platform: "As stated in the 1976 and 1980 platforms, the Democratic Party recognizes and supports the established status of Jerusalem as the capital of Israel. As a symbol of this stand, the U.S. Embassy should be moved from Tel Aviv to Jerusalem."

What the platform did not say was that, during his four years as president, Jimmy Carter—the Democratic candidate elected on the 1976 platform—did nothing to move the embassy. On the contrary, in his official letters to President Sadat and Prime Minister Begin accompanying the September 1978 Camp David accords, Carter reaffirmed the American position on Jerusalem that had been enunciated by American diplomats at the United Nations following the 1967 war. In effect this stated that the United States would not accept unilateral actions by Israel as defining the status of Jerusalem, which would ultimately have to be determined in peace negotiations. In contrast to Carter, who had questioned the wisdom of the platform plank even before his election, Mondale said that, if elected, one of his first actions would be to move the American embassy to Jerusalem. During the primary campaign in New York, Senator Hart, who initially had been noncommittal on the matter, also made a strong public statement backing the move, in an appearance before the Conference of Presidents of Major American Jewish Organizations.

The leader in the campaign to move the embassy was Sen. Daniel Patrick Moynihan (D.,N.Y.). On October 31, 1983, Moynihan had introduced a bill (S.2031) in the Senate stipulating that "notwithstanding any other Act, the United States Embassy in Israel and the residence of the American Ambassador in Israel shall hereafter be located in the city of Jerusalem." In a statement before the Senate Foreign Relations Committee on February 23, 1984, Moynihan criticized the "unprecedented and bewildering practice" by the United States government, in official publications, of designating Tel Aviv as the location of the U.S. embassy in the country of Israel, while treating Jerusalem as if it were a separate country, with its own consular "post" reporting to Washington. He also criticized the United States for its failure to veto a UN Security Council resolution of August 20, 1980, that called on all member nations to withdraw their embassies from Jerusalem, which was designated as among "Arab territories occupied by Israel." Moynihan said that these American actions had undermined international law and given "succor and encouragement to avowed enemies of the State of Israel."

Moynihan went on to suggest that President Reagan privately shared his view, and that it was only "State Department policy" that inhibited him from moving the embassy. If Congress mandated such action, Moynihan continued, the president would be enabled to act "without fear of his action being misunderstood in other capitals." Moynihan said he would "dismiss with a measure of contempt" the proposition that standing with Israel in this matter would cause grave damage to America's relations with other states in the region. Only the previous August, he noted, the government of Kuwait had refused to receive an experienced career officer as our ambassador there on the grounds that he had once been the American consul general "in what our State Department Telephone Directory describes as the 'country' of Jerusalem. What do we gain, then," Moynihan asked, "for having kept our embassy out of Jerusalem?" (To compound the irony, the diplomat in question, Brandon Grove, had, during his service in Jerusalem, drawn fire from right-wing Israeli and American Jewish groups for maintaining close personal contacts with nationalistic Palestinians on the West Bank.)

Moynihan stressed that Israel was the only country whose own choice of capital the United States failed to accept. The Kingdom of Saudi Arabia, he noted, which had until recently declined to have embassies located in its capital of Riyadh, had now reversed its position and requested that embassies be located there. Consequently, Moynihan pointed out, "the United States government, in the normal way that applies to every country in the world save one, is now proceeding to build an embassy in that capital."

By early March, the Moynihan bill had attracted 34 cosponsors; a parallel bill in the House, introduced by Tom Lantos (D.,Calif.) and Benjamin A. Gilman (R.,N.Y.), had 180 cosponsors. At a press conference in Washington on February 22 announcing the measure, Lantos stressed that this was not simply "a symbolic gesture" but that "we will make a full-court press" to have the legislation quickly approved by Congress so as to "present the President with this legislation for his signature well before the November elections." Although the five congressmen participating in the press conference stressed the bipartisan support for the measure, Rep. Robert Mrazek (D.,N.Y.) noted that this was the "one year" when the president could be expected to sign it. Should the president veto the legislation, however, Lantos and the others warned that they would tie the embassy move to an appropriations bill.

Shultz Presents Administration Opposition to Jerusalem Law

Sen. Charles H. Percy (R.,Ill.), chairman of the Committee on Foreign Relations, had asked the executive branch for a coordinated statement of its position in advance of hearings on the Moynihan bill, which began on February 23. Secretary of State Shultz responded in a letter of February 13. The administration opposed the proposed legislation, he explained, as part of the "consistent" U.S. position that "the final status of Jerusalem must be resolved among the parties concerned, in the context of a comprehensive, just, and lasting Middle East settlement." Pending such a negotiated settlement, "our Embassy and the Ambassador's residence remain in Tel Aviv, a recognized part of the state of Israel." The change called for in the Senate bill would be "extremely harmful at a critical juncture" in the peace process, he added, noting that there was "a renewed opportunity" to resume and broaden the negotiations called for by the president's September 1982 initiative. "A precipitous transfer" of U.S. diplomatic facilities to Jerusalem, Shultz warned, would seriously undercut the ability of the United States to play "a facilitative role in promoting a negotiated settlement."

Secretary Shultz also criticized the Moynihan bill because it raised "serious constitutional questions of a separation of powers nature." In the administration's view, he said, "the President's exclusive constitutional power" to conduct foreign relations was "beyond the proper scope of legislative action." Congressman Lantos rejected this argument, saying that Congress had the right to be included in the "formulation of policy." Moreover, he said, Congress had frequently taken action relating to consulates, as for example, preventing a previous administration from closing some.

State Department officials in the Middle East also echoed Secretary Shultz's warning that, in the current environment, "a move of our embassy would certainly fan Islamic extremism, possibly inciting a wave of violence against our citizens, diplomats, and installations." When Nicholas A. Veliotes, the ambassador to Egypt, visited Washington for consultations, he told some senators he hoped they would give him advance notice before they voted to move the embassy so that he and his staff could be evacuated from Cairo first. Told by a reporter of the State Department's concern about violence, Senator Moynihan responded, "If the United States can be deterred from taking a normal, legal, everyday act by the threat of mob violence, what kind of country have we become?"

American Jewish Organizations Support Jerusalem Bill

Kenneth Bialkin, chairman of the Anti-Defamation League of B'nai B'rith and current chairman of the Conference of Presidents of Major American Jewish Organizations, testified in support of the bill and also accused the U.S. government of giving in to fear of Arab reaction. "It is time to end several generations of U.S. surrender to intimidation and threats from our so-called friends in Arab lands," he said. Also testifying on behalf of the bill were spokespersons for the International Christian Embassy in Jerusalem and the Moral Majority. Joining the administration in opposing the pending legislation were representatives of the Episcopal and Orthodox churches, the U.S. Catholic Conference, and David Sadd, executive director of the National Association of Arab Americans. At the hearing on February 23, Senator Percy noted that this was the first time the Congress had ever formally considered the issue. In a briefing for the Jewish media, Thomas Dine, executive director of AIPAC, said that this fact constituted a "precedent" and that no matter what happened to the current bill, the issue would continue to be raised.

Embassy Issue Poses Dilemma for Israel

Even though the Reagan administration and the supporters of the Jerusalem bill seemed to be heading for a showdown, there was in fact a strong desire to avoid a full-scale confrontation. Israeli officials were caught in a dilemma. While they were naturally committed to the idea that united Jerusalem was the eternal capital of Israel, and they welcomed international acceptance of this fact, they did not wish to embarrass the Reagan administration. Apart from the fact that they were working to forge increasingly close economic, strategic, and military ties with Washington, they did not wish to appear to be interfering in American domestic politics, especially in a presidential election year. American Jewish supporters of Israel faced a similar dilemma. They did not wish to undercut Senator Moynihan's positive initiative, but they also did not wish to contribute to a potential backlash in anti-Israel feeling by the administration. Consequently, while both sides publicly proclaimed that they were sticking to their respective positions, behind-the-scenes efforts were under way to work out a face-saving compromise. An administration offer in March to drop the sale of Stinger missiles to Jordan and Saudi Arabia in exchange for abandonment of the Jerusalem bill was turned down by supporters of the Moynihan bill. (When the trade-off was rejected, the administration dropped the sale anyway, following Hussein's critical remarks.)

In an appearance on NBC's "Meet the Press" on April 1, Secretary Shultz was asked whether President Reagan would, as he had hinted, veto the Jerusalem legislation. While refusing to predict what Reagan would do, Shultz stressed that he knew both from the president's public statements and from private conversations with him that "the President is very much opposed" and "will not move that embassy" even if Congress passed the legislation. However, he added, "my impression is that people in the Congress are more and more having second thoughts about this and looking around for some ways in which they might defuse this issue."

President Reagan himself remained adamant on the issue. When asked by reporters during his flight home from China on May 1 whether the administration was considering a compromise, he replied, "No, I feel very strongly that this is not something we should do. . . . Jerusalem has to be part of the negotiations if we're going to have peace talks."

Meanwhile, the legislation was gaining supporters in both houses of Congress. Following the Senate hearings, additional joint hearings were held by the House Foreign Affairs Subcommittee on Europe and the Middle East and the Subcommittee on International Operations. In testimony on May 1, Howard Friedman, president of the American Jewish Committee, pointed out that the American position was not consistent with general American practice. He cited as an example the fact that "our embassy in East Germany is located in East Berlin, though that city is not recognized by the U.S. as the capital." Responding to Shultz's argument that the embassy could not be moved until the status of Jerusalem had been finally settled, Friedman contended that situating the embassy in Jerusalem would not preclude negotiations called for under the Camp David accords.

Turning to the expressed fear of hostile Arab reaction, the American Jewish Committee leader suggested that the Arabs' bark was worse than their bite: "When the American-Israeli strategic cooperation agreement was announced, Arab states voiced their opposition but took no retaliatory action against the United States." In contrast to "that substantive agreement," he noted, moving the embassy to Jerusalem "would be a symbolic act." But, he concluded, it would be an important step, since it would provide another "unmistakable sign that the United States is committed to having firm, unambiguous relations with Israel."

On June 21 Under Secretary of State for Political Affairs Michael H. Armacost reiterated the administration's reasons for opposing the embassy move. In reviewing the historical record, he noted that as early as 1949, when Israel began relocating some government ministries to Jerusalem, the United States had said that it could not accept this unilateral move. Again in 1960 "we informed Jordan of our opposition to its making the eastern part of the city Jordan's second capital." He stressed that "we would not have achieved the Camp David Accords—which led to Israel's first peace treaty with an Arab state—if the United States had adopted the position of either Israel or Egypt on the subject of Jerusalem." He said he realized "the frustrations" many feel because of the administration's position, but urged them to look at the long term. He was convinced that "in the long term it is peace for Israel that will bring with it a solution to the problem of the status of Jerusalem."

Congress Backs Away from Confrontation

Meanwhile, the House sponsors of the Jerusalem bill had expressed a readiness to defer a vote on the issue until the following year—if Reagan were to indicate that he would not oppose it after the election. The president refused. Despite administration opposition, on October 2 the two House subcommittees approved nonbinding resolutions declaring it to be "the sense of the Congress" that the embassy be moved "at the earliest possible date." With Congress scheduled to adjourn in a few days, however, there was little prospect of the resolutions being voted upon by the full House, and in the Senate the measure had not even been put to a vote. Supporters of the bill claimed a moral victory, nevertheless, since their position had not been defeated, and vowed to bring up the issue again in the future. The president's political advisers were grateful that by avoiding the need for a presidential veto, the unresolved issue would not cost them dearly with Jewish voters, and the State Department was relieved that it had been spared another complicating factor in U.S. relations with the Arab and Islamic worlds.

One political figure who did suffer fallout from the episode was Senate Foreign Relations Committee chairman Percy, an opponent of the Jerusalem bill. Percy told a Chicago radio audience on October 5 that his Democratic opponent, Rep. Paul Simon (D., Ill.), "brings the house down when he debates against me in a temple" and calls for moving the American embassy in Israel to Jerusalem. "Jewish people are the most intelligent people I've ever known," Percy said. "But they are also extraordinarily emotional, and on that particular issue they are wrong, wrong, wrong!" Jewish votes in Illinois and financial support for Simon from pro-Israel political-action committees around the country helped Simon to defeat Percy in the November senatorial race.

Mondale Warns of Reagan "Surprises" for Israel

Walter Mondale, the Democratic nominee, tried to play upon Jewish fears of what a second-term Reagan administration would do. In a speech to some 200 Jewish supporters in Washington on September 17, Mondale said that on the issue of the Middle East, "Mr. Reagan has been essentially absent," and that others less sympathetic to Israel, including Defense Secretary Weinberger, "have taken charge." Mondale warned that a Reagan reelection might bring "December surprises" for Israel, such as more arms sales to Saudi Arabia and other Arab states, increased pressure on Israel to accept a reactivated Reagan plan, and possible resumption of secret talks with the PLO. He charged that the administration had already conducted "400 hours of so-called unofficial talks with Yasir Arafat and the PLO."

Mondale said that instead of the Reagan plan, which "made concessions to the Arabs at Israel's expense before talks even started," he would "give the new Israeli government time to develop its own policies toward the Arabs." At the same time, he would strengthen strategic cooperation and end "the fiction that Jerusalem is not the capital of that good country" by moving the U.S. embassy to that city. Emphasizing his firm commitment to America's "special relationship" with Israel, he concluded that "I would rather lose with your support than win without it."

Mondale was to get his wish. Although Reagan won reelection by a national landslide, Jews were among the few groups (blacks and persons earning less than $10,000 per annum were the others) that gave a majority of their votes to the Democratic contender. While the Republicans continued to make inroads in the traditionally Democratic Jewish vote—obtaining roughly one out of every three Jewish votes—some political analysts had predicted a better showing among Jews, especially in light of the Democrats' mishandling of the Jackson-Farrakhan issue. In the end, though, other factors apparently carried more weight than did mistrust of Jesse Jackson. Concern over U.S. policy toward Israel was undoubtedly one, though to what extent it is hard to determine. Probably most significant was growing Jewish discomfort with Ronald Reagan's closeness to Christian right-wing conservatives, whose views on church-state separation and on America as "a Christian nation" he evidently shared. (See "Intergroup Relations" article in this volume.)

Reagan Administration Strengthens Ties with Israel

While Mondale may have succeeded in arousing fears among some Jewish voters about a second Reagan administration, the president took every opportunity to let his record on the Middle East make its own case. In a speech to the B'nai B'rith International convention in September, Reagan asserted that "our administration has strengthened the American-Israeli alliance in three crucial ways." He listed these areas: upgraded and formalized strategic cooperation, including cooperation in military research and development, procurement, and logistics; the marked increase in economic assistance to Israel from 1981 to 1984, including the changeover from loans to grants; and the initiation of negotiations for an unprecedented Free Trade Area (FTA) between the two countries. In actuality, these actions enjoyed bipartisan support—for example, the legislation to authorize the president to negotiate and conclude the FTA was passed in the House by a vote of 416 to 6 and in the Senate by a vote of 96 to 0—but Reagan could take credit for initiating them.

The president could also point to his successful rounds of meetings with Foreign Minister Shamir and Prime Minister Peres. At a joint press conference with Peres in the White House rose garden on October 9, Reagan said that he was "impressed by the bold and wide-ranging steps" the new Israeli national unity government was undertaking to revitalize the economy and announced plans to establish a joint economic development group of officials and private experts from both countries to help Israel overcome its severe economic problems. Reagan concluded that the recent discussions with Shamir and Peres "reconfirm the close friendship, the mutual respect, and the shared values that bind our countries. Our ties remain unbreakable, [they] continue to grow." In his response, Prime Minister Peres declared that "I found in the White House a true friend of Israel" and expressed his gratitude to the president for the fact that "the relations between the United States and Israel have reached a new level of harmony and understanding."

Probably the most significant development in the relationship was the president's success in overcoming traditional hesitations in the Defense Department and in the Near East bureau of the State Department to close and *public* U.S.-Israeli cooperation in the military area. Robert McFarlane, the president's national security adviser, told the national convention of Hadassah—in San Francisco on August 28— that because the Reagan administration was convinced that "Israel and the U.S. are allies in the defense of freedom in the Middle East and throughout the world," it had accomplished "long-lasting structural changes" to strengthen the U.S.-Israeli relationship. Among these, McFarlane said, were strategic cooperation; expanded and more sophisticated levels of diplomatic cooperation; procurement of Israeli high-technology equipment for the American military; and U.S. assistance for Israel in building its new Lavi fighter and SAAR patrol boat.

After Secretary of Defense Weinberger visited Israel in mid-October for two days of discussions that were described by both sides as "extremely warm and friendly," he announced that the Reagan administration would give Israel access to the advanced American technology needed to produce its ultramodern Lavi fighter. (Weinberger had reportedly opposed U.S. aid earlier, because the Lavi would compete with the American-made Northrop F-20.) The secretary of defense also said that a joint U.S.-Israeli working team would study Israel's requests to acquire three American diesel submarines as well as offers by Israel to sell 120-millimeter mortars to the U.S. Army. (It was subsequently revealed that the submarines would be jointly produced and that the U.S. Navy had decided to purchase Israeli-manufactured Kfir fighters to simulate Soviet MIGs in training exercises for American pilots.)

On December 11 the Defense Department announced the start of joint antisubmarine exercises in the eastern Mediterranean by ships and aircraft of the U.S. and Israeli navies. Pentagon officials said that except for a medical evacuation drill the previous summer, this was the first time the two countries had practiced military maneuvers since the president had agreed to increase military cooperation with Israel.

To friends of Israel, all these developments were hopeful signs that whatever storm clouds might lie ahead on the Middle East diplomatic horizon, the American-Israeli strategic relationship would continue to gain strength during the second Reagan era.

GEORGE E. GRUEN

Communal

Attitudes of American Jews Toward Israel: Trends Over Time

ALMOST EVERY STUDY of American Jewry includes references to the place of Israel in the lives of American Jews. Similarly, works on the history of Israel and American-Israeli relations discuss the contributions of American Jewry in helping to sustain the Jewish state. It is widely recognized and accepted that the two largest contemporary Jewish communities have a special relationship.

This article examines continuities and changes in the attitudes of American Jews toward Israel, as they have been expressed in public-opinion surveys over a period of some four decades. The specific dimensions measured are the overall strength of American-Jewish attachment to Israel, attitudes toward U.S. governmental and private Jewish aid to Israel, and opinions about various aspects of the Arab-Israeli conflict.

Data Sources

The article is based on data from a number of surveys carried out under both general and Jewish auspices, beginning in 1948. Methodologically, the studies represent a variety of sampling approaches.[1] The earliest surveys of Jewish attitudes were conducted in cities with easily identifiable Jewish neighborhoods. The first such

Note: The author acknowledges the support of the Leonard Davis Institute for International Relations at the Hebrew University in the preparation of this article. He also thanks Herbert Kelman, Mordechai Gazit, Milton Himmelfarb, and Chaim Waxman for valuable comments on an earlier draft.

[1]Problems of design and sampling in surveys of American Jewry are discussed in Harold S. Himmelfarb, "Research on American Jewish Identity and Identification: Progress, Pitfalls and Prospects," in Marshall Sklare (ed.), *Understanding American Jewry* (New Brunswick, N.J., 1982), esp. pp. 66–73; Samuel C. Heilman, "The Sociology of American Jewry: The Last Ten Years," *Annual Review of Sociology,* Vol. 8 (1982), pp. 135–160; and Egon Mayer, *From Suburb to Shtetl: The Jews of Boro Park* (Philadelphia, 1979).

survey was carried out in Baltimore in May 1948, just a few days after the creation of Israel, by the National Opinion Research Center (NORC), on behalf of the American Jewish Committee.[2]

In 1952 and 1957–1958 the American Jewish Committee conducted surveys of Jews living in two different types of communities. The first was an East Coast city of 130,000, with a Jewish population of 8,500, identified only as "Riverton."[3] The second community studied, a Midwestern suburb of 25,000 people, of whom approximately 8,000 were Jews, was named "Lakeville."[4] While the Riverton sample of 200 Jewish families was considered representative of about a third of American Jewry (excluding the Jews of New York City), the Lakeville sample of 432 individuals was seen as "representing to a greater or lesser extent the experiences of most American Jews."

Additional surveys conducted in the late 1960s and early 1970s targeted more specific samples. In 1969 Charles Liebman investigated the views of rabbis and presidents of synagogues affiliated with Orthodox, Conservative, and Reform Judaism, while in 1970 Leonard Fein and others conducted a major survey of Reform Jews.[5] In two separate studies, initiated in 1965 and 1972, Simon Herman investigated the attitudes of several hundred American students who were spending a year at the Hebrew University of Jerusalem.[6]

In the early 1980s the major polling organizations—Harris,[7] Gallup,[8] and

---

[2]Marshall Sklare and Benjamin B. Ringer, "A Study of Jewish Attitudes Toward the State of Israel," in Marshall Sklare (ed.), *The Jews: Social Patterns of an American Group* (Glencoe, Ill., 1958), pp. 437–450.

[3]Marshall Sklare and Marc Vosk, *The Riverton Study: How Jews Look at Themselves and Their Neighbors* (New York, 1957).

[4]Marshall Sklare and Joseph Greenblum, *Jewish Identity on the Suburban Frontier* (New York, 1967).

[5]Charles Liebman, "The Role of Israel in the Ideology of American Jewry," *Dispersion and Unity*, Vol. 10 (Winter 1970), pp. 19–26; Leonard J. Fein et al., *Reform Is a Verb: Notes on Reform and Reforming Jews* (New York, 1972).

[6]Simon N. Herman, *American Students in Israel* (Ithaca and London, 1970); *Jewish Identity: A Social Psychological Perspective* (Beverly Hills, Calif., 1977).

[7]In July 1980 the Harris organization conducted a comprehensive survey of both Jews and non-Jews, using personal interviews. The Jewish sample consisted of 1,030 respondents. Louis Harris, *A Study of the Attitudes of the American People and the American Jewish Community Toward Anti-Semitism and the Arab-Israeli Conflict in the Middle East,* Study No. 804011, August 1980.

[8]The Gallup organization preferred telephone interviews. In September 1981, for example, they interviewed a sample of 522 Jews and in August 1982 a national sample of 605 adults and an additional cross-section of 258 American Jews. Gallup claimed a margin of error of $\pm$ 8 percentage points for the September 1981 poll and $\pm$ 8 percentage points for the August 1982 survey. These margins of error are somewhat larger than those normally accepted for national samples. See *Newsweek*, September 14, 1981, and October 4, 1982.

Yankelovich[9]—carried out comprehensive polls of American-Jewish opinion, primarily on issues surrounding the Arab-Israeli conflict. At the same time, Steven M. Cohen produced four national surveys of American Jews (1981–1982, 1982, 1983, 1984), carried out under the auspices of the American Jewish Committee.[10] Sample size in these surveys ranged between 500 and 1,000.

In 1984 Deborah Lipstadt, Charles Pruitt, and Jonathan Woocher administered lengthy questionnaires to participants in a United Jewish Appeal conference for young leaders. This effort produced the American Jewish Young Leadership Survey, whose sample of 750 had a median age of 33.[11]

While the surveys that form the basis of this study used a variety of sampling and interviewing approaches, the fact that important questions and themes were repeated over time provides a sufficient basis for trend analysis.

Attitudes Toward Israel

AMERICAN-JEWISH ATTACHMENT TO ISRAEL

In September 1945, a few months after the end of World War II, the Roper organization asked a cross-section sample of American Jews to state their views about the following proposal:

> "A Jewish state in Palestine is a good thing for the Jews and every possible effort should be made to establish Palestine as a Jewish state or commonwealth for those who want to settle there."[12]

Some 80 percent of the respondents approved of this statement, while 10 percent disapproved. In response to another question, more than 80 percent rejected the notion that "Jews are a religious group only and not a nation, and it would be bad for the Jews to try to set up a Jewish state in Palestine or anywhere else." The Roper organization commented that the decision to support or oppose the establishment

---

[9]In February 1981 the Yankelovich organization conducted a major survey of Jews and non-Jews about their beliefs on Israel and other issues. It was based on 1,215 interviews, of which 174 were with Jews. Gregory Martire and Ruth Clark, *Anti-Semitism in the United States* (New York, 1982).

[10]Steven M. Cohen, "The 1981–1982 National Survey of American Jews," AJYB, Vol. 83, 1983, pp. 89–110 and "What American Jews Believe," *Moment,* July-August 1982, pp. 23–27; "After the War and Before the Peace: A Survey of American Jewish Public Opinion in the Aftermath of the Israeli/PLO War in Lebanon" (New York, September 1982); *Attitudes of American Jews Toward Israel and Israelis: The 1983 National Survey of American Jews and Jewish Communal Leaders* (New York, 1983); *The 1984 National Survey of American Jews: Political and Social Outlooks* (New York, 1984). Cohen used a mail-back questionnaire which was sent to a national sample of households with distinctive Jewish surnames (DJN).

[11]Deborah Lipstadt, Charles Pruitt, and Jonathan Woocher, "What They Think," *Moment,* June 1984, pp. 13–17.

[12]AJYB, Vol. 48, 1946–47, pp. 243–255.

of Israel was taken with a high "degree of firmness," and that supporters "were evenly distributed through all economic levels." Two months later a Gallup Poll found overwhelming support in the American Jewish community (90 to 10 percent) for the proposal to allow Jews to settle in Palestine.[13]

In May 1948, just a few days after the birth of Israel, NORC put this question to Jews in Baltimore:

"The Jews have set up a new Jewish state in part of Palestine. Do you approve or disapprove of this action by the Jews?"[14]

Ninety percent approved of the establishment of Israel and a similar percentage thought that the United States was right to recognize Israel.

All in all, the initial surveys of American Jewish opinion were highly favorable toward Israel. By a ratio of 90 to 10 percent, American Jews supported the establishment of Israel, Jewish immigration to Israel, the Israeli declaration of independence, and the decision by President Truman to grant recognition to Israel immediately after its founding.

Since the establishment of Israel, American Jewry has consistently held highly favorable feelings toward it (Table 1). In these surveys conducted between 1957 and 1983, all but one of the pro-Israel scores rank above 90 percent. The breakdown of the last score, for 1983, shows an enormous affinity for Israel, both among the public and the leaders of the Jewish community. Of the 91 percent expressing favorable feelings toward Israel, 43 percent said that they were "very pro-Israel," while 48 percent were "pro-Israel." The combined score for all the remaining categories— "neutral," "anti-Israel," and "very anti-Israel"—was less than 10 percent.

TABLE 1. OVERALL ATTITUDES TOWARD ISRAEL, 1957–1983 (PERCENT)

Date	Poll	Favorable Pro-Israel	Unfavorable Anti-Israel	Neutral	(n)
1957	Riverton	94	5	1	(200)
1972	Herman	91	9	—	(269)
1981	Yankelovich	96	4	—	(174)
1981	NSAJ	94	1	6	(673)
1982	Cohen Post-Lebanon	88	1	11	(500)
1983	NSAJ	91	3	6	(640)

Sources: Riverton—footnote 3; Herman—footnote 6; Yankelovich—footnote 9; NSAJs and Cohen Post-Lebanon—footnote 10.

---

[13]George H. Gallup, *The Gallup Poll, Public Opinion, 1935–1971*, Vol. 1, 1935–1948 (New York, 1972), p. 554.

[14]Sklare and Ringer, op. cit., p. 441.

Because Israel has faced a large, hostile Arab world since its inception, the question of its very survival has been a source of concern. In the 1981 Yankelovich survey, 93 percent of the respondents said that "the continuation of Israel as a Jewish state is important," while only 5 percent held the opposite opinion.[15]

Even stronger evidence of Israel's importance to American Jews is found in the responses to a query regarding the hypothetical destruction of Israel (Table 2). The great majority of those questioned said they would feel a sense of great personal loss if Israel were destroyed. The figures for 1981, 1982, and 1983 are particularly striking since participants were asked to agree or disagree with the assertion that the loss of Israel would be the "greatest personal tragedy" in their lives: 83, 83, and 77 percent of respondents, respectively, answered in the affirmative.

In May-June 1967, when the hypothetical situation of Table 2 turned suddenly into the frightening reality of the Six Day War, American-Jewish political activity in behalf of Israel was coupled with an outpouring of volunteers and money, all of which testified better than any public-opinion poll to the strong attachment of American Jews to Israel. Polls taken after the war basically confirmed the high levels of concern and action shown during the crisis.

Marshall Sklare, chief author of the 1957–1958 Lakeville studies, returned to Lakeville in the early months of 1968 to "learn something about the response" of American Jewry "to the Israeli crisis, to the war, and to its aftermath."[16] Sklare called his mission "a reconnaissance effort," and indeed was able to interview only 17 residents of Lakeville, 11 of whom were from the original study sample of 432. He found that, during the crisis, most of the respondents were very concerned about

TABLE 2. HYPOTHETICAL DESTRUCTION OF ISRAEL, 1957–1983 (PERCENT)

Date	Poll	Yes	No	Not Sure	(n)
Q. "Would feel a personal sense of loss if Israel were destroyed."					
1957	Lakeville	90	10	—	(432)
1975	Harris	94	6	—	NA
Q. "Would feel as if I had suffered the greatest personal tragedy of my life if Israel were destroyed."					
1981	NSAJ	83	13	5	(673)
1982	Cohen Post-Lebanon	83	9	8	(500)
1983	NSAJ	77	10	13	(640)

Sources: Lakeville—footnote 4; Harris—footnote 7; NSAJs and Cohen Post-Lebanon—footnote 10.

[15]Martire and Clark, op. cit., p. 87.
[16]Marshall Sklare, "Lakeville and Israel/The Six Day War and Its Aftermath," *Midstream,* October 1968, pp. 3–21.

the survival of Israel. They strongly supported Israel's position and increased their financial contributions to the state. The decisive Israeli victory not only relieved them of tension and anxiety, it gave them a sense of pride and confidence. These feelings were shared even by those who claimed to be anti-Zionists.

In this same period, Simon Herman was investigating the feelings of Jewish identity of American-Jewish students studying in Israel.[17] Since these students were experiencing the pressures of the war directly, their reactions were, not surprisingly, even more intense than those of their compatriots in the United States. Statements like the following, cited by Herman, well represent the students' feelings: "I'd say the biggest impact of the Six Day War on me was the realization (the knowledge was there before June 1967) that the destruction of Israel meant the end of our sign of hope in modern Jewish existence. American Jews couldn't live without Israel." According to Herman, 87 percent of the respondents indicated that they had been reminded of the Holocaust during the Six Day War.

Similar attitudes and behavior emerged during the 1973 Yom Kippur War as during the Six Day War, thus making clear the depth of American Jewish commitment to Israel's survival.

Zionism and Pro-Israelism

Analysis of the data cited above reveals the strong emotional attachment of American Jews to Israel. But do the data also point to a clear Zionist commitment? A few months after the Yom Kippur War, Norman Podhoretz, the editor of *Commentary* magazine, argued as follows: "If Zionism means supporting the idea of a sovereign Jewish state in Palestine, then most American Jews have been Zionist since the end of World War II."[18] Podhoretz's equation of Zionism with "support" of a sovereign Jewish state did not go unchallenged. Columbia University professor David Sidorsky maintained that American Jews rejected both Zionist and non-Zionist ideologies, adding:

> Support of Israel in a non-ideological way without a philosophy of Jewish history or a coherent set of principles, but with a sense of moral purpose and pragmatic policies, has become a major aspect of the American Jewish consensus. The obvious question to put to the thesis is whether the distinction between pro-Israel consensus and a Zionist ideology is a distinction with a difference.[19]

Sidorsky did not provide a direct answer to his question, but others did. Simon Herman and Chaim Waxman argued that there was a major difference between

---

[17]Herman, *American Students in Israel.*

[18]Norman Podhoretz, "Now, Instant Zionism," *New York Times Magazine,* February 3, 1974, p. 11.

[19]David Sidorsky, "The End of Ideology and American Jewry," *Betfuzot Hagolah* (Hebrew), No. 85/86, Summer 1978, p. 114.

Zionism and pro-Israelism. In Herman's view, Zionism "represents an all-encompassing approach to the problems of the Jewish people," not just positive attitudes toward Israel or even readiness to emigrate to Israel. Waxman asserted that from a true Zionist perspective, Israel was the spiritual and cultural center of Judaism. "A Zionist is one for whom Israel plays a central role in his own personal life, in his identity and very existence." By contrast, Waxman said, a pro-Israel American Jew is one "who lives in the U.S. and supports Israel economically, politically, and even emotionally, but whose primary source of Jewish identification is derived from, and oriented to, the American Jewish community."[20]

The lack of clarity on the theoretical issue was reflected in popular attitudes as well. The 1983 National Survey of American Jews showed 39 percent of the public and 50 percent of the leadership identifying themselves as Zionist. In the same period, several major non-Zionist organizations joined the Jewish Agency and the World Zionist Organization. All this, however, needs to be viewed in the broader context of the time. In the mid-1970s the Arab bloc, the Communist nations, and the Third World countries sought to delegitimize Israel via the denunciation of Zionism, an effort that culminated in the 1975 UN General Assembly resolution equating Zionism with racism. This resolution was seen by Jews everywhere as a direct assault on world Jewry, no less so than the State of Israel. Thus, favorable statements about Zionism made during the mid and late 1970s do not provide an accurate measure of the true feelings of American Jewry on this subject.

It is clear that in earlier surveys American Jews did not equate support of Israel with support of Zionism (Table 3). Within each of the groups studied, individuals assigned far more importance to supporting Israel than to supporting Zionism as essential or desirable to being a "good Jew."

Classical Zionism defines the condition of Jews in the Diaspora as permanently insecure, and consequently views settlement in Israel as essential. American Jews, however, have never accepted these assumptions. As far back as the 1948 Baltimore study, only 5 percent of the respondents said that they would like to emigrate to Israel; in the 1952 Riverton survey, 7 percent expressed an interest in moving to Israel. Results in more recent studies are slightly higher, but do not alter the basic trend. In the 1981–1982 National Survey of American Jews, 12 percent of the respondents agreed with the statement "Each American Jew should give serious thought to settling in Israel," while 82 percent disagreed. The 1983 National Survey of American Jews reported that only 17 percent of American Jews had "ever seriously considered living in Israel."

---

[20]Chaim I. Waxman, "The Centrality of Israel in American Jewish Life: A Sociological Analysis," *Judaism,* Vol. 25, Spring 1976, p. 177.

For more extensive discussion on the question of Zionism and pro-Israelism, see Steven M. Cohen, *American Modernity and Jewish Identity* (New York, 1983), pp. 162–163; Jonathan S. Woocher, "The Civil Judaism of Communal Leaders," AJYB, Vol. 81, 1981, pp. 149–169 and Chaim I. Waxman, *America's Jews in Transition* (Philadelphia, 1983).

TABLE 3. PRO-ISRAELISM VS. ZIONISM, 1957, 1970 (PERCENT)

	Support Israel		Support Zionism	
	Lakeville (n = 432)	Reform Jews (n = 864)	Lakeville (n = 432)	Reform Jews (n = 864)
Percent who believe that to be a "good Jew" the item:				
Is essential	21	37	7	13
Is desirable	47	45	23	30
Makes no difference	32	—	59	—
Is essential not to do	—	1	9	—
Rank order of item, of 22 total items	14	5	17	16
Rank order of item, of 14 items of specifically Jewish content	7	2	9	9

Sources: Lakeville—footnote 4; Reform Jews—footnote 5.

Economic and Military Assistance

The extensive economic assistance that American Jewry has given to Israel over the years can undoubtedly be viewed as one of the most impressive measures of American-Jewish attachment to Israel.[21] All surveys of American Jews show overwhelming majorities expecting the U.S. government to aid Israel, but American Jews themselves even more so. In the 1948 Baltimore survey, 76 percent of the respondents supported American aid to Israel, but a much larger majority, 95 percent, said that American Jews should assist Israel even if the U.S. government did not. Preference was shown for assistance in the form of money, food, and clothing (Table 4); least support was given to the sending of soldiers, although about half of the respondents still expected American Jews to volunteer for military service in Israel's behalf.

The 1957–1958 Lakeville survey also found substantial support for Jewish economic aid to Israel. Of six different types of possible Jewish support, "raising money for Israel" was approved by 93 percent of the sample.

In general, insufficient data have been generated to assess accurately the percentage of American Jews who have contributed money to Israel. A few sources of information are available, however. In a July 1980 Harris survey, 83 percent of the respondents said that they had contributed financially to "an organization which supports Israel." In the 1981–1982 National Survey of American Jews, almost half

---

[21]See Marc Lee Raphael, *A History of the United Jewish Appeal, 1939–1982,* Brown Judaic Studies 34 (Providence, R.I., 1982).

TABLE 4. TYPES OF AID TO ISRAEL: U.S. GOVERNMENTAL OR JEWISH, MAY 1948 (PERCENT)

Type of Aid	NORC-Baltimore Survey (n=230)	
	Favor U.S. Government Aid	Favor Jewish Aid
Food and clothing	59	93
Money	62	91
Arms and ammunition	51	80
Sending soldiers	23	51

Source: NORC-Baltimore—footnote 2.

the respondents said that they had contributed directly to "Israeli educational or charitable institutions"; the same survey in 1983 found 34 percent of the respondents reporting that they "have given the UJA $100 or more in the last twelve months." One of the best indicators of American Jewry's attitude regarding financial contributions to Israel is a Harris survey (1974–1975) in which 87 percent of the respondents agreed that "Jews who live in the U.S. have special obligations to support Israel with funds and other aid."[22]

Between 1971 and 1985, Israel received some $30 billion worth of military and economic aid from the United States. Even as Israeli financial needs grew, and increased demands for aid were made, surveys of American Jews yielded consistent support for official U.S. aid in the range of 91 to 96 percent (Table 5). Almost half of American Jews also approved of American diplomatic and military assistance to Israel, even at the risk of the United States becoming involved in a Middle East war. More than half of the respondents supported sending American troops to defend Israel in case of extreme danger.

Attitudes Toward the Arab-Israeli Conflict

BASIC ISSUES

The American-Jewish community has been concerned about the Arab-Israeli conflict since the beginning of Israel's existence. This concern is heightened in times of crisis and war, when it is channeled into massive financial and political support. American Jews have generally agreed with fundamental Israeli positions in the conflict. Recently, however, they have begun to express reservations about certain policies, especially those which have also generated controversy in Israel.

---

[22]Quoted in Seymour Martin Lipset and William Schneider, "Carter Vs. Israel: What the Polls Reveal," Commentary, November 1972, p. 27.

TABLE 5. U.S. ECONOMIC AND MILITARY ASSISTANCE, 1971–1983 (PERCENT)

Date	Poll	Question	Yes	No	Don't Know/ No Opinion
1971	*Newsweek*-Gallup	The U.S. should help Israel with diplomatic support & military equipment	95	2	3
1974/75	Harris	Agree-disagree: U.S. sending military support & supplies to Israel	96	2	2
1980	Harris	" "	96	2	2
1981	Yankelovich	The U.S. should increase (continue at same level, cut back) military aid to Israel. (Increase & continue=yes, cut=no)	93	2	5
1981	Yankelovich	The continuation of U.S. support to Israel is important	95	2	3
1981	NSAJ	U.S. support for Israel is in America's interest	93	2	5
1983	NSAJ	" "	91	3	6
1971	*Newsweek*-Gallup	U.S. should help Israel with diplomatic support and military equipment, even at risk of becoming involved in a war	49	32	19
1980	Harris	If it looked as though Israel were going to be overrun by the Arabs in another war, the U.S. should be willing to send troops to support Israel	56	27	17

Sources: Newsweek-Gallup—*Newsweek,* March 1, 1971; Harris—footnote 7; Yankelovich—footnote 9; NSAJ—footnote 10.

During the 1950s the vast majority of American Jews blamed the Arab side for failure to resolve the Arab-Israeli conflict. In November 1955, for example, 69 percent said that the Arabs were more to blame for the conflict, while none said that Israel alone was at fault.[23] In April 1957, following the Sinai campaign, 83 percent held the Arabs responsible for the conflict, while only 2 percent saw Israel as responsible.

Various surveys of American Jews conducted since 1967 reveal consistent support for Israel's position overall as well as for specific policies (Table 6). During the 1967 Six Day War, 99 percent of American Jews who were polled said that Israel was "more right" than the Arabs. Successive polls taken before and after the signing of the Israeli-Egyptian peace treaty in 1979 indicated a strong belief in Israel's peaceful intentions. In both the 1981–1982 National Survey of American Jews and Steven Cohen's post-Lebanon study, approximately three-quarters of the respondents held the view that Israel's policies were neither "too hawkish" nor "too dovish," but "about right."

Cohen's 1982 study included items specifically related to the war in Lebanon. Two of the given choices referred to the controversial invasion of West Beirut and Israel's actions there. Forty-nine percent of the respondents believed that Israel was right to "try and expel the PLO military forces," and 27 percent thought "Israel should have attacked and destroyed" those forces. Only 5 percent said Israel should never have gone into Lebanon, and 13 percent thought "Israel should have gone into Lebanon, but should have stopped after 25 miles."

THE PALESTINIAN PROBLEM

Questions on the Palestinian issue—couched in various forms—have been asked by several investigators. The findings help to clarify the range of American-Jewish opinion on the matter, while at the same time making clear the limitations of public-opinion polls.

Most probing of the Palestinian issue focuses on two specific matters: Israeli-PLO negotiations and the establishment of an independent Palestinian state on the West Bank. In the years 1980–1984 pollsters approached the issue of Israeli-PLO negotiations by asking respondents to agree or disagree with two different propositions (Table 7). One was the actual Israeli official position of nonnegotiation; the second was a hypothetical situation: Israel should talk to the PLO, contingent upon PLO recognition of Israel and renunciation of terrorism. A comparison of the responses to the two questions reveals a distinct contrast. As long as the PLO was seen as adhering to the goals stated in its National Covenant and was employing terrorism, American Jewry overwhelmingly supported Israel's refusal to negotiate with PLO

---

[23]Hazel Erskine, "The Polls: Western Partisanship in the Middle East," *Public Opinion Quarterly,* Vol. 33, Winter 1969/70, pp. 633–634.

TABLE 6. POSITIONS AND POLICIES IN THE ARAB-ISRAELI CONFLICT, 1967–1982
(PERCENT)

Date	Poll	Question	Yes	No	Don't Know
1967	Harris	Israel was more right than the Arabs in the Six Day War	99	—	1
1975	Harris		89	5	6
1976	Harris	Israeli leadership is reasonable and will really work for a just settlement	94	3	3
1980	Harris		87	8	5
1980	Harris	Israel really wants peace with Egypt	92	5	3
1981	Yankelovich	Israeli attitudes toward a Palestinian state in the West Bank are reasonable	71	17	12
1981	Yankelovich	Israel's refusal to give back the Golan Heights is reasonable	78	13	9
1981	Yankelovich	Israel has the right to make Jerusalem its capital	74	14	12
1981	NSAJ	Israeli policies are about right (not too hawkish, not too dovish) or too dovish	77	23[a]	—
1982	Cohen Post-Lebanon		81	19[a]	—
1982	Cohen Post-Lebanon	Israel was right to send forces to expel the PLO from West Beirut; Israel should have attacked and destroyed the PLO in West Beirut (responses combined)	76	18[b]	7

Sources: Harris 1967—Erskine, footnote 23; Harris 1974, 1976, 1980—footnote 7; Yan-kelovich—footnote 9; NSAJ and Cohen Post-Lebanon—footnote 10.
[a]"Israeli policies too hawkish."
[b]Of this 18 percent, 5 percent said "Israel never should have gone into Lebanon in the first place," and 13 percent said "Israel should have stopped after the first 25 miles."

TABLE 7. ISRAELI–PLO NEGOTIATIONS, 1980–1984 (PERCENT)

Date	Poll	Yes	No	Don't Know/ No Opinion	(n)
Q. "Israel is right in refusing to negotiate with the PLO [because it is a terrorist organization that wants to destroy Israel]."[a]					
1980	Harris	90	7	3	(1,030)
1981	Yankelovich	62	28	10	(174)
1981	NSAJ	74	18	8	(673)
1982	Cohen Post-Lebanon	76	15	9	(640)
Q. "Israel should talk to the PLO if the PLO recognizes Israel [and renounces terrorism]."[a]					
1980	Harris	53	34	13	(1,030)
1981	*Newsweek*-Gallup	69	23	8	(522)
1982	Cohen Post-Lebanon	66	23	10	(500)
1983	NSAJ	70	17	13	(640)
1984	AJYLS	66	24	9	(756)

Sources: Harris—footnote 7; Yankelovich—footnote 9; NSAJ and Cohen Post-Lebanon—footnote 10; *Newsweek*-Gallup—footnote 8; AJYLS—footnote 11.
[a]The bracketed phrases did not appear in the Yankelovich survey.

representatives. However, given the possibility of PLO recognition of Israel and renunciation of terrorism, a sizeable majority of American Jews and their leaders indicated readiness to approve PLO-Israeli talks.

A similar picture emerges in relation to attitudes toward the establishment of a Palestinian state (Table 8). When the idea of an independent Palestinian state was presented in a humanitarian context (question "a"), almost half the respondents supported the idea. However, when the context was broadened to include other elements, such as Israel's security and the PLO, the outcome was totally different. The prospect of a Palestinian state that would include Yasir Arafat and the PLO (question "b"), for example, elicited enormous opposition (86 to 6 percent). In polls by Harris and the National Survey of American Jews, when respondents were asked to choose between two alternatives—Israeli annexation of the West Bank or the establishment there of a Palestinian state (question "c")—they showed significant support for Israeli annexation, in one case by a margin of 54 to 20. An item (question "d") affirming both Palestinian rights and Israel's security needs produced mixed results, in this case, perhaps, due to the composition of the samples.

While inconsistent opinions on the matter of a Palestinian state most likely reflect the objective complexity of the issues, they may also be attributed to the conflict between wishful thinking and realistic expectations among those interviewed. In the

TABLE 8. PALESTINIAN STATE, 1980–1984 (PERCENT)

Q.	Date	Poll	Context	For	Against	Don't Know
(a)	1980	Harris	Humanitarian	49	36	15
(b)	1980	Harris	Under PLO	6	86	8
(c)	1980	Harris	Israeli Security	20	54	26
(c)	1981	NSAJ	Israeli Security	28	42	30
(d)	1983	NSAJ	Rights & Israeli Security	48	26	27
(d)	1984	AJYLS	"	34	46	19

Questions:
  (a) "The Palestinian people are now homeless and deserve their own independent state, just as much as the Jews deserved a homeland after World War II."
  (b) "Arafat and the PLO should be given the West Bank and allowed to form an independent Palestinian state."
  (c) "If the alternatives are permanent Israeli annexation of the West Bank or an independent Palestinian state, then an independent Palestinian state is preferable."
  (d) "Palestinians have a right to a homeland in the West Bank and Gaza, so long as it doesn't threaten Israel."

Sources: Harris—footnote 7; NSAJ—footnote 10; AJYLS—footnote 11.

July 1980 Harris survey, a 59-to-25-percent plurality of respondents agreed with the following statement: "There must be a way to guarantee Israel's security and also give the Palestinians an independent state on the West Bank." Yet, in the same Harris survey, 63 percent of the respondents agreed with the following statement: "If the West Bank became an independent Palestinian state, the Russians would soon use it as a launching pad for them to destroy Israel and to take over the entire oil-rich Middle East." A similar proportion, 64 percent, agreed with the following statement, which was presented in the 1981–1982 National Survey of American Jews: "If the West Bank became an independent Palestinian state, it would probably be used as a launching pad to endanger Israel."

On a related issue—whether Israel should take permanent control of the West Bank—42 percent of respondents in the 1983 National Survey of American Jews and 48 percent of the respondents in the 1984 poll of United Jewish Appeal young leadership favored such action. Even higher pluralities emerged in polls conducted by *Newsweek*-Gallup: 61 percent of the respondents in 1981 and 58 percent of the respondents in 1982 favored Israeli sovereignty over the West Bank—with or without civil control by local Palestinians. Only between 7 and 9 percent of the respondents, respectively, supported the establishment of a Palestinian state (Table 9).

Conclusion

The bulk of American Jewry is concerned with the survival and well-being of Israel and has supported it both politically and economically. The great majority of American Jews share the larger American consensus about the need for economic and military aid to Israel, on the grounds, primarily, that it serves both American and Israeli interests. At the same time, most American Jews do not consider themselves Zionist in the classical sense, and only a few have expressed the wish to settle in Israel.

American Jews have traditionally supported basic Israeli positions and strategies in the Arab-Israeli conflict, mobilizing to assist Israel during times of war and crisis. Regarding the Palestinian problem, American Jews have opposed negotiations with the PLO and the establishment of an independent Palestinian state on the West Bank. However, they have shown readiness to revise these opinions in the event that the PLO changes its ideology and tactics, and if the establishment of a Palestinian state no longer threatens the security of Israel.

The most striking conclusion to be drawn from the data cited in this study is that the attitudes of American Jews toward Israel have been remarkably stable and

TABLE 9. SOLUTIONS TO THE PALESTINIAN PROBLEM, 1981–1982 (PERCENT)

Proposals	Newsweek-Gallup Poll	
	Sept. '81 (n=522)	Sept. '82 (n=258)
Q: "The Camp David accords call for negotiations on Palestinian autonomy over the Israeli-occupied West Bank. Which of these proposals for the West Bank would you prefer to see implemented?"		
Israeli sovereignty with military & civil control by Israel	29	19
Israeli sovereignty with military control by Israel but civil control by the Palestinians themselves	32 }61	39 }58
Returning the West Bank to Jordanian sovereignty and making it a demilitarized zone	14	16
An independent Palestinian state	9	7
Don't know	16	19

Source: Newsweek, October 4, 1982.

consistent. Still, while the likelihood is strong that American-Jewish support for Israel will continue, there is some evidence that older, less educated, and more religious individuals have been more committed to Israel than those who are younger and better educated, and who cannot remember a time when there was no Israel.[24] This means that the bonds between Israel and American Jewry must not be taken for granted, but rather should be closely guarded and cultivated.

EYTAN GILBOA

---

[24]See Steven M. Cohen, "Romantic Idealism to Loving Realism: The Changing Place of Israel in the Consciousness of American Jews," in William Frankel (ed.), *Survey of Jewish Affairs 1985* (Madison, N.J., 1985), pp. 169–182.

Los Angeles Jewry: A Demographic Portrait

As a city, Los Angeles is quite unlike New York. New York is concentrated and urban, while Los Angeles is spread out over hundreds of square miles. As a Jewish center, too, Los Angeles differs from New York. New York has the Lower East Side as a visible link to the Jewish immigrant past; Los Angeles is a continent away from such links. Moreover, in New York, "Jewish" is a conspicuous ethnic identity; in Los Angeles it is easy for Jews to get lost.

Still, Los Angeles has developed a Jewish community with identifiably Jewish neighborhoods, an impressive range of institutions, and a dynamic cultural life. For older communities in the Southwest, and especially for a host of new "pioneering" communities, Los Angeles has become the great Jewish center.

This article presents a portrait of the Los Angeles Jewish community: its development since earliest days, its demographic characteristics, and the patterns of participation by Jews in community activities and institutions. Data for the study come from three primary sources: a 1979 survey carried out by the author for the Jewish Federation Council of Greater Los Angeles, three earlier surveys (1951, 1959, 1967) conducted by Fred Massarik, and the 1980 U.S. population census.

GROWTH OF THE LOS ANGELES JEWISH COMMUNITY

Early History

Unlike the major urban centers of the East and Midwest, Los Angeles was never a city of direct disembarkation for immigrants during the nineteenth century. Since it did not emerge as a city until the beginning of the twentieth century, its Jewish community is relatively young. While there were some German Jews living in Los Angeles in the nineteenth century, San Francisco was the center of population in California for Jews and non-Jews alike.[1] The dramatic growth of the Los Angeles Jewish community occurred as part of the growth of

---

[1]Robert E. Levinson, *The Jews in the California Gold Rush* (New York, 1978), p. 7.

Los Angeles itself and can only be understood within that context. (Table 1 traces the growth of both the Jewish and the general populations over a 100-year period.*)

In the 1870s Los Angeles began making the transition from a dusty frontier town —not much larger than the original Spanish pueblo—to the second-largest city in the United States. Between 1870 and 1880 the population grew by 101 percent, and by another 213 percent between 1880 and 1890. As the general population of Los Angeles County increased, so did the number of Jews, except that the Jewish population grew at a faster rate. During the last two decades of the nineteenth century, when the general population of Los Angeles County grew fivefold, the Jewish population increased almost 20 times: from 136 Jews in 1880 to 2,500 at the dawn of the new century.

Even before the Southern Pacific Railroad had arrived in Los Angeles, speculators were busy turning open land into new towns. The "SP" itself was busy promoting southern California through excursions from the East and Midwest, and even sold plots of land in the city.[2] As Los Angeles journalist and social historian Carey McWilliams has noted:

> Every city has its booms, but the history of Los Angeles is the history of its booms. Actually, the growth of Southern California since 1870 should be regarded as one continuous boom punctuated at intervals with major explosions. Other American cities have gone through a boom phase and then entered upon a period of normal growth. But Los Angeles has always been a boom town, chronically unable to consolidate its gains or to integrate its new population.[3]

A "bust" in 1888 following a boom in 1887 caused growth to slow down in the 1890s, but it resumed again after the turn of the century. The first two decades of the twentieth century saw the general population of Los Angeles County multiply fivefold and the Jewish population twelvefold. While great waves of Eastern European Jewish immigrants continued to settle in New York, Philadelphia, and Chicago, smaller but still significant numbers made their way across the continent. In addition to the attraction of expanding business opportunities, the area's mild climate drew sufferers from tuberculosis and the other respiratory ailments that were common among the sweatshop workers of the East.

Not until the 1920s did the growth rate for the county as a whole (135 percent) catch up to and even surpass that of the Jewish population (128 percent). The 1920–1930 period, which included a major land boom in 1923, brought over 200,000 people to California, the majority (72 percent) to the southern part of the state. According to McWilliams, "The migration to Southern California in this decade has been characterized as the largest internal migration of the American people."[4] By

---

*See Appendix for tables.

[2]Carey McWilliams, *Southern California; An Island on the Land* (Layton, Utah, 1973), pp. 125–126.

[3]Ibid., p. 114.

[4]Ibid., p. 135.

the end of the decade, the Jewish community of Los Angeles had become the sixth largest in the country (just behind Detroit).

Although both Jewish and general growth rates slowed during the Great Depression, Jewish growth between 1930 and 1940 remained almost twice the general rate: 44 percent as compared with 27 percent.

Wartime and Postwar Period

The decade of greatest expansion for Los Angeles Jewry was the 1940s. During the war, the entire Pacific coast, and the southland in particular, gained strategic importance as a staging area for the Pacific theater and also as an aircraft manufacturing center. The combination of a land boom in 1943 and a burgeoning economy sparked a new cycle of growth. Once again the Jewish rate surpassed that of the overall population, and by the end of the decade the proportion of Jews in the county had risen from 4 to 7 percent.

Between 1940 and 1950 more than 168,000 Jews came to Los Angeles—more Jews than came in any decade before or after, and more Jews than lived in Detroit, Boston, Cleveland, or Baltimore in 1950. Many of these were servicemen who had been stationed in California—or had passed through en route to the Pacific—liked what they saw, and decided to make it their home. As a result of this migration, the size of the Jewish community almost tripled in the space of a few years. Indeed, by 1955 the Los Angeles Jewish community had become the second largest in the United States.[5]

In the 1950s Jewish growth slowed to the same rate as that of the county—if a growth rate of 50 percent can be called "slow"!— and has remained close to the county rate ever since. During the 1960s the rate of Jewish growth fell behind that of Los Angeles County, while in the 1970s the Jewish growth rate was higher. This is noteworthy because the decade of the 1970s also brought large-scale immigration of Mexicans, Central Americans, and Asians to the area.

The dramatic growth of Jewish Los Angeles, as seen in the population figures, can be explained only partially by the general westward migration to California. Many factors undoubtedly served to attract Jews in such large numbers, among them the promise of unparalleled business and professional opportunities, a benign climate, the casual and glamorous lifestyle depicted in the movies, and ease of social integration. Perhaps there was a greater willingness among those who came to pull up roots and start over again and perhaps, too, a greater desire to break with the past and start afresh in a place that seemed to embody the ultimate American dream.

Changing Jewish Residential Patterns Within Los Angeles

With growing population movement into Los Angeles, urban boundaries were forced to expand, and the city's physical appearance underwent radical change.

---

[5]As reported in the AJYB, Vol. 57, 1956, pp. 126–130.

Hollywood, for example, which was largely rural as late as 1915, became entirely urban within the succeeding ten years. During the various boom decades of Los Angeles' growth, the nature of Jewish settlement also changed, with Jewish neighborhoods springing up in newer and more distant areas. Since World War II was a watershed in the community's development, the discussion of changing residential patterns falls naturally into two main periods: 1900–1940 and 1940–1980. (The areas referred to in the discussion that follows are shown on maps A-1 and A-2, pp. 130–131.)

1900–1940

At the turn of the century Los Angeles Jews lived in the area now known as "downtown," with two additional concentrations in the nearby Westlake and University districts.[6] As Los Angeles changed from a frontier town to a city in the early decades of the century, the Jewish population began to spread. Between 1910 and 1926, the percentage of Jews living in the older Jewish settlement shrank from 30 to 3 percent, while two nearby areas succeeded "downtown" as Jewish centers: Temple Street (near what is now the new downtown Civic Center) in the teens, and Central Avenue (south of what is now "Little Tokyo") in the twenties. However, since both areas were close to what was then "downtown" (and are in fact considered part of the contemporary downtown), Jews remained essentially urban, even as the city itself was moving further outward. The real departure from "downtown" began only during the boom years of the 1920s, with the development of two important migration trends: east across the Los Angeles River to Boyle Heights, and west to the neighborhoods of Fairfax, Hollywood, and West Adams.

From the point of view of urban development, Boyle Heights can be considered similar to areas of second settlement in older cities. Like the Roxbury section in Boston, for example, Boyle Heights was built in the late nineteenth century as a "streetcar" suburb, in the first ring of settlement outside the boundaries of the "walking city."[7] As happened elsewhere, upwardly mobile Jews replaced upper-class Protestants, and Boyle Heights became a transition area between the ethnic neighborhoods of the inner city and the residential urban mainstream.[8] Unlike Boston, however, Los Angeles had no immigrant "ghetto," and newcomers to Boyle Heights were predominantly newcomers to Los Angeles. Boyle Heights, then, functioned simultaneously as an area of first and second settlement for Jewish Los Angeles.

---

[6]Max Vorspan and Lloyd Gartner, *History of the Jews of Los Angeles* (Philadelphia, 1970), p. 117; Mitchell Gelfand, "Progress and Prosperity: Jewish Social Mobility in Los Angeles in the Booming Eighties," *American Jewish History*, June 1979, p. 414.

[7]Sam Bass Warner, *Street Car Suburbs: The Process of Growth in Boston, 1870–1900* (New York, 1972), p. 58.

[8]Robert A. Woods and Albert J. Kennedy, *The Zone of Emergence: Observations of the Lower Middle and Upper Working Class Communities of Boston, 1905–1914* (Cambridge, Mass., 1962), pp. 31–35.

MAP A-1
Los Angeles County:
Geographic Areas

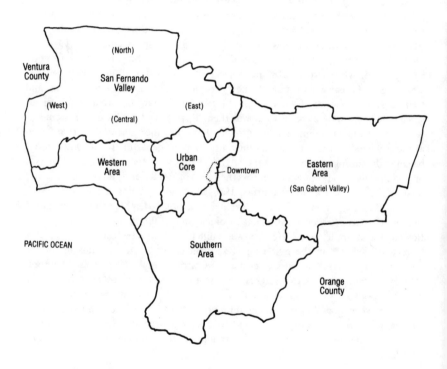

MAP A-2
Los Angeles County: Communities

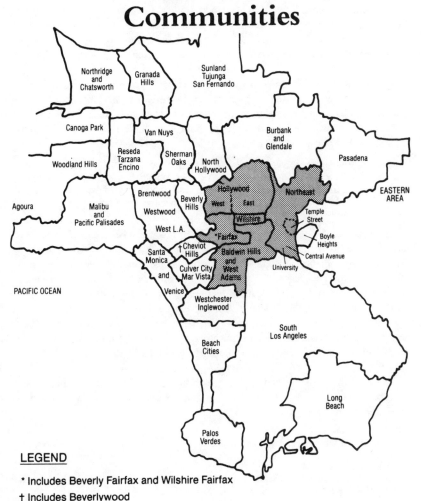

LEGEND

* Includes Beverly Fairfax and Wilshire Fairfax

† Includes Beverlywood

░ Urban Core

Boyle Heights grew from 1,800 Jewish households in 1920 to more than 10,000 in 1930, and to more than 14,000 by 1938.[9] It was the first visibly Jewish neighborhood in Los Angeles: "On the main streets of Boyle Heights were stores where Jews bought and sold, Yiddish was freely used, and Saturdays and Jewish holidays were marked by festive appearances and many closed businesses. Such was Boyle Heights of the late 1920s and the years following as mass immigration created a large-scale Jewish environment."[10]

Although numerically small as compared to the great Jewish urban enclaves of the East and Midwest, Boyle Heights had an immense psychological impact on Los Angeles Jewry. For Jews experiencing the inevitable anomie of the dislocated, Boyle Heights was a link to communities left behind. Jews who lived in Boyle Heights during the '20s, '30s, and '40s exhibit a nostalgic affection for "the Heights" to this day.

At the same time that Boyle Heights was undergoing its period of rapid growth, important changes were taking place in newly developed neighborhoods on the westside of Los Angeles, neighborhoods that had not even existed ten years earlier. Los Angeles Jews, like other Angelenos, flocked to these new areas of the city. According to Vorspan and Gartner:

> More prosperous and acculturated Jews settled westward in such areas as Wilshire, West Adams and Hollywood. Affluent Wilshire, with about 310 Jewish households in 1914, had 2,410 in 1926. Hollywood, still sylvan in 1914, had hardly any; by 1926 there were about 3,287. West Adams rose during the same period from 143 to 1,534.[11]

As a result of the population movement that took place between 1920 and 1940, there emerged two sides to Jewish Los Angeles: the Yiddish, Orthodox, working-class eastside and the more affluent and acculturated westside, with its two main centers in Beverly Fairfax and West Adams. The difference in socioeconomic status between eastside and westside can be documented from the 1940 U.S. census. Five census tracts were notably Jewish (using the "Russian stock" population to identify Jews): three in Beverly Fairfax and West Adams and two in Boyle Heights. Using occupation, education, and rent as indicators, the Beverly Fairfax and West Adams tracts were of middle social rank, while the Boyle Heights tracts were of low social rank.[12]

By 1940, the westside had replaced the older eastside as the leading Jewish neighborhood of Los Angeles. In the meantime, a new "westside" was forming in more affluent areas.

---

[9]Vorspan and Gartner, op. cit., pp. 118, 203.

[10]Ibid., p. 119.

[11]Ibid., p. 118.

[12]Eshref Shevky and Marilyn Williams, *The Social Areas of Los Angeles: Analysis and Typology* (Berkeley and Los Angeles, 1949), p. 70.

1940–1980

As the population of Los Angeles mushroomed during the 1940s, the scope of Jewish settlement widened beyond what Fred Massarik has termed the "Urban Core" areas, described above, to include two new areas: the San Fernando Valley and the Western Area.[13] Between 1950 and 1980 the new areas expanded and the Urban Core declined, with the result that by 1980 there were almost equal numbers of Jewish households in the San Fernando Valley, the Western Area, and the Urban Core.

A few geographical definitions will be helpful at this point. The Urban Core begins with Beverly Fairfax, Wilshire Fairfax, and West Hollywood and extends eastward to Boyle Heights. The Western Area begins with Beverly Hills and Cheviot Hills-Beverlywood and extends west to the ocean, taking in the exclusive hillside communities of Westwood and Brentwood, the flats of West Los Angeles, Mar Vista, and the ocean communities of Venice, Marina Del Rey, Santa Monica, Pacific Palisades, and Malibu. While both the Western Area and Urban Core are separated from the San Fernando Valley by mountains, they are divided from each other by socioeconomic rather than geographic barriers.

The "westside" of Los Angeles—wherever its location in any particular decade —has always been the most prestigious section of the city. Beverly Hills, legally an independent city, is considered part of the westside by virtue of its affluence and international social status. South of Beverly Hills are the communities of Cheviot Hills and Beverlywood, which developed after the boom years of the twenties. Their modern single-family dwellings on winding streets contrast markedly with the older homes and many apartment buildings, laid out on square blocks, that characterize Beverly Fairfax, Wilshire Fairfax, and West Hollywood—the three neighborhoods that border Beverly Hills and Cheviot Hills-Beverlywood. Thus, the Western Area can be distinguished from the Urban Core by neighborhoods that are more affluent and less urbanized.

The San Fernando Valley lies to the north of the Western Area and Urban Core and is separated from them by the Santa Monica Mountains. Ecologically, historically, and logistically it is entirely separate from the rest of Los Angeles. In the early decades of the century, when the Valley was largely agricultural, it was accessible only through the Cahuenga Pass (where the Hollywood Bowl is located). Even today access to the Valley is limited to four winding canyon roads and three freeways.

Two sections of Los Angeles have remained Jewishly marginal: the Eastern Area, consisting of the San Gabriel and Pomona Valleys, and the Southern Area, extending south from Los Angeles International Airport, the Fox Hills and Baldwin Hills

---

[13]Fred Massarik, *The Jewish Population Indicator Reports, 1971–1974*, Community Planning Department, Jewish Federation Council of Greater Los Angeles, mimeo, 1976.

areas, to San Pedro and the Palos Verdes Peninsula. These areas, which together have never accounted for more than 15 percent of the Jewish population of Los Angeles, are discussed separately below.

Beginning in 1951, Fred Massarik began to collect and publish estimates of the number of Jewish households in over 20 named communities in Los Angeles. As a result, it is possible to study population shifts both among and within the three major Jewish areas—the San Fernando Valley, the Western Area, and the Urban Core—during the period 1950–1980 (Tables 2A,B,C).

In 1951 Jewish Los Angeles was still largely urban; over half (61 percent) of all Jewish households were located in the Urban Core. The Western Area, the second largest in the city, had fewer than half the number of Jewish households found in the Urban Core. (Beverly Fairfax, now included in the Urban Core, was still considered at that time to be on the "westside," as evidenced by the naming of the "Westside Jewish Community Center" in the early 1950s.[14]) The San Fernando Valley, just beginning to open up to Jewish settlement, had less than half again as many households as the Western Area (Table 2C).

In 1959 the Jewish community was still urban, but less so than it had been just a few years earlier. The Urban Core entered a period of decline in the 1950s, while the San Fernando Valley grew by 125 percent, increasing its share of Jewish households from 9.5 to 19 percent. The Western Area, which grew by a more modest 25 percent, particularly in Santa Monica and Cheviot Hills-Beverlywood, was just barely maintaining its position as the second-largest Jewish area (Tables 2B, C).

Jewish residential trends established in the 1950s continued throughout the 1960s. Overall, the Urban Core lost another 9 percent of its Jewish households, the San Fernando Valley grew by another 80 percent, and growth in the Western Area accelerated to 53 percent. The result was that by 1970, the number of Jewish households was almost evenly divided among the three major areas: 33 percent in the Urban Core; 28 percent in the Western Area; and 26 percent in the San Fernando Valley.

The rapid growth of Jewish population in the San Fernando Valley and the Western Area was part of the postwar suburban growth that characterized all American cities. It was also associated with economic changes and the movement of minorities within the city.

The changing economic fortunes of the Valley, Western Area, and Urban Core have been plotted over a 30-year period by the City of Los Angeles, using U.S. census data from 1940, 1950, 1960, and 1970.[15] Based on information on income, education, and home value, all Los Angeles census tracts were assigned economic ranks from "1" (the highest) to "4" (the lowest). The 30-year period 1940–1970 saw

---

[14]Located two blocks east of the intersection of Olympic Boulevard and Fairfax Avenue.
[15]*1980 Los Angeles County Forecast,* Appendix A, Community Development Department, Community Analysis and Planning Division, City of Los Angeles, Sept. 1977.

a marked decline in the socioeconomic status of the Fairfax area. Whereas in 1940 census tracts in Beverly Fairfax, Wilshire Fairfax, and West Hollywood had all been either in the first ("upper economic") or second ("above average") ranks, by 1950 only three tracts were in the first rank, and by 1960 only one. Beginning in the 1960s, tracts which had formerly been in the second ("above average") rank had fallen to the third ("below average") rank. Only the exclusive hillside areas of West Hollywood remained in the first rank.

Even more dramatic change occurred in the San Fernando Valley. In 1940, when all the census tracts in and around Fairfax were in the first or second rank, most Valley tracts were in the second and third ranks—none were in the first. Little change took place in the San Fernando Valley between 1940 and 1950. By the 1960 census, however, a number of second-ranked census tracts had moved to the first rank, and a number of third-ranked tracts had moved to the second. This economic upgrading took place primarily in a strip of communities hugging the Santa Monica Mountains "south of the Boulevard" (i.e., Ventura Boulevard): Encino, Sherman Oaks, and Tarzana. Particularly notable improvement took place in Woodland Hills (West Valley), which moved, between 1940 and 1960, from the third to the first rank, and in Northridge (North Valley), sections of which moved, between 1950 and 1970, from the third to the first or second rank. Census tracts in North Hollywood, the original area of San Fernando Valley settlement, either declined or remained stable during this period.

By 1970, the areas in the Valley with the highest economic standing were also those that had experienced the most Jewish growth: the North Valley and West Valley (including Granada Hills, Woodland Hills, and Northridge), Encino, and Sherman Oaks. Thus the move to the Valley, which in the 1940s and early 1950s had commonly been a move to affordable single-family housing, became two decades later a move upward in socioeconomic status.

Even more so did the shift to the Western Area reflect a movement of upward social mobility. Beginning in the 1940s, Cheviot Hills came to occupy the first rank, as did Westwood and Brentwood. Beverlywood, on the eastern slope of the Cheviot Hills, was consistently in the second rank.

These trends continued until the mid-1970s. Between 1970 and 1974 the Urban Core declined an additional 17 percent, losing more Jewish households in five years (8,681) than it had in the previous ten (4,962). By contrast, the Valley gained an additional 10,309 Jewish households and the Western Area an additional 7,745.

Beginning in the post-World War II period, the movement of Jews to the west and the north was accompanied by a movement of blacks into the areas that the Jews were vacating.[16] The impact of this change was felt first in West Adams, in the late

---

[16]*An Ethnic Trend Analysis of Los Angeles County, 1950–1980,* Community Development Department, Community Analysis and Planning Division, City of Los Angeles, mimeo, Dec. 1977.

1940s, after restrictive housing covenants were struck down by the Supreme Court. When the extent of black migration into West Adams became apparent, the Jewish Community Centers Association canceled plans for additional building that had been contemplated in that area.[17]

Just to the west of West Adams, Baldwin Hills—which was the primary residential area for Sephardic Jews from Greece and Turkey[18]—attracted growing numbers of upwardly mobile, middle-class blacks, and by 1970 blacks had moved just east of Beverlywood and just south of Wilshire Fairfax, adding to the black student population of the two "Jewish" high schools—Fairfax and Hamilton.[19] The same year, after a major earthquake destroyed the predominantly black Los Angeles High School, situated in the district just east of Fairfax, a number of black students were transferred to Fairfax. In response to these changes, Beverly Fairfax, Wilshire Fairfax, and West Hollywood lost Jewish households for the first time since the 1920s, thereby reversing a half century of growth. Cheviot Hills-Beverlywood, located in the Hamilton High School district, experienced no change, ending a period of growth that had begun before 1950. In contrast, neighboring Beverly Hills, with its independent school district, grew by 30 percent in the years 1970–1974.

By 1974 it appeared that the Urban Core would eventually be eclipsed entirely by the San Fernando Valley and the Western Area. However, a housing speculation boom in the late 1970s dramatically reversed the trend. The recession at the beginning of the decade had caused a slump in housing starts, even as the population continued to grow. As a result of increased demand, existing housing appreciated rapidly, with prices fueled by heavy speculation. As housing costs became prohibitive in more desirable neighborhoods, more Jewish families (and even single persons) bought houses and rented apartments in what had been declining, and therefore less expensive, neighborhoods. Thus, the Urban Core, which had consistently lost Jewish households through 1974, showed a 40-percent increase by 1979 (for a net increase of 16.8 percent during the decade 1970–1979) (Table 2B). For every household that moved out of Beverly Fairfax between 1974 and 1975, more than two new ones moved in.[20] The turnaround in the area was so complete that by 1981 a report commissioned by the Young Israel Community Development Corporation in the Fairfax area warned that small shopkeepers and low-income residents were in danger of being forced out by escalating rental charges.

---

[17]Fred Massarik, *The Jewish Population of the West Adams Area: A Tentative Report,* Jewish Centers Association, mimeo, 1948.

[18]Eliezer Chammou, "Migration and Adjustment: The Case of Sephardic Jews in Los Angeles," Ph.D. dissertation, Dept. of Social Geography, University of California, Los Angeles, 1976.

[19]*An Ethnic Trend Analysis of Los Angeles County, 1950–1980,* op. cit.; map "1980 Ethnic Clusters."

[20]Bruce A. Phillips, *Los Angeles Jewish Community Survey: Overview for Regional Planning,* Planning and Budgeting Department, Jewish Federation Council of Greater Los Angeles, 1980, p. 30.

In contrast to the Urban Core, growth in the Western Area, during 1974–1979, slowed to 6 percent, but the picture was far from uniform. All the growth was concentrated in the Brentwood-Westwood area, in which the number of Jewish households more than doubled.[21] The Valley continued to grow, but in new ways. Expensive areas such as Encino and Tarzana (ranked as "1" even in 1970) lost Jewish households, while less desirable communities such as Van Nuys, Reseda, and North Hollywood gained Jewish households.[22] Communities in the West Valley and North Valley that were in the first rank but further out from the urban center gained new households as well.

SOUTHERN AND EASTERN AREAS

The Eastern and Southern Areas have always had an insignificant share of the Jewish population of Los Angeles County. The San Gabriel Valley to the east never held much attraction, probably for two reasons. First, it is geographically isolated from the rest of Los Angeles, not only by mountains but by bumper-to-bumper commuter traffic on the freeways. Second, the San Gabriel Valley as a whole is of lower socioeconomic status than the rest of Los Angeles.

The Southern Area can be divided into three separate sections: the beach cities, the midcities inland from the beach communities, and the promontory of the Palos Verdes Peninsula. The midcities, located on the flat plains of South Los Angeles and of lower socioeconomic status, have never attracted Jewish settlement. Nor have the beach cities (Hermosa Beach, Redondo Beach, Playa Del Rey), though Jews did move to other beach communities, such as Santa Monica and Venice, early on. The probable reason for Jews avoiding the Southern Area is that these beach cities not only did not welcome Jews but were the headquarters for a number of overtly antisemitic organizations.[23] The exclusive and expensive Palos Verdes area was largely off-limits to Jews until the 1960s, but has since experienced growing Jewish settlement.

Distribution of Jewish Households in 1979

A striking feature of the Jewish population of Los Angeles is that it is widely spread out, but also highly localized. If Jews were randomly distributed throughout the county, any given community in 1979 would have had a Jewish density of about

---

[21]Ibid. Although Cheviot Hills had been in the first rank economically in 1970, the continued movement of the black population in its direction reduced its desirability. By the 1980s, high prices in Westwood made Cheviot Hills once again attractive to Jewish home buyers.

[22]Valley neighborhoods that are south of Ventura Boulevard are more desirable and expensive because they are either in or adjacent to the foothills. Reseda, Van Nuys, and North Hollywood are all on the floor of the Valley.

[23]Information communicated to the author by John Babcock, author of a forthcoming history of Jewish Los Angeles.

MAP B
JEWISH DENSITY
BY ZIP CODE
LOS ANGELES COUNTY, 1979

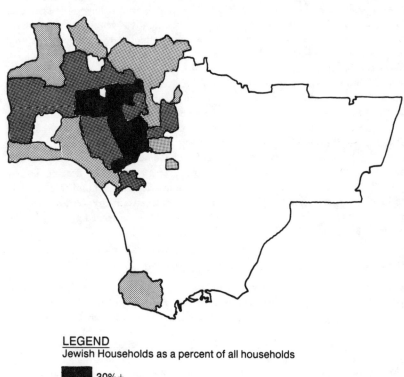

LEGEND
Jewish Households as a percent of all households

30%+

15-29%

7-14%

0-6%

7 percent (the percentage of Jews in the population). Even if only those communities outside the black concentrations of Watts, Compton, and South-Central Los Angeles are considered, a random distribution would have produced approximately 10-percent Jewish density. In actuality, more than half of all Jewish households were concentrated in 32 zip-code areas that had Jewish densities of at least 14 percent —twice that of the overall Jewish density for Los Angeles.

Map B illustrates the concentration of Jews throughout Los Angeles County in 1979. More than 30,000 phone calls from a random-digit-dialing survey were used to estimate the size of the Jewish population and its distribution by zip codes. (See "Sociodemographic Profile," below.) The zip-code percentages were then assigned to four strata: the first with 30 percent or more Jewish households; the second with 15 to 29 percent Jewish households; the third with 7 to 14 percent Jewish households; the fourth with less than 7 percent Jewish households.

The pattern that emerged was one of concentric rings of decreasing Jewish density. The area of highest density—the darkest on the map, shaped like a T with a fat base—included both Valley and city (i.e., Western Area and Urban Core) zip codes. The south, or city, side of this first stratum included Beverly Hills, Beverly Fairfax, Beverlywood, and West Hollywood. These formed the stem of the T. The Valley part of the first stratum, or the cross of the T, consisted of Encino, Van Nuys, Sherman Oaks, Studio City, and North Hollywood. Thus, the Valley zip codes of the first stratum were directly north over the hills from the city zip codes, indicating that the most Jewish parts of the Valley were those closest to the city.

While the city had a smaller Jewish population, it was more densely Jewish than the Valley, which occupied an extensive land area and offered a large selection of acceptable places to live in. All but one of the first-stratum zip codes in the city had Jewish densities of 40 percent or more, as contrasted with the Valley, where all but one of the first-stratum zip codes had Jewish densities of less than 40 percent. An interesting feature of the distribution is that in both city and Valley, the first stratum consisted of both newer affluent areas and contiguous older areas (e.g., Beverly Fairfax and Beverly Hills in the city, North Hollywood and Sherman Oaks in the Valley).

In both Valley and city, the most densely Jewish areas included the communities generally regarded as most desirable. These were Woodland Hills, Encino, Brentwood, Pacific Palisades, and, slightly lower in status, West Wilshire—including Beverly Fairfax and West Hollywood—and West Los Angeles. An analysis of census-tract characteristics in the 1970 census identified the residents of these communities as having the highest per capita income and the most years of college education, as well as homes with the highest real-estate values and rental costs.[24]

---

[24]*A Trend Analysis of Los Angeles County, 1950–1970,* Community Analysis Bureau, Office of the Mayor, City of Los Angeles, mimeo, June 1, 1976.

SOCIODEMOGRAPHIC PROFILE OF LOS ANGELES JEWRY

Sampling Methodology

The sociodemographic profile of Los Angeles Jews that is presented here is based on a telephone survey of 800 randomly selected Jewish households that was conducted in spring 1979.[25] A random-digit-dialing sample was stratified by area (with an oversampling of the Southern and Eastern Areas due to need for planning) and by the distribution of residential phone numbers within the area. The sample included all of Los Angeles County (except for predominantly black areas in South-Central Los Angeles) and those areas of Ventura County that are contiguous to and form a Jewish extension of the West Valley (e.g., Agoura, Thousand Oaks, Newbury Park, etc.).

A minimum of five calls was made to each phone number in the sample, at random intervals including evenings and Sundays. Interviews were conducted in English, Spanish, Arabic, Hebrew, Parsi (Persian), Yiddish, and Hungarian. All persons answering the phone were read a short explanation of the survey based on standard protocols used at the Survey Research Center of the Institute for Social Science Research at UCLA. The purpose of the initial screening was to eliminate nonresidential phone numbers from the sample. If the phone number was determined to be a residence, the respondent was read a further explanation of the study and asked whether any Jewish persons lived in the household.

In addition to the 1979 survey data, comparable data are introduced into the discussion from Jewish population surveys conducted in 1951, 1959, and 1967 (referenced in Table 3) as well as the 1980 U.S. census for Los Angeles County.[26] With the help of the older surveys it is possible to evaluate the extent of social change that has taken place among Los Angeles Jews. The comparison with the non-Hispanic white population made possible by the availability of data from the 1980 census highlights similarities and differences between Los Angeles Jews and other whites in the population.[27]

---

[25]The study was funded by the Jewish Federation Council of Greater Los Angeles and conducted by the author as Research Director of the Planning and Budgeting Department. (See Phillips, op. cit.)

[26]Special tabulations for the non-Hispanic white population in Los Angeles County were ordered from the California State Demographic Office, from Summary Tape File #4, Part B, as described in *1980 Census of Population and Housing, User's Guide Part A. Text*, PHC80-R1-A, Mar. 1973; and *User's Guide Part C. Index to Summary Tape Files 1 to 4*, PHC80-R1-C, Sept. 1983, U.S. Department of Commerce, Bureau of the Census.

[27]The effect of the one-year difference between the 1979 Jewish population study and the 1980 census is minimal. The validity of the comparison was enhanced by including only non-Hispanic whites in the analysis. Although many Hispanics classify themselves as white in the census, they constitute a distinct linguistic, cultural, and ethnic group. Because of significant differences in family size and socioeconomic status between Hispanic and

Impact of Mobility on the Jewish Population

Los Angeles has long been described as a community without roots, and this is true of Jewish Los Angeles as well. In every decade there have been significant numbers of Jewish newcomers who have been living in Los Angeles less than ten years (Table 3). The proportion of new arrivals rose to its highest in 1951, after the population explosion of the 1940s. At that time the majority (62 percent) of Jewish households reported being in the city five years or less; a mere 16 percent of Jewish households in Los Angeles in 1951 had lived in that city before World War II. In effect, a whole new community came into being in the space of a decade.

In the 20 years following 1959, newcomers constituted a small but sizeable element in the city. In that period, between one-fifth and one-quarter of all Jewish households had been in Los Angeles less than a decade. The significance of this can be highlighted by noting the proportion of Jewish households in 1979 that were resident in Los Angeles when earlier population surveys were conducted: 75 percent in 1967; 55 percent in 1959; and 25 percent in 1951. Another indicator of the youthfulness of the community is the proportion of households in 1979 that had been in the city 21 years or longer (Table 3)—55 percent. The comparable figure for a more established community, such as Milwaukee, was 75 percent.[28]

While all the Jewish areas within Los Angeles benefited from movement into the city, it was not evenly distributed in terms of either period or rate (Table 4). The Urban Core, for example, experienced an upsurge between 1974 and 1979—20 percent newcomers as compared with a citywide newcomer rate of 14 percent. The San Fernando Valley, which experienced major growth in the 1950s and 1960s, saw a tapering off in the 1970s. In Santa Monica, Pacific Palisades, and Malibu, which were relatively new areas of Jewish settlement, 45 percent of Jewish households had moved in just in the ten years prior to 1979. By contrast, the populations of Beverly Hills and other Western Area communities were older and more stable; in Beverly Hills, 68 percent of Jewish households had been in the city 20 years or longer, as compared with 55 percent citywide.

As might be expected in a community made up largely of newcomers, relatively few Jewish adults were native-born Angelenos. Between 1951 and 1979 the

---

non-Hispanic whites, inclusion of the former can either spuriously accentuate, or accidentally mask, the differences between Jews and other whites, making it harder to evaluate the extent to which Jews are "blending in" to mainstream American society.

Because the census does not ask about religion and there is no way of identifying Jews, Jews are included in the data for the non-Hispanic white population (of which they constitute about 10 percent in Los Angeles County). The effect of comparing the Jewish population with a larger population that includes them is to underestimate differences between Jews and non-Jews. Thus, if a comparison could be made between the Jewish population and the non-Hispanic white, *non-Jewish* population, the differences would be even greater than those reported here.

[28]Bruce A. Phillips and Eve Weinberg, *The Milwaukee Jewish Population: Report of a Survey,* Milwaukee Jewish Federation, Jan. 1984, p. I-25.

proportion of Jewish adults born in Los Angeles increased from 8 to 14 percent—almost doubling but still remaining relatively small (Table 5). The effect of post-World War II migration is to be seen in the fact that 39 percent of 18–29-year-olds —those born since 1950—were native-born (Table 6). With regard to the future, assuming that in-migration remains constant, as the current cohort of 18–29-year-olds ages, and as children under 18—three-quarters of whom are native Californians (Table 8)—become adults, native-born Angelenos will come to predominate in the community.

While the proportion of foreign-born Jews in Los Angeles decreased from 37 percent in 1951 to 29 percent in 1979 (Table 5), the late 1970s brought a new wave of immigration from abroad. Fully one-third of all born-Jewish respondents who arrived in Los Angeles between 1974 and 1979 had been born in other countries (Table 7). Included in this immigration were three particularly visible groups: Soviet and Iranian Jews and Israelis.

There were an estimated 12,000 to 15,000 Israelis living in Los Angeles in 1979. While popular estimates generally put this number much higher—anywhere from 50,000 to 150,000—the 1979 estimate was corroborated by a study of immigration data from the Immigration and Naturalization Service[29] that was later confirmed informally by statisticians from the Central Bureau of Statistics in Israel.

In comparison with the white population as a whole, Jews were more likely to have been born either outside of California or out of the United States (Table 8). Jews were more than twice as likely as all American-born whites to have been born in the Northeast (comprising the Mid-Atlantic and New England regions).

Age and Household Type

AGE

Jewish demographers and federation planners tend to focus on the oldest and youngest ends of the age distribution in order to track the extent to which the American Jewish population is aging—thanks to increased life expectancy—and declining in numbers—due to low fertility. Surprisingly, the common assumptions about these demographic indicators were not confirmed—or at least not totally—for Los Angeles Jewry. Thus, while Jewish fertility had declined, it was actually slightly ahead of the rate for non-Hispanic whites. Similarly, while the proportion of the aged had increased over several decades, by 1979 it had leveled off. Indeed, the proportion of the aged was higher among non-Hispanic whites in Los Angeles than among Jews.

Following the baby boom of the 1950s, the proportion of children (aged 0–19) in the Jewish population rose from 27 percent in 1951 to 35 percent in 1959 (Table

---

[29]Pini Herman and David LaFontaine, "In Our Footsteps: Israeli Migration to the U.S. and Los Angeles," master's thesis, University of Southern California School of Social Work and Hebrew Union College, Los Angeles, 1983.

9). With the end of the baby boom and the start of a trend away from childbearing, the proportion of children dropped to 32 percent in 1967 and to a low of 23 percent in 1979. The change was most dramatically apparent in the proportion of children under age 10, which declined from 20 to 10 percent between 1959 and 1979. While the drop in fertility was a cause for concern, the Jewish fertility rate was actually slightly ahead of the non-Hispanic white rate (Table 10), as reflected in the proportion of the population under 5 years of age.

On the national level, Jewish planners work on the assumption that the Jewish population is becoming increasingly aged.[30] In Los Angeles, however, Jews are not older than the non-Hispanic white population. In fact, in 1979 non-Hispanic whites as a group had a greater proportion of the elderly (60 and older) than did the Jews: 20.2 as against 16.4 percent (Table 10). Moreover, Jews and non-Hispanic whites had nearly identical proportions of children aged 0–9 and 10–19. The only significant differences were in the higher proportion of Jews aged 30–39 and the lower proportion aged 20–24. The latter may well be accounted for by the large number of Jews attending college and graduate school outside the county.

HOUSEHOLD TYPE AND DISTRIBUTION

While the overall contours of household type and family structure of the non-Hispanic white and Jewish populations were similar, Jews were more likely to be married, to have children, and to be married with children (Table 11). Thus, 58 percent of all Jewish households contained married couples as against 50 percent of non-Hispanic white households; 28 percent of all Jewish households had children as against 25 percent of non-Hispanic white households; and 24 percent of all Jewish households contained married couples with children as against 20 percent of non-Hispanic white households.

As would be expected from the preceding figures, fewer Jewish households were headed by single persons (42 vs. 50 percent), and far fewer were single-parent families (non-Hispanic white households were 1.4 times as likely as Jewish households to be single-parent families). This was not because Jews did not divorce, for the percentage of divorced persons in the Jewish population rose steadily from 1951 on.[31] However, 22 percent of all ever-married Jews under age 54 had been divorced, as compared with 33 percent of non-Hispanic whites (Table 12). Jews were also more likely to be remarried. Approximately one-third of all married persons had gone through divorce, yet more Jews than non-Jews were currently married.

As with the geographical distribution of the total Jewish population, Jewish household types were not homogeneously distributed throughout the city. Rather, particular household types were more numerous in some areas than in others. The analysis of the distributions is complicated, however. An attempt was made to

---

[30]See, for example, *Jewish Environmental Scan to 1990,* Council of Jewish Federations, Long Range Strategic Planning Committee, mimeo, Oct. 1984, p. 2.
[31]Phillips, op.cit., p. 9.

include as many separate communities as possible, even while bearing in mind that small subsamples have large variances which are reflected in over-large or -small proportions of particular household types. Two typologies were employed for the analysis: "household type," combining the marital status of the respondent with the presence or absence of children; and "family-cycle stage," grouping households according to the ages of respondents and children.

The Valley and the Eastern Area had higher proportions of married couples with children (37 and 30 percent respectively) than any of the other areas or the Jewish community overall (24 percent) (Table 13). Conversely, never-married households were least likely to be found in the San Fernando Valley.

The San Fernando Valley, with a Jewish population ten times as large as that of the Eastern Area, was the premier family area in Los Angeles. Over half (56 percent) of the Jewish married couples with children lived in the San Fernando Valley, the majority (58 percent)[32] concentrated in the North Valley and West Valley (running from Woodland Hills and Agoura north through Granada Hills and Northridge). In fact, a majority of Jewish households in these two areas consisted of married couples with children: 53 percent as compared with 24 percent in Los Angeles overall (Table 14).

The communities contiguous with the North Valley and West Valley—Encino, Tarzana, and Sherman Oaks—would have been expected to have the next highest concentrations of married couples with children, but this was not the case. These communities actually had the lowest proportions of married couples with children, and it was the Central Valley that contained the next highest (30 percent) proportion of married couples with children in the San Fernando Valley. Since Encinco, Tarzana, and Sherman Oaks were the most expensive areas in the San Fernando Valley, it is likely that they were too costly for younger families. This observation is confirmed by looking at the ages of the children in the households (Table 15). The less expensive Central Valley had the highest proportion of families with children under age 6 of any area either in the San Fernando Valley or Los Angeles.

While the area breakdown shows the Urban Core and the Western Area as having the lowest proportions of married couples with children and the highest proportions of never-married and divorced household heads, closer analysis reveals a more complex picture. The Western Area, for example, includes such disparate communities as Beverly Hills and Venice–Mar Vista–Culver City. Beverly Hills, renowned for its excellent school system, had the highest percentage of married couples with children in Los Angeles (35.1 percent), while Venice–Mar Vista–Culver City, an area with many small apartments near the beach, had the lowest (6.7 percent).

The figures for Beverly Fairfax–West Hollywood may also be misleading. These Urban Core communities, which experienced a rejuvenating influx of young families, showed the third-lowest proportion of married couples with children. However,

---

[32]Ibid.

these were largely families with young children. If only households with children under the age of 6 are considered, the Urban Core proportion (7.4 percent) was almost the same as that in the North Valley and West Valley (10 percent), which were highly suburban areas, strongly identified as family centers.

Just as the Eastern Area was identified as being family-oriented, so the Southern Area stood out as having large numbers of single-parent families. Single-parent families were relatively rare (4 percent) in the Los Angeles Jewish community as a whole, but they accounted for 13 percent of all Jewish households, and 36 percent of all households with children, in the Southern Area. While there were numerically more single-parent families in the Western Area and Urban Core, this is explained by their much larger Jewish populations. Only the Central Valley came close to having the same proportion of single-parent families as that in the Southern Area —8 percent of all households and 22 percent of all households with children. What these two areas had in common was availability of apartments and relatively low housing costs.

Marriage and Divorce

The 12 years between the 1967 and 1979 surveys saw the rise of a new marital pattern—Jews delaying marriage longer, in many cases not marrying until their 30s. Although the 1979 survey questionnaire did not include an item on age at first marriage, by comparing the relationship between age and marital status in 1967 and 1979 it is possible to document the dramatic shift that took place (Table 16A).

The most striking difference is found in the cohort aged 30–39. In 1967 only 6.2 percent of 30-year-olds had never been married, whereas in 1979 the proportion had more than doubled (16 percent). Tracing this shift in detail is made difficult by the use of ten-year intervals in the 1967 survey, which masks significant five-year changes. That five-year intervals are important can be seen from Table 16B, which presents data from 1979 only, but broken down into five-year cohorts. The percent never-married in 1979 drops by half (from 80 to 38 percent) after age 25, and then again by three-fourths (from 23 to 8 percent) after age 35.

Changing patterns of divorce since 1967 are also striking, particularly in the 30- and 40-year-old age groups. In 1979 the percentage of Jews aged 30–39 who had been divorced was three times as high as in 1967 (12.6 as against 3.9 percent), while the percentage of those aged 40–49 was twice as high (13.6 as against 6.8 percent). Overall, the percentage of divorced persons more than doubled during the period.

Intermarriage

Religious intermarriage (defined as marriage to a non-Jew by birth who has not converted to Judaism) dramatically increased in the decade of the 70s. This can be seen by comparing the percentage of born Jews married to non-Jews in different age groups (Table 17). Whereas 13 percent (an average of the male and female figures) of those in the 30–39 age group had non-Jewish spouses, some 30 percent of Jews under age 30 had non-Jewish spouses. Thus, the individual intermarriage rate for Jews under age 30 was nearly one-third. As against this, the couple intermarriage rate for the same age group was 49 percent, or one-half (Table 18). The difference in the two rates is due to the method of reporting. When individuals are counted, each born-Jew counts as one. When a tabulation is made of all *couples,* however, two Jews who marry persons not born Jewish are counted as two marriages, but two Jews who marry each other are counted as one. This reduces the total (the denominator) on which the percentage is taken and results in the higher rate.

Sex differences in intermarriage show no consistent patterns, although overall a slightly higher percentage of females was intermarried. In the 30–39 age range, Jewish males were 50 percent more likely to be married to non-Jews than were Jewish females. Under age 30, however—the age group in which intermarriage rates increased sharply—Jewish females were 35 percent more likely to be married to non-Jews than were Jewish males. Similarly, Jewish females in their 40s were more likely to be married to non-Jews than were Jewish males of the same age.

The relationship between conversion and intermarriage is characterized by a sharp break between the over-40 and under-40 age groups (Table 18). While in absolute numbers conversion was on the increase—because the total number of exogamous marriages (marriage to a born non-Jew who may or may not have converted) was increasing—the proportion of convert marriages to the total of all intermarriages actually showed a steep decline, dropping from 31.4 percent for 40–49-year-olds to 11 percent for those under 40. Thus, the rate of conversion declined as the intermarriage rate increased.

That the intermarriage rate for couples under age 40 was in fact higher than in the past is borne out by a comparison with earlier studies (Table 19). First, however, a methodological problem has to be clarified, involving the computation base used in earlier studies. Whereas in 1979 intermarriage was computed against a base of *all current marriages* (couples)—the standard practice—in 1951, 1959, and 1967 intermarriage was reported as a percentage of all *households.* The number of total households is always greater than the number of married couples, since the former includes single as well as married household heads. A comparison between the 1979 and earlier studies cannot proceed, then, without a common denominator of households. Because married couples made up 58 percent of all households in 1979 (Table 13), the 20 percent of all couples who were intermarried (Table 18) is equivalent to 11.7 percent of all Jewish households.

A comparison using a consistent intermarriage rate essentially confirms the expected rise. The 11.7-percent household intermarriage rate reported for 1979 represents a 100-percent increase over the 1967 rate of 5.4 percent and a 125-percent increase over the 4.8-percent rate reported in 1951. The one apparent inconsistency in the figures—a decline from 6.3 percent in 1959 to 5.4 percent in 1967—is a methodological artifact.[33] Given the tendency toward later marriage, it is probable that the 1979 figures do not reflect the full magnitude of the trend toward increased intermarriage. As more of the 20-year-olds who were surveyed in 1979 marry in their late 20s and early 30s, an even more dramatic increase in the intermarriage rate is likely to be seen.

Socioeconomic Status

EDUCATION

Jewish males and females in 1979 were better educated than non-Hispanic whites. Across all age groups, Jewish males were between 40 and 50 percent more likely than non-Hispanic white males to have gone beyond high school, and twice as likely to be college graduates (Table 20). Jewish females, too, had more education than non-Hispanic white females. Jewish women under age 65 were twice as likely to have gone beyond high school, and between 50 and 60 percent more likely to be college graduates.

Among Jewish males, educational attainment was inversely related to age. The percentage of those who had attended college jumped from 43 percent among those aged 65 and over to 75 percent in the 45–64 age group. The increase in college attendance was less pronounced, but still steady, for males under age 45, 90 percent of whom had attended college. College attendance among Jewish females showed a similar pattern—increasing from 30 percent of the over-65 age cohort to 59 percent of the cohort aged 40–49, to 79 percent of the cohort aged 25–44. The biggest gain among Jewish females was in the proportion graduating from college: those under age 45 were twice as likely as those aged 45–64 to have graduated from college, while the latter, in turn, were twice as likely to have completed college as those over age 65.

The educational gap between Jewish males and Jewish females narrows with age, though never completely closing. Jewish males over age 65 were 1.4 times as likely to have gone beyond high school as Jewish females of the same age group; Jewish males aged 45–64 were 1.3 times as likely to have gone beyond high school, and

---

[33]When intermarriage is calculated as the proportion of all households—as was the case in the 1951, 1959, and 1967 studies—single household heads are counted as if they were in-married couples. As long as the proportion of single-headed households stays constant over time, this does not present a problem. In 1959, however, the percentage of single-headed households was 50 percent lower than in 1951 and 25 percent lower than in 1967. Thus, the high intermarriage rate reported in 1959 reflects the lower proportion of singles, rather than a lower proportion of in-married households. See Fred Massarik, *A Report on the Jewish Population of Los Angeles, 1959,* Research Service Bureau, Jewish Federation Council of Greater Los Angeles, November 1959; and *A Report on the Jewish Population of Los Angeles, 1968,* Research Service Bureau, Jewish Federation Council of Greater Los Angeles, 1968.

Jewish males under age 45 were 1.14 times as likely to have gone beyond high school. Similarly, Jewish males over age 65 were 2.6 times as likely to be college graduates as Jewish females of the same age; Jewish males aged 45–64 were 2.1 times as likely to be college graduates; and Jewish males under age 45 were 1.4 times as likely to be college graduates.

OCCUPATIONAL STRUCTURE

As would be expected, increased education was accompanied by an increase in professionalization, most conspicuously in the years between 1951 and 1967 (Table 21). The proportion of males employed professionally grew by 63 percent between 1951 and 1959, and then by another 42 percent over the next ten years. Beginning in 1967 the professions were the modal category for employed males, although the percentage dropped slightly over the next 12 years. The percentage in the category of "proprietors, managers, and officials" was lower than it had been in the 1950s and 1960s, but was slightly higher than in 1967. The employment of Jewish males in clerical and sales positions declined during the 1950s but leveled off at about 21 percent after 1967. The proportion of males employed in skilled, craft, and unskilled occupations also decreased after the 1950s.

Jewish males worked in higher-status occupations than non-Hispanic white males, with the greatest differences appearing in the professional and retail categories (Table 22). Just as Jewish males were twice as likely as non-Hispanic white males to be college graduates, so also were they twice as likely to be professionals: 32 as against 17 percent. As to choice of profession, Jewish males were more likely to be working in the health area (e.g., as physicians and dentists) and in law, while non-Hispanic white males were more likely to be employed as engineers (Table 23).

The biggest difference between Jews and non-Hispanic whites was in the category of retail business, with Jewish males almost 8 times as likely as non-Hispanic white males to be in self-employed retail management and proprietorship.[34] Still, retail ownership was not a primary Jewish occupation in Los Angeles. More Jewish males worked in the professions than in any other category, followed by managerial (21 percent) and sales positions (exclusive of self-employed retail managers and proprietors) (18.2 percent). One out of every five employed Jewish males worked in a clerical, service, skilled, semiskilled, or unskilled position.

Since no occupational data were reported for working females in earlier studies, it is not possible to chart employment trends for Jewish females in Los Angeles. However, in 1979 the differences reported between Jewish and non-Hispanic white males applied to females as well, with the exception of managerial positions and sales

---

[34]The U.S. census reports "Retail self-employed managers" separately from "Supervisor, self-employed," in Sales, as shown in Table 23. The two categories are reported together in Table 22, "Retail-mgr./proprietor."

employment, where the proportions of Jewish and non-Jewish females were about the same (Table 22). Like Jewish males, Jewish females were more likely to be employed in the professions and in retail ownership than their non-Hispanic white counterparts.

Although Jewish females were most likely to be employed as professionals, they tended toward such traditionally female professions as teaching (13.1 percent), librarianship (3.4 percent), and social work (5.5 percent) (Table 23). However, they were also clustered in two "male" professional areas: lawyers and judges (4 times as likely as non-Hispanic whites) and "writers, artists, and athletes" (2.3 times as likely as non-Hispanic whites).

After the professions, Jewish females were next most frequently employed in clerical (i.e., "administrative support") occupations, but less so than non-Hispanic white females, for whom clerical work was the largest category. Jewish females were also much less likely than non-Hispanic white females to be employed in service occupations (5 as against 12 percent) or in skilled, unskilled, and craft positions (5 as against 9 percent).

The biggest difference between Jewish and non-Hispanic white females was in self-employed retail management and proprietorship—Jewish females were 5.4 times as likely to be so employed. Overall, however, only 2.7 percent of working Jewish females were self-employed retail managers and proprietors. They were more likely to be employed in sales (exclusive of self-employed proprietorship), where their rate of participation (14 percent) was almost the same as that of non-Hispanic white females. Within this occupational category, however, Jewish females were more likely to be salaried supervisors and financial representatives than cashiers or retail workers.

Despite differences in occupation and education, the labor-force-participation rates of Jewish females were virtually identical to those of non-Hispanic white females (Table 24). Married females with children in both groups were equally likely to be in the labor force, and in both cases females with children aged 6–17 were more likely to be working than females with children aged 5 and under. In both groups employment was highest among single mothers—78 percent for non-Hispanic white females and 81 percent for Jewish females.

PATTERNS OF PARTICIPATION IN JEWISH COMMUNAL LIFE

Except for the neighborhoods around Fairfax Avenue, the Jewish community of Los Angeles is largely invisible. It is the formal institutions and organizations of the community that provide it with its structure. For that reason, it makes sense to employ institutional affiliation as the measure of Jewish identity. Formal affiliation is defined here as participation in one or more of three major types of associations: synagogues, Jewish organizations, and the local Federation.[35]

Findings

Of all Jewish households in Los Angeles, 44 percent had some kind of formal affiliation, and 56 percent had none (Table 25). If a Jewish household was formally affiliated, it most likely had a single kind of affiliation. Only 12 percent of Jewish households had two affiliations, and only 5 percent had all three kinds.

Although the Federation is the largest, wealthiest, and most visible Jewish organization in Los Angeles, it was the synagogues and Jewish organizations that were the primary points of formal affiliation. Among Jewish households with one or more affiliations, 39 percent belonged to a synagogue or a Jewish organization (or both), as compared to 14 percent who gave to the Federation. If a household had only one affiliation, it was much more likely to be a synagogue (11 percent) or an organization (12 percent) than the Federation (4 percent). Similarly, those households with two affiliations were much more likely to belong to both a synagogue and an organization (7 percent) than to either of these two and the Federation (2 and 3 percent).

Membership in synagogues and Jewish organizations was divided almost equally between those who were affiliated with either of the two and those who were affiliated with both. Of the 39 percent of Jewish households that claimed membership in either a synagogue or a Jewish organization, 13 percent belonged to a synagogue and not to an organization, 14 percent belonged to a Jewish organization and not to a synagogue, and 12 percent belonged to both. Stated another way, just under half of all synagogue members (48 percent) belonged to a Jewish organization, and just under half (46 percent) of Jewish organization members belonged to a synagogue.

Over the years, the level of synagogue affiliation has remained at about one-quarter of all Jewish households: 24 percent in 1951;[36] 27 percent in 1967;[37] and 25 percent in 1979. When the growing rate of intermarriage is taken into consideration, the synagogue affiliation rate may actually be seen as increasing since 1967. Intermarriage increased 100 percent between 1967 and 1979, and only 7 percent of intermarried couples had a congregational membership. Thus, if the overall rate of congregational membership remained stable in the face of rising intermarriage, the affiliation rate of in-married couples must have increased. The unusually high rate of congregational membership of 34 percent[38] observed in 1959 is linked to the

---

[35]For a more extensive discussion of affiliation and Jewish identity in Los Angeles, see Neil C. Sandberg, *Jewish Life in Los Angeles: A Window to Tomorrow* (Washington, D.C., forthcoming).

[36]Massarik, *Report on the Jewish Population of Los Angeles, 1959*, p. 31.

[37]Massarik, *Report on the Jewish Population of Los Angeles, 1968*, Table 20.

[38]Massarik, *Report on the Jewish Population of Los Angeles, 1959*, p. 31.

higher marriage rate found in that study, corroborating the positive relationship between marriage and synagogue affiliation that is discussed below.

Federation giving was closely related to other forms of affiliation. Only 4 percent of Los Angeles Jewish households claimed Federation giving as their only formal affiliation, and less than a third (31 percent) of all Federation givers had no other affiliation. Exactly half of all Federation givers were synagogue members, and just over half (53 percent) belonged to an organization. The vast majority (68 percent) of Federation givers were affiliated either with a synagogue or with a Jewish organization.

Respondents could name up to five separate Jewish organizations to which they or their spouses belonged. When the individual Jewish organizations were grouped into eight categories, the most popular in terms of membership (11.7 percent of all households) was that of clubs and social organizations. This category included a diverse range of associations, from Jewish community center groups to groups for singles, young adults, and seniors, and a Jewish Masonic lodge. The next most popular category was women's organizations, such as Hadassah, ORT, Mizrachi Women (now AMIT Women), and the National Council of Jewish Women; 10.4 percent of all Jewish households claimed a membership in a women's organization.

The other categories were all named by less than 5 percent of households. Thus, 4 percent were affiliated with Jewish health and welfare organizations, such as Jewish Big Brothers, Cedars-Sinai Hospital, and the Jewish Home for the Aged. This category was followed by Israel-oriented organizations, such as Habonim, Histadrut (Labor Zionists), ARZA (Reform Zionists), and support groups for Israeli hospitals and universities, which were mentioned by 2.5 percent of the respondents. Jewish "defense" organizations, such as the American Jewish Committee, the Anti-Defamation League, and the American Jewish Congress, drew 1.8 percent of households, followed by voluntary activities in the Los Angeles Federation, such as working for the Welfare Fund or participation in a Federation committee. Educational and cultural groups were mentioned by 0.8 percent of respondents, and special-interest groups, such as Jewish Marriage Encounter and Jewish homosexual organizations, were mentioned by 0.4 percent.

Affiliation Variables

Affiliation with the Jewish community is related to two sets of social variables: those relating to the type of family or household, and those relating to the place of the household in the social structure of the Los Angeles Jewish community. The family and household variables examined here are age, household type, family-cycle stage, and Jewish status of the spouse (i.e., intermarriage status). The two social-structure variables considered are length of residence in Los Angeles and income.

Family and Household Variables

AGE

Synagogue membership was only loosely related to age: households with respondents aged 36–50 were the most likely to belong; households with respondents 18–35 years old were the least likely to belong; and households with respondents over age 50 were in the middle (Table 26). Organizational membership, on the other hand, was very much related to age—the older the respondents, the greater was the probability of one or more memberships. Federation giving, too, was related to age, with respondents over the age of 36 being between 4.6 and 9 times as likely to give as those under age 36.

Overall patterns of affiliation increased with age, from 26 percent for those under age 36, to 44 percent for those aged 36–50, 58 percent for those aged 51–65, and 68 percent for those aged 65 and over (Table 27). The sharpest increase in affiliation (one, two, and three affiliations) occurred with a move into the 36–50 age group.

HOUSEHOLD TYPE

Single parents, separated or divorced persons, and the never-married were the least likely to be affiliated with any institution (Table 29). Married couples with children and widowed household heads were the most likely to be affiliated. Married couples with children were the most likely to have all three kinds of affiliation (8 percent) as well as two out of the three (21 percent).

Married couples with children were the most likely to belong to a synagogue (44 percent), followed by married couples without children (24 percent), and widows (23 percent) (Table 28). Married couples with children were also the most likely to be Federation givers, along with married couples without children (22 and 20 percent). Widows and widowers were the most likely to belong to a Jewish organization (45 percent), followed by both kinds of married couples (31 percent).

FAMILY-CYCLE STAGE

Synagogue affiliation was lowest for families with no children and a household head under age 40 and highest for families with children aged 6–17 (with a slight dip for families with only teenagers) (Table 30). Synagogue membership was 44 percent higher for families with children of bar-mitzvah age than for families with children under age 6 only. (This is undoubtedly related to the desire for bar-mitzvah preparation, which is a significant—often the only—inducement for Jewish education.)

Although married couples with children were the most likely to belong to a synagogue, fewer than half of them actually did so, and fewer than half (42 percent) of Jewish children aged 6–13 were receiving any Jewish education. Among children past bar-mitzvah age, religious-school enrollment dropped to 18 percent; in the San Fernando Valley, where most Jewish children lived, only 7 percent of teenagers were enrolled in a Jewish educational program.[39]

Although children tend to leave Hebrew and religious school after bar mitzvah, their parents apparently maintain ties to the sponsoring synagogue. Synagogue affiliation was the same for families whose children were all past bar-mitzvah age as for those with 6–13-year-olds. Moreover, Jewish families with only teenage children were the most likely to belong to a Jewish organization (43 percent) and to give to the Federation (36 percent).

Among households with no children, those with household heads over age 40 were more likely to be affiliated than those with under-40 heads; the over-40 household heads were almost twice as likely to belong to a synagogue, 6 times as likely to belong to a Jewish organization, and more than 12 times as likely to be Federation givers.

Families with only teenage children were the most likely to have all three kinds of affiliation (20 percent), and households without children with a head under age 40 were the least likely (only 15 percent had any affiliation at all) (Table 31).

INTERMARRIAGE

Intermarried couples had very little formal connection with the Jewish community (Table 32). Only 8 percent belonged to a synagogue (as compared with 42 percent of in-married couples), and only 1.5 percent held membership in a Jewish organization (as compared with 27 percent of in-married couples). None of the intermarried couples in the survey were Federation givers. Overall, the total rate of formal affiliation among intermarried couples was only 8 percent, as compared with 53.2 percent for in-married couples (Table 33).

The affiliation patterns of convert couples are puzzling because they differ substantially from those of in-married couples. The convert couples were more organizationally than congregationally involved, 37 percent claiming affiliation with a Jewish organization and only 10 percent with a synagogue. Also, while a much larger proportion of convert couples than of in-marrieds had all three affiliations, their overall affiliation rate was lower than that of in-married couples. Since the number of convert marriages in the sample was small, the anomalous patterns may simply be a reflection of sample size.

Social-Structure Variables

LENGTH OF RESIDENCE IN LOS ANGELES

The number of years lived in Los Angeles was a significant factor in affiliation. For synagogue membership, 6 and 11 years of residence were thresholds at which

---

[39]Phillips, op. cit., p. 20.

membership increased (by 44 percent and 80 percent respectively) (Table 34). The threshold for membership in a Jewish organization were 6 and 31 years of residence; after 5 years in Los Angeles, organizational membership doubled, from 10 to 20 percent, and after 30 years it increased another 80 percent. For Federation giving, 11 and 31 years were the thresholds, with the giving rate increasing by 55 percent after 10 years, and by 51 percent after 30 years.

The overall rate of affiliation was also related to length of residence, increasing in the first 20 years, declining in the 21–30-year range, and climbing to its highest in the 31-years-and-over range. Whereas just over one-fifth (22 percent) of Jewish households present in Los Angeles for fewer than 6 years were affiliated, one-third (32 percent) of those in the community 6–10 years, one-half (51 percent) of those in the community between 11 and 20 years, and 57 percent of those in the community 30 years and over had at least one affiliation (Table 35).

HOUSEHOLD INCOME

The relationship between household income and Jewish participation is clearly evident in Los Angeles, with $30,000 being the threshold figure (Table 36). At $30,000, synagogue membership increased by 56 percent, organizational membership by 87 percent, and Federation giving by over 400 percent. The number of affiliations also increased with income (Table 37). Households with incomes of $50,000 and over were the most likely to have all three kinds of affiliation, followed by households with incomes between $30,000 and $49,000. Interestingly, households with incomes under $20,000 were more likely to belong to a Jewish organization, give to the Federation, and have all three affiliations than households with incomes between $20,000 and $29,000. This was due to the higher proportion of older persons in the lowest income category, with older people being more likely to participate in community activities.

Mean Affiliation Score

Table 38 summarizes the mean level of affiliation for the family and social-structure variables discussed above with a mean affiliation score. Households were coded as "0" for no affiliation, "1" for one type of affiliation, "2" for two types of affiliation, or "3" for three types of affiliation. The mean affiliation score does not give the average number of total affiliations, but rather the average number of *types* of affiliation. If all Jewish households had one type of affiliation each, the mean affiliation score would be "1." Similarly, if every household had all three kinds of affiliation, the mean affiliation score would be "3." The mean affiliation score for all Jewish households in Los Angeles was 0.065, less than 1, because there were more Jewish households with no affiliations whatsoever—56 percent—than there were with two or three types of affiliation—16.8 percent (Table 25).

Only three groups had mean affiliation scores of 1.00 or higher—married couples with children (1.00); households with only teenage children (1.25); and born Jews married to converts (1.05). Another 12 groups had mean affiliation scores of 0.70 or higher: born Jews married to born Jews (0.98); households headed by persons 51 years of age or older (0.89 and 0.98); households headed by widow(er)s (0.86); households with children aged 6–13 (0.85); households in Los Angeles 31 years or longer (0.84); households with incomes over $30,000 (0.80 and 0.84); households without children, where the respondent was 40 years and over (0.83); households in Los Angeles between 11 and 20 years (0.78); households headed by persons aged 36–50 (0.71); and married couples with no children (0.71).

Because several of the variables related to affiliation are also related to each other, it is difficult to tell which are the most weighty. Age, for example, is related to marital status (Table 16A), and also, among married couples, to the Jewish status of the spouse (Table 17). Which of the variables discussed, then, are most strongly associated with affiliation? A multiple-regression model was created to deal with this question.

Multiple regression is a statistical technique that measures the degree of correlation between a single dependent variable and a number of independent variables, using a linear equation. The dependent variable that was employed for this analysis is the mean level of affiliation discussed above, and called AFFILIATION in the regression model.

Seven independent variables, based on the variables discussed above, were entered into the equation as follows: *AGE*—Age was used as a continuous variable running from 18 to 95. *INCOME*—The 13 categories for income used in the questionnaire were entered into the regression equation rather than the 4 categories used in the discussion above and in Tables 37 and 38. *MARRIED*—Married was entered as a dummy variable based on marital status of the respondent; a married household head was coded "1" and a single household head as "0." *WIDOW*—Widows were seen to have particularly high organizational affiliation, so widowhood was entered as a dummy variable with "1" coded for widow(er) and "0" for all other marital-status categories. *KIDCYCLE*—The family-cycle typology used above was altered to emphasize both the presence and ages of children. Households with no children were coded as "0," households with children only under age 6 were coded as "1," households with children between ages 6 and 13 were coded as "2," and households with children only aged 14 and over were coded as "3." *LAYEARS*—The number of years in Los Angeles was coded as a continuous variable starting with "0" for households that had moved to Los Angeles in 1979. *MARRIAGE*—Marriages between two born Jews and between a born Jew and a convert were coded as "1"; intermarried couples and single household heads were coded as "0."

The stepwise regression model that was used for the analysis orders the independent variables in order of correlation, starting with the variable that has the highest individual correlation. Each subsequent variable is entered into the equation controlling for the effect of the previous variable(s). The results of the multiple regression are found in Table 39. The simple R in the table is the independent correlation coefficient, or the correlation between the independent variable and AFFILIATION, without controlling for the other variables. The beta is the coefficient used in the regression equation for predicting the value of the dependent variable. The R-Square is the amount of variance explained by the individual variable combined with all the previous variables. An independent variable that contributes to our understanding of the dependent variable is one that adds to the R-Square. In other words, including it in the equation explains additional variance in the dependent variable.

The variable called *MARRIAGE* is the first-ranked variable in the equation, with the highest individual correlation (.36). In other words, being married to another Jew (as opposed to not being married or being married to a non-Jew) is the factor most predictive of affiliation. *AGE* is the next best predictor, followed by *KIDCYCLE*, which takes into account the presence and ages of the children. These are the three most important variables because, taken together, they explain 21 percent of the variance in AFFILIATION.

The remaining four variables, *MARRIED, INCOME, WIDOW,* and *LA-YEARS,* together explain only an additional 2.4 percent of the variance in AFFILIATION. In other words, being married to a born Jew is more important for affiliation than simply being married. Similarly, being elderly (as reflected in *AGE*) is a better predictor of affiliation than the particular marital status of widowhood.

The biggest surprise of the regression analysis is the fifth-place rank and relatively low correlation of *INCOME* with AFFILIATION. Once the family variables (marital status, type of marriage, and ages of children in the household) are held constant, the correlation between *INCOME* and AFFILIATION is greatly reduced.

In summary, although all the variables were found to be associated with the degree of affiliation presented first in the cross-categorical analysis (i.e., combinations of affiliation with the Federation, a synagogue, and Jewish organizations), it is the family-related variables that are the best predictors of affiliation. In-married families with older children in the household had the greatest degree of formal affiliation with the Los Angeles Jewish community.

IS LOS ANGELES DIFFERENT?

To round out the analysis, it would be well to take a brief look at Los Angeles Jews in the broader context of American Jewry. Toward that end, Los Angeles is here compared with the other "big three" Jewish communities of New York, Chicago, and Philadelphia. The comparison is based on three dimensions: age and family structure, intermarriage, and affiliation.

Age and Family Structure

Given the popular images of hedonistic, freewheeling California, one would expect there to be proportionately fewer Jewish families in Los Angeles than elsewhere. This is partly true (Table 40). Los Angeles has a lower proportion of Jewish married couples with children than does either New York or Chicago (24 percent in Los Angeles vs. 30 percent in New York and 36 percent in Chicago), but it has almost the same proportion as Philadelphia (26 percent). Thus, Los Angeles can be said to be part of a larger demographic pattern rather than to stand by itself.

When age is taken into account, Los Angeles appears even less deviant, for it has the same proportion of children as New York, Philadelphia, and Chicago (Table 41). Los Angeles, however, has a larger share of the young-adult cohort (aged 30–39)—17 percent of Los Angeles Jews as against 14 percent of New York and Philadelphia Jews—a difference that may help to explain the smaller percentage of married couples with children. As noted above (see Table 16A), since 16 percent of the 30–39-year-olds in Los Angeles have never been married, and another 13 percent have been separated or divorced, 30 percent (including 0.8 percent who are widowed) of this age cohort are single. With most of these individuals living in single-person households, the effect is to lower the proportion of households with children.

Los Angeles also has fewer elderly Jews than the other three communities: 22 percent of New York Jews and 23 percent of Philadelphia Jews are 60 and over, as compared with only 16 percent of Los Angeles Jews. Or, put another way, there are 1.4 elderly Jews in New York and Philadelphia for every 1 elderly Jew in Los Angeles. In Chicago, 15 percent of the Jewish population is 65 and over as compared with 11 percent in Los Angeles—again a ratio of almost 1.4 to 1.

The lower percentage of the elderly and the higher percentage of young adults in Los Angeles are both associated with migration. Since Los Angeles is not the retirement city that Miami is, migrants have tended to be younger rather than older. Further, since half of all Jewish household heads have come to Los Angeles only since 1959, they have not resided there long enough to become elderly.

Intermarriage

The intermarriage rate has historically been higher in the West than in the Midwest or East. A study using data from 1964 found that Jews born in the West were up to 2.6 times as likely to intermarry as Jews born in the Northeast and almost twice as likely to intermarry as Jews born in the North Central states.[40] Reviewing more recent community studies (i.e., since 1979), Charles Silberman found that

---

[40]Fred Solomon Sherrow, "Patterns of Religious Intermarriage Among American College Students," Ph.D. dissertation, Columbia University (University Microfilm #72-28, 099), 1971, p. 103.

intermarriage rates continued to be higher in the West than anywhere else in the country.[41]

Within the West, Los Angeles has the lowest intermarriage rate of any community studied thus far (Table 42). For those under the age of 30—the cohort in which intermarriage is highest—the intermarriage rates (for couples) are 66 and 60 percent in Denver and Phoenix respectively, as compared with 49 percent in Los Angeles. For the 30–39 age group, the couple intermarriage rate in Denver is 40 percent, nearly twice as high as the 21-percent rate in Los Angeles.

Affiliation

Statistics on affiliation show that Los Angeles Jews are less likely to belong to Jewish organizations than are Chicago Jews, and are much less likely to do so than Philadelphia Jews (Table 43). Only 25 percent of Los Angeles Jewish households belong to a synagogue, as compared with 41 percent or more in Philadelphia, New York, and Chicago. The statistics on Federation giving follow the same pattern: only 14 percent of Los Angeles Jewish households gave to the Federation as compared with 26 percent in New York.[42]

To sum up: it is clear that the Los Angeles Jewish community is different from the large Jewish communities of the Midwest and the East in certain key aspects. Its population is younger overall, it has a higher intermarriage rate, and its Jews are much less likely to be affiliated with the organized community than Jews elsewhere. At the same time, marriage and family patterns of Los Angeles Jews closely resemble those in other communities.

Looking to the Future

If New York symbolizes continuity with the Jewish past, Los Angeles represents the emergence of a new Jewish America in the Sunbelt, particularly in the West. This second Jewish America is distinctive in that it has no significant European roots, its cultural heritage is more Wild West than Lower East Side, and its members

---

[41]Charles E. Silberman, *A Certain People: American Jews and Their Lives Today* (New York, 1985), p. 294.

A direct comparison of Western with Eastern and Midwestern cities is not feasible either because the intermarriage data have not been published or because they are not clearly comparable. However, to provide some basis for comparison, it is worthwhile to report estimates of the individual intermarriage rate for the under-35 population, as cited by Silberman, based on correspondence with various study directors: New York Metropolitan Area, 13 percent; St. Louis, 14 percent; Chicago, 20 percent; Philadelphia, 24 percent; Cleveland, 24 percent.

[42]The Federation's estimate of the number of givers is higher, but at any rate is not higher than the giving rate in New York. See also Paul Ritterband and Steven M. Cohen, "The Social Characteristics of the New York Area Jewish Community, 1981," AJYB, Vol. 84, 1984, p. 133.

have few cultural reference points in common. Nevertheless, there is a growing community in the West, with Los Angeles its acknowledged capital. This fact has been recognized by the three main religious groups in Jewish life, which have established branches of their schools of higher learning in Los Angeles.[43]

For Jewish communities in the West, the issues of intermarriage, migration, and affiliation are particularly acute. Rather than counting on affiliation as part of the natural course of the Jewish life cycle, the organized Jewish community is increasingly thinking in terms of outreach. The Hebrew Union College, for example, is developing a museum-outreach center situated in the Sepulveda Pass between the westside and the Valley. The Council on Jewish Life of the Jewish Federation Council sponsors a task force on synagogue affiliation as well as a commission on outreach to intermarrieds.

Additional help may come from an unexpected quarter. Situated as it is on the eastern shore of the "Pacific rim," Los Angeles has attracted growing numbers of Asian immigrants—Japanese, Chinese, Thais, Filipinos, Koreans, Laotians, Cambodians, and Samoans. In addition, because it is only a two-hour drive from Mexico, Los Angeles is a natural destination for Spanish-speaking immigrants—both documented and undocumented. (Los Angeles is already the second-largest Spanish-speaking city in the world, after Mexico City.) Immigration has had such an impact on Los Angeles that *Time* magazine recently called it "the New Ellis Island."[44] As the population of Los Angeles becomes increasingly varied, ethnicity could easily become the city's dominant cultural motif. Such a development might spur Los Angeles Jews to strengthen their own sense of identity and community as part of the expanding ethnic mosaic.

Whatever the future holds, one thing is clear. Los Angeles will remain the largest Jewish community as well as the Jewish institutional center of a rapidly growing western region. This includes Dallas, Houston, Denver, Phoenix, San Francisco, and Orange County—all with Jewish communities that have doubled their populations over the last decade. These communities represent the new face of American Jewry.

BRUCE A. PHILLIPS

---

[43]These are the West Coast branch of the Hebrew Union College, representing the Reform movement; the University of Judaism, which is the West Coast branch of the Jewish Theological Seminary; and Yeshiva University of Los Angeles.

[44]*Time,* June 13, 1983, pp. 18–27.

APPENDIX

TABLE 1. GENERAL AND JEWISH POPULATION GROWTH IN LOS ANGELES
COUNTY, 1880–1980: ABSOLUTE NUMBERS, GROWTH RATE, AND
JEWISH DENSITY

	General		Jewish		Jewish
Year	Population Size	Growth[a] (Percent)	Population Size	Growth[a] (Percent)	Density[b] (Percent)
1880	33,381	—	136	—	0.4
1890	101,454	200	No estimate	—	—
1900	170,298	68	2,500	—	1.5
1910	489,322	180	9,000	260	1.8
1920	880,862	80	31,500	250	3.6
1930	2,066,460	135	72,041	128	3.5
1940	2,621,372	27	103,634	44	4.0
1950	3,900,920	49	272,100	163	7.0
1960	5,615,748	44	400,000	47	6.8
1970	6,579,585	17	444,934	11	6.8
1980	7,116,066	8	503,000	13	7.1

Sources: U.S. Census of Population (not including Long Beach). Jewish population estimates
for 1880 to 1920 are from Max Vorspan and Lloyd Gartner, *History of the Jews of Los Angeles*
(Philadelphia, 1970). Estimates for 1930, 1940, 1950, and 1960 are extrapolated from the
AJYB figures for 1927, 1937, 1944, 1948, 1954, 1959, and 1964. The 1970 estimate was
provided by Dr. Fred Massarik in an unpublished report to the Jewish Federation Council of
Greater Los Angeles. The 1980 estimate is from Bruce A. Phillips, *Los Angeles Jewish Community Survey: Overview for Regional Planning,* Planning and Budgeting Department, Jewish
Federation Council of Greater Los Angeles, 1980.
[a]Relative to the previous decade, for example:

$$\text{Change}_{1960-1970} = \frac{(\text{Population}_{1970} - \text{Population}_{1960})}{\text{Population}_{1960}}$$

[b]Jewish households as a percent of Los Angeles County households, minus Long Beach
households.

TABLE 2A. DISTRIBUTION OF JEWISH HOUSEHOLDS BY GEOGRAPHIC AREA AND
NAMED COMMUNITY, 1951–1979

Area & Community	1951	1959	1970	1974	1979
Urban Core	64,818	56,699	51,737	43,056	60,405
Wilshire Fairfax	8,446	9,294	9,188	8,790	9,890
Beverly Fairfax	8,627	9,371	11,725	8,547	13,619
Hollywood	18,096	15,337	23,517	21,509	23,416
Central Wilshire	7,815	5,308	3,149	1,256	5,642
Northeast-Downtown	2,228	5,228	764	1,256	3,852
East Los Angeles	8,069	4,967	743	159	0
Baldwin Hills-West Adams	8,728	5,813	2,131	1,053	1,915
Jefferson-University	2,809	1,381	520	486	2,071
Western Area	23,068	28,993	44,294	52,039	54,877
B.W.-C.H.-M.V.-C.C.[a]	9,853	13,124	20,596	21,840	15,244
Beverly Hills	10,929	6,563	7,705	10,050	8,890
Westwood-Brentwood	incl. above	5,038	9,112	10,299	22,626
Santa Monica	2,286	4,268	6,881	9,850	8,117
San Fernando Valley	10,165	22,827	40,997	51,286	72,136
North & West Valley	incl. above	3,776	7,975	10,287	13,537
Reseda-Encino	" "	3,767	9,992	14,113	14,043
Van Nuys-Sherman Oaks	" "	4,157	10,743	12,722	19,900
North Hollywd-Burbank	" "	6,456	10,007	10,405	16,168
Sunland-Glendale	" "	4,671	2,280	3,759	8,488
Eastern Area	2,067	4,859	9,350	8,305	11,893
San Gabriel Valley	1,553	4,345	7,700	7,000	9,665
Pasadena-Altadena	514	514	1,650	1,305	2,228
Southern Area	6,780	6,982	10,200	8,670	20,805
Westchester-Inglewood	2,075	2,139	4,010	1,890	2,862
South Los Angeles	3,498	3,386	3,780	3,420	8,590
Beach Cities & South	1,207	1,457	2,410	3,360	9,353
Total	106,898	120,360	156,578	163,356	220,116

Sources (2A, 2B, 2C): Fred Massarik, *A Report on the Jewish Population of Los Angeles,* Los
Angeles Jewish Community Council, January 1953; Fred Massarik, *A Report on the Jewish
Population of Los Angeles, 1959,* Research Service Bureau, Jewish Federation Council of
Greater Los Angeles, Nov. 1959; Fred Massarik, *Jewish Population Indicator Reports I, II, III,
IV, and Special Analysis Memo Number 4,* Jewish Federation Council Community Planning
Department, mimeo, 1976; Bruce A. Phillips, *Analysis of the 1974 Jewish Population Indicator
Reports,* Jewish Federation Council Community Planning Department, mimeo, 1976; Bruce
A. Phillips, *Los Angeles Jewish Community Survey: Overview for Regional Planning,* Planning
and Budgeting Department, Jewish Federation Council of Greater Los Angeles, 1980.
[a]Beverlywood, Cheviot Hills, Mar Vista, & Culver City

TABLE 2B. CHANGES IN DISTRIBUTION OF JEWISH HOUSEHOLDS, BY GEO-
GRAPHIC AREA AND NAMED COMMUNITY, 1951–1979 (PERCENT)

Area & Community	Percent Change				
	1951–59	1959–70	1970–79	[1970–74	1974–79]
Urban Core	−12.5	−8.8	16.8	[−16.8	40.3]
Wilshire Fairfax	10.0	−1.1	7.6	[−4.3	12.5]
Beverly Fairfax	8.6	25.1	16.2	[−27.1	59.3]
Hollywood	−15.2	53.3	−0.4	[−8.5	8.9]
Central Wilshire	−32.1	−40.7	79.2	[−60.1	349.2]
Northeast-Downtown	134.6	−85.4	404.2	[64.4	206.7]
East Los Angeles	−38.4	−85.0	−100.0	[−78.6	−100.0]
Baldwin Hills-West Adams	−33.4	−63.3	−10.1	[−50.6	81.9]
Jefferson-University	−50.8	−62.3	298.3	[−6.5	326.1]
Western Area	25.7	52.8	23.9	[17.5	5.5]
B.W.-C.H.-M.V.-C.C.a	33.2	56.9	−26.0	[6.0	−30.2]
Beverly Hills	6.1	17.4	15.4	[30.4	−11.5]
Westwood-Brentwood	incl. above	80.9	148.3	[13.0	119.7]
Santa Monica	86.7	61.2	18.0	[43.1	−17.6]
San Fernando Valley	124.6	79.6	76.0	[25.1	40.7]
North & West Valley	incl. above	111.2	69.7	[29.0	31.6]
Reseda-Encino	" "	165.3	40.5	[41.2	−0.5]
Van Nuys-Sherman Oaks	" "	158.4	85.2	[18.4	56.4]
North Hollywd-Burbank	" "	55.0	61.6	[4.0	55.4]
Sunland-Glendale	" "	−51.2	272.3	[64.9	125.8]
Eastern Area	135.1	92.4	27.2	[−11.2	43.2]
San Gabriel Valley	179.8	77.2	25.5	[−9.1	38.1]
Pasadena-Altadena	0.0	220.8	35.0	[−20.9	70.7]
Southern Area	3.0	46.1	104.0	[−15.0	40.0]
Westchester-Inglewood	3.1	87.5	−28.6	[−52.9	51.4]
South Los Angeles	−3.2	11.6	127.2	[−9.5	151.2]
Beach Cities & South	20.7	65.4	288.1	[39.4	178.4]

aBeverlywood, Cheviot Hills, Mar Vista, & Culver City

TABLE 2C. JEWISH POPULATION OF GEOGRAPHIC AREAS AND NAMED COMMUNITIES AS A PERCENTAGE OF TOTAL LOS ANGELES JEWISH POPULATION, 1951–1979

Area & Community	1951	1959	1970	1974	1979
Urban Core	60.6	47.1	33.0	26.4	27.4
Wilshire Fairfax	7.9	7.7	5.9	5.4	4.5
Beverly Fairfax	8.1	7.8	7.5	5.2	6.2
Hollywood	16.9	12.7	15.0	13.2	10.6
Central Wilshire	7.3	4.4	2.0	0.8	2.6
Northeast-Downtown	2.1	4.3	0.5	0.8	1.7
East Los Angeles	7.5	4.1	0.5	0.1	0.0
Baldwin Hills-West Adams	8.2	4.8	1.4	0.6	0.9
Jefferson-University	2.6	1.1	0.3	0.3	0.9
Western Area	21.6	24.1	28.3	31.9	24.9
B.W.-C.H.-M.V.-C.C[a]	9.2	10.9	13.2	13.4	6.9
Beverly Hills	10.2	5.5	4.9	6.2	4.0
Westwood-Brentwood	incl. above	4.2	5.8	6.3	10.3
Santa Monica	2.1	3.5	4.4	6.0	3.7
San Fernando Valley	9.5	19.0	26.2	31.4	32.8
North & West Valley	incl. above	3.1	5.1	6.3	6.1
Reseda-Encino	" "	3.1	6.4	8.6	6.4
Van Nuys-Sherman Oaks	" "	3.5	6.9	7.8	9.0
North Hollywd-Burbank	" "	5.4	6.4	6.4	7.3
Sunland-Glendale	" "	3.9	1.5	2.3	3.9
Eastern Area	1.9	4.0	6.0	5.1	5.4
San Gabriel Valley	1.5	3.6	4.9	4.3	4.4
Pasadena-Altadena	0.5	0.4	1.1	0.8	1.0
Southern Area	6.3	5.8	6.5	5.3	9.5
Westchester-Inglewood	1.9	1.8	2.6	1.2	1.3
South Los Angeles	3.3	2.8	2.4	2.1	3.9
Beach Cities & South	1.1	1.2	1.5	2.1	4.2
Total	100.0	100.0	100.0	100.0	100.0

[a]Beverlywood, Cheviot Hills, Mar Vista, & Culver City

TABLE 3. LENGTH OF RESIDENCE OF JEWISH HOUSEHOLD HEADS IN LOS AN-
GELES BY YEAR OF SURVEY, 1951–1979 (PERCENT)

Years in Los Angeles	Year of Survey			
	1951	1959	1967	1979
0–5	61.7	12.3	14.2	13.9
6–10	22.8	15.1	6.9	12.9
11–15	[15.6]	25.9	16.0	[17.9]
16–20	[ ]	[46.7]	19.2	[ ]
21–30	[ ]	[ ]	26.2	26.7
30 +	[ ]	[ ]	23.9	28.5
Total	100.0	100.0	100.0	100.0
Percentage in Los Angeles 10 years or more:	15.6	72.6	78.9	73.2

Sources: Fred Massarik, *A Report on the Jewish Population of Los Angeles,* Los Angeles Jewish
Community Council, Jan., 1953; Fred Massarik, *A Report on the Jewish Population of Los
Angeles, 1959,* Research Service Bureau, Jewish Federation Council of Greater Los Angeles,
Nov., 1959; Fred Massarik, *A Report on the Jewish Population of Los Angeles, 1968,* Research
Service Bureau, Jewish Federation Council of Greater Los Angeles, 1968; Bruce A. Phillips,
Los Angeles Jewish Community Survey: Overview for Regional Planning, Planning and Budget-
ing Department, Jewish Federation Council of Greater Los Angeles, 1980.

TABLE 4. LENGTH OF RESIDENCE OF JEWISH HOUSEHOLD HEADS IN LOS ANGELES BY COMMUNITY, 1979 (PERCENT)

Years in Los Angeles	Beverly Fairfax W.Hollywood	Silverlake Los Feliz Hollywood	Beverly Hills	Santa Monica Palisades Malibu	Venice Mar Vista Culver	Cheviot W.L.A. Bevwood	Westwood Brentwood
0–5	20.0	20.8	11.2	26.3	26.9	9.9	10.8
6–10	6.0	8.5	6.5	18.6	10.7	12.6	18.6
11–20	18.2	23.3	14.4	17.5	18.2	15.0	12.5
21–30	19.5	7.6	36.0	14.6	27.4	29.3	18.1
30 +	35.5	39.8	31.8	23.0	16.8	33.1	40.1
Total	100.0	100.0	100.0	100.0	100.0	100.0	100.0

Years in Los Angeles	North & West Valley	Central Valley	Encino Tarzana Sh. Oaks	North Hollywood	Southern Area	Eastern Area
0–5	12.4	6.6	10.0	4.6	14.7	11.6
6–10	15.8	18.2	16.6	24.8	11.4	3.4
11–20	17.1	20.2	18.9	24.7	20.3	17.9
21–30	26.3	39.6	28.3	33.9	29.9	37.0
30 +	28.4	15.3	26.2	12.1	23.7	30.2
Total	100.0	100.0	100.0	100.0	100.0	100.0

Source: Bruce A. Phillips, *Los Angeles Jewish Community Survey: Overview for Regional Planning,* Planning and Budgeting Department, Jewish Federation Council of Greater Los Angeles, 1980.

TABLE 5. PLACE OF BIRTH OF BORN JEWS 18 AND OVER BY YEAR OF SURVEY, 1951–1979 (PERCENT)

Place of Birth	Year of Survey			
	1951	1959	1967	1979
Los Angeles	8.3	11.8	not	14.1
Other U.S.	52.1	53.6	available	57.3
Foreign born	39.6	34.6		28.6
Total	100.0	100.0		100.0

Source: Fred Massarik, *A Report on the Jewish Population of Los Angeles, 1959,* Research Service Bureau, Jewish Federation Council of Greater Los Angeles, Nov., 1959: Table 18 compares 1959 and 1951; Bruce A. Phillips, *Los Angeles Jewish Community Survey: Overview for Regional Planning,* Planning and Budgeting Department, Jewish Federation Council of Greater Los Angeles, 1980.

TABLE 6. PLACE OF BIRTH OF BORN JEWS 18 AND OVER BY AGE, 1979 (PERCENT)

Place of Birth	Age				
	18–29	30–39	40–49	50+	All
New England	2.5	2.2	3.5	4.5	3.7
Mid-Atlantic	15.2	34.3	39.2	27.8	28.8
East North-Central	15.2	14.2	15.1	19.3	16.8
West North-Central	2.9	3.4	1.0	3.6	3.0
South Atlantic	2.9	3.0	0.5	3.2	2.6
E. & W. South-Central	1.5	1.9	0.0	0.0	0.7
Mountain	0.5	0.7	0.5	0.8	0.8
Pacific	0.0	0.7	0.5	0.2	0.3
Los Angeles	39.2	17.9	14.1	2.8	14.1
Other California	2.5	3.0	0.5	0.8	1.5
U.S. not specific	2.9	0.4	3.5	2.1	2.1
Foreign born	14.7	18.3	21.6	35.0	25.6
Total	100.0	100.0	100.0	100.0	100.0

Source: Bruce A. Phillips, *Los Angeles Jewish Community Survey: Overview for Regional Planning,* Planning and Budgeting Department, Jewish Federation Council of Greater Los Angeles, 1980.

TABLE 7. PLACE OF BIRTH OF BORN JEWS 18 AND OVER BY LENGTH OF RESI-
DENCE IN LOS ANGELES, 1979 (PERCENT)

Place of Birth	Years in Los Angeles				
	5 or Less	6–10	11–20	21–30	30+
New England	5.5	7.6	1.6	2.0	3.2
Mid-Atlantic	29.5	36.2	41.9	24.1	25.1
East North-Central	13.3	21.6	14.2	16.3	17.6
West North-Central	4.4	2.1	0.7	2.8	3.7
South Atlantic	3.9	2.3	3.4	3.4	1.7
E. & W. South-Central	0.0	0.0	0.6	1.4	0.0
Mountain	1.1	0.5	0.0	0.5	1.1
Pacific	0.0	0.0	1.0	0.4	0.3
Foreign born	33.0	20.4	28.4	17.5	21.3
U.S. not specific	3.1	1.1	1.0	1.0	1.7
California	6.2	8.3	7.2	29.9	25.3
Total	100.0	100.0	100.0	100.0	100.0

Source: Bruce A. Phillips, *Los Angeles Jewish Community Survey: Overview for Regional Planning,* Planning and Budgeting Department, Jewish Federation Council of Greater Los Angeles, 1980.

TABLE 8.   PLACE OF BIRTH OF WHITE AND JEWISH POPULATIONS OF LOS ANGELES COUNTY, 1979–1980 (PERCENT)

Place of Birth	All Whites[a]	Jewish Population Only		
		All Ages	Adults	Children
Born in California	41.2	29.9	16.0	73.6
Out of state	40.3	48.0	58.0	15.4
Northeast	(10.4)	(26.8)	(33.5)	(5.8)
North Central	(16.8)	(17.3)	(20.4)	(7.7)
South	(7.6)	(3.0)	(3.4)	(1.8)
Other Mountain & Pacific	(5.4)	(0.9)	(1.2)	(0.0)
Foreign born	18.5	22.1	25.6	11.0
Total	100.0	100.0	100.0	100.0

Sources: Summary Tape File #4, PB-25; Bruce A. Phillips, *Los Angeles Jewish Community Survey: Overview for Regional Planning,* Planning and Budgeting Department, Jewish Federation Council of Greater Los Angeles, 1980.
[a]All whites, including Hispanics and Jews, are incorporated in this tabulation.

TABLE 9. AGE DISTRIBUTION OF JEWISH POPULATION BY YEAR OF SURVEY, 1951–1979 (PERCENT)

Age	Year of Survey			
	1951	1959	1967	1979
0–4	8.2	10.0	7.1	4.3
5–9	7.7	10.4	7.4	5.5
10–14	5.8	8.7	10.3	6.3
15–19	5.3	6.4	8.3	7.2
20–24	4.9	3.5	4.5	6.2
25–29	6.8	5.0	3.9	10.4
30–34	8.0	8.0	4.7	9.2
35–39	11.0	8.6	7.7	8.1
40–44	9.1	8.1	8.9	5.3
45–49	7.1	7.0	6.0	6.8
50–54	6.4	6.5	5.0	6.8
55–59	6.2	5.2	5.0	7.5
60–64	5.3	4.4	. 4.2	5.3
65–69	[ ]	4.1	3.8	4.2
70–74	[6.9]	2.1	[ ]	3.1
75–79	[ ]	1.1	[8.4]	1.9
80 +	[ ]	0.8	[ ]	1.9
Total	100.0	100.0	100.0	100.0

Sources: Fred Massarik, *A Report on the Jewish Population of Los Angeles,* Los Angeles Jewish Community Council, Jan. 1953; Fred Massarik, *A Report on the Jewish Population of Los Angeles, 1959,* Research Service Bureau, Jewish Federation Council of Greater Los Angeles, November 1959; Fred Massarik, *A Report on the Jewish Population of Los Angeles, 1968,* Research Service Bureau, Jewish Federation Council of Greater Los Angeles, 1968; Bruce A. Phillips, *Los Angeles Jewish Community Survey: Overview for Regional Planning,* Planning and Budgeting Department, Jewish Federation Council of Greater Los Angeles, 1980.

TABLE 10. AGE DISTRIBUTION OF NON-HISPANIC WHITE AND JEWISH POPULA-
TIONS BY 5-, 10-, AND 15-YEAR COHORTS, 1979–1980 (PERCENT)

Age	5-Year Cohorts		Age	10- & 15-Year Cohorts	
	White	Jewish		White	Jewish
0–4	4.7	4.3	0–9	9.4	9.8
5–9	4.7	5.5	10–19	13.6	13.5
10–14	6.0	6.3	20–29	18.0	16.6
15–19	7.6	7.2	30–39	14.9	17.3
20–24	9.1	6.2	40–49	10.9	12.1
25–29	8.9	10.4	50–59	13.2	14.3
30–34	8.2	9.2	60–69	10.6	9.5
35–39	6.6	8.1	70+	9.6	6.9
40–44	5.4	5.3			
45–49	5.4	6.8	Total	100.0	100.0
50–54	6.3	6.8			
55–59	6.8	7.5			
60–64	5.8	5.3	0–19	23.0	23.3
65–69	4.8	4.2	20–35	26.2	25.8
70–74	3.7	3.1	35–50	17.5	20.2
75–79	2.7	1.9	50–65	18.9	19.6
80+	3.2	1.9	65+	14.4	11.1
Total	100.0	100.0	Total	100.0	100.0

Sources: Summary Tape File #4, PB-1; Bruce A. Phillips, *Los Angeles Jewish Community Survey: Overview for Regional Planning,* Planning and Budgeting Department, Jewish Federation Council of Greater Los Angeles, 1980.

TABLE 11.   HOUSEHOLD TYPES, NON-HISPANIC WHITE AND JEWISH, 1979–1980
             (PERCENT)

Household Type	White	Jewish
Married couple	50.1	57.6
With children	19.8	24.3
No children	30.4	33.3
Single-headed	49.9	42.4
With children	5.5	4.0
No children	44.4	38.4
Percent of all households that include children:	25.3	28.3

Sources: Summary Tape File #4, computed from Tables PB2, PB3, PB7, PB8, and PB18;
Bruce A. Phillips, *Los Angeles Jewish Community Survey: Overview for Regional Planning,*
Planning and Budgeting Department, Jewish Federation Council of Greater Los Angeles,
1980.

TABLE 12.   MARITAL HISTORY OF ALL EVER-MARRIED PERSONS, AGED 15–54,
             NON-HISPANIC WHITE AND JEWISH, 1979–1980 (PERCENT)

Marital History	White	Jewish
Never widowed or divorced	64.4	74.6
Widowed only	2.3	3.7
Ever divorced	33.3	21.7
Total	100.0	100.0

Sources: Summary Tape File #4, PB23; Bruce A. Phillips, Los Angeles Jewish Population
Study, 1979.

TABLE 13. JEWISH HOUSEHOLD TYPES BY GEOGRAPHIC AREA, 1979 (PERCENT)

Household Type	Geographic Area					
	Urban Core	Western Area	S.F. Valley	Southern Area	Eastern Area	All Areas
Married couple with children	11.4	16.3	37.4	22.5	29.5	24.3
Married couple no children	29.7	36.4	33.2	36.9	29.2	33.3
Single parent	1.8	4.3	3.8	12.5	2.7	4.0
Never married	25.4	23.6	7.7	16.6	16.2	17.2
Widow(er)	16.5	7.7	9.1	3.5	12.5	10.2
Sep./div.	15.1	11.8	8.8	8.1	10.0	11.0
Total	100.0	100.0	100.0	100.0	100.0	100.0

Source: Bruce A. Phillips, Los Angeles Jewish Population Study, 1979.

TABLE 14. JEWISH HOUSEHOLD TYPES BY COMMUNITY, 1979 (PERCENT)

Household Type	Beverly Fairfax W.Hollywood	Silverlake Los Feliz Hollywood	Beverly Hills	Santa Monica Palisades Malibu	Venice Mar Vista Culver	Cheviot W.L.A. Bevwood	Westwood Brentwood
Married couple with children	13.7	0.0	35.1	20.4	6.7	7.9	13.3
Married couple no children	27.0	43.3	40.3	23.9	38.2	37.4	41.3
Single parent	2.2	0.0	0.0	8.6	5.9	2.6	4.3
Never married	22.3	41.0	9.2	25.7	34.2	30.3	19.7
Widow(er)	18.1	8.5	11.0	8.6	0.0	10.4	7.3
Sep./div.	16.7	7.2	4.5	12.9	15.0	11.3	14.1
Total	100.0	100.0	100.0	100.0	100.0	100.0	100.0

Household Type	North & West Valley	Central Valley	Encino Tarzana Sh. Oaks	North Hollywood	Southern Area	Eastern Area	All Areas
Married couple with children	53.0	29.7	21.5	26.7	22.5	29.5	24.3
Married couple no children	30.5	35.4	26.4	42.5	36.9	29.2	33.3
Single parent	1.2	8.3	3.8	3.5	12.5	2.7	4.0
Never married	4.0	6.5	17.8	8.6	16.6	16.2	17.2
Widow(er)	5.0	7.6	14.9	15.5	3.5	12.5	10.2
Sep./div.	6.3	12.5	15.5	3.2	8.1	10.0	11.0
Total	100.0	100.0	100.0	100.0	100.0	100.0	100.0

Source: Bruce A. Phillips, Los Angeles Jewish Population Study, 1979.

TABLE 15. JEWISH FAMILY-CYCLE STAGE BY COMMUNITY, 1979 (PERCENT)

Family-Cycle Stage	Beverly Fairfax W.Hollywood	Silverlake Los Feliz Hollywood	Beverly Hills	Community Santa Monica Palisades Malibu	Venice Mar Vista Culver	Cheviot W.L.A. Beywood	Westwood Brentwood
Children							
Under 6 only	7.4	0.0	2.7	2.1	2.1	1.7	0.0
6–13	5.3	0.0	23.4	19.3	9.9	8.0	6.6
14–17 only	3.5	0.0	9.9	7.5	3.3	1.0	9.2
No Children							
Head under 40	26.7	49.1	12.3	39.7	55.6	37.8	38.8
Head over 40	57.2	50.9	51.7	31.4	29.1	51.5	45.4
Total	100.0	100.0	100.0	100.0	100.0	100.0	100.0

Family-Cycle Stage	North & West Valley	Central Valley	Encino Tarzana Sh. Oaks	North Hollywood	Southern Area	Eastern Area	All Areas
Children							
Under 6 only	10.0	17.7	0.0	12.2	5.3	4.7	6.3
6–13	36.2	14.9	11.4	13.8	20.4	18.1	15.6
14–17 only	8.0	6.1	15.1	5.2	7.9	7.1	6.4
No Children							
Head under 40	14.8	22.5	21.6	22.4	31.0	34.3	28.6
Head over 40	30.9	38.7	51.8	46.4	35.4	35.9	43.1
Total	100.0	100.0	100.0	100.0	100.0	100.0	100.0

TABLE 16A. MARITAL STATUS OF JEWS BY 10-YEAR COHORTS, 1967 AND 1979
(PERCENT)

| Marital | Cohort and Year | | | |
| | 20–29 | | 30–39 | |
Status	1967	1979	1967	1979
Never married	50.9	58.8	6.2	16.1
Married	43.6	34.0	87.8	70.5
Widow(er)	0.0	0.0	2.1	0.8
Sep./div.	5.5	7.2	3.9	12.6
Total	100.0	100.0	100.0	100.0

| Marital | 40–49 | | 50–59 | |
Status	1967	1979	1967	1979
Never married	4.8	3.7	1.0	0.9
Married	86.5	81.2	91.1	83.1
Widow(er)	2.0	1.6	4.2	8.2
Sep./div.	6.8	13.6	3.7	7.8
Total	100.0	100.0	100.0	100.0

| Marital | 60 + | | All Ages | |
Status	1967	1979	1967	1979
Never married	3.5	2.2	19.7	18.2
Married	68.7	61.9	69.3	64.2
Widow(er)	22.7	28.2	6.6	8.1
Sep./div.	4.4	7.7	4.4	9.5
Total	100.0	100.0	100.0	100.0

Sources: Fred Massarik, *A Report on the Jewish Population of Los Angeles, 1968,* Research
Service Bureau, Jewish Federation Council of Greater Los Angeles, 1968, Table 5; Bruce A.
Phillips, Los Angeles Jewish Population Study, 1979.

TABLE 16B. MARITAL STATUS OF JEWS BY 5- AND 10-YEAR COHORTS, 1979 (PERCENT)

Marital Status	Cohort			
	18–24	25–29	30–34	35–39
Never married	80.1	38.0	23.0	8.3
Married	12.6	54.8	63.5	78.5
Widow(er)	0.0	0.0	0.8	0.8
Sep./div.	7.3	7.2	12.7	12.4
Total	100.0	100.0	100.0	100.0

Marital Status	40–49	50–59	60–69	70 +
Never married	3.7	0.9	1.4	3.3
Married	81.2	83.1	72.1	48.4
Widow(er)	1.6	8.2	19.7	39.5
Sep./div.	13.6	7.8	6.8	8.8
Total	100.0	100.0	100.0	100.0

Source: Bruce A. Phillips, Los Angeles Jewish Population Study, 1979.

TABLE 17. INTERMARRIAGE STATUS OF SPOUSES OF CURRENTLY MARRIED BORN JEWS BY AGE AND SEX, 1979 (PERCENT)

Status of Spouse	Age and Sex of Born Jew					
	18–29		30–39		40–49	
	Male	Female	Male	Female	Male	Female
Born Jew	70.4	60.2	82.8	88.5	90.1	88.7
Convert	3.4	4.6	2.7	0.7	6.1	0.9
Non-Jew	26.2	35.3	14.5	10.8	3.9	10.5
Total	100.0	100.0	100.0	100.0	100.0	100.0

Status of Spouse	50 +		All Ages	
	Male	Female	Male	Female
Born Jew	90.8	92.4	87.3	85.2
Convert	2.0	1.6	3.1	1.7
Non-Jew	7.0	6.0	9.6	13.1
Total	100.0	100.0	100.0	100.0

Source: Bruce A. Phillips, Los Angeles Jewish Population Study, 1979.

TABLE 18. INTERMARRIAGE STATUS OF MARRIED COUPLES WITH AT LEAST ONE BORN-JEWISH SPOUSE, BY AGE OF RESPONDENT, 1979 (PERCENT)

Status of Couple	Age of Respondent[a]				All Ages
	18–29	30–39	40–49	50+	
Born Jew–born Jew	44.8	76.5	80.6	83.9	75.5
Born Jew–convert	6.3	2.6	6.1	3.6	4.2
Born Jew–non-Jew	48.9	20.8	13.3	12.5	20.1
Total	100.0	100.0	100.0	100.0	100.0
Conversion rate[b]	11.4	11.1	31.4	22.4	17.3

Source: Bruce A. Phillips, Los Angeles Jewish Population Study, 1979.
[a]The intermarriage rates by age in Tables 17 and 18 do not correspond exactly. Table 18 is based only on the age of the respondent, Jew or non-Jew. Table 17 includes the ages of all Jewish spouses, males and females, either of whom may have been counted as the respondent in Table 18.
[b]Marriages to converts as a percentage of all exogamous marriages (i.e., marriages to converts + marriages to non-Jews).

TABLE 19. INTERMARRIAGE RATE (BORN JEW MARRIED TO NON-JEW) BY YEAR OF SURVEY, 1951–1979

	Year of Survey			
	1951	1959	1967	1979
Percentage of Households with Intermarried Couple	4.8	6.3	5.4	11.7

Sources: Fred Massarik, *A Report on the Jewish Population of Los Angeles,* Los Angeles Jewish Community Council, Jan. 1953; Fred Massarik, *A Report on the Jewish Population of Los Angeles, 1959,* Research Service Bureau, Jewish Federation Council of Greater Los Angeles, Nov. 1959; Fred Massarik, *A Report on the Jewish Population of Los Angeles, 1968,* Research Service Bureau, Jewish Federation Council of Greater Los Angeles, 1968; Bruce A. Phillips, Los Angeles Jewish Population Study, 1979.

TABLE 20. EDUCATION OF NON-HISPANIC WHITE AND JEWISH POPULATIONS BY AGE AND SEX, 1979–1980 (PERCENT)

	Males					
	White			Jewish		
Education	25–44	45–64	65+	25–44	45–64	65+
Elementary	2.2	7.8	25.8	0.5	0.9	17.9
Some h.s.	6.7	12.3	17.6	1.4	3.2	7.1
H.S. grad.	25.5	31.3	26.5	7.8	20.6	32.1
Some college	29.5	21.4	15.1	20.7	19.3	10.7
College grad.	36.1	27.2	15.0	69.6	56.0	32.2
Total	100.0	100.0	100.0	100.0	100.0	100.0
Jewish/White Ratio[a]						
Some college				1.4	1.5	1.4
Some college & college grad.				1.9	2.1	2.1

	Females					
	White			Jewish		
Education	25–44	45–64	65+	25–44	45–64	65+
Elementary	2.2	6.8	25.6	0.4	2.7	19.4
Some h.s.	8.1	13.8	18.0	0.7	4.1	6.8
H.S. grad.	35.9	43.7	32.5	19.9	34.5	44.3
Some college	29.3	22.3	14.7	28.5	32.3	17.0
College grad.	24.4	13.4	9.2	50.5	26.4	12.5
Total	100.0	100.0	100.0	100.0	100.0	100.0
Jewish/White Ratio[a]						
Some college				2.1	2.0	1.4
Some college & college grad.				1.5	1.6	1.2

Sources: Summary Tape File #4, PB48; Bruce A. Phillips, Los Angeles Jewish Population Study, 1979.

[a]Jewish/White Ratio $= \dfrac{\% \text{ of Jews}}{\% \text{ of whites}}$

TABLE 21. OCCUPATIONS OF EMPLOYED JEWISH MALES BY YEAR OF SURVEY, 1951–1979 (PERCENT)

Occupational Category	Year of Survey			
	1951	1959	1967	1979
Professional & semiprofessional	15.3	24.9	35.4	33.7
Proprietors, managers, officials	35.5	30.5	23.5	28.8
Clerical and sales occupations	28.3	24.2	20.8	21.5
Skilled, crafts, and unskilled	19.2	17.5	16.6	13.6
Service occupations	1.7	2.9	3.8	4.2
Total	100.0	100.0	100.0	100.0

Sources: Fred Massarik, *A Report on the Jewish Population of Los Angeles,* Los Angeles Jewish Community Council, Jan. 1953; Fred Massarik, *A Report on the Jewish Population of Los Angeles, 1959,* Research Service Bureau, Jewish Federation Council of Greater Los Angeles, Nov. 1959; Fred Massarik, *A Report on the Jewish Population of Los Angeles, 1968,* Research Service Bureau, Jewish Federation Council of Greater Los Angeles, 1968; Bruce A. Phillips, Los Angeles Jewish Population Study, 1979.

TABLE 22. OCCUPATIONS OF EMPLOYED NON-HISPANIC WHITE AND JEWISH POPULATIONS BY SEX: SUMMARY, 1979–1980 (PERCENT)

Occupational Category[a]	Males		Females	
	White	Jewish	White	Jewish
Managerial-excl. retail props.	16.8	21.0	11.4	11.6
Professional	16.5	31.5	15.4	35.7
Retail-mgr./prop.	1.0	7.8	0.5	2.7
Technicians	3.6	2.2	2.8	0.3
Sales-excl. retail superv.	10.9	18.2	12.1	13.7
Administrative support	7.8	3.3	36.2	26.5
Service	6.8	4.2	12.0	4.6
Skilled, unskilled, & craft	36.4	13.6	9.2	4.9
Total	100.0	100.0	100.0	100.0

Source: Summary Tape File #4, PB57; Bruce A. Phillips, Los Angeles Jewish Population Study, 1979.
[a]Full and part-time employed males and females.

TABLE 23.   OCCUPATIONS OF NON-HISPANIC WHITE AND JEWISH POPULATIONS
BY SEX: DETAILED, 1979–1980 (PERCENT)

Occupational Category[a]	Males		Females	
	White	Jewish	White	Jewish
Executive, Administ., & Managerial				
Public administration	0.2	1.1	0.1	2.7
Manufacturing	4.1	3.3	1.2	0.6
[Retail, self-employed]	0.3	2.6	0.2	0.6
Retail, salaried	1.6	1.1	1.1	0.9
Other	7.1	8.6	5.2	5.2
Management-related	3.9	6.6	3.8	2.1
Professional				
Architects	0.3	3.1	0.0	0.3
Engineers	4.1	0.0	0.3	0.0
Surveyors	0.0	3.3	0.0	0.3
Nat. sci., math, computer sci.	0.9	1.3	0.5	0.3
Health, diagnosis	1.6	7.7	0.3	0.9
Health, assessment	0.5	1.3	3.3	3.7
Teachers, elem. & second.	1.5	1.3	5.1	13.1
Other teach. & librarians	1.3	1.1	1.8	3.4
Social scientists	0.3	0.9	0.4	0.6
Social, rec. & relig. wrkrs.	0.6	0.4	0.7	5.5
Lawyers & judges	1.6	7.0	0.4	1.5
Wrtr-Artst-Entrtnr-Athlte	3.6	4.0	2.7	6.1
Technicians				
Health, excl. nurses	0.3	0.7	0.8	0.3
Lic. nurses	0.0	1.5	0.7	0.0
Other	3.3	0.0	1.3	0.0
Sales				
[Supervisor, self-employed]	0.7	5.1	0.3	2.1
Supervisor, Salaried	1.5	3.5	0.9	2.7
Representatives:				
-finance	3.2	4.0	2.8	5.5
-commodities, excl. retail	2.5	3.1	0.9	0.6
Workers:				
-retail	2.7	5.5	4.5	2.1
-non-retail	0.4	0.7	0.4	0.0

Continued on next page

TABLE 23—*(Continued)*

Occupational Category[a]	Males		Females	
	White	Jewish	White	Jewish
Cashiers	0.6	0.2	2.6	1.8
Sales-related	0.0	1.3	0.0	0.9
Administrative Support				
Supervisors	1.1	0.9	1.9	1.2
Computer operators	0.4	0.9	0.7	0.9
Secretaries & typists	0.2	0.9	12.6	16.5
Bookkeepers & accts.	0.5	0.2	4.8	4.6
Financial processors	0.1	0.0	0.9	0.0
Mail & message distrib.	0.9	0.0	0.5	0.0
Material recording	2.0	0.4	1.7	0.3
Other	2.6	0.0	13.3	3.0
Service				
Household	0.1	1.3	0.6	0.3
Police-firefighters	0.9	0.7	0.1	0.0
Guards	0.9	0.9	0.3	0.0
Other protective	0.4	0.0	0.0	0.0
Food	2.0	0.4	5.0	1.2
Health	0.3	0.0	2.2	0.3
Building cleaners	1.6	0.4	0.6	0.6
Personal	0.8	0.0	3.2	2.1
Farming, Fishing, etc.				
Farm mgrs.	0.1	0.0	0.0	0.6
Other farm	0.1	0.0	0.1	0.0
Related agriculture	0.6	0.0	0.2	0.0
Forest & logging	0.0	0.0	0.0	0.0
Fishing, hunting, trapping	0.1	0.0	0.0	0.0
Craft & Repair				
Auto mechanics	1.6	1.8	0.0	0.0
Other mechanics	3.9	0.2	0.3	0.0
Carpenters	1.5	0.7	0.0	0.0
Other construction	4.7	2.4	0.2	0.0
Extractors	0.1	0.0	0.0	0.0

Continued on next page

TABLE 23—*(Continued)*

Occupational Category[a]	Males		Females	
	White	Jewish	White	Jewish
Precision Production				
Supervisors	2.7	0.2	0.7	0.0
Metal workers	2.0	0.0	0.2	0.3
Plant & syst. operators	0.3	0.0	0.0	0.0
Other	1.3	0.0	0.9	1.5
Operators				
Machine excl. precision	3.6	1.1	1.8	1.2
Fabricators, assembl.	1.5	0.4	1.0	0.6
Product inspectors	0.5	0.0	0.6	0.0
Transport & Material Movers				
Vehicle operators	3.8	1.1	0.4	0.3
Other transport	0.2	0.0	0.0	0.0
Material movers	0.7	0.0	0.1	0.0
Handlers, Helpers, & Laborers				
Helpers	3.6	0.7	1.8	0.0
Construct. laborers	0.6	0.0	0.0	0.0
Handlers	1.4	0.0	0.4	0.3
Cleaners	0.1	0.2	0.0	0.0
Misc. manual	1.5	0.0	0.6	0.0
Total	100.0	100.0	100.0	100.0

Sources: Summary Tape File #4, PB57; Bruce A. Phillips, Los Angeles Jewish Population Study, 1979.
[a]Full- and part-time employed males and females.

TABLE 24. LABOR-FORCE PARTICIPATION OF NON-HISPANIC WHITE AND JEW-
ISH FEMALES BY FAMILY AND MARITAL STATUS, 1979–1980 (PER-
CENT)

Family and Marital Status of Female	White	Jewish
Married, husband present		
With own children 0–5 yrs.	41.9	42.2
With own children 6–17 yrs.	59.8	60.4
Without own children[a]	46.9	52.4
Other marital status		
With own children 0–17 yrs.	77.7	80.5
Without own children[a]	54.4	57.4

Sources: Summary Tape File #4, PB23; Bruce A. Phillips, Los Angeles Jewish Population
Study, 1979.
[a]"Children" refers to children under 18 only.

TABLE 25. PATTERNS OF AFFILIATION, 1979 (PERCENT)

Number of Different Types of Affiliation	Percent of Households	Particular Type of Affiliation	Percent of Households
Three	4.8	Synagogue (current)	25.1
Two	12.0		
Syn. & org.	(7.2)		
Syn. & Fed.	(2.2)	One or more Jewish	
Org. & Fed.	(2.6)	organizations	26.1
One	26.8	Federation	
Syn. only	(10.9)	(as a giver)	14.0
Org. only	(11.5)		
Fed. only	(4.4)		
None	56.3		
Total[a]	100.0		

OVERLAP AMONG TYPES OF AFFILIATION
Percent of synagogue members who
    Belong to a Jewish organization   47.8
    Give to Federation   27.9
Percent of Jewish organization members who
    Belong to a synagogue   45.8
    Give to Federation   28.2
Percent of Federation givers who
    Belong to a synagogue   50.0
    Belong to a Jewish organization   52.9

Source: Bruce A. Phillips, Los Angeles Jewish Population Study, 1979.
[a]The total refers to the underlined percentages. The percentages in parentheses are subtotals under the patterns of combined affiliations.

TABLE 26. TYPES OF AFFILIATION BY AGE OF RESPONDENT, 1979 (PERCENT)

Type of Affiliation	Age of Respondent			
	18–35	36–50	51–65	65 +
Synagogue member (current)	20.0	32.8	26.6	28.6
Member of Jewish organization	13.0	25.8	36.9	44.7
Gives to Federation	3.7	17.0	24.1	20.1

Source: Bruce A. Phillips, Los Angeles Jewish Population Study, 1979.

TABLE 27. PATTERNS OF AFFILIATION BY AGE OF RESPONDENT, 1979 (PERCENT)

Number of Different Types of Affiliation	Age of Respondent			
	18–35	36–50	51–65	65 +
Three	0.6	6.7	8.8	6.3
Two	8.9	13.3	12.8	17.4
Syn. & org.	(7.1)	(7.0)	(6.1)	(9.8)
Syn. & Fed.	(0.6)	(4.0)	(2.9)	(2.2)
Org. & Fed.	(1.2)	(2.3)	(3.8)	(5.4)
One	16.8	24.0	36.4	44.0
Syn. only	(11.0)	(12.8)	(8.0)	(11.8)
Org. only	(4.5)	(7.1)	(19.8)	(26.0)
Fed. only	(1.3)	(4.1)	(8.6)	(6.2)
None	73.6	56.1	41.9	32.3
Total[a]	100.0	100.0	100.0	100.0

Source: Bruce A. Phillips, Los Angeles Jewish Population Study, 1979.
[a]The total refers to the underlined percentages. The percentages in parentheses are subtotals under the patterns of combined affiliations.

TABLE 28.   TYPES OF AFFILIATION BY HOUSEHOLD TYPE, 1979 (PERCENT)

	Household Type					
	Married Couple		Single Household Head			
Type of	With	No	Single	Never	Widow/	Sep./
Affiliation	Children	Children	Parent	Married	Widower	Div.
Synagogue member (current)	44.1	23.5	19.8	14.6	23.3	15.3
Member of Jewish organization	31.1	31.4	21.3	7.2	44.9	15.3
Gives to Federation	21.5	19.6	4.0	2.5	12.4	6.6

Source: Bruce A. Phillips, Los Angeles Jewish Population Study, 1979.

TABLE 29.   PATTERNS OF AFFILIATION BY HOUSEHOLD TYPE, 1979 (PERCENT)

	Household Type					
	Married Couple		Single Household Head			
Number of Different	With	No	Single	Never	Widow/	Sep./
Types of Affiliation	Children	Children	Parent	Married	Widower	Div.
Three	7.6	6.7	1.5	0.0	4.8	1.6
Two	20.5	11.6	10.4	3.9	12.2	8.3
Syn. & org.	(12.3)	(5.5)	(7.9)	(2.7)	(10.1)	(5.0)
Syn. & Fed.	(4.9)	(1.8)	(2.5)	(0.6)	(1.0)	(0.8)
Org. & Fed.	(3.3)	(4.3)	(0.0)	(0.6)	(1.1)	(2.5)
One	33.1	28.1	20.9	16.0	47.1	15.7
Syn. only	(19.7)	(7.1)	(7.1)	(10.8)	(9.4)	(6.6)
Org. only	(7.6)	(14.1)	(13.8)	(3.9)	(32.2)	(7.4)
Fed. only	(5.8)	(6.9)	(0.0)	(1.3)	(5.5)	(1.7)
None	38.9	53.6	67.3	80.0	36.0	74.5
Total[a]	100.0	100.0	100.0	100.0	100.0	100.0

Source: Bruce A. Phillips, Los Angeles Jewish Population Study, 1979.
[a]The total refers to the underlined percentages. The percentages in parentheses are subtotals under the patterns of combined affiliations.

TABLE 30. TYPES OF AFFILIATION BY FAMILY-CYCLE STAGE, 1979 (PERCENT)

| Type of Affiliation | Family-Cycle Stage | | | | |
| | Children | | | No Children | |
	Under 6 Only	6–13	14–17 Only	Head under 40	Head 40 +
Synagogue member (current)	30.7	44.3	44.1	13.0	24.8
Member of Jewish organization	25.5	26.9	42.6	6.2	36.9
Gives to Federation	9.7	15.8	35.7	1.5	19.1

Source: Bruce A. Phillips, Los Angeles Jewish Population Study, 1979.

TABLE 31. PATTERNS OF AFFILIATION BY FAMILY-CYCLE STAGE, 1979 (PERCENT)

| Number of Different Types of Affiliation | Family-Cycle Stage | | | | |
| | Children | | | No Children | |
	Under 6 Only	6–13	14–17 Only	Head under 40	Head 40 +
Three	0.0	3.6	19.9	0.8	6.3
Two	17.2	20.5	18.5	3.0	13.5
Syn. & org.	(7.5)	(15.3)	(7.8)	(3.0)	(7.0)
Syn. & Fed.	(2.2)	(5.2)	(5.6)	(0.0)	(2.2)
Org. & Fed.	(7.5)	(0.0)	(5.1)	(0.0)	(4.3)
One	32.8	32.7	28.2	11.1	34.5
Syn. only	(21.3)	(19.5)	(12.1)	(8.4)	(7.8)
Org. only	(11.5)	(6.3)	(10.9)	(1.9)	(20.2)
Fed. only	(0.0)	(6.9)	(5.2)	(0.8)	(6.5)
None	50.1	43.2	33.4	85.3	45.8
Total[a]	100.0	100.0	100.0	100.0	100.0

Source: Bruce A. Phillips, Los Angeles Jewish Population Study, 1979.
[a]The total refers to the underlined percentages. The percentages in parentheses are subtotals under the patterns of combined affiliations.

TABLE 32. TYPES OF AFFILIATION BY INTERMARRIAGE STATUS, 1979 (PERCENT)

Type of Affiliation	Born Jew Married to		
	Born Jew	Convert	Non-Jew
Synagogue member (current)	41.1	10.2	7.9
Member of Jewish organization	27.2	36.9	1.5
Gives to Federation	11.9	30.2	0.0

Source: Bruce A. Phillips, Los Angeles Jewish Population Study, 1979.

TABLE 33. PATTERNS OF AFFILIATION BY INTERMARRIAGE STATUS, 1979 (PERCENT)

Number of Different Types of Affiliation	Born Jew Married to		
	Born Jew	Convert	Non-Jew
Three	2.0	10.2	0.0
Two	23.0	20.0	1.5
Syn. & org.	(15.9)	(0.0)	(1.5)
Syn. & Fed.	(4.1)	(0.0)	(0.0)
Org. & Fed.	(3.0)	(20.0)	(0.0)
One	28.2	6.7	6.4
Syn. only	(19.1)	(0.0)	(6.4)
Org. only	(6.3)	(6.7)	(0.0)
Fed. only	(2.8)	(0.0)	(0.0)
None	46.8	63.1	92.1
Total[a]	100.0	100.0	100.0

Source: Bruce A. Phillips, Los Angeles Jewish Population Study, 1979.
[a]The total refers to the underlined percentages. The percentages in parentheses are subtotals under the patterns of combined affiliations.

TABLE 34.   TYPES OF AFFILIATION BY LENGTH OF RESIDENCE IN LOS ANGELES, 1979 (PERCENT)

Type of Affiliation	Number of Years Respondent in Los Angeles				
	Less than 6	6–10	11–20	21–30	31 +
Synagogue member (current)	13.0	18.7	33.5	29.7	27.4
Member of Jewish organization	9.9	20.4	28.8	25.1	37.2
Gives to Federation	6.5	8.1	14.6	13.1	21.1

Source: Bruce A. Phillips, Los Angeles Jewish Population Study, 1979.

TABLE 35.   PATTERNS OF AFFILIATION BY LENGTH OF RESIDENCE IN LOS ANGELES, 1979 (PERCENT)

Number of Different Types of Affiliation	Number of Years Respondent in Los Angeles				
	Less than 6	6–10	11–20	21–30	31 +
Three	0.0	2.8	4.6	5.3	7.8
Two	8.1	11.9	18.0	10.3	11.7
Syn. & org.	(5.7)	(8.6)	(11.9)	(6.0)	(5.4)
Syn. & Fed.	(2.2)	(1.5)	(3.1)	(1.0)	(3.1)
Org. & Fed.	(0.2)	(1.8)	(3.0)	(3.3)	(3.2)
One	13.4	16.8	28.5	28.8	37.5
Syn. only	(5.7)	(6.9)	(14.6)	(15.9)	(8.8)
Org. only	(3.5)	(7.9)	(10.0)	(9.3)	(21.6)
Fed. only	(4.2)	(2.0)	(3.9)	(3.6)	(7.1)
None	78.4	68.4	48.9	55.7	43.0
Total[a]	100.0	100.0	100.0	100.0	100.0

Source: Bruce A. Phillips, Los Angeles Jewish Population Study, 1979.
[a]The total refers to the underlined percentages. The percentages in parentheses are subtotals under the patterns of combined affiliations.

TABLE 36. TYPES OF AFFILIATION BY COMBINED HOUSEHOLD INCOME, 1979 (PERCENT)

Type of Affiliation	Combined Household Income			
	Less than $20,000	$20,000–$29,000	$30,000–$49,000	$50,000 and over
Synagogue member (current)	20.4	21.2	33.0	34.0
Member of Jewish organization	21.9	15.9	29.7	27.9
Gives to Federation	8.1	4.1	21.2	26.9

Source: Bruce A. Phillips, Los Angeles Jewish Population Study, 1979.

TABLE 37. PATTERNS OF AFFILIATION BY COMBINED HOUSEHOLD INCOME, 1979 (PERCENT)

Number of Different Types of Affiliation	Combined Household Income			
	Less than $20,000	$20,000–$29,000	$30,000–$49,000	$50,000 and over
Three	3.7	2.2	6.8	9.8
Two	7.9	8.5	16.2	16.6
Syn. & org.	(5.9)	(6.9)	(9.3)	(2.4)
Syn. & Fed.	(0.7)	(1.1)	(0.4)	(7.9)
Org. & Fed.	(1.3)	(0.5)	(6.5)	(6.3)
One	24.0	18.4	27.3	21.6
Syn. only	(9.8)	(10.5)	(15.0)	(10.4)
Org. only	(11.7)	(7.5)	(4.5)	(8.3)
Fed. only	(2.5)	(0.4)	(7.8)	(2.9)
None	64.4	71.1	49.7	52.0
Total[a]	100.0	100.0	100.0	100.0

Source: Bruce A. Phillips, Los Angeles Jewish Population Study, 1979.
[a]The total refers to the underlined percentages. The percentages in parentheses are subtotals under the patterns of combined affiliations.

TABLE 38. MEAN AFFILIATION SCORE BY SELECTED VARIABLES

Mean Affiliation Score[a]

Age		Household Type	
18–35	0.37	Married couple w/children	1.00
36–50	0.71	Married couple, no children	0.71
51–65	0.89	Single-parent family	0.46
65 +	0.98	Never married	0.24
		Widow/widower, sep./div.	0.86

Family-Cycle Stage		Household Income	
Children			
Under 6 only	0.67	Under $20,000	0.51
6–13	0.85	$20,000–$29,000	0.42
14–17 only	1.25	$30,000–$49,000	0.80
		$50,000 and over	0.84
No Children			
Head under 40	0.19		
Head 40 +	0.83		

Number of Years in L.A.		Jewish Status of Spouse	
5 or less	0.30	Born Jew	0.98
6–10	0.49	Convert	1.05
11–20	0.78	Non-Jew	0.18
21–30	0.65		
30 +	0.84		

[a]The mean affiliation score is computed from a score of "3" if the household has all three kinds of affiliation (i.e., synagogue membership, organizational membership, and Federation giving), a "2" if it has two out of three kinds of affiliation, a "1" if it has a single affiliation, and a "0" if it has no affiliation.

TABLE 39. MULTIPLE REGRESSION EQUATION FOR AFFILIATION

Variable	Correlation Coefficient (Simple R)	Beta	R-Square	F-Test	Significance
MARRIAGE	0.365	0.375	0.132	95.35	.001
AGE	0.276	0.180	0.180	66.86	.001
KIDCYCLE	0.241	0.172	0.211	54.15	.001
MARRIED	0.234	−0.138	0.218	42.27	.001
INCOME	0.195	0.112	0.227	35.54	.001
WIDOW	0.086	0.095	0.232	30.41	.001
LAYEARS	0.152	0.064	0.235	26.51	.001

TABLE 40. JEWISH HOUSEHOLD TYPES IN 4 CITIES, 1979–1984 (PERCENT)

Household Type	Los Angeles (1979)	Phila- delphia (1984)	New York (1981)	Chicago (1981)
Married couple w/children	24.0	26.0	30.0	36.0
Single-parent family	4.0	4.0	5.0	n/a

Sources: Bruce A. Phillips, Los Angeles Jewish Population Study, Overview for Regional Planning, Jewish Federation Council of Greater Los Angeles, 1980, p. 10; Federation of Jewish Agencies of Greater Philadelphia, Summary Report of the Jewish Population Study of Greater Philadelphia, June 1985, p. 18; Jewish Federation of Metropolitan Chicago, Metropolitan Chicago Jewish Population, 1981, p. 4; Federation of Jewish Philanthropies of New York, The Jewish Population of Greater New York: A Profile, 1984, p. 15.

TABLE 41. JEWISH AGE DISTRIBUTION IN 4 CITIES, 1979–1984 (PERCENT)

Age (by Decade)	Los Angeles (1979)	Phila- delphia (1984)	New York (1981)	Age (by Life-Cycle Stage)[a]	Chicago (1981)	Los Angeles (1979)
0–9	9.8	9.0	11.0	0–17	[21.0]	[20.4]
10–19	13.5	14.0	12.0		[ ]	[ ]
20–29	16.6	15.5	17.0	18–39	[35.0]	[36.8]
30–39	17.3	13.5	14.0		[ ]	[ ]
40–49	12.1	13.5	12.0	40–64	[30.0]	[31.7]
50–59	14.3	14.0	11.0		[ ]	[ ]
60–69	9.5	12.0	12.0	65 +	[15.0]	[11.1]
70+	6.9	9.5	11.0			
Total	100.0	100.0	100.0	Total	100.0	100.0

Sources: Bruce A. Phillips, Los Angeles Jewish Population Study, Overview for Regional Planning, Jewish Federation Council of Greater Los Angeles, 1980, p. 7; Federation of Jewish Agencies of Greater Philadelphia, Summary Report of the Jewish Population Study of Greater Philadelphia, June 1985, p. 13; Jewish Federation of Metropolitan Chicago, Metropolitan Chicago Jewish Population, 1981, p. 3; Federation of Jewish Philanthropies of New York, The Jewish Population of Greater New York: A Profile, 1984, p. 19.
[a]Based on different reporting method in Chicago study.

TABLE 42. INTERMARRIAGE RATE (BORN JEW MARRIED TO NON-JEW) IN 3
WESTERN CITIES, 1979–1983

	Percentage of Households with Intermarried Couple		
Age of Household Head	Los Angeles (1979)	Phoenix (1983)	Denver (1981)
18–29	48.9	60.3	66.0
30–39	20.8	25.8	40.0
40–49	13.3	23.7	13.3

Sources: Bruce A. Phillips, *Denver Jewish Population Study,* Allied Jewish Federation of
Denver, 1982, p. 47; Bruce A. Phillips and William S. Aron, *The Greater Phoenix Jewish
Population Study,* Jewish Federation of Greater Phoenix, 1984, p. 11.

TABLE 43. AFFILIATION RATE IN 4 CITIES, 1979–1984

	Percentage of Affiliated Households			
Type of Affiliation	Los Angeles (1979)	Phila- delphia (1984)	New York (1981)	Chicago (1981)
Synagogue member	25.1	41.0	41.0	44.0
Member of Jewish organization	26.1	70.0	n/a	34.0
Gives to Federation	14.0	n/a	26.0	n/a

Sources: Bruce A. Phillips, *Los Angeles Jewish Community Survey: Overview for Regional
Planning,* Planning and Budgeting Department, Jewish Federation Council of Greater Los
Angeles, 1980; Federation of Jewish Agencies of Greater Philadelphia, *Summary Report of the
Jewish Population Study of Greater Philadelphia,* June 1985, p. 25 (includes data for other
communities); Jewish Federation of Metropolitan Chicago, *Metropolitan Chicago Jewish Population, 1981,* p. 18; Federation of Jewish Philanthropies of New York, *The Jewish Population
of Greater New York: A Profile,* 1984, pp. 23, 31.

California Jews: Data from the Field Polls

As CALIFORNIA GOES—according to the common wisdom—so goes the rest of America. This is true not only in the cultural and political spheres but also in terms of demographic patterns. Such trends as decreased and delayed marriage, increased divorce and remarriage, childless marriage, high geographic mobility, and low institutional religious participation first became evident in California. It is natural to wonder how the sizeable Jewish population of that state fits into the picture. Are California Jews like other Californians—setting the pace for the rest of American Jewry in social-cultural and demographic developments?

According to the most recent estimates, the Jewish population of California numbers over 790,000, qualifying it to be the second-largest Jewish "state" in the country.[1] At present, one out of every seven Jews in the United States lives in California. Given the significant upswing in Jewish migration to the Sunbelt in recent years, that proportion is bound to increase.

The bulk of the Jewish population lives in southern California, primarily in metropolitan Los Angeles. With just over half a million Jews,[2] Los Angeles emerges as the second-largest Jewish community both in the United States and in the world. It is home to the second-largest Israeli population outside of Israel and one of the largest Russian-Jewish communities outside of the Soviet Union. While Jews constitute less than 4 percent of the state's population, they can significantly affect the outcome of statewide (and thus national) elections, and they have high visibility in the media.

Methods

The data selected for the present study come from Field Polls, which have been conducted statewide in California since 1947.[3] Use of the early polls (up to 1958)

Note: This project was aided by a Social and Behavioral Science Dean's Award, California State University Dominguez Hills, and a grant from the American Jewish Committee. Cooperation and help were extended by Mark DiCamillo of the Field Institute and Lynn Anderson of the Computer Center, CSUDH.

[1]AJYB, Vol. 85, 1985, p. 180.
[2]Ibid., p. 183.
[3]To study American Jews, social scientists have turned increasingly to the use of general survey data, such as that provided by the Gallup Poll or the Institute for Social Research at the University of Michigan. General surveys are considered to produce more representative samples than studies directed solely at the Jewish population (which may overcount affiliated, and undercount nonaffiliated, Jews). However, the number of Jews even in a large national sample is too small to be useful. To overcome this difficulty, at least four separate investigators have employed the technique of aggregating responses across several studies in order to create

presents certain problems in that they were conducted infrequently, suffered from small sizes, and used an abbreviated, irregular list of demographic questions, which sometimes omitted religion. In the late 1950s the situation took a positive turn: sampling procedures were improved, the number of questions was increased, and the demographic items became more standardized. Since 1960, polling has been conducted four times a year during nonelection years and six times a year during election years, with minor deviations.

Like most major polls, Field uses primarily random-digit telephoning within geographical clusters (proportionate to telephone and population density), reaching a sample of about 1,150 (California) respondents 18 years of age and older. Recent research has been increasingly accepting of telephone polling, even though it does eliminate people without phones, as well as those who are homeless or in institutions.[4] Many of these individuals belong to the lower socioeconomic classes; in California, many are foreign born, particularly Hispanics. The resultant bias produces a telephone sample that has higher socioeconomic status, with more "Anglos" (including Jews), more American-born, and more citizens than the general population. (In election years, a few polls also screen out people who admit to not being registered to vote.)

The biases, however, are mitigated by several factors. First, census data are available to weight against. Second, the Field organization has incorporated adjustments into the sampling and weighting to ensure the fit of age, sex, and region within California. Last—and in the present context, most importantly—the distortions are much smaller for Jews than for other Californians because Jews have higher incomes, are better educated, and are more likely to be American-born citizens and registered to vote.

The data cited in this article are from 1958 through 1984. Data are either not available or are without religious identification (with up to one exception per year) for the years 1959, 1965–1968, and 1973. The total number of polls is 106, averaging 5 per year for those years in which data are available. The median Jewish subsample is 43, compared with a total median sample of 1,073 per poll. Since demographic change tends to be relatively slow, and the small subsample size is a critical issue, polls are generally aggregated over three-to-four-year periods, with some adjustments made to compensate for uneven subsample sizes and inaccessible polls. The

a respectable Jewish sample. These studies are, in chronological order: Bernard Lazerwitz, "A Comparison of Major United States Religious Groups," *Journal of the American Statistical Association,* Sept. 1961, pp. 568–579; John Shelton Reed, "Needles in Haystacks: Studying Rare Populations by Secondary Analysis of National Sample Surveys," *Public Opinion Quarterly,* Winter 1975–76, pp. 514–522; Steven M. Cohen, "The American Jewish Family Today," AJYB, Vol. 82, 1982, pp. 136–154; Alan M. Fisher, "The National Gallup Polls and American Jewish Demography," AJYB, Vol. 83, 1983, pp. 111–126.

[4]Robert M. Groves and Robert L. Kahn, *Surveys by Telephone: A National Comparison with Personal Interviews* (New York, 1979) and James H. Frey, *Survey Research by Phone* (Beverly Hills, 1983).

aggregated Jewish samples of 550–950 yield an approximate error margin of $\pm$ 5.4 to $\pm$ 2.6 percentage points. (In comparison, the average Field Poll—like most major media polls—has an average error margin of approximately $\pm$ 3.3 percentage points.)[5]

Even though the error margin is relatively large for demographic studies—which means that the data can be regarded only as rough indicators—it needs to be stressed that the Field Polls provide a rich source of data on California Jews. The Field sampling methodology is superior to—less biased than—that of almost all Jewish community studies, most of which have also employed telephone interviews.[6] In addition, because the Field data allow for religious identification, it is possible to compare Jews with non-Jewish Californians as two mutually exclusive populations.

The sociodemographic findings covered here fall into four basic categories: place of residence; achieved status (education, income, occupation); marital status and family size; and ascribed status (race, gender, age). The first data section presents various comparisons of California Jews with Jews nationwide (the 1970–1971 National Jewish Population Study and Gallup Poll studies), as well as with New York Jews (the 1981 Greater New York Jewish Population Survey), in order to examine regional differences. The next section compares Jews and non-Jews in California in the early 1980s. A third section looks at trends in California over the last 20 years. Finally, there is a brief summary discussion of the data including projections for the immediate future.

Comparative Jewish Perspectives

Findings from the Field Poll have been specially aggregated for two separate time periods in order to compare them with the 1970–1971 National Jewish Population Study (NJPS) and the 1981 New York study; where appropriate and available, national Gallup Poll data about Jews have also been introduced.[7] Some of the differences among the four studies are attributable to differences in response categories. In Table 1, for example, the lower level of graduate education shown by Field

---

[5]The error margins, based on a significance level of .05, are only approximate, since they depend upon both exact proportions and sampling methods. The standard formula of s.e.= $1.96\sqrt{p(1-p)/n}$ applies to purely random sampling and is minimized as the distribution moves from 50-50 to 100-0.

[6]For a review of communal studies, see Gary Tobin and Alvin Chenkin, "Recent Jewish Community Population Studies: A Roundup," AJYB, Vol. 85, 1985, pp. 154–178; Sidney Goldstein, "Jews in the United States: Perspectives from Demography," AJYB, Vol. 81, 1981, pp. 3–59; and Sidney Goldstein, "American Jewry, 1970: A Demographic Profile," AJYB, Vol. 72, 1971, pp. 3–88.

[7]NJPS data are from Fred Massarik and Alvin Chenkin, "United States National Jewish Population Study: A First Report," AJYB, Vol. 74, 1973, pp. 264–306; New York data from Paul Ritterband and Steven M. Cohen, "The Social Characteristics of the New York Area Jewish Community, 1981," AJYB, Vol. 84, 1984, pp. 128–163; Gallup data from Fisher, op. cit.

reflects the inclusion of a small number of respondents too young (18-20) to have finished advanced degrees.

ACHIEVED STATUS

In the period 1969–1972, California Jews were not dramatically different from Jews across the country in achievement: a slightly smaller percentage of California Jews had a high-school education or less and a smaller percentage had achieved graduate degrees (Table 1). On the other hand, a larger percentage of California Jews had some college, undoubtedly a reflection of the extensive statewide system of two-year community colleges.

By the early 1980s, California Jews had achieved significantly higher educational levels than Jews across the country (Table 2). Even if the data overstate education, it is clear that relatively few California Jews had less than a high-school degree, and the large majority (81 percent) had at least some college. At the highest level, postgraduate study, the distribution is similar to that of New York Jews.

TABLE 1. EDUCATIONAL LEVELS OF JEWS IN CALIFORNIA (1969–1972) AND NATIONAL (1970–1971) POLLS (PERCENT)

Education	California[a]	NJPS[b,c]
Less than high school	16.0	15.9
High-school graduate[d]	24.1	30.6
Some college[d]	31.8	20.4
College graduate	15.3	14.5
M.A. and beyond[e]	12.8	18.6
Total[f]	100.0 (N=752)	100.0 (N=c.7,500)

Sources: California Field Polls; NJPS (recalculated), AJYB, Vol. 74, 1973, p. 278.
[a]Based on respondents 21 and older for 1969–70, and 18 and older for 1970–72.
[b]Based on respondents aged 25 and older.
[c]The category for no response eliminated and the numbers recalculated as a percentage of legitimate responses.
[d]The original NJPS category of "other" (1.6 percent) is divided in two and half (0.8) added here.
[e]The original NJPS category of professional degree (6.4 percent) is included here.
[f]Errors in column total due to rounding.

TABLE 2. EDUCATIONAL LEVELS OF JEWS IN CALIFORNIA (1980–1982), NEW YORK (1981), AND NATIONAL (1979) POLLS (PERCENT)

Education	California	New York	Nation
High school graduates and lower	20	30	44
Some college	35	17	
College degree	23	32	56
Graduate degree	23	21	
Total[a]	100	100	100
	(N=745)	(N=c. 4,500)	(N=991)

Sources: California Field Polls; Greater New York Jewish Population Study, AJYB, Vol. 84, 1984, p. 156; National Gallup Polls, AJYB, Vol. 83, 1983, p. 123.
[a]Errors in column total due to rounding.

Generally parallel findings occur for another measure of personal achievement, income. One must be careful, however, about aggregating income in the late 1970s and very early 1980s, because of high inflation rates and high unemployment, which made yearly differences greater than those in more stable periods. Other problems in the Field Poll findings are the lack of one standardized set of income categories and a change in minimum respondent age.

In 1970 the income of California Jews was only moderately larger than that of all American Jews in the Gallup data, and almost equal to that shown in the NJPS figures. By the early 1980s the Jews of California were remarkably similar in income to the Jews of New York and, according to Gallup data, were far ahead of Jews nationwide (Table 3). While individual community studies show Los Angeles Jews as not differing much from Jews in other large communities,[8] the Gallup data may well be the more accurate because not just Jews, but California and New York non-Hispanic whites overall, made more money than other Americans.

Differences in the incidence of poverty among New York and California Jews and those elsewhere in the country, as shown in Table 3, may be overstated, due both to the bias of telephone polling and variance in the cost of living. At the upper levels, however, the geographical differences likely reflect not only sampling differences and higher cost of living in the Los Angeles and New York areas but the greater job opportunities and related higher educational and occupational levels of Jews in those cities.

Comparable results obtain for occupation. California Jews in 1970 had higher occupational status—a greater percentage of professionals and a smaller percentage

---

[8]Tobin and Chenkin, op. cit., p. 169.

TABLE 3. HOUSEHOLD INCOME OF JEWS IN CALIFORNIA (1980–1982), NEW YORK (1981), AND NATIONAL (1979) POLLS (PERCENT)

Income	California	New York	Nation
Less than $10,000	12	11	25
$10,000–19,999	17	16	25
$20,000–29,999	19	20	} 49
$30,000+	52	53	
Total[a]	100	100	100
	(N=664)	(N=c. 4,500)	(N=991)

Sources: California Field Polls; Greater New York Jewish Population Study, AJYB, Vol. 84, 1984, p. 158; National Gallup Polls, AJYB, Vol. 83, 1983, p. 125.
[a]Errors in column total due to rounding.

of salespeople/clerks—than did Jews in both the NJPS and Gallup studies, and the differences increased a little in the early 1980s.

MARITAL STATUS AND FAMILY SIZE

While the proportion of married California Jews in the early 1970s closely matched that of Jews in the national Gallup data, Jews in the NJPS were significantly more likely (79:68) to be married (Table 4).

Some of the difference undoubtedly results from the sampling strategy of the NJPS, which, by starting with known Jewish families, found an inflated proportion of marrieds. Much of the difference in marital rates is real, however, reflecting the fact that Californians were less likely than other Americans to be married at the time and more likely never to have married. (Examination of the combined categories of divorced/separated and widowed reveals no important differences.) A comparison of marital status among California and other Jews in 1981, using both the NJPS and New York data as standards, shows the differences persisting: a smaller percentage of California Jews were married and a larger percentage had never married.

Since California Jews were less likely to marry, they were more likely to live alone or with friends. Comparison of average family or household size across studies is made difficult by a lack of identical questions, the use of different categories, and the availability of only partially published data. However, taking all the difficulties into account, a comparison of figures indicates that household size for California Jewish families has been consistently smaller—smaller than for Jewish families nationwide in 1970 (NJPS); and smaller than for New York families in 1981, if the adjusted figure (2.78) based on similar categories is employed (Table 5).

TABLE 4. MARITAL STATUS OF JEWS IN CALIFORNIA (1970–1972) AND NATIONAL (1970–1973) POLLS (PERCENT)

Marital Status	California[a]	NJPS (1970–71)[b]	Nation (1973)[c]
Never married	16.7	6.2	19.9
Married	67.8	78.6	67.6
Separated/ divorced	0.7 / 4.2	} 5.1	0.3
Widowed	10.7	10.0	} 12.2
Total[d]	100.0	100.0	100.0
	(N=600)	(N=c. 7,500)	(N=571)

Sources: California Field Polls; NJPS (recalculated), AJYB, Vol. 74, 1973, p. 275; National Gallup Polls, AJYB, Vol. 83, 1983, p. 114.
[a]Based on respondents 18 and older (N=489) and 21 and older (N=111).
[b]Based on head of household. The category for "no response" (0.4 percent) eliminated and the figures recalculated as a percentage of legitimate responses.
[c]Based on respondents 18 and older.
[d]Errors in column total due to rounding.

TABLE 5. MEAN HOUSEHOLD SIZE OF NEW YORK JEWS (1981), CALIFORNIA JEWS, AND CALIFORNIA NON-JEWS (1980–1982)

Household Size	California Jews[a,b]	California Non-Jews[b]	New York Jews[c]	New York Jews[a]
	2.54	2.87	2.49	2.78
	(N=648)	(N=15,662)	(N=c. 4,500)	(N=c. 4,500)

Sources: California Field Polls; Greater New York Jewish Population Study, AJYB, Vol. 84, 1984, p. 141.
[a]Both Jewish and non-Jewish household members counted for Jewish respondents. Calculation for New York estimated by 0.66K(J), where K is the proportion of households (including non-Jews/Jews only) found in the Washington, D.C. community study (2.7/2.3) and J is the mean size for New York households with only Jews.
[b]Families with more than 6 members counted as having 7.77 members.
[c]Only Jewish household members counted.

Confirmation of the California figure can be found in the 1979 community study of Los Angeles.[9]

ASCRIBED STATUS

Neither the NJPS nor the New York study provides information about race or Hispanic subethnicity. The Gallup Poll, which does include such information, shows a very low (about 0.5 percent) but consistent figure for nonwhite (primarily black) Jews, and this matches the Field Polls.

Gender produces fewer surprises. Because it is relatively easy to control for in sampling and weighting, the male-female ratio regularly hovers around 49–51 percent in all the major surveys.

Since the Field Polls provide no systematic accounting for people under 18 (under 21 before 1970), age distribution is shown for adults only (Table 6). Comparison with the NJPS is complicated by the use of different respondent categories, but in 1970 all three studies of Jews (NJPS, Gallup, and Field) showed a notably similar age distribution. By the 1980s, however, the relative age distribution had changed noticeably. A picture compiled from the Gallup Polls, New York data, and other recent community studies—as well as projections from earlier ones—shows that California (adult) Jews were younger: a larger percentage were under age 30 and a smaller percentage were over age 65. (This difference can be seen, also, in a comparison of the Los Angeles and other community studies.)[10] While Table 6

TABLE 6.   AGES OF JEWS IN CALIFORNIA (1980–1982), NEW YORK (1981), AND NATIONAL (1979) POLLS (PERCENT)

Age	California	New York	Nation
18–29	27	24	22
30–49	39	31	34
Over 50	35	45	43
Total[a]	100	100	100
	(N=743)	(N=c. 4,500)	(N=991)

Sources: California Field Polls; Greater New York Jewish Population Study, AJYB, Vol. 84, 1984, p. 149; National Gallup Polls, AJYB, Vol. 83, 1983, p. 120.
[a]Errors in column total due to rounding.

---

[9]Bruce A. Phillips, Los Angeles Jewish Community Survey: Overview for Regional Planning (Planning and Budgeting Department, Jewish Federation Council of Greater Los Angeles, Los Angeles, 1980).
[10]See Tobin and Chenkin, op.cit., and Goldstein, op. cit. (1971 and 1981), as well as individual community studies, especially that of Los Angeles—Phillips, op. cit., p. 7.

probably magnifies the differences at the extremes by 1 or 2 percentage points—because of the particular years selected—the differences are still significant. The explanation is probably related to migration dynamics, i.e., a relatively high movement of young people to California in the 1970s and 1980s.

Contemporary California: Jews and Non-Jews

PLACE OF RESIDENCE

Within California, the geographical distribution of Jews is heavily weighted toward two regions, Los Angeles–Orange counties and the San Francisco–Bay Area (Table 7). These two areas contain more than eight out of ten Jews in the state, six of whom live in the greater Los Angeles area.

The AJYB allocations for city and metropolitan areas, as shown in Table 7, have been redistributed according to the Field configuration. Because the Field Poll is broken down into so many (10) categories, each one contains a smaller number of people, thus increasing the margin of error. (In order to increase the sample size, this is the only table which includes data from 1985.) At the same time, for the AJYB there are questions about two subareas in the Los Angeles basin which may have been double counted.[11]

While both sources find overwhelming concentrations of Jews in Los Angeles–Orange counties and the San Francisco–Bay area, there are noticeable differences. The Field data report Jews slightly more dispersed, with more Jews in San Francisco and fewer in Los Angeles than in the AJYB estimates. The difference probably reflects both migration dynamics and sampling bias. Jews who move to largely non-Jewish areas tend to be more marginal than those moving to Jewishly identified regions, e.g., Los Angeles. Whereas the methods employed in community studies —organizational membership lists, personal references, and Jewish name indexes— make it easier to sample publicly identified and affiliated Jews in Jewish areas, the less stratified random-dialing techniques of the Field Poll are as likely to reach a Jew in a mountain cabin as one in the middle of the Fairfax ghetto—provided that each has one telephone number and neither denies being Jewish.

The AJYB updated several of its population counts in the mid-1980s, bringing them closer to the Field data than they had been in 1981. Based on a number of factors—too many to be analyzed here—it appears that the AJYB figures are more accurate, especially for Los Angeles–Orange counties. They are not exact, however, and where the Field data differ, correction needs to be made in the direction of the latter.

---

[11]For a comprehensive overview, see Jack Diamond, "A Reader in the Demography of American Jews," AJYB, Vol. 77, 1977, pp. 251–319.

TABLE 7. GEOGRAPHICAL DISTRIBUTION OF CALIFORNIA JEWS AND NON-JEWS (1980–1985) (PERCENT)

Region[a]	Jews, 1980–85 (Field)	Jews, 1984 (AJYB)	Non-Jews, 1980–85 (Field)	State Population, 1980 (Census)
Oregon Border	0.2	0.0	0.7	1.0
Sacramento Valley	2.0	0.9	5.3	5.1
Northern Sierras	0.6	0.0	1.6	2.3
San Francisco– Bay Area	22.5	17.1	25.4	21.9
Monterey– Coast	1.3	0.4	3.1	2.8
San Joaquin Valley	1.1	0.6	7.0	8.7
Santa Barbara– Ventura	3.7	1.3	4.5	3.5
Los Angeles– Orange[b]	59.5	74.2	38.1	39.8
San Diego	6.1	4.3	8.1	7.9
Riverside– San Bernadino– Desert[b]	3.0	1.3	6.3	7.0
Total[c]	100.0 (N=1,220)	100.0	100.0 (N=31,923)	100.0

Sources: California Field Polls; AJYB, Vol. 85, 1985, p. 170; U. S. Census, *California: General Population Characteristics,* Part 6, pp. 17–18.
[a]Composition of the counties as spelled out in "California Field Poll Codebook," April 1984, p. 90.
[b]AJYB figure for the Pomona Valley (3,500) is divided into Los Angeles–Orange (2,900) and San Bernadino (600).
[c]Errors in column total due to rounding.

As the distribution makes clear, Jews were not scattered randomly throughout the state; nor did they live in rural regions. California Jews lived primarily in urban areas with sizeable Jewish populations.

On the related item of housing—not shown in the tables—the Field Polls indicate that California Jews were nearly as likely as non-Jews (61:63) to own their own homes. In the past, the gap had been larger—close to 8 percentage points.

ACHIEVED STATUS

In matters pertaining to personal achievement, the differences are consistently sharp, although the exact figures are distorted by the sampling procedure. In the early 1980s, only one out of five California Jews had no college experience, compared with one out of three non-Jews (Table 8). Jews were also significantly more likely than others to have extended their education beyond the four-year baccalaureate.

The high educational attainment of Jews makes it likely that they will be well represented among professionals and will enjoy relatively high income. This is borne

TABLE 8. EDUCATIONAL LEVELS OF CALIFORNIA JEWS AND NON-JEWS (1981– 1984) (PERCENT)

Education	Jews	Non-Jews
5th grade or less	0.8	2.4
Some high school	1.8	7.0
High-school graduate	16.1	24.5
Trade school	1.7	2.6
Some college	31.6	36.6
4-year-college graduate	17.4	12.8
Some graduate school	5.9	4.3
M.A.	12.7	5.7
More than M.A.	12.2	4.0
(More than B.A.)	(30.8)	(14.0)
Total[a]	100.0 (N=901)	100.0 (N=22,433)

Source: California Field Polls.
[a]Errors in column total due to rounding.

out, in fact, by the data (Table 9). By the early 1980s, about three-fifths of employed Jewish household heads worked primarily as professionals (44 percent) or as managers (17 percent). Combining all levels of labor and service jobs yields only about 12 percent of employed Jews (compared with 34 percent of non-Jews). Slightly more than one-third of employed Jewish household heads worked for themselves, double the figure for non-Jews (Table 10).

TABLE 9. OCCUPATIONS OF WORKING CALIFORNIA JEWS AND NON-JEWS (1981–1984) (PERCENT)

Occupation[a]	Jews	Non-Jews
Professional	44.1	29.5
Managerial	16.7	17.3
Clerical	7.6	10.4
Sales	19.2	9.3
Skilled labor	6.4	15.9
Semi-skilled labor	1.7	7.4
Service	2.7	7.3
Farm and unskilled labor	1.5	2.9
Total[b]	100.0	100.0
	(N=657)	(N=15,795)

Source: California Field Polls.
[a]Based only on chief wage earner.
[b]Errors in column total due to rounding.

TABLE 10. SELF-EMPLOYMENT OF WORKING CALIFORNIA JEWS AND NON-JEWS (1981–1984) (PERCENT)

Employment Status[a]	Jews	Non-Jews
Self-employed	36.4	19.7
Work for other	63.6	80.3
Total	100.0	100.0
	(N=662)	(N=15,915)

Source: California Field Polls.
[a]Based on chief wage earner.

In line with Jewish educational and occupational attainment, Jewish family income was significantly higher than that of other Californians (Table 11). The superior earning power of Jews was not a function of the presence of more wage earners per family. In the early 1980s a direct question on the number of wage earners produced the following results: Jewish households were slightly more likely than non-Jewish households to have one and particularly two breadwinners, but were less likely to have more than two—reflecting smaller Jewish household size. (See Table 18.)

Although there are no direct data on the subject of working women, related data indirectly suggest that Jewish women were more likely than non-Jewish women to be employed. Jewish households were smaller, and fewer of them consisted of married couples—yet more Jewish households had two working adults. This is most likely explained by a large proportion of working women, an inference that is further reinforced by the considerably higher educational levels of Jewish women compared with non-Jewish women.[12]

At the lower end of the income scale, relative differences between Jews and non-Jews were smaller than in the highest income category. About 10 percent of California Jewish households reported an income of $10,000 or less, compared with 14 percent of other Californians. However, since poor, foreign-language-speaking, and institutionalized individuals are all underrepresented in telephone surveys, the figures for both Jews and non-Jews should probably be increased by at least 3–4 percentage points.

TABLE 11. HOUSEHOLD INCOME OF CALIFORNIA JEWS AND NON-JEWS (1981–1984) (PERCENT)

Income	Jews	Non-Jews
Less than $7,000	5.3	6.6
$7,000–$9,999	4.9	7.8
$10,000–$14,999	5.7	9.7
$15,000–$19,999	8.6	13.3
$20,000–$29,999	20.8	23.8
More than $30,000	54.6	38.8
Total[a]	100.0	100.0
	(N=853)	(N=21,383)

Source: California Field Polls.
[a]Errors in column total due to rounding.

[12]Alan M. Fisher and Curtis K. Tanaka, "Jewish Demography in California: The Use of Aggregated Survey Data," in Papers in Jewish Demography 1985 (Jerusalem, forthcoming).

MARITAL STATUS AND FAMILY SIZE

Differences in marital status between Jews and non-Jews were small, although significant and in the same direction found in the Gallup studies: Jews were more likely never to have been married and slightly less likely to be currently married (Table 12). Since California Jews were not younger than other Californians, these differences cannot be attributed to age.

Rates for divorce, separation, and widowhood are similar. One-seventh of California adults were separated or divorced. (Since people who had been divorced and were currently married counted as married, the figures for "divorced" and "separated" are only partial indicators of the total incidence of divorce.)

The notion of widespread singledom in California has some basis in fact. Indeed, there were higher proportions of one-person households and single-parent families in California than in the rest of the nation. Still, among all Californians, married adults significantly outnumbered the unmarried. Among Jews, although a smaller percentage were married or had ever been married, the majority were in fact married.

In the early 1980s, about one-fifth of Jewish households consisted of only one person, variously defined as divorced, separated, widowed, but primarily never-married (Table 13). The addition of single parents raises the number of one-adult households to one-quarter of all Jewish households. (This figure is not shown in the table, in which "two persons" may be a parent and child or two adults.) Furthermore, almost six out of ten California Jewish households consisted of no more than one or two people—primarily couples (married and unmarried), but also single

TABLE 12. MARITAL STATUS OF ADULT CALIFORNIA JEWS AND NON-JEWS (1983–1984) (PERCENT)

Marital Status[a]	Jews	Non-Jews
Never married	25.4	21.1
Married	54.6	57.7
Separated/ divorced	14.0	13.8
Widowed	6.1	7.4
Total[b]	100.0	100.0
	(N=394)	(N=9,876)

Source: California Field Polls.
[a]Based on respondents 18 and older.
[b]Errors in column total due to rounding.

TABLE 13.   HOUSEHOLD SIZE OF CALIFORNIA JEWS AND NON-JEWS (1981–1984)
(PERCENT)

Number of Persons per Household	Jews	Non-Jews
1	21.4	18.0
2	38.3	33.2
3	18.0	18.7
4	13.2	17.2
5	6.2	7.8
6	1.7	3.0
7 or more	1.1	2.1
Total[a]	100.0	100.0
	(N=809)	(N=19,763)

Source: California Field Polls.
[a]Errors in column total due to rounding.

parents with one child and unrelated roommates. Not only were Jewish households significantly smaller overall than those of non-Jews, but the sampling bias against the poor and the foreign-born suggests that the real differences were even greater than they appear.

Married couples with at least one child at home—the traditional family—constituted a distinct minority, both among Jews and other Californians, and represented a smaller percentage than in the past. Although there is no single measure of the total number of children living at home, a partial picture can be obtained by looking at numbers of children in three age groupings: 0–5, 6–12, 13–17 (Table 14). For each age category, more than four-fifths of all California households (including Jews) showed no children at all. (An indirect measure of the declining Jewish birthrate is the fact that a slightly smaller percentage had very young children at home than had children aged 6–12, and a smaller percentage had 6–12-year-olds than had teenagers.) For all three age groups, Jews were more likely than non-Jews to have no children at home, and for those who did have children, Jews were more likely than others to have only one.

ASCRIBED STATUS

In matters of ascribed status, the Field findings are weighted for one measure (gender), are completely one-sided for a second (race), and are expected for the third (age).

TABLE 14. NUMBER OF CHILDREN IN CALIFORNIA JEWISH AND NON-JEWISH HOUSEHOLDS, BY AGES OF CHILDREN (1981–1984) (PERCENT)

Number of Children	Children's Ages, Jewish Households		
	0–5	6–12	13–17
0	90.4	88.0	84.5
1	8.4	8.3	11.4
2	1.2	3.5	3.5
3	0.0	.2	.5
4	0.0	0.0	0.0
5	0.0	0.0	0.0
Total[a]	100.0	100.0	100.0
	(N=809)	(N=809)	(N=809)

Number of Children	Children's Ages, Non-Jewish Households		
	0–5	6–12	13–17
0	83.5	81.6	82.5
1	11.3	12.1	11.9
2	4.4	5.2	4.4
3	.7	.9	1.0
4	.1	.2	.2
5	0.0	.1	0.0
Total[a]	100.0	100.0	100.0
	(N=19,714)	(N=19,683)	(N=19,614)

Source: California Field Polls.
[a]Errors in column total due to rounding.

The distribution of gender within the Jewish community is not apparently much different from the rest of the population, but this is one of the only variables for which the sampling-error margin precludes any confidence in the findings.

As is commonly known, almost all Jews are white—almost 98 percent, according to the polls of the early 1980s. Among California Jews, 0.4 percent were Asian, 0.6 percent black, and 1.2 percent "other." Since Eskimos and Native Americans are not plentiful in the Jewish community, "other" probably signifies primarily the offspring of interracial marriages. It is noteworthy that both the Field and Gallup Polls have found small but consistent traces of nonwhite Jews. Since California is one of the most racially heterogeneous states in the country, it is not surprising that the figures are higher there.

A separate question turns up a small proportion (3.4 percent) of California Jews who claim Latin descent, a larger number than in the past. This probably reflects the increased antisemitism and economic instability in some Latin American countries, leading to emigration.

For age, the California findings of the early 1980s duplicate the general pattern found across the country, but with more moderate differences: a smaller percentage of young (adult) Jews and a larger percentage of older ones than in the population at large (Table 15). In the middle of the age spectrum, differences are minimal. (See also Table 19.) This is explainable by the declining size of Jewish families, i.e., more people who have never married and fewer children for married couples, hence a smaller proportion of young people. This is partly balanced by an immigration weighted toward younger people.

TABLE 15. AGES OF ADULT CALIFORNIA JEWS AND NON-JEWS (1981–1984) (PERCENT)

Age[a]	Jews	Non-Jews
18–20	5.1	5.7
21–29	20.1	21.6
30–39	21.6	23.6
40–49	15.4	15.2
50–59	14.7	13.8
60–69	13.5	12.4
70+	9.4	7.8
(60+)	(22.9)	(20.2)
Total[b]	100.0	100.0
	(N=901)	(N=22,349)

Source: California Field Polls.
[a]Based only on population 18 and older.
[b]Errors in column total due to rounding.

Change Over Two Decades

ACHIEVED STATUS

How have California Jews and other Californians changed over the last quarter of a century? The most dramatic change has been in educational attainment. The proportion of California Jewish adults who were college graduates or higher doubled —from 24 percent in the 1958–1961 period to 48 percent in the early 1980s (Table 16). The percentage having at least some college experience rose from 49 to 79 in

TABLE 16. EDUCATIONAL LEVELS OF CALIFORNIA JEWS (1958–1984) (PER-
CENT)

Education	1958–61	1962–64	1968–72	1974–77	1978–80[a]	1981–84[a]
Less than 8th grade	13.9	8.0	7.6	3.1	1.3	0.8
Some high school	11.5	6.6	8.2	5.6	2.5	1.8
High-school graduate	25.8	26.6	23.5	23.1	17.0	17.8
Some college	25.0	22.8	33.6	26.4	33.9	31.0
College graduate	15.3	23.2	13.7	23.1	16.9	17.4
Post-graduate work	8.3	12.8	13.4	18.8	28.5	30.7
Total[b]	100.0	100.0	100.0	100.0	100.0	100.0
	(N=503)	(N=561)	(N=801)	(N=576)	(N=629)	(N=901)

Source: California Field Polls.
[a]Trade school included as high-school graduate.
[b]Errors in column total due to rounding.

the same time span. By 1982 the proportion of Jews going on to graduate school was greater than the proportion that had finished college 20 years earlier.

The proportion of non-Jewish adults in California with at least some college rose from 38 to 63 percent—almost proportional to the Jewish increase—and the proportion of college graduates increased from 15 to 27 percent.

Changes in occupation and income follow those in education. The proportion of Jews working as professionals rose from 25 percent (1958–1961) to 44 percent (1981–1984), with some leveling off between the late 1970s and the early 1980s. The most significant decreases were for managers and clerical workers, attributable largely to increasing education and a focus on the professions. There were few physical laborers in the early 1960s, and even fewer in the early 1980s. (See Table 9.)

For non-Jewish Californians, the pattern of change closely parallels that of Jews, including a rise in the proportion of professionals. For many years the proportion of non-Jews who were professionals was between 60 and 67 percent of the comparable figure for Jews. The fact that this proportion was higher in the 1980s than in the 1960s suggests a possible trend toward less differentiation.

The proportions of Jews working for others and those working for themselves remained generally stable. The proportion of self-employed individuals was about 37 percent from the early 1960s on. Among non-Jewish Californians, there was a slight increase in the percentage of self-employed from the early 1970s to the early 1980s, but the figure (15–20 percent) always remained lower than that for Jews.

A noteworthy change that occurred among Jews between 1972 and 1982 was in the number of wage earners (Table 17). The proportion of households without any wage earner declined (from 23 to 16 percent), as did the proportion of households with only one wage earner (from 49 to 43 percent). There was a complementary increase in the number of households with two or more working people, from 28 to 42 percent. The wage-earner trend for other Californians was similar, though the percentage of non-Jewish families with no working member remained the same over the years.

The increasing number of working couples—combined with higher educational levels and a rise in vocational status—led to much higher levels of income. Although part of this increase obviously reflected inflation, real income rose strikingly. Whereas in the late 1960s about two-fifths of Jews had a family income of over $15,000, by the early 1980s more than one-half earned above $30,000.

A comparative study of income produces mixed findings. From 1969 to 1984 the proportion of Jews in the highest income category (which increases to $40,000 in 1981) was about double the proportion of other Californians, although there was a slight decline over time. Keeping the top category at $30,000 (see Table 11), however, the relative proportion decreases considerably, from 204 to 144 (with 100 as parity). At the lowest income levels the figures are much closer. According to Table 11, for example, the relative proportion of Jews making less than $7,000 per year was almost equal (0.80) to the comparable figure for non-Jews. The persistence over time of a poor Jewish element is linked to the relatively high (and growing) percentage of elderly within the community (though this percentage was lower in California for both Jews and non-Jews than elsewhere).

TABLE 17. NUMBER OF WAGE EARNERS IN CALIFORNIA JEWISH HOUSEHOLDS (1971–1984) (PERCENT)

Number of Wage Earners	1971–72	1974–77	1978–81	1982–84
0	22.8	18.8	14.2	15.8
1	49.0	54.4	49.1	42.6
2	25.1	24.4	32.2	34.5
3	3.1	2.4	4.6	7.1
Total[a]	100.0	100.0	100.0	100.0
	(N=382)	(N=463)	(N=696)	(N=707)

Source: California Field Polls.
[a]Errors in column total due to rounding.

MARITAL STATUS AND FAMILY SIZE

The picture with regard to marital status is somewhat blurred; in the past the question appeared irregularly in the Field Poll, and the statewide findings for 1970 differ from the census by 5 percentage points. By contrast, in the 1980s the figures corresponded more closely.

Jews match and even slightly surpass other Californians in the percentage increase in those never-married as well as in the percentage decrease in those currently married. (Dramatic changes in Jewish marital rates can be seen by comparing Tables 4 and 12.) Rates for widows remain about the same, whereas those for the separated and divorced increase.

Changes in household or family size are harder to detect than changes in marital status because the ranges are narrow. Californians in general start at a low level, and the 1970 findings are biased by use of a minimum age of 21 rather than 18. Nevertheless, there was a small but noticeable diminution in the number of people living at home with family. In the 1969–1972 period, 35 percent of Jewish households had at least four family members, whereas ten years later the figure was 23 percent (Table 18). During the same period, the proportion of single-person families increased gradually from 17 to 21 percent. The modal two-person household climbed from 33 percent in 1969–1972 to a relatively stable 38 percent from 1975 onward.

The proportion of Jewish households with any child younger than six dropped from 13.2 percent in 1970–1972 to 9.6 percent in 1981–1984, while the proportion of those with more than one young child dropped from 4.9 to 1.2 percent. Jewish

TABLE 18. HOUSEHOLD SIZE OF CALIFORNIA JEWS (1969–1984) (PERCENT)

Number of Persons per Household	1969–72	1974–77	1978–80	1981–84
1	16.6	19.0	22.4	21.4
2	32.7	36.9	41.0	38.3
3	15.7	14.9	14.2	18.0
4	20.7	18.4	14.8	13.2
5	10.5	6.3	4.8	6.2
6	2.8	3.0	2.0	1.7
7	0.9	1.5	0.8	1.1
Total[a]	100.0	100.0	100.0	100.0
	(N=667)	(N=463)	(N=393)	(N=809)

Source: California Field Polls.
[a]Errors in column total due to rounding.

families were not the only ones becoming smaller, however. Similar patterns obtain for California in general.

For the state as a whole—Jews excepted—dramatic changes in racial composition were brought about by the immigration of large groups of Koreans, Hong-Kong Chinese, and Vietnamese. The proportion of whites (including Latinos) in the Field statewide sample dropped from 95 percent in 1960 to 88 percent in the early 1980s, while for Jews it remained almost exactly the same—99 to 98 percent. There was no noticeable change with regard to gender for either group.

Changes in age distribution reflect the singular dynamics of California's population. According to census data for the United States as a whole, the proportion of adults (18+) aged 65 and over jumped from 13.7 to 16.0 percent between 1960 and 1984. In California, however, the increase was from 13.6 to 14.0 percent—one-sixth of the increase for the country as a whole.

The Field findings resemble census figures in that age is weighted against them and the error margin is narrowed. In order to facilitate observation over time, the initial (Field) age divisions have been kept, with 21 as the minimum and senior status set at age 60 and above. Fluctuations—which arise even in the three-year time periods—have been moderated by combining two such periods. Because the findings in the available polls from 1969 through 1976 present a disconcerting interruption in the flow from the earlier period to the mid-1980s, we treat the middle period as containing some minor sampling aberrations, although there are some consistent developments as well. The most striking change in age distribution is the increase in the percentage of people in their 20s (Table 19). Also noteworthy is the relatively modest increase in adults (21+) aged 60 and above—for Jews from 20.9 to 22.2 percent and for non-Jews from 19.9 to 20.9 percent. Like other Californians, Jews, as a group, have not appreciably aged. This is due primarily to migration of mostly younger people, from other parts of the United States and from overseas (including Israel, the Soviet Union, and Iran).

Future Trends

California is a trendsetter, a place where change starts and then spreads. While this has been less true in Jewish life, where New York City is still the pivot, the signs of change are there: New York is losing Jewish population, while California is gaining; New York Jews are becoming older and many of them poorer, while California Jews, on the whole, are maintaining their relative youthfulness and becoming wealthier.

For several of the demographic characteristics examined in this article, California Jews are more like other Jews than other Californians. They are more likely to live in cosmopolitan areas; are more highly educated, of higher vocational status, have

TABLE 19. AGES OF CALIFORNIA JEWS AND NON-JEWS (1958–1984) (PERCENT)

Age	Jews		
	1958–64	1969–76[a]	1977–84
21–29	16.5	19.9	22.4
30–39	24.6	17.5	25.2
40–49	22.1	19.2	15.4
50–59	15.9	18.0	14.7
60+	20.9	25.3	22.2
Total[b]	100.0	100.0	100.0
	(N=1,314)	(N=1,628)	(N=1,477)

Age	Non-Jews		
	1958–64	1968–76[a]	1977–84
21–29	17.1	22.4	23.5
30–39	24.9	21.3	24.4
40–49	22.0	19.2	16.2
50–59	16.1	16.5	14.9
60+	19.9	20.7	20.9
Total[b]	100.0	100.0	100.0
	(N=26,551)	(N=40,463)	(N=36,208)

Source: California Field Polls.
[a]Data for 1973 are missing.
[b]Errors in column totals due to rounding.

higher incomes, and are more likely to be self-employed; they are also more likely to be single or to have smaller families. Since these traits also characterize the Jews who are currently moving to California, they are likely to persist in the near future.

But the Jews do not live in a vacuum; demographically, they have not escaped the currents of California life. There is no single demographic trait for which Jews have moved in a direction different from other Californians. Thus, increasing educational levels result not only from an influx of educated migrants but also from a higher educational system that is open to all Californians. The same factors that have created stress for non-Jewish marriages have led to fewer successful Jewish marriages. Even in racial composition Jews have not been insulated from societal change, acquiring a small but growing number of black and Asian Jews, or some mixture thereof, as well as Hispanic Jews.

The future is likely to bring more of the same for both Jews and non-Jews in California. Immigration of Anglos, which had slowed in the late 1970s, will continue, especially for Jews, centering upon the young and upwardly mobile, but also including some of the elderly. Jews will continue to succeed in socioeconomic terms, being disproportionately represented among the most highly educated and economically comfortable segments of California society.

It may perhaps be that California has passed the peak of a demographic upheaval like that which occurred on the East Coast in the 30 years prior to 1920. When the process is finished, the California Jewish community will be more numerous and powerful than ever before. After that, the numbers will depend primarily on rates of birth and assimilation, and prosperity will continue to be tied to education and the general economic condition of the state.

ALAN M. FISHER
and
CURTIS K. TANAKA

Jewish Population in the United States, 1985

T HE JEWISH POPULATION in the United States in 1985 is estimated to be 5.835 million. This figure is approximately the same as that reported for 1984, and reflects the absence of demographic factors making for population increase.

The basic population units are the fund-raising areas of local Jewish federations, which may represent one county or an aggregate of several counties. In Table 3, those communities shown with two asterisks have indicated changes in their Jewish populations in 1985; those with a single asterisk have submitted current estimates, but have indicated no changes in numbers. While less than a quarter of all communities have supplied population estimates for 1985, the total population of the responding communities accounts for more than 90 percent of the estimated total population of Jews in the United States in 1985.

The state and regional totals shown in Table 1 and Table 2 are derived by summing individual community estimates, shown in Table 3, and then making three adjustments. First, communities of less than 100 are added. Second, duplications within states are eliminated. Third, communities falling within two or more states (e.g., Washington, D.C., and Kansas City, Missouri) are distributed accordingly.

In almost every instance, local estimates refer to "Jewish households," i.e., households in which one or more Jews reside. As a consequence, non-Jews are included in the count, their percentage of the total being estimated (based on the 1970 National Jewish Population Study and a number of current studies) as between 6 and 7 percent. Assuming this proportion, the number of individuals in "Jewish households" who identify themselves as Jewish in 1985 would be approximately 5.425 million.

Based on recent studies, three communities reported significant changes from their 1984 estimates. Atlanta and Phoenix showed increases: Atlanta from 33,500 to 50,000; Phoenix from 35,000 to 50,000. Philadelphia lowered its estimate from 295,000 to 240,000. These changes, which are reflected in the state and regional totals, are part of the continuing trend toward geographical redistribution that has been evident over the past decade. The Jewish population in the Northeast is decreasing as a proportion of the total Jewish population, while the South's and the West's proportions are increasing.

ALVIN CHENKIN

APPENDIX

TABLE 1. JEWISH POPULATION IN THE UNITED STATES, 1985

State	Estimated Jewish Population	Total Population*	Estimated Jewish Percent of Total
Alabama...............	9,400	3,990,000	0.2
Alaska................	960	500,000	0.2
Arizona...............	68,285	3,053,000	2.2
Arkansas	2,975	2,349,000	0.1
California.............	793,065	25,622,000	3.1
Colorado..............	48,565	3,178,000	1.5
Connecticut	105,400	3,154,000	3.3
Delaware	9,500	613,000	1.6
District of Columbia.....	24,285	622,823	3.9
Florida	570,320	10,976,000	5.2
Georgia...............	58,570	5,837,000	1.0
Hawaii	5,550	1,039,000	0.5
Idaho	505	1,001,000	0.1
Illinois	262,710	11,511,000	2.3
Indiana...............	21,335	5,498,000	0.4
Iowa	5,570	2,910,000	0.2
Kansas	11,430	2,438,000	0.5
Kentucky	12,775	3,723,000	0.3
Louisiana	17,405	4,462,000	0.4
Maine	9,350	1,156,000	0.8
Maryland	199,415	4,439,000	4.5
Massachusetts	249,370	5,798,000	4.3
Michigan	86,125	9,075,000	0.9
Minnesota.............	32,240	4,162,000	0.8
Mississippi	3,130	2,598,000	0.1
Missouri	64,690	5,008,000	1.3
Montana..............	645	824,000	0.1
Nebraska	7,865	1,606,000	0.5
Nevada...............	18,200	911,000	2.0
New Hampshire.........	5,980	977,000	0.6
New Jersey............	430,570	7,515,000	5.7
New Mexico...........	5,155	1,424,000	0.4
New York	1,915,145	17,735,000	10.8

State	Estimated Jewish Population	Total Population*	Estimated Jewish Percent of Total
North Carolina	14,990	6,165,000	0.2
North Dakota	1,085	686,000	0.2
Ohio	138,935	10,752,000	1.3
Oklahoma.	6,885	3,298,000	0.2
Oregon	11,050	2,674,000	0.4
Pennsylvania	353,045	11,901,000	3.0
Rhode Island	22,000	962,000	2.3
South Carolina.	8,095	3,300,000	0.2
South Dakota.	635	706,000	0.1
Tennessee	19,445	4,717,000	0.4
Texas	78,655	15,989,000	0.5
Utah	2,850	1,652,000	0.2
Vermont	2,465	530,000	0.5
Virginia.	60,185	5,636,000	1.1
Washington	22,085	4,149,000	0.5
West Virginia.	4,265	1,952,000	0.2
Wisconsin.	31,190	4,766,000	0.7
Wyoming	310	511,000	0.1
U.S. TOTAL	**5,834,655	236,031,000	2.5

N.B. Details may not add to totals because of rounding.
*Resident population, July 1, 1984, provisional. (Source: *Provisional Estimates of the Population of Counties: July 1984,* Bureau of the Census, series P-26, No. 84-52-C, March 1985.)
**Exclusive of Puerto Rico and the Virgin Islands, which previously reported Jewish populations of 1,800 and 510, respectively.

TABLE 2. DISTRIBUTION OF U.S. JEWISH POPULATION BY REGIONS, 1985

Region	Total Population	Percent Distribution	Jewish Population	Percent Distribution
Northeast:	49,728,000	21.1	3,093,330	53.0
New England	12,577,000	5.3	394,555	6.8
Middle Atlantic	37,151,000	15.7	2,698,760	46.3
North Central:	59,118,000	25.0	663,810	11.4
East North Central ..	41,602,000	17.6	540,300	9.3
West North Central..	17,516,000	7.4	123,515	2.1
South:	80,667,000	34.2	1,100,295	18.9
South Atlantic	39,541,000	16.8	949,625	16.3
East South Central...	15,028,000	6.4	44,750	0.8
West South Central ..	26,098,000	11.1	105,915	1.8
West:	46,538,000	19.7	977,220	16.8
Mountain...........	12,554,000	5.3	144,515	2.5
Pacific	33,984,000	14.4	832,710	14.3
TOTALS.............	236,031,000	100.0	5,834,655	100.0

N.B. Details may not add to totals because of rounding.

TABLE 3. COMMUNITIES WITH JEWISH POPULATIONS OF 100 OR MORE, 1985
(ESTIMATED)

State and City	Jewish Population	State and City	Jewish Population	State and City	Jewish Population
ALABAMA		Eureka	250	Tulare & Kings County	
Anniston	100	Fontana	165	(incl. in Fresno)	
*Birmingham	4,500	*Fresno	2,000	Vallejo	400
Dothan	205	Kern County	850	Ventura County	6,000
Gadsden	180	Lancaster (incl. in			
Huntsville	550	Antelope Valley)		**COLORADO**	
*Mobile	1,250	*Long Beach	13,500	Colorado Springs	1,000
**Montgomery	1,650	*Los Angeles Metropoli-		**Denver	46,800
Selma	210	tan Area	500,870	Pueblo	375
Tri-Cities[a]	150	Merced	100		
Tuscaloosa	315	Modesto	260	**CONNECTICUT**	
		Monterey	1,500	*Bridgeport	18,000
ALASKA		Oakland (incl. in		Bristol	250
Anchorage	600	Alameda & Contra		Colchester	525
Fairbanks	210	Costa Counties)		*Danbury (incl. New Mil-	
		Ontario (incl. in Pomona		ford)	3,500
ARIZONA		Valley)		**Greenwich	5,000
**Phoenix	50,000	*Orange County	60,000	*Hartford (incl. New	
*Tucson	18,000	*Palm Springs	4,950	Britain)	26,000
		Pasadena (also incl. in		Lebanon	175
ARKANSAS		Los Angeles Metropol-		Lower Middlesex	
Fayetteville	120	itan Area)	2,000	County (incl. in	
Ft. Smith	160	Petaluma	800	New London)[d]	
Hot Springs (incl. in		Pomona Valley[c]	3,500	Manchester (incl. in	
Little Rock)		Riverside	1,200	Hartford)	
**Little Rock	1,400	**Sacramento	8,500	Meriden	1,400
Pine Bluff	175	Salinas	350	Middletown	1,300
Southeast		San Bernardino	1,900	Milford (incl. in	
Arkansas[b]	140	**San Diego	35,000	New Haven)	
Wynne-Forest		*San Francisco	80,000	Moodus	150
City	110	*San Jose	18,000	*New Haven	22,000
		San Luis Obispo	450	New London	3,500
CALIFORNIA		San Pedro	300	Newtown (incl. in	
*Alameda & Contra		Santa Barbara	3,800	Danbury)	
Costa Counties	35,000	Santa Cruz	1,000	*Norwalk	4,000
Antelope Valley	375	Santa Maria	200	Norwich	2,500
Bakersfield (incl. in Kern		Santa Monica	8,000	Putnam	110
County)		Santa Rosa	750	Rockville (incl. in	
El Centro	125	**Stockton	1,500	Hartford)	
Elsinore	250	Sun City	800	*Stamford	12,000

State and City	Jewish Population	State and City	Jewish Population	State and City	Jewish Population
Torrington	450	Tallahassee	1,000	Quincy	200
Valley Area[e]	700	*Tampa	10,500	Rock Island (incl. in	
Wallingford	440			Quad Cities)	
**Waterbury	2,700	GEORGIA		*Rockford	975
Westport	2,800	Albany	525	**Southern Illinois[h]	900
Willimantic	400	Athens	250	*Springfield	1,100
Winsted	110	**Atlanta	50,000	Sterling-Dixon	110
		*Augusta	1,500	Waukegan	1,200
DELAWARE		Brunswick	120		
*Wilmington (incl. rest of		*Columbus	1,000	INDIANA	
state)	9,500	Dalton	235	Anderson	105
		Fitzgerald-Cordele	125	Bloomington	300
DISTRICT OF COLUMBIA		Macon	900	Elkhart (incl. in	
*Greater Washing-		*Savannah	2,600	South Bend)	
ton[f]	157,335	Valdosta	145	Evansville	1,200
				**Ft. Wayne	1,170
FLORIDA		HAWAII		Gary (incl. in Northwest	
*Boca Raton-		Hilo	100	Indiana-Calumet	
Delray	40,000	Honolulu	5,000	Region)	
Brevard County	2,250	Kona	150	**Indianapolis	11,000
*Daytona Beach	2,000	Kuaii	100	*Lafayette	600
**Fort		Maui	200	Marion	170
Lauderdale	110,000			**Michigan City	450
Fort Pierce	270	IDAHO		Muncie	175
Gainesville	1,000	Boise	120	**Northwest	
*Hollywood	60,000			Indiana-Calumet	
*Jacksonville	6,800	ILLINOIS		Region[i]	3,000
Key West	170	Aurora	400	Richmond	110
Lakeland	800	Bloomington	125	Shelbyville	140
**Lee County (incl. Ft.		*Champaign-		*South Bend	1,900
Myers)	3,000	Urbana	2,000	Terre Haute	450
Lehigh Acres	125	*Chicago Metropolitan			
*Miami	253,340	Area	248,000	IOWA	
*Orlando	15,000	Danville	240	Cedar Rapids	330
*Palm Beach County		Decatur	350	Council Bluffs	245
(excl. Boca		East St. Louis (incl.		Davenport (incl. in Quad	
Raton)	45,000	in So. Ill.)		Cities, Ill.)	
Pensacola	725	Elgin	830	**Des Moines	3,200
Port Charlotte	150	Galesburg (incl. in		Dubuque	105
**Sarasota	8,500	Peoria)		Fort Dodge	115
St. Augustine	100	*Joliet	800	Iowa City	750
*St. Petersburg (incl.		Kankakee	260	Mason City	110
Clearwater)	9,500	**Peoria	1,500	Muscatine	120
		**Quad Cities[g]	1,750	Ottumwa	150

State and City	Jewish Population	State and City	Jewish Population	State and City	Jewish Population
**Sioux City	785	**MASSACHUSETTS**		**MICHIGAN**	
Waterloo	450	Amherst	750	Ann Arbor (incl. all	
		Athol	110	Washtenaw	
KANSAS		Attleboro	200	County)	3,000
Topeka	500	Beverly	1,000	Battle Creek	245
*Wichita	1,000	*Boston (incl.		Bay City	650
		Brockton)	170,000	Benton Harbor	650
KENTUCKY		Fall River	1,780	*Detroit	70,000
**Lexington	2,000	Fitchburg	300	**Flint	2,765
*Louisville	9,200	*Framingham	10,000	*Grand Rapids	1,500
Paducah	175	Gardner	100	Iron County	160
		Gloucester	400	Iron Mountain	105
LOUISIANA		Great Barrington	105	Jackson	375
Alexandria	700	Greenfield	250	Kalamazoo	1,000
**Baton Rouge	1,400	Haverhill	1,650	**Lansing	2,100
Lafayette	600	Holyoke	1,100	Marquette	
Lake Charles	250	Hyannis	1,200	County	175
**Monroe	425	**Lawrence	3,600	Mt. Clemens	420
*New Orleans	12,000	*Leominster	750	Mt. Pleasant	100
**Shreveport	1,200	Lowell	2,000	Muskegon	235
		*Lynn (incl. Beverly,		**Saginaw	400
MAINE		Peabody, and		South Haven	100
Augusta	215	Salem)	19,000		
Bangor	1,300	Medway (incl. in Fra-		**MINNESOTA**	
Southern Maine (excl.		mingham)		Austin	125
Portland)	950	Milford (incl. in Fra-		*Duluth	1,100
Calais	135	mingham)		Hibbing	155
**Lewiston-Auburn	500	Mills (incl. in Framing-		**Minneapolis	23,000
*Portland	5,500	ham)		Rochester	240
Waterville	300	*New Bedford	2,700	*St. Paul	7,500
		Newburyport	280	Virginia	100
MARYLAND		North Berkshire	675		
Annapolis	2,000	Northampton	700	**MISSISSIPPI**	
*Baltimore	92,000	Peabody	2,600	Biloxi-Gulfport	100
Cumberland	265	**Pittsfield (incl. all Berk-		Clarksdale	160
Easton Park Areaʲ	100	shire County)	3,100	Cleveland	180
Frederick	400	Plymouth	500	Greenville	500
Hagerstown	275	Salem	1,150	Greenwood	100
Hartford County	500	Southbridge	105	Hattiesburg	180
Howard County	4,000	**Springfield	11,250	**Jackson	700
Montgomery and		Taunton	1,200	Meridian	135
Prince Georges		Webster	125	Natchez	140
Countyᶠ	99,500	*Worcester	10,000	Vicksburg	260
Salisbury	300				

State and City	Jewish Population
MISSOURI	
Columbia	350
Joplin	115
**Kansas City	19,000
Kennett	110
Springfield	230
St. Joseph	343
*St. Louis	53,500
MONTANA	
Billings	160
NEBRASKA	
Lincoln	750
*Omaha	6,500
NEVADA	
*Las Vegas	17,000
Reno	1,200
NEW HAMPSHIRE	
Claremont	130
Concord	350
Dover	425
Keene	105
Laconia	150
*Manchester	3,000
Nashua	450
Portsmouth	1,000
NEW JERSEY	
*Atlantic City (incl. Atlantic County)	12,000
Bayonne	4,500
*Bergen County[k]	100,000
Bridgeton	375
*Camden[l]	28,000
Carteret	300
Elizabeth (incl. in Union County)	
Englewood (incl. in Bergen County)	
*Essex County[m]	111,000

State and City	Jewish Population
Flemington	875
Gloucester County[n]	165
Hoboken	350
**Jersey City	4,000
**Middlesex County[o]	39,350
Millville	240
*Monmouth County	33,600
Morris-Sussex Counties[p] (incl. in Essex County)	
Morristown (incl. in Morris County)	
Mt. Holly	300
Newark (incl. in Essex County)	
New Brunswick (incl. in Raritan Valley)	
North Hudson County[q]	7,000
*North Jersey[r]	32,500
**Ocean County	9,000
**Passaic-Clifton	7,800
Paterson (incl. in North Jersey)	
Perth Amboy (incl. in Middlesex County)	
Plainfield (incl. in Union County)	
Princeton	2,600
Salem	230
**Somerset County[s]	4,300
Somerville (incl. in Somerset County)	
Toms River (incl. in Ocean County)	
Trenton[t]	8,500
*Union County	32,000
**Vineland[u]	3,290
Wildwood	425
Willingboro (incl. in Camden)	

State and City	Jewish Population
NEW MEXICO	
*Albuquerque	4,500
Las Cruces	100
Santa Fe	300
NEW YORK	
*Albany	12,000
Amenia	140
Amsterdam	595
Auburn	315
Batavia	165
Beacon	315
*Binghamton (incl. all Broome County)	3,000
Brewster (also incl. in Danbury, Ct.)	300
*Buffalo	18,500
Canandaigua	135
Catskill	200
Corning	125
Cortland	440
Dunkirk	150
Ellenville	1,450
*Elmira	1,100
Geneva	300
*Glens Falls	800
Gloversville	535
Herkimer	185
Highland Falls	105
Hudson	470
Ithaca	1,000
Jamestown	185
*Kingston	3,000
Liberty	2,100
Loch Sheldrake-Hurleyville	750
Monroe	400
Monticello	2,400
Mountaindale	150
*New York City Metropolitan Area	1,742,500
New Paltz	150

State and City	Jewish Population	State and City	Jewish Population	State and City	Jewish Population
Newark	220	Hendersonville	105	**OREGON**	
Newburgh-		High Point	400	Corvallis	140
Middletown	8,950	Raleigh	1,375	Eugene	1,500
**Niagara Falls	600	Rocky Mount	110	**Portland	8,950
Norwich	120	Whiteville Zone^v	160	Salem	200
Olean	140	Wilmington	500		
Oneonta	175	Winston-Salem	440	**PENNSYLVANIA**	
Oswego	100			Aliquippa	400
Parksville	140	**NORTH DAKOTA**		Allentown	4,980
Pawling	105	Fargo	500	*Altoona	580
Plattsburg	275	Grand Forks	100	Ambridge	250
Port Jervis	560			Beaver (incl. in	
Potsdam	175	**OHIO**		Pittsburgh)	
Poughkeepsie	4,900	*Akron	6,000	Beaver Falls	350
*Rochester	19,600	**Canton	2,750	Berwick	120
**Rockland		*Cincinnati	22,000	Bethlehem	960
County	60,000	*Cleveland	70,000	Braddock	250
Rome	205	*Columbus	15,000	Bradford	150
Saratoga Springs	500	*Dayton	6,000	Brownville	150
Schenectady	5,400	East Liverpool	300	Butler	300
Sharon Springs	165	Elyria	275	Carbon County	125
South Fallsburg	1,100	Hamilton	560	Carnegie	100
*Syracuse	9,000	Lima	168	Central Bucks	
Troy	1,200	Lorain	1,000	County	400
*Utica	2,100	Mansfield	600	Chambersburg	340
Walden (incl. in New-		Marion	150	Chester	2,100
burgh-Middletown)		Middletown	140	Coatesville	305
Warwick	100	New Philadelphia	140	Connellsville	110
Watertown	250	Newark	105	*Delaware Valley	
White Lake	425	Piqua	120	(Lower Bucks	
Woodbourne	200	Portsmouth	120	County)^w	23,000
Woodridge	300	Sandusky	150	Donora	100
		Springfield	340	Easton	1,300
NORTH CAROLINA		**Steubenville	200	Ellwood City	110
**Asheville	1,100	*Toledo	6,300	**Erie	855
**Chapel Hill-		Warren	500	Farrell	150
Durham	2,400	Wooster	200	Greensburg	300
*Charlotte	4,000	**Youngstown	5,000	*Harrisburg	6,500
Fayetteville (incl. all		Zanesville	350	Hazleton	481
Cumberland				Homestead	300
County)	500	**OKLAHOMA**		Indiana	135
Gastonia	220	Muskogee	120	*Johnstown	550
Goldsboro	120	**Oklahoma City	2,325	Kittanning	175
**Greensboro	2,500	*Tulsa	2,900		

State and City	Jewish Population
Lancaster	1,800
Lebanon	425
Lock Haven	140
McKeesport	2,000
Monessen	100
Mt. Pleasant	120
New Castle	400
New Kensington	560
*Norristown	1,500
North Penn	200
Oil City	165
Oxford-Kennett Square	180
**Philadelphia Metropolitan Area	240,000
Phoenixville	340
**Pittsburgh	45,000
Pottstown	700
Pottsville	500
*Reading	2,800
Sayre	100
*Scranton	3,400
Sharon	330
State College	450
Stroudsburg	410
Sunbury	200
Uniontown	240
Upper Beaver	500
Washington (incl. in Pittsburgh)	
Wayne County	210
West Chester	300
**Wilkes-Barre	4,200
Williamsport	415
*York	1,600

RHODE ISLAND

State and City	Jewish Population
*Providence (incl. rest of state)	22,000

SOUTH CAROLINA

State and City	Jewish Population
*Charleston	3,500

State and City	Jewish Population
**Columbia	2,000
Florence	350
Greenville	600
Orangeburg County	105
Spartanburg	295
Sumter	190

SOUTH DAKOTA

State and City	Jewish Population
**Sioux Falls	125

TENNESSEE

State and City	Jewish Population
*Chattanooga	2,000
Johnson City[x]	210
Knoxville	1,350
**Memphis	10,000
**Nashville	5,120
Oak Ridge	240

TEXAS

State and City	Jewish Population
Amarillo	300
**Austin	3,800
Baytown	300
Beaumont	400
Brownsville	160
*Corpus Christi	1,200
*Dallas	22,000
De Witt County[y]	150
**El Paso	4,700
*Ft. Worth	3,600
Galveston	630
*Houston	28,000
Laredo	420
Longview	185
Lubbock	350
McAllen	295
Odessa	150
Port Arthur	260
*San Antonio	9,000
Texarkana	100
Tyler	450
**Waco	385

State and City	Jewish Population
Wharton	170
Wichita Falls	260

UTAH

State and City	Jewish Population
Ogden	100
**Salt Lake City	2,750

VERMONT

State and City	Jewish Population
Bennington	120
Burlington	1,800
Rutland	350
St. Johnsbury	100

VIRGINIA

State and City	Jewish Population
Alexandria (incl. Falls Church, Arlington County, and urban Fairfax County)	33,550
Arlington (incl. in Alexandria)	
Charlottesville	800
Danville	180
Fredericksburg	140
Hampton (incl. in Newport News)	
Harrisonburg	115
Hopewell	140
Lynchburg	275
Martinsville	135
*Newport News (incl. Hampton)	2,575
*Norfolk (incl. Virginia Beach)	11,000
Petersburg	600
*Portsmouth (incl. Suffolk)	1,100
*Richmond	8,000
**Roanoke	710
Williamsburg	120
Winchester	110

WASHINGTON

State and City	Jewish Population
Bellingham	120

State and City	Jewish Population	State and City	Jewish Population	State and City	Jewish Population
Bremerton (incl. in Seattle)		Parkersburg	155	Manitowoc	115
*Seattle	19,500	Weirton	150	*Milwaukee	23,900
*Spokane	1,000	Wheeling	650	Oshkosh	150
Tacoma	750	WISCONSIN		**Racine	375
		Appleton	250	Sheboygan	250
WEST VIRGINIA		Beloit	120	Superior	165
Bluefield-Princeton	250	Eau Clair	120	Waukesha (incl. in Milwaukee)	
Charleston	1,075	Fond du Lac	100	Wausau	155
Clarksburg	205	*Green Bay	280		
*Huntington	450	**Kenosha	240	WYOMING	
Morgantown	200	*Madison	4,500	Cheyenne	255

---

*Denotes estimates submitted in current year.

**Estimates submitted in current year; represents change from previous estimate.

ᵃFlorence, Sheffield, Tuscumbia.

ᵇTowns in Chicot, Desha, Drew Counties.

ᶜIncludes Alta Loma, Chino, Claremont, Cucamonga, La Verne, Montclair, Ontario, Pomona, San Dimas, Upland.

ᵈCenterbrook, Chester, Clinton, Deep River, Essex, Killingworth, Old Lyme, Old Saybrook, Seabrook, Westbrook.

ᵉAnsonia, Derby-Shelton, Oxford, Seymour.

ᶠGreater Washington includes urbanized portions of Montgomery and Prince Georges Counties, in Maryland; Arlington County, Fairfax County (organized portion), Falls Church, Alexandria, in Virginia.

ᵍRock Island, Moline (Illinois); Davenport, Bettendorf (Iowa).

ʰTowns in Alexander, Bond, Clay, Clinton, Crawford, Edwards, Effingham, Fayette, Franklin, Gallatin, Hamilton, Hardin, Jackson, Jasper, Jefferson, Jersey, Johnson, Lawrence, Mascoupin, Madison, Marion, Massac, Montgomery, Perry, Pope, Pulaski, Randolph, Richland, St. Clair, Saline, Union, Wabash, Washington, Wayne, White, Williamson Counties.

ⁱIncludes Crown Point, East Chicago, Gary, Hammond, Munster, Valparaiso, Whiting, and the Greater Calumet region.

ʲTowns in Caroline, Kent, Queen Annes, Talbot Counties.

ᵏAllendale, Elmwood Park, Fair Lawn, Franklin Lakes, Oakland, Midland Park, Rochelle Park, Saddle Brook, Wykoff also included in North Jersey estimate.

ˡIncludes Camden and Burlington Counties.

ᵐIncludes Morris & Sussex Counties & contiguous areas in Hudson, Somerset & Union Counties.

ⁿIncludes Clayton, Paulsboro, Woodbury. Excludes Newfield; see Vineland.
ᵒIncludes in Somerset County, Kendall Park, Somerset; in Mercer County, Hightstown.
ᵖSee footnote (m).
ᑫIncludes Guttenberg, Hudson Heights, North Bergen, North Hudson, Secaucus, Union City, Weehawken, West New York, Woodcliff.
ʳIncludes Paterson, Wayne, Hawthorne in Passaic County, and nine towns in Bergen County. See footnote (k).
ˢExcludes Kendall Park and Somerset, which are included in Middlesex County.
ᵗIncludes Mercer County in New Jersey; and Lower Makefield, Morrisville, Newtown, and Yardley in Pennsylvania.
ᵘIncludes in Cumberland County, Norma, Rosenheim, Vineland; in Salem County, Elmer; in Gloucester County, Clayton, Newfield; in Cape May County, Woodbine.
ᵛElizabethtown, Fairmont, Jacksonville, Lumberton, Tabor City, Wallace, Warsaw, and Loris, S.C.
ʷBensalem Township, Bristol, Langhorne, Levittown, New Hope, Newtown, Penndel, Warington, Yardley. Also includes communities listed in footnote (u).
ˣIncludes Kingsport and Bristol (including the portion of Bristol in Virginia).
ʸIncludes communities also in Colorado, Fayette, Gonzales, and La Vaca Counties.

Canada

As the midpoint of the decade approached, the Jews of Canada generally continued in directions that had been established for some time. The community was well organized and exhibited a strong sense of Jewish identity. Its formal operations were conducted mainly through the Canadian Jewish Congress (CJC) and the federations, as well as B'nai B'rith and the Canadian Zionist Federation (CZF), all of which continued to enjoy broad support. The community displayed a high profile in its relations with the general population and with the government in confronting such issues as public debate over the war in Lebanon, the demands for the prosecution or deportation of alleged Nazi war criminals living in Canada, and public manifestations of anti-Semitism.

National Affairs

Politically, the highlight of the 1983–1984 period was the general election, held in September 1984. Progressive Conservative leader Brian Mulroney won a landslide victory over Prime Minister John Turner, who had taken over the reins of the Liberal party a mere two months earlier, following the resignation of Pierre Elliott Trudeau. Mulroney's victory brought a decisive end to the Trudeau era (1968–1984), and opened the way for new emphases in public policy.

During the election campaign, Mulroney ignored the customary assumption of Jewish loyalty to the Liberal party and made a strenuous effort to attract Jewish support—an effort that met with some success.

In the new House of Commons, Jews were represented in the caucuses of the three parties: Gerry Weiner of Quebec—Progressive Conservatives; David Orlikow of Manitoba—New Democratic party; and Herb Gray and Robert Kaplan of Ontario and David Berger and Sheila Finestone of Quebec—Liberals. Weiner was later named parliamentary secretary to the secretary of state for external affairs. Jerry Lampert of Ottawa, who served as codirector of operations for the Progressive Conservatives during the campaign, was later appointed national director of the party.

Canada entered a new political era under the recently adopted constitution, which contained the country's first Charter of Rights and Freedoms. The Jewish community generally welcomed the charter as a progressive step.

231

In Quebec, despite the fact that the secessionist Parti Québécois remained in charge of the provincial government, all survey evidence indicated that public support for sovereignty was weak. The Jews of Montreal, virtually all of whom preferred to keep Canada intact, were somewhat reassured by the reduction in separatist agitation.

Although the economy had begun to recover from the 1981–1982 recession, the pace of recovery lagged behind that in the United States. While inflation had dropped considerably by the end of 1984, unemployment remained at a disturbing level. Continued demand for government services and inadequate growth of revenues resulted in record federal government deficits. The nation's economic plight was paralleled in the organized Jewish community, with federation budgets experiencing intensified pressure.

JEWISH COMMUNITY

Demography

The 1981 census reported 296,425 Jews, categorized by religion. (The Canadian Jewish total in 1984 was estimated to be 310,000.) Historical patterns of concentration persisted, with about 250,000 Jews in the two central provinces of Ontario and Quebec. The Jewish populations of the major metropolitan areas were Toronto—123,730; Montreal—101,365; Winnipeg—15,350; Vancouver—12,865; Ottawa—8,365; and Calgary—5,575. Communities of between 1,000 and 5,000 were found in Edmonton, Halifax, London, Kitchener, St. Catharines, and Windsor.

A major trend that emerged from the data was the movement of Jewish population from Montreal to Toronto, evidently in response to political and economic difficulties in Quebec. Montreal's Jewish community declined by about 8,000 between 1971 and 1981, and probably dropped by several thousand more since 1981. In contrast, the greater Toronto Jewish community grew by about 22,000 between the two censuses. The feeling in Montreal was that even the defeat of the Parti Québécois would not stem the Jewish population outflow, thereby ensuring that the already distorted age distribution of the city's Jews, with its large proportion of elderly, would continue. In a report issued early in 1984, the Long-Range Planning Committee of the Allied Jewish Community Services (AJCS)—Montreal's federation—concluded that an urgent situation existed and called for action to maintain the community's viability. A critical concern was the prospect of a severe financial crisis and its impact on services for the aging population. Suggested recommendations focused on encouraging young Jews to remain in Montreal, attracting immigrants from overseas, and finding new ways to provide services to the elderly.

Another notable feature of Jewish demography was the decline of Jewish life in very small communities. For example, the future of the 35 remaining Jewish families in Quebec City was in doubt, and the synagogue was put up for sale. The community had been in existence for over 200 years, but its members gradually drifted away. The last Jewish family in Shawinigan, Quebec, moved away in 1984. The only synagogue in Newfoundland, with its membership reduced to 28 families, gave up its rabbi and was considering selling its building. In New Brunswick and Nova Scotia, Jewish life remained vigorous, if limited in scope. Representatives of the communities in the two provinces expressed determination to carry on despite the inherent difficulties of living far away from the main centers of Jewish activity.

Canadian Jews were concerned about the increasing rate of intermarriage, which, along with low levels of fertility, threatened the long-term viability of the community. According to one recent estimate, about one-half of the new marriages involving Jews in Montreal were of a mixed nature. In response, the Canadian Jewish Congress (CJC) established a Jewish Introduction Service, functioning on a national basis.

Communal Activities

The Canadian Jewish community prided itself on the breadth and complexity of its organizational structure, and on its ability to resolve internal conflicts through consensus. Thus, there was great consternation when a lockout of teachers began at four Montreal Hebrew day schools just after Passover 1984. The school administrations, feeling squeezed by limited revenues and increasing costs, had attempted to extract concessions from the teachers' union during protracted negotiations. The teachers, generally supported by their counterparts in the public sector, resisted giving up the gains of previous contracts. The situation was exacerbated by personal animosities that developed. The lockout ended the school year two months early for nearly 4,000 students, even though classes were resumed for a short time in June. When contracts were finally signed, neither side could claim victory. After the teachers resumed work, there were fears that residual bitterness would cause long-term damage to the quality of Jewish education in Montreal.

When the new school year began in August 1984, the Jewish People's and Peretz School in Montreal opened a new building for its Bialik High School, which enrolled over 500 students. The decision to construct the building was seen as an affirmation of the Jewish community's future in Montreal.

In Toronto, the Jewish community failed to secure government financial support for day schools. Community leaders met with Ontario premier William Davis and with the leaders of the two opposition parties, but were unable to obtain the commitments they sought. A decision to extend government support to Catholic high schools stimulated renewed Jewish demands for equitable treatment.

In Calgary, Alberta, the status of Jewish day schools was also at issue. When a Calgary school-board election brought to power commissioners who opposed public aid to religious schools, Jewish schools were required to leave the public-school system, through which they had been receiving public funds. Subsequently, the schools were allowed to affiliate with the Catholic board, thereby restoring most of the funding. However, the agreement with the Catholic schools was only for two years and did not guarantee long-term stability. A hopeful move toward that end was the recommendation by a provincial government committee permitting private schools—including the Jewish day schools—that met certain conditions to be integrated into the public-school system.

Schools were not the only institutions with financial problems. Rampant inflation exacerbated by a recession produced a serious fiscal squeeze for federations and national organizations. One of the hardest hit was the CJC, which found that unanticipated demands necessitated an increase in expenditures. The resulting deficit led, in turn, to vigorous action to institute financial controls, consolidate or even eliminate some operations, and reduce the number of employees.

Milton Harris was elected president of the CJC at the Triennial Congress Plenary Assembly, held in Montreal in May 1983. Other national officers who were elected by acclamation included Dorothy Reitman of Montreal, chairman of the national executive; Laurence Bessner of Montreal, treasurer; and Edward Waitzer of Toronto, honorary counsel. In contested elections, Barbara Stern of Montreal became associate chairman of the national executive and Harry Steiner of Toronto won the post of secretary. Delegates to the plenary reviewed matters of national and international concern as well as organizational problems.

Another major convention was the General Assembly of the Council of Jewish Federations of North America, held in Toronto in November 1984, and attended by some 2,500 delegates. Among the highlights of the convention were an unofficial demonstration in behalf of Ethiopian Jewry, which disrupted the opening session, and, later, an official rally in support of Soviet refuseniks. While hosting the gathering, Toronto also celebrated the opening of its new community complex, the Lipa Green Building for Community Services, located in suburban Willowdale. The complex housed the Toronto Jewish Congress, the Jewish public library and archives, social service agencies, the board of Jewish education, several national offices, and a Jewish museum and Holocaust memorial. The location of the complex in Willowdale reflected the northward movement of Toronto's Jewish population over the past two decades.

An important Jewish population trend was the growing proportion of Sephardim in both Toronto and Montreal. In Toronto an Ontario Sephardic Federation was formed, while in Montreal the Communauté Sepharade du Québec had been in existence for some years. Representatives of both Sephardic communities expressed concern that Ashkenazi-dominated federations and community organizations were not doing enough to integrate the Sephardim fully into community life.

A study carried out under the auspices of the CJC concluded that Jewish women were underrepresented in positions of power in Jewish organizations. While women were overrepresented in less highly paid positions, they held only a little over one-third of policy-making posts. Measures to rectify the imbalance were being considered by groups concerned with the status of women. It should be noted that during the two years prior to the study Dodo Heppner had been elected president of AJCS in Montreal, while Anne Gross became chairman of the Canada-Israel Committee (CIC).

A study carried out by Yogev Tzuk of decision-making patterns in AJCS, the Montreal federation, produced some interesting findings. Tzuk, an independent researcher, interviewed both lay and professional leaders to evaluate the respective roles played by major donors to the annual campaign—who were not necessarily officials of AJCS, and by the officers and board members—who were not necessarily big givers. Tzuk found that access to positions of leadership and power did not necessarily depend on personal wealth. Tzuk also found that a new generation of professionals had achieved power in community affairs, based on personal talent and commitment.

One of the perennial issues in the Montreal community—the possible merger between AJCS and the Quebec Region of the CJC—was still under consideration, especially in light of similar mergers that had taken place in Winnipeg and Toronto. As of the end of 1984, no concrete decisions had been reached.

A major community initiative in Montreal was the Youth Retention Project, a job-placement service of the Jewish Vocational Service that was designed to stem the exodus of young Jews from Montreal. The project showed signs of modest success, eliciting growing interest from both employers and job seekers and making some 100 job placements in its first two years.

Nazi War Criminals and Neo-Nazism

A major concern of Canada's Jews during 1983–1984 was the fate of accused Nazi war criminals living in Canada. The CJC and other organizations made the matter a priority, putting great pressure on the federal government to take action against former Nazis who had apparently entered Canada as the result of lax immigration procedures after World War II. Various remedies were proposed, including trials in Canada, deportation, and extradition. The situation was complicated by the possibility that former Nazis who had acquired Canadian citizenship might be protected from deportation by the new Charter of Rights.

One major case involved Albert Helmut Rauca, a naturalized Canadian citizen wanted in West Germany for the murder of over 11,000 Jews in Lithuania. After an Ontario court issued an extradition order in 1982, Rauca filed an appeal to the highest Ontario court in 1983. The CJC was allowed to intervene in the appeal, to present legal arguments concerning Rauca's constitutional rights. The government, which had initiated the proceedings against Rauca, maintained that extradition was a reasonable limitation on a citizen's right to remain in Canada. The appeals court did eventually uphold the government's position, and Rauca was extradited to West Germany to stand trial. He died of natural causes, while in a German jail, before his case was heard.

The CJC continued to press for action against other accused war criminals, with President Milton Harris arguing for revocation of citizenship and deportation.

Despite strong pressure, however, the government seemed slow to act, and by the end of 1984 no additional legal proceeding had been undertaken.

An equally troubling issue was the propagation of Nazi-like ideas in Canada, with attention focused on Ernest Zundel in Toronto and James Keegstra in Eckville, Alberta. Zundel, a German citizen living in Canada as a landed immigrant, published antisemitic and Holocaust-denial literature for distribution in Canada and abroad. A first measure taken against him, at the request of the West German government, was a ban on mailing privileges, but it was subsequently rescinded.

Efforts to stop Zundel came to a head when Sabina Citron of Toronto, a survivor and founder of the Canadian Holocaust Remembrance Association, formally requested that Zundel be charged under Section 177 of the Criminal Code, which defined as a crime the willful publication of a false statement likely to cause injury to a public interest. Various preliminary proceedings were held during 1984, with the judge in the Ontario provincial court setting a trial date for early 1985. Zundel's appetite for publicity threatened to convert the proceedings into a media circus.

The case against James Keegstra, in Alberta, centered on his career as a social-studies teacher in Eckville, a town that he also served as mayor. Keegstra had been dismissed from his teaching job in December 1982, after a parent revealed that antisemitism was central to his teaching and enlisted other parents in a protest. In 1983 Keegstra was defeated for reelection as mayor, because of adverse publicity. In June 1984, after a lengthy investigation, the government charged him with violating Section 281.2 of the Criminal Code by willfully promoting hatred against an identifiable group. During a preliminary hearing, former students testified that Keegstra had taught that Jews caused both world wars, the French and Russian revolutions, the U.S. Civil War, and the Great Depression; Keegstra also questioned the reality of the Holocaust. Defense attorney Douglas Christie—who took over the Zundel defense as well—invoked the principle of freedom of speech in his client's behalf, but to no avail. The judge committed Keegstra to trial, which was to take place in 1985. While the prosecution was pursuing the case with determination, widespread concern was expressed over the following: that Keegstra had been allowed to teach his hate message for over a decade; that even after his dismissal some Alberta political figures were reluctant to take a strong stand against him; and that many of his fellow citizens in Eckville expressed support for him as a teacher and seemed insensitive to the larger issues.

In a related matter, a book purporting to demonstrate that the Holocaust was a myth was banned from importation into Canada by the government, largely due to strenuous efforts by the League for Human Rights of B'nai B'rith. The book, *The Hoax of the Twentieth Century,* by Arthur Butz, had been published in the United States by the Institute for Historical Review, an organization actively engaged in denying the reality of the Holocaust.

Community Relations

While the major focus in community relations was on war criminals and anti-semitism, there were other important issues as well. One of these was the question of Sunday closing laws. Most businesses in Canada were required to close on the Christian Sabbath by virtue of the federal Lord's Day Act or similar provincial laws. The implications for Jewish Sabbath observers were such that Jewish organizations actively sought changes in the laws—either abolition or guaranteed exceptions for those who observed the Sabbath on a day other than Sunday. Particular concern developed in Quebec, where the provincial government amended its law to increase penalties for violation but failed to include an exception for Saturday Sabbath observers. Both the League for Human Rights and the CJC vigorously lobbied with the authorities on the issue, but to no avail. A concession to small businesses that close from Friday sundown to Saturday sundown was put into the Quebec regulations, but the law itself remained unchanged. There was dismay in the Jewish community when the CJC was asked by the provincial government to certify the religious bona fides of applicants for the exemption.

In September 1984 the federal Lord's Day Act was declared unconstitutional by the Ontario Court of Appeal. The decision, which was based on concepts of freedom of religion and multiculturalism in the new Charter of Rights and Freedoms, was subject to a future definitive judgment in the Supreme Court of Canada.

Jews in Montreal continued to face problems arising from the Quebec government's increasing intervention in matters traditionally outside its purview. One key issue was language, which had come under government regulation through passage of Quebec's drastic language law in 1977. Particularly nettlesome to the Jewish community were restrictions on access to English-language education, such that people moving into the province were required to send their children to French schools. Since the law had discouraged English-speaking people from settling in Quebec, it had been a major factor affecting the decline of Montreal's Jewish population after 1976. Without such restrictions, community leaders maintained, Jews from other parts of Canada, from the United States, and from other parts of the English-speaking world would be more likely to move to Montreal. In 1984 a long-awaited Supreme Court decision confirmed the supremacy of the federal constitution over the Quebec law, thereby guaranteeing English education to children of Canadian citizens from any part of the country. Immigrants, however, including English-speaking ones, were still required to attend French schools. For the Jewish community, the law's existence meant continued difficulty in recruiting newcomers, especially professional personnel needed to serve the Jewish community.

In a more subtle maneuver, a Quebec government agency sponsored public lectures designed to make the case to Jews that its so-called Francization policy (forcing more extensive use of French at the expense of English in the business world and public life) was roughly analogous to the process by which Hebrew had become the dominant language in Israel. Generally the arguments were greeted with skepticism, not least because the compulsion of state power was a crucial feature of language policy in Quebec.

Another troubling matter was the Quebec government's effort to reorganize the delivery of social services in the province under centralized direction. Jewish Family Services, a federation agency, fought the plan because it would make it more difficult to maintain a specific Jewish focus in programming.

A positive effect of government intervention was the granting of over $500,000 to various Jewish groups over a three-year period. Nearly half the funds were used to help construct three community centers to serve the growing Sephardic community.

In May 1984 Rabbi Meir Kahane was denied permission to enter Canada to make a speech to a Jewish Defense League meeting in Toronto. The decision, which was defended by two cabinet ministers, was based on his criminal record in the United States, charges then pending against him in Israel, and his association with acts of violence. Supporters of Kahane charged the government with adherence to a double standard, whereby Palestine Liberation Organization officials were permitted entry but Kahane was barred. While not denying the charge, the government spokesman noted that Reverend Hilarion Capucci, a PLO supporter who had been convicted in Israel on gun-running charges, had been barred from Canada early in the year.

When Pope John Paul II visited Canada in 1984, arrangements were made for representatives of the Jewish community to meet briefly with him, in Montreal, for a discussion of topics of mutual concern.

Zionism and Israel

The fact that Canada's foreign policy over the years had been generally supportive of Israel was a matter of pride and satisfaction to Canadian Jews. Thus, they found it troubling when support for the Palestinian cause began to be openly expressed in Canadian public life. Early in 1983 two MPs attended a PLO National Council meeting in Algiers and had their picture taken with Yasir Arafat. A year later, seven MPs traveled to Jordan to meet with Arafat and hear his plea that Canada recognize the PLO. Both major party leaders disassociated themselves from the latter action.

On broader policy questions, the Canada-Israel Committee (CIC)—the Jewish community's voice on Middle East issues—was critical of Canadian government positions on a possible Palestinian homeland, Israeli settlements in the territories, and the long-term status of Jerusalem. While the government was praised for maintaining a policy of nonrecognition of the PLO, it was also found wanting. It seemed willing to condemn Israeli actions without a full understanding of their context, and Canada's UN voting policy was ambiguous and inconsistent. In addition, there was a growing perception that Israel was not getting fair treatment in the Canadian media.

Canadian attitudes toward the Middle East may well have been affected by endorsements of Palestinian rights put forward by the Parti Québécois and the

Ontario Federation of Labor. In August 1983 a major meeting of the World Council of Churches in Vancouver passed a resolution blaming Israel for a host of ills and strongly backing the Palestinian cause. As for the campus scene, there were anti-Israel polemics in student newspapers, attacks on Jewish student organizations, and other such incidents at the universities of Calgary, Waterloo, Ottawa, and McMaster.

On the positive side, a public-opinion poll commissioned by the League for Human Rights showed more support for Israel than for the Arabs among Canadians, although most people questioned had no opinion on the matter or did not know enough about it to respond. The degree of support for Israel was markedly higher among Anglophones than among Francophones. Subsequent to the appearance of the poll, a French newspaper columnist and commentator on public affairs, Pierre Bourgault, returned from a trip to Israel with a very positive report that was widely circulated.

The CIC maintained an ongoing program to influence Canadian foreign policy in a manner favorable to Israel. The centerpiece of this effort was an annual dinner for parliamentarians and members of the community at which party leaders were given an opportunity to explain their policy stands on the Middle East. In 1983 the question of support for the PLO was a major topic. Jake Epp, representing the then-opposition Progressive Conservatives, noted that supporters of the PLO position were now found in each of the three national parties, a development that gave the PLO a certain "aura of legitimacy" in Ottawa. External Affairs Minister Allan MacEachen spoke frankly about Canada's contacts with the PLO but reaffirmed the government's position of not recognizing the group. A representative of the New Democratic party sought to deal with the accusation that his party had moved close to the PLO position.

A general look at Canadian foreign policy in the Middle East was undertaken by a committee of the Senate, a rather weak body within the Canadian parliamentary system. Controversy erupted when the senators invited Zehdi Terzi, the PLO representative at the United Nations, to testify. The committee's report was expected in 1985.

The PLO issue created a controversy in Montreal when it was revealed that the main Quebec teachers' union was attempting to distribute pro-PLO propaganda in the public schools. The union leader, Yvon Charbonneau, was known to be a virulent anti-Zionist, with close ties to Libya. In June 1983 a demonstration against him was organized, at about the same time that anti-Zionist elements staged a protest against the visit of Ariel Sharon to Montreal to speak at a fund-raising dinner. The situation was decidedly tense during that period.

The Canadian Zionist Federation (CZF) elected new leadership in 1984. Prior to its convention in Montreal a deal was worked out between two of the candidates for the presidency, Neri Bloomfield and David Azrieli, both of Montreal, to share the office, with Bloomfield to serve for three years and Azrieli to become president in 1987. The third candidate in the race, Rabbi Michael Stroh of Toronto, representing Kadimah, the Reform Zionist organization, protested vigorously against the arrangement, which was nonetheless approved by the delegates to the CZF convention. Major issues discussed at the convention included relations between Zionists and fund-raisers and religious pluralism in Israel.

Economic relations between Canada and Israel benefited from changes in Canadian banking laws, with several prominent Israeli banks establishing Canadian subsidiaries.

Eliashiv Ben-Horin assumed the post of Israel's ambassador to Canada in 1984.

Soviet and Ethiopian Jews

Canadian Jews were active in various ways in behalf of oppressed Jews, especially those in the Soviet Union and Ethiopia. There was particular interest in the case of Anatoly Shcharansky, whose attorney was McGill University law professor Irwin Cotler. Shcharansky's 35th birthday in 1983 was observed as a day of protest; his wife, Avital, visited Canada shortly thereafter to press her husband's cause.

Several dozen Canadians attended the third International Conference on Soviet Jewry in Jerusalem in 1983. The delegation included members of Parliament from all three parties as well as representatives of the parliamentary spouses' group. Further evidence of the interest of MPs in the plight of Soviet Jewry was the trip of three members, representing the three parties, to the Soviet Union in 1984. Accompanied by Alan Rose, executive vice-president of the CJC, and Barbara Stern, head of a key activist group, the MPs met with numerous refuseniks to learn firsthand about their problems.

The plight of Ethiopian Jews was a matter of deep concern to the Jews of Canada. The Canadian Association for Ethiopian Jews sent its president, Barry Weinrib, of Toronto, to Ethiopia, to check on the situation and deliver medical supplies. Later in 1984, two community leaders joined an American fact-finding mission, which concluded that while the situation was grim, Jews were not necessarily worse off than other Ethiopians. These leaders even speculated that relief earmarked for Jews might produce a backlash that could create serious problems. The observation reflected tension between mainline community organizations and the Canadian Association for Ethiopian Jews, which had criticized the Jewish establishment and Israel for allegedly committing insufficient resources to aid Ethiopian Jews. Despite differing views, as the dimensions of the evacuation effort known as Operation Moses became public, Canadian Jews responded enthusiastically to requests for funds.

Holocaust Observances

Canadian Jews continued to stress the importance of commemorating the Holocaust. The 1983 observances in Montreal featured an address by Nazi-hunter Beate

Klarsfeld. In addition, the Holocaust Memorial Center of the Jewish public library in Montreal sponsored a major exhibit devoted to Jewish resistance. The 1984 exhibit was devoted to the story of the Lodz ghetto.

In Toronto, a Holocaust memorial museum was under construction as part of the new community complex. One key exhibit would be an audiovisual display called Gates of Hope, funded in part by a grant from the Canadian government.

In 1984 the Canadian Broadcasting Corporation telecast an original drama, "Charlie Grant's War," based on the true story of a non-Jewish Canadian who was in Vienna during the period leading up to World War II. Grant arranged to obtain papers and exit visas for Jews trapped in Austria and was reputed to have saved some 600 individuals by his efforts. Eventually he was arrested and interned in a labor camp.

Religion

The 1983–1984 period saw a marked increase in tension between the three main religious groupings. This could be attributed to a variety of causes, including the Reform decision on patrilineal descent and the Conservative move toward religious equality for women, especially the granting of rabbinical ordination.

The role of women in Judaism became an issue in a Toronto court case when an Orthodox synagogue was sued for establishing an egalitarian *minyan* downstairs as a monthly supplement to its regular Sabbath service upstairs. Several members of the congregation challenged this on the grounds that the *minyan* contravened the Orthodox character of the synagogue. The court ruled against them.

At the Reform Holy Blossom Temple in Toronto, one of the leading congregations in the country, Rabbi Dov Marmur became senior rabbi, while Rabbi Elyse Goldstein accepted an appointment as assistant rabbi. In Winnipeg, Rabbi Tracy Guren Klirs became the first woman to occupy the main rabbinical post at a Canadian congregation when she was appointed to lead Temple Shalom.

For many Jews in Toronto and Montreal the visit of Israeli Sephardic chief rabbi Mordechai Eliyahu in December 1984 was an inspiring occasion. In addition to events within the Jewish community—including visits to day schools and the official opening of the Centre Sepharade Rabbinique Maghen David in Montreal, a community center—Rabbi Eliyahu met with political leaders in Quebec and Ontario. In a meeting with Premier Davis of Ontario, Rabbi Eliyahu stressed the importance of Jewish education, a message of particular relevance in a province where the issue of government financial aid to Jewish day schools remained unresolved.

Jewish Culture

While Jewish culture in Canada functioned on a small scale, it was actively pursued. Writing, both in Yiddish and English, was a traditional area of strength.

Two books by Montreal writers, Yehuda Elberg and Chava Rosenfarb, were included in a collection of Yiddish works distributed to subscribers by the World Council for Yiddish. Elberg received the Prime Minister of Israel's award for literature in 1984, in recognition of his many literary accomplishments. His novel *The Empire of Kalman the Cripple* was awarded the Fernando Jeno Prize for fiction by the Jewish community of Mexico.

In Montreal the Jewish public library opened an archive for material pertaining to people who were active in culture and the arts. The family of Rachel Korn, a noted writer and poet, donated her personal papers to the archive, which also contained material from 18 other collections.

In 1984 the city library of Lachine, Quebec, was officially named the "Bibliothèque Municipale Saul Bellow," in honor of the Nobel Laureate, who was born in the Montreal suburb and lived there and in Montreal for nine years before his family moved to Chicago. In addition to the official ceremony at the library, there were other festive events, including a literary brunch attended by well-known Canadian writers and a street fair where Bellow autographed books.

Former Montrealer David Roskies, now a professor at the Jewish Theological Seminary in New York, returned to his hometown to lecture on Jewish artistic and literary reactions to Jewish suffering, primarily in Europe. Montreal photographer Edward Hillel exhibited his photographs at a show entitled "The Main—A Portrait of Life Around St. Lawrence Blvd.," the area where Jewish immigrants traditionally settled. Cable television in Montreal presented a three-month series on the Jewish heritage early in 1983. The series was produced by Stanley Asher, using films obtained from the CJC.

Publications

Viewpoints, a periodical dealing with Jewish literary, religious, cultural, and political matters, adopted a new format early in 1983 and began distribution as a supplement to the *Canadian Jewish News*; it was edited by William Abrams. A new Montreal monthly publication was *Tribune juive,* edited by Ghila Benesty-Sroka, which planned to cover Israel, community events, and cultural matters. *Jonathan* was the more established French-language Jewish journal, edited for the Quebec-Israel Committee by Victor Teboul; its purpose was to portray Quebec Jewry and Israel in realistic terms to the Quebec intelligentsia. In Winnipeg, the venerable *Jewish Post* was purchased by its editor, Matt Bellan, his brother, Bernie Bellan, and advertising manager Gail Frankel.

Publication of material of Jewish interest in Canada was considerably aided by the emergence of Lester & Orpen Dennys as a successful publishing house. One of its best-known efforts was *None Is Too Many,* by Harold Troper and Irving Abella, which documented Canada's exclusion of Jewish refugees during the Nazi period. The book, which had a major impact in Canada, won a National Jewish Book Award in the United States in 1983.

Vengeance, by George Jonas of Toronto, was a controversial book claiming to be the personal account of the leader of an Israeli hit team that set out to avenge the Munich massacre of 1972. While some critics disputed the veracity of the story, Jonas insisted that it was authentic.

David Bercuson, a history professor at the University of Calgary, published *The Secret Army,* an account of the volunteers from abroad who joined the Israeli military effort during the War of Independence. A revealing work was *The Strangest Dream: Canadian Communists, the Spy Trials, and the Cold War,* by Merrily Weisbord. Canadian Communists were by no means all Jews, but a number were involved, most notably former MP Fred Rose, who died recently in Poland, where he had settled after his release from prison. Weisbord raised questions about due process in connection with Rose's trial. She also discussed the impact of Khrushchev's revelations about Stalin on Jewish Communists in Canada.

An unusual Holocaust-related book was *The Visitors,* written by Suzanne Filiatrault, a non-Jew who taught French for a time in a Montreal Jewish day school, became intrigued by the Holocaust, and spent several years carrying out research on the subject. Her book is an account of a trip made to Germany and Poland with a Jewish friend, a survivor, and their visits to extermination camps. Published in French and English, the book was written to make non-Jews, especially French Canadians, more aware of the horrors of the Holocaust.

A moving memoir of Budapest Jewry during the Holocaust is *Broken Silence,* by Andre Stein, a Hungarian Jew who settled in Toronto after the war.

The Institut Québécois de Recherche sur la Culture, a body supported by the provincial government, published its second volume on the Jews of Quebec—*Juifs et réalités juives au Québec,* edited by Pierre Anctil and Gary Caldwell, a collection of essays examining various aspects of the Jewish community from a social-science perspective. *Montreal Judaica,* by Ghila Benesty-Sroka, published by the B'nai B'rith Hillel Foundation, was designed as a practical guide to Jewish living in Montreal.

Rabbi Stuart Rosenberg's *The Real Jewish World: A Rabbi's Second Thoughts* is a combination of autobiography and analysis of contemporary trends in Judaism. Rosenberg's long career at Toronto's largest synagogue, Beth Tzedec, ended acrimoniously.

Victor Teboul, director of the Quebec-Israel Committee, published *The Emergence of Liberalism in Modern Quebec.*

Leonard Cohen, the poet and singer, produced an unusual volume, *His Book of Mercy,* a type of literary prayer book using decidedly Jewish motifs.

Seymour Mayne, a younger Canadian Jewish writer with a number of poetry collections to his credit, spent 1983–1984 on sabbatical in Israel, where he published *Vanguard of Dreams,* a volume of poetry in Hebrew translation.

Among other recently published books by Canadian Jewish writers were *The Spanish Doctor,* by Matt Cohen of Toronto; *The Mikveh Man,* by Sharon Drache of Ottawa; and *Stefanesti: Portrait of a Romanian Shtetl,* by Ghitta Sternberg of

Montreal. Nomi Berger of Montreal published a paperback novel, *Devotions,* in the United States.

Dan Nimrod, of the Montreal suburb of Dollard des Ormeaux, operated a publishing house, Dawn Books, that was a source of many books and pamphlets on various issues relating to the Arab-Israeli conflict. In 1983 he published a book by a former Montrealer now living in Israel, Mordechai Nisan, entitled *American Middle East Foreign Policy.* Nimrod himself wrote a polemic against those whom he perceived as advocates of dangerous policies, *Peace Now: Blueprint for National Suicide.*

Personalia

Robert Kaplan of Toronto, Herb Gray of Windsor, and Sen. Jack Austin of Vancouver lost their federal cabinet positions when the Liberals went down to defeat in the 1984 election. In the new Progressive Conservative government, Gerry Weiner of Dollard des Ormeaux, Quebec, was appointed a parliamentary secretary. Stephen Lewis, former leader of the Ontario New Democratic party, became ambassador to the United Nations. Earlier, Leo Kolber of Montreal and Jerry Grafstein of Toronto were appointed to the Senate.

Mickey Cohen was named deputy minister of finance, but resigned after serving only about two years. Gerald Caplan was appointed national secretary of the NDP.

In the judiciary, Alan Gold was named chief justice of the Superior Court of Quebec, the first Jew to hold that position. Harold Lande and Irving Halperin were appointed judges of the same court, while Sam Filer was appointed to a judgeship on the Ontario county court.

The nation's highest honor, the Order of Canada, was bestowed upon Naim Kattan, Jacob Lowy, Victor Goldbloom, Naomi Bronstein, Albert Cohen, and Sheila Kussner.

A number of members of the community attained positions of note. Haviva Hosek became chairman of the National Advisory Council on the Status of Women. Jeff Rose was elected president of the Canadian Union of Public Employees. Moshe Safdie, the noted architect, was commissioned to design the National Gallery of Canada building in Ottawa. David Bloom became president of Shoppers Drug Mart; Daniel Oberlander assumed the same position with CN Hotels. Justice Allen Linden of the Ontario High Court of Justice took a seven-year leave of absence to head the Law Reform Commission of Canada. Phil Gold was appointed physician-in-chief of the Montreal General Hospital. Steven Applebaum became dean of Commerce and Administration at Montreal's Concordia University. Eric Maldoff, a young Montreal lawyer, headed Alliance Québec, the English rights group. Rabbi W. Gunther Plaut, rabbi emeritus of the Holy Blossom Temple in Toronto and former president of the CJC, was asked by the federal government to recommend policy changes with regard to handling applications for refugee status. Rabbi Plaut was also elected president of the Central Conference of American Rabbis.

In the Jewish community, the following individuals assumed new posts: Charles Bronfman as chairman and Morton Brownstein, followed by Allan Offman, as presidents of the United Israel Appeal of Canada; Morley Wolfe as president of B'nai B'rith; Steven Ain as executive director of the Toronto Jewish Congress; Shira Herzog Bessin as associate director of the CIC; Ted Greenfield as chairman of the Quebec-Israel Committee; Cecily Peters as president of Hadassah-WIZO; John Fishel as director of planning and then executive director of Allied Jewish Community Services in Montreal; Thomas Hecht as president of Israel Bonds; Manuel Prutschi as national director of community relations for the CJC, succeeding Ben Kayfetz, whose distinguished service spanned many years. Jim Archibald served for a time as executive director of the CJC but later resigned.

At the Maccabi Pan Am Games held in São Paulo, Brazil, Daniel Fedder won six gold medals and one silver, as a gymnast, while Gordon Orlikow won four gold and two silver medals in track and field. A former Olympic athlete, Abigail Hoffman, became director of Sport Canada. Jeremy Fraiberg of Montreal won the Canadian junior squash championship.

Irving Layton, the noted author, moved back to Montreal after an absence of 14 years.

Simcha Jacobovici, a young filmmaker, produced a documentary on the Jews of Ethiopia, which was televised nationally on the CBC network.

Among those who died in 1983–1984 were the following: Bora Laskin, chief justice of the Supreme Court of Canada, eminent legal scholar, and champion of human rights, aged 71; Rabbi Harry J. Stern, a leading Reform rabbi in Montreal noted for his interfaith activities, aged 87; Louis Bloomfield, international lawyer and philanthropist, aged 78; Bernard Bloomfield, business executive and philanthropist, aged 80; Nathan Steinberg, one of the Steinberg brothers who built their mother's Montreal grocery store into a major supermarket chain, aged 76; Hyman Pascal, former president of J. Pascal Inc., a large hardware and furniture chain, aged 80; Sam Maislin, founder of Maislin Transport, Ltd., one of the largest North American carriers, aged 64; Sam Shopsowitz, proprietor of the famous Shopsy's delicatessen in Toronto and benefactor of charitable causes, aged 63; Judge Harry Batshaw, the first Canadian Jew to be appointed to the Quebec Superior Court and a leader of the Canadian Friends of Alliance Israélite Universelle, aged 81; Jack Posluns, leading apparel manufacturer, aged 54; Cecil Solin, emeritus professor of mathematics and former dean of students at McGill University, aged 67; Fred Rose, a former Communist MP, later convicted of spying, aged 76; Norman Caplan, lawyer and agent for athletes and celebrities, aged 40; Daniel Mettarlin, legal scholar, aged 46; Rabbi David Klein, noted linguist and a member of the Order of Canada, aged 83; Rabbi Albert Pappenheim, former president of the Toronto Board of Rabbis, aged 62; James Senor, Jewish civil servant who headed the Toronto Israel Bonds office and was executive vice-president of the Canadian Society for the Weizmann Institute of Science, aged 62; Alexander Brown, Toronto educator, who served the board of Jewish education and the Jewish Teachers' Seminary, aged 75;

Max Wershof, one of Canada's first Jewish ambassadors, who headed embassies in Denmark and Czechoslovakia, aged 74; Stephen Barber, former executive director of the Canada-Israel Chamber of Commerce and founding president of Reconstructionist Congregation Dorshei Emet in Montreal, aged 72; and Toronto composer and teacher Samuel Levitan, aged 64.

HAROLD M. WALLER

Western Europe

Great Britain

National Affairs

Dominating all else on the British national scene in 1984 was the strike by the National Union of Mineworkers (NUM), begun in March, over the right of the National Coal Board to close uneconomic pits. Despite the refusal of the Nottinghamshire miners—approximately 20 percent of the industry's work force—to join the strike, and a lack of support from other labor sectors and the general public, the strike was still in force at year's end.

While the strike had only minor repercussions economically, politically it proved a serious embarrassment to the Labor party, particularly to Labor leader Neil Kinnock. His failure to take a clear position weakened his standing with all sides. Conversely, Prime Minister Margaret Thatcher's determination to stand up to the most powerful union in Great Britain won widespread support.

The Irish Republican Army's campaign of violence found new targets during the year. A bomb exploded in October in the Grand Hotel, Brighton, where ministerial delegates to the Conservative conference were staying, including the prime minister and her husband. Five senior Conservative party members were killed and many more were seriously injured.

A government White Paper published in February sought to deter extremist candidates from running in future parliamentary elections by raising the deposit for candidature from £150 to £1,000. The measure's effectiveness was weakened, however, by its lowering of the percentage of votes required to qualify from 12½ to 5.

Activities of the extreme right-wing National Front (NF) included a march and rally in Stoke-on-Trent, in April, prior to local elections, and a march and rally in Brighton, in September, protesting kosher slaughter. Permission to hold demonstrations in Birmingham and Salford was refused by local authorities. Demonstrations at North London Polytechnic, by left-wing students against NF student organizer Patrick Harrington, resulted in legal action against the pickets themselves. In November Harrington was elected to the NF's directorate.

In October Jacob Gewirtz, executive director of the defense and group relations committee of the Board of Deputies of British Jews, reported that while antisemitic incidents had increased since 1979, most did not involve violence, nor were they on the scale of racist attacks directed against the Asian community. Five Jews had been assaulted, two seriously, in antisemitic attacks in the previous four months, board figures showed.

An average of 20–25 antisemitic incidents a month had been fomented by extreme right-wing groups during the previous two years, according to "Racial Harassment in London," a report published in May by the Greater London Council's (GLC) police committee. The report was the work of a panel of inquiry that had been set up in August 1982.

In January a fire attributed to arson destroyed Auschwitz relics that were on exhibit in Birmingham. In the same month, fire damaged a North London office building owned by the Central Council for Jewish Social Services. In May arson was thought to be responsible for damage to the North Manchester Synagogue. A fire that totally destroyed West Ham and Upton Park Synagogue, however, was attributed to an electrical fault.

Relations with Israel

A certain amount of strain was evident throughout the year, arising from the government's efforts to maintain good relations with both Israel and the Arabs. In January Foreign Secretary Geoffrey Howe, visiting in Saudi Arabia, criticized Israel's West Bank policy. His remarks, which coincided with reports of projected British arms sales to Middle East countries, were criticized by the Board of Deputies and the Conservative Friends of Israel (CFI), as well as by Yehuda Avner, the Israeli ambassador in London. In response, Howe claimed that his comments reflected the same "balanced" approach adopted by the government in the June 1980 Venice declaration of the European Economic Community (EEC). He went on to urge the Palestinians to give unequivocal recognition to Israel's right to a secure existence.

Tension was created by Queen Elizabeth's visit to Amman in March, during which she praised King Hussein's "efforts to obtain a negotiated settlement" in the Middle East and made other remarks judged favorable to the Arabs. A visit to Great Britain by Israeli president Chaim Herzog later the same month, during which he met with the queen and other prominent personalities, helped to clear the atmosphere. In June the government welcomed Israel's assurance that it did not intend to retain territory in Lebanon, but took the opportunity to repeat its earlier condemnation of the 1982 invasion. In July Foreign Office official Richard Luce said that "a clear statement by the PLO of Israel's right to exist within secure boundaries, and a clear renunciation of terrorism" would help the peace process.

In October Foreign Secretary Howe, on a visit to Israel, reiterated his government's "unwavering support for Israel's rights and security," while at the same time stating that "the basic insight of EEC's Venice declaration remained as relevant as ever." Howe regarded Prime Minister Shimon Peres's offer to negotiate with Jordan as a step in the right direction, but asked Israel for more concrete demonstrations of goodwill, including a freeze on new West Bank settlements and an easing of restrictions on West Bank Palestinians. On the subject of the Palestinian right to self-determination, Howe said that while it was not for others to tell the Palestinians whom to choose to represent them, these representatives "would have to commit themselves to finding a solution not by violence, but by peaceful means."

In October Defense Secretary Michael Heseltine visited Jordan and Egypt for talks about the sale of British defense equipment and—with Egypt—about possible collaboration in military production.

In July Prime Minister Thatcher accepted the presidency of CFI's North London Area Council, evoking sharp protest from the Council for the Advancement of Arab-British Understanding. In October CFI director Michael Fidler reported that his group was the largest special-interest group in Parliament, with 155 MPs, including eight cabinet ministers, and a total of 222 parliamentarians, including peers and members of the European Parliament. A planned mission to Israel in November, under CFI auspices, had to be canceled when over half the scheduled participants became victims of the Brighton bombing. In December a chair in chemistry at the Weizmann Institute was endowed in Prime Minister Thatcher's name.

The British labor movement continued to be divided about the issue of the Israel-Arab conflict. In April the Association of Cinematograph, Television, and Allied Technicians approved a resolution condemning Israel. In August Trade Union Friends of Palestine invited Rev. Jesse Jackson to participate in a London seminar organized in conjunction with the Palestine Trade Union Federation and the PLO. By contrast, in September nearly two hundred trade-union leaders attended a Trade Union Friends of Israel (TUFI) meeting at which strong support for the Histadrut, Israel's labor federation, was expressed. By October six major unions were affiliated with TUFI.

Controversy surrounded the Labor-led Greater London Council (GLC). On the one hand, the council provided funds to several Jewish groups, including Agudath Israel, the Jewish Association for the Physically Handicapped, the Jewish Social Responsibility Council, the Lubavitch Foundation, and the Jewish Museum. In addition, it aided the Jewish Socialists Group in launching its Jewish Cultural and Anti-Racist Project. In September the GLC reported that it was financing a £15,000 survey into the needs of London's Hackney Orthodox community. On the other hand, GLC members continually angered the Jewish community with allegedly anti-Zionist remarks, and GLC leader Ken Livingstone—"Red Ken"—persisted in making a distinction between "anti-Zionism" and "antisemitism." The GLC's funding of a Palestine Solidarity Campaign conference on the theme of anti-Arab racism, in October, brought the controversy to a head. The Board of Deputies asked GLC's auditor to examine what it described as a "misuse" of GLC money, which, it claimed, was being used to foment prejudice against London's Jewish community. In December the board protested the use of GLC's County Hall for a miners' rally that featured a PLO representative.

JEWISH COMMUNITY

Demography

The Jewish population of Great Britain was estimated to be 350,000. Leading Jewish population centers were London, Manchester, Leeds, and Glasgow.

According to the annual report of the Board of Deputies' research unit, 1,180 synagogue marriages took place in 1983, up slightly from the 1,110 recorded in 1982. Of the total, 772 were under modern-Orthodox auspices; 188 were Reform, 104 were traditionalist-Orthodox, 71 were Liberal, and 45 were Sephardi. A slight increase over the previous two years in the number of people married in London suggested that the movement of young people to the London area and the Home Counties was continuing. The number of burials and cremations under Jewish religious auspices (4,715) was about the same as in 1982 (4,846).

Some 400 Jewish couples divorced in 1983, according to "Children and Family Break-Up in Anglo-Jewry," published in September by the West Central Counseling and Communal Research Organization, in conjunction with the Anglo-Jewish Divorce and Conciliation Project.

Communal Activities

"The Anglo-Jewish Research Report," issued in December, concluded that communal fund-raising priorities needed immediate adjustment in favor of domestic concerns. The report, which had been commissioned by seven leading communal figures, showed that domestic needs accounted for only 40 percent of the £40 million raised annually, while the remainder went to Israel. The major problem areas, according to Melvyn Carlowe, Jewish Welfare Board (JWB) executive director, were the increasingly aged community (by the year 2000, Carlowe estimated, one in five British Jews would be over 65) and the heavy dependence on government aid, with no alternative provision if it ceased. Of the £20 million currently spent each year on social services to Jews, £13.1 million came in the form of direct government grants, subsidized rents, and statutory payments, while the Jewish community provided the balance of £6.6 million. Following up on the fund-raising report, Carlowe announced in June that the four leading social-service agencies, backed by the Central Council for Jewish Social Service, would cooperate in researching community needs, establishing priorities, and developing machinery for the delivery of services.

As of July, communal housing-association waiting lists contained over 500 names. Westlon opened its second project in July—Deborah Rayne House in Hendon, North London—and began work on a third, in Ealing, West London, to accommodate 34 elderly Jews. In August representatives of seven Orthodox, Reform, and Liberal synagogues in the South-West London region formed a housing society to plan sheltered accommodation for the elderly. In December the Industrial

Dwellings Society opened a building of sheltered flatlets in Grants Hill, Essex, its first project.

The Jewish Blind Society (JBS), which announced plans in April to expand services in the provinces, later in the year joined with the Manchester JBS in sponsoring a £250,000-appeal for a new day center in that city for the visually handicapped and elderly. In the course of the year, with a budget of almost £2 million, JBS assisted some 2,000 people.

Ravenswood entered the field of community care for the mentally handicapped, adopting a program, in conjunction with the Jewish Society for the Mentally Handicapped, to open sheltered hostels for young adults in areas with large Jewish populations. Haven Foundation announced the imminent opening of its own second group home for mentally handicapped individuals.

The Jewish Marriage Council (JMC) moved to new North London premises in November, primarily in order to accommodate its growing marriage-counseling service.

Soviet Jewry

Major efforts were directed toward obtaining the release of prisoner of conscience Anatoly Shcharansky. In February a group of 41 leading British doctors signed a letter to Soviet party chief Yuri Andropov expressing concern over Shcharansky's failing health. Also in February children at Ilford Jewish Primary School celebrated Shcharansky's birthday. In March a group of 87 MPs from all parties wrote to Soviet ambassador Viktor Popov asking for a meeting to discuss Shcharansky's case. In July two seats at the Manchester Jewish Museum, which had opened in March, were dedicated in the names of Avital and Anatoly Shcharansky. In October Prime Minister Thatcher, in a statement expressing concern for the difficulties facing the Jewish community in the Soviet Union, reminded Russian leaders of their obligations under the Helsinki accords. In July Foreign Secretary Howe, visiting Moscow, made particular mention of Shcharansky as exemplifying Soviet Jewry's plight.

Members of all parties assisted the campaign on behalf of Soviet Jews. In January Liberal leader David Steel agreed to raise the issue of Soviet Jewry in general, and Shcharansky in particular, when visiting the Soviet Union as a guest of the parliamentary group of the Supreme Soviet. In February a plea on behalf of refusenik Yosif Begun was sent to Ambassador Popov by 27 members of the GLC, including leader Ken Livingstone. In April several MPs met refusenik leaders in Moscow, the first time a group of MPs had been granted visas to enter Russia for such a purpose. In December Labor leader Neil Kinnock undertook to raise the question of human rights with Soviet leader Gorbachev, who was visiting London.

At the first meeting of the Inter-Parliamentary Conference on Soviet Jewry, held in London in June, a group of 75 parliamentarians from 15 European countries agreed to step up their campaign in support of rights for Soviet Jews.

Religion

Recommendations for upgrading the status of rabbis, approved by the honorary officers of the United Synagogue (US) and by the Council of Ministers, were placed before the US council for consideration. The proposals called for higher salaries, greater participation by rabbis in communal affairs, a regular review of placements, and the awarding of tenure within the US after the first review.

In November newly elected US president Victor Lucas articulated what he saw as the major tasks facing the organization: improving communications between the various US communal bodies; developing a first-class Jewish civil service with competitive salary scales and working conditions; and promoting greater public awareness of the role played by the US in the community. He also called for measures to meet the needs of the large numbers of families who had moved to outlying London areas, such as Borehamwood, Bushey, Belmont, Chigwell, and Newbury Park.

One of London's oldest synagogues, the Bayswater and Maida Vale, closed in December. At the same time, the US council approved a grant for a new synagogue at Borehamwood and Elstree and agreed to purchase property for the future development of the Pinner Synagogue.

The executive director of the chief rabbi's office, Moshe Davis, resigned in May, after 11 years in his post, for reasons of ill health. In August Rabbi Maurice Unterman became special adviser to the chief rabbi's office, assigned to liaison with the US president and honorary officers. Dayan Chanoch Ehrentreu was appointed head of the London Beth Din.

In December Chief Rabbi Immanuel Jakobovits urged rabbis not to sanction activities which could be construed as according legitimacy to "nontraditional" Judaism. He also advised the US council that the Board of Deputies, as the representative body of Anglo-Jewry, should not be permitted to serve as a vehicle for the expression of minority views that violated the *halakhic* norms of the majority, as defined by the board's ecclesiastical authorities. In December the board increased the power of these ecclesiastical authorities by making their guidelines mandatory.

The new headquarters of the Reform Synagogue of Great Britain (RSGB) and affiliated institutions had its official opening in June, in London's East Finchley, in the presence of Prime Minister Thatcher. The "Sternberg Center for Judaism," named for benefactor Sir Sigmund Sternberg, housed, in addition to the RSGB, the Leo Baeck College, the postgraduate training school for Progressive rabbis; the Akiva School, Britain's first Progressive primary day school; the independent New North London Synagogue; the Michael Goulston Educational Foundation; and the Jewish East End Museum and Research Center. A program to train doctors as *mohelim* had been introduced because of the Initiation Society's reluctance to circumcise children of Progressive converts.

A program for reaching British Jews who were unaffiliated with any religious movement—approximately 20 percent of Anglo-Jewry—was proposed in December by RSGB chairman Maurice Michaels. The movement's 32 synagogues and 5 associate congregations had 38,000–40,000 members, only 15 percent of the total Jewish religious population. Michaels indicated, however, that while Anglo-Jewry as a whole was declining by some 2,000 individuals a year, the Reform movement was growing at an annual rate of 2½ percent.

In April RSGB's largest congregation, located at Edgware, Middlesex, insisted that any association with the Union of Liberal and Progressive Synagogues (ULPS) be made conditional on the ULPS's acceptance of minimum RSGB *halakhic* standards.

Britain's first Conservative synagogue opened in November in Stanmore, Middlesex.

Declining sales of kosher meat were the subject of February meetings of both the London Board for Shechita and the Licensed Retail Kosher Butchers' Association. The number of kosher butcher shops in London, it was reported, had dropped from some 300 in the mid-1950s to the present 50. Kedassia, the Union of Orthodox Hebrew Congregations' *shehitah* body, reported that sales in the six shops it maintained had dropped during the previous six or seven years by 11 percent. In an effort to increase competition among kosher meat retailers and thus benefit consumers, the London Board for Shechita licensed a new wholesaler to operate from an abattoir at Waltham Abbey.

It was announced in December that the Kashrus Commission would move to the same premises as the London Beth Din, of which it would henceforth be a division.

Jewish Education

Of the estimated 55,000 Jewish children of school age in Great Britain, reported the *Jewish Chronicle*, 14,500 were currently attending Jewish nursery, primary, or secondary schools. Some 13,000 children were enrolled in part-time religion classes, while 2,500 were in released-time classes or receiving private instruction. It appeared that around 10,000 young people had stopped their Jewish education with bar or bat mitzvah; 15,000 children received no Jewish education at all.

In September the London Board for Jewish Religious Education reported that nearly half the headmasters in its program of religion classes had been replaced over the preceding two and a half years. The changes had affected such major centers as Stanmore (about 400 pupils), Borehamwood (300), Bushey (over 200), and Essex Regional (over 220).

To help improve teaching standards, intensified training courses were inaugurated by the new Institute of Jewish Education at Jews' College. The institute was run cooperatively by the Board for Jewish Religious Education, the Torah Department of the World Zionist Organization, Jews' College, and the Jewish Educational Development Trust.

Rabbi Jonathan Sacks was appointed principal and Irving Jacobs named dean of Jews' College, which moved to new premises in Hendon, North London, in October.

In addition to preparing students for *semikhah*, the college offered B.A. and B.Ed. courses, part-time courses in Jewish studies, and training programs for teachers and communal leaders.

In November it was announced that the future of London's Hillel House, threatened with closure in 1983, was, for the time being, secure.

Publications

The Harold H. Wingate Prize for a book of broad Jewish interest was awarded to Naomi Shepherd for *Wilfred Israel: German Jewry's Secret Ambassador*.

Ownership of the *Jewish Chronicle* was transferred from private hands to the Kessler Foundation in November. The move was designed to secure the newspaper's future independence and integrity.

Books on Judaism and Jewish history published during the year included *Human Rights in Jewish Law* by Justice Haim Cohn and *Ascend the Mountain: A Guide to the Torah for Teenagers* by Rabbi E. S. Rabinowitz; *The Slaughter of Sacred Cows* by S. J. Goldsmith; *Hebrew Illuminated Manuscripts in the British Isles: Vol. 1, The Spanish and Portuguese Manuscripts* by B. Narkiss; and the *Leo Baeck Institute Year Book*, Vol. 28, published in memory of Robert Weltsch.

Works on contemporary history included *The New Diplomacy* by Abba Eban; *The Jews of Hope: The Plight of Soviet Jewry Today* by Martin Gilbert; *Hasidic Tales of the Holocaust* by Yaffa Eliach; *Britain's Internees in the Second World War* by Miriam Kochan; *The War of the Doomed: Jewish Armed Resistance in Poland, 1942–1944* by Shmuel Krakowski; *Atlas of the Jewish World* by Nicholas de Lange; *To Make Them English* by Cyril P. Hershon, an examination of Liverpool's Jewish school system; and *Birmingham Jewry: More Aspects, 1740–1930*, edited by Zoe Josephs.

Books on Israel and Zionism included *1948 and After: Aspects of Israeli Fiction* by Leon I. Yudkin and *If Only My People . . .* by Chief Rabbi Immanuel Jakobovits.

The category of autobiography and biography included *Begin: A Biography* by Eric Silver; *Josephus* by Tessa Rajak; *Barnett Janner* by Elsie Janner; and two works of Rothschild reminiscences, *Random Variables* by Lord Rothschild and *Milady Vine: The Autobiography of Philippe de Rothschild* by Joan Littlewood. The publication of *Sir Moses Montefiore: A Symposium*, lectures given at the Oxford Center for Post-graduate Hebrew Studies, edited by Vivian D. Lipman, was pegged to the upcoming commemoration of the centennial of Montefiore's death. Two volumes of women's reminiscences were *You'd Prefer Me Not to Mention It* by the Jewish Women's History Group and *Heritage of the Kaiser's Children: An Autobiography* by Ruth Michaelis-Jena.

Works of fiction included *Rose of Jericho* by Rosemary Friedman, a sequel to her *Proofs of Affection*; *A Sense of Place* by Maisie Mosco; *Something Out There* by Nadine Gordimer; *The Border* by Elaine Feinstein; *Peeping Tom* by Howard Jacobson; *The Devil in Texas* by Wolf Mankowitz; and *Dancing Bear* by Chaim Bermant.

Among new poetic works were two collections by Ruth Fainlight, *Fifteen to Infinity* and *Climates; Years at the Ending: Poems, 1892–1982* by Joseph Leftwich; *A Lifelong House* by Lottie Kramer; and *Selected Poems* and *Chapter and Verse* by Laurence Lerner. *The Poetry of Danny Abse,* edited by Joseph Cohen, was a festschrift; *God and the Poets* contained David Daiches' Gifford lectures. Michael Horovits published *Frances Horovits: A Celebration,* in memory of the poet who had died the previous year.

Of great interest was Roman Vishniac's masterly collection of pre-World War II photographs, *A Vanished World.*

Personalia

Argentine-born Cesar Milstein, a Cambridge University molecular biologist, was co-winner of the 1984 Nobel Prize in medicine.

Knighthoods went to David Wolfson for political service; Raymond Hoffenberg, president of the Royal College of Physicians; Geoffrey Finsberg, MP, for political and public service; Arthur Abraham Gold, president of the European Athletics Association, for service to sports; and Eric Sharp, chairman and chief executive of Cable and Wireless.

Among British Jews who died in 1984 were Alfred Woolf, former United Synagogue president, in January, aged 86; Harris Shoerats, Britain's oldest man, in February, aged 111; Leslie Edgar, emeritus rabbi of London's Liberal Jewish Synagogue, in February, aged 78; Solomon Schonfeld, founder of the Jewish secondary-school movement and noted rabbinic scholar, in February, aged 72; Bernard Schlesinger, pediatrician, in February, aged 87; Lewis Olsover, local historian, in February, aged 81; Joseph Asulay, rabbi of Southend and Westcliff, in February, aged 84; Joyce Weiner, distinguished literary agent, in February; Lionel Land, Kashrus Commission secretary for 30 years, in February, aged 67; Marcus M. Kaye, pilot, engineer, judo expert, and sculptor, in March, aged 85; Joel Slutsky, communal leader, in March, aged 87; Lou Simmons, band leader, in March, aged 77; Samuel Weiser, Zionist-Revisionist leader, in March, aged 81; David Mellows, youth organizer and for 23 years secretary of the London Spanish and Portuguese Jewish Congregation, in March, aged 73; Zalman Plitnick, former Liverpool communal rabbi, in March, aged 90; Janus Cohen, Zionist leader, in April, aged 84; Clive Gaventa, communal worker and chairman of British Herut, in April, aged 55; Celina Sokolow, daughter of Nahum Sokolow, in May, aged 97; George Silver, Oxford communal figure, film star, and restaurateur, in June, aged 67; Anna Mayerson, artist, in June, aged 77; Arnold Shaw, Labor politician, in June, aged 74; Maurice Levinson, author, in June, aged 73; Jacob Sonntag, writer and translator, founder-editor of the *Jewish Quarterly,* in July, aged 79; Flora Solomon, communal worker, in July, aged 89; Bernard King, journalist and *Jewish Chronicle* art editor, in July, aged 92; Ralph Yablon, financier and philanthropist, in July, aged 78; Harry Bidney, founder of the antifascist "43 group," in August, aged 62; Aida Foster, theater school director, in August, aged 89; Yakov Maitlis, historian, folklorist, and Yiddishist, in August, aged 84; Solomon Wald, noted physician, in September, aged 85; Louis Saipe, historian, lecturer, and Leeds communal worker, in October, aged 87; Benno Schotz, the queen's Sculptor in Ordinary for Scotland, in October, aged 93; Gabriella Gros-Galliner, glass expert and singer, in October, aged 61; Helen Rosenau, art historian, in November, aged 84; Gerald I. Ronson, industrialist and philanthropist, in November; Louis Rosenhead, emeritus professor of mathematics, Liverpool University, Zionist and communal worker, in November, aged 78; Ivor Montagu, third son of the second Lord Swaythling, in November, aged 80; Peter Brent, author and playwright, in December, aged 53; Leonard Goss, communal worker, in December, aged 59; Nathan Barnett, journalist, in December, aged 90; Oswald M. Stroud, Bradford industrialist and communal benefactor, in December, aged 87.

LIONEL AND MIRIAM KOCHAN

France

National Affairs

IN 1984—THE HALFWAY mark of President François Mitterrand's seven-year term of office—there was a continued decline in the popularity of the Socialist regime, primarily due to dissatisfaction over the economy. It was a year that also saw growing support for the extreme-right National Front movement; further losses for the Communists; a change of prime minister; unrest over a proposed schooling bill; continued racial violence; and a lessening of anti-Israel sentiment.

The loss of support for the Left was evidenced dramatically in the June election of representatives to the European Parliament, in which the Socialists won only 20.8 percent of the vote (down from 37.5 percent in the 1981 legislative elections), and the Communists (who had polled 14 percent in 1981) attracted only 11 percent—their lowest in half a century. The one group that showed a significant gain in strength was the extreme-right National Front movement, which received almost the same percentage as the Communists—this, for a group whose influence had been negligible when Mitterrand came to power in 1981. The National Front's campaign, led by Jean-Marie Le Pen, focused mainly on the problem of immigrant workers, who were blamed for France's economic woes. The National Front advocated the expulsion of the immigrants.

The Socialists' weak showing in the European Parliament election was seen as a poor omen for their prospects in the 1986 elections to the National Assembly. It came as no surprise, therefore, when Prime Minister Pierre Mauroy and his cabinet resigned on July 17. Shortly thereafter the Communists announced their withdrawal from the government. President Mitterrand appointed as Mauroy's successor 38-year-old Laurent Fabius, who had been budget minister, and then industry minister, in the previous government. (Fabius was the son of a well-to-do Jewish family that had converted to Christianity after World War II. His wife was Jewish and he was considered to be friendly to Israel.)

The appointment of Fabius signaled to many observers the end of one phase in Mitterrand's presidential career and the start of another. Whereas Mitterrand, in coming into office, had pledged to carry out a program of socialist reform, economic necessity forced a gradual retreat from that position. An austerity plan introduced in 1983 had entailed severe budget cutbacks, higher taxes, and the closing down of unproductive industries, leading to widespread job layoffs. To the Communists, a policy carried out at the expense of workers had become increasingly untenable. The same applied to Mauroy, who was identified with the old-style Left. Fabius, who appeared more committed to pragmatism than to ideology, was considered by many observers to embody the shift in the Mitterrand approach away from orthodox socialism and toward a moderate social-democratic outlook. Early evidence of this was the announcement of tax cuts aimed at the middle class and business and measures seeking to encourage investment and high-tech industry, moves likely to broaden the base of Mitterrand's support. At the same time, while the Communists were out of the government, their control of several unions, including the country's largest, the Confédération Générale du Travail (CGT, General Confederation of Labor), meant that they would continue to play a crucial role in the political and economic spheres.

Even before the change in government, Mitterrand had already conceded defeat on an issue that had been a cornerstone of his original electoral program. This was a measure to place "free" parochial and private schools under state control—a measure that was viewed by many French citizens as an infringement of basic freedoms. Following a spate of protest demonstrations—including one in Paris that was described as the largest since the liberation of France in 1945—the president announced the bill's withdrawal.

With the prospect of an opposition victory in 1986 looming as a very real possibility, political circles were already concerned about the issue of "cohabitation": how would a National Assembly dominated by the Right get along with a left-wing president for the two years until the 1988 presidential election? Such a division of power was permitted by the constitution but had never occurred since Charles de Gaulle ushered in the Fifth Republic in 1958. Many Frenchmen feared that "cohabitation" would condemn the country to a period of weak parliamentary democracy and a succession of short-lived coalitions.

Controversy continued over the volatile situation in New Caledonia, a French territory in the South Pacific. Mitterrand had been advocating a policy of gradual progress toward self-determination for the territory. When the largely Socialist separatist movement there carried out an insurrection in November, establishing a provisional government, Mitterrand was accused by Gaullists of betraying the 37 percent of New Caledonians who are European, most of whom opposed independence.

Mitterrand made several visits to foreign countries during the year, the most important being: to the United States, March 21–28; to the USSR, where he publicly discussed the case of Andrei Sakharov, June 20–23; to Jordan, July 9–11; and to Syria, November 26–28. Israeli prime minister Shimon Peres paid an official visit to France during the first week in December.

A two-hour television documentary shown on national television in November revived the controversy surrounding Marshal Philippe Pétain, the wartime leader of Vichy France, who was later convicted of collaborating with the Nazis. The previous summer, Pétain's lawyer, Jacques Isorni, had placed a full-page advertisement in *Le Monde* arguing that "Pétain [had] accepted the bad in order to avoid the worse," i.e., to lessen the harshness of Nazi rule. A response placed in the paper a few days later by the Association of Sons and Daughters of Deported French Jews refuted Isorni's claims, describing the persecution of Jews in Vichy France and the mass deportations to Auschwitz.

Attitudes Toward Israel

The harsh anti-Israel atmosphere that had prevailed in the country following the war in Lebanon lost considerable force during 1984. Contributing to the change of attitude were divisions within the Arab world, the war between Iran and Iraq, dissidence within the PLO, and Yasir Arafat's loss of prestige after his expulsion from Lebanon. French pro-Arab agitators, such as the France-Pays Arabes (France-Arab Nations) group, found themselves unable to function effectively due to internecine conflicts. Two positive results of the confusion were a lessening of pro-Palestinian agitation in high schools and universities and a marked reduction in the painting of anti-Israel graffitti on Paris walls and subways.

Jewish leftist supporters of the Palestinian cause, such as Trotskyist Alain Krivine —who had called for the destruction of the Zionist regime in Israel—and Maoist Alain Geismar—one of the first people to use the term "Nazi" in connection with Zionism—greatly toned down their rhetoric. Indeed, Geismar displayed a repentant attitude.

There was a noticeable difference in the tone of news reports and feature articles about Israel in the major newspapers and periodicals, with expressions of overt hostility generally being abandoned. This was certainly true of *Le Monde,* despite the long-standing hostility of its Jerusalem correspondent to the Israeli Right.

Seeking to gain political advantage from these developments, the opposition parties, led by the very popular Simone Veil, a Jew, assumed strongly pro-Israel positions. According to an authoritative source, the opposition groups planned to close the PLO's Paris office if they came to power in the 1986 elections.

Racism and Antisemitism

Racism was on the rise in France, though this fact was rarely acknowledged even in sympathetic "new Right" circles. The victims of racist abuse were mostly immigrant workers, especially Arabs and Kabyles from North Africa, and, less frequently, blacks. North Africans who were arrested and interrogated by the police were often beaten; many were wounded and some even killed. Indeed, anti-Arab prejudice was widespread in the police force, especially among those who had fought in the Algerian war. The same kind of racism could be found among the poorer elements of the working class, who lived in squalid conditions in the industrial centers.

Many incidents, some of them dramatic, highlighted the critical situation and made it the subject of continuing debate. Most shocking were murders motivated purely by racism, such as the killing of an Algerian citizen by several French youths; the Algerian was killed in a railroad train compartment and thrown out the window.

Some time after this act of racist savagery, an elderly Jewish woman in Cannes was killed by a young man whom she had befriended; he turned out to be an avid reader of Nazi literature.

The National Front's relative success at the polls was unquestionably attributable to its campaign of xenophobia. In the suburbs of larger cities, for example, Le Pen attracted low-income French families who resented the growing numbers of foreign pupils attending elementary schools—children who were seen as lowering the quality of education.

Meanwhile, a new generation of rootless people had come into being, as young North Africans born in France became adults. While legally French citizens, they were not really viewed as such by the authorities, by other Frenchmen, or even by themselves. The most gifted and most intellectual of the North Africans refused to assimilate, thereby arousing widespread hostility, since France lacks any tradition of cultural pluralism.

In the winter of 1984, North Africans staged a mass protest march on foot, with banners flying, from the south all the way to Paris, where a delegation was received by President Mitterrand. Among those who joined the protesters along the route —out of sympathy and feelings of solidarity—were groups of young Jews. They soon realized, however, that not a few of the demonstrators were ostentatiously wearing Palestinian headdresses as a sign of identification with the PLO.

Overt incidents of antisemitism were relatively few and minor in 1984. In Lille, for example, a city in northern France, a Communist municipal councilman was fined for making defamatory remarks about Jews. Two organizations devoted to the struggle against antisemitism—the pro-Zionist Ligue Internationale Contre l'Antisémitisme et Racisme (LICRA, League Against Antisemitism and Racism) and the Communist-influenced Mouvement Contre le Racisme et pour l'Amitié des Peuples (MRAP, Movement Against Racism and for Friendship Among Peoples) —were active on the legal front in bringing suit over such incidents as the refusal by owners of cafés and restaurants to serve Arabs, racist slurs, and discrimination in employment. However, even when sentences were handed down for violating laws against racial or religious discrimination, they were considered too light to serve as a deterrent.

In 1984 it seemed unlikely that large numbers of French citizens could be mobilized to fight against racism. LICRA did organize several important protest demonstrations, but the participants were mostly Jews, chiefly concerned about antisemitism. The MRAP recruited participants for its intermittent demonstrations from Communist groups and the Communist-dominated General Confederation of Labor. The antiracist movement was hampered both by intellectual and organizational confusion, however. The General Confederation of Labor, for example, viewed racism as purely a "fascist" phenomenon, but the definition of fascism varied with events and the Communist party's tactics of the day. Under some circumstances, conservatives and moderate liberals were labeled fascists; at other times, when relations between the Communists and Socialists were especially tense, the

Socialists were so designated. Because the antiracism movement consisted of a loose coalition of special-interest groups, confusion of aims was often in evidence. Arabs, for example, were perfectly capable of marching in demonstrations against anti-semitism, holding banners that proclaimed "Jews and Arabs, the same struggle," yet at the same time shouting "antiracist" slogans against Israel, Zionism, and, by extension, all Jews.

JEWISH COMMUNITY

Demography

The Jewish population of France was estimated to be 530,000. Leading Jewish population centers were Paris, Marseilles, Nice, Lyons, and Toulouse.

Communal Activities

There continued to be a small but perceptible increase in the number of Jews from assimilated or dejudaized backgrounds who were "searching for their roots" and seeking some form of identification with authentic Judaism. This trend only partially compensated, however, for the decline of Jewishness among Jews who were as-similating "unconsciously"—without being assimilationists on principle—and losses through intermarriage.

Membership in the Consistory, the organized religious body of French Jewry, remained shockingly low, considering the size of the Jewish population. (The Paris Consistory, for example, had only 9,000 members.) However, these figures were not a wholly reliable estimate of the number of religiously affiliated Jews in France, since many synagogues and communities, mostly Orthodox and ultra-Orthodox, did not belong to the Consistory.

In principle, Consistory synagogues were Conservative—what is called "Lib-eral" in other European countries, especially Germany—but in recent years there has been an "orthodoxization" of the Consistory constituency. This development was strongly influenced by the arrival of large numbers of religious Jews from North Africa, Jews who had never been identified with an Orthodox movement as such but who were decidedly traditionalist in their observance. What some re-ferred to as the "radicalization" of Jewish religious life in France was attributed to the leadership of Chief Rabbi René Samuel Sirat, who, since his election in 1980, had been pressing for a more committed and energetic Judaism. (Rabbi Sirat came to France from Algeria in 1948, before the mass influx of North Afri-cans in the 1950s and 1960s. He was ordained at the Séminaire Israélite de France, and earned a doctorate at the University of Strasbourg.) Rabbi Sirat's efforts were ably assisted by the Consistory's new president, Emile Touati, also from North Africa.

During the year several new Consistory synagogues were organized in the suburbs and the provinces, and courses in religion were offered by a number of institutions. In addition, stricter controls were instituted over the granting of *kashrut* certificates to butcher shops and restaurants.

Five old synagogues were declared "monuments of national historic importance" by the French Ministry for Cultural Affairs. This meant that while the buildings could not be altered, they were eligible to receive government help for restoration. The synagogues were located in Nancy, Mulhouse, Soultz, Colmar, and Guebwiller.

Pressure exerted by religious groups on the social and cultural body of French Jewry, the Fonds Social Juif Unifié (FSJU, United Jewish Philanthropic Fund), to place greater emphasis on religious activities, provoked considerable controversy. While secularists argued for the exclusion of religion from the organization's programs, their opponents charged that this omission was incompatible with the very nature of Jewish existence. Professor Ady Steg, an eminent French Jew who favored a religious emphasis in all Jewish social and educational activities, resigned as a director of the FSJU at the end of the year.

In April French Jewry celebrated the 40th anniversary of the founding of the Conseil Représentatif des Institutions Juives de France (CRIF, Representative Council of French Jewish Institutions), the quasi-official umbrella organization of French Jewry comprising 50 major Jewish groups. The council was created by members of the Jewish underground in German-occupied France in 1944 as a symbol of their determination to survive and to rebuild the Jewish institutions destroyed by the Nazis. The principal ceremonies were held in Lyons, where Klaus Barbie, the wartime Gestapo chief there, was in prison awaiting trial for crimes against humanity. The festivities were attended by, among others, Cardinal Albert Decourtray, the archbishop of Lyons, and Defense Minister Charles Hernu. There were also ceremonies in the village of Izieu where, in 1944, 44 Jewish children were arrested for deportation on Barbie's orders.

CRIF intervened on several occasions with government officials, primarily in connection with the plight of Soviet refuseniks and prisoners. CRIF president Théo Klein accompanied President Mitterrand to Moscow, where Klein attended synagogue services and presented a prayer book to the rabbi. The next day, a Saturday, he flew to the Crimea, for which he was sharply criticized in Jewish religious circles in Paris.

Two Jewish political groups, espousing different viewpoints, sought to gain support in the community. Socialisme et Judaïsme (Socialism and Judaism) supported the Mitterrand regime, while Judaïsme et Liberté (Judaism and Freedom), which advocated the policies of the opposition, was supported by Jewish deputies Claude-Girard Marcus and Simone Veil. Though both groups stressed their Jewish character, quoting traditional sources to validate their views, it became all too obvious that they were merely propaganda conduits for the respective parties they supported.

On the Zionist front, Youth Aliyah had a successful year, thanks to the Israeli emissary of the Jewish Agency, Elie Cohen, who demonstrated verve and intelligence in his work and succeeded in attracting a sizeable number of young people to the Youth Aliyah program. Overall, however, Israel's difficult economic situation negatively affected *aliyah* from France.

Education and Culture

An estimated 8,000 youngsters, 8 percent of the Jewish school-age population, attended Jewish schools full time. Other students were enrolled in ORT technical schools and in one-day-a-week religious classes that met on Wednesdays, when French schools were closed. While both the absolute number and the percentage of students receiving full-time Jewish education were low compared with figures for other Western European countries—e.g., Italy—they actually represented an increase over previous years, when such enrollment stood at only 5 percent. Parental indifference was undoubtedly a factor, but many families who wanted to place their children in full-time Jewish schools were unable to do so because of a shortage of schools and qualified teachers. One of the reasons for the school shortage was financial—government subsidies covered only a small part of private school expenses, with parents' associations required to cover the rest.

Jewish cultural activities of varying quality were offered during the year. These included radio and television programs devoted to various aspects of Jewish life and tradition: folk songs, ritual chants, historical sketches, the Israeli scene, and food. There was even a matchmaking program for people seeking to meet prospective mates. Significant broadcast time was devoted to political news and comment as well. A TV program that continued to attract millions of Jewish and non-Jewish viewers was presented by Rabbi Josy Eisenberg. The program dealt with both traditional teachings and contemporary topics of interest.

There were several groups engaged in serious basic study of Talmud and, even more, of Kabbalah. An important intellectual trend was the growing interest in religious rationalism, a philosophy based largely on the work of Emmanuel Levinas, a Lithuanian-born "post-phenomenologist" and talmudist, a retired Sorbonne professor who remained active as a writer and lecturer. Levinas had attracted many ardent disciples, including non-Jews among the French intelligentsia; his writings brought Judaism unprecedented prestige among French philosophers.

Despite the impressive variety of Jewish cultural and educational activities offered throughout the country, the number of Jews taking advantage of them remained relatively small.

Books

Among new novels with Jewish characters or themes, the best were translations from other languages. Of these, the most noteworthy was *Il fait beau aujourd'hui à Paris* ("The Weather in Paris Is Beautiful Today," Stock) by Fred Uhlman, a British Jew of German origin. The translation of one of his earlier books, *L'ami retrouvé* ("The Rediscovered Friend," Stock) had already won him an appreciative audience. A new novel by the well-known Israeli author Amos Kenan, *Le chemin d'Ain Harod* ("The Ain Harod Road," Albin Michel), distressed both critics and readers because of its mocking, nihilistic tone.

A notable new nonfiction work was *L'antisémitisme français aujourd'hui et demain* ("French Antisemitism Today and Tomorrow," Laffont) by Simon Epstein, a French Jew living in Israel. The Jewish press paid almost no attention to this book, which criticized the Jewish community leadership of France for underestimating the problem of antisemitism and fostering the view that propaganda alone can alleviate it.

A book characterized by uncompromising views was *Le Retour d'Israel* ("Israel's Return," Du Rocher/Monaco) by Abraham Livni, a French Christian convert to Judaism who had been living in Israel for many years. The volume is a vigorous political and theological defense of the mystical nationalism of Rabbi Zvi Yehuda Kook, Livni's mentor. Reviewers contrasted Livni's position with the conciliatory outlook of Amitiés Judeo-Chrétiennes ("Jewish-Christian Friendship Group").

The Verdier publishing house continued to earn praise for its editions of Jewish classical texts translated from Hebrew and Aramaic into French by Charles Mopsik, a learned young translator. Mopsik's most recent publication was an anthology based on the Babylonian Talmud.

Another new nonfiction work deserving of mention was *L'humour juif dans la littérature: de Job à Woody Allen* ("Jewish Humor in Literature: From Job to Woody Allen," Presses Universitaires) by Judith Storo-Sandor.

Personalia

Manès Sperber, famous as a novelist and memoirist, and also as a psychologist who had been an assistant to Alfred Adler, died in Paris on February 4, aged 78. Born in eastern Galicia and raised in Vienna, he had lived in Berlin for many years before coming to France, where he wrote in both German and French. His lovely *Qu'une larme dans l'océan* ("A Tear in the Ocean," Calmann-Levy) won him special praise in Jewish literary circles. Sperber, a friend of Arthur Koestler, spent a good part of his life in the Communist movement, which he left at the beginning of World War II. He became a French citizen, served as editor of foreign books for Calmann-Levy, and became a friend of André Malraux and Raymond Aron. Sperber eventually returned to Jewish life and in the end became an effective defender of the State of Israel.

France's highest award, the infrequently given Grand Officer of the Legion of Honor, was bestowed on two prominent French Jews: Léo Hamon, a former cabinet minister and law professor, and Marcel Bleustein-Blanchet, dean of France's advertising and broadcasting industries. Hamon, 76, a professor of law at the Paris Sorbonne, served as minister of information under the late president Georges Pompidou and was a personal aide to Gen. Charles de Gaulle during World War II. He led a pro-Socialist Gaullist party that backed Mitterrand in the 1981 presidential elections.

Bleustein-Blanchet, 78, headed "Publicis," the country's largest privately owned advertising agency. He pioneered radio broadcasting in France in the early 1920s by creating the private company "Radio Paris." He was active in Jewish affairs and a generous contributor to local Jewish charities.

The rank of Commander in the Legion of Honor was awarded to Jules Braunschvig, president of the Alliance Israélite Universelle. Rabbi Josy Eisenberg, 52, France's "TV rabbi," was named to the Legion of Honor for "improving relations between Jews and Christians." Bulgarian-born concert pianist Alexis Weisenberg was named to the Legion of Honor for his contribution to France's musical life.

ARNOLD MANDEL

Central Europe

Federal Republic of Germany

Domestic Affairs

IN POLITICAL AND ECONOMIC terms, 1984 was relatively stable, although not without its share of troubling events. On the economic front, the gross national output rose by 2.6 percent, while the cost-of-living increase—2.4 percent —was the lowest since 1969. Unemployment, however, stood at 9 percent. The slight upward trend of the West German economy was slowed by lengthy strikes during the second quarter of the year.

A scandal involving high government officials plagued the government of Chancellor Helmut Kohl throughout much of the year, producing considerable public unrest. Investigations by a parliamentary committee and the public prosecutor led to allegations of bribery, influence peddling, and tax evasion involving the huge Flick industrial concern and major political figures. West German economics minister Otto Graf Lambsdorff resigned in June, just before being indicted for accepting bribes from Flick to arrange tax waivers. (He was succeeded by his Free Democratic party colleague Martin Bangemann.) Bundestag president Rainer Barzel resigned in October, in the wake of similar accusations. (Philipp Jenninger, also a Christian Democratic leader, was elected his successor in November.) Court proceedings were initiated against other leading personalities, in business as well as politics.

In connection with public criticism of Flick's substantial political payoffs, spokesmen for Nazi victims and anti-Nazi groups recalled that the Flick concern had made large donations to the Nazi party and had refused to pay indemnity to World War II slave laborers.

In May former mayor of West Berlin and Christian Democratic leader Richard von Weizsäcker was chosen as the sixth president of the Federal Republic, succeeding Karl Carstens, who had been elected in 1979.

Elections in the Federal Republic for the European Parliament on June 17 saw the Christian Democratic Union (CDU) emerge as the winner with 37.5 percent of the vote, with the Social Democrats (SPD) a close second (37.4 percent), followed by the Christian Social Union (CSU) (8.5 percent), the Greens (8.2 percent), the Free Democrats (FDP) (4.8 percent), the Peace List (1.3 percent), the National

Democratic party (NPD) (0.8 percent), the Center party (0.4 percent), and the Women's party (0.4 percent). In state elections in Baden-Württemberg the CDU won 51.9 percent of the vote, followed by the SPD (32.4 percent), the Greens (8.0 percent), and the FDP (7.2 percent). Elections to the communal parliaments in Bavaria saw the CSU an easy winner, with the SPD a distant second. The CDU was the winner in communal elections in Rhineland-Palatinate, while the SPD won the races in North Rhine-Westphalia and Saarland.

Pacifist groups opposed to the deployment of U.S. nuclear missiles in West Germany experienced some loss of impetus over the year, with public support of their cause beginning to dwindle. As a result, the U.S. missile deployment program was able to proceed almost completely unhindered. Public criticism of NATO, U.S. policy, and West Germany's political position was limited in the main to an organized minority made up of SPD and Communist supporters and the Greens. In December the Federal Constitutional Court rejected a complaint by the Greens that the stationing of U.S. nuclear missiles in West Germany violated German law.

The Greens, despite internal strife over political and personal issues, continued to consolidate their position on the federal and state political levels. In June Holger Börner was elected head of the Hesse state government with the support of the Greens, but in November the party withdrew its support.

The 40th anniversary of the plot to kill Hitler was commemorated in July. Chancellor Kohl, paying tribute at a ceremony in West Berlin to the "bravery and righteousness" of the group of plotters, said that the planned assassination showed the world that the German people as a whole had not been Hitler's collaborators. The chancellor and other West German leaders, joined by Howard Friedman, president of the American Jewish Committee, laid wreaths at a memorial for the conspirators executed after the plot's failure. Friedman praised the courage and determination of the plotters and said it was important for American Jews today to acknowledge that from the ruins of an evil regime a free society had arisen, one committed to preserving the values of Western civilization and democratic society. At another ceremony, however, Dr. Albert H. Friedlander, rabbi of the Westminster Synagogue in London, warned against seeing the plotters as representative of the entire German people. In reality, he asserted, the majority had followed Hitler's lead. This viewpoint was echoed at an international conference of historians held in West Berlin on the anniversary of the plot.

Discord among the West German political parties over the proposed bill to punish public denial or minimization of Nazi mass crimes continued to prevent legislative action on the issue.

In the fall, public criticism was voiced over the appointment of former members of the Nazi Waffen-SS to leading positions in the news media and political life. Asked why it was not possible to fill important positions with persons who had not actively supported the Nazi regime, officials offered the opinion that SS membership at age 20 was not sufficient cause to prevent the appointment of men who were otherwise qualified.

In a poll of viewers' reactions to a series of television programs on the Nazi epoch, shown in 1982–1983, about one-third of those who responded to the telephone survey complained of being "overfed" by these programs, voicing concern that too much public attention to the Nazi regime might foster neo-Nazi tendencies. About half of this group of viewers expressed pro-Nazi attitudes, including antisemitic and anti-Israel statements. Of those who expressed their views in writing, about one-fourth made pro-Nazi statements, while over a third welcomed the programs as providing valuable information on an important chapter of German history.

Extremism

According to the annual government report on extremism, no dramatic change occurred in the area of domestic security in 1984, or in the membership of extremist organizations. West German interior minister Friedrich Zimmermann, warning that political extremism had to be watched carefully, reiterated the official view that left-wing extremism was far more dangerous than that of the right. During the year, left-wing extremists were responsible for 1,269 acts of violence, including 11 terrorist attacks.

State agencies warned against growing left-wing extremism, which included terrorist acts against NATO bases and nuclear installations on German soil. Leftist groups and individuals committed numerous attacks on U.S. army installations and personnel during the year. Foremost among the groups were the Rote Armee-Fraktion (Red Army Faction, RAF) and the Revolutionäre Zellen (Revolutionary Cells, RZ). At Stuttgart, in May, former RAF member Peter-Jürgen Book was given three lifetime sentences for murders committed in 1977.

Ultraright groups, according to the government, numbered 89, with 22,100 members. The largest organization, the Deutsche Volksunion (German People's Union), led by Gerhard Frey, editor of the weekly *Deutsche National-Zeitung*—whose circulation of 100,000 made it one of Germany's biggest weeklies—increased its membership from 11,000 to 12,000 during the year. The National Democratic party (NPD) had a membership of 6,100.

There were 34 neo-Nazi groups with 1,350 members. Twelve of these groups were composed of former members of the recently outlawed Aktionsfront Nationaler Sozialisten (Action Front of National Socialists, ANS). Half of all the groups had fewer than ten members; most had between 15 and 25. Neo-Nazis were responsible for a total of 1,137 offenses (as against 1,347 in 1983), of which 191 had an antisemitic character.

During the year police seized large quantities of neo-Nazi propaganda material as well as firearms, ammunition, and explosives. Among those arrested was Michael Kühnen, head of the disbanded ANS, who had fled to France but was extradited to West Germany. Among neo-Nazis indicted for various crimes were followers of the American Gary Lauck; they were charged with circulating antidemocratic and antisemitic materials that had been shipped from the United States.

Several hundred members of democratic and antifascist groups demonstrated at the NPD's congress held in Munich in November, at which the 20th anniversary of the party's formation was celebrated. Protests from Germany and abroad did not succeed in halting rallies of former members of the Nazi Waffen-*SS*, held in various places, including Oberaula and Marktheidenfeld. Social Democratic party chairman Willy Brandt stated that he shared the indignation of those who deplored *SS* veterans' rallies, since they glorified the Nazi regime and encouraged the revival of Nazism. Other political leaders, while critical of the rallies, defended the participants' constitutional rights of free expression and freedom of assembly. State and municipal agencies claimed they were not authorized to ban such rallies.

At the end of June, over 300 West German neo-Nazis met at Diksmuiden, in Belgium, with some 600 neo-Nazis from Belgium, Denmark, France, Great Britain, Italy, the Netherlands, Austria, Sweden, Switzerland, and Spain. Most of the Germans belonged to such groups as the NPD and its youth division, Junge Nationaldemokraten (Young National Democrats); the Wiking-Jugend (Viking Youth); the Hilfsorganisation für nationale politische Gefangene und deren Angehörige (Organization in Aid of National Political Prisoners and Their Families), and the ANS. About 40 "skinheads," as well as 20 members of a far-right soccer fan club, "Borussenfront," who tried to join the neo-Nazi rally, were prevented from doing so by the Belgian police. Contacts and sometimes cooperation between "skinheads," "punks," and soccer fans, on the one hand, and neo-Nazi groups on the other, were a growing phenomenon in several West German centers.

According to government sources, foreign extremist groups operating in West Germany had a total of 116,000 members, including about 3,550 Arabs. Palestinian groups were largely inactive in 1984, probably because of internal strife within the Palestine Liberation Organization.

Antisemitism

Jubilee performances of the controversial Passion play staged at the Bavarian village of Oberammergau drew 470,000 spectators from all over the world between May and September. As in the past, the play's producers and the village council rejected charges of antisemitism leveled by Jewish critics. They blamed the American Jewish Committee and the Anti-Defamation League of B'nai B'rith for mounting an international campaign against the religious pageant. The play's organizers insisted that the text had been cleared of all purportedly antisemitic passages and stressed that no more alterations would be made.

Jewish groups criticized as antisemitic and anti-Zionist the film *Hotel Polan und seine Gäste* ("Hotel Polan and Its Guests"), based on a novel by Jewish author Jan Koplowitz, who also wrote the screenplay. The film, made in East Germany, was purchased for television in the Federal Republic and Austria by the Sender Freies Berlin station, which claimed that all passages thought to be insulting to Jews had been cut before its screening. Another controversy centered on a stage play, *Ghetto,* written by Israeli author Joshua Sobol and performed by a German cast on a West Berlin stage. The work was judged by Jewish and other circles as unsuitable for German audiences, on the grounds that it could cause confusion about Jewish attitudes under Nazi rule and exonerate Nazi criminals.

At least 28 Jewish cemeteries were desecrated during the year, including those at Mönchengladbach, Hamburg-Ohlsdorf, Tübingen/Reutlingen, Essen, and Flehingen. A small former synagogue at Düsseldorf-Gerresheim was destroyed in a fire set by a 24-year-old neo-Nazi.

A textbook on antisemitism, the first of its kind in the country, was published by the state agency for political education for use in West German schools. The work was prepared by the Center for Research on Antisemitism, which was established in 1982 at the West Berlin Technical University and was headed by Herbert A. Strauss of New York.

Following antisemitic incidents at the West Berlin police college, visits to Nazi concentration-camp sites were incorporated in the curriculum. The aim was to broaden students' knowledge of the Nazi period and reduce anti-Jewish attitudes.

Nazi Trials

At the start of 1984, West German legal authorities were investigating 1,542 persons suspected of involvement in Nazi crimes, and were carrying out preliminary investigations of another 110 cases. According to the Central Agency for the Investigation of Nazi Crimes at Ludwigsburg, since the end of World War II, West German prosecutors had investigated more than 88,000 suspects, of whom 6,469 were convicted and received sentences. In February Adalbert Rückerl, head of the agency since 1966, was succeeded by chief prosecutor Alfred Streim.

The number of court proceedings against Nazi suspects continued to drop, due in large measure to the aging and failing health of the accused, poor memory on the part of witnesses, and lack of evidence. As a result, an increasing number of proceedings ended in acquittal.

Landau: In June 72-year-old former police officer Albert Eichelis was sentenced to six years in prison for the murder of Jews in Latvia.

Fulda: In February 74-year-old former concentration-camp inmate Hermann Ebender was acquitted of the murder of 17 Jewish prisoners.

Heidelberg: In October Clemens Druschke, former Gestapo chief at Jesenice in Yugoslavia, was acquitted of the murder of a Yugoslav partisan by torture.

Itzehoe: In March 75-year-old former concentration-camp inmate Kurt Vogel was acquitted of the attempted murder of three fellow prisoners.

Bonn: In April a local court stopped proceedings against 66-year-old former doctor Helmut Rühl, for complicity in the murder of concentration-camp prisoners by medical experiments, on account of the accused's ill health.

Frankfurt: In June the local high court stopped the state's case against 72-year-old former SS sergeant Hubert Gomerski, for health reasons. Convicted in 1950 of the murder of Jewish prisoners at Sobibor and sentenced to life imprisonment, Gomerski was released in 1973 and given a retrial. This ended with a 15-year prison sentence which was subsequently annulled by the West German supreme court. A third trial, in 1981, was stopped because of Gomerski's ill health.

Oldenburg: In July the local high court refused to permit the start of court proceedings against 75-year-old former security police chief at Angers, France, Hans-Dietrich Ernst, because of insufficient evidence and the failing health of the accused. Ernst had been charged with complicity in the deportation and murder of 824 French Jews.

Hamburg: In April retrial began before a local jury of 69-year-old former Gestapo official Harri Schulz, who was charged with the murder of seven Jews and complicity in the murder of over 5,000 Jews deported to Auschwitz.

Düsseldorf: In August retrial opened of 67-year-old Heinz-Günter Wisner, former SS chief sergeant and medical aide at the Riga-Kaiserwald concentration camp, who was charged as an accomplice in the murder of at least five Jewish prisoners. In 1983 a local jury had sentenced Wisner to six years in prison for these offenses, but the sentence had been annulled by the West German supreme court.

Bochum: In November, at the local trial of 68-year-old Helmut Georg Krizons, former officer in the Jewish affairs department of the Gestapo in Lodz, Poland, the public prosecutor demanded eight and a half years of imprisonment for complicity in the murder of thousands of Jews.

Karlsruhe: In June the local West German supreme court rejected appeals by seven former SS guards who had been convicted of atrocities at the Majdanek concentration camp in Poland by a Düsseldorf jury in 1981. Five men and a woman who had been sentenced to prison terms of 3 to 12 years had based their appeals on alleged procedural errors. The seventh convict, Hermine Ryan-Braunsteiner, who became a U.S. citizen after the war, had claimed that the court lacked jurisdiction because she was no longer a German citizen. She had been sentenced to life imprisonment for murder. In November West German television networks screened a five-hour documentary on the Majdanek trial, showing the proceedings in detail.

In May 77-year-old former SS colonel Walter Rauff, who had been sought by West German authorities for the murder of 97,000 Jews in mobile gas chambers, died in Santiago, Chile, of lung cancer. He had lived in Chile since 1958, protected against West German, French, and Israeli extradition requests by Chile's statute of limitations.

Arthur Rudolph, a 78-year-old former rocket and space-aviation expert and postwar U.S. citizen, left the United States in March and relinquished U.S. citizenship in May, after publication of charges that he had tormented Jewish slave laborers in a Nazi rocket factory. Rudolph was one of a group of 118 Nazi rocket experts who came to the United States after the war; he became director of the Saturn V program. Rudolph denied ever having been involved in Nazi brutality, and West German legal authorities announced that they as yet had no incriminating evidence against him.

In September the West Berlin prosecutor completed the indictment against Paul Reimers, a former judge at the infamous Nazi People's Court, charging him with murder for his part in numerous death sentences handed down by that court. The ex-judge committed suicide a short time after.

Foreign Affairs

On the occasion of the visit to Bonn in October of Hosni Mubarak, president of Egypt, Chancellor Kohl promised the European community's assistance in helping the parties involved in the Middle East conflict to resume peace negotiations. At the same time, the German leader rejected Soviet plans for a Middle East conference under United Nations' auspices as unrealistic, since both Israel and the United States were against it. Kohl voiced his hope that the new Israeli government of Shimon Peres would help advance peace efforts, and welcomed the resumption of diplomatic ties between Egypt and Jordan. Kohl also said he was convinced that withdrawal of Israeli troops from Lebanon would improve the political climate in the region and ease the way for new peace moves. Foreign Minister Hans-Dietrich Genscher reaffirmed the official West German position calling for Palestinian self-determination, including establishment of a national home.

West German arms exports to Saudi Arabia and other Arab states remained a controversial issue both on the domestic scene and internationally. Among those protesting possible arms deliveries to the Arabs were SPD and church leaders, the German-Israel Society, other groups active in German-Israeli relations, and noted publisher Axel Springer. Israeli political leaders also appealed to the Bonn government not to allow the sale of arms to the enemies of the Jewish state. In March meetings between Chancellor Kohl and leading representatives of Jewish organizations in the United States, the German chancellor promised that arms sales would be limited to defensive weapons and that precautions would be taken so that no arms would fall into the hands of radical Arab states or Arab terrorists. Later in the year, Chancellor Kohl announced that West Germany's most modern tank, the Leopard II, would not be sold to any state outside the North Atlantic Treaty Organization.

Answering a query by the Greens in March, the government could not explain how small arms of West German make, seized by Israeli troops in Lebanon in 1983, had come into Palestinian hands. The Greens charged that the government had lost control over arms exports, pointing out that Saudi Arabia had refused to accept any restrictions on the use of arms supplied by West Germany. Another infringement of government policy was revealed when, following U.S. intervention, the West German trade ministry suspended the sale of 30,000 bullet-proof jackets by a West

German firm to Syria—a transaction that had already received the ministry's approval.

Relations with Israel

Relations between the Federal Republic and Israel were highlighted by Chancellor Kohl's visit to the Jewish state on January 24–29, which began with a ceremony at Yad Vashem and included extensive talks with Prime Minister Yitzhak Shamir and other political leaders. Kohl reiterated his government's support for Palestinian self-determination and for the security of all nations in the region. Criticizing as barriers to peace both Israel's settlement activity in the occupied areas and the Arab refusal to recognize the Jewish state, the chancellor called upon all parties to the conflict to agree to direct peace talks.

In a statement to the federal parliament upon his return to West Germany, Chancellor Kohl said he had gone to Israel as a friend and left the country as a friend, and hoped to build continued cooperation, particularly among the younger generations of both countries. "Behind ourselves and Israel stands a horrible past for which we Germans bear a historic responsibility. But behind us also stands the achievement of patient development of contacts, relations and ties which was begun by Konrad Adenauer and David Ben-Gurion and carried on by all federal governments. . . ."

In parliamentary debate that followed Kohl's statement the coalition parties hailed his determination to strive for good relations with both Israel and the Arab states. CDU/CSU faction leader Alfred Dregger thanked Kohl for not having bowed to "unobjective pressure" from Israel with regard to German arms sales. Speakers for the opposition parties, however, sharply criticized Kohl's stand on the arms-export issue, as well as statements made by him in Israel on historical and political questions, charging him with insensitivity to sentiment within the Jewish state. Both SPD and Greens speakers questioned the inclusion of 72-year-old Kurt Ziesel in Kohl's entourage, because of his past as a pro-Nazi journalist. The chancellor responded that Ziesel had made a fresh start after the war and repented his Nazi past.

German-Israeli cooperation continued to flourish on many levels, as evidenced by a stream of visitors to Israel and by the holding of numerous joint conferences. Among German visitors to the Jewish state were: federal agriculture minister Ignaz Kiechle, to discuss agricultural cooperation; federal research and technology minister Heinz Riesenhuber, to consider ways of extending and consolidating scientific cooperation; federal education minister Dorothee Wilms, to review occupational education programs; head of the Baden-Württemberg state government Lothar Späth, for talks on political and economic issues; a delegation of the FDP to attend the World Congress of Liberal Parties in Tel Aviv; and General Dietrich Genschel of the federal defense ministry, to study military operations, particularly women's integration into the armed forces.

A delegation of the Greens party interested in Israeli policy in the occupied areas also visited the country. Expressing support for their hosts, the Jewish-Arab Progressive Peace list, the Greens rejected charges of antisemitism, stressing that they were against all forms of racism.

The Deutsch-Israelische Gesellschaft (German-Israel Society, DIG) and its Israeli counterpart met for a four-day conference with about 200 participants in Bonn in November. Earlier in the year, the two groups and their partner organizations, the Austrian-Israel Society and the Swiss-Israel Society, at a meeting in Vienna, denounced efforts to equate Zionism with racism and colonialism, and asked their respective governments to resist defamation of the Jewish state by international bodies. The meeting also called upon the Egyptian government to resume talks with Israel on Palestinian autonomy.

Problematic aspects of German-Jewish and German-Israeli relations, past and present, were discussed at several academic and professional meetings: a conference of German and Israeli historians at the newly established Institute for German History and Culture at Haifa University; a gathering of German and Israeli experts at the Hebrew University in Jerusalem; and a conference of German, Israeli, Arab, and Palestinian publicists, scientists, and artists at the Evangelische Akademie Arnoldshain. A symposium on youth exchange programs was sponsored by the Evangelical church in the Rhineland, at Bendorf. In addition to government-financed exchange programs, which by the end of 1984 had enabled over 70,000 youths to visit Israel and Germany, there were a growing number of privately arranged exchange programs.

Cooperation between West Germany and Israel in science and technology continued to expand. Cooperative agreements were concluded between the Haifa Technion and Berlin Technical University, Tel Aviv University and Munich University, and the Hebrew University and Hamburg University. During his visit to the Hebrew University in January, Chancellor Kohl announced the establishment of a Bonn-financed chair in international finance and politics, named for former German-Jewish economist and jurist Carl Melchior. The Volkswagenwerk Foundation donated one million DM to the Weizmann Institute of Science in honor of the 50th anniversary of the institute's founding.

Israeli enterprises were represented at numerous international trade fairs in the Federal Republic. The West Berlin film company Chronos-Film donated 50 hours of film documenting the history of European Jewry in the first half of this century to the Nahum Goldmann Museum in Tel Aviv, Israel's State Film Archives, the Ghetto Fighters' House, and Israel television.

The number of German tourists to the Jewish state rose by 20 percent in 1984, to over 130,000, making Germany first among European countries in tourism to Israel.

Yad Vashem again honored a number of West German citizens as "Righteous Gentiles," some of them posthumously, for their role in the rescue of persecuted Jews: Jean Jülich, Bartholomäus Schink, Michael Jovy, Konrad David, Käthe

Hauschild, Wilhelm Hammann, Helene Jacobs, Willi Kulka, Maria Kulka, Willi Otto, Aenne Otto, and Johanna Schallschmidt.

JEWISH COMMUNITY

Demography

On January 1, 1984, the 65 local Jewish communities in the Federal Republic and West Berlin had 27,791 members—14,193 males and 13,598 females. A year later the communities registered 27,561 members—14,024 males and 13,537 females. An additional 25,000 unaffiliated Jews were estimated to be living in the Federal Republic and West Berlin.

In 1984 the Central Welfare Agency of Jews in Germany, located in Frankfurt, recorded 361 immigrants and 305 emigrants, 69 births and 377 deaths, and 35 conversions to Judaism. The largest Jewish communities, as of January 1, 1985, were West Berlin (6,177), Frankfurt (4,784), Munich (4,019), Düsseldorf (1,659), Hamburg (1,373), and Cologne (1,222).

Communal Activities

Calling the Jewish community a "small but loyal" part of German society, the Zentralrat der Juden in Deutschland (Central Council of Jews in Germany) emphasized in its annual Rosh Hashanah message the basically positive outlook for Jewish life in postwar Germany. At the same time, the council underscored the need for eternal vigilance to guard against antisemitism and extremism. Two additional themes sounded in the message were the importance of passing on Jewish knowledge and the Jewish way of life to the young, and unfailing love and support for Israel.

During the year, communal representatives from all parts of the country convened at two plenary meetings of the Central Council to discuss a broad array of subjects. The council's seventh Youth and Culture Congress at Mannheim brought together over 200 young Jews, including guests from other European countries and Israel. Adult Jewish representatives at the gathering expressed dismay at the lack of interest in Jewish life shown by many young Jews. Several communities organized special dialogues between groups of parents and young people to analyze the situation and suggest ways to improve it.

A four-day seminar on the Holocaust and its aftermath was organized for youth leaders by the Youth and Hechalutz Department of the World Zionist Organization in conjunction with the British Zionist Federation Education Trust; it was held in Munich. Youths from all parts of the country attended a symposium on Middle East events that was sponsored by the Zionist Youth Organization in West Berlin. Young Jews from Germany and other German-language countries attended a seminar on problems of Jewish identity at Grindelwald in Switzerland.

The Bundesverband Jüdischer Studenten in Deutschland (Union of Jewish Students in Germany, BJSD) continued to expand its activities and established several new local branches. Among the activities were seminars on various aspects of Jewish life, actions against antisemitic and anti-Israel propaganda, demonstrations in support of Soviet Jews, and publication of the periodical *Cheschbon.*

A truly historic occasion was the Maccabiah that took place in April, the first to be held in Germany since before World War II. Over 300 members of nine Maccabiah groups from various West German centers participated in the event at Augsburg. Willi Weyer, president of the Deutscher Sportbund (German Sports Union), and Franz Josef Strauss, head of the Bavarian state government, saw in the event a symbol of Jewish renewal in Germany. The Munich Maccabiah club, the most successful in the competition, received a special award from the federal interior ministry. To many observers the Munich victory seemed to have symbolic significance, as it called to mind the massacre of Israeli athletes by Arab terrorists at the 1972 Olympics. In September that tragic event was commemorated by the City of Munich and the Jewish community there.

Moshe Elat, professor of Jewish history at the Hebrew University of Jerusalem, was appointed rector of the Academy for Jewish Studies at Heidelberg, succeeding Shemaryahu Talmon, also of the Hebrew University. The academy also cooperated with Jewish institutions in the United States.

At the invitation of the Anti-Defamation League of B'nai B'rith, a group of former soldiers of the U.S. 442nd Regiment, which had liberated Dachau in April 1945, visited the site of the former Nazi concentration camp there.

A new Jewish community center opened in Nuremberg in September, and the cornerstone for a new center was laid in Frankfurt in November. Also in November, the Jewish community center on Fasanenstrasse in West Berlin and the synagogue in the Ruhr city of Essen celebrated the 25th anniversaries of their opening.

Christian-Jewish Cooperation

On the occasion of Rosh Hashanah 5745, West German president Richard von Weizsäcker, president of the Bundestag (federal parliament) Rainer Barzel, Chancellor Kohl, and other political as well as religious leaders sent messages to the Jewish community praising Jewish contributions to German life and underlining support of the State of Israel. Annemarie Renger, SPD vice-president of the Bundestag and head of the pro-Israel group of German parliamentarians, thanked Jewish citizens for their readiness to stretch out their hands in reconciliation, despite their awareness of past horrors.

During the year, various Christian groups met to evaluate their roles during the Nazi period and their relations with Jews and Judaism in the present. Former Berlin bishop Kurt Scharf, a noted Evangelical church leader in postwar Germany, criticized Christians for failing to stem the rise of antisemitism. The West Berlin synod of the Evangelical church issued a paper acknowledging the Christian role in the

Holocaust, recalling the common origins of Christians and Jews, and promising to work for a new understanding with Jews in both Germany and Israel. For the first time, the organization of West German Baptists criticized its own behavior during the Nazi period, stating, "It grieves us that we often succumbed to the ideological enticement of that time and did not evince more courage in professing truth and justice."

The German Catholic Congress held in Munich in July included speeches, workshops, and symposia dealing with aspects of the Jewish religion, Christian antisemitism before and during the Nazi period, and Christian-Jewish understanding. Christian and Jewish participants held joint religious services, and the Munich Jewish community gave a reception for leading Catholic representatives at the congress.

The theme of 1984 brotherhood week, organized by the German Coordinating Council of Associations for Christian-Jewish Cooperation and its affiliates in all parts of the country, was "Jewish Heritage in Germany—Message and Challenge." The Coordinating Council's 1984 Buber and Rosenzweig Medal, presented at a televised ceremony held in Worms on March 11, went to DDR citizens Siegfried Arndt, a Protestant pastor, and Helmut Eschwege, a Jewish historian, for their personal contributions to Christian-Jewish dialogue and cooperation. Rabbi Henry G. Brandt, Rev. Eckhard von Nordheim, and Father Hans Hermann Henrix were elected new joint chairmen of the council.

The Institute of Contemporary History at Munich started a comprehensive research and documentation project on the history of German Jews during the Nazi era. The state agency for political education in Baden-Württemberg held a seminar on Jewish and Israeli issues for non-Jewish teachers and educators. The Holocaust was the subject of an international meeting of historians, with Israeli, British, and German participants, held at Stuttgart in May. The conference was arranged by the local university, the Library of Contemporary History, and the German Committee of the International Society for the History of World War II. Germania Judaica, the library of German-Jewish history in Cologne, with 34,000 volumes, celebrated its 25th anniversary. It had been awarded the 1983 Walter Meckauer medal for furthering German-Jewish understanding. The 1984 Meckauer medal went to the New York German-language weekly *Aufbau* ("Reconstruction").

Exhibitions shown in various West German centers during the year dealt with the history of Jews in Cologne, Badenia, Württemberg, and Hanover as well as with other Jewish subjects. In Worms, the 950th anniversary of Germany's oldest synagogue was marked by two exhibitions, one on the history of the famous local Jewish community, the other on Jewish contributions to German literature and science, both arranged by the Worms municipality. A history of Jewish Worms was published for the anniversary, and a commemorative coin showing the Rashi Synagogue was offered for sale by a local savings bank.

Exhibits relating to the German-Jewish literary historian Walter A. Berendsohn and to composer Richard Wagner and his relations with Jews were presented. An exhibit of special interest featured photographs of the Warsaw ghetto taken by a Nazi soldier, Joe J. Heydecker. Jewish sections were opened in the Berlin Museum and the museum of the Hesse provincial town of Hofgeismar. An international symposium on Jewish and Christian art in the Middle Ages was held at Wolfenbüttel. A seminar on "Jews in Books for Children and Adolescents since 1750" was arranged by the German Academy of Child and Youth Literature at Volkach. Jewish cultural and film weeks were arranged at Frankfurt and Erlangen, and a Yiddish song festival was held in Wuppertal.

The European premiere of the documentary film *Genocide*, produced by the Simon Wiesenthal Center of Los Angeles, took place at the Dachau camp memorial site in May.

A delegation from the American Jewish Committee, headed by president Howard Friedman, visited the Federal Republic at the invitation of the Konrad Adenauer Foundation in Bonn. The group held extensive talks with non-Jewish and Jewish representatives.

B'nai B'rith's gold medal for "distinguished leadership and services to humanity" was conferred on leading German industrialist Rolf Rodenstock, president of the Union of German Industries.

For helping to rescue persecuted Jews during the Nazi regime, the Service Cross of the German Order of Merit was awarded to Carola Müller, Ilse Schwersensky, and Gerhard Schwersensky. Jews, Catholics, and Protestants honored Oskar Schindler, the late German rescuer of over 1,200 Jews, at a ceremony in Frankfurt.

A Raoul Wallenberg Committee was set up in Düsseldorf to help clarify the fate of the Swedish diplomat and to publicize his rescue work.

Publications

New books dealing with aspects of the German-Jewish situation included Saul Friedländer, *Kitsch und Tod: Der Widerschein des Nazismus* ("Kitsch and Death: Reflections of Nazism"; Hanser); Leon Brandt, *Menschen ohne Schatten: Juden zwischen Untergang und Untergrund 1938 bis 1945* ("Men Without Shadows: Jews Between Extinction and Underground 1938–1945"; Oberbaum); Konrad Kwiet/ Helmut Eschwege, *Selbstbehauptung und Widerstand: Deutsche Juden im Kampf um Existenz und Menschenwürde 1933–1945* ("Self-Assertion and Resistance: German Jews in Their Fight for Existence and Human Dignity 1933–1945"; Christians); Paul Assall, *Juden im Elsaß* ("Jews in Alsace"; Elster Verlag Moos); Erhard R. Wiehn, *Kaddisch: Totengebet in Polen, Reisegespräche und Zeitzeugnisse gegen Vergessen in Deutschland* ("Kaddish: Death Prayer in Poland, Travel Conversations and Contemporary Testimonies Against German Forgetfulness"; Darmstädter Blätter); Günther B. Ginzel, ed., *Jüdischer Alltag in Deutschland 1933 bis 1945: Fotografierte Zeitgeschichte* ("Everyday Jewish Life in Germany 1933–1945: Photographs of Contemporary History"; Droste); Herman Dicker, *Aus Württembergs jüdischer Vergangenheit und Gegenwart* ("From Württemberg's Jewish Past and

Present"; Bleicher); Ludwig Marum, *Briefe aus dem Konzentrationslager Kislau* ("Letters from the Kislau Concentration Camp"; C.F. Müller); Arthur Prinz, *Juden im deutschen Wirtschaftsleben: Soziale und wirtschaftliche Struktur im Wandel 1850 bis 1914* ("Jews in German Economic Life: Changing Social and Economic Structure 1850–1914"; Mohr); Alphons Silbermann, *Was ist jüdischer Geist ? Zur Identität der Juden* ("What Is Jewish Spirit? On Jewish Identity"; Fromm); Fritz Reuter, *Warmaisa: 1000 Jahre Juden in Worms* ("Warmaisa: 1000 Years of Jews in Worms"; Der Wormsgau, Worms); Léon Poliakov, Christian Delacampagne, and Patrick Girard, *Über den Rassismus: Sechzehn Kapitel zur Anatomie, Geschichte und Deutung des Rassenwahns* ("On Racism: 16 Chapters on Anatomy, History, and Definition of Racial Mania"; Klett-Cotta-Ullstein); Naftali Herbert Sonn and Otto Berge, *Schicksalswege der Juden in Fulda und Umgebung* ("Roads of Destiny of Jews in Fulda and Neighborhood"; Cre-art); Peter Dudek and Hans-Gerd Jaschke, *Entstehung und Entwicklung des Rechtsextremismus in der Bundesrepublik: Zur Tradition einer besonderen politischen Kultur* ("Rise and Development of Right-Wing Extremism in the Federal Republic: On the Tradition of a Special Political Culture"; Westdeutscher Verlag); Wolfgang Benz, ed., *Rechtsextremismus in der Bundesrepublik: Voraussetzungen, Zusammenhänge, Wirkungen* ("Right-Wing Extremism in the Federal Republic: Preconditions, Contexts, Consequences"; Fischer); Giovanni di Lorenzo, *Stefan, 22, deutscher Rechtsterrorist: Mein Traum ist der Traum von vielen* ("Stefan, 22, German Right-Wing Terrorist: My Dream Is the Dream of Many"; Rowohlt); Jürgen Weber and Peter Steinbach, eds., *Vergangenheitsbewältigung durch Strafverfahren? NS-Prozesse in der Bundesrepublik Deutschland* ("Coming to Grips with the Past Through Criminal Proceedings? Nazi Trials in the German Federal Republic";Olzog); Michael Jovy, *Jugendbewegung und Nationalsozialismus: Zusammenhänge und Gegensätze.* ("Youth Movement and National Socialism: Contexts and Contrasts;" Lit); György Ranki, *Unternehmen Margarethe: Die deutsche Besetzung Ungarns* ("Operation Margarethe: The German Occupation of Hungary"; Böhlau); Henri Jacob Hempel, ed., *Wenn ich schon ein Fremder sein muß: Deutsch-jüdische Emigranten in New York* ("If I Have to Be an Alien: German-Jewish Emigrants in New York"; Ullstein); Georg Denzler and Volker Fabricius, eds., *Die Kirchen im Dritten Reich: Christen und Nazis Hand in Hand?* ("The Churches in the Third Reich: Christians and Nazis Hand in Hand?"; Fischer); Y.Ahren, C. B. Melchers, W.Seifert, and W.Wagner, eds., *Das Lehrstück "Holocaust": Wirkungen und Nachwirkungen eines Medienereignisses* (" 'Holocaust'; A Didactic Drama: Effects and Repercussions of a Media Event"; Westdeutscher Verlag); Fabian von Schlabrendorff, *Offiziere gegen Hitler* ("Officers Against Hitler"; Siedler); Ulrich von Hassel, *Vom anderen Deutschland: Tagebuchaufzeichnungen 1938–1944* ("On the Other Germany: Notes from a Diary 1938–1944"; Siedler); Gerhard Ritter, *Carl Goerdeler und die deutsche Widerstandsbewegung* ("Carl Goerdeler and the German Resistance Movement"; Deutsche Verlagsanstalt); Richard Löwenthal and Patrick von zur Mühlen, eds., *Widerstand und Verweigerung in Deutschland 1933–1945* ("Resistance and Refusal in Germany 1933–1945"; Dietz); Rudolf Lill and Heinrich Oberreuter, eds., 20.Juli: Portraits des Widerstandes ("July 20: Portraits of the Resistance";Econ); Ingrid Weckert, Feuerzeichen: Die "Reichskristallnacht," Anstifter und Brandstifter, Opfer und Nutznießer ("Fire Signals: The 'Reich Crystal Night,' Instigators and Arsonists, Victims and Profiteers"; Grabert); Walter N. Sanning, "Die Auflösung" des osteuropäischen Judentums: Eine technische Studie zur demographischen Entwicklung der Juden der Neuzeit ("The Disintegration of East European Jewry: A Technical Study on the Demographic Development of Jewry in Modern Times";Grabert); Karl-Dietrich Bracher, ed., Das Gewissen steht auf: Lebensbilder aus dem deutschen Widerstand ("The Rising of Conscience: Biographical Data of the German Resistance"; Hase & Koehler); Hans-Jochen Markmann, Der deutsche Widerstand gegen den Nationalsozialismus 1933–1945: Modelle für den Unterricht ("German Resistance Against National Socialism 1933–1945: Models for Instruction"; Hase & Koehler); Heiner Lichtenstein, Im Namen des Volkes? Eine persönliche Bilanz der NS-Prozesse ("In the People's Name? A Personal Balance Sheet of Nazi Trials"; Bund).

New publications on Israel and on Middle East issues included Yohanan Aharoni, Das Land der Bibel: Eine historische Geographie ("The Land of the Bible: A Historical Geography"; Neukirchener); Peter Gradenwitz, Das Heilige Land in Augenzeugenberichten deutscher Pilger, Kaufleute und Abenteurer vom 10. bis zum 19.Jahrhundert ("The Holy Land in Eyewitness Accounts of German Pilgrims, Merchants, and Adventurers from the 10th to the 19th Century"; Deutscher Taschenbuchverlag); Michael Wolffsohn, Israel: Politik, Gesellschaft und Wirtschaft ("Israel: Policy, Society, and Economy"; Leske); Chaim Herzog, Kriege um Israel: Von 1948 bis 1984 ("Israel's Wars: 1948–1984"; Ullstein); Daniel Wiener, ed., Shalom: Israels Friedensbewegung ("Shalom: Israel's Peace Movement"; Rowohlt); Walter Ackerman, Arye Carmon, and David Zucker, eds., Erziehung in Israel ("Education in Israel"; Klett-Cotta); Gernot Müller-Serten, Palästinas feindliche Brüder: Der endlose Konflikt am Jordan und seine Geschichte ("Palestine's Hostile Brothers: The Unending Conflict on the Jordan and Its History"; Econ).

New volumes on Judaism and Jewish history included Jürgen Stemmler, Erlebtes Israel: Eine biblisch-geschichtliche Reise ("Israel Witnessed: A Biblical-Historical Journey"; Goertz); Joseph Ehrlich, Schabbat: Religion und Ritus einer polnischen Judenfamilie ("Shabbat: Religion and Rites of a Polish-Jewish Family"; Trikont-Dianus); Rudolf Sussmann, ed., Zeugnisse jüdischer Vergangenheit in Unterfranken ("Testimonies of a Jewish Past in Lower Franconia"; Bayerische Verlagsanstalt); Walter Kickel, Das gelobte Land: Die religiöse Bedeutung des Staates Israel in jüdischer und christlicher Sicht ("The Promised Land: The Religious Importance of the State of Israel in Jewish and Christian Perspective"; Kösel); Jacob Neusner, Das pharisäische und talmudische Judentum: Neue Wege zu seinem Verständnis ("Pharisaic and Talmudic Judaism: New Roads to Understanding"; Mohr); Günther B. Ginzel, ed., Antisemitismus: Erscheinungsformen und Motive des Judenhasses gestern und heute ("Antisemitism: Manifestations and Motives of Hatred

Against the Jews Yesterday and Today"; Lambert Schneider); Heinz Gstrein, *Jüdisches Wien* ("Jewish Vienna"; Herold); Johannes Lehmann, *Moses—Der Mann aus Ägypten: Religionsstifter, Gesetzgeber, Staatsgründer* ("Moses—The Man from Egypt: Legislator, Founder of Religion and State"; Hoffmann und Campe); Hans Liebeschütz, *Synagoge und Ecclesia: Religionsgeschichtliche Studien über die Auseinandersetzung der Kirche mit dem Judentum im Hochmittelalter* ("Synagogue and Ecclesia: Religious History Studies of the Conflict Between the Church and Judaism in the High Middle Ages"; Lambert Schneider); Elie Wiesel, *Geschichten gegen die Melancholie: Die Weisheit der chassidischen Meister* ("Stories Against Melancholy: The Wisdom of the Chassidic Masters"; Herder); Laurenz Volken, *Jesus der Jude und das Jüdische im Christentum* ("Jesus the Jew and the Jewish in Christianity"; Patmos); Hans-Joachim Schoeps, *Judentum und Christentum in der Auseinandersetzung um die Wahrheit: Jüdisch-christliches Religionsgespräch in neunzehn Jahrhunderten* ("Jews and Christians in Their Fight for Truth: Jewish-Christian Dialogue During Nineteen Centuries"; Jüdischer Verlag Athenäum); Clemens Thoma, *Die theologischen Beziehungen zwischen Christentum und Judentum* ("The Theological Relations Between Christians and Jews"; Wissenschaftliche Buchgesellschaft Darmstadt); Abraham Joshua Heschel, *Der Mensch fragt nach Gott* ("Man's Quest for God"; Neukirchener); Abraham Joshua Heschel, *Gott sucht den Menschen: Eine Philosophie des Judentums* ("God in Search of Man: A Philosophy of Judaism"; Neukirchener); Franz J. Bautz, ed., *Geschichte der Juden: Von der biblischen Zeit zur Gegenwart* ("History of the Jews: From Biblical Times to the Present"; Beck).

New titles in the fields of literature and biography included Reinhard Bendix, *Von Berlin nach Berkeley: Deutsch-jüdische Identitäten* ("From Berlin to Berkeley: German-Jewish Identities"; Suhrkamp); Wilhelm Unger, *Wofür ist das ein Zeichen? Auswahl aus veröffentlichten und unveröffentlichten Werken des Kritikers und Autors* ("What Does This Signify? A Selection of Published and Unpublished Texts by the Critic and Author"; DuMont); Renate Heuer, *Bibliographia Judaica: Verzeichnis jüdischer Autoren deutscher Sprache* ("Bibliographia Judaica: A Catalog of German-Language Jewish Authors"; Campus); Leo Nadelmann, *Jiddische Erzählungen von Mendele Mojcher Sforim, Jitzhak Lejb Perez, Sholem Alejchem* ("Yiddish Stories by Mendele Mocher Sforim, Yitzhak Leib Peretz, Sholem Aleichem"; Manesse); Thomas B. Schumann, *Asphaltliteratur: 45 Aufsätze und Hinweise zu im Dritten Reich verfemten und verfolgten Autoren* ("Asphalt Literature: 45 Essays and Annotations on Authors Outlawed and Persecuted in the Third Reich"; Guhl); Sidney Alexander, *Marc Chagall: Eine Biographie* ("Marc Chagall: A Biography"; Kindler); Rose Ausländer, *Hügel/aus Äther/unwiderruflich: Gedichte und Prosa 1966 bis 1975* ("Hills/Of Ether/Irrevocable: Poems and Prose 1966–1975"; Fischer); Rose Ausländer, *Im Aschenregen/die Spur deines Namens: Gedichte und Prosa 1976* ("In the Rain of Ashes/The Trace of Your Name: Poems and Prose 1976"; Fischer); Berndt W.Wessling, *Max Brod: Ein Portrait zum 100.Geburtstag* ("Max Brod: A Portrait on His 100th Birthday"; Bleicher);Ruth Dinesen and

Helmut Müssener, eds., *Briefe der Nelly Sachs* ("Letters of Nelly Sachs"; Suhrkamp); Bernd Sösemann, ed., *Theodor Wolff: Tagebücher 1914–1919* ("Theodor Wolff: Diaries 1914–1919"; Boldt); Jakob Wassermann, *Schläfst du, Mutter?— Meistererzählungen* ("Are You Sleeping, Mother?—Master Stories"; Langen-Müller); Hans Dieter Hellige, ed., *Walther Rathenau/Maximilian Harden: Briefwechsel 1897–1930* ("Walther Rathenau/Maximilian Harden: Correspondence 1897–1930"; Müller-Schneider); Gerhard Hecker, *Walther Rathenau und sein Verhältnis zu Militär und Krieg* ("Walther Rathenau and His Attitude on the Armed Forces and War"; Boldt); Bernd Sösemann, ed., *Theodor Wolff: Die Juden. Ein Dokument aus dem Exil 1942/43* ("Theodor Wolff: The Jews, A Document from Exile 1942/43"; Jüdischer Verlag Athenäum); Gunter E.Grimm and Hans-Peter Bayerdörfer, eds., *Im Zeichen Hiobs: Jüdische Schriftsteller und deutsche Literatur im 20. Jahrhundert* ("In the Name of Job: Jewish Authors and German Literature in the 20th Century"; Jüdischer Verlag Athenäum); Franz Kobler, ed., *Dreihundert Jahre jüdische Geschichte im deutschen Sprachraum: Juden und Judentum in deutschen Briefen aus drei Jahrhunderten* ("Three Hundred Years of Jewish History in the German-Language Region: Jews and Judaism in German Letters from Three Centuries"; Jüdischer Verlag Athenäum); Jürgen Schebera, *Kurt Weill: Leben und Werk* ("Kurt Weill: Life and Work"; Jüdischer Verlag Athenäum); Sammy Gronemann, *Hawdoloh und Zapfenstreich: Erinnerungen an die ostjüdische Etappe 1916–18* ("Havdalah and Tattoo: Memories of the Eastern Jewish Rear Area 1916–18"; Jüdischer Verlag Athenäum); Rosa Luxemburg, *Ich umarme Sie in großer Sehnsucht: Briefe aus dem Gefängnis 1915–1918* ("I Embrace You with Great Longing: Letters from Prison 1915–1918"; Dietz); Konrad Feilchenfeldt, Uwe Schweikert, and Rahel E. Steiner, eds., *Rahel Varnhagen: Gesammelte Werke* ("Rahel Varnhagen: Complete Works"; Matthes & Seitz); Joseph Schupack, *Tote Jahre. Eine jüdische Leidensgeschichte* ("Dead Years: A Story of Jewish Suffering"; Katzmann); Werner Lansburgh and Frank-Wolf Matthies, *Exil: Ein Briefwechsel. Mit Essays, Gedichten und Dokumenten* ("Exile: A Correspondence, with Essays, Poems and Documents"; Bund); Salomo Friedlaender-Mynona, *Briefe aus dem Exil 1933–1946* ("Letters from Exile 1933–1946"; Hase & Koehler); Klaus Wagenbach, *Franz Kafka: Bilder aus seinem Leben* ("Franz Kafka: Pictures from His Life"; Wagenbach); Hans Schafgans, *Die Insel* ("The Island"; Bleicher); Herbert Freeden, *Der Vorhang fiel im November* ("The Curtain Dropped in November"; Bleicher); Antonia Bruha, *Ich war keine Heldin* ("I Was No Heroine"; Europa); Walter Tetzlaff, *2000 Kurzbiographien bedeutender deutscher Juden des 20.Jahrhunderts* ("2000 Short Biographies of Important German Jews of the 20th Century"; Asknia); M. and J. Papst, eds., *Die schönsten jüdischen Liebesgeschichten* ("The Most Beautiful Jewish Love Stories"; Diogenes); Marek Halter, *Abraham: Wege der Erinnerung* ("The Book of Abraham"; Kübler Akselrad); Silvia Tennenbaum, *Straßen von gestern* ("Streets of Yesterday"; Knaus); Alexander Eliasberg, ed. and trans., *Wie Baal Schem ins Heilige Land kam und andere ostjüdische Legenden* ("How Baal

Shem Came into the Holy Land and Other Eastern Jewish Legends"; Insel); Georg Langer, *Der Rabbi, über den der Himmel lachte: Die schönsten Geschichten der Chassidim* ("The Rabbi Who Made the Sky Laugh: The Most Beautiful Chassidic Stories"; Scherz); Hans Lamm, *Deutsch-jüdischer Publizist: Ausgewählte Aufsätze 1933–1983* ("A German-Jewish Publicist: Selected Texts 1933–1983"; Saur); Wilhelm von Sternburg, *Lion Feuchtwanger: Ein deutsches Schriftstellerleben* ("Lion Feuchtwanger: The Life of a German Author"; Jüdischer Verlag Athenäum); Rudolf Wolff, ed., *Lion Feuchtwanger: Werk und Wirkung* ("Lion Feuchtwanger: Work and Impact"; Bouvier); Volker Skierka and Stefan Jaeger, eds., *Lion Feuchtwanger: Eine Biographie* ("Lion Feuchtwanger: A Biography"; Quadriga); Wolfgang Jeske and Peter Zahn, *Feuchtwanger oder der arge Weg der Erkenntnis: Eine Biographie* ("Feuchtwanger or the Hard Way of Recognition: A Biography"; Metzler); Reinhold Jaretzky, *Lion Feuchtwanger: Monographie* ("Lion Feuchtwanger: A Monograph"; Rowohlt).

Personalia

Robert M.W. Kempner, 85, Frankfurt lawyer and former U.S. deputy prosecutor-general at the Nuremberg war crimes tribunal, received the Great Service Cross with star and ribbon of the West German Federal Order of Merit, the country's highest honor. Max Kampelman, U.S. diplomat and former head of the U.S. delegation at the Madrid Conference on Security and Cooperation in Europe, received the Great Service Cross with star. Adolph Lowe, 91, a founder of the New School for Social Research (University in Exile) in New York, who returned to Germany in 1983, received the Great Service Cross of Merit.

Israeli citizens awarded the Great Service Cross for their contributions to German-Israeli understanding were: Akiva Lewinsky, treasurer of the Jewish Agency and World Zionist Organization; Ernest J. Japhet, chairman of the board of the Bank Leumi; and Joseph Cohn, director of the European office of the Weizmann Institute of Sciences, in Zurich. The Federal Service Cross was awarded to Yehudit Huebner, Israeli diplomat; Nissan Harpaz, Jerusalem Histadrut secretary-general; Raya Jaglom, president of the Women's International Zionist Organization (WIZO); Shalom Levin, president of the Israeli teachers' union; Yehuda Erel, head of Tel Aviv's municipal department for international affairs and tourism; Adin Talbar, cofounder of the Israeli-German Chamber of Commerce and founder of the Jerusalem section of the Israeli-German Society; Eliahu Ben-Yehuda, who had been active in the field of Israeli-German youth exchange; and journalist and historian Werner David Melchior.

The Service Cross was also awarded to Ernst Ludwig Ehrlich, philosopher, author, and director of the European district of B'nai B'rith, in Switzerland; Julius Spokojny, head of the Jewish community in Augsburg; Oskar Althausen, leader of the Mannheim Jewish community; Jakob Safier, prominent member of the Munich

Jewish community; Jakob J. Petuchowski, professor of Jewish-Christian Studies at Hebrew Union College in Cincinnati, Ohio; and Rolf Simon, journalist and author, of San Francisco, California.

American historian and author Walter Laqueur received the 1984 Award for Literature and the Fine Arts given by InterNationes, a Bonn state institution promoting international relations. Marcel Reich-Ranicki, journalist, author, and literary editor of the *Frankfurter Allgemeine Zeitung* since 1973, received the Goethe Medal of the Frankfurt municipality. The state-financed Andreas Gryphius Prize was awarded to Dresden-born poet, author, critic, and translator Hans Sahl, in New York. The 1984 literary prize of the Bavarian Academy of Fine Arts was awarded to poet Rose Ausländer, of Düsseldorf.

Alfred Weichselbaum, director of the Central Welfare Agency of Jews in Germany at Frankfurt and a leading figure in postwar German-Jewish life, died on February 8, 1984, at the age of 61.

FRIEDO SACHSER

German Democratic Republic

O F THE 600 registered Jews living in the German Democratic Republic (DDR), 200 were in East Berlin and the balance in Dresden, Halle, Karl-Marx-Stadt, Leipzig, Magdeburg, Schwerin, and Erfurt. There were thought to be several thousand other Jews in East Germany who were not affiliated with the organized Jewish communities. About two-thirds of the Jews in the DDR were over 60 years of age.

The East Berlin community, without a rabbi or cantor since 1969, received help in ritual matters from the West Berlin community and from Jewish communities in other Soviet bloc countries, particularly for high holy day services. The only kosher slaughterhouse in the country, located in East Berlin, brought a *shoḥet* from Budapest every fortnight to slaughter meat—not only for the Jewish community but also for Seventh Day Adventists and Muslim diplomats living in East Berlin.

Financial support from the East German government amounting to M 170,000 was used by the East Berlin Jewish community for cultural and social activities and for the maintenance of the only Jewish home for the aged in the DDR. Maintenance of Jewish cemeteries in East Berlin, including the Weissensee—with 115,000 graves the largest in Europe—was financed by an additional M 150,000. The activities of the remaining Jewish communities were financed by the state with an additional sum of approximately M 250,000.

On the occasion of the 35th-anniversary celebration of the establishment of the DDR, in October, Jewish representatives expressed pride in being citizens of a country where they could live unmolested and loyal to their faith. Helmut Aris, president of the Federation of Jewish Communities in the DDR, stressed the communities' sense of security and their awareness that fascism, antisemitism, and war-mongering had no breeding ground in the DDR. In a message to Mr. Aris on the occasion of the Jewish New Year, the DDR government praised the Jewish community for its active participation in the successful upbuilding of the socialist state.

On the 40th anniversary of the anti-Hitler plot, DDR representatives laid a wreath paying homage "to the victims of July 20, 1944" at the memorial site of the former Nazi concentration camp at Sachsenhausen. A wreath was laid on the same site by the head of the West German diplomatic standing mission in East Berlin, Hans Otto Bräutigam. In September a museum documenting opposition to the Nazi regime opened on the site of the former Nazi concentration camp at Ravensbrück, the women's camp where more than 92,000 women and children perished.

The community welcomed a number of foreign visitors, including German-born U.S. rabbi Ernest Lorge, who conducted Rosh Hashanah services at the Rykestrasse synagogue in East Berlin. Services were conducted there in May by Rabbi Zalman Schachter, who came with a delegation from Temple University in Philadelphia, together with rabbis Alan Mittleman and Lewis Eron and Christian representatives.

Kurt Cohn, member of the East Berlin Jewish community and a former judge of the DDR supreme court, received the state's highest honor, the Golden Star of Friendship Between Nations. Karin Mylius, head of the Jewish community in Halle, received the Fatherland's Order of Merit in Bronze. From the hands of West Berlin Jewish leader Heinz Galinski, Marie Grünberg of East Berlin received the Yad Vashem medal and citation, "Righteous Gentile." On the occasion of the 50th anniversary of the murder of writer and politician Erich Mühsam at the Oranienburg concentration camp, the DDR publishing house Volk und Welt released a volume of hitherto unknown texts by the author, *Pamphlets & Literary Leftovers*.

The DDR continued its anti-Israel, pro-Arab policy. State and party chief Erich Honecker, at a reception for Farouk Al-Khaddoumi, head of the political section of the Palestine Liberation Organization, called the PLO "the only legitimate representative of the Palestinian people." Cooperation between the DDR and the PLO was underscored by Honecker's meeting with Yasir Arafat in Bucharest in August. DDR criticism of Israeli policy was voiced before international agencies debating Middle East issues, particularly the United Nations.

FRIEDO SACHSER

Eastern Europe

Soviet Union

Domestic Affairs

AFTER only 15 months in office—the shortest tenure of any Soviet leader up to that point—Yuri Andropov died on February 9, 1984, at the age of 69. He had been out of the public view for the previous six months, during which time —official denials notwithstanding—he had been gravely ill. Andropov was succeeded as both first secretary of the Communist party and as head of the Soviet state by 72-year-old Konstantin Chernenko, who had been Andropov's major rival for the succession following the death of Leonid Brezhnev in November 1982. Chernenko, a protégé of Brezhnev, had spent his entire career in the party apparatus, largely involved in the areas of ideology and culture, and had served as head of the General Department of the Central Committee.

While Andropov's tenure had been brief, he managed to make his mark on Soviet society, especially in his attempts to tighten discipline in the economic, political, and cultural spheres. Despite Chernenko's close association with Brezhnev, under whom corruption and inefficiency had reached levels which Andropov was not ready to tolerate, the new leader did not renounce Andropov's anticorruption campaign. Rather he continued it at a more moderate pace.

Just before Andropov's death, and after much public discussion, the USSR adopted a major program of school reform. The first of its two main goals was to insure that non-Russian nationality groups acquire better knowledge of the Russian language; the second was to encourage more Soviet young people to pursue technological and industrial vocations rather than going on to university education. At the time the reform program was announced, about 40 percent of the student population spent the last two years of its schooling in technical-vocational institutions; the goal of reform was to raise this figure to 60 percent. The implications for nationalities with strong traditional aspirations to higher education, such as Jews, Armenians, and Georgians, were clearly negative.

More disturbing in the short run was the passage of a law in February requiring prison terms for anyone caught passing economic, scientific, technical, or other official *("sluzhebnye")* secrets to foreigners, with the definition of "secret" being determined solely by the state and party. Another new law required Soviet citizens with foreign house guests to register them with the local authorities. Measures like these, together with the continued crackdown on dissidents and the further harassment of scientist Andrei Sakharov and his wife, Elena Bonner, signaled a continued, and perhaps even stepped-up, tightening of the political reins.

In the economic sphere, agriculture continued to be a major problem. The officially planned harvest of 240 million metric tons fell short by some 60 million tons. The U.S. Department of Agriculture estimated that the USSR would have to import 43 million tons of grain in 1984, only slightly less than the record 46 million tons imported in 1982. Oil production also fell short, a development that had been predicted by some Western observers, based on the declining output of the Tiumen fields.

Under Andropov there had been expectations that tightened discipline and the imposition of a stronger work ethic would reverse the economic slowdown. Chernenko, however, offered no such hope. He was very much part of the Brezhnev group, which, in the last decade, had emphasized "stability of cadres," opposing all efforts that threatened to disturb the equilibrium of society.

The new faces introduced into the party leadership by Andropov continued in their positions under Chernenko. At the same time, some of the old guard began to slip away. Thus, the minister of defense, Marshal Ustinov, died of a stroke in December at the age of 76.

In the elections to the Supreme Soviet of the USSR in March, eight Jews—two more than in 1979—won seats. Of the eight, three were from Birobidzhan, the official Jewish autonomous region, which sent only five deputies altogether to the Supreme Soviet. In point of fact, Birobidzhan Jews accounted for only 5.3 percent of that region's population—and only half of 1 percent of the entire Soviet Jewish population.

Foreign Affairs

Soviet-American relations deteriorated further in 1984. The main issues dividing the two countries were the Soviet military effort in Afghanistan, human rights and emigration concerns, differences over the Middle East and Central America, and arms control. Tensions between the two superpowers were reflected in a number of minor incidents, including an assault on an American vice-consul in the USSR, the harassment of tourists in Leningrad—to the point where the American government issued a warning to tourists traveling there—and the beating and temporary jailing of a marine guard stationed at the U.S. embassy.

The most troubling episode of the year was the USSR's announcement in May that it would not participate in the summer Olympic Games in Los Angeles, on the grounds that the U.S. government could not guarantee the safety of its athletes. Several private groups in the United States had announced their intention to demonstrate at the Olympics against the violation of human rights in the USSR, and some had promised aid to any Soviet athlete who would defect. Whether the Soviets were motivated by these actions or by the desire to retaliate for the U.S. boycott of the 1980 Moscow Olympics was not clear. All of the USSR's East European allies except Rumania stayed away from Los Angeles, and a competing set of games was held in Moscow, largely for those athletes whose countries did not participate in the American games.

The two superpowers did make some conciliatory gestures during the year: agreement was reached on modernizing the "hot line" between Moscow and Washington; the 1980 ban on Soviet fishing in U.S. waters was lifted; and the ceiling was raised on Soviet purchases of American grain.

Some sectors of the American public that were becoming increasingly alarmed over the deterioration of U.S.-Soviet relations attempted to revive contacts with the Soviet public and leadership. A delegation of 266 church leaders, sponsored by the National Council of Churches, toured the Soviet Union. The group issued a statement praising freedom of religion there, while condemning the American role in the arms race.

In early November the daughter of Joseph Stalin, Svetlana Alliluyeva, returned to the USSR after many years in the West, declaring that she was disillusioned with life there and wanted to be reunited with the Soviet branch of her family.

JEWISH COMMUNITY

Demography

Because the published findings of the 1979 census were not as detailed as those of the previous two censuses (1959 and 1970), there was less information available about the current Jewish population. Still, the volume based on the 1979 census, published in 1984, did contain some revealing data. According to the 1979 census, there were 1,810,876 Jews in the USSR, down from 2,151,000 in 1970. The largest concentration continued to reside in the Russian republic (700,651) and the second largest in the Ukraine (634,154), where Jews were the third-largest nationality.

Some 14.2 percent of Soviet Jews declared Yiddish as their mother tongue *(rodnoi iazyk)*. There was, however, substantial geographical variation. In the Ukraine, for example, 19 percent of the Jews residing in Vinnitsa *oblast* declared Yiddish as their mother tongue, whereas in Donetsk and Dnepropetrovsk *oblasti*—which were more heavily urbanized and industrialized—only 4.1 and 4.5 percent, respectively, did so. Of the Jews in Birobidzhan, only 13.4 percent claimed Yiddish as their first language. In Lithuania, 41 percent of the Jews declared Yiddish as their mother tongue, but this figure may be misleading. The Jewish population of that republic had declined from 24,000 in 1970 to 15,000 in 1979, due largely to emigration, and the remaining Jews were presumably older and Yiddish-speaking.

While there are no precise figures on intermarriage in the Soviet Union, estimates can be developed indirectly from census findings. Data are provided on average family size, by nationality, for each republic. While families are defined as people living in the same household, it is not clear how the nationality of a family is defined. In the Russian republic (RSFSR)—to offer one example—there were 2.9 people in the average "ethnically homogeneous" Jewish family. Multiplying the number of Jewish families in the RSFSR (127,281) by average family size (2.9) yields 369,115 Jews living in homogeneously Jewish families. When this figure is subtracted from the total number of Jews in the RSFSR (700,651), the remainder is the number of Jews living in families with a non-Jewish member (331,536), or 47.3 percent of the republic's Jewish population. Of course, when a family is listed as "mixed," we cannot tell how many non-Jews there are in the family or which member or members are not Jewish. Despite these shortcomings, however, the extrapolation does provide some inkling of the proportion of mixed families among Russian Jews. In the Ukraine this proportion was about one-third and in Belorussia slightly less than 30 percent. These data confirm the general impression that intermarriage is highest in the Russian republic and lower in the areas formerly in the Pale of Settlement. It is undoubtedly still lower in Georgia, Central Asia, and Moldavia, areas where Jewish tradition and religion have been stronger than in the Slavic republics.

Emigration

The number of Jewish emigrants continued to decline in 1984. For the first time since the late 1960s fewer than a thousand Jews were allowed to leave the country; whereas 1,314 had left in 1983, only 894 did so in 1984. Emigration of ethnic Germans and Armenians was also reduced. At a press conference of the Anti-Zionist Committee of the Soviet Public, held at the Foreign Ministry on May 15 (Israeli Independence Day), Prof. S.L. Zivs, a well-known Soviet spokesman on political and ideological matters, declared that "the process of reuniting separated families is practically over." This was one of several official rationales offered by the authorities to explain the closing off of emigration.

Antisemitism and Jewish Resistance

There was no change in the status of Jews within Soviet society. The Soviet media continued to attack Zionism and Israel, as well as the Jewish religion, usually making it quite clear that all of these were associated with Jews as individuals. In the Ukraine alone, nearly a dozen books attacking Zionism were published. Boris Kravtsov's *Flight from the Ghetto,* purporting to be based on the testimony of a Soviet Jew who had emigrated first to Israel and then to the United States before returning to the Soviet Union, was published in Leningrad in 330,000 copies. The well-known anti-Zionist writer V. Bol'shakov published a book, in an edition of 100,000, titled *Aggression Against Reason,* which included a chapter on Zionism, the "shock brigade" of imperialism. L.E. Berenshtain's *Zionism—Enemy of Peace and Social Progress* contained chapters entitled "Expansionism and Terror—the Face of Zionism" and "Zionism—Racism in Action." In Odessa, a book titled *Zionism in the Service of World Reaction* was published in an edition of 25,000. One of the recurring themes in this literature was the alleged collaboration between the Zionists and the Nazis, even at the height of the Holocaust.

The campaign against Zionism was not confined to "agitation and propaganda" but was also expressed in harassment and persecution of would-be emigrants to Israel. Anatoly Shcharansky, sentenced in 1978 to three years in prison and ten years in labor camps, and again in 1981 to three more years of labor, was said to be in declining health. Despite intercession by several international figures, Soviet authorities gave no sign of allowing him to emigrate or even of commuting his sentence.

Prominent as well as relatively unknown Jewish activists continued to be arrested and sentenced to prison and labor camps, often on trumped-up charges. Yosef Bernshtain was sentenced to four years in a labor camp for "resisting arrest"; Yuli Edelshtain was sentenced to three years in a prison camp for "illegal trafficking in drugs," after the authorities apparently planted some in a matchbox in his home. Alexander Kholmiansky was jailed for "hooliganism," as was Rabbi Moshe Abramov of Samarkand. Zakhar Zunshain was given a three-year sentence for "defaming" the Soviet system and state, and Mark Niepomniashchy was sentenced on similar charges. Yakov Mesh of Odessa was arrested for "resisting the police" and refusing to testify against another Odessa activist, Yakov Levin, who had been accused of anti-Soviet slander. Others were imprisoned on charges of embezzlement, forgery, "parasitism," or draft evasion.

In July Ephraim Katzir, a distinguished scientist and former president of the State of Israel, attempted to meet with refuseniks while attending a scientific congress in Leningrad. He was first held and interrogated by the KGB; later he and four other Israelis attending the biochemistry meeting were expelled from the country.

Even while continuing its policy of anti-Zionism, the Soviet Union was careful to retain some low-level contacts with Israel. In March a four-man Soviet Peace Committee delegation visited the Jewish state, and in May seven Soviet citizens traveled to Israel, under the auspices of the Israel-Soviet Friendship Committee, to participate in commemorations of the defeat of Nazism.

Jewish Religion

The rabbi of the Moscow Choral Synagogue, Adolf Shayevich, toured the United States at the invitation of the National Council of Churches. He reported a rise in synagogue attendance, which he attributed to an increased desire on the part of Soviet Jews "to identify with one's roots."

Chief Rabbi René Sirat of France visited the USSR, the first time in almost a decade that the Soviet government had permitted an official visit of a high-ranking Jewish figure from the West.

Jewish Culture

The Jewish collection in the Leningrad State Museum was described in an article by Tatiana Gelfman in the Yiddish monthly *Sovetish haimland* (1984, No. 2). The 1,100 objects in the museum that are related to Judaism formed part of that institution's section on the "history of religion and atheism." Included were items from the antireligious campaigns of the 1920s and 1930s as well as Torah scrolls, crowns, paintings, amulets, candlesticks, and other objects. According to the author of the article, "The purpose of the museum is to preserve and teach about the monuments of the past, using them for scholarly, atheistic and educational purposes."

An interesting feature article on contemporary Yiddish theater, published in *Sovetish haimland* (1984, Nos. 6, 7), focused on the six existing companies. The Moscow Yiddish Dramatic Ensemble, established in 1962 by survivors of the theatrical group that had been dissolved in 1948, was staffed largely by younger graduates of Moscow theater schools. The ensemble, which had only two plays in its repertoire, employed a considerable amount of Russian it its performances, in order to have "sufficient contact with the general audience." The group staged its work in Siberia, Birobidzhan, and the Baltic, but not Leningrad or Moldavia.

Yuri Sherling, director of the Birobidzhan Jewish Musical Chamber Theater, founded in 1977, related how he had grown up in an assimilated family but had become attracted to Yiddish culture. Like the Moscow ensemble, his group did not perform exclusively in Yiddish. "Our actors are young, and the theater is for them a school for learning the Yiddish language and culture," he explained. With five productions in its repertoire, the group traveled widely in the USSR and even performed in the German Democratic Republic. Sherling was working on an opera based on the life of the second-century Jewish hero Bar Kokhba.

The Vilnius (Vilna) Dramatic Amateur Collective, which originated in 1956, included some 120 participants, among them more than 50 children under the age of 15. Its director disagreed with his colleagues in Moscow and Birobidzhan about the use of Russian. "I believe the language of the Jewish stage should be Yiddish," he argued. "I'm aware of the attempt by the Moscow ensemble to go the route of bilingualism, but I don't agree. And this is the opinion [in] my environment, Lithuanian Jews [being] less assimilated, especially linguistically, than the Jews of Moscow."

The director of the Kaunas (Kovno) amateur theater, which was smaller than the one in Vilnius, suggested that in light of the shrinking number of people familiar with Yiddish language and culture, "we ought to consider establishing a center for preparing creative cadres for Soviet Jewish art."

The long-awaited Russian-Yiddish dictionary, containing 40,000 entries, was published in March in an edition of 20,000. This monumental work had been initiated in 1935 at a Jewish research institute in Kiev. Although ready for publication in 1948, the manuscript was put aside when its editor, I.G. Spivak, was arrested and executed, in 1952. Work on the project resumed in 1965, and the manuscript was finally given to a publisher in January 1982. Of the three individuals listed as editors—M.A. Shapiro, I.G. Spivak, and M.Ia. Shulman—only the last was still alive when the work appeared.

On the occasion of the observance of the 125th birthday of Sholem Aleichem, it was reported that his works had appeared in 542 editions in 24 languages, with a total of 9.5 million copies printed.

Birobidzhan

On May 7, 1934, the Birobidzhan Jewish national *raion* (district) was elevated to *oblast* (province) status. The 50th anniversary of that event was celebrated with a government award to the province, much publicity in *Sovetish haimland*—which published an article by Lev Shapiro, first secretary of the provincial Communist party committee—and a half-hour television special. Despite the region's official designation as "Jewish," there appeared to be little in the way of Jewish cultural activity there. The only Yiddish newspaper in the USSR was published in Birobidzhan, but it carried few items of specifically Jewish interest. The director of the Birobidzhan Folk Theater could name only 16 participants, 10 of them "veterans."

Personalia

Iosif Amusin, noted historian and expert on the Dead Sea Scrolls, died at the age of 74. Yankl Elkis, poet, died at the age of 89. Khane Blushchinska, a Yiddish actress active in Minsk and Moscow and the widow of the noted Yiddish poet Motl Grubian, died at the age of 69. Prior to her death she had been teaching Yiddish to young actors in Moscow.

ZVI GITELMAN

Israel

Political Affairs

NEARLY ALL OF 1984 was taken up with the elections to the 11th Knesset and surrounding events: the opposition's successful attempts to bring down the government; the precampaign selection of party lists; the actual campaign, culminating in the July 23rd election; and, finally, protracted interparty negotiations which produced a government unlike any that coalition-rich Israel had ever seen. By the time this last event had occurred, the year was three-quarters over.

TOWARD AN ELECTION

Early in the year the Labor Alignment, encouraged by polls that showed it well ahead of the ruling Likud party, intensified its efforts to topple the government of Prime Minister Yitzhak Shamir. The government coalition, reeling under the double burden of an economy threatening to lurch out of control and continuing guerrilla warfare in Lebanon, was also wracked by personal feuding within the two main components of the Likud bloc, Herut and the Liberal party. This state of affairs was reflected in the polls, which showed the prime minister trailing former president Yitzhak Navon as the "person most suited" to lead the country; more concretely, it seriously hampered the government's day-to-day functioning. Thus, in mid-January the coalition lost three Knesset votes in one week, including one on an issue central to the Likud government's ethos: a motion regarding a freeze on settlements in the administered areas.

On January 25 the government coalition barely survived three no-confidence motions. These grew out of threats by the Tami party, whose three votes were crucial for the coalition, to bolt unless its demands were met. The ethnic-oriented Tami party (which was back to full strength after its leader, MK Aharon Abuhatzeira, had served a three-month jail sentence on fraud charges) was making political capital of a recently issued report showing the spread of poverty in the country. Essentially, Tami wanted greater social benefits for the large, low-income families which presumably formed its constituency, and was not deterred in its demands by the Treasury's near bankruptcy. In the event, Tami fell into line—having wrung secret economic pledges from the finance minister and other coalition leaders—and the government survived.

The unsavory spectacle surrounding this affair led Minister Without Portfolio Mordechai Ben-Porat to threaten resignation. At the January 29 cabinet meeting, Ben-Porat pledged to support the government in principle, but said that he would judge each issue "on its own merits." With Tami making waves, and the support of Ben-Porat and former finance minister MK Yigael Hurvitz (who abstained on the no-confidence motion) wavering, the coalition, with an ostensible majority of 64-56, found itself in a precarious position.

PREPARING FOR THE CAMPAIGN

On March 22 the Knesset voted on a motion for the agenda, submitted by the Alignment, calling for the dissolution of parliament and early elections. Labor had played its hand well. Tami, riding high, so it believed (the voters were to judge differently), on the crest of the social-welfare concessions it had extracted from the Treasury, and stung by reports that the party's Swiss patron, Nessim Gaon, had been refused financial concessions by that same Treasury, announced that it would vote for the Alignment bill. Not even the hurried return of a parliamentary delegation from Argentina in the midst of a key mission (see "Israel and World Jewry") could help the government stave off defeat, since both MK Ben-Porat and MK Yitzhak Berman (Likud-Liberal), another maverick, had also decided to cast their votes with the opposition. An 11th-hour maneuver by the Likud—getting the House Committee to approve a secret ballot—was ruled out by Speaker Menahem Savidor after consultation with the attorney general. (Savidor was later dropped by the Liberals from their Knesset list for his pains.) Reinforced by the coalition defectors, the opposition pushed through the vote 61-58. The one uncast vote belonged to former prime minister Menachem Begin, who continued to remain in seclusion.

About a week later Prime Minister Shamir met with Labor party leader Peres and the two agreed on July 23 as election day. Peres came under criticism from within Labor and from the left-of-center parties for having consented to this date, the conventional wisdom (which proved to be correct) being that a late July poll would cost the Labor Alignment and its natural allies votes, since supporters of this bloc constituted a disproportionate number of the Israelis who went abroad during the summer.

As the traditional parties geared up for the campaign, they were joined by some new faces, whose impact was to be considerable. On the eve of the crucial Knesset vote, Ezer Weizman, a highly popular former air force commander who had served as defense minister in the first Begin government and had played a key role in bringing about the peace treaty with Egypt, announced that he was forming a centrist party. Weizman believed that he could better the performance of Yigael Yadin's Democratic Movement for Change (DMC) in 1977, and, by siphoning off votes from both the Likud and the Alignment, emerge as a major Knesset force. Two other new lists formed around this time: the Sephardi Torah Guardians (Shas), an ultra-Orthodox religious (rather than ethnic) list that had already scored impressive gains in municipal elections in Bnei Brak and Jerusalem and was to prove a surprise factor in the Knesset elections as well, challenging the Ashkenazi hegemony in the religious-political sphere; and the Progressive List for Peace (PLP), an Arab-Jewish list (50-percent representation for each nationality) that was also to do well, its primary challenge being to the long-established Democratic Front for Peace and Equality, Israel's Communist party, and like it drawing its votes almost exclusively from Israel's Arab citizens.

In the Labor party, victory was considered virtually a foregone conclusion, given the economic crisis—labor unrest, runaway inflation, and panicky economic behavior by a public fearful of drastic postelection measures—and the seemingly unresolvable situation in Lebanon, where Israeli casualties mounted, with nothing to show in return. For Labor, then, the unstated slogan was "don't rock the boat." Thus, on March 30 both Yitzhak Navon and Yitzhak Rabin, Shimon Peres's former arch rival in the party, announced that they would not contest the party leadership.

The Likud's precampaign road was less smooth. Although Deputy Prime Minister David Levy, who had mounted a fairly strong challenge to Shamir for the Herut party leadership the previous September, following Menachem Begin's resignation, announced (April 4) that as a "personal sacrifice" in the interest of party unity he would not contest the top spot, Minister Without Portfolio Ariel Sharon proved less altruistic. (Sharon had been forced to resign as defense minister in February 1983 following the publication of the Kahan Commission of Inquiry report into the massacre at two Beirut refugee camps the previous September.) On April 12 Sharon obtained a surprising 42.2 percent of the vote in Herut's Central Committee against Shamir. However, a month later, when the Central Committee met to finalize the party's list, the second slot (after Shamir) went to David Levy, followed by Defense Minister Moshe Arens. Sharon was placed fourth.

Two events in May seriously harmed Herut's image. One was a squabble with its Likud partner, the Liberal party, regarding the order of candidates on the final combined list. The second was former prime minister Begin's decision not to stand in the honorary 120th slot on the Likud list. Begin was also evasive about whether he would campaign on behalf of the party. (In the event, he did not, although he did make a donation to the Likud's campaign chest.)

No fewer than 26 lists were initially approved by the Central Elections Committee after the May 31 registration deadline had passed. Thirteen of them were entirely new, including Ezer Weizman's Yahad party; Shas; the PLP; Morasha (headed by Rabbi Haim Druckman, who had earlier broken with the National Religious party); Yigael Hurvitz's Ometz list; and the "Lova Eliav for the Knesset" list, headed by a former Labor-party secretary-general who had quit the party when he felt that Labor was swinging too far rightward. (Eliav could not be dissuaded from running by the argument that he would not obtain enough votes for a Knesset seat and would only draw off votes from the dovish left—which is precisely what transpired, in an election where every vote made a difference.)

Some of the lists were very narrowly focused, such as the Tenants Protection League, the Organization for the Disabled, and a one-man list—the Movement for the Abolition of the Income Tax. Also running was former MK Shmuel Flatto-Sharon, who was sentenced by the Supreme Court, at the end of June, to 18 months' imprisonment (of which 15 months were suspended), following his appeal of a lower-court conviction on charges stemming from electoral offenses, including bribery, in the 1977 election campaign, when he was elected to the Knesset. Even though the start of his jail sentence was deferred by 45 days, Flatto-Sharon's hope of staying out of prison under parliamentary immunity regulations was dashed when he failed even to cross the election threshold, placing 23rd out of the 26 lists.

Uncertainty about the final lists resulted when, on June 1, the legal adviser to the Defense Ministry announced that Defense Minister Arens was considering outlawing the newly founded PLP under the Defense (Emergency) Regulations of 1945. The PLP viewed this threat as retaliation for efforts by the Labor Alignment and two other parties to have Rabbi Meir Kahane's Kach list disqualified on the grounds that its platform was racist. Although Arens finally decided not to outlaw the PLP, the Defense Ministry announced that after having made a "detailed examination" of the facts, it was "convinced" that the PLP harbored "subversive elements" and that "central people" on it identified with "enemies of the state." Encouraged by these charges, the Likud and its allies, notably the Tehiya party, requested the Central Elections Committee to disqualify the PLP. On June 17 the committee (composed of representatives of all the parties with seats in the outgoing Knessset) voted 18-10, with seven abstentions, to disqualify Kach; the committee's chairman, Supreme Court justice Gavriel Bach, voted for disqualification, as did some of the Likud representatives. The following day, in tit-for-tat fashion, the committee voted 17-12, with four abstentions (Bach among them), to disqualify the PLP as well. Both lists petitioned the Supreme Court to overturn the decision, and on June 28 five justices ruled unanimously that both parties could take part in the elections.

THE CAMPAIGN

With memories of the stormy and traumatic 1981 election campaign still vivid, the Likud and the Alignment, prodded by Justice Bach, on June 11 signed an agreement to run a fair, clean campaign. Barred were "physical violence, threats of violence or incitement to violence," references to people's national or ethnic origin or religious affiliation, "degrading" caricatures, and organized attempts to disrupt election rallies. The Alignment, being given as many as 55 seats by the polls at this stage, with another 11 going to parties of the left and center, proceeded on the assumption that a heated campaign would only play into the hands of the Likud. This proved to be sound reasoning, as the Alignment's unwillingness to be drawn into the kind of invective-laden rhetoric that had marked the two previous elections hampered the

Likud's ability to get its campaign off the ground. With the economy and the Lebanon war ruled out as issues for it to run on, and the Jewish settlement theme set back by the arrest of the Jewish terrorist organization that had operated in the territories, the Likud turned, as in the past, to *ad hominem* attacks on Shimon Peres. Peres's image as an opportunistic wheeler-dealer, a cliché of Israeli political folklore, was mercilessly played up, particularly in television commercials. In a subtle variation on this theme, the Likud claimed that "the neighborhoods"—meaning the low-income groups of oriental origin—had been imbued with a "new pride" during the Likud's years in power because the Likud had put an end to "Mapai protectionism."

Hoping to attract disaffected Likud supporters, Labor opted for a "soft-sell" approach. However, by trying to avoid giving offense to voters on the Right, the campaign team opened itself to charges of hiding the real issues of the election. Whether the tactic ultimately swayed any Likud voters is moot. What cannot be gainsaid is that it alienated potential Labor voters, as manifested in the swing to center and left-of-center parties in traditional Labor strongholds, notably the kibbutzim.

ELECTION RESULTS AND ANALYSIS

The biggest losers in the campaign were the pollsters. So unanimous were they in their predictions of a substantial Alignment victory that even though the gap between the two major parties narrowed perceptibly at the very end of the campaign —as "floating" voters cast anchor and errant Likud supporters decided to "come home"—the actual result of the vote took everyone by surprise. (See table below.) Voters reacted to the lackluster campaigns of the two major parties by turning to the smaller lists, where the issues were clearly enunciated. The upshot was that the Alignment and the Likud, which between them accounted for 95 seats in the outgoing 10th Knesset, were reduced to 85 seats in the newly elected parliament; concomitantly, there was a 50-percent increase in the number of lists represented in the Knesset, from 10 in 1981 to no fewer than 15 three years later.

ELECTIONS TO THE 11TH KNESSET (July 23, 1984) AND 10TH KNESSET (June 30, 1981)

	1984	1981
Eligible voters	2,654,613	2,490,140
Valid votes cast[a]	2,073,321	1,937,366
Valid votes cast for parties not qualifying[a]	58,978	99,903
Valid votes counting in allocation of seats[b]	2,014,343	1,837,463
Quota per Knesset seat[b]	16,786	15,312

| Party | Popular Vote (%) | | Net Gain | Knesset Seats | | Net Gain |
	1984	1981	or Loss	1984	1981	or Loss
Alignment	724,074 (34.9)	708,536 (36.6)	−(1.7)	44	47	−3
Likud	661,302 (31.9)	718,941 (37.1)	−(5.2)	41	48	−7
Tehiya-Tzomet	83,037 (4.0)	44,700 (2.3)	+(1.7)	5	3	+2
National Religious ...	73,530 (3.5)	95,232 (4.9)	−(1.4)	4	6	−2
Democratic Front for Peace and Equality .	69,815 (3.36)	64,918 (3.46)	−(0.1)	4	4	—
Sephardi Torah Guardians	63,605 (3.06)	— —	—	4	—	+4
Shinui	54,747 (2.6)	29,837 (1.5)	+(1.1)	3	2	+1
Citizens Rights and Peace Movement ..	49,698 (2.4)	27,921 (1.4)	+(1.0)	3	1	+2
Yahad	46,302 (2.2)	— —	—	3	—	+3
Progressive List for Peace	38,012 (1.8)	— —	—	2	—	+2
Agudat Israel	36,079 (1.7)	72,312 (3.7)	−(2.0)	2	4	−2
Morasha	33,287 (1.6)	— —	—	2	—	+2
Tami	31,103 (1.5)	44,466 (2.3)	−(0.8)	1	3	−2
Kach	25,907 (1.2)	5,128 (0.3)	+(0.9)	1	—	+1
Ometz	23,845 (1.15)	— —	—	1	—	+1
Lova Eliav for the Knesset	15,348 (0.7)	— —	—	—	—	—
Organization for the Disabled	12,329 (0.6)	— —	—	—	—	—
Renewal (Mordechai Ben-Porat)	5,876 (0.3)	— —	—	—	—	—
Immigration and Youth	5,794 (0.27)	— —	—	—	—	—
Shiluv	5,499 (0.26)	— —	—	—	—	—
Atzma'ut	4,887 (0.2)	4,710 (0.2)	—	—	—	—
Tenants Protection League	3,195 (0.15)	— —	—	—	—	—
Flatto-Sharon	2,430 (0.1)	10,823 (0.6)	−(0.5)	—	—	—
Movement to Abolish Income Tax	1,472 (0.07)	503 (0.03)	+(0.04)	—	—	—
Homeland	1,415 (0.07)	— —	—	—	—	—
Amcha	733 (0.035)	460 (0.02)	+(0.015)	—	—	—

[a]Only lists receiving at least 1 percent of the valid votes cast—i.e., 20,733 in 1984—are entitled to share in the allocation of seats.
[b]The quotient for one Knesset seat is the number of valid votes cast for the lists qualifying —i.e., 2,014,343 in 1984—divided by 120 (the number of Knesset seats). Thus the quotient in 1984 was 16,786.

Because coalition arithmetic was so complex, with neither major party able to put together a narrow-based coalition, pundits termed the election results "inconclusive." Yet from a long-term perspective, the electorate had spoken very conclusively indeed. Primarily, the vote demonstrated that in the years since 1977 the Likud had carved out a solid electoral base on which it could rely even if its immediate record was uninspiring. At the same time, the results ruled out the possibility that Yitzhak Shamir could consolidate his position as undisputed leader of Herut and heir to Menachem Begin. Challenges to his position within Herut, such as that by Sharon prior to the election, were bound to intensify. In the other political camp, Labor's attempt to project itself as all things to all people proved untenable. Patently, the party would have to stake out its own ground more precisely if it wished to retain the support of its ideological constituency.

What also emerged conclusively from the election—the handwriting had been on the wall for a long time—was the radicalization of the Israeli polity. This was manifested most strikingly on the Right, where Tehiya increased its strength significantly, and where Rabbi Meir Kahane, having failed in several previous attempts, won a Knesset seat. Since Kahane had run on an unabashedly racist platform— several of his television ads were disqualified by Justice Bach because they were of an inflammatory nature—his election confirmed the worst fears of those who had been warning against growing trends of "Jewish fascism" in the country. Further confirmation came on the day after his election, when Kahane and about 200 of his followers staged a "victory march" through the streets of Jerusalem. As they moved through the Old City, they vandalized Arab-owned shops, keeping up a constant shout of "Death to the Arabs!" and "Arabs out!"

Although condemned by all shades of political opinion, Kahane (who summed up his credo when he told reporters after the elections that "the Torah is above and beyond the laws of the state," and that his first act in the Knesset would be to submit a bill aimed at expelling all of the country's Arabs) had obviously touched a responsive chord among certain sections of the populace. Although Kahane received only about 1.2 percent of the vote overall, 2.5 percent of the votes cast in the army went to him. Moreover, as public opinion analyst Hanoch Smith pointed out in the *Jerusalem Post,* not only did Kahane draw fully 3.3 percent of the votes cast in small development towns, he did almost as well in religious moshavim—where the population is overwhelmingly of Asian/African origin—and in disadvantaged neighborhoods in Jerusalem. Even in certain fairly large towns, such as Beersheba and Ashkelon, he polled 2 percent of the vote. By contrast, Kahane had almost no support in older cities and neighborhoods where the population is largely of Western (and Ashkenazi) origin. It seemed obvious to many observers that the residents of the development towns, being estranged from the reigning political culture and resentful of the persistent economic and social gap between themselves and Israelis of European origin, were ripe for the appeal of a demagogue offering a convenient scapegoat. Now that Kahane had been "legitimized" by being elected to the Knesset, the likelihood was that some who had previously hesitated to vote for him for fear of wasting their ballots would give him the nod at the next opportunity. Postelection polls did in fact show Kahane capable of winning as many as five seats. (See also "Political and Religious Extremism.")

A somewhat analogous phenomenon occurred among Israeli Arabs. Here the shift was to the potent ideology of nationalism. According to a voting analysis published in *Ha'aretz*, Arab turnout at the polls increased by about 8 percent as compared with 1981, from 68 to 76 percent. That this substantial rise could be attributed almost entirely to the appearance of the Progressive List for Peace was evident in the dramatic change in outcome. Three years earlier, in 1981, nearly two-thirds (63 percent) of the Arab vote had gone to parties clearly identified as Zionist, while the remaining 37 percent went to the Communist list. In 1984 a majority of the country's Arab voters (52 percent) opted for non-Zionist lists—the Communists and the PLP.

A combination of factors seemed to have come into play in this area: an ongoing sense of disaffection vis-à-vis the country's governing establishment, particularly among young Arabs; the cumulative effect of contact between Israeli Arabs and the Palestinian population across the pre-1967 "green line"; and an echoing response, again chiefly among the young, to the growing nationalism among Israel's Jewish population. Nor can the Israeli Arabs' blatant disappointment in the Labor party be overlooked; Labor placed only one Arab in a "safe" position on its list, with Mapam adding one more in the combined Alignment list. This evidence of Labor's "take them for granted" attitude toward its traditional supporters helped account for the drastic falloff in votes for the Alignment in the Arab sector. In 1984 Labor obtained less than one-quarter of the Arab vote (23 percent), as compared with 41 percent (29 percent directly and 12 percent via affiliated Arab lists) three years earlier. In the Knesset, then, the two lists that were oriented toward, and drew their strength from, the Arab population (notwithstanding the presence of Jews on them) obtained six seats, two more than in 1981. Analysts suggested that such a trend could, if continued, give Arab lists control of up to 10 percent of the Knesset within the foreseeable future. Indeed, some maintained that it was precisely the fear of such a development within the Jewish political and security establishments that accounted for the abortive attempts, first by the Defense Ministry and then by the right-wing and religious parties, to force the PLP out of the election campaign.

Whatever the case, the election was held in an atmosphere of intensifying nationalism, at times spilling over into xenophobia among Jews and Arabs both, and fueled to a degree in both nations by religious revivalism.

FORMING A COALITION

The vote had produced a virtually unprecedented situation, with neither of the two large parties able to form a narrow-based coalition without engaging in severe political contortions. Theoretically, the Labor Alignment could have created a coalition with the support—even tacit—of the Communists and the PLP. However, a majority in the Alignment itself, along with a good number of the potential participants in such a coalition—the religious lists in particular—viewed those two parties with unfeigned abhorrence, a posture which could only confirm the country's Arabs in their sense of alienation from the mainstream.

On August 1, the day after the Central Elections Committee published the official results of the vote, President Chaim Herzog began meeting with delegations of the lists elected to the Knesset in order to determine whom to charge with the task of forming a government. (Breaking with precedent, the president refused to invite Meir Kahane for consultations because, according to an official statement, the president would "not countenance insults to the feelings and honor of many minority citizens—civilians and soldiers, Moslems, Druze, and Christians.") On August 5 Shimon Peres, as the head of the largest Knesset faction, was named to form the new government. The president urged the creation of a "government of national unity," citing—as Peres also did in accepting the nomination—the economic situation and the need to mend social and political rifts in the nation.

With almost two weeks of intensive, unofficial give-and-take already behind him, Peres now embarked on the formal government-making process, which was to take 40 more arduous, crisis-ridden days. (By law, the person entrusted with forming the government has 21 days in which to accomplish this task, although the president may grant him an additional 21 days if he deems it necessary.) Adding to Peres's problems, the Likud let it be known that while it would agree to enter into talks on a possible unity government, it would simultaneously proceed with efforts to form a government under its own leadership. The Likud took this step, which both flouted the constitutional process and showed contempt for the president's decision, in the not unreasonable belief that despite its second-place finish and 14-percent decrease in Knesset representation (from 48 seats to 41), its prospects of forming a government were equal to if not better than the Alignment's. It was axiomatic that, overall, the religious parties found the Likud a more congenial coalition partner than Labor, and it was assumed that Ezer Weizman would, whether out of opportunism or nostalgia, support a Likud-led coalition as well.

The Alignment, too, paralleled its unity-government efforts with (legitimate) attempts to form a government on its own, courting the National Religious party in particular. The NRP had been reduced to 4 seats, down from 6 in 1981 and 12 in 1977. The fact that the religious vote was so fragmented, with six parties (including Tami and Kach) splitting 13 Knesset seats, made the coalition talks all the more difficult, since each list had its own set of demands, and all of them sought to outdo one another in winning "achievements" for the religious camp.

At all events, on August 9 Likud and Alignment leaders met at the King David Hotel in Jerusalem to explore the possibility of forming a national unity government. However, this and subsequent meetings were generally viewed as merely a public relations ploy intended to satisfy the president and the growing popular sentiment for a unity government, at the same time concealing intensive behind-the-scenes efforts by each party to form a narrow-based coalition. In the meantime, the 11th

Knesset was formally inaugurated on August 13 with the traditional presidential speech. As some 2,000 persons demonstrated outside the Knesset building against Meir Kahane and called for the enactment of a law barring racism in Israel, the president told the new parliament that its test would lie in how firmly it shored up democracy and safeguarded the "principles of justice and the supremacy of the law" in the country.

It was only in the third week of Peres's first 21-day period that the Likud began to negotiate in earnest, spurred by the dropping of a bombshell by Ezer Weizman into the desultory unity talks. Bitterly disappointed at having won only three seats, but mollified somewhat by his emergence as coalition kingmaker, Weizman announced on August 20 that he and MK Yigael Hurvitz would refuse to participate in a narrow-based Likud-led coalition. A formal parliamentary cooperation agreement signed two days later by Weizman and Peres, which all but brought the Yahad list into the Alignment, still did not assure the Alignment of being able to form its own government, but the loss of the four seats controlled by Weizman and Hurvitz did rule out a Likud government.

On August 24 Peres and Shamir met privately—the first in a series of such conversations—to consider the avenues open to them. The unstated bond between them was forged by their desire to break the political impasse without resort to new elections, since both men were keenly aware that their future political careers were on the line. Peres, having already led his party to two previous defeats, would not be given a fourth chance. Nor would Shamir, at age 68, and with David Levy and Ariel Sharon breathing down his neck, get another opportunity to lead either his party or the country.

With these developments as a backdrop, on August 26 Shimon Peres requested and was granted a further three weeks to form a government.

The Likud having moved to block any possible remaining Alignment option of forming a narrow-based government by signing a parliamentary agreement-in-principle with the two-man ultra-Orthodox Agudat Israel party—as it was to do shortly thereafter with the party largely responsible for halving the Agudah's Knesset representation, Shas—Peres and Shamir met on August 29 for the third time in three days and managed to overcome the outstanding major obstacles to the formation of a national unity government. They decided on a rotating premiership that would change hands at the midpoint of the 50-month government, with Peres to hold the post first (the Likud having come to terms with the inevitable in this regard). They further agreed that the defense portfolio would be held by Labor's Yitzhak Rabin for the entire tenure of the national unity government, this being a *sine qua non* for Peres, who had to deliver the Defense Ministry to Rabin or see the feud between them, now quiescent, erupt again.

Yet it was only after another full week of talks and three more Peres-Shamir meetings (September 4, 5, 6) that the final details of the unprecedented agreement were hammered out. In the interim, David Levy and Ariel Sharon once more asserted themselves in Herut, forcing Shamir to inject an entirely new element into the negotiations. This was a demand that the unity government establish no fewer than 28 settlements in the territories, settlements which the outgoing government had approved but which were still on paper only. Peres balked at this, and only a threat by the NRP that it would seriously consider entering a narrow-based Labor government was able to budge the Likud. So the fifth week of the coalition negotiations ended, their protracted nature in stark counterpoint to the urgency demanded by the deteriorating economic situation and the casualty-ridden stalemate in Lebanon.

Resentment was expressed in both parties over the proposed allocation of ministries. Labor members were dismayed by the assignment of the major economic portfolios to the Likud, especially by the awarding of the industry and trade portfolio to Ariel Sharon, architect of the Lebanon war, who would, ironically, secure "public rehabilitation" under a Labor prime minister. In the Likud there was anger that the coveted defense portfolio would remain in Alignment hands for the entire 50-month span of the government. The other major portfolio, foreign affairs, would continue to be held by Shamir, who would also serve as "vice prime minister" for the first 25 months, at which time he and Peres would switch posts.

Shamir survived another mutiny in his party's ranks, though not without a further erosion of authority, when Levy and Sharon demanded a secret ballot by the Herut Central Committee to choose Herut's ministers, rather than leave the selection in Shamir's hands. Peres, on August 10, obtained a 70-percent majority in Labor's Central Committee vote on forming a national unity government. However, the price he paid was heavy. Mapam's Central Committee, declaring that the proposed government would prove incapable either of solving the "burning" socioeconomic issues facing the country or of advancing the peace process, on August 9 voted almost unanimously to dissolve the Labor Alignment, which had been created prior to the 1969 elections. On the same day, maverick MK Yossi Sarid bolted the Labor party and joined the Citizens Rights and Peace Movement.

Just as the coalition agreement seemed to have been settled, Ariel Sharon precipitated a new crisis. He insisted that the Likud honor its agreement with Shas by ensuring that that party receive the religious affairs portfolio; this in the face of an identical Alignment pledge to the NRP. Finally, after almost nonstop negotiations in the sixth and final week left to Peres, he and Shamir decided in the early morning hours of September 13 that both the religious affairs and interior portfolios—the latter also demanded by the NRP—would be entrusted to the prime minister for a month, during which period an acceptable solution would be sought.

The agreement, which was at last signed by six representatives each from the Likud and the Alignment in the afternoon of September 13, spelled out the technical arrangements for the national unity government. Its first principle stipulated not only an equal number of cabinet ministers from each party but "creation of a balance when other factions join, such that neither camp achieves a majority over the other," with the NRP representative in the cabinet considered to belong to neither "camp" and thus effectively having the tie-breaking vote. The highly personal nature of the

THE NATIONAL UNITY CABINET
(installed on September 14, 1984)

Prime Minister	Shimon Peres (Alignment-Labor)
Vice Prime Minister & Minister of Foreign Affairs	Yitzhak Shamir (Likud-Herut)
Deputy Prime Minister & Minister of Education and Culture	Yitzhak Navon (Alignment-Labor)
Deputy Prime Minister & Minister of Construction and Housing	David Levy (Likud-Herut)
Agriculture	Aryeh Nachamkin (Alignment-Labor)
Communications	Amnon Rubinstein (Shinui)
Defense	Yitzhak Rabin (Alignment-Labor)
Economy and Planning	Gad Ya'akobi (Alignment-Labor)
Energy and Infrastructure	Moshe Shahal (Alignment-Labor)
Finance	Yitzhak Modai (Likud-Liberals)
Health	Mordechai Gur (Alignment-Labor)
Immigrant Absorption	Ya'akov Tzur (Alignment-Labor)
Industry and Trade	Ariel Sharon (Likud-Herut)
Interior	Shimon Peres[a]
Justice	Moshe Nissim (Likud-Liberals)
Police	Haim Bar-Lev (Alignment-Labor)[b]
Religious Affairs	Shimon Peres[a]
Science and Development	Gideon Patt (Likud-Liberals)
Tourism	Avraham Sharir (Likud-Liberals)
Transport	Haim Corfu (Likud-Herut)
Without Portfolio	Moshe Arens (Likud-Herut)
	Yosef Burg (NRP)[a]
	Yigael Hurvitz (Ometz)
	Yitzhak Peretz (Shas)[a]
	Yosef Shapira (Morasha)[c]
Minister in the Prime Minister's Office	Ezer Weizman (Alignment-Yahad)

[a]Prime Minister Peres held the interior and religious affairs portfolios until December 24, when Yitzhak Peretz and Yosef Burg took them over, respectively, following Knesset approval.
[b]The Ministry of Police was formally separated from the Interior Ministry by Knesset vote on September 24.
[c]Not a Knesset member.

accord was pointed up by another key clause which stated that if either Peres or Shamir proved "unable to perform his task for any reason," the party involved would choose someone to take his place "*with the agreement of the other side*" (emphasis added). The implication was that if "the other side" were to refuse its assent, the agreement would be rendered null and void. Because of the unwieldy size of the cabinet—no fewer than 25 ministers would eventually be part of that body —and to smooth ruffled feathers, the coalition agreement provided for the creation of a so-called inner cabinet, consisting of five Likud and five Alignment ministers, which would be empowered to decide on "policy, defense, and settlement issues." As for the innovative rotation of the premiership, the agreement stipulated that

> Mr. Shimon Peres will resign from his post as prime minister [under Israeli law, the prime minister's resignation is tantamount to the resignation of the entire government] toward the end of the first 25 months of the government's tenure, and the Alignment and the Likud will together recommend to the president to charge Mr. Yitzhak Shamir with the task of forming a government. The new government will be established at the conclusion of the first 25 months.

All ministers other than Peres and Shamir would retain their portfolios for the full four-year term of the 11th Knesset. Since the coalition was not dependent on the religious parties for a Knesset majority, the normally vexatious religious issue was resolved in the laconic declaration that "the preservation of the status quo on religious matters will be ensured."

With respect to policy, the new government's "basic guidelines" included "continuing and extending the peace process in the region; consolidating the peace with Egypt; and withdrawing the IDF [Israel Defense Forces] from Lebanon while ensuring the security of the northern settlements"; a reaffirmation that "Jerusalem, Israel's eternal capital, is one indivisible city under Israeli sovereignty"; a call to Jordan to enter peace negotiations and a pledge by the government to "consider proposals raised by Jordan in the negotiations"; and opposition to the establishment of "an additional Palestinian state" in the Gaza Strip or "in the area between Israel and Jordan," as well as to any negotiations between Israel and the PLO. As for the highly contentious issue of the territories, there would be "no change in the sovereignty over Judea, Samaria, and the Gaza District except with the consent of the Alignment and the Likud." Settlements already established would have their "existence and development" assured, while "five [or] six settlements will be established within a year."

In the crucial economic sphere, the goals included curbing inflation and renewing economic growth, *inter alia* "by reducing the proportion of public and administrative services." Also to be reduced were public expenditure and private consumption. A "socioeconomic agreement" was to be worked out with the Histadrut (General Federation of Labor). Section 26 added, almost as an afterthought, that the government's economic policy would be "based on a comprehensive program," something conspicuously lacking in earlier attempts to heal the economy.

THE NEW GOVERNMENT

In the evening hours of September 13, the new Speaker of the Knesset, the Alignment's Shlomo Hillel (elected to the post the previous day by a vote of 60-46 over the Likud's Meir Cohen-Avidov), called on Shimon Peres to present his new government and its basic guidelines for a vote of confidence. Although the outcome of that vote was a foregone conclusion, an atmosphere of tense expectancy prevailed as Peres took the podium. This was generated not only by curiosity about the new hybrid government but also by the fact that, when all was said and done, a Labor government was taking the reins of power again after seven years. There was admiration, too, which cut across party lines, for the tenacity shown by Shimon Peres, who had finally achieved the post he had coveted openly ever since Golda Meir's resignation as prime minister following publication of the Agranat Commission of Inquiry report in 1974.

Taking as his theme the need for reconciliation at home and conciliation with Israel's neighbors in the region, Peres pledged to introduce "a new and beneficent style" of government that would try to overcome the divisions in the country. The first of the "pressing and demanding" challenges confronting the government, he said, was the "crisis in the economy." This would be dealt with, he promised, "not by imposing harsh measures but by maintaining a constant dialogue" between Histadrut, private employers, farmers, and government. Regarding Lebanon, the objective was "to guarantee the safety of the Galilee settlements and to bring our soldiers home."

Peres called on King Hussein to enter negotiations with Israel, "in order to attain genuine peace," and said his government would endeavor to resolve amicably its differences with Egypt. Reaffirming that "the friendship of the American people is very precious" to Israel, Peres expressed the hope for continued "mutual trust and close cooperation" between Israel and the United States. The prime minister-designate called on Moscow to renew its diplomatic relations with Israel and to "open its gates to our people." Elsewhere in the international arena, he said, Israel would pursue its diplomatic efforts in Africa, improve ties with Europe and Latin America, and "we shall once again knock on great China's door."

Yet, Peres continued, it was domestically that "our principal effort must be made." The urgent task was "to root out enmity, violence, incitement, discrimination, and intolerance in our good land." The government would devote special efforts to education and would seek to inculcate the principle of mutual respect based on the equality of all citizens before the law. The country's Arab and Druze minorities would be helped to further their development, Peres pledged. Finally, referring to the relations between Israel and the Diaspora, he declared: "We believe that the place of every Jew is ultimately in the homeland of our people; but we also believe that Israel has an interest in the fate of every Jew and every Jewish Diaspora wherever it may be."

A lively debate, lasting until well after midnight, was followed by a vote of confidence of 89–18 and one abstention. Thus, on Friday, September 14, 1984, Shimon Peres, 61, became Israel's eighth prime minister. The national unity government commanded the support of no fewer than 97 of the 120 Knesset members, the

Alignment (now reduced to 40 seats, including Yahad's 3) and the Likud (41) having been joined in the coalition by the NRP (4), Shas (4), Shinui (3), Morasha (2), Agudat Israel (2), and Ometz (1).

The first meeting of the new cabinet, on September 16, was devoted largely to procedural matters and only partially to the economic situation, but a second meeting four days later, lasting eight hours, was entirely given over to that subject. (See "Economic Developments.") The remainder of the year is best described as a breaking-in period for the new government. Foreign Minister Shamir, under growing pressure within his own party as Peres began to assert himself in the premiership, declared on October 25 that the Likud was remaining in the government "with teeth gritted." About a week later a group of Likud ministers met in what was intended to be the inaugural gathering of a permanent forum to parallel Labor's so-called *sarenu* ("our ministers") group—reminiscent of Golda Meir's "kitchen cabinet"— which met faithfully once a week to discuss the political situation in general and to coordinate positions for the Sunday cabinet meeting. At the Likud meeting, which turned out to be the first and last of its kind, the ministers averred that Peres was going "too fast" on certain foreign policy issues, notably the dispute with Egypt regarding Taba and his intentions vis-à-vis the West Bank.

More serious than these rumblings of discontent was a full-fledged crisis that began to simmer in late November and erupted in December, threatening to topple the government. At issue was the division of the interior and religious affairs portfolios between the NRP and Shas, which was to have been resolved within one month of the government's installation but was allowed to drag on. Shas leader MK Rabbi Yitzhak Peretz actually submitted his resignation from the government in protest at the delay—with the Likud, which was committed to backing Shas, threatening to follow suit—but withdrew it when Peres announced on November 30 that Shas would receive the interior portfolio. However, a new crisis arose when the NRP demanded that certain of the functions (and budgets) of the Interior Ministry—its traditional preserve—be transferred to the Religious Affairs Ministry. Shas balked at this, the NRP was adamant, and Rabbi Peretz had in fact resigned by the time a compromise solution was worked out. Under the compromise, 60 percent of the budgets for the country's religious councils would be channeled through the Interior Ministry and the remainder through the Religious Affairs Ministry. Thus, on December 24 Yitzhak Peretz was confirmed by the Knesset as minister of the interior and Yosef Burg as minister of religious affairs. The national unity government had survived its first crisis.

A poll conducted at year's end, marking Prime Minister Peres's first 100 days in office, gave him a 42-percent popularity rating, up from 18 percent on the eve of the elections and nearly four times the rating enjoyed by Yitzhak Shamir. In an interview in *Ha'aretz* on December 18, Peres said the Likud had shown "mismanagement" of both the economy and the peace process during its years in power. Peres told the interviewer, "I believe in a modern economy which will bring us economic independence, and I believe we have what to talk about with the Arabs.

I want a different governing style: one without hatred, a cultured style, with responsibility." He was, he confessed, "an optimist."

Economic Developments

With the Shamir government unable to implement its own budget-paring decisions and the country plunged into an election atmosphere and campaign for over half of 1984, followed by nearly two months of virtual political paralysis, it was only toward the end of September, after the formation of the national unity government, that a concerted effort was begun to check Israel's rapid descent into economic chaos.

During the first quarter of the year a veritable war of attrition was waged within the government itself over the budget, with the leadership vacillating and ministers wrangling over proposed budget cuts. A growing crisis of public confidence in the entire economic system was fueled by this and other factors: widespread labor unrest as wages, even though ostensibly index-linked, failed to keep pace with spiraling inflation, and a mid-January report of the National Insurance Institute confirming statistically that poverty in the country was increasing. On February 22 the government presented a budget of IS 4.36 trillion (approximately $32 billion at the time) that called for a 7-percent drop in the standard of living, upped the cost of government services, and provided for a personnel cut of 5,000 from the bloated public-service sector. By the time the Knesset passed the budget bill (March 28) it had already voted to dissolve itself, and it was clear that in an election year many budget clauses would not be implemented.

On May 17 a new two-year cost-of-living-increment accord was signed by employers and the Histadrut. Taking into account Israel's new inflationary reality, the agreement stipulated that the increment would henceforth be paid on a monthly, rather than on a quarterly, basis if the consumer price index climbed by at least 12 percent in any one month (as it did ten times in 1984). A special payment was provided for in the event of a one-month inflation rate of 25 percent or more. The agreement was finalized two days after the announcement of the second-highest monthly inflation rate in Israel's history (at that time)—20.6 percent for April. During the first quarter of the year the government raised the prices of subsidized basic goods by some 30 percent and introduced measures—among them a reduction of one-third (to $2,000) in the amount of foreign currency Israelis going abroad could purchase—to help stem the rapid depletion of the country's foreign currency reserves.

A momentary bright light in the economic gloom came in May when some 600 persons, including 400 from 20 foreign countries, gathered for the Jerusalem Economic Conference, organized by Minister of Economic Coordination Ya'acov Meridor. Some of the international community's leading industrialists, financiers, and businessmen were present, and, according to Meridor, over 100 contacts for joint ventures were established.

In June the battered dam holding back massive government spending burst in several places in a replay, albeit in more muted fashion, of the 1981 "election economics" foisted on the country by then finance minister Yoram Aridor. With the Likud well behind in the polls, the cabinet approved wage increases for sections of the civil service, along with various other benefits, at a cost to the Treasury of nearly IS 30 billion. Nevertheless, as the election campaign entered its final stage, the country was wracked by a series of strikes and slowdowns involving tens of thousands of workers in the public services. Further complicating the situation were rumors that a major devaluation of the shekel was in the offing immediately after the elections and that restrictive measures would be introduced on the dollar-linked "Patam" accounts that Israelis were allowed to maintain. These fears triggered a massive buying of foreign currency by the public, legally and on the black market, with the result that Israel's foreign currency reserves plunged by at least $350 million in June alone. The gap between the shekel's official dollar rate and the black-market rate soared to nearly 40 percent, allowing for profiteering on a vast scale.

On July 2, three weeks before election day, the Knesset met in special session and passed into law a bill to protect the public's savings, aiming in this manner both to stem the foreign currency drain by putting an end to speculative behavior and to gain electoral points. Not one vote was cast against the measure. Also passed were a bill granting various education, employment, and housing benefits to discharged soldiers following their compulsory military service, and an amendment to the Income Tax Ordinance granting tax breaks to certain groups. A few days earlier a two-year wage agreement signed between the Histadrut and the government, granting a 15-percent pay rise, had effectively put a halt to labor disputes involving some 240,000 workers. Finally, with just one week to go before election day, the Histadrut and the private-sector associations also signed a new wage accord.

No sooner were the elections over than the government imposed additional levies on Israelis going abroad and barred foreign currency transfers to dependents residing abroad. Although the governor of the Bank of Israel, Moshe Mandelbaum, declared that "urgent" economic action was required, only patchwork attempts were made to deal with the economy during the lengthy coalition negotiations, including freezes on hiring in the public sector and on government contracts. Mandelbaum's own credibility was called into question when it was revealed that the Bank of Israel had engaged in a "bookkeeping maneuver" to conceal the fact that in the immediate preelection period the country's foreign currency reserves were depleted by nearly $700 million, or double the officially announced figure. This, coupled with a record "injection" into the economy—the traditional euphemism in Israel for printing money—of IS 95 billion, or about $360 million, in the month of July, attested to the fact that the government had to all intents and purposes lost control of the economy.

In September it was announced that unemployment had risen to 6 percent (about 85,000 persons), that yet another money-printing record had been set (IS 135 billion) in August, and that the month had also seen a further $200-million drop in the foreign currency reserves. With only about $2 billion remaining in the coffers, or $1 billion below the "red line" level, it was clear that the crisis moment had arrived: Israel's economic viability now depended on an emergency dollar injection from the United States. It was not an auspicious moment for a new government to take office.

At its very first meeting (September 16) the new cabinet authorized Finance Minister Yitzhak Modai to trim the budget by $1 billion immediately. Four days later the cabinet held a special eight-hour meeting at which the finance minister explained his plans for economic recovery. The initial measures decided on at the cabinet meeting of September 23 (following a 9-percent shekel devaluation on September 17) included a drastic price hike of 18 to 55 percent on subsidized basic commodities. While this was a major step toward the phasing out of subsidization, it was harshly criticized for being implemented just days before the Jewish New Year and the onset of the fall holidays. Other actions announced (though these required Knesset approval) included a tax on automobiles and luxury pleasure craft, an education fee, a tax on the monthly child allowance, and a levy on certain pensions. Price control was imposed on a range of goods, though only after—indeed, because—manufacturers had already raised their prices inordinately in anticipation of just such controls. In an interview with the *Jerusalem Post,* Prime Minister Peres said the nation had to be made aware of "our painful economic reality," which had come to pass because "we have been living well beyond our means." He expressed the hope that "within a year" the worst would be over and Israel would be embarked on "a future of growth and development."

On October 2 the cabinet met in another special session and placed a six-month import ban on about 50 "luxury items," among them ovens, large refrigerators, air conditioners, cars, soft and hard drinks, most furniture, and certain cosmetics. In addition, with Israel's foreign currency reserves having fallen by a further $323 million in September, and now sufficient for no more than 40 days of essential imports of raw materials and other goods, the amount of foreign currency Israelis could take abroad was halved, to $1,000. Adoption of these latest measures, coming just a few days before Prime Minister Peres left for the United States on October 7, enabled him to present a more convincing case to administration leaders, who were urging Israel to take more stringent steps. (See also "Foreign Relations.")

One day after the prime minister's return from the United States, the announcement that the September consumer price index had risen by 21.4 percent—the highest increase in the country's history (at that time)—sent the Ministerial Economic Committee into a round of intensive deliberations. A special task force, set up by the finance minister to make recommendations for curbing inflation, submitted its proposals. Some commentators compared the economic situation in Israel to that of the Weimar Republic in the early 1920s. The skyrocketing inflation, now poised on the brink of hyperinflation, meant that wages were worth 20 percent less in real terms than they had been just three months earlier.

In what many observers viewed as a symptomatic case, the long-established Haifa-based Ata textiles plant, employing some 3,000 workers, announced that it was virtually bankrupt and would have to shut its doors. As furious workers, many of whom had been with the company for 30 or even 40 years, demanded a government bailout, the Histadrut said it would give them its full backing as part of its efforts to combat incipient unemployment. Prime Minister Peres threw his weight behind efforts to find a buyer for the firm, which was losing $1 million each month, because, as he said, the company was "a byword in Israel."

The major economic breakthrough of 1984 came at the beginning of November (following a further 24-percent price increase in subsidized staples), when the private-sector employers and the government signed an agreement on a so-called package deal (November 2), to which the Histadrut appended its signature the following day. After approving the final terms of the accord at its November 4 session, the cabinet announced that a three-month freeze on all goods and services was in effect as of that day. Emergency regulations were invoked under which prices had to be displayed in shekels and could not be raised above a fixed level. Penalties for violators included a prison term of up to three years and a stiff fine. All prices that had been quoted in dollars were frozen at the shekel rate of November 2 ($1 =IS 527) for the three-month period. A complicated set of calculations for the forthcoming cost-of-living increments (based on the assumption that the December inflation rate would be below 12 percent) meant that January 1985 wages, paid at the beginning of February, would be eroded by a further 20 percent in real terms as compared with October salaries. A follow-up committee was set up to ensure that what was officially known as the Agreement to Stabilize the Economy was fully implemented. The hope was that the three-month respite, aimed at dealing a death blow to inflation, which was running at an annualized rate approaching 1,000 percent, would enable the government to take the next essential step, one which had proved the bane of previous economic amelioration plans: effecting a deep cut in the state budget.

As the package deal staggered through its first week, marked by confusion, bureaucratic bungling, and criticism that Prime Minister Peres was moving too gradually in the face of the urgent crisis, preliminary budget-trimming negotiations got under way between the Treasury and the ministries. Peres rejected calls by economics professors for a $2-billion budget cut, pointing out that nearly half of the budget was already earmarked for debt servicing (Israel was now defraying both interest and principal on its loans), leaving no more than $11.6 billion to finance all government operations. As for the ministers, balk as they might at cuts in their domains, they could hardly remain sanguine in the face of the announcement (on November 15) that the consumer price index had risen by a staggering 24.4 percent in October, sending annualized inflation into the 1,300-percent range.

In the meantime, price stabilization efforts began to have an impact—of which the psychological aspect was not the least important—especially as they were backed up by quick trials for violators of the emergency regulations. At the same time, police cracked down on black-market dealers in foreign currency in Tel Aviv, and new regulations were issued to prevent Israelis from conducting foreign currency transactions with the numerous "money changers" operating legally in East Jerusalem.

However, efforts to lop even $550 million from the budget (down from the originally proposed $1 billion) hit a snag, largely due to the resistance of Defense Minister Yitzhak Rabin, who told the cabinet that the Treasury's demand for a further $150-million cut in defense spending, above the $300 million already agreed on, would endanger the country's security. Calls to scrap the prodigiously expensive Lavi jet-fighter project were rejected on the grounds that virtually all the current funding came from the United States, and that dropping the project would throw thousands of engineers out of work and jeopardize the future of Israel's sophisticated technological industries. Strong opposition to any trimming of their budgets was also voiced by the ministers of health, education, labor, and housing. Finally, on November 30, the cabinet decided on a total budget cut of no more than $375 million, of which $100 million would come from the defense budget. Since this was less than the rock-bottom $395-million figure recommended by a ministerial committee composed of Modai, Ya'akobi, Weizman, and Arens, the disgruntled finance minister, Modai, signaled his protest by refusing to take part in the vote. Defense Minister Rabin, who abstained, told Israel Television that the IDF's ability to defend the country in war would be impaired, ongoing security needs would suffer, and army reserve stocks were liable to fall to the level of the eve of the Yom Kippur War. It was decided to reopen discussion of the defense budget in a cabinet meeting to be held at general-staff headquarters.

But even as the ministers haggled, the public was responding favorably to a state of affairs that had not been seen for nearly a decade: a situation of stable prices, quoted in shekels, and one which, as the deputy director-general of the Ministry of Industry and Trade told the *Jerusalem Post,* seemed to have done away with "the dreaded buy-today-because-tomorrow-it-will-cost-more syndrome that has been plaguing us for too long." The November inflation rate, though still extremely high, showed a downward trend—19.5 percent. Looking ahead, the prime minister urged a "year-long stabilization of wages and prices."

In December the country registered the first monthly single-digit rise in the consumer price index in well over a year—3.7 percent. Overall, however, 1984 saw an inflation rate of no less than 444.9 percent, more than double the previous high set just one year earlier. During the year the shekel was once again devalued against the dollar at a rate higher than that of the consumer-price-index increase, this time by nearly 50 percentage points (492.6 percent), the highest of any foreign currency. On the bright side, a decrease was registered in the balance-of-payments deficit, down by 5.5 percent as compared with 1983. However, the country's gross foreign debt remained over $20 billion, while foreign currency reserves tumbled dangerously by year's end to below the $2-billion mark. The GNP registered zero growth in fixed prices, and work productivity actually fell by 1 percent, following stability in the previous two years.

On the personal level, private consumption was down by 6 percent in 1984, following increases of 7 percent in each of the two preceding years. The level of per capita consumption in 1984 declined by 3 percent, only the second time since 1950 that such a phenomenon had occurred (the previous instance was in 1980). The most dramatic falloff occurred in the sphere of durable goods, where purchases were off by fully one-third; purchases of private automobiles fell by 42 percent. All told, the standard of living in Israel declined by some 7.5 percent in 1984, with unemployment approaching 7 percent at the end of the year.

Thus, as the economy seemed to be cooling down in the final quarter, there was place for guarded optimism. Indeed, not even the release on December 31 of the long-awaited state comptroller's report on the bank-shares collapse of 1983—a report highly critical of the country's banking and financial establishment—could undermine the feeling that, after a period of drift and deterioration, the Israeli economy was embarked on the road to recovery, however painful that road might turn out to be for the individual Israeli.

The War in Lebanon

It was only at the tail end of 1984, following the installation of the new government, that a serious new effort was launched to break the impasse in Lebanon and to find a way, in accordance with the national unity government's basic guidelines, of "withdrawing the IDF [Israel Defense Forces] from Lebanon while ensuring the security of the northern settlements." Although Israeli casualties tapered off during the year, thanks largely to the September 1983 pullback to the Awali River line, on average nearly one IDF soldier was killed every week in Lebanon in 1984. In addition, the year saw the emergence of intense Shi'ite resistance to the Israeli presence in southern Lebanon.

Indeed, the rise of this new element was acknowledged at the year's very outset, with a concentrated Israel Air Force (IAF) bombing (January 4) of a Syrian-backed Shi'ite terrorist base near Baalbek. At the same time, efforts were under way by the IDF's liaison unit to cultivate relations with the Shi'ites in the south, who comprised some 80 percent or more of the population in the area immediately north of Israel. As it turned out, however, this move was a case of too little and too late. Israel's almost exclusively Christian orientation in Lebanon had caused bitter hostility on the part of the Shi'ites, who were now being tagged as the emerging power in Lebanon's Byzantine military-political complex. In the meantime, U.S. special envoy Donald Rumsfeld met on January 6 with Prime Minister Shamir as part of his efforts to try to effect a disengagement-of-forces agreement in Lebanon. However, American resolve vis-à-vis Lebanon had become the victim of Washington's vacillating policy, and the efforts of Rumsfeld and, later, Assistant Secretary of State Richard Murphy proved singularly ineffectual.

On January 14 Major Sa'ad Haddad, commander of the Israeli-backed Christian militia in southern Lebanon, died of cancer, aged 46. Hospitalized for a period at

Rambam Hospital in Haifa, Haddad was sent home at the beginning of the year when the disease reached an irreversible point. Prime Minister Shamir, who attended Haddad's funeral in his home village of Marjayoun along with other Israeli leaders and ranking security personnel, termed him "a great patriot and a true friend of Israel." On April 14, following behind-the-scenes negotiations with Israel, Antoine Lahad, 55, who held the rank of major general when he retired from the Lebanese army in 1983, formally took command of Haddad's 1,200-man force. Lahad, a Christian, launched a drive to double the strength of the militia and to recruit more Shi'ites into it. The new commander's background held out hope that the militia could be incorporated into the Lebanese army as part of a scenario in which Beirut would take responsibility for the south. (Haddad, a defector from the Lebanese army, had been anathema in Beirut.)

Domestic opposition to the war was highlighted by the announcement on January 20 that a suspect had been arrested in the killing of Emil Grunzweig at a 1983 Peace Now demonstration in Jerusalem. (See AJYB, Vol. 85, 1985, pp. 281–282.) Police Minister Yosef Burg and ranking police officers told a press conference that the arrest of Yona Avrushmi, 28, on suspicion of having thrown the grenade that took the life of Grunzweig and wounded ten others, marked the end of a year-long investigation, "the most complicated and most intensive" ever conducted by the Israel Police. In a demonstration commemorating the first anniversary of the incident, some 50,000 people marched through Jerusalem to the spot where the murder had occurred. On February 10, exactly one year after the killing, Avrushmi was formally charged in a Jerusalem court with having murdered Grunzweig "in cold blood" and "with malice aforethought." (Avrushmi denied all the charges against him when the trial opened on March 27. As the trial proceeded, it became clear that the suspect had acted alone; he had been enraged by what he considered to be "unpatriotic" actions of the Israeli Left in general, and Peace Now in particular. By year's end the court had recessed and a verdict was being awaited.)

As political disagreement in Israel over the Lebanon war continued unabated, U.S. president Ronald Reagan announced a decision in February to evacuate the marine detachment stationed in Beirut. This move further weakened Israel's position by enhancing Syrian prestige, which in turn enabled Damascus to exert greater leverage on Lebanese president Amin Gemayel. On February 9, two days after the Reagan announcement, three Katyusha rockets landed near Metullah in the Galilee panhandle. No one was hurt, but inhabitants of the area went to their bomb shelters for the first time since the Israeli incursion into Lebanon in June 1982. The following day the IAF struck again at terrorist bases in Lebanon.

Another in the series of Israel–United States policy disagreements over Lebanon developed when Washington signaled Jerusalem that for the sake of saving the Gemayel government—in the face of mounting Syrian political and other pressure on Beirut—Israel should make no objection if Lebanon decided to abrogate its May 17, 1983, accord with Israel, to which Washington itself was also a signatory. Prime Minister Shamir implicitly criticized this U.S. message as well as the U.S. decision to leave Lebanon when he told Israel Radio (February 11): "There may be some in the United States who believe that Gemayel has no choice but to give in to Syrian aggression. But such a view is the result of weakness or error. I believe that the United States knows, as we do, that aggression is not enfeebled when one gives in to it." Shamir, who warned Lebanon that its abrogation of the agreement would also release Israel from its commitments, also shrugged off the significance of the Katyusha attack, explaining that "what we have prevented, and will continue to prevent, are the systematic barrages of Katyusha and rocket fire which used to occur." This was actually a modification of former prime minister Begin's blanket assertion that no more Katyushas would ever again fall on Galilee.

Israel itself could do no more than issue a verbal condemnation when, on March 5, Lebanon finally succumbed to Syrian pressure and abrogated the May 1983 agreement. Syria, a statement issued by the Prime Minister's Office read, had forced Lebanon "to surrender to a *diktat* which is tantamount to a death sentence on Lebanese independence." As for Israel, the statement continued, it had no recourse but to come up with its own "suitable means for protecting its security," Lebanon having reneged on its international commitments.

A few days later, expectations of an imminent IDF pullback were raised by Deputy Prime Minister David Levy, who told Israel Radio that such a move was needed in order to end the present state of affairs in which the IDF was "stuck in the midst of a hostile civilian population." However, the anticipation generated by Levy's remarks proved premature, and the situation he had described continued to take its toll: 11 soldiers were wounded on March 4 (one of whom later died) when three separate bomb blasts rocked the port of Sidon. In the days following, two civilian workers of the public works department were killed in ambushes while engaged in road work for the IDF in southern Lebanon. Two others had been killed earlier in the year. At home, the Knesset rejected by a vote of 42–33 a Mapam motion for the agenda calling for the establishment of a commission of inquiry into the entire course of the Lebanon war. The motion was submitted following the publication of two best-selling books by leading Israeli journalists: *Israel's Lebanon War* by Ze'ev Schiff and Ehud Ya'ari, and *Operation Peace for Galilee* by Shimon Shiffer. Their message, backed up by a wealth of newly revealed details, was, as Mapam MK Ya'ir Tzaban put it, that the Lebanon war had been "conceived in deceit and born in duplicity."

On April 7 the IAF struck at a base of the Democratic Front for the Liberation of Palestine at Bahamdoun in retaliation for a terrorist attack in Jerusalem earlier that week. According to army sources, the base had been used by terrorists who were connected with the attack, in which one person was killed and 47 wounded. (See also "Terrorism.") In the meantime, after two more Katyushas hit Israeli territory, landing near the border kibbutz of Misgav Am, IDF artillery shelled PLO bases in the eastern Beka'a Valley for the first time in a year.

In what seemed to be turning into an annual spring ritual, the Syrian media in April began to sound warnings about an alleged imminent Israeli preemptive strike, throwing in charges of U.S. collusion for good measure. One explanation adduced for the rash of Syrian pronouncements was an apparent power struggle under way in Damascus. In any event, Prime Minister Shamir told the Reuters news agency on April 24 that Israel was not contemplating any military operations against Syria, nor was any Syrian buildup of forces discernible. However, he added, in view of the fact that the two countries had fought five wars since 1948, the IDF would continue its vigilance.

One week later (May 1), Syrian troops in Lebanon seized three members of the Israeli liaison unit at Dbaiyeh, north of Beirut. The three, who had evidently driven their car into Syrian-held territory by mistake, were initially branded "saboteurs" and "spies" by the Syrians and taken to Damascus for interrogation. Jerusalem breathed a bit easier when Syria announced that the three would be treated "as prisoners of war according to the Geneva international conventions." (Coincidentally or not, it was not long after this incident that Lebanon asked Israel to close the Dbaiyeh office. After some initial resistance to the move by Israel the office was shut down on July 25—yet another Syrian triumph and the loss, for Israel, of a key site for monitoring developments in Lebanon.) The three errant Israelis were not returned until June 28, as part of an overall Israeli–Syrian prisoner exchange. Israel received at the same time three soldiers captured by the Syrians during the fighting in Lebanon in the summer of 1982, including an air force pilot. The Syrians also transferred five coffins to Israel, two of which were found to contain the remains of Israeli soldiers killed in the Lebanon fighting; the other three could not be identified as Israelis (although three Israelis were still listed as missing in action). In return, the Syrians received 291 prisoners of war, among them 23 officers, as well as 20 civilian security prisoners and the bodies of 70 Syrian soldiers. According to former justice minister Shmuel Tamir, the chief Israeli negotiator in the talks that led up to the prisoner exchange, three Israeli soldiers were still being held by Ahmed Jibril's terrorist organization (it admitted to having only two), while Nayif Hawatmeh's organization was holding one Israeli.

On June 9 some 30,000 persons marked the second anniversary of Israel's incursion into Lebanon by staging a protest march, organized by Peace Now, in Tel Aviv. Speaking in the Knesset on June 12, Yitzhak Rabin, Labor's candidate for defense minister, excoriated the Likud government for its Lebanon policy. With the war now in its third year, Rabin pointed out, Lebanon was under virtual Syrian control, the Beirut government was inimical to Israel, there were 20,000 terrorists in Lebanon, and "Shi'ite Khomeinist terrorism" had emerged as a factor against Israel. Rabin went on to call for a two-stage IDF withdrawal from Lebanon within six months, with UNIFIL (the United Nations Interim Force in Lebanon) and a beefed-up Southern Lebanon Army (SLA), the successor to the Haddad militia, to take the place of Israeli troops and to prevent terrorist infiltration.

Meanwhile, as the election campaign at home gained momentum, Israeli forces in Lebanon continued to sustain heavy casualties. On June 16 five soldiers were wounded near Sidon when a suicide driver blew up his car as he drove by an IDF convoy. Earlier that week four soldiers were wounded when a roadside bomb went off near Tyre, and three more were hurt when their vehicle was hit by light-arms fire from an ambush south of the Zaharani River. On June 13 two Katyushas landed just north of the Israeli border.

On June 28 the Israel Navy sank a terrorist boat off Tripoli. The following day an Israeli gunboat intercepted a Cyprus–Beirut ferryboat on the high seas and towed it into Haifa port. Rejecting allegations of "piracy," the Foreign Ministry in Jerusalem issued a statement saying that the seizure of the boat was an act of self-defense and part of Israel's "unending war against PLO terrorism." Moreover, it was "the duty of every civilized nation" to assist in that war, the statement added. The boat and most of its passengers were soon released, and by mid-July Israel continued to hold only two of the passengers. With attacks on Israeli forces intensifying, on August 1 the IDF used helicopter gunships, supported by offshore naval vessels, to attack PLO targets in a refugee camp north of Tripoli. In southern Lebanon, with Shi'ite resistance mounting, the IDF forbade the public display of pictures of the Ayatollah Khomeini and other extremist religious figures.

As the coalition talks in Israel were concluding in mid-September, it was "business as usual" in Lebanon. On September 10 the IAF bombed a terrorist site at Bahamdoun, its fourth raid over Lebanon within six weeks. On September 12, the day before the new government was presented in the Knesset, one Israeli soldier was killed while dismantling a roadside bomb and a second died of wounds he had sustained in an attack two days earlier. The Parents Against Silence group held a silent vigil outside the Knesset and dispatched cables to all the newly installed cabinet ministers, asserting that the country's most urgent problem was not the economy but the need to withdraw the IDF from Lebanon.

This was certainly the top priority for Israel's new defense minister, Yitzhak Rabin, a former prime minister and chief of staff. In his first public address after taking up his new duties, Rabin signaled a dramatic Israeli policy shift when he told a United Jewish Appeal leadership conference in Jerusalem that the IDF's presence in Lebanon was not a *sine qua non* for an untroubled Galilee. He intimated that an IDF withdrawal was a matter of "months not years." Two days of talks between Israeli leaders and U.N. undersecretary-general Brian Urquhart (September 19–20) seemed to reinforce Rabin's prognosis, with Urquhart telling reporters that his current regional swing through Israel, Syria, and Lebanon had shown him that a "mood of realism" now prevailed.

Lebanese reality was driven home when, on September 20, Druze members of the SLA massacred 13 residents of a village where 4 Druze had been killed in an ambush. (The same day also saw the terrorist bombing of the U.S. embassy in Beirut, killing 23 persons, with responsibility claimed by an extremist Shi'ite group.) After meeting with SLA commander General Lahad, the IDF's liaison officer in southern Lebanon, Brig. Gen. Shlomo Iliya, described the massacre as a private act of revenge and said the incident did not compromise the SLA's ability to defend southern Lebanon.

In a by-now-standard Middle East pattern, incipient diplomatic activity evoked intensified anti-Israel action. On September 23 an Israel Navy gunboat spotted a rubber dinghy bound for Israeli waters from the north. Returning to the Lebanese shore, the occupants of the dinghy ran into an Israeli ambush. In the exchange of fire three terrorists were killed (one of them a French woman) and two others were captured. Later that day five Israeli soldiers were wounded when the convoy they were traveling in came under light-arms fire near Nabatiyeh. Three of the ambushers were killed by SLA troops following a chase. In a third incident on the same day, another three Israelis were wounded when a roadside bomb went off as their vehicle passed about two kilometers from the border crossing at Metullah. The following day an Israeli soldier and a member of the General Security Service were killed when their vehicle was ambushed in the eastern sector.

On October 4 Defense Minister Rabin told a memorial service for fallen para-troopers that negotiations for an Israeli withdrawal were already under way. Rabin indicated that the intention was to reach an understanding, perforce tacit, with the Syrians, by which they would prevent terrorist infiltration into southern Lebanon following an Israeli withdrawal. Visiting Washington in the second week of October, Prime Minister Peres set a timetable for withdrawal, albeit a sketchy one, when he told reporters that the cabinet would make decisions on the Lebanon issue within a month, and that Israel would "unilaterally" pull out of Lebanon within six to nine months after that. In a meeting with UN secretary-general Javier Pérez de Cuéllar in New York on October 12, Peres presented Israel's ideas concerning the role that UNIFIL could play in helping stabilize southern Lebanon. (The UN Security Council subsequently extended UNIFIL's mandate for a further six months, until April 19, 1985.)

On October 17 the first detailed official public announcement of the new govern-ment's position was issued in the form of a statement released by the Prime Minis-ter's Office, following talks between Peres and visiting U.S. secretary of defense Caspar Weinberger. Although Israel was "firmly resolved" to bring the IDF home "soon," there would be no compromise over security arrangements in the north, the statement said. According to the official communiqué, Peres had told Weinberger that the "framework for an arrangement in Lebanon" entailed "a political under-standing with the Syrians and a military accord with the Lebanese." Peres then went on to list four specific terms for an IDF withdrawal: "A Syrian commitment not to expand the deployment of its forces into the areas to be evacuated by the IDF; a Syrian undertaking to prevent terrorist infiltration from the territory under Syrian army control; the continued existence of the SLA under General Lahad's command, and its deployment in the southern area contiguous with the Israel border; and the deployment of UNIFIL units in the zone north of the SLA strip, from the Mediter-ranean in the west to the Syrians' lines of deployment in the east." Israel, the statement concluded, would "welcome the good offices of the United States in mediating between the sides." Three days later, on October 20, the 835th day of the war, a rocket-propelled grenade fired at an Israeli vehicle in southern Lebanon took the life of Corp. Alon Tzur, a 30-year-old reservist from Kibbutz Shamir in Upper Galilee. He was the 600th Israeli soldier to die in Lebanon.

On November 8 talks on an IDF withdrawal opened between Israel and Lebanon when military delegations from the two countries (a concession by Israel, which had sought civilian talks) met at Nakoura, in southern Lebanon, under UN auspices. About a week earlier, Prime Minister Peres had explained to the Knesset's Defense and Foreign Affairs Committee that the government was going to give diplomacy two or three months to effect a withdrawal agreement.

Unlike the 1983 talks that had produced the May 17 agreement (which had already been abrogated), and despite Israel's declared wish for American mediation, the United States was pointedly absent from the Nakoura talks, another trenchant reminder of its abrupt disengagement from the Lebanese arena. Indeed, the invisible presence hovering above the Nakoura talks was that of the undisputed victor in Lebanon, the Syrians, who had been able to delay the start of the negotiations at will before giving their tacit consent to Beirut to proceed with them. Nor was the Gemayel government immune to pressure from within. Less than 48 hours after the talks began, Gemayel, bowing to pressure from Nabih Berri, head of the Shi'ite Amal militia, suspended the negotiations. The reason was Israel's arrest of the Amal commander in Sidon following the death of one Israeli soldier and the wounding of four others in that city on November 7, the day before the talks opened, when an IDF convoy was ambushed.

Little progress was discernible in the opening round of the talks. Israel outlined its plan for a two-part security zone, with the southern section to be controlled by the SLA and the area immediately to its north by UNIFIL. For its part, Lebanon insisted that its army must take control of any areas evacuated by the IDF, a patently unfeasible notion since the Lebanese army was barely in control of large parts of Beirut itself. The talks resumed on November 15, one week after their suspension, and the following day Israel released the Amal commander—his interrogation had been completed, the IDF said—and expelled him from southern Lebanon. To some, the Israeli move, which was clearly part of a deal, was yet one more demonstration of Israel's weakened resolve where Lebanon was concerned. With the positions of both sides now on the table, the talks continued in a desultory manner on a twice-weekly basis, against a backdrop of continuing attacks on Israeli forces. On December 13, in what seemed to mark the onset of a new policy vis-à-vis anti-IDF activity in southern Lebanon, Israeli forces conducted a sweep of nine villages there, in the course of which 2 local residents were killed, 7 were wounded, and 30 terrorist suspects were detained. The Israeli operation touched off a general strike by both Moslems and Christians.

The 608th Israeli soldier to die in Lebanon, the third since the start of the Nakoura talks, and the last in 1984, fell on December 16 in a clash between an IDF patrol and a local guerrilla force. Later in the week, on December 19 and 20, the final rounds of the Nakoura talks for 1984 took place. They were scheduled to reconvene in January 1985, but it was evident by then that they held little promise.

Looking ahead, Prime Minister Peres and, more guardedly, Defense Minister Rabin said they favored a full unilateral IDF withdrawal when and if the talks broke down. However, Vice Prime Minister and Likud leader Shamir told the *Jerusalem Post* late in December that "unless there are satisfactory arrangements on the border, the IDF will stay in Lebanon in one form or another." The national unity government had just survived a coalition crisis set off by what, in comparison with Lebanon, was a minor affair involving the allocation of two ministries (see "Political Affairs"). Now it would have to decide how to proceed regarding a war which, as Defense Minister Rabin put it shortly after assuming his post in September, "has brought about a divisiveness that I cannot recall in any of [Israel's previous] wars."

Foreign Relations

THE UNITED STATES

Israeli–U.S. relations in 1984 showed a marked improvement over recent years. This was due largely to the collapse of American policy in Lebanon and the physical withdrawal of the marines from Beirut, accompanied by Israel's professed desire to get out of Lebanon. Attention now shifted to two areas: the evolving strategic cooperation between the two countries, carried out within the framework of the joint political-military committee created during Prime Minister Shamir's Washington talks at the end of 1983 (its first meeting was held in the U.S. capital in January 1984); and, with the advent of the national unity government in September, Israel's economic situation.

In February Israel's plans to build its own jet fighter for the 1990s, the Lavi, received a shot in the arm when the Reagan administration announced that Israel would be allowed to spend the $250 million allocated for related research and development projects in Israel itself. A growing controversy in Israel about the economic feasibility of the Lavi project was partially muted by the fact that the funds were coming from Washington. Later in the year, Defense Secretary Caspar Weinberger reported that the United States would release technology required by Israel for the Lavi's development. While in Israel in mid-October for a 36-hour visit, Weinberger promised that red tape would be cut for direct sales of Israeli weapons systems to the U.S. military, as long as the Israeli products were "competitive both in price and technology" with their American-made counterparts.

The American commitment to Israel's security was reaffirmed in April by Vice-President George Bush. Speaking at the annual policy conference of AIPAC (American Israel Public Affairs Committee) in Washington, Bush asserted that Israel was America's "foremost strategic friend in the Middle East." The ongoing talks and growing strategic bonds between the two countries were a manifestation, he continued, of "America's long-standing commitment to ensure Israel's qualitative edge in armaments over any potential combination of adversaries." Regarding a perennial source of discord between Jerusalem and Washington—U.S. plans to sell advanced weaponry to what were regarded as "moderate" Arab regimes, notably Saudi Arabia and Jordan—Bush said that such deals would not be allowed to threaten Israel's security. Explaining the U.S. position on another contentious issue, the proposal to move the U.S. embassy in Israel to Jerusalem, Bush told the AIPAC meeting: "While Jerusalem must remain undivided, its final status can only be resolved in negotiations, not through unilateral acts."

In May a senior Pentagon official took the lid off some of the ideas and concepts that were being discussed by the joint political-military committee. Speaking to an American Jewish Congress meeting in Washington, Dov Zakheim, assistant under secretary of defense for policy and resources, said that one of the first concrete steps in the strategic cooperation sphere would be a joint medical evacuation exercise aimed at putting into practice a December 1983 agreement "to share medical support in the event of some disaster or emergency." (The exercise was in fact held in June, with 44 "wounded" American servicemen being airlifted by helicopter from their Sixth Fleet home ship to two Israeli hospitals. About three months later four Americans were flown to a Tel Aviv hospital following the car-bombing of the U.S. embassy in Beirut. A year earlier, under similar circumstances, the United States had refused to hospitalize wounded personnel in Israel.) In general, Zakheim said, the joint committee was considering "combined planning, exercises, access, and possible requirements for prepositioning of U.S. equipment" in Israel.

Yet another manifestation of growing strategic cooperation was a series of port calls at Haifa by U.S. Sixth Fleet warships, including a battleship and an amphibious helicopter carrier. In May it was confirmed that the U.S. Navy had purchased highly advanced pilotless reconnaissance aircraft (drones) from Israel, which was able to outbid a U.S. firm for the contract. It was subsequently revealed that the navy had also acquired Israeli-made air-launched gliders for release as decoys in aerial combat.

Visits to the United States by Israel's two ranking defense officials helped cement the emerging strategic relationship. At the end of May Defense Minister Arens met at the Pentagon with Defense Secretary Weinberger for a *tour d'horizon*. Arens told reporters that U.S.–Israeli military relations were at their "best-ever" level. The latest possible hitch in those relations, Washington's plan to sell the Saudis 400 shoulder-fired Stinger antiaircraft missiles, to which Israeli officials had expressed low-key opposition, did not feature prominently in the Arens-Weinberger meeting. Three months later Israel's chief of staff, Lt. Gen. Moshe Levy, visited the United States for an extensive tour of military facilities and meetings with top military brass. In a meeting with Israeli correspondents, Levy effectively dissociated Israel from statements made by various American spokesmen, including President Reagan, who had said a week earlier that he did not regard the Soviet Union as Israel's enemy. The Jewish state, Levy said, had "specific enemies" against whom it had to buttress its security.

While Levy was in the United States, Secretary of the Navy John Lehman announced (August 31) that the U.S. Navy was leasing 12 Israeli-made Kfir jet fighters, which would be used to simulate MIG-21 aircraft in training navy pilots for aerial combat. Israel Aircraft Industries (IAI) received a $68-million contract, for a three-and-a-half-year period, to service the planes in the United States. In return for the loan of the planes, Israel was to receive unspecified services and equipment of equivalent value. The first three of the Kfirs were formally handed over to the United States on September 19 in a ceremony at IAI. In December the navies of the two countries held a week-long antisubmarine exercise in the Mediterranean.

In October Prime Minister Peres (accompanied by Vice Prime Minister Shamir) told Weinberger that in the immediate future the focus in the IDF would be on upgrading quality rather than augmenting quantity. Peres, who was in the United States for a week-long visit, requested an increase of some $300 million in military grants, to a level of $1.7 billion, to help Israel offset the cost of the arms and matériel it was seeking within the framework of a four-year procurement plan that was submitted to the Pentagon.

Both Peres's visit and the advent of the national unity government in Israel signaled a shift—at least in public perception—from concentration on military matters to concentration on economic strategy in Jerusalem-Washington relations. This shift was symbolized by the creation during the Peres visit (October 7–13) of a joint economic committee, in contrast to the political-military committee that had been set up a year earlier. Concretely, Peres reportedly asked for an emergency aid injection of $750 million in each of the two coming fiscal years. Washington agreed, in the interim, to transfer an already approved $1.2 billion in civilian aid immediately because of the critical status of Israel's foreign currency reserves. President Reagan also established what Peres later dubbed an economic "safety net" for Israel by assuring the American—and international—financial community that "the U.S. government will work closely with the Israeli government to avert" any balance-of-payments crunch that might arise. Speaking to reporters after his October 9 meeting with the president, Prime Minister Peres said: "I found in the White House a true friend of Israel who understands our problems and dilemmas."

As the year drew to a close, Washington was increasingly prone to use its economic leverage on Jerusalem to compel the national unity government to take steps the United States deemed essential for Israeli economic stability. When an Israeli economic delegation to Washington in mid-December submitted a record Israeli aid request of about $4.1 billion for fiscal 1986, plus $800 million in emergency aid for the current (1985) fiscal year, it was told bluntly that Israel must adopt more stringent economic measures. On December 21 a State Department spokesman said that a final decision on whether to grant Israel supplementary economic assistance was being deferred, "pending Israel's adoption of an effective stabilization program and a determination of the utility of such U.S. assistance in supporting such a program." (Washington regarded the "Agreement to Stabilize the Economy" that Israel implemented in November as insufficiently comprehensive and too gradual.)

Following publication in *Ha'aretz* on December 24 of a letter from Secretary of State Shultz to Prime Minister Peres, once more urging Israel to implement more rigorous economic steps, Minister of Economy and Planning Gad Ya'akobi was quoted in the press as having said that Israel had no need of "moralizing" by the United States. Applying immediate damage control, Peres termed Shultz "one of Israel's best friends in Washington," adding that the letter was "the advice of a friend, without pressure and without insult."

The bottom line in this area was well summed up in a *Jerusalem Post* editorial (December 26) calling on Israel to approve a U.S. request to construct a powerful Voice of America relay station in the country to enhance its broadcasts to the Soviet Union. Concluded the editorial: "But the clinching argument in favor of letting the station be built is simply that Israel cannot possibly say no to the Americans in a matter that does not touch on truly vital Israeli interests. Not when the United States is Israel's most—and sometimes only—trusted friend in the world arena. And especially not when this country is critically dependent on the United States for its sheer economic survival."

EGYPT

The rhetoric in the relations between Israel and Egypt took a positive turn following the installation of Shimon Peres as prime minister in mid-September. However, there was no accompanying breakthrough in the "cold peace" that had prevailed between the two countries ever since Egypt's recall of its ambassador from Tel Aviv following the Sabra-Shatilla massacre in September 1982.

In talks at the beginning of February with the commander of the Sinai Multinational Force and Observers (MFO), Lt. Gen. Fredrik Bull-Hansen, and the force's director-general, Leamon Hunt (who was gunned down in Rome just days later), Israel requested that the MFO carefully monitor Egyptian military infrastructure construction in Zone A in Sinai. However, in mid-March, summing up his tenure as MFO commander (he was replaced by another Norwegian, Lt. Gen. Egil Ingebrigsten), Bull-Hansen told reporters that in the five years since the signing of the Israel-Egypt peace treaty the MFO had detected only minor violations of its provisions.

Prime Minister Shamir sent what were described as "warm and friendly" greetings to Egyptian president Hosni Mubarak on the occasion of the fifth anniversary of the treaty, expressing the hope for continuing and expanding peaceful relations between the two countries. His message was sent less than three weeks after he excoriated the Egyptians in the Knesset (March 7), asserting that Egypt's behavior "impairs the credibility of agreements and commitments it has undertaken." Shamir was particularly outraged over the blatantly anti-Semitic propaganda being disseminated in the "institutionalized" Egyptian press, as he termed it. Shamir's harsh words notwithstanding, two days later Industry and Trade Minister Gideon Patt attended the opening of the annual Cairo International Fair in which Israel participated. This proved to be the only visit to Egypt by an Israeli cabinet minister in 1984—a visit that was not reciprocated.

In April MK Abba Eban (Alignment-Labor) was given a red-carpet welcome in Cairo, even as Defense Minister Arens was reiterating, to Israel Radio, the complaint that had already been lodged with the MFO earlier in the year, namely, that Egypt was effectively violating the peace treaty by its extensive military construction in Sinai. Eban, who was received by President Mubarak in his private residence on April 5 for a 75-minute talk, was told that the Israeli presence in Lebanon was the main obstacle to a thaw in the relations between the two countries. Following his two-day stay in Cairo, during which he also met with other Egyptian leaders, Eban told reporters that Mubarak had expressed his country's commitment to the peace treaty. Yet, in an interview with the *Jerusalem Post,* Eban's official host in Egypt, Secretary of State for Foreign Affairs Butros Ghali, declared that as far as his country was concerned, Israel had "betrayed the whole peace process" by its behavior in the West Bank and its actions in Lebanon.

Matters were not helped by Egypt's decision, in April, to break diplomatic relations with El Salvador and Costa Rica for returning their embassies in Israel to Jerusalem. Egypt's chargé d'affaires in Israel, Mohamed Bassiouny, was called in to the Foreign Ministry in Jerusalem and told of Israel's "profound astonishment" at Cairo's move, the more so as this "intervention" in Israel's foreign relations constituted a violation of the peace treaty. Another Foreign Ministry statement around this time objected to a remark by Butros Ghali that Israel's treatment of the Palestinians under its control was "armed terror without parallel in human history." Terming such comments "hostile propaganda," an Israeli spokesman said they "encourage terrorism, and are contrary to the peace treaty."

A case of mixed messages occurred again on June 4 when the chairman of the Knesset's Defense and Foreign Relations Committee, Eliahu Ben-Elissar (Likud-Herut), who also served as Israel's first ambassador to Egypt, paid a surprise visit to Cairo to convey a message from Prime Minister Shamir to President Mubarak. On the very same day, the Israeli press headlined charges by the IDF's chief of military intelligence, Maj. Gen. Ehud Barak, to the effect that Egypt was engaged in a military buildup in Sinai and was liable to rejoin the "active circle of hostility against Israel." Although the Ben-Elissar visit was widely regarded as an election ploy aimed at arranging a Shamir-Mubarak meeting like the Begin-Sadat summit that took place on the eve of the 1981 elections, it was made in response to what was said to have been a positive message from Mubarak to Shamir at the end of April. The comments of General Barak, an embarrassment in light of the diplomatic moves being made, were disclaimed by the prime minister. Speaking on Israel Radio, Shamir said the press had overblown Barak's remarks, and that while Egypt was apparently engaged in a military buildup, Israel faced no danger from that quarter. Ben-Elissar reported to Shamir on his talks on June 5, perhaps just at the time when Israeli diplomat Zvi Kedar was being shot and wounded outside his Cairo residence. A Palestinian organization claimed responsibility for the attack.

The advent of Shimon Peres as prime minister brought a spurt of diplomatic activity. In the final week of September he received the Egyptian chargé d'affaires three times in as many days. The Egyptian official handed Peres a message from Mubarak and briefed him on Egypt's resumption of diplomatic relations with Jordan, a move Israel welcomed. In a *Jerusalem Post* interview, Peres cited Lebanon and Taba—the disputed tiny stretch of coastline south of Eilat—as the chief obstacles to a thaw in the cool relations between the two countries. As for the former, he said, Cairo was aware that Israel was serious in its intention to terminate its presence in Lebanon; and as for Taba, that was under study, with a view to resolving the dispute without resorting to international arbitration.

The year ended on a relatively up-beat note when Israel's ambassador to Egypt, Moshe Sasson, was received by Prime Minister Kamal Hassan Ali, who told him that Egypt remained committed to peace with Israel. This was followed by Prime Minister Peres's confirmation on November 11 of reports that he had proposed a summit meeting with Mubarak. While this was not rejected outright, the Egyptian leader said that the ground for such an encounter had to be prepared. What this meant in concrete terms was explained a few days later by Mubarak's foreign policy adviser, Osama al-Baz. He told the *New York Times* that "we have to be certain that a summit would produce meaningful and concrete progress not only on bilateral relations, but also with respect to the Palestinian question and the situation in Lebanon."

OTHER MIDDLE EAST COUNTRIES

The question of Israeli arms sales to Iran received considerable attention in 1984. In March an Israeli spokesman, responding to reports in Bonn, said there had been no Israeli arms deliveries to Iran for the past three years. In May assertions by Minister Without Portfolio Ariel Sharon, who was in the United States, that Israel was in fact providing the Khomeini regime with arms were denied by the prime minister's spokesman. In June, this time in the wake of a remark by former U.S. ambassador to Saudi Arabia James Akins, Defense Minister Arens himself rejected charges that Israel was supplying arms to Iran. The Israeli embassy in Washington disavowed a report in a local newsletter which intimated that Israel was providing Iran with spare parts for its Phantom jet fighters.

As for the Iran-Iraq war itself, Prime Minister Shamir told *Ma'ariv* in April that "wars between our enemies work in our favor; they give us, at least, more time, which is the essential thing we need now." Iraq, he pointed out, could not move against Israel as long as it was bogged down in its conflict with Iran, and even though Baghdad was receiving large stocks of combat matériel, that equipment was "being used up in battle." Shamir put it still more bluntly in an Israel Radio interview in June: "Let those two crazy countries destroy each other," he said, explaining that Israel's attitude was one of neutrality in the conflict.

Israel's attitude toward nuclear installations in the Middle East—a subject of major interest since the air force's destruction of the Iraqi nuclear station in 1981 —was formally expressed by Prime Minister Shamir in May. He stated that Israel advocated international arrangements that would guarantee immunity for peaceful nuclear power plants in the region. Reinforcing this posture, the director-general of the Israel Atomic Energy Commission, Uzi Eilam, notified the International Atomic Energy Agency in June of Israel's position that all peaceful nuclear installations should be "inviolable from military attack." Israel itself, Eilam added, would not interfere with any nuclear facility operating for peaceful purposes.

An event that seemed to hold out hopeful prospects for the future took place in May when a group of some 35 Israelis, including 11 Knesset members, local officials, and journalists, visited Morocco within the framework of a two-day conference there of world Jewish communities. During this first-ever official visit by an Israeli delegation to the North African state, the head of the Israeli group, Moroccan-born MK Rafi Edri (Alignment-Labor), invited the host country to send a reciprocal delegation to visit Israel. Addressing the delegation, Moroccan minister of state Moulay Ahmed Alaoui told the Israelis that King Hassan II was willing and able to act as a mediator between Israel and the Palestinians. In Israel, Prime Minister Shamir described the reception given the visitors to Morocco as "one more expression of the growing acceptance by the Arab world of the independent existence of the State of Israel."

Shamir's optimism was tempered, however, in a speech he delivered in the Knesset a week later (May 21). "Ideological and practical inertia," he said, prevented the Arabs from "responding to Israel's willingness to sit at the negotiating table with any Arab state." In one of his final policy statements as prime minister, Shamir declared as unacceptable a Middle East peace plan published by the Soviet news agency Tass on July 29, one which centered on the convening of an international conference. Shamir told the cabinet in August that the plan would be unwieldy and unworkable.

The main thrust of Prime Minister Peres's thinking was, as expected, in the direction of a possible breakthrough with Jordan. Welcoming the resumption of Egyptian-Jordanian diplomatic relations (announced September 25), Peres said he hoped this move augured a similar renewal of regional peace efforts.

That peace, however, was not around the corner was demonstrated on October 1 when King Hussein, evidently on the defensive in the Arab world following his resumption of relations with Egypt, launched a scathing attack on the new Israeli government and presented a hard-line posture with respect to the peace process. Responding within hours of the king's remarks, Prime Minister Peres rejected Hussein's preconditions for talks, adding that Israel's declared desire for negotiations was not a "tactical ruse" but was based on the "real and serious need" for peace in the region.

In late November attention focused on the meetings in Amman of the 17th Palestine National Council (PNC), regarded by Palestinians as their "parliament in exile." While the meetings were noteworthy for bringing about reconciliation between King Hussein and Yasir Arafat, they did not produce an agreement by the PLO leader to join Hussein in seeking a negotiated peace with Israel. In his speech opening the PNC, King Hussein called for an international peace conference in which the PLO would be a participant, and for a political settlement based on the principle of "peace for territories." Prime Minister Peres's spokesman, in a statement issued the day after the speech, expressed skepticism about a possible PLO shift to the diplomatic path, but reiterated Jerusalem's call to the Jordanian monarch to commence direct negotiations with Israel, without prior conditions on either side. Peres's views served to highlight the divisions within the government of national unity—which some dubbed the "government of national paralysis"—since Foreign Minister Shamir was known to be opposed to talks with Jordan. Declaring that he was "not enthusiastic about this slogan of 'peace for territories,'" Shamir explained that "Hussein understands it as meaning a total [Israeli] withdrawal to the 1967 borders, while Arafat's interpretation is that it would be the first stage in the liquidation of Israel." About a week later, Peres himself termed the PNC meeting "more of a psychological than a political event," one which would not produce concrete results because of its ambivalent message.

In the meantime, on November 28 a Katyusha rocket fired from Jordan hit the Jordan Valley, the second such attack in a month. Defense Minister Yitzhak Rabin told Israel Television on November 30 that Israel had warned Jordan not to allow the kind of PLO buildup that had taken place in the 1960s. Israel's information, Rabin said, was that growing numbers of PLO personnel were converging on Amman in the wake of the organization's expulsion from Beirut.

In an episode related to the PNC meetings, MK Abdel Wahab Darousha (Alignment-Labor) on November 27 left secretly for Cyprus where he hoped to obtain a visa to enter Jordan, there to address the council in a dramatic peace gesture. When an Israeli news magazine revealed the story while Darousha was still in Cyprus, the Labor party tried frantically to contact him and convince him to call off the trip. Foreign Minister Shamir reflected Likud thinking when he termed the move "grave, hostile, and dangerous." As things turned out, Darousha returned to Israel on November 29, which was also the final day of the PNC meeting, having failed to receive a visa to enter Jordan. He told reporters that he had no regrets, averring that he had taken "the first step in the right direction—toward an Israeli-Palestinian peace."

A peace move of a different sort—less dramatic but perhaps ultimately more effective—was shown to reporters during a tour of the Jordan Rift Valley that took place near the end of the year. Pointing to the lush green valley visible across the Jordan River, Agriculture Minister Aryeh Nachamkin noted that it had been totally barren before 1967. The Jordanian region had been developed, he said, with the help of Israeli-trained advisers and with state-of-the-art equipment purchased from Israel. Nachamkin explained that Israeli agricultural goods, such as drip-irrigation devices, were being exported (without Israeli markings) to various Arab lands via the Jordan River bridges. The government had decided to allow this indirect form of aid to proceed, he said, because "it has made the border quiet."

WESTERN EUROPE

Following a trend already visible in 1983, Israel's relations with the nations of Western Europe continued to improve, to the pre-Lebanon-war level or better. A major event was the visit to Israel by West German chancellor Helmut Kohl, the first such visit by a German chancellor while in office. (Originally scheduled for September 1983, the visit was at that time postponed in the wake of Prime Minister Begin's resignation.) Kohl's six-day visit, which began January 24, included a ceremony at the Yad Vashem Holocaust Memorial in Jerusalem and meetings with leading Israelis in politics, industry, and higher education. Israel requested Bonn's assistance in offsetting agricultural competition caused by the entry of Spain and Portugal into the European Economic Community (EEC). However, the key issue in the talks was a mooted West German arms sale to Saudi Arabia, a move which Israel strenuously opposed, as much on moral as on practical grounds. As Prime Minister Shamir told a West German paper: "We don't want Jewish blood to be spilled again by German arms." Shamir told Kohl that implementation of the arms sale would have serious repercussions for the "special relationship" between Germany and Israel. For his part, the German chancellor said at a press conference at the conclusion of his visit that, while he was well aware of Germany's "historic responsibility" vis-à-vis the Jewish people, the final decision on the arms sale would be made in Bonn, "based on our conviction and our responsibility."

Other important European visitors to Israel in 1984 included the president of the European Parliament, Pieter Dankert, from the Netherlands, who, in an address to the Knesset in February, termed Israeli settlement policy in the West Bank "counter-productive to an overall peaceful solution in the region"; France's minister for research and industry, Laurent Fabius, whose March visit produced a decision to create a joint Franco-Israeli body for coordination of industrial research; the political director of the Greek Foreign Ministry, in a rare visit (mid-April) by a ranking Greek official, who indicated his country's readiness to improve relations in various fields, if not yet to exchange ambassadors; French foreign minister Claude Cheysson, who was in Israel for a lightning 24-hour stay on July 11–12, within the framework of a Middle East junket by President Mitterrand, and reported to Shamir and Peres on the French president's talks in Egypt and Jordan; British foreign secretary Sir Geoffrey Howe in an intensive 24-hour visit at the end of October, during which he obtained, according to a British official, "a better understanding of Israel's preoccupation with its security needs"; and a year-end four-day visit by Italian defense minister Giovanni Spadolini for discussions of Italy's role in UNI-FIL and Italian-Israeli cooperation in combating terrorism. Earlier in December, Prime Minister Peres had announced that he was postponing a scheduled January

1985 visit to Rome because of a meeting between Italian premier Benito Craxi and PLO chief Yasir Arafat.

The major visit to Europe by an Israeli was that paid by Prime Minister Peres to France (December 5–8), the first such visit since David Ben-Gurion was received by Charles de Gaulle over two decades earlier. Peres told a press conference in the French capital that the "extraordinary reception" he had been accorded by the president and the government "was a manifestation of profound friendship." Among the practical matters discussed were French help in negotiating an Israeli withdrawal from Lebanon and the possible acquisition by Israel of French-built nuclear power stations. Peres said France had pledged not to supply Arab states with nuclear plants possessing military potential (as France had done in supplying Iraq with the reactor destroyed by Israel in 1981).

Earlier in the year, Prime Minister and Foreign Minister Shamir visited Brussels and The Hague (in February), his chief purpose being to alert officials of the EEC to Israel's deep concern about the possible ramifications of Spain and Portugal's entry into the Common Market. Industry and Trade Minister Gideon Patt told Israel Radio that the EEC, recognizing the country's economic problems, had agreed to allow Israel to continue customs levies on imported European products until 1989, instead of the originally scheduled 1987.

Defense Minister Moshe Arens met with his British counterpart, Michael Heseltine, in London, on June 4, reportedly proposing joint arms development projects in which Israel would provide the technology and Britain the financing.

That a new atmosphere prevailed in Israeli-European relations was perhaps best indicated by the fact that the Foreign Ministry was able to welcome—albeit with reservations—a statement issued by the leaders of the EEC in December regarding the Middle East. The Foreign Ministry reacted positively to the EEC's call for "direct negotiations among the parties themselves—the Arab states, Israel, and the Palestinian people—which must recognize mutually each other's existence and rights." However, the ministry also expressed "regret" at the EEC leaders' assertion that "the PLO must be associated with the peace negotiations."

OTHER FOREIGN RELATIONS

President Herzog, who also paid two state visits to Europe during the year (to Britain and the Netherlands), helped cement Israel's growing formal ties with African nations when he paid a week-long visit to Zaire and Liberia in January. The president told reporters upon his return to Israel that the reception accorded him and Mrs. Herzog was "beyond all our expectations." In February Liberian finance minister Maj. J. Irving Hones visited Israel and concluded agreements on Israeli training of civil pilots and bank officials. In mid-August two Nigerian dignitaries, one a tribal king and the other an emir, were in Israel as the guests of an Israeli businessman. The two, who were the first ranking Nigerians to visit the country since Lagos broke diplomatic relations in 1973 (although economic bonds between the two countries continued uninterrupted), paid courtesy calls on the president and the prime minister. In September and again in December senior officials from Swaziland were in Israel for talks on various aid and cooperation projects.

Israel's ties with South Africa were in the news in 1984. In April the Israeli ambassador to that country, Eliahu Lankin, denied what he termed a "tendentious" and "distorted" report in the London *Sunday Times* on Israeli–South African military cooperation. Specifically, Lankin denied that Israeli personnel were training South African troops and that South Africa was a partner in the Lavi jet-fighter project. In November Israel sought to downplay a visit by South African foreign minister Roelof Botha. Although the visit was termed "not official," Botha was met at the airport by Foreign Minister Shamir, who also acted as his host and held a working session with him at the Foreign Ministry. Botha also met with Defense Minister Rabin; however, virtually all Labor cabinet ministers and MKs boycotted a reception for the South African official at the Knesset.

Relations with Asian countries saw improvement during the year. Talks between Australian foreign minister Bill Hayden and Prime Minister Shamir during the former's five-day visit in January centered on the future of Australia's contingent in the Sinai peacekeeping force. In February Israel was accepted into the Asian region of the International Labor Organization (ILO) by a vote of 32–16 in a secret ballot at the ILO's Geneva headquarters. On May 27 Prime Minister Shamir told the cabinet that Israel and Sri Lanka were resuming diplomatic ties after 14 years, this amid press reports that Sri Lanka was receiving Israeli assistance in counterinsurgency techniques. Prime Minister Peres cabled Israel's condolences to Rajiv Gandhi following his mother's assassination in October, even though Israel and India had no diplomatic relations.

In the East European bloc, ties with Rumania were expanded when Industry and Trade Minister Gideon Patt and Histadrut secretary-general Yeruham Meshel visited Bucharest in February and met with President Ceaucescu. A protocol was signed doubling Israeli-Rumanian annual trade to $90 million, and Meshel said the Histadrut would open an office in the Rumanian capital to help promote commercial ties. There was no breakthrough, however, in Israeli-Soviet relations, severed since 1967. In February, following the assumption of power in the Kremlin by Konstantin Chernenko, Prime Minister Shamir called on the Soviet leader to reexamine his country's policy toward the Middle East and toward Soviet Jewry. (See also "Israel and World Jewry.") In October, acting in his capacity as foreign minister, Shamir met with his Soviet counterpart, Andrei Gromyko, in New York, during the UN General Assembly session. The "serious and businesslike" meeting, as it was termed by an official of Israel's UN mission, which lasted 90 minutes, was the first of its kind in three years. Shamir also met in New York with Polish foreign minister Stefan Olszowski, their discussion reportedly centering on ways to expand economic and cultural ties between the two countries. In another high-level meeting, Israel's ambassador to the United States, Meir Rosenne, met with his Soviet counterpart, Anatoly Dobrynin, at a "neutral" embassy in Washington, though again no diplomatic breakthrough resulted.

Relations with Latin America were expanded during the year, with the Foreign Ministry announcing on September 6 that diplomatic ties were to be established between Israel and Belize. In April El Salvador became the second country (following Costa Rica) to return its embassy to Jerusalem, following its transfer to Tel Aviv in 1981. In December Foreign Minister Shamir visited Panama and Venezuela, but his visit was cut short because of an urgent call to return home in the wake of a coalition crisis. The same fate befell a parliamentary fact-finding mission to Argentina in March. (See also "Israel and World Jewry.")

In June UN secretary-general Javier Pérez de Cuéllar visited Israel as part of a Middle East tour, his talks centering on Lebanon, possible prisoner-of-war exchanges, and the Middle East situation in general. Foreign Ministry director-general David Kimche told the visitor of Israel's "discontent and disillusion" with the United Nations, a feeling that was reinforced during the year when Iran once again led a drive to unseat the Israeli delegation. Prime Minister Peres reciprocated Pérez de Cuéllar's visit by calling on him at UN headquarters in New York during a visit to the United States in October.

Terrorism

The year 1984 saw a sharp rise in Arab terrorism inside Israel, together with increased manifestations of Jewish counterterrorism. A crackdown by the authorities on Jewish vigilantes led to the roundup of several underground groups, including one major organization based in Jewish settlements in the administered territories.

During the year there were 350 attacks by Arabs—an average of 1 a day—in which 5 Jews were killed and 108 wounded.

As in the past, Jerusalem was the scene of some of the worst of the terrorist outrages, including the planting of 15 bombs in various parts of the city, most of which were discovered by passersby before they went off. One major disaster was averted when 12 kilograms of explosives hidden inside a car parked in downtown Jerusalem were neutralized by police bomb-disposal experts on August 15. However, 21 persons were hurt when two of four grenades hidden in a plastic bag exploded in the city's downtown area on February 28; responsibility was claimed by Nayif Hawatmeh's Democratic Front for the Liberation of Palestine. What police termed an attack "of an entirely new nature" occurred on April 2, close to Jerusalem's main downtown intersection, when three gunmen opened fire at passersby on the street. Forty-eight persons were wounded, one of whom later died, in what became a veritable "wild West" shoot-out, as civilians carrying pistols opened fire on the fleeing terrorists. Two of them were captured and one killed. (The Israel Air Force carried out a retaliation strike for the attack later in the week.) On

November 22 the two captured terrorists raised their fists in defiance as they were led off after being sentenced to life imprisonment.

Buses were involved in several terrorist acts during the year. On March 7 three persons were killed and eight wounded when a booby-trapped hand grenade exploded on a bus in Ashdod; responsibility was claimed by the Abu Nidal organization. On September 17 a bus plying the Jerusalem–Kiryat Arba route was fired on near the Dehaishe refugee camp. Five Jewish passengers on the bus were wounded, as were two Arabs traveling in a car behind the bus. On December 19 three persons, including a three-year-old boy, were lightly wounded when a grenade was thrown at a bus adjacent to the wholesale fruit and vegetable market in Tel Aviv; a Gaza teenager employed at the market was arrested in connection with the attack two days later.

However, it was during the 11 hours beginning at 6:20 P.M. on April 12 that the year's most dramatic terrorist attack took place. Four Arabs boarded the No. 300 Tel Aviv–Ashkelon bus at the central bus station in Tel Aviv. As the bus passed the Ashdod junction the suspicious behavior of the four alerted one of the passengers, who told the driver he was feeling ill and wanted to get off. Just after the man left, the four Arabs took command of the bus, brandishing what were apparently homemade bombs and holding a knife to the driver's throat. The hijackers let a second person disembark when she began screaming hysterically. She and the first man hitchhiked to a nearby gas station and called the police. Following a wild chase along the highway, with police and army personnel trying to shoot out the bus's tires, the bus crashed through a barrier, roared through Gaza, and finally came to a halt, its tires blown out, near the town of Deir al-Balah, about 35 kilometers from the Egyptian border.

Although some passengers managed to escape in the confusion, about 25 still remained on board, as security forces surrounded the bus and sealed off the area. When the defense minister and the chief of staff arrived on the scene, the terrorists indicated that they were attached to George Habash's Popular Front for the Liberation of Palestine and demanded the release of 500 security prisoners in exchange for the hostages. Just before dawn, IDF soldiers stormed the bus. One Israeli, a 19-year-old woman soldier, was killed, and seven civilians were wounded, by the soldiers' gunfire. (It was later discovered that the hijackers had no firearms.) The IDF spokesman said that two of the terrorists were killed when the bus was seized by the army, while the other two died shortly afterwards of their wounds, one of them while en route to the hospital.

The incident soon took a new and unexpected turn. The *New York Times* reported that two of the hijackers had actually been led away under their own steam by security forces after the bus was stormed, and that photographs existed to prove it. On April 30 an Israeli tabloid, *Hadashot,* was shut down for three days by the military censor for reporting, in violation of censorship, that the defense minister had set up an internal commission of inquiry to determine how the four terrorists had died. A month later (May 28) the report of the commission of inquiry, headed by Maj. Gen. (Res.) Meir Zorea, was released. In dry, clinically detached language, it concluded that two of the terrorists died when the bus was stormed, "as a result of the attacking force's gunfire," while the two others died of skull fractures caused by blows to their heads by blunt instruments, presumably rifle butts. Since these findings raised "suspicions that some security forces personnel broke the law," a full investigation was to be carried out by the Israel Police and the Military Police in conjunction with the State Attorney's Office. On May 29 *Hadashot* devoted its entire front page to the photograph that had touched off the story, and which it was now allowed to print, though with the faces of the Israeli security personnel involved blacked out, giving rise to new speculation about a cover-up. The entire incident, besides completely overshadowing the original terrorist attack, further undermined the credibility of the IDF Spokesman's Office (already at a low point following the Lebanon war) and raised disturbing questions about the use to which military censorship had been put.

Several brutal killings of individuals that occurred during the year aroused public demand for harsher treatment of apprehended terrorists. On August 10 the body of Moshe Tamam, a 19-year-old soldier, was found in an orchard near Nablus; he had been shot through the chest. Hawatmeh's DFLP claimed responsibility. On October 22 two Hebrew University students were murdered while walking in the woods near the Cremisan Monastery between Jerusalem and Bethlehem. They had been tied to a tree and shot through the head. Arrested within days on suspicion of having killed the two was a 22-year-old resident of the Dehaishe refugee camp just south of Bethlehem. It was unclear whether the alleged murderer had acted on his own or on orders from a terrorist organization.

On December 11 the body of a 20-year-old woman soldier, Hadass Kedmi, was found on Mount Carmel. Hundreds of volunteers had been searching for the young woman, who had been missing since November 29, when she was seen hitchhiking to her home in a Haifa-area kibbutz. The autopsy revealed that she had been repeatedly raped during her captivity before being strangled. As calls for the death penalty for terrorists mounted, the Citizens Rights and Peace Movement submitted a bill in the Knesset which would deprive persons convicted of "murder in the first degree" of all prison privileges. The "first degree" charge would be applicable in cases of kidnap-and-murder and if there was maltreatment of the victim for nationalist, racial, or religious reasons.

A number of Arab terrorists faced court trials during the year. At the beginning of March eight West Bank and Jerusalem Arabs went on trial in Nablus military court, accused of having organized an underground terrorist cell, based on Islamic fundamentalist tenets, in order "to overthrow the Jewish state and establish a Moslem theocracy in its place." They were charged with the fatal stabbing of a yeshivah student, Aharon Gross, in Hebron in July 1983. On May 21 four of the men were sentenced to life imprisonment; the others received jail terms of from 10 to 25 years. (In March the trial also opened, in Jerusalem, of six Jewish settlers accused of torching the Hebron marketplace in retaliation for the murder of Aharon Gross.)

Two Kalkilya residents were sentenced in June to 25- and 15-year prison terms for having attempted twice to plant a bomb in a Kfar Sava schoolyard. In July seven persons received prison terms of 7 to 15 years from a Gaza military court for throwing grenades at Israelis and at local residents earlier in the year. Also in July, a 22-year-old Bedouin from a Judean township was given life imprisonment for the murder, two years earlier, of an Israeli who was shopping in Bethlehem. In the same month the Lod military court handed down a 25-year sentence to each of two men from the Nablus area who planted five bombs in and around Petah Tikva and Kfar Sava in 1982. On September 4 a panel of five judges in a military appeals court commuted to life imprisonment the sentences of two Israeli Arabs who had been sentenced to death the previous December for the murder of an Israeli soldier in 1980. In December five members of yet another Islamic fundamentalist terrorist cell, this time in Gaza, were sentenced to prison terms ranging from 9 to 13 years.

Two foreign nationals operating for Arab terrorist organizations were also convicted and sentenced. A 22-year-old West German man who was recruited by the PLO in Europe received a five-year prison term in February for attempting to set fire to fuel pumps at a Tel Aviv police facility in 1983. In March a French citizen was given a four-year term for gathering information in a PLO plot to blow up Israel's tallest building six years earlier. (The man, whose part in the scheme came to light in PLO documents seized by the IDF in Beirut, was pardoned on December 6 by President Herzog and deported to France on the eve of Prime Minister Peres's visit to that country.)

Acts of terrorism committed by Jews against Arabs revealed the growing boldness of Jewish underground groups. At the same time, vigorous action by police and legal authorities indicated that the government would not tolerate unlawful behavior on the part of any citizen, Arab or Jew.

On March 5 four American nationals said to be followers of Rabbi Meir Kahane's Kach movement were arrested and charged with opening automatic-weapons fire, just hours earlier, on an Arab bus traveling near Ramallah, wounding seven passengers. On November 11 Yehuda Richter, the number-two man on Kahane's Knesset list, was given five years' imprisonment and a three-year suspended sentence for his part in the bus attack, following plea bargaining. Two other members of the squad were earlier sentenced to lighter prison terms. The Kach movement paid the legal expenses of the defendants.

Also on March 5 three persons were arrested in Jerusalem in connection with an abortive attempt in January to blow up the Moslem holy places on the Temple Mount in Jerusalem and with various other attacks on non-Jewish holy sites in the city. Purportedly members of a messianic sect, the three lived in the ruins of the Arab village of Lifta at the western entrance to Jerusalem. There police found an extensive cache of arms and high explosives. The alleged leader of the sect, Shimon Barda, who had avoided arrest in March, was detained by police on June 25.

On April 9 police announced that they had in custody four members of another mystically oriented Jewish terrorist band whose operations, together with those of the Lifta group, evidently accounted between them for all the attacks in 1983 and the beginning of 1984 perpetrated by the "TNT" (Hebrew acronym for "terror against terror") gang. The four, two of whom were brothers and a third their cousin, resided in Jerusalem's Ein Karem quarter. On November 20, following plea bargaining, three of them, including the two brothers, Amram and David Der'i, aged 26 and 23 respectively, were sentenced to six years' imprisonment and a three-year suspended sentence. The series of attacks they carried out, mainly against Moslem and Christian holy sites in Jerusalem, wounded a number of persons and caused property damage.

On October 28 a LAW antitank rocket was fired into an Arab bus near the Old City of Jerusalem, killing one person and wounding ten. The suspected perpetrator, an 18-year-old soldier, was arrested five days after the attack. Found next to the rocket launcher was a note claiming that the attack was in retaliation for the murder a few days earlier of two Hebrew University students at Cremisan.

On January 26 a member of the Elon Moreh settlement was charged in Tel Aviv district court with the murder of an 11-year-old Nablus girl near the end of 1983; a second member of the settlement was charged with being an accomplice after the fact. Before their trial got under way, at the beginning of June, yet a third Elon Moreh member, the settlement's security chief, was sentenced to 3 months' imprisonment and a 33-month suspended sentence for having destroyed evidence relating to the case.

The year's most sensational episode of Jewish terrorism began to unfold on April 27 when police and General Security Service (GSS) personnel arrested a number of Jewish activists, nearly all of them from settlements in the West Bank and Golan Heights, following the discovery that bombs had been placed beneath six Arab-owned buses in the Jerusalem area. Had the devices detonated as planned, hundreds of tourists and passersby, as well as passengers, would probably have been killed. The arrests, which were followed by additional detentions of Jewish settlers, proved to be the culmination of an investigation of suspected Jewish terrorists that had been under way for over two years. While the immediate motive for the plan to blow up the buses was evidently retaliation for the bus hijacking at Ashdod earlier in the month, it soon became apparent that all or some of those detained had been responsible for a number of "vigilante" terrorist acts in the territories. Among these were the 1980 attack that left two leading West Bank mayors crippled and the 1983 operation against the Islamic College in Hebron in which three students were gunned down. Prime Minister Shamir, the official to whom the GSS was responsible and who had given the order for the round-up of suspects, said their arrest had "prevented a catastrophe."

Condemnation was not universal, however. Science and Development Minister Yuval Ne'eman, leader of the far-right Tehiya party, touched off a public furor when he drew a distinction between the different acts allegedly committed by those in detention. The attack on the mayors, he said, had, without killing anyone, brought about the dissolution of the National Guidance Committee, "which was effectively the PLO's official representation in Judea and Samaria and flourished with the encouragement of then-defense minister Ezer Weizman." By contrast, he said, the raid on the Islamic College and the abortive Jerusalem bus attack were "acts of blind terrorism." The Tehiya leader's remarks reflected an emerging debate in the Jewish settlements and among their advocates, particularly within the Gush Emunim ("Bloc of the Faithful") movement, as to the validity, moral and otherwise, of the detainees' acts. One Gush Emunim spokesman who was far from apologetic was Rabbi Moshe Levinger, leader of the Jewish settlement in Hebron, who asserted that responsibility lay with "shortcomings of the government." Levinger himself was soon taken into custody for about ten days for questioning in connection with one or more of the acts attributed to the suspects. His release was followed by the detention of Rabbi Eliezer Waldman, director of the Kiryat Arba yeshivah and the number-four candidate on the Tehiya Knesset list for the July elections. He too was released after several days of questioning.

On May 23 an indictment was handed down in Jerusalem district court against 27 persons on six counts, each relating to one or more of the defendants. The defendants' names were still, at this stage, barred from publication and remained so for over three weeks more, a delay that gave rise to fierce criticism and even a front-page threat by *Ha'aretz* to take the matter to the Supreme Court.

The charge sheet stated that between 1978 and 1981, 11 of the defendants "joined together in a terrorist organization whose aim was to perpetrate violent acts that could cause death or injury." Among those acts were: a conspiracy to blow up the Dome of the Rock on the Temple Mount; an attack on members of the National Guidance Committee in June 1980, as a result of which Nablus mayor Bassam al-Shaka lost both legs and Ramallah mayor Karim Khalaf lost one leg, while a border policeman was blinded in both eyes when one of the charges blew up in his face (the man, a bomb-disposal expert, was bitter when he testified at the end of June, it having emerged that two of the defendants, both army officers, had watched him approach what they knew to be a booby-trapped garage of a West Bank mayor without warning him); the premeditated murder of 3 students and the wounding of 33 more at the Islamic College in Hebron in July 1983, in revenge for the murder of yeshivah student Aharon Gross in Hebron a month before; the booby-trapping of six Arab-owned buses in and around Jerusalem in April 1984 "with the intention of causing the death and injury of passengers on the buses"; and the planting of grenades at two Hebron mosques and a Hebron schoolyard, all of which had gone off, causing injury. If convicted, the defendants faced severe penalties, ranging from a mandatory life sentence for murder, to 20 years for "activity in a terrorist organization" or attempted murder, and 10 years for "illegal possession and bearing of arms."

The prosecution obtained its first conviction even before the trial formally opened when Noam Yinon, 27, from a Golan Heights moshav, pleaded guilty on May 29 to illegal possession of arms, following plea bargaining. The sentence he received, an 18-month prison term and an 18-month suspended sentence, was appealed by both Yinon and the prosecution. A more important guilty plea, again after plea bargaining, was that of Gilad Peli, defendant number 9, who on June 13 admitted to being a member of a terrorist organization and to conspiring to blow up the Dome of the Rock—thereby establishing that such an organization and such a conspiracy had indeed existed. The 30-year-old Peli, also from a Golan Heights moshav, was a graduate of the Mercaz Harav Yeshivah in Jerusalem, Gush Emunim's spiritual center, and the son of one of Yitzhak Shamir's colleagues in the prestate LEHI underground. Peli received a ten-year sentence, which stunned his family and the settlement movement in the territories, and led Gush Emunim to issue a statement (in English) expressing the movement's position vis-à-vis the trial and the Jewish terrorist organization. After condemning the "extraordinary . . . harshness" of the sentence and maintaining that it was "influenced by public opinion created by the media"—as witnessed by the fact that PLO members received "five years or less" for "similar or more severe crimes"—the statement moved to its ideological heart:

> It was not the Jewish people who opened the violent feud that has continued on this land. The Jewish nation in Israel has been subjected to terrorist atrocities since its inception, and reaction to these atrocities, albeit not handled in the correct fashion, was the result of an insufficient and desperate security situation. To equate these individuals with terrorists such as the PLO, who are committed to Israel's destruction, is morally abominable.

Peli later appealed the sentence. On June 14, defendant number 17, Yosef Tzuria, 25, was convicted after plea bargaining of, *inter alia,* complicity in the Temple Mount episode. He was given a three-year prison term with two years suspended, which both he and the prosecution appealed.

When the names and biographies of the other defendants were finally released on June 18, they turned out to include some of the leading figures of the Jewish settlement movement in the territories. Defendant number 1, the alleged leader of the Jewish terrorist organization, was Menachem Livni, 36, secretary of the Association for the Rehabilitation of the Jewish Quarter in Hebron, where he resided. An engineering corps battalion commander in the reserves, Livni was an explosives expert. Yehuda Etzion, 33, defendant number 2, was among the founders of Gush Emunim and of the key settlement of Ofrah, in Samaria, where he made his home. He was a member of the Gush Emunim secretariat and author of a number of its publications. Defendant number 4, Yeshua Ben-Shoshan, 34, a rabbi, was a recipient of the Medal of Valor for heroism in the Yom Kippur War. Also among those in detention were the sons-in-law of Rabbis Moshe Levinger and Eliezer Waldman; a father, his son, and the father's brother; and another pair of brothers.

On June 27 the trial of 20 of the defendants formally opened (three had already been sentenced and two more plea-bargaining cases were pending; the trial of the two army officers had been separated from the rest); all pleaded not guilty. Proceedings were deferred until after the summer recess of the courts (and, coincidentally, until after the Knesset elections), but in the meantime the two other plea-bargainers were sentenced: defendant number 20, Yehuda Cohen, 25, on July 15, to 18 months' imprisonment and two years' suspended sentence (his appeal was rejected by the

Supreme Court in November); and defendant number 16, Avinoam Katrieli, 23, on August 26, to 15 months in prison and 33 months' suspended sentence, which he appealed. A week before the trial resumed, defendant number 22, Moshe Zar, 47, a major land dealer in the West Bank, was released on bail due to ill health. When the trial finally did reopen, on September 16, it began with a "mini-trial" to determine whether statements given to police and GSS investigators by the suspects immediately following their arrests were admissible. The defendants contended that the statements had been extracted illegally, by a combination of trickery and pressure.

Speaking on the occasion of Jerusalem Day (May 30) to a group from the Bnei Akiva religious youth movement, President Chaim Herzog expressed what many—though by no means all—in the country felt about the affair. Actions such as the defendants were charged with, he said, "lower us to the subhuman depths of the terrorist organizations that operate against us." Noting that such crimes violated not only the commandment against murder but also the precepts proscribing "false messianism" and "rebellion against the kingdom," Herzog quoted a leading Gush Emunim rabbi who had expressed concern at the mounting extremism and tendency toward isolationism among certain circles of religious Zionist youth. The president assailed these trends, "especially at a time when the entire nation needs, as we need the air we breathe, a bridge across the yawning divide, mutual understanding, reconciliation, and tolerance."

The Administered Areas

For the Jewish settlement movement in the territories, 1984 was largely a year of marking time. For various reasons—the economic slide, the security problems that were relentlessly dinned into the public's consciousness by the settlers themselves, the uncovering of the Jewish terrorist organization in the territories, and the ramifications of the so-called Karp report (see below), which was made public near the beginning of the year—the momentum of the settlement drive slowed considerably. A poll published in the *Jerusalem Post* in February showed that nearly 18 percent of the public would be willing to cede all of Judea and Samaria (though not East Jerusalem) in return for peace with Jordan, while a further 44 percent said they would give up parts of those areas for peace.

Even the advent of a general election proved unable to generate the kind of momentum that had been witnessed just three years earlier. Although some 10 to 15 settlements were approved in the weeks and days prior to the July 23 vote, and several inaugural ceremonies were actually held for new settlements at various sites, a *Jerusalem Post* editorial of July 18 was probably not far off the mark when it termed "the eleventh-hour settlement drive in the territories" an "electoral fraud." The number of persons involved was "negligible," the paper said, and the settlements "are being rushed into place without any budgets and without any adequate planning for the future." The actuality of the slowdown was starkly confirmed during postelection coalition negotiations when Herut insisted that the new government pledge to establish no fewer than the 28 settlements that had been approved by the outgoing government but that existed only on paper. The fact that the final coalition agreement called for the creation of only "five [or] six" new settlements within a year spoke for itself.

Also finally allowed to speak for itself, as it were, was the text of the Karp report, the broad outlines of which had already been published by the press in 1983 (see AJYB, Vol. 85, 1985, pp. 292–293) and which was officially published in full on February 7. The report, produced by a committee chaired by Deputy Attorney General Yehudit Karp, confirmed the worst suspicions of those who opposed Jewish settlement in the territories and was rejected as "biased and irrelevant" by the settlement movement. Entitled "Investigation of Suspicions Against Israelis in Judea and Samaria—Report of the Inquiry Team," and bearing the date May 25, 1982 (when it had been submitted to the attorney general), the document was essentially an examination of how the Israeli authorities in the territories had dealt with some 70 complaints by Arabs against Jews during the one-year period preceding the report's submission. The committee found that 53 of the cases had been given such protracted treatment that they were effectively closed, 33 of them on the ground of "offender unknown." A random check turned up 15 cases in which "investigation was either poor or substantially flawed."

One of the most shocking cases detailed in the report was the killing of a boy in the village of Bani Na'im, near Kiryat Arba, by an Israeli civilian in March 1982. In this and in two other instances "of unnatural deaths" the committee found that "the appropriate energy and efficiency required in investigations of this kind were not in evidence." In the Bani Na'im affair, Jewish settlers told the police that they would not cooperate in the investigation "unless they received instructions [to do so] from the political echelon."

What emerged from the report was that what some termed "two systems of justice" had developed in the territories under Israeli control since 1967, one for Jews, the other for Arabs. Because Arabs were in many cases loath to complain about harassment of various kinds by Jews, the committee discovered, "a vicious circle" had been created "in which events are not investigated for lack of complaint, while complaints are not lodged because of an absence of proper investigation." One of the main problems in this regard was the poor cooperation between the civil and military police, a state of affairs that was detrimental to the functioning of both bodies. Moreover, the committee found that there was often "external intervention [in investigations] by military government personnel." Singling out behavior of Kiryat Arba and Hebron area settlers, the committee said that their insistence on having investigations carried out exclusively by military-government authorities was "tantamount to civil revolt" and the "calumniation of the civilian echelons of the Israel Police, the State Attorney's Office and the courts of the State of Israel."

When the minister of justice conveyed the report to the Knesset's Constitution, Law, and Justice Committee, nearly two years after its submission to him, he appended to it a "List of Unsolved Attacks Against Jews" in the territories and Israel, from June 1982–December 1983, naming 23 Israeli Jews who had been killed and 227 wounded. This tit-for-tat approach, which would emerge shortly as the underlying rationale for the activities of the Jewish terrorist organization in the territories, was regarded by many as a less-than-adequate response to the Karp committee's call for inculcating the "basic concept of the rule of law in its broadest and most profound sense."

Two days before the report's publication, and with a view to its release, the cabinet, under pressure from the settlers' lobby, issued a new set of guidelines intended to curb Arab violence in the West Bank. More personnel and other resources would be assigned to track down offenders, the cabinet communiqué said, and the prosecution would demand stiffer penalties in military trials of rock-throwers and others. Some four months later, Military Order No. 1108 was issued by the Israeli authorities in Judea-Samaria. Under its provisions, persons throwing "an object, including a rock," at a "moving vehicle" could face a prison term of up to 20 years. Even the throwing of a stone liable to hit passing traffic could carry with it a ten-year term for a convicted offender.

One of the focal points in the settlers' fight against the increasing number of stone-throwing incidents was the Dehaishe refugee camp on the Jerusalem-Hebron road. In the very first week of 1984 Defense Minister Moshe Arens told the Likud Knesset caucus that the IDF would demolish houses situated near highways, in refugee camps—particularly Dehaishe—from which passing Jewish traffic was regularly stoned. Such warnings had little effect, however. Finally, in October, following a rash of stone throwing that was evidently triggered by the announcement of renewed diplomatic relations between Jordan and Egypt, Dehaishe was placed under curfew for three days. A visit to the camp by MK Meir Kahane shortly after the imposition of the curfew led to renewed stone throwing, this time at IDF soldiers who responded by firing in the air. Inside the camp, Kahane uttered the afternoon prayers next to a mosque and told journalists that the purpose of his visit was "to clean away the filth." While the curfew was in progress, the IDF sealed off several paths that had been used as escape routes by stone-throwing youths. About a month later, following the arrest of a Dehaishe man for the murder of two students near Jerusalem, and yet another spate of stone throwing in which three persons were hurt, Rabbi Moshe Levinger, leader of the Jewish settlement in Hebron, began a one-man vigil opposite the camp, with the aim of bringing about its dismantlement. In the final week of the year, hundreds of Gush Emunim members joined Levinger in demanding that the refugee camp be closed.

Educational institutions were another focus of unrest, and three leading West Bank universities were closed down for varying periods during the year. On February 2 the old campus of Bir Zeit University was ordered shut for three months following a demonstration by students in which the Palestinian flag was raised. On July 30 An-Najah National University in Nablus was closed for four months after security forces confiscated a large quantity of "nationalistic and provocative" material from a campus exhibition. At the beginning of November Bethlehem University, which operates under Vatican auspices, was closed down for four days after students engaged in stone throwing. That such punitive actions were for the most part ineffective was demonstrated yet again when Israeli troops opened fire at Bir Zeit students on November 21 and the following day in Ramallah—in each case killing one demonstrator and wounding a total of five—in the wake of unrest generated by the Palestine National Council meeting in Amman. (Jordan Television broadcast the sessions live, virtually emptying the streets in the West Bank and Gaza during the evenings for the entire week of the PNC deliberations, as local residents were glued to their television screens.)

Violence was not limited to refugee camps and college campuses. On January 1 troops shot and killed a Jenin resident who tried to evade an IDF patrol. On January 28 a Border Police patrol opened fire on a crowd in Nablus that was stoning them; a 17-year-old youth was killed. Five persons were wounded in violent clashes with Israeli forces during unrest throughout the West Bank on March 30 and 31, as demonstrations and riots occurred in solidarity with the Land Day rallies held by Israel's Arabs (though the latter were peaceful).

With a Labor party prime minister in power as of mid-September, Palestinians hoped for significant political moves, or at least new attitudes toward the territories. These expectations were fulfilled to a degree during the first three months of the Peres government. Five days after assuming his new post, Defense Minister Yitzhak Rabin told Kiryat Arba settlers who had asked to meet with him following an attack on a Jerusalem–Kiryat Arba bus (see "Terrorism") that he did not favor expulsions of Arabs from the territories. He also rejected a contention by settlers in Hebron that an enhanced Jewish presence there would upgrade security, adding that he was opposed to the entire notion of Jewish settlement in the city. However, Rabin refused to accede to a request by Peace Now to bar Simhat Torah festivities in Hebron, and some 7,000 persons turned out for the celebrations on October 18.

Minister of Police Haim Bar-Lev agreed to grant some of the demands of hunger-striking prisoners at the Jnaid prison facility near Nablus, after visiting there on October 1; in return, the prisoners agreed to end their 12-day strike. Also at the beginning of October, Prime Minister Peres, acting in his temporary capacity as minister of the interior, intervened to prevent the possible closure on security grounds of the Jerusalem-based Palestine Press Service, run by Ramallah journalist Raymonda Tawil. On October 31 Defense Minister Rabin gave expression to the government's policy of "improving the quality of life" in the territories (a long-standing desire of the United States) when he told the Knesset that approval in principle had been given for the establishment of an Arab bank there. However, he stressed, even though local residents would operate the bank, it would be under the close supervision of the Bank of Israel.

The year ended on an optimistic note, in verbal and symbolic terms at least, when Prime Minister Peres visited Bethlehem on Christmas Eve. Peres, the first prime minister of Israel ever to visit the city while in office, was accompanied by Minister of Police Bar-Lev and Jerusalem mayor Teddy Kollek. Exchanging greetings with Bethlehem mayor Elias Freij, he expressed the hope that "mutual respect, coexistence, and understanding will prevail among all of us."

According to official figures—generally considered to be a good deal lower than the reality—some 90,000 persons from the West Bank and the Gaza Strip—37 percent of the entire work force there—were employed in Israel in 1984. About half worked in construction, while the rest worked mainly in low-level service occupations. Some observers applauded the economic opportunities available to Arabs. Others, however, deplored Israel's growing dependence on Arab labor as well as a developing pattern of relationships in which menial tasks were carried out exclusively by Arabs.

Political and Religious Extremism

In 1984 there was perceptible growth in the phenomenon known as "Kahanism" —the anti-Arab activism propounded by American-born Rabbi Meir Kahane— notably after his election to the Knesset in July. His growing appeal was generally attributed to the public's deepening frustration and despair over seemingly insoluble problems: the ongoing economic crisis, Israel's continued rule of 1.3 million Palestinians in the territories, and the Arab-Israeli conflict itself, as brought home most forcefully in recent years by the Lebanon war and an upsurge in Arab terrorism.

Soon after the election, MK Kahane began putting his campaign promises into action. On August 29, accompanied by a few of his followers, he traveled to Israel's largest Arab "village," Umm al-Faham (population 24,000), for the express purpose of urging the inhabitants to emigrate from the country. Alerted to his coming, a crowd of some 5,000 persons, including Knesset members, leading figures on the political left, and other Jewish supporters, awaited Kahane just outside the village. Although police had barred him from entering the village, some 26 persons, among them 13 policemen, were injured when angry village youths began throwing stones, leading the police to use force to disperse the crowd.

Seeking to block Kahane's influence at another level, the Knesset's House Committee authorized the Speaker to strike from the protocol any racist remarks made from the podium, to expel an MK from the chamber for uttering such remarks, and to block private members' bills which were racist in nature. Speaker Shlomo Hillel made use of his new prerogative within ten days: he disqualified a Kahane bill that would have made it mandatory for a Jew serving a prison term for a security offense to be released whenever a non-Jewish security prisoner was freed before serving out his full prison term.

In an effort to help counteract the effects of Kahane's rhetoric on the Arab population, and to demonstrate solidarity with the country's Arab citizens, Prime Minister Peres announced in mid-December a plan to close the development gap between Arab and Jewish locales. Peres told Arab and Druze Labor-party activists that the government would earmark IS 1 billion for Arab local councils and that in future local funding for Arabs and Jews would be equal. He also promised that all Arab villages in the country would be hooked up to the electricity grid and would have their internal roads paved.

At about the same time, Attorney General Yitzhak Zamir joined the battle against extremism in an article in the *Jerusalem Post* (based on remarks he had made to the Knesset's House Committee) entitled "The Danger of Kahanism." Pulling no punches, Zamir called Kahanism "a shameful, loathsome, and dangerous phenomenon" that "contravenes international law," distorts Judaism, "is in conflict with the Zionist idea," undermines the foundations of the Knesset and of Israeli democracy, and "lacks any human feeling." In the attorney general's view, because Kahanism posed "a clear and present danger to Israel's social order . . . we must uncompromisingly join battle" against it. To that end, Zamir said, the Justice Ministry was preparing two amendments to existing law in order to help in "an effective battle against racism."

On December 18 the House Committee voted to recommend to the Knesset plenum that Kahane's freedom of movement, as granted under his parliamentary immunity, be restricted. Voting in favor were the representatives of Labor, Mapam, Shinui, the CRPM, and the Communists; against were the Likud, Tehiya, and the NRP. On December 25 the Knesset, by a vote of 58–36 in a secret ballot, effectively rendered Kahane an ordinary citizen in terms of his ability to ignore police restrictions and to engage in racist agitation. The new policy was put into practice the very next day, when police barred Kahane and some of his yellow-shirted supporters from entering the village of Taibeh, where they planned to protest Arab-Jewish intermarriage. Despite this apparent defeat for Kahane, widespread media coverage of the incident, both local and international, gave Kahane the attention he sought. It was becoming increasingly evident that attempts to write off Kahane as a fringe figure were unduly optimistic. The growing sense in the country that "Kahane is only saying out loud what most people think" appeared to pose, as the attorney general believed, an urgent threat to the delicate fabric of Israeli society.

Another major social problem in the country—the intensifying schism between Orthodox Jews and the nonobservant—exploded into an open conflict in Petah Tikvah. In February, following the Petah Tikvah municipal council's vote to permit places of entertainment and restaurants to open on the Sabbath and holidays, a local movie theater began showing films on Friday night. Week after week thereafter, hundreds of Orthodox men gathered outside the theater on Friday evening to protest the film showings and to try and prevent moviegoers from entering. On Friday evening, March 9, scores of religious demonstrators stormed a packed café, smashing furniture, breaking windows, and dumping food and coffee on clients. The following morning, as hundreds of demonstrators tried to disrupt a panel discussion at the town hall, Petah Tikvah's chief rabbi was arrested on suspicion of having led the Friday-night rampage. He was released that evening after questioning, and no charges were filed against him. On Friday, June 22, in one of the year's largest Orthodox demonstrations, some 15,000 men held a prayer rally outside the city's main synagogue to protest a rock concert scheduled for that evening in the movie theater. Not only were their attempts to prevent the audience from entering the theater foiled by police and Border Police troops, but the music, amplified by 12 big speakers, was clearly audible outside. In the meantime, the Petah Tikvah municipality petitioned the High Court of Justice to order the minister of the interior to show cause why he should not approve the municipal bylaw responsible for the uproar, which he had thus far refrained from doing for over half a year.

Orthodox extremism was manifested in March when the body of a woman who had been identified as not Jewish by certain Orthodox circles was removed from her grave in a Jewish cemetery in Rishon LeZion and crudely reburied in an Arab cemetery in Ramleh. (The woman had been interned in a concentration camp during World War II, where she met her husband, and had lived as a Jew since settling in the country after the war.) The body was subsequently reinterred in the original grave by order of the High Court of Justice. In November two Orthodox men, both employees of the Rishon LeZion burial society, were sentenced to three-month prison terms, plus a three-month suspended sentence, for having done the deed. The sentence, whose leniency touched off rejoicing among Orthodox spectators in the court, was handed down by a majority opinion of the magistrate's court. The court's president had actually urged a much stiffer penalty as a deterrent, the maximum possible sentence for the offense being 13 years.

That religious intolerance was not aimed exclusively at the nonreligious was demonstrated on the first Sabbath in June, when Orthodox MK Rabbi Menachem Porush was severely beaten in the synagogue of a Jerusalem hotel of which he was the owner. According to witnesses, several dozen Orthodox men, who were said to be from a rival Hasidic group, burst into the synagogue, attacked Porush, and vandalized the synagogue itself. The Agudat Israel MK, however, refused to file a complaint or to press charges, with the result that no investigation was undertaken and no one was charged.

An incident occurred in September that outraged members of Masorti (Conservative) and Reform congregations in Jerusalem, many of them recent immigrants from North America. A pamphlet circulated in the neighborhood where the Masorti movement had its center declared non-Orthodox forms of Judaism an "alien growth" and urged Jews not to attend the forthcoming high holy day services in Conservative or Reform synagogues. The pamphlet, which had been authorized by the chief rabbis of Israel and Jerusalem, also infuriated Jerusalem mayor Teddy Kollek, who assailed Jerusalem's Ashkenazi chief rabbi at a meeting between the two, accusing him of fostering intolerance and extremism. In the meantime, the country's first autonomous non-Orthodox rabbinical seminary opened in Jerusalem under the auspices of the Masorti movement.

Israel and World Jewry

In March a week of "national identification" with Soviet Jewry was proclaimed. Prime Minister Shamir issued a statement demanding that the Soviet leadership "stop the anti-Semitic war against the Jewish people" and allow Jewish emigration.

In August the prime minister called on the international community to help secure the release of prisoner of Zion Yosif Begun from his Soviet prison, noting that his health had deteriorated badly. In September Jewish Agency chairman Arye Dulzin, returning to Israel from attending a session in London of the presidium of the World Conference on Soviet Jewry, said that Israel and world Jewry as a whole must step up their activity on behalf of Russia's Jewish community. Many Soviet Jews, he said, had the feeling that their fellow Jews in Israel and elsewhere had forgotten them. In what had become almost an annual ritual, Immigrant Absorption Minister Ya'akov Tzur replied in the Knesset on October 24 to four motions for the agenda regarding the plight of Soviet Jewry. Tzur branded as "shameful" the apathetic attitude of Israeli society to the fate of Soviet Jewry. On November 11 the subject finally received the attention that many thought was long overdue when the cabinet, for the first time in years, held a discussion on the situation of Soviet Jewry. In its resolution the cabinet called on Moscow to cease its harassment and detention of *aliyah* activists, to permit them to teach Hebrew, and to allow all who wished to leave the country to do so. A highlight of the year's activities on behalf of Soviet Jewry was a Russian Jewry Solidarity Week held throughout the country in December, to coincide with Hanukkah. (Despite these efforts, the situation remained gloomy, as fewer than a thousand Jews were allowed to emigrate from the Soviet Union in 1984, and of these only 390 chose to settle in Israel.)

In February a Jewish Agency spokesman, responding to allegations by two anthropologists that the growing numbers of Ethiopian immigrants in the country were being pressured into artifical integration into Israeli society, said that immigration authorities had "developed a project especially geared to the Ethiopians," and that the agency was "consciously avoiding" the mistakes that had been made in the 1950s in the absorption of immigrants from Islamic lands. Later in the month, Education Minister Zevulun Hammer pledged greater cultural and educational help to offset the culture shock the Ethiopians faced in Israel. Nevertheless, a potentially serious situation began to emerge when the Chief Rabbinate ruled that all Ethiopians would have to undergo ritual immersion in order to dispel doubts about their Jewishness. Calling the ruling "humiliating," leaders of the Ethiopian community expressed shock that their Jewishness should be called into question, after they had experienced 2,000 years of exilic suffering.

In June about a thousand Ethiopian immigrants staged a demonstration outside a meeting of the Zionist General Council in Jerusalem to protest what they said was the Israeli government's failure to spur immigration from their native land. Like their Soviet Jewish counterparts in the country, they insisted that greater publicity would only benefit their cause. In mid-August the Israel Association of Ethiopian Jews organized a prayer-and-fast day for their brethren in Ethiopia who, they said, were suffering from disease and persecution. However, a statement issued in November by the Israeli embassy in London seemed to hold out little hope for improvement in the situation. According to the embassy release, "Ethiopians, including Jews of that country, are not free to leave." Noting that "thousands of Jews from Ethiopia" had nevertheless, "after much hardship," managed to reach Israel in recent years, the statement went on to express the hope that the Ethiopian regime would allow all Jews there to leave. Israel itself, the statement said, was "urgently and solemnly committed" to helping the Jews of Ethiopia find a haven in the Jewish state.

The fate of several other Jewish communities was also of concern during the year. In January the cabinet expressed "shock and outrage" at the "brutal murder" of a pregnant Jewish woman and her two children in Aleppo, Syria. The cabinet urged "enlightened opinion" everywhere to exert pressure on Damascus to alleviate the plight of Syria's 4,500 Jews and to allow those who wished to leave to do so.

Speaking in the Knesset in March, Prime Minister Shamir, in reply to a parliamentary question, said that the government believed it had a duty to intervene on behalf of Argentinian Jews who had disappeared or been tortured in recent years. He said there was "no doubt that they were made to suffer more because of their Jewishness," even if they had not necessarily been detained solely because they were Jewish. A three-member Knesset delegation visited Argentina to look into the fate of the missing Jews, but was forced to return home before completing its mission in order to take part in the Knesset vote on early elections on March 22. MK Uzi Baram (Alignment-Labor) termed the recall a "disgrace," adding that the hasty departure of the three MKs had dumbfounded their hosts.

In April the Knesset Immigration and Absorption Committee was told that the remaining thousand Jews in Yemen were being harassed, and that information was hard to come by because mail contacts between the Jews in Yemen and their Israeli relatives had been broken off.

Several leading Diaspora organizations held conferences in Israel in 1984. In January about 200 Jewish activists from North America, Latin America, and elsewhere took part in an international Israel Bonds leadership conference. Conspicuously, their itinerary did not include a visit to the site of the projected Mediterranean–Dead Sea canal for which the Bonds campaign had already raised about $100 million in "seed money," but whose future in post-Begin Israel was far from certain. The Conference of Presidents of Major American Jewish Organizations met in Israel for only the second time in its 29-year history and for the first time in a decade. During the February visit, participants were briefed by senior Israeli officials on the regional situation and sat in on a meeting of the Knesset's Defense and Foreign Affairs Committee.

Speaking to the World Leadership Conference for Jewish Education, held in Jerusalem in June, Prime Minister Shamir put his finger on a major dilemma facing contemporary Jewry when he spoke of the "strange paradox" that even though Jewish existence was physically "more secure than at any other time within living memory," the Jewish nation's "spiritual quality" was "in jeopardy and declining at an alarming rate." Shamir called on Diaspora educators to combat assimilation by emphasizing Israel's centrality in Jewish life and by fostering the study of Hebrew.

In October the board of governors of the European Council of Jewish Communities assembled in Israel, also for the first time in ten years. At the conclusion of their meeting they signed a pact with the mayors of 30 development towns in Israel to establish ties through Jewish educational and student exchanges.

At the end of October Prime Minister Peres convened a conference in Jerusalem of Israel Bond organization workers and other community and fund-raising leaders from abroad. On November 1 the 40 participants signed what was termed "a dramatic agreement to jointly mobilize the human and financial resources of the Jewish world, in support of Israel's economic growth." To that end, the declaration said, "world Jewish leadership will meet at once" to determine how best to proceed, the prime minister would "at the earliest possible date" convene a meeting of Diaspora leaders in Israel, and a "task force will be established, to plan and implement programs aimed at business development."

Other Domestic Matters

Israel's population at the end of 1984 stood at approximately 4,235,000, of whom 3,500,000 (about 83 percent) were Jews. As in 1983, the Jewish population grew by 1.9 percent and the non-Jewish population by 2.8 percent. Data gleaned from the mid-1983 general population census showed that the declared policy of population dispersal remained no more than a declaration, since 90 percent of the country's inhabitants were urban dwellers, 25 percent of them residing in the three largest cities—Jerusalem, Tel Aviv, and Haifa. In October the Central Bureau of Statistics, basing itself on the census, reported that Jews were now a minority in Galilee, this situation the result of a higher non-Jewish birthrate combined with persistent Jewish migration away from the area.

At the end of May a crowd estimated at nearly half a million jammed Tel Aviv's Hayarkon Park for the annual Philharmonic-in-the-Park concert. The Spanish soprano Montserrat Caballé appeared with the Israel Philharmonic Orchestra under the baton of maestro Zubin Mehta. Yet it was Jerusalem that provided the highlight of the cultural year when it hosted the Israel Festival during the month of June; at the same time the local Cinematheque presented an international film festival, and art lovers enjoyed a citywide exhibition entitled "80 Years of Sculpture in Israel." The festival itself was pronounced a major success, with most events sold out and 20 extra performances added to meet the demand.

In September an Israeli film dealing with Arab-Jewish relations, *Beyond the Walls,* was awarded the International Film Critics' Prize at the Venice Film Festival. Subtitled in Arabic (along with English) for local showing, the film was seen by thousands of Arabs from Israel and the territories during its highly successful Israeli run.

Personalia

On April 18 Judges Eliezer Goldberg and Avraham Halima were installed as Supreme Court justices. Israel Kessar, 53, was elected new Histadrut (General

Federation of Labor) secretary-general on May 15, replacing Yeruham Meshel, who retired after a decade at the head of the labor federation. On September 16 the cabinet approved the appointment of Binyamin Netanyahu as Israel's ambassador to the United Nations.

Personalities who died during the year included Rabbi Yisrael Abuhatzeira, spiritual head of North African Jewry, on January 8, aged 94; Paul Ben-Haim, celebrated composer, on January 14, aged 86; *Schwester* Selma Mayer, after a lifetime of service and devotion at Jerusalem's Shaare Zedek Hospital, on February 5, two days after celebrating her 100th birthday; David Hacohen, a founder and longtime leader of Israel's labor movement, on February 19, aged 85; Ya'acov Levinson, banker and financier, who propelled Bank Hapoalim to international standing, a suicide, on February 23, aged 52; Recha Freier, founder of Youth Aliyah, on April 2, aged 92; Ze'ev Sharef, a former cabinet minister and Israel's first cabinet secretary, on April 18, aged 78; Marcel Janco, a founder of the Dada art movement, on April 21, aged 89; Zelda Schneerson Mishkowsky, a noted Hebrew poet who signed her work with her first name only, on April 29, aged 72; Miriam Yalan-Stekelis, Israel Prize laureate for children's literature, on May 9, aged 83; Alfred Witkon, former Supreme Court justice and noted legal scholar, on May 20, aged 74; Yigael Yadin, eminent archaeologist, Israel's second chief of staff (1949–1952) and former deputy prime minister (1977–1981), on June 28, aged 67; Moshe Pinhas Feldenkrais, physical education pioneer, on July 1, aged 80; Avraham Even-Shoshan, lexicographer, who compiled the authoritative contemporary dictionary of the Hebrew language, on August 8, aged 78; Amir Gilboa, distinguished Hebrew poet and Israel Prize laureate, on September 2, aged 70; Daniel Recanati, longtime chairman and managing director of Israel Discount Bank, on September 9, aged 63; Pinhas Ben-Matzliah Halevi, high priest of the Samaritan community, on October 20, aged 86; and Baharan Baruch, known as Uri Ben-Baruch, spiritual leader of the Ethiopian immigrant community in Israel, on December 22, aged 84.

RALPH MANDEL

World Jewish Population, 1984

Updated Estimates

THIS ARTICLE PRESENTS updates, as of 1984, of the Jewish population estimates for 1982 which were first published in the 1984 AJYB and reprinted in a condensed version in the 1985 AJYB. The estimates reflect some of the results of a prolonged and ongoing effort to study scientifically the demography of contemporary world Jewry.[1] Data collection and comparative research have benefited from the collaboration of scholars and institutions in many countries, including replies to direct inquiries regarding current estimates. Also, population censuses taken around 1980 have yielded useful information on the Jews of some countries. It should be emphasized, however, that the elaboration of a worldwide set of estimates for the Jewish populations of the various countries is beset with difficulties and uncertainties. The reader has been given some information on the quality of the estimate for each country by an accuracy rating, using a simple scale explained below.

About 95 percent of world Jewry is concentrated in nine countries, with approximately 100,000 or more Jews each. The aggregate of these nine major Jewish population centers virtually determines the assessment of the size of total world Jewry. The figures for 1982 have been updated to 1984 in accordance with the intervening changes—natural (i.e., births and deaths), affiliative, and migratory. In addition, some corrections have been introduced in the light of newly accrued information from recent population censuses and Jewish surveys. Analogous corrections have also been applied retrospectively to the 1982 figures, which appear below in revised summary (see Table 1), so as to allow for comparison with the 1984 estimates.

Jewish Population Trends[2]

Diaspora Jews are highly dispersed. In most countries their number is now rather small and they constitute no more than a minute fraction of the entire population.

---

[1]Many of these activities have been carrried out by, or in coordination with, the Division of Jewish Demography and Statistics at the Institute of Contemporary Jewry, the Hebrew University of Jerusalem.

[2]A fuller discussion of the subject can be found in U.O. Schmelz, "Jewish Survival: The Demographic Factors," AJYB, Vol. 81, 1981, pp. 61–117.

Consequently, though Jews tend to cluster in large cities, they are greatly exposed to assimilation. While the assimilatory process leads to demographic losses for the Jewish population, there may also be gains through affiliation of persons who were born as non-Jews. It is the net balance of the affiliative changes that matters demographically; in the longer run, the cohesion of a Diaspora population may be affected as well.

The Jews in most countries of the Diaspora are demographically characterized by very low fertility, considerable out-marriage (which may involve losses of children to the Jewish population),[3] some other net assimilatory losses, and great aging. Since an increased proportion of elderly in the population usually implies not only many deceased but also a reduced proportion of persons of reproductive age—and therefore relatively fewer births—the aging factor has the effect of reducing the birthrate and raising the death rate. There are differences in the levels of these demographic factors among the Jews in various regions and countries of the world. In all the major Diaspora populations the joint balance of the natural and affiliative changes is now close to nil or outrightly negative, with the Jewish deceased frequently outnumbering newborn Jews. These negative tendencies have been taken into account in updating the estimates of Jews in many countries.

With regard to the balance of external migrations, there is no regularity among the various Diaspora populations or even in the same population over time. Where the migratory balance is positive—e.g., in North America—it counteracts or even outweighs any numerically negative influence of internal demographic developments. Where the migratory balance is negative, it may cause, or aggravate, the decrease of a Jewish population. In 1983–1984, the overall volume of international migrations of Jews was rather restricted, primarily because of the virtual cessation of Jewish emigration from the Soviet Union.

In contrast, Jews in Israel incur virtually no out-marriages and direct assimilatory losses. Moreover, they have so far had a positive migration balance almost continually. They have a younger age structure than Diaspora Jews and the general population of the developed countries and exhibit a fairly high level of fertility. The previously substantial fertility differentials between Jews in-gathered in Israel from Asia-Africa and Europe-America are no longer in evidence. Remarkably, European Jews in Israel have not participated in the drastic fertility decline that has characterized the developed nations and Diaspora Jews during the last few decades, but have actually raised their fertility. In recent years, both major origin groups among Israel's Jews have displayed a fertility level surpassing not only the vast majority of Diaspora Jewry but also the general populations in the developed countries.

In the overall demographic balance of world Jewry, the natural increase of Israel has, until recently, made up for losses in the Diaspora. But such compensation will not be possible for much longer. As a consequence of the intensifying demographic

---

[3]If less than half of the children of the out-married are themselves Jews.

deficit in the Diaspora, a trend for some reduction in the total number of the world's Jews may soon be setting in.[4]

Difficulties in Estimating Jewish Population Size in the Diaspora[5]

Some of the difficulties involved in estimating the size of Jewish Diaspora populations are common to all aspects of the study of Diaspora demography. They are mainly due to the great geographical scattering of Jews (a factor that makes multiple data collection mandatory but also hinders its feasibility); their unusually strong demographic dynamics in many respects—migrations, social mobility, family formation patterns (including out-marriage), etc.; and to lacunae of available demographic information, which is deficient in both quantity and quality.

More specific difficulties in estimating the up-to-date size of Jewish populations are due to conceptual and measurement problems.

When mixed couples and households are not infrequent, it is necessary to distinguish between the "actually Jewish population" and the "enlarged Jewish population." The latter comprises also the non-Jewish household members (spouses, children, etc.) of the Jews. However socially significant the non-Jewish household members (and more distant non-Jewish relatives) of the Jews may be, they should not be included in a count of Jews. The paradoxical situation that exists is that growth of an enlarged Jewish population may be associated with contraction of the respective actually Jewish population.

Another vexing problem is affiliative changes among Jews. Under present conditions, there are Jews who have not formally embraced another religion, yet are either very estranged ("marginal") or have even become resolutely alienated from Judaism and the Jewish community and, if questioned, disclaim being Jews any longer. When a census or survey is taken which inquires into religion or ethnicity, these individuals have an opportunity to define their current status subjectively.[6] In general, the practice of self-determination is followed in all relevant censuses and surveys. This applies to marginal individuals, converts to Judaism (although some of the conversions may be contested between the various ideological trends—Orthodox, Conservative, and Reform), and to all other persons who claim to be Jews. In estimating the size of a Jewish population, it is usual to include, in principle, all marginal individuals who have not ceased to be Jews.[7]

Not a few Jews (like other persons) have some residential status in more than one country.[8] This may be due to business requirements, professional assignments in

---

[4]*Aliyah* and *yeridah*—immigration to, and emigration from, Israel—obviously constitute only internal transfers within the global Jewish framework.

[5]Reliable figures are currently forthcoming for the Jews of Israel from official statistics.

[6]Misreporting of Jews in official censuses is a different issue; see below.

[7]Even persons who disclaim being Jews at some stage of life may change their minds later.

[8]The problem is even more acute with regard to residential status in more than one locality of the same country, but this does not affect the population estimates for entire countries.

foreign countries, climatic differences between countries, migrants staying temporarily in prolonged transit, etc. The danger of double-counting or omissions is inherent in such situations. As far as possible we have tried to account for such persons only once, giving precedence to the usual country of residence.

Figures on Jews from population censuses are unavailable for most Diaspora communities. Even where census statistics on Jews are forthcoming, they are usually scant, because the Jews are a small minority. There have been instances where detailed tabulations on Jews have been undertaken, through Jewish initiative, from official census material; examples are Canada, South Africa, and Argentina. In some countries serious problems exist, or are feared to exist, in the reporting of Jews as such: individuals may prefer not to describe themselves as Jews, or non-Jews may be erroneously included as Jews (as has happened in Latin American countries). These problems require statistical evaluation whose feasibility and conclusiveness depend on the relevant information available.

Surveys are the only way of obtaining comprehensive information on Jewish populations in the absence of official censuses. Jewish-sponsored surveys have the additional advantage of being able to inquire into matters of specifically Jewish interest, e.g., Jewish education, observances, and attitudes. However, since they address themselves to a small and scattered minority with identification problems, they are not easy to conduct competently and may encounter difficulties with regard to both coverage and response, especially with regard to marginal Jews. Again, these aspects require evaluation. Countrywide surveys have been undertaken in the United States, South Africa, France, Italy, Netherlands, etc. Local surveys have been carried out in many U.S. cities, in the United Kingdom, Latin America, Australia, etc. However, these local initiatives have so far been uncoordinated with regard to content and method.

Many estimates of Jewish populations for which no solid data from censuses or surveys exist are regrettably of unspecified or dubious source and methodology.

Besides the conceptual and measurement difficulties affecting the figures for a Jewish population at any base date, similar problems recur with regard to the updating information which should account for all the various types of changes in the time elapsed since that base date. For natural and affiliative changes, age-sex-specific models can be of use; these may be applied after studying the evolution of the respective or similar Jewish populations. With regard to the migratory balance in any updating interval, concrete information must be gathered, because of the above-mentioned irregularity, over time, in the intensity of many migratory streams.

Presentation of Data

The detailed estimates of Jewish population distribution in each continent (Tables 2–6 below) refer to residents in countries with at least 100 Jews. A residual estimate of "other" Jews living in smaller communities, or staying temporarily in transit accommodations, supplements some of the continental totals. For each of the reported countries, the four columns in the table provide the United Nations estimate of mid-year 1983 total population,[9] the estimated end-1984 Jewish population, the proportion of Jews per 1,000 total population, and a rating of the accuracy of the Jewish population estimates.

There is wide variation in the quality of the Jewish population estimates for different countries. For many Diaspora countries it would be best to indicate a range (minimum-maximum) rather than a definite figure for the number of Jews. It would be confusing, however, for the reader to be confronted with a long list of ranges; this would also complicate the regional and world totals. Yet, the figures actually indicated for most of the Diaspora countries should be understood as being the central value of the plausible range. The relative magnitude of this range varies inversely with the accuracy of the estimate.

The three main elements which affect the accuracy of each estimate are the nature of the base data, the recency of the base data, and the method of updating. A simple code, combining these elements, is used to provide a general evaluation of the reliability of the Jewish population figures reported in the detailed tables below. The code indicates different quality levels of the reported estimates: (A) base figure derived from countrywide census or relatively reliable Jewish population survey; updated on the basis of full or partial information on Jewish population movements in the intervening period; (B) base figure derived from less accurate but recent countrywide Jewish population investigation; partial information on population movements in the intervening period; (C) base figure derived from less recent sources, and/or unsatisfactory or partial coverage of Jewish population in country; updating according to demographic information illustrative of regional demographic trends; and (D) base figure essentially conjectural; no reliable updating procedure. In categories (A), (B), and (C), the years in which the base figures or important partial updates were obtained are also stated.

For countries whose Jewish population estimate of 1984 was not only updated but also revised in the light of improved information, the sign "X" is appended to the accuracy rating.

Distribution of World Jewish Population by Major Regions

Table 1 gives an overall picture for 1984 as compared to 1982. For 1982, the originally published estimates are presented along with somewhat revised figures that take into account, retrospectively, the corrections made in 1984 in certain country estimates, in the light of improved information. These corrections resulted in a net reduction of world Jewry's estimated size by 44,700 or 0.3 percent, mainly due to Israel and Great Britain (explanations for these two countries are given below).

---

[9]These were the latest official estimates available at the time of writing. See United Nations, Department of International Economic and Social Affairs, Statistical Office, *Population and Vital Statistics Report; Data Available as of January 1, 1985.* Statistical Papers, Series A, Vol. 37, No. 1, New York, 1985.

TABLE 1.   ESTIMATED JEWISH POPULATION, BY CONTINENTS AND MAJOR GEO-
GRAPHICAL REGIONS, 1982 AND 1984

Region	1982 Original	1982 Revised Abs. Nos.	1982 Revised Percent	1984 Abs. Nos.	1984 Percent	% Change 1982–1984
Diaspora	9,614,300	9,594,300	74.1	9,491,600	73.2	− 1.1
Israel	3,374,300	3,349,600	25.9	3,471,700	26.8	+ 3.6
World	12,988,600	12,943,900	100.0	12,963,300	100.0	+ 0.2
America, Total	6,477,700	6,477,600	50.1	6,469,000	49.9	− 1.3
North[a]	6,013,000	6,015,000	46.5	6,015,000	46.4	—
Central	46,800	46,800	0.4	47,300	0.4	+ 1.1
South	417,900	415,800	3.2	406,700	3.1	− 2.2
Europe, Total	2,842,700	2,825,100	21.8	2,758,600	21.3	− 2.6
West	1,070,900	1,053,300	8.1	1,048,900	8.1	− 1.0
East & Balkans[b]	1,771,800	1,771,800	13.7	1,709,700	13.2	− 3.5
Asia, Total	3,417,200	3,392,500	26.2	3,509,300	27.1	+ 3.4
Israel	3,374,300	3,349,600	25.9	3,471,700	26.8	+ 3.6
Rest[b]	42,900	42,900	0.3	37,600	0.3	−12.4
Africa, Total	172,000	169,700	1.3	147,400	1.1	−13.3
North	21,250	19,950	0.2	16,700	0.1	−17.5
South	120,250	119,250	0.9	119,100	0.9	− 0.1
Rest[c]	30,500	30,500	0.2	11,600	0.1	−62.0
Oceania	79,000	79,000	0.6	79,000	0.6	—

[a]U.S.A. and Canada.
[b]The Asian territories of USSR and Turkey are included in "East Europe and Balkans."
[c]Including Ethiopia.

The size of world Jewry is assessed at slightly below 13 million. According to the revised figures, the estimated growth between 1982 and 1984 was negligible—about one-tenth of a percent annually. Despite all the imperfections in the estimates, it is clear that world Jewry is in the state of "zero population growth," with the natural increase in Israel compensating for the demographic losses in the Diaspora.

While the number of Jews in Israel rose from a revised figure of 3,349,600 in 1982 to 3,471,700 at the end of 1984, Diaspora Jewry declined from 9,594,300 (according to the revised figures) to approximately 9,491,600. By the end of 1984, Israel's Jews constituted nearly 27 percent of total world Jewry.

About half of the world's Jews reside in the Americas, with 46 percent in North America. Twenty-seven percent live in Asia (excluding the Asian territories of the USSR and Turkey), nearly all of them in Israel. Europe (including the Asian territories of the USSR and Turkey) accounts for 21 percent of the total. The proportions of the world's Jews who live in Africa and Oceania are very small.

Among the major geographical regions listed in Table 1, Israel—and, in consequence, total Asia—increased by more than 3 percent in the two-year span 1982–1984. The total number of Jews estimated for North America, South Africa, and Oceania virtually did not change. With the probable exception of Central America, all the other regions sustained decreases in Jewish population size.

Individual Countries

THE AMERICAS

In 1984 the total number of Jews in the American continents was somewhat less than six and a half million. The overwhelming majority (about 93 percent) reside in the United States and Canada, less than 1 percent live in Central America (including Mexico), and about 6 percent live in South America, where Argentina and Brazil have the largest Jewish communities (see Table 2).

The Jewish population in the United States is estimated to have increased from 5,690,000 in 1980 to 5,705,000 in 1982, as a consequence of immigration. Several local surveys taken in recent years provide evidence of very low "effectively Jewish" birthrates and of increasing aging among the Jewish population. Thus, it is possible that the influence of internal evolution on the size of U.S. Jewry may be negative, though there is no consensus with regard to this assessment. Any negative internal balance in U.S. Jewry was more than offset for several years by an undoubtedly positive balance of external migrations. This latter has been greatly reduced, however, by the virtual cessation of Soviet Jewish immigration. Pending further research, we have repeated for 1984 the figure of 5,705,000 already reported for 1982.[10] This figure does not include non-Jewish members of Jewish households, who are included in the detailed U.S. Jewish population estimates which are reported elsewhere in this volume.

In Canada an official population census held in 1981 enumerated 296,425 Jews according to religion. If the persons are added who responded "Jewish" (as a single reply) to the census question on ethnic groups, while not indicating any religious affiliation (i.e., they were not Christians, etc.), the figure rises to 306,375. There were additional persons who did not indicate religion but mentioned "Jewish" as part of a multiple response to the question on ethnic groups; however, the full number of these people was not published. It is likely that some of them were merely thinking in terms of ancestry but did not actually consider themselves as Jews at the time

---

[10]For derivation of the estimate for U.S. Jewry from the National Jewish Population Study (NJPS) of 1970–1971, see U.O. Schmelz, *World Jewish Population: Regional Estimates and Projections* (Jerusalem, 1981), pp. 32–36. For a discussion of U.S. Jewish population dynamics and perspectives, see U.O. Schmelz and Sergio DellaPergola, "The Demographic Consequences of U.S. Jewish Population Trends," AJYB, Vol. 83, 1983, pp. 141–187.

TABLE 2. ESTIMATED JEWISH POPULATION DISTRIBUTION IN THE AMERICAS, 1984

Country	Total Population	Jewish Population	Jews per 1,000 Population	Accuracy Rating
Canada	24,907,000	310,000	12.4	A 1981 X
United States	234,496,000	5,705,000	24.3	B 1971–83
Total Northern America		6,015,000		
Bahamas	222,000	500	2.2	C 1970
Costa Rica	2,379,000	2,500	1.0	C 1984
Cuba	9,884,000	700	0.1	D
Dominican Republic	5,962,000	100	0.0	D
Guatemala	7,932,000	800	0.1	A 1983
Haiti	5,201,000	100	0.0	D
Jamaica	2,258,000	800	0.1	B 1982
Mexico	75,103,000	35,000	0.5	C 1980
Netherlands Antilles	256,000	700	2.7	D
Panama	2,089,000	3,800	1.8	D
Puerto Rico	3,350,000	2,500	0.7	D
Other		300		D
Total Central America		47,300		
Argentina	29,627,000	228,000	7.7	C 1960–75
Bolivia	6,082,000	600	0.1	C 1984 X
Brazil	129,662,000	100,000	0.8	B 1980
Chile	11,682,000	17,000	1.5	C 1982 X
Columbia	27,515,000	7,000	0.2	C 1977
Ecuador	9,251,000	1,000	0.1	C 1982
Paraguay	3,472,000	900	0.3	C 1984 X
Peru	18,707,000	5,000	0.3	C 1982
Surinam	351,000	200	0.6	B 1984
Uruguay	2,988,000	27,000	9.1	D
Venezuela	16,394,000	20,000	1.2	D
Total Southern America		406,700		
Total		6,469,000		

of the census. By making some allowance for others who considered themselves as Jews but were identified in the census by multiple ethnicity only, a round total of 310,000 is arrived at for 1981, as compared to the previous 1982 estimate of 308,000 for Canadian Jewry. The figure of 310,000 was also adopted for 1984, as a migratory surplus may have roughly offset the probably negative balance of internal evolution since the census.

The estimate for Mexico has been kept unchanged at 35,000. While the official Mexican censuses have given widely varying figures—(1950) 17,574; (1960) 100,750; (1970) 49,277; (1980) 61,790—it is generally admitted that the last three censuses erroneously included many thousands of non-Jews among the Jews.

The Jewish population of Argentina is marked by a negative balance in both internal evolution and external migrations. The estimate has been reduced, therefore, from 233,000 in 1982 to 228,000 in 1984, allowing for some return migration since the present democratic regime came to power.

The official population census of Brazil in 1980 showed a figure of 91,795 Jews, thus confirming the lower order of magnitude of the authors' estimates as compared to the exaggerated figures previously circulated. Since it is possible that some Jews failed to declare themselves as such in the census, the estimate for 1984 has been kept at the round figure of 100,000. On the strength of fragmentary information that is accumulating, the admittedly quite tentative estimates for Uruguay and Chile have been revised downward, while that for Venezuela has not been changed.[11]

EUROPE

Of Europe's estimated 2,759,000 Jews, 38 percent live in Western Europe and 62 percent in Eastern Europe and the Balkan countries (including the Asian territories of the USSR and Turkey).

France has the largest Jewish population in Western Europe, estimated at 530,000, as in 1982.[12] Monitoring of the plausible trends in the internal evolution and the external migrations of Jews in France renders it likely that there has been little net change in this two-year interval. A reestimation of the size of British Jewry was carried out by the research unit of the Board of Deputies, based on an analysis of Jewish deaths during 1975–1979. The revised population figure for 1977, first announced as 354,000, was later amended to 336,000, with a margin of error of

---

[11]For a more detailed discussion of the region's Jewish population trends, see U.O. Schmelz and Sergio DellaPergola, "The Demography of Latin American Jewry," AJYB, Vol. 85, 1985, pp. 51–102.

[12]This estimate is empirically based on the detailed analysis of the French Jewish Population Study. See Doris Bensimon and Sergio DellaPergola, *La population juive de France: socio-démographie et identité* (Jerusalem and Paris, 1984).

TABLE 3. ESTIMATED JEWISH POPULATION DISTRIBUTION IN EUROPE, 1984

Country	Total Population	Jewish Population	Jews per 1,000 Population	Accuracy Rating
Austria	7,549,000	6,500	0.9	A 1981
Belgium	9,856,000	32,200	3.3	D
Bulgaria	8,939,000	3,300	0.4	C 1965
Czechoslovakia	15,415,000	8,500	0.5	D
Denmark	5,114,000	6,800	1.3	C 1984
Finland	4,863,000	1,000	0.2	A 1984
France	54,652,000	530,000	9.7	B 1972–78
Germany, East	16,699,000	800	0.0	D
Germany, West	61,421,000	33,000	0.5	B 1984
Gibraltar	29,000	600	20.1	A 1981
Great Britain	56,377,000	330,000	5.8	B 1984 X
Greece	9,848,000	5,000	0.5	B 1984
Hungary	10,690,000	61,500	5.7	D
Ireland	3,508,000	2,300	0.7	A 1984 X
Italy	56,836,000	32,000	0.6	B 1982
Luxemburg	366,000	700	1.9	C 1970
Netherlands	14,362,000	26,200	1.8	C 1984
Norway	4,129,000	1,000	0.2	A 1982
Poland	36,571,000	4,600	0.1	D
Portugal	10,099,000	600	0.1	D
Rumania	22,553,000	26,000	1.1	B 1984
Spain	38,228,000	12,000	0.3	D
Sweden	8,329,000	15,000	1.8	C 1982
Switzerland	6,505,000	19,000	2.9	A 1980
Turkey[a]	47,279,000	20,000	0.4	C 1984
USSR[a]	272,500,000	1,575,000	5.8	B 1979
Yugoslavia	22,800,000	5,000	0.2	B 1980
Total		2,758,600		

[a]Including Asian regions.

± 34,000.[13] Allowing for an excess of deaths over births, some assimilatory losses, and emigration, the update for 1984, as elaborated by the board's research unit,

[13]S. Haberman, B. A. Kosmin, and C. Levy, "Mortality Patterns of British Jews 1975–79: Insights and Applications for the Size and Structure of British Jewry," *Journal of the Royal Statistical Society*, Ser. A, Vol. 146, Pt. 3 (1983), pp. 294–310.

came to 330,000. Western Germany, Belgium, Italy, and the Netherlands each have Jewish populations ranging around 30,000. There is an internal tendency toward shrinkage of all these Jewries, but in some instances this is offset partly or perhaps even wholly (Italy) by immigration. Switzerland's Jews are estimated at below 20,000, on the strength of the 1980 census. While there is evidence of a negative balance of births and deaths (connected *inter alia* with great aging) and of frequent out-marriage, in this instance, also, immigration may have offset the internal losses.

By far the largest Jewish population in Eastern Europe is concentrated in the Soviet Union, including its Asian territory. Only about 2,000 Jews were permitted to leave for abroad in 1983–1984, but the heavy deficit of internal population dynamics continued and even grew, due to the great aging which prevailed. Under these circumstances the estimate has been reduced from 1,630,000 in 1982 to 1,575,000 in 1984. The Jewish populations in Hungary and Rumania and the small remnants extant in Czechoslovakia, Poland, East Germany, and Bulgaria are all reputed to be very overaged. Their inevitable numerical decline, accelerated by relatively large emigration in the case of Rumania, is reflected in reduced estimates. The Jewish population of Turkey is being eroded by both emigration and a probable deficit of births versus deaths.

ASIA

Israel accounts for 99 percent of all the Jews in Asia, excluding the Asian territories of the USSR and Turkey. Israel held its fourth national population census in June 1983. After evaluation of the results by the Central Bureau of Statistics, in light of all available information the benchmark figure (which serves as the base of subsequent updating until the next census) for the Jewish population as of census date was placed at 3,371,000. This represented a downward revision by some 20,000, or 0.6 percent, of the "old" estimate of 3,392,400 (ultimately based on the previous census, taken in 1972). The corresponding figure for end of 1982 was revised from 3,374,300 to 3,349,600, and the bureau's current estimate for the end of 1984 was 3,471,700. Israel's Jewish population grew over those two years by more than 120,000; 81 percent of this growth was due to natural increase. The Jewish population of Iran continued to dwindle.

AFRICA

Somewhat fewer than 150,000 Jews are estimated to remain now in Africa. The Republic of South Africa accounts for an ever-increasing share (81 percent in 1984) of total Jews in that continent.

According to the 1980 census of the Republic of South Africa, the final figure for Jews (by religion, among the white population) was 117,963. Pending analysis of the

TABLE 4.   ESTIMATED JEWISH POPULATION DISTRIBUTION IN ASIA, 1984

Country	Total Population	Jewish Population	Jews per 1,000 Population	Accuracy Rating	
Hong-Kong	5,313,000	1,000	0.2	C 1980	
India	732,256,000	4,300	0.0	C 1971	
Iran	42,071,000	25,000	0.6	D	X
Iraq	14,654,000	200	0.0	D	
Israel	4,200,000a	3,471,700	826.6	A 1984	
Japan	119,259,000	1,000	0.0	C 1984	
Lebanon	2,635,000	100	0.0	D	
Philippines	52,055,000	100	0.0	C 1982	
Singapore	2,502,000	300	0.1	C 1984	
Syria	9,611,000	4,000	0.4	D	
Thailand	49,459,000	300	0.0	C 1980	
Yemen	6,232,000	1,000	0.2	D	X
Other		300		D	
Total		3,509,300			

aEnd 1984.

TABLE 5.   ESTIMATED JEWISH POPULATION DISTRIBUTION IN AFRICA, 1984

Country	Total Population	Jewish Population	Jews per 1,000 Population	Accuracy Rating	
Egypt	45,915,000	200	0.0	D	
Ethiopia	33,680,000	10,000	0.3	D	
Kenya	18,774,000	100	0.0	B 1984 X	
Morocco	22,109,000	13,000	0.6	D	X
South Africa	30,802,000	118,000	3.8	B 1980	
Tunisia	6,886,000	3,500	0.5	C 1982	
Zaire	31,151,000	200	0.0	D	
Zambia	6,242,000	300	0.0	D	
Zimbabwe	7,740,000	1,100	0.1	D	
Other		1,000		D	
Total		147,400			

data from this census, the 1984 estimate is still given as 118,000 Jews. While the Jews of Ethiopia were affected by calamitous conditions, more than 10,000 succeeded in reaching Israel. In the absence of solid information, the number of those still in Ethiopia is estimated at 10,000. The remnant of Moroccan Jewry continued to shrink through emigration. It should be pointed out, though, that not a few Jews have a foothold both in Morocco (or Tunisia) and in France, and their geographical attribution is uncertain.

OCEANIA

The major country of Jewish residence in this geographical region is Australia, where 95 percent of the estimated total of somewhat below 80,000 Jews live.

TABLE 6. ESTIMATED JEWISH POPULATION DISTRIBUTION IN OCEANIA, 1984

Country	Total Population	Jewish Population	Jews per 1,000 Population	Accuracy Rating
Australia	15,369,000	75,000	4.9	B 1981
New Zealand	3,203,000	4,000	1.2	B 1981
Total		79,000		

The figures for Australia and New Zealand have not been changed from 1982 to 1984, since a migratory surplus may have largely offset an internal deficit caused by low fertility, aging, and out-marriage.

Dispersion and Concentration

Table 7 demonstrates the magnitude of Jewish dispersion. The individual countries listed above as each having at least 100 Jews are scattered over five continents. More than half (40 out of 74 countries) have fewer than 5,000 Jews apiece.

In relative terms, too, the Jews are now thinly scattered nearly everywhere in the Diaspora. There is not a single Diaspora country where they amount even to 3 percent of the total population. In most countries they constitute a far smaller fraction. Probably only three Diaspora countries have 10–25 Jews per 1,000 of total population; and only nine countries have more than 5 Jews per 1,000 of population. The respective nine countries are, in descending order of the proportion—but regardless of the absolute number—of their Jews: United States (24.3), Gibraltar (20.1), Canada (12.4), France (9.7), Uruguay (9.1), Argentina (7.7), USSR (5.8), Great Britain (5.8), Hungary (5.7). This list includes all the Diaspora countries with Jewries of 100,000 or more, except for South Africa and Brazil (in the latter's large population the Jews form only 0.8 per 1,000). In the State of Israel, by contrast, the Jewish majority amounted to 82.7 percent in 1984.

While Jews are widely dispersed, they are also concentrated to some extent (Table 8). In 1984 over 95 percent of world Jewry lived in the nine countries with the largest Jewish populations, each comprising about 100,000 Jews or more; 83 percent lived in the three countries that have at least a million Jews each (United States, Israel,

TABLE 7. DISTRIBUTION OF THE WORLD'S JEWS, BY NUMBER AND PROPORTION (PER 1,000 POPULATION) IN VARIOUS COUNTRIES

Number of Jews in Country	Jews per 1,000 Population					
	Total	Below 1	1–5	5–10	10–25	25 and over
	Number of Countries					
Total	74a	50	14	6	3	1
Below 1,000	23	19	3	—	1	—
1,000–5,000	17	14	3	—	—	—
5,000–10,000	7	6	1	—	—	—
10,000–50,000	16	10	5	1	—	—
50,000–100,000	2	—	1	1	—	—
100,000–1,000,000	6	1	1	3	1	—
1,000,000 and over	3	—	—	1	1	1

	Jewish Population Distribution (Absolute Numbers)					
Total	12,963,300	389,500	333,400	2,751,500	6,015,600	3,471,700
Below 1,000	11,000	6,900	1,900	—	600	—
1,000–5,000	41,900	31,600	10,300	—	—	—
5,000–10,000	43,800	37,000	6,800	—	—	—
10,000–50,000	362,400	214,000	121,400	27,000	—	—
50,000–100,000	136,500	—	75,000	61,500	—	—
100,000–1,000,000	1,616,000	100,000	118,000	1,088,000	310,000	—
1,000,000 and over	10,751,700	—	—	1,575,000	5,705,000	3,471,700

	Jewish Population Distribution (Percent of World's Jews)					
Total	100.0	3.0	2.6	21.2	46.4	26.8
Below 1,000	0.1	0.0	0.0	—	0.0	—
1,000–5,000	0.3	0.2	0.1	—	—	—
5,000–10,000	0.3	0.3	0.0	—	—	—
10,000–50,000	2.8	1.6	0.9	0.2	—	—
50,000–100,000	1.1	—	0.6	0.5	—	—
100,000–1,000,000	12.5	0.8	0.9	8.4	2.4	—
1,000,000 and over	82.9	—	—	12.1	44.0	26.8

aExcluding countries with fewer than 100 Jews.

TABLE 8. COUNTRIES WITH LARGEST JEWISH POPULATIONS (100,000 JEWS AND ABOVE), 1984

| | | | % of Total Jewish Population | | | |
| | | | In the Diaspora | | In the World | |
Rank	Country	Jewish Population	%	Cumulative %	%	Cumulative %
1	United States	5,705,000	60.1	60.1	44.0	44.0
2	Israel	3,471,700	—	—	26.8	70.8
3	Soviet Union	1,575,000	16.6	76.7	12.1	82.9
4	France	530,000	5.6	82.3	4.1	87.0
5	Great Britain	330,000	3.5	85.8	2.5	89.5
6	Canada	310,000	3.3	89.1	2.4	91.9
7	Argentina	228,000	2.4	91.5	1.8	93.7
8	South Africa	118,000	1.2	92.7	0.9	94.6
9	Brazil	100,000	1.0	93.7	0.8	95.4

Soviet Union). Similarly, the United States alone accounted for 60 percent of total Diaspora Jewry; two countries (United States and Soviet Union) for 77 percent; and the eight Diaspora countries with 100,000 Jews or more together comprised 94 percent of the Diaspora Jewish population.

U. O. SCHMELZ
SERGIO DELLAPERGOLA

Directories
Lists
Necrology

National Jewish Organizations[1]

UNITED STATES

Organizations are listed according to functions as follows:

COMMUNITY RELATIONS

AMERICAN COUNCIL FOR JUDAISM (1943). 298 Fifth Ave., NYC 10001. (212)947-8878. Bd. Chmn. Clarence L. Coleman, Jr.; Pres. Alan V. Stone. Seeks to advance the universal principles of a Judaism free of nationalism, and the national, civic, cultural, and social integration into American institutions of Americans of Jewish faith. *Issues of the American Council for Judaism; Special Interest Report.*

AMERICAN JEWISH ALTERNATIVES TO ZIONISM, INC. (1968). 133 E. 73 St., NYC 10021. (212)628-2727. Pres. Elmer Berger; V. Pres. Mrs. Arthur Gutman. Applies Jewish values of justice and humanity to the Arab-Israel conflict in the Middle East; rejects nationality attachment of Jews, particularly American Jews, to the State of Israel as self-segregating, inconsistent with American constitutional concepts of individual citizenship and separation of church and state, and as being a principal obstacle to Middle East peace. *Report.*

AMERICAN JEWISH COMMITTEE (1906). Institute of Human Relations, 165 E. 56 St., NYC 10022. (212)751-4000. Pres. Howard I. Friedman; Exec. V. Pres. David M. Gordis. Seeks to prevent infraction of civil and religious rights of Jews in any part of the world; to advance the cause of human rights for people of all races, creeds, and nationalities; to interpret the position of Israel to the American public; and to help American Jews maintain and enrich their

---

[1]The information in this directory is based on replies to questionnaires circulated by the editors.

Jewish identity and, at the same time, achieve full integration in American life; includes Jacob and Hilda Blaustein Center for Human Relations, William E. Wiener Oral History Library, Leonard and Rose Sperry International Center for the Resolution of Group Conflict. AMERICAN JEWISH YEAR BOOK (with Jewish Publication Society of America); *Commentary; Present Tense; AJC Journal.*

AMERICAN JEWISH CONGRESS (1918). Stephen Wise Congress House, 15 E. 84 St., NYC 10028. (212)879-4500. Pres. Theodore R. Mann; Exec. Dir. Henry Siegman. Works to foster the creative cultural survival of the Jewish people; to help Israel develop in peace, freedom, and security; to eliminate all forms of racial and religious bigotry; to advance civil rights, protect civil liberties, defend religious freedom, and safeguard the separation of church and state. Maintains the Martin Steinberg Center for Jewish arts and artists. *Congress Monthly; Judaism; Boycott Report; Jewish Arts Newsletter.*

ANTI-DEFAMATION LEAGUE OF B'NAI B'RITH (1913). 823 United Nations Plaza, NYC 10017. (212)490-2525. Chmn. Kenneth J. Bialkin; Dir. Nathan Perlmutter. Seeks to combat antisemitism and to secure justice and fair treatment for all citizens through law, education, and community relations. *ADL Bulletin; Face to Face; Fact Finding Report; International Reports; Law Notes; Rights; Law; Research and Evaluation Report; Discriminations Report; Litigation Docket; Dimensions; Middle East Notebook; Nuestro Encuentro.*

ASSOCIATION OF JEWISH CENTER WORKERS (1918). 15 E. 26 St., NYC 10010. (212)532-4949. Pres. George Korobkin; Exec. Dir. Herman L. Zimmerman. Seeks to enhance the standards, techniques, practices, scope, and public understanding of Jewish community-center and kindred work. *Kesher.*

ASSOCIATION OF JEWISH COMMUNITY RELATIONS WORKERS (1950). 155 Fifth Ave., NYC 10010. (212)533-7800. Pres. Muriel Berman; Exec. Dir. Ann Plutzer. Aims to stimulate higher standards of professional practice in Jewish community relations; encourages research and training toward that end; conducts educational programs and seminars; aims to encourage cooperation between community relations workers and those working in other areas of Jewish communal service. Quarterly newsletter.

CENTER FOR JEWISH COMMUNITY STUDIES (1970). 1017 Gladfelter Hall, Temple University, Philadelphia, PA 19122. (215)787-1459. Jerusalem office: Jerusalem Center for Public Affairs. Pres. Daniel J. Elazar. Worldwide policy-studies institute devoted to the study of Jewish community organization, political thought, and public affairs, past and present, in Israel and throughout the world. Publishes original articles, essays, and monographs; maintains library, archives, and reprint series. *Jerusalem Letter/Viewpoints; Tefutsot Israel; Iggeret.*

COMMISSION ON SOCIAL ACTION OF REFORM JUDAISM (1953, under the auspices of the Union of American Hebrew Congregations). 838 Fifth Ave., NYC 10021. (212)249-0100. Chmn. Harris Gilbert; Dir. Albert Vorspan; Assoc. Dir. David Saperstein. Develops materials to assist Reform synagogues in setting up social-action programs relating the principles of Judaism to contemporary social problems; assists congregations in studying the moral and religious implications in social issues such as civil rights, civil liberties, church-state relations; guides congregational social-action committees. *Briefings.*

COMMITTEE TO BRING NAZI WAR CRIMINALS TO JUSTICE IN U.S.A., INC. (1973). 135 W. 106 St., NYC 10025. (212)866-0692. Pres. Charles H. Kremer; Treas. Albert Sigal; Sec. Paul Schwarzbaum. Compiles and publicizes records of Nazi atrocities and labors to bring to justice the perpetrators of those crimes. Remains committed to preserving the memory of all victims of the Holocaust, and actively opposes antisemitism wherever and however it is found.

CONFERENCE OF PRESIDENTS OF MAJOR AMERICAN JEWISH ORGANIZATIONS (1955). 515 Park Ave., NYC 10022. (212)-752-1616. Chmn. Kenneth J. Bialkin; Exec. V. Chmn. Yehuda Hellman. Coordinates the activities of 38 major American Jewish organizations as they relate to American-Israeli affairs and problems affecting Jews in other lands. *Annual Report; Middle East Memo.*

CONSULTATIVE COUNCIL OF JEWISH ORGANIZATIONS-CCJO (1946). 135 William St., NYC 10038. (212)349-0537. Cochmn.

Basil Bard, Jules Braunschvig, Joseph Nuss; V. Chmn. Arnold Franco; Sec.-Gen. Moses Moskowitz. A nongovernmental organization in consultative status with the UN, UNESCO, ILO, UNICEF, and the Council of Europe; cooperates and consults with, advises and renders assistance to the Economic and Social Council of the UN on all problems relating to human rights and economic, social, cultural, educational, and related matters pertaining to Jews.

COORDINATING BOARD OF JEWISH ORGANIZATIONS (1947). 1640 Rhode Island Ave., NW, Washington, DC 20036. (202)857-6545. Pres. Gerald Kraft (B'nai B'rith), Greville Janner (Board of Deputies of British Jews), David K. Mann (South African Jewish Board of Deputies); Exec. V. Pres. Daniel Thursz (U.S.). As an organization in consultative status with the Economic and Social Council of the UN, represents the three constituents (B'nai B'rith, the Board of Deputies of British Jews, and the South African Jewish Board of Deputies) in the appropriate UN bodies for the purpose of promoting human rights, with special attention to combatting persecution or discrimination on grounds of race, religion, or origin.

COUNCIL OF JEWISH ORGANIZATIONS IN CIVIL SERVICE, INC. (1948). 45 E. 33 St., NYC 10016. (212)689-2015. Pres. Louis Weiser. Supports merit system; combats discrimination; promotes all Jewish interest projects; sponsors scholarships; is member of Coalition to Free Soviet Jews, Jewish Labor Committee, America-Israel Friendship League, NY Jewish Community Relations Council, NY Metropolitan Coordinating Council on Jewish Poverty. *CJO Digest.*

INSTITUTE FOR JEWISH POLICY PLANNING AND RESEARCH (*see* Synagogue Council of America)

INTERNATIONAL CONFERENCE OF JEWISH COMMUNAL SERVICE (*see* World Conference of Jewish Communal Service)

JEWISH LABOR COMMITTEE (1934). Atran Center for Jewish Culture, 25 E. 21 St., NYC, 10010. (212)477-0707. Pres. Herb Magidson; Exec. Dir. Martin Lapan. Serves as a link between the Jewish community and the trade union movement; works with the AFL-CIO and others to combat all forms of racial and religious discrimination in the United States and abroad; furthers labor support for Israel's security and Soviet Jewry, and Jewish communal support for labor's social and economic programs; supports Yiddish cultural institutions. *JLC News.*

——, NATIONAL TRADE UNION COUNCIL FOR HUMAN RIGHTS (1956). Atran Center for Jewish Culture, 25 E. 21 St., NYC 10010. (212)477-0707. Chmn. Sol Hoffman; Exec. Sec. Martin Lapan. Works with trade unions on programs and issues affecting both labor and the Jewish community.

——, WOMEN'S DIVISION OF (1947). Atran Center for Jewish Culture, 25 E. 21 St., NYC 10010. (212)477-0707. Natl. Chmn. Eleanor Schachner. Supports the general activities of the Jewish Labor Committee; provides secondary-school and college scholarships for needy Israeli students; participates in educational and cultural activities.

——, WORKMEN'S CIRCLE DIVISION OF (1939). Atran Center for Jewish Culture, 25 E. 21 St., NYC 10010. (212)477-0707. Promotes aims of, and raises funds for, the Jewish Labor Committee among the Workmen's Circle branches; conducts Yiddish educational and cultural activities.

JEWISH PEACE FELLOWSHIP (1941). Box 271, Nyack, NY 10960. (914)358-4601. Pres. Naomi Goodman. Unites those who believe that Jewish ideals and experience provide inspiration for a nonviolent philosophy and way of life; offers draft counseling, especially for conscientious objection based on Jewish "religious training and belief"; encourages Jewish community to become more knowledgeable, concerned, and active in regard to the war/peace problem. *Shalom/Jewish Peace Letter.*

JEWISH WAR VETERANS OF THE UNITED STATES OF AMERICA (1896). 1811 R St., NW, Washington, DC 20009. (202)265-6280. Natl. Comdr. Samuel Greenberg; Natl. Exec. Dir. Harris B. Stone. Seeks to foster true allegiance to the United States; to combat bigotry and prevent defamation of Jews; to encourage the doctrine of universal liberty, equal rights, and full justice for all; to cooperate with and support existing educational institutions and establish new ones; to foster the education of ex-servicemen, ex-servicewomen, and members in the ideals and principles of Americanism. *Jewish Veteran.*

————, NATIONAL MEMORIAL, INC; NATIONAL SHRINE TO THE JEWISH WAR DEAD (1958). 1811 R St., NW, Washington, DC 20009. (202)265-6280. Pres. Ainslee R. Ferdie. Maintains a national archives and museum commemorating the wartime service of American Jews in the Armed Forces of the U.S.; maintains *Golden Book* of names of the war dead; *Routes to Roots.*

NATIONAL CONFERENCE ON SOVIET JEWRY (formerly AMERICAN JEWISH CONFERENCE ON SOVIET JEWRY) (1964; reorg. 1971). 10 E. 40 St., Suite 907, NYC 10016. (212)679-6122. Chmn. Morris B. Abram; Exec. Dir. Jerry Goodman. Coordinating agency for major national Jewish organizations and local community groups in the U.S., acting on behalf of Soviet Jewry through public education and social action; stimulates all segments of the community to maintain an interest in the problems of Soviet Jews by publishing reports and special pamphlets, sponsoring special programs and projects, organizing public meetings and forums. *Newsbreak; Annual Report; Wrap-Up Activities Report.*

————, SOVIET JEWRY RESEARCH BUREAU. Chmn. Charlotte Jacobson. Organized by NCSJ to monitor emigration trends. Primary task is the accumulation, evaluation, and processing of information regarding Soviet Jews, especially those who apply for emigration.

NATIONAL JEWISH COMMISSION ON LAW AND PUBLIC AFFAIRS (COLPA) (1965). 450 Seventh Ave., Suite 2203, NYC 10001. (212)563-0100. Pres. Allen L. Rothenberg; Exec. Dir. Dennis Rapps. Voluntary association of attorneys whose purpose is to represent the observant Jewish community on legal, legislative, and public affairs matters.

NATIONAL JEWISH COMMUNITY RELATIONS ADVISORY COUNCIL (1944). 443 Park Ave. S., 11th fl., NYC 10016. (212)-684-6950. Chmn. Bennett Yanowitz; Exec. V. Chmn. Albert D. Chernin; Sec. Raymond Epstein. Consultative, advisory, and coordinating council of 11 national Jewish organizations and 108 local Jewish councils that seeks the promotion of understanding of Israel and the Middle East; freedom for Jews in the Soviet Union; equal status and opportunity for all groups, including Jews, with full expression of distinctive group values and full participation in the general society. Through the processes of the Council, its constituent organizations seek agreement on policies, strategies, and programs for most effective utilization of their collective resources for common ends. *Guide to Program Planning for Jewish Community Relations.*

NEW JEWISH AGENDA (1980). 149 Church St., Suite 2N, NYC 10007. (212)227-5885. Cochmn. Christie Balka and Andy Rose; Exec. Dir. Reena Bernards. Founded as "a progressive voice in the Jewish community and a Jewish voice among progressives." Works for nuclear disarmament, peace in Central America, Arab-Jewish reconciliation, and economic justice, and against antisemitism and racism.

NORTH AMERICAN JEWISH YOUTH COUNCIL (1965). 515 Park Ave., NYC 10022. (212)751-6070. Exec. Dir. Donald Adelman. Provides a framework for coordination and exchange of programs and information among national Jewish youth organizations to help them deepen the concern of American Jewish youth for world Jewry; represents Jewish youth in the Conference of Presidents, United States Youth Council, etc.

STUDENT STRUGGLE FOR SOVIET JEWRY, INC. (1964). 210 W. 91 St., NYC 10024. (212)799-8900. Natl. Dir. Jacob Birnbaum; Natl. Coord. Glenn Richter; Chmn. Avraham Weiss. Provides information and action guidance to adult and student organizations, communities, and schools throughout the U.S. and Canada; assists Soviet Jews by publicity campaigns; helps Russian Jews in the U.S.; aids Rumanian Jews seeking emigration; maintains speakers bureau and research documents. *Soviet Jewry Action Newsletter.*

UNION OF COUNCILS FOR SOVIET JEWS (1970). 1411 K St., NW, Suite 402, Washington, DC 20005. (202)393-4117. Pres. Morey Schapira; Exec. Dir. Mark A. Epstein. A confederation of 38 grass-roots organizations established in support of Soviet Jewry. Works on behalf of Soviet Jews through public education, representations to the administration and Congress, letter-writing assistance, tourist briefing, speakers bureau, Adopt-A-Family, Adopt-A-Prisoner, Bar/Bat Mitzvah twinning, Tarbut, congressional vigil, congressional briefings, and publications programming; affiliations include Soviet Jewry Legal Advocacy Center and Medical Mobilization for Soviet Jewry. *Alert; UCSJ Quarterly Report.*

WORLD CONFERENCE OF JEWISH COMMUNAL SERVICE (1966). 15 E. 26 St., NYC 10010. (212)532-2526. Pres. Irving Kessler; Sec.-Gen. Solomon H. Green. Established by worldwide Jewish communal workers to strengthen their understanding of each other's programs and to communicate with colleagues in order to enrich the quality of their work. Conducts quadrennial international conferences in Jerusalem and periodic regional meetings. *Proceedings of International Conferences; Newsletter.*

WORLD JEWISH CONGRESS (1936; org. in U.S. 1939). 1 Park Ave., Suite 418, NYC 10016. (212)679-0600. Pres. Edgar M. Bronfman; Chmn. N. Amer. Branch Sol Kanee; Chmn. Amer. Sect. Frieda Lewis; Exec. Dir. Israel Singer. Seeks to intensify bonds of world Jewry with Israel as central force in Jewish life; to strengthen solidarity among Jews everywhere and secure their rights, status, and interests as individuals and communities; to encourage development of Jewish social, religious, and cultural life throughout the world and coordinate efforts by Jewish communities and organizations to cope with any Jewish problem; to work for human rights generally. Represents its affiliated organizations —most representative bodies of Jewish communities in more than 70 countries and 32 national organizations in Amer. section—at UN, OAS, UNESCO, Council of Europe, ILO, UNICEF, and other governmental, intergovernmental, and international authorities. Publications (including those by Institute of Jewish Affairs, London): *Christian Jewish Relations; Coloquio; News and Views; Boletín Informativo OJI; Batfutsot; Gesher; Patterns of Prejudice; Soviet Jewish Affairs.*

CULTURAL

AMERICAN ACADEMY FOR JEWISH RESEARCH (1920). 3080 Broadway, NYC 10027. Pres. Isaac Barzilay; V. Pres. Franz Rosenthal; Treas. Arthur Hyman. Encourages Jewish learning and research; holds annual or semiannual meeting; awards grants for the publication of scholarly works. *Proceedings of the American Academy for Jewish Research; Texts and Studies; Monograph Series.*

AMERICAN BIBLICAL ENCYCLOPEDIA SOCIETY (1930). 24 W. Maple Ave., Monsey, NY 10952. (914)352-4609. Pres. Leo Jung; Exec. V. Pres. Irving Fredman; Author-Ed. Menachem M. Kasher. Fosters biblical-talmudical research; sponsors and publishes *Torah Shelemah* (Heb., 38 vols.), *Encyclopedia of Biblical Interpretation* (Eng., 9 vols.), *Divrei Menachem* (Heb., 4 vols.), and related publications. *Noam.*

AMERICAN FEDERATION OF JEWISH FIGHTERS, CAMP INMATES AND NAZI VICTIMS, INC. (1971). 823 United Nations Plaza, NYC 10017. (212)697-5670. Pres. Solomon Zynstein; Exec. Dir. Ernest Honig. Seeks to perpetuate the memory of victims of the Holocaust and make Jewish and non-Jewish youth aware of the Holocaust and resistance period. *Martyrdom and Resistance.*

AMERICAN JEWISH HISTORICAL SOCIETY (1892). 2 Thornton Rd., Waltham, MA 02154. (617)891-8110. Pres. Morris Soble; Dir. Bernard Wax. Collects, catalogues, publishes, and displays material on the history of the Jews in America; serves as an information center for inquiries on American Jewish history; maintains archives of original source material on American Jewish history; sponsors lectures and exhibitions; makes available historic Yiddish films and audio-visual material. *American Jewish History; Heritage.*

AMERICAN JEWISH PRESS ASSOCIATION (1943). c/o St. Louis Jewish Light, 12 Millstone Campus Dr., St. Louis, MO 63146. (314)432-3353. Pres. Robert A. Cohn. Seeks the advancement of Jewish journalism, the attainment of the highest editorial and business standards for members, and the maintenance of a strong Jewish press in the U.S. and Canada.

AMERICAN SOCIETY FOR JEWISH MUSIC (1974). 155 Fifth Ave., NYC 10010. (212)-533-2601. Pres. Paul Kavon; V. Pres. David Lefkowitz; Sec. Hadássah B. Markson. Seeks to raise standards of composition and performance in Jewish liturgical and secular music; encourages research in all areas of Jewish music; publishes scholarly journal; presents programs and sponsors performances of new and rarely heard works and encourages their recording; commissions new works of Jewish interest. *Musica Judaica.*

ASSOCIATED AMERICAN JEWISH MUSEUMS, INC. (1971). 303 LeRoi Road, Pittsburgh, PA 15208. Pres. Walter Jacob; V. Pres. William Rosenthall; Sec. Robert H. Lehman; Treas. Jason Z. Edelstein. Maintains regional collections of Jewish art, historical and ritual objects, as well as a central catalogue of such objects in the collections of Jewish museums throughout the U.S.; helps Jewish museums acquire, identify, and classify objects; arranges exchanges of collections, exhibits, and individual objects among Jewish museums; encourages the creation of Jewish art, ceremonial and ritual objects.

ASSOCIATION FOR THE SOCIOLOGICAL STUDY OF JEWRY (1971). Dept. of Sociology, Brooklyn College, Brooklyn, NY 11210. (718)780-5315. Pres. Egon Mayer; V. Pres. Abraham Lavender; Sec.-Treas. Walter Zenner. Arranges academic sessions and facilitates communication among social scientists studying Jewry through meetings, newsletter, and related materials. *Contemporary Jewry: A Journal of Sociological Inquiry; The ASSJ Newsletter.*

ASSOCIATION OF JEWISH BOOK PUBLISHERS (1962). 838 Fifth Ave., NYC 10021. (212)-249-0100. Pres. Bernard I. Levinson. As a nonprofit group, provides a forum for discussion of mutual problems by publishers, authors, and other individuals and institutions concerned with books of Jewish interest. Provides national and international exhibit opportunities for Jewish books. *Combined Jewish Book Catalogue.*

ASSOCIATION OF JEWISH LIBRARIES (1965). c/o National Foundation for Jewish Culture, 122 E. 42 St., NYC 10168. (212)-490-2280. Pres. Hazel B. Karp; V. Pres. Edith Lubetski. Seeks to promote and improve services and professional standards in Jewish libraries; serves as a center for the dissemination of Jewish library information and guidance; promotes publication of literature in the field; encourages the establishment of Jewish libraries and collections of Judaica and the choice of Jewish librarianship as a vocation. *Judaica Librarianship; AJL Newsletter.*

B'NAI B'RITH KLUTZNICK MUSEUM (1956). 1640 Rhode Island Ave. NW, Washington, DC 20036. (202)857-6583. Chmn. Museum & Art Comm., David and Jane Greene; Dir. Linda Altshuler. A center of Jewish art and history in nation's capital, maintains exhibition galleries, permanent collection of Jewish ceremonial and folk art, B'nai B'rith International reference archive, outdoor sculpture garden, and museum shop. Provides exhibitions, tours, educational programs, research assistance, and tourist information. *Quarterly Newsletter.*

CENTER FOR HOLOCAUST STUDIES, INC. (1974). 1610 Ave. J, Brooklyn, NY 11230. (718)338-6494. Dir. Yaffa Eliach. Collects and preserves documents and memorabilia, oral histories, and literary works on the Holocaust period for purposes of documentation and research; arranges lectures, exhibits, drama and music performances, and exhibitions of Holocaust art; conducts outreach programs to schools; maintains speakers bureau, oral history publication series, and audiovisual department. *Newsletter.*

CENTRAL YIDDISH CULTURE ORGANIZATION (CYCO), INC. (1943). 25 E. 78 St., NYC 10021. (212)535-4320. Pres. Noah Singman. Promotes and publishes Yiddish books; distributes books from other Yiddish publishing houses throughout the world; publishes annual bibliographical and statistical register of Yiddish books, and catalogues of new publications. *Zukunft.*

CONFERENCE ON JEWISH SOCIAL STUDIES, INC. (formerly **CONFERENCE ON JEWISH RELATIONS, INC.**) (1939). 2112 Broadway, Rm. 206, NYC 10023. (212)724-5336. Pres. Jeannette M. Baron; Hon. Pres. Salo W. Baron; V. Pres. Joseph L. Blau. Publishes scientific studies on Jews in the modern world, dealing with such aspects as antisemitism, demography, economic stratification, history, philosophy, and political developments. *Jewish Social Studies.*

CONGREGATION BINA (1981). 600 W. End Ave., NYC 10024. (212)873-4261. Pres. Elijah E. Jhirad; Exec. V. Pres. Samuel M. Daniel. Serves the religious, cultural, charitable, and philanthropic needs of the Jews of India who reside in the U.S. Works to foster and preserve the ancient traditions, music, and folklore of Indian Jewry. *Kol Bina.*

HEBREW ARTS SCHOOL (1952). 129 W. 67 St., NYC 10023. (212)362-8060. Bd. Chmn. Abraham Goodman; Pres. Leonard P. Shaykin; Dir. & Founder Tzipora H. Jochsberger; Sec. Lewis Kruger. Chartered by the Board of Regents, University of the State of New York. Offers instruction in music, dance, theater, and art to children and adults, combining studies in Western cultural traditions with the heritage of the Jewish people; provides instrumental, vocal, dance, theater, and art classes on all levels, classes in music and art for preschool children and their parents, music workshops for teachers, ensemble workshops; sponsors the Hebrew Arts Chorale, a community chorus; presents, in its Merkin Concert Hall and Ann Goodman Recital Hall, Heritage Concerts, Tuesday Matinees, Music Today, On Original Instruments, Twilight Concerts of Jewish Music, Boston Camerata, Concerts Plus, the American Jewish Choral Festival, Young Musicians' Concerts, Adventures in Jewish Music for the Young; sponsors resident ensembles: Musica Camerit, Mendelssohn String Quartet, Hebrew Arts Concert Choir. *Newsletter.*

HEBREW CULTURE FOUNDATION (1955). 515 Park Ave., NYC 10022. (212)752-0600. Chmn. Milton R. Konvitz; Sec. Herman L. Sainer. Sponsors the introduction and strengthening of Hebrew language and literature courses in institutions of higher learning in the United States.

HISTADRUTH IVRITH OF AMERICA (1916; reorg. 1922). 1841 Broadway, NYC 10023. (212)581-5151. Pres. Rabbi Joseph Sternstein; Exec. V. Pres. Aviva Barzel. Emphasizes the primacy of Hebrew in Jewish life, culture, and education; aims to disseminate knowledge of written and spoken Hebrew in the Diaspora, thus building a cultural bridge between the State of Israel and Jewish communities throughout the world. *Hadoar; Lamishpaha.*

HOLOCAUST CENTER OF GREATER PITTSBURGH (1980). 242 McKee Pl., Pittsburgh, PA 15213. (412)682-7111. Dir. Isaiah Kuperstein; Chmn. Sidney N. Busis. Develops programs and provides resources to further understanding of the Holocaust

and its impact on civilization. Maintains a library, archive; provides speakers, educational materials; organizes community programs.

JWB JEWISH BOOK COUNCIL (1942). 15 E. 26 St., NYC 10010. (212)532-4949. Pres. Blu Greenberg; Dir. Paula Gribetz Gottlieb. Promotes knowledge of Jewish books through dissemination of booklists, program materials; sponsors Jewish Book Month; presents literary awards and library citations; cooperates with publishers of Jewish books. *Jewish Book Annual; Jewish Books in Review; Jewish Book World.*

JWB JEWISH MUSIC COUNCIL (1944). 15 E. 26 St., NYC 10010. (212)532-4949. Chmn. Leonard Kaplan; Coord. Paula Gribetz Gottlieb. Promotes Jewish music activities nationally; annually sponsors and promotes the Jewish Music season; encourages participation on a community basis. *Jewish Music Notes* and numerous music resource publications for national distribution.

JEWISH ACADEMY OF ARTS AND SCIENCES, INC. (1926). 136 W. 39 St., NYC 10016. (212)725-1211. Hon. Pres. Leo Jung; Pres. Abraham I. Katsh. An honor society of Jews who have attained distinction in the arts, sciences, professions, and communal endeavors. Encourages the advancement of knowledge; stimulates scholarship, with particular reference to Jewish life and thought; recognition by election to membership and/or fellowship; publishes papers delivered at annual convocations.

JEWISH INFORMATION BUREAU, INC. (1932). 250 W. 57 St., NYC 10019. (212)-582-5318. Dir. Steven Wise; V. Chmn. Ruth Eisenstein. Serves as clearinghouse of information for inquiries regarding Jews, Judaism, Israel, and Jewish affairs; refers inquiries to communal agencies. *Index.*

JEWISH MUSEUM (1904, under auspices of Jewish Theological Seminary of America). 1109 Fifth Ave., NYC 10028. (212)860-1888. Chmn. Bd. of Trustees James Weinberg; Dir. Joan Rosenbaum. A nonprofit organization, the main repository in the U.S. for art and artifacts representing Jewish culture, and the largest museum devoted to creating changing exhibitions which relate to Jewish culture. Collection of 15,000 works in all media, including Biblical archaeology, numismatics, fine arts, and ethnography. Answers inquiries;

conducts tours of special exhibitions and permanent installations; gives lectures, film showings, and concerts. Special classes and a program for children are conducted by the Education department. *Special exhibition catalogues.*

JEWISH PUBLICATION SOCIETY OF AMERICA (1888). 1930 Chestnut St., Philadelphia, PA 19103. (215)564-5925. Pres. Charles R. Weiner; Editor David Rosenberg; Exec. V. Pres. Nathan Barnett. Publishes and disseminates books of Jewish interest for adults and children; titles include contemporary literature, classics, art, religion, biographies, poetry, and history. AMERICAN JEWISH YEAR BOOK (with American Jewish Committee).

JUDAH L. MAGNES MUSEUM—JEWISH MUSEUM OF THE WEST (1962). 2911 Russell St., Berkeley, CA 94705. (415)849-2710. Pres. Jacques Reutlinger; Exec. Dir. Seymour Fromer. Serves as museum and library, combining historical and literary materials illustrating Jewish life in the Bay Area, the Western states, and around the world; provides archives of world Jewish history and Jewish art; repository of historical documents intended for scholarly use; changing exhibits; facilities open to the general public. *Magnes News; special exhibition catalogues.*

JUDAICA CAPTIONED FILM CENTER, INC. (1983). P.O. Box 21439, Baltimore, MD 21208-0439, Voice (301)922-4642 TDD (301)655-6767. Pres. Lois Lilienfeld Weiner. Developing a comprehensive library of captioned and subtitled films and tapes on Jewish subjects; distributes them to organizations serving the hearing-impaired on a free-loan, handling/shipping-charge-only basis. *Quarterly Newsletter.*

LEAGUE FOR YIDDISH, INC. (1935). 200 W. 72 St., Suite 40, NYC 10023. (212)787-6675. Pres. Sadie Turak; Exec. Dir. Mordkhe Schaechter. Promotes the development and use of Yiddish as a living language. *Afn Shvel.*

LEO BAECK INSTITUTE, INC. (1955). 129 E. 73 St., NYC 10021. (212)744-6400. Pres. Ismar Schorsch; Sec. Fred Grubel. A library, archive, and research center for the history of German-speaking Jewry. Offers lectures, exhibits, faculty seminars; publishes a series of monographs, yearbooks, and journals. *LBI Bulletin; LBI News; LBI Year Book.*

MARTYRS MEMORIAL & MUSEUM OF THE HOLOCAUST (1963). 6505 Wilshire Blvd., Los Angeles, CA 90048. (213)651-3175. Chmn. Abraham Spiegel; Dir. Michael Nutkiewicz. Seeks to commemorate the events and victims of the Holocaust and to educate against future reoccurrences; maintains permanent and traveling exhibits, sponsors public lectures, offers school curricula and teacher training. West Coast representative of Israel's Yad Vashem; affiliated with the Jewish Federation Council of Greater Los Angeles.

MEMORIAL FOUNDATION FOR JEWISH CULTURE, INC. (1964). 15 E. 26 St., NYC 10010. (212)679-4074. Pres. Philip M. Klutznick; Exec. Dir. Jerry Hochbaum. Supports Jewish cultural and educational programs around the world, in cooperation with universities and established scholarly organizations. *Biennial Report.*

NATIONAL FOUNDATION FOR JEWISH CULTURE (1960). 1512 Chanin Bldg., 122 E. 42 St., NYC 10168. (212)490-2280. Pres. Marver Bernstein; Exec. Dir. Abraham Atik. Provides consultation and support to Jewish community organizations, educational and cultural institutions, and individuals for Jewish cultural activities; awards fellowships and publication grants to individuals preparing for careers in Jewish scholarship; presents awards for creative efforts in Jewish cultural arts and for Jewish programming in small and intermediate communities; publishes guides to national Jewish cultural resources, traveling exhibitions, and plays; serves as clearinghouse of information on American Jewish culture; administers Joint Cultural Appeal on behalf of nine national cultural organizations; administers Council for Archives and Research Libraries in Jewish Studies and Council of American Jewish Museums.

NATIONAL HEBREW CULTURE COUNCIL (1952). 1776 Broadway, NYC 10019. (212)247-0741. Pres. Frances K. Thau; Exec. Dir. Judah Lapson. Cultivates the study of Hebrew as a modern language in American public high schools and colleges, providing guidance to community groups and public educational authorities; annually administers National Voluntary Examination in Hebrew Culture and Knowledge of Israel in the public high schools, and conducts summer seminar and tour of Israel for teachers and other educational personnel of the public school system, in cooperation with Hebrew University and WZO. *Hebrew in Colleges and Universities.*

NATIONAL YIDDISH BOOK CENTER (1980). P.O. Box 969, East Street School, Amherst, MA 01004. (413)253-9201. Pres. Joseph Marcus; Exec. Dir. Aaron Lansky. Collects used and out-of-print Yiddish books to distribute to individuals and libraries; offers courses in Yiddish language, literature, and cultural activities; publishes bimonthly *Catalogue of Rare and Out-of-Print Yiddish Books,* listing over 100,000 volumes for sale. *Der Pakntrege; Afn Veg.*

NEW YORK CITY HOLOCAUST MEMORIAL COMMISSION (1981). 111 W. 40 St., NYC 10018. (212)221-1574. Cochmn. George Klein, Hon. Robert M. Morgenthau; Exec. Dir. David L. Blumenfeld. Seeks to create a major "living memorial" center in New York City consisting of a museum, library, archives, and lecture/conference facilities which will commemorate the lives of the Jewish victims of Nazi Germany by creating a record of their cultural and societal lives in Europe, restoring to memory the close affinity between the Jews of Europe and the large Jewish immigrant population of New York City, educating future generations on the history and lessons of the Holocaust, and providing appropriate commemoration honoring the memory of those who died in the Holocaust. *Times to Remember.*

RESEARCH FOUNDATION FOR JEWISH IMMIGRATION, INC. (1971). 570 Seventh Ave., NYC 10018. (212)921-3871. Pres. Curt C. Silberman; Sec. Herbert A. Strauss. Studies and records the history of the migration and acculturation of Jewish Nazi persecutees in the various resettlement countries. *International Biographical Dictionary of Central European Emigrés, 1933–1945; Jewish Immigrants of the Nazi Period in the USA.*

ST. LOUIS CENTER FOR HOLOCAUST STUDIES (1977). 12 Millstone Campus Dr., St. Louis, MO 63146. (314)432-0020. Chmn. Lois Gould-Rafaeli; Dir. Rabbi Robert Sternberg. Develops programs and provides resources and educational materials to further an understanding of the Holocaust and its impact on civilization. *Audio Visual Guide.*

SEPHARDIC HOUSE (1978). 8 West 70 St., NYC 10023. (212)873-0300. Dir. Rabbi Marc D. Angel. Works to foster the history and culture of Sephardic Jewry by offering classes, programs, publications, and resource people; works to integrate Sephardic studies into the curriculum of Jewish schools and adult education programs; offers advice and guidance to individuals involved in Sephardic research. *The Sephardic House Newsletter.*

SKIRBALL MUSEUM, Los Angeles, CA (see Hebrew Union College-Jewish Institute of Religion)

SOCIETY FOR THE HISTORY OF CZECHOSLOVAK JEWS, INC. (1961). 87-08 Santiago St., Holliswood, NY 11423. Pres. Lewis Weiner; Sec. Joseph Abeles. Studies the history of Czechoslovak Jews, collects material and disseminates information through the publication of books and pamphlets. *The Jews of Czechoslovakia* book series: Vol. I (1968), Vol. II (1971), Vol. III (1984). *Annual reports and pamphlets.*

YESHIVA UNIVERSITY MUSEUM (1973). 2520 Amsterdam Ave., NYC 10033. (212)-960-5390. Dir. Sylvia A. Herskowitz. Collects, preserves, interprets, and displays ceremonial objects, rare books and scrolls, models, paintings, and decorative arts expressing the Jewish religious experience historically, to the present. Major exhibition for 1985–1986 is "The Art of Celebration and Ashkenaz: The German Jewish Heritage." Changing exhibits of contemporary artists and historical subjects; programs for adults and children. *Annual illustrated exhibition catalogue.*

YIDDISHER KULTUR FARBAND—YKUF (1937). 1123 Broadway, Rm. 305, NYC 10010. (212)691-0708. Pres. Itche Goldberg. Publishes a monthly magazine and books by contemporary and classical Jewish writers; conducts cultural forums; exhibits works by contemporary Jewish artists and materials of Jewish historical value; organizes reading circles. *Yiddishe Kultur.*

YIVO INSTITUTE FOR JEWISH RESEARCH, INC. (1925). 1048 Fifth Ave., NYC 10028. (212)535-6700. Pres. Arthur A. Cohen; Exec. Dir. Samuel Norich. Engages in social and humanistic research pertaining to East European Jewish life; maintains library and archives which provide a major international, national, and New York resource used by institutions, individual scholars, and laymen; trains graduate students in Yiddish, East European, and American Jewish studies; offers exhibits, conferences, public programs; publishes books. *Yedies fun Yivo—News of the Yivo; Yidishe Shprakh; Yivo Annual of Jewish Social Science; Yivo Bleter.*

——, MAX WEINREICH CENTER FOR ADVANCED JEWISH STUDIES (1968). 1048 Fifth Ave., NYC 10028. (212)535-6700. Act. Dean Marvin I. Herzog. Trains scholars and nonacademics in the language, history, folklore, and literature of East European Jewry; sponsors lecture series and exhibits; offers courses for credit in conjunction with Columbia University; conducts a summer Yiddish-language program. *Working papers in Yiddish and East European Jewish studies.*

OVERSEAS AID

AMERICAN ASSOCIATION FOR ETHIOPIAN JEWS (1974). 2789 Oak St., Highland Park, IL 60035. (312)433-8150. Pres. Nate Shapiro. Provides relief, rescue, and resettlement of Ethiopian Jews in Israel.

AMERICAN FRIENDS OF THE ALLIANCE ISRAÉLITE UNIVERSELLE, INC. (1946). 135 William St., NYC 10038. (212)349-0537. Pres. Arnold C. Franco; Exec. Dir. Jack Kantrowitz. Helps and supports the Alliance network of Jewish schools, remedial programs, and teacher training in Israel, North Africa, the Middle East and Europe. *Alliance Review; AF Notes.*

AMERICAN JEWISH JOINT DISTRIBUTION COMMITTEE, INC.—JDC (1914). 60 E. 42 St., NYC 10165. (212)687-6200. Pres. Heinz Eppler; Exec. V. Pres. Saul B. Cohen. Organizes and finances rescue, relief, and rehabilitation programs for imperiled and needy Jews overseas; conducts wide range of health, welfare, rehabilitation, education programs and aid to cultural and religious institutions; programs benefiting 500,000 Jews in over 30 countries overseas. Major areas of operation are Israel, North Africa, and Europe. *JDC Annual Report; JDC World.*

AMERICAN JEWISH PHILANTHROPIC FUND (1955). 386 Park Ave. S., NYC 10016. (212)684-1525. Pres. Charles J. Tanenbaum. Provides resettlement and retraining assistance to Jewish refugees primarily

through programs administered by the International Rescue Committee at its offices in Western Europe and the U.S.

AMERICAN ORT FEDERATION, INC.—ORGANIZATION FOR REHABILITATION THROUGH TRAINING (1924). 817 Broadway, NYC 10003. (212)677-4400. Pres. Alvin L. Gray; Exec. V. Pres. Donald H. Klein. Teaches vocational skills in 30 countries around the world, maintaining 800 schools for over 120,000 students annually, with the largest program of 80,000 trainees in Israel. The teaching staff numbers 4,000. Annual cost of program is about $99 million. *ORT Bulletin; ORT Yearbook.*

——, AMERICAN AND EUROPEAN FRIENDS OF ORT (1941). 817 Broadway, NYC 10003. (212)677-4400. Pres. Simon Jaglom; Chmn. Exec. Com. Jacques Zwibak. Promotes the ORT idea among Americans of European extraction; supports the Litton ORT Auto-Mechanics School in Jerusalem and the ORT School of Engineering in Jerusalem. Promotes the work of the American ORT Federation.

——, AMERICAN LABOR ORT (1937). 817 Broadway, NYC 10003. (212)677-4400. Chmn. Edward Schneider. Promotes ORT program of vocational training among Jews through activities of the ILGWU and the Amalgamated Clothing & Textile Workers Union. Promotes the work of the American ORT Federation.

——, BUSINESS AND PROFESSIONAL ORT (formerly YOUNG MEN'S AND WOMEN'S ORT) (1937). 817 Broadway, NYC 10003. (212)677-4770. Pres. Rose Seidel Kalich; Exec. Sec. Helen S. Kreisler. Promotes work of American ORT Federation.

——, NATIONAL ORT LEAGUE (1914). 817 Broadway, NYC 10003. (212)677-4400. Pres. Judah Wattenberg; First V. Pres. Tibor Waldman. Promotes ORT idea among Jewish fraternal *landsmanshaften* and individuals. Promotes the work of the American ORT Federation.

——, WOMEN'S AMERICAN ORT (1927). 315 Park Ave. S., NYC 10010. (212)505-7700. Pres. Gertrude S. White; Exec. V. Pres. Nathan Gould. Represents and advances the program and philosophy of ORT among the women of the American Jewish community through membership and educational activities; materially supports the vocational training operations of World ORT; contributes to the American Jewish community by encouraging participation in ORT campaigns and through general education to help raise the level of Jewish consciousness among American Jewish women; through its American Affairs program, cooperates in efforts to improve the quality of education and vocational training in the U.S. *Facts and Findings; Highlights; Insights; The Merchandiser; Women's American ORT Reporter.*

A.R.I.F.—ASSOCIATION POUR LE RÉTABLISSEMENT DES INSTITUTIONS ET OEUVRES ISRAÉLITES EN FRANCE, INC. (1944). 119 E. 95 St., NYC 10028. (212)-876-1448. Pres. Baroness Robert de Gunzburg; Sec.-Treas. Simon Langer. Helps Jewish religious and cultural institutions in France.

CONFERENCE ON JEWISH MATERIAL CLAIMS AGAINST GERMANY, INC. (1951). 15 E. 26 St., Rm. 1355, NYC 10010. (212)-696-4944. Pres. Israel Miller; Sec. and Exec. Dir. Saul Kagan. Monitors the implementation of restitution and indemnification programs of the German Federal Republic (FRG) arising from its agreements with FRG. Administers Hardship Fund, which distributes DM 400,000,000 appropriated by FRG for Jewish Nazi victims unable to file timely claims under original indemnification laws. Also assists needy non-Jews who risked their lives to help Jewish survivors. *Periodic reports.*

HIAS, INC. (HEBREW IMMIGRANT AID SOCIETY) (1880; reorg. 1954). 200 Park Ave. S., NYC 10003. (212)674-6800. Pres. Robert L. Israeloff; Exec. V. Pres. Karl D. Zukerman. International Jewish migration agency with headquarters in the U.S. and offices, affiliates, and representatives in Europe, Latin America, Canada, Australia, New Zealand, and Israel. Assists Jewish migrants and refugees from Eastern Europe, the Middle East, North Africa, and Latin America. Via U.S. government-funded programs, assists in the resettlement of Indo-Chinese and other refugees. *HIAS Annual Report; HIAS Reporter; Quarterly Statistical Abstract.*

JEWISH RESTITUTION SUCCESSOR ORGANIZATION (1947). 15 E. 26 St., NYC 10010. (212)696-4944. Sec. and Exec. Dir. Saul Kagan. Acts to discover, claim, receive,

and assist in the recovery of Jewish heirless or unclaimed property; to utilize such assets or to provide for their utilization for the relief, rehabilitation, and resettlement of surviving victims of Nazi persecution.

THANKS TO SCANDINAVIA, INC. (1963). 745 Fifth Ave., Rm. 603, NYC 10151. (212)-486-8600. Natl. Chmn. Victor Borge; Pres. and Exec. Officer Richard Netter. Provides scholarships and fellowships at American universities and medical centers to students and doctors from Denmark, Finland, Norway, and Sweden in appreciation of the rescue of Jews from the Holocaust. Informs current and future generations of Americans and Scandinavians of these singular examples of humanity and bravery. *Annual Report.*

UNITED JEWISH APPEAL, INC. (1939). 99 Park Ave., NYC 10016. (212)757-1500. Pres. Stanley Horowitz; Chmn. Bd. of Trustees Robert E. Loup; Natl. Chmn. Alexander Grass. Channels funds for overseas humanitarian aid, supports immigration, Youth Aliyah, and rural settlements in Israel, through the United Israel Appeal; provides additional humanitarian assistance in 30 countries around the world through the American Jewish Joint Distribution Committee. *Newsbrief.*

———, FACULTY ADVISORY CABINET (1975). 99 Park Ave., NYC 10016. (212)-757-1500. Chmn. Seymour Martin Lipset; Dir. Richard A. Davis. Promotes faculty leadership support for local and national UJA campaigns through educational and personal commitment; uses faculty resources and expertise on behalf of UJA and Israel.

———, RABBINIC CABINET (1972). 99 Park Ave., NYC 10016. (212)757-1500. Chmn. Rabbi Haskel Lookstein; Dir. Oscar Groner. Promotes rabbinic leadership support for local and national UJA campaigns through education and personal commitment; uses rabbinic resources on behalf of UJA and Israel.

———, UNIVERSITY PROGRAMS DEPT. (1970). 99 Park Ave., NYC 10016. (212)-757-1500. Student Advisory Board Chmn. Alan Semal. Crystallizes Jewish commitment on the campus through an educational fund-raising campaign involving various programs, leadership training, and opportunities for participation in community functions.

——, WOMEN'S DIVISION OF (1946). 99 Park Ave., NYC 10016. (212)757-1500. Pres. Harriet Zimmerman; Chmn. Judith A. Levy; Dir. Nan Goldberg. Strengthens communities to raise funds for Israel and Jews worldwide. *Campaign Network Newsletter.*

——, YOUNG LEADERSHIP CABINET (1977). 99 Park Ave., NYC 10016. (212)-757-1500. Exec. Dir. Michael Reiner; Chmn. Michael M. Adler. Committed to the creative survival of Jews, Judaism, and Israel through dialogues with leading scholars and writers, and through peer exchanges at retreats, conferences, missions to Israel, and special programs. *In Process; Judaica series.*

——, YOUNG WOMEN'S LEADERSHIP CABINET (1977). 99 Park Ave., NYC 10016 (212)757-1500. Chmn. Ann-Louise Levine. Focuses on bringing more career women into the UJA campaign; features a career women's Campaign Institute, special missions to Israel, and in-depth Israel experience for top women executives and leaders. A training and service organization offering the opportunity to enhance skills and put those skills to use through UJA programs, regional and national seminars, speaking engagements, and heightened local involvement. *Showcase.*

WOMEN'S SOCIAL SERVICE FOR ISRAEL, INC. (1937). 240 W. 98 St., NYC 10025. (212)666-7880. Pres. Ursula Merkin; Sec. Dory Gordon. Maintains in Israel subsidized housing for self-reliant older people, old-age homes for more dependent elderly, Lichtenstadter Hospital for chronically ill, subsidized meals, distribution of clothing collected in U.S. All-volunteer group in New York. *Annual Journal.*

RELIGIOUS AND EDUCATIONAL

AGUDATH ISRAEL OF AMERICA (1912). 5 Beekman St., NYC 10038. (212)791-1800. Pres. Rabbi Moshe Sherer; Exec. Dir. Rabbi Boruch B. Borchardt. Mobilizes Orthodox Jews to cope with Jewish problems in the spirit of the Torah; sponsors a broad range of constructive projects in religion, education, children's welfare, protection of Jewish religious rights, outreach, and social services. *Jewish Observer; Dos Yiddishe Vort.*

——, CHILDREN'S DIVISION—PIRCHEI AGUDATH ISRAEL (1925). 5 Beekman St.,

NYC 10038 (212)791-1800. Pres. Shimon Katz; Dir. Joshua Silbermintz. Educates Orthodox Jewish children in Torah; encourages sense of communal responsibility; communal celebrations, learning groups, and welfare projects. *Darkeinu; Leaders Guide.*

——, GIRLS' DIVISION—BNOS AGUDATH ISRAEL (1921). 5 Beekman St., NYC 10038. (212)791-1800. Coord. Sara Zimmerman. Educates Jewish girls to the historic nature of the Jewish people as the people of the Torah; encourages greater devotion to and understanding of the Torah. *Kol Bnos.*

——, WOMEN'S DIVISION—N'SHEI AGUDATH ISRAEL OF AMERICA (1940). 5 Beekman St., NYC 10038. (212)227-5715. Pres. Esther Bohensky, Aliza Grund. Organizes Jewish women for philanthropic work in the U.S. and Israel and for intensive Torah education. Seeks to train Torah-guided Jewish mothers.

——, YOUTH DIVISION—ZEIREI AGUDATH ISRAEL (1921). 5 Beekman St., NYC 10038. (212)791-1820. Pres. Yisroel Greenwald; Exec. Dir. Labish Becker. Educates Jewish youth to realize the historic nature of the Jewish people as the people of the Torah and to seek solutions to all the problems of the Jewish people in Israel in the spirit of the Torah. Carries out projects in religious, educational, and community-welfare fields. *The Zeirei Forum; Am Hatorah; Daf Chizuk; Yom Tov Publications.*

AGUDATH ISRAEL WORLD ORGANIZATION (1912). 5 Beekman St., NYC 10038. (212)-791-1800. Cochmn. Rabbi Moshe Sherer, Rabbi Yehudah Meir Abramowitz. Represents the interests of Orthodox Jewry on the national and international scenes. Sponsors projects to strengthen Torah life worldwide.

AMERICAN ASSOCIATION OF RABBIS (1978). 350 Fifth Ave., Suite 3308, NYC 10001. (212)244-3350. Pres. Rabbi David L. Dunn; Sec. Rabbi Robert Chernoff. An organization of rabbis serving in pulpits, and in the fields of education and social work. Provides rabbinical fraternity and placement services. *Quarterly Newsletter.*

ASSOCIATION FOR JEWISH STUDIES (1969). Widener Library M., Harvard University, Cambridge, MA 02138. (617)495-2985.

Pres. Nahum M. Sarna; Exec. Sec. Charles Berlin. Seeks to promote, maintain, and improve the teaching of Jewish studies in American colleges and universities by sponsoring meetings and conferences, publishing a newsletter and other scholarly materials, setting standards for programs in Jewish studies, aiding in the placement of teachers, coordinating research, and cooperating with other scholarly organizations. *AJS Review; Newsletter.*

ASSOCIATION OF HILLEL/JEWISH CAMPUS PROFESSIONALS (1949). 2615 Clifton Ave., Cincinnati, OH 45220. (513)221-6728. Pres. Abie Ingber; V. Pres. Paul Golomb. Seeks to promote professional relationships and exchanges of experience, develop personnel standards and qualifications, safeguard integrity of Hillel profession; represents and advocates before National Hillel Staff, National Hillel Commission, B'nai B'rith International, Council of Jewish Federations. *AHJCP Bulletin.*

ASSOCIATION OF JEWISH CHAPLAINS OF THE ARMED FORCES (1946). 15 E. 26 St., NYC 10010. (212)532-4949. Pres. Rabbi Alvin I. Lieberman; Sec. Rabbi Jacob Greenberg. An organization of former and current chaplains of the U.S. armed forces which seeks to enhance the religious program of Jewish chaplains in the armed forces and in Veterans Administration hospitals.

ASSOCIATION OF ORTHODOX JEWISH SCIENTISTS (1947). 1373 Coney Island Ave., Brooklyn, NY 11219. (718)338-8592. Pres. Sheldon Kornbluth; Bd. Chmn. Nora Smith. Seeks to contribute to the development of science within the framework of Orthodox Jewish tradition; to obtain and disseminate information relating to the interaction between the Jewish traditional way of life and scientific developments—on both an ideological and practical level; to assist in the solution of problems pertaining to Orthodox Jews engaged in scientific teaching or research. Two main conventions are held each year. *Intercom; Proceedings; Halacha Bulletin; Newsletter.*

BETH MEDROSH ELYON (ACADEMY OF HIGHER LEARNING AND RESEARCH) (1943). 73 Main St., Monsey, NY 10952. (914)356-7065. Bd. Chmn. Emanuel Weldler; Treas. Arnold Jacobs; Sec. Yerachmiel Censor. Provides postgraduate courses and research work in higher Jewish studies; offers scholarships and fellowships. *Annual Journal.*

B'NAI B'RITH HILLEL FOUNDATIONS, INC. (1923). 1640 Rhode Island Ave., NW, Washington, DC 20036. (202)857-6560. Chmn. B'nai B'rith Hillel Comm. Edwin Shapiro; Internatl. Dir. Larry S. Moses. Provides a program of cultural, religious, educational, social, and counseling content to Jewish college and university students on more than 400 campuses in the U.S., Australia, Canada, England, Israel, Europe, and S. America. Also sponsors Academic Associates, National Jewish Law Students Network, and Student Secretariat. *Jewish Life on Campus; Igeret; NJLSN Newsletter; Chadashot-Secretariat Newsletter.*

B'NAI B'RITH YOUTH ORGANIZATION (1924). 1640 Rhode Island Ave., NW, Washington, DC 20036. (202)857-6633. Chmn. Youth Com. Aaron Grossman; Internatl. Dir. Sidney Clearfield. Helps Jewish teenagers achieve self-fulfillment and make a maximum contribution to the Jewish community and their country's culture; helps members acquire a greater knowledge and appreciation of Jewish religion and culture. *BBYO Advisor; Monday Morning; Shofar; Hakol; Kesher.*

BRAMSON ORT (1977). 44 E. 23 St., NYC 10010. (212)677-7420. Dir. Ira L. Jaskoll. A two-year technical college offering certificates and associate degrees in high technology and business fields, as well as Jewish studies. Houses the Center for Computers in Jewish Education. *Jewish Computer Newsletter.*

BRANDEIS-BARDIN INSTITUTE (1941). 1101 Peppertree Lane, Brandeis, CA 93064. (818)348-7201. Pres. Ira Weiner. Maintains Brandeis Camp Institute (BCI), a Jewish student leadership program for college-age adults; Camp Alonim for children 8–16; introductory and membership House of the Book weekends for adults 25+, in an effort to instill an appreciation of Jewish cultural and spiritual heritage and to create a desire for active participation in Jewish communities. *Brandeis-Bardin Institute News.*

CANTORS ASSEMBLY (1947). 150 Fifth Ave., NYC 10011. (212)691-8020. Pres. Saul Z. Hammerman; Exec. V. Pres. Samuel Rosenbaum. Seeks to unite all cantors who adhere to traditional Judaism and who serve as full-time cantors in bona fide congregations, to conserve and promote the musical traditions of the Jews and to elevate the status of the cantorial profession. *Annual Proceedings; Journal of Synagogue Music.*

CENTRAL CONFERENCE OF AMERICAN RABBIS (1889). 21 E. 40 St., NYC 10016. (212)684-4990. Pres. Rabbi Jack Stern; Exec. V. Pres. Rabbi Joseph B. Glaser. Seeks to conserve and promote Judaism and to disseminate its teachings in a liberal spirit. *Journal of Reform Judaism; CCAR Yearbook.*

CENTRAL YESHIVA BETH JOSEPH RABBINICAL SEMINARY (in Europe 1891; in U.S. 1941). 1427 49 St., Brooklyn, NY 11219. Pres. and Dean Jacob Jofen. Maintains a school for teaching Orthodox rabbis and teachers, and promoting the cause of higher Torah learning.

CLEVELAND COLLEGE OF JEWISH STUDIES (1964). 26500 Shaker Blvd., Beachwood, OH 44122. (216)464-4050. Pres. David Ariel; Bd. Chmn. Dan Polster. Provides courses in all areas of Judaic and Hebrew studies to adults and college-age students; offers continuing education for Jewish educators and administrators; serves as a center for Jewish life and culture; expands the availability of courses in Judaic studies by exchanging faculty, students, and credits with neighboring academic institutions; grants bachelor's and master's degrees.

COALITION FOR ALTERNATIVES IN JEWISH EDUCATION (CAJE) (1976). 468 Park Ave. S., Rm. 904, NYC 10016. (212)696-0740. Chmn. Stuart Kelman; Dir. Eliot G. Spack. Brings together Jews from all ideologies who are involved in every facet of Jewish education, and are committed to transmitting Jewish knowledge, culture, and experience; serves as a channel of communication for its membership to share resources and methods, and as a forum for exchange of philosophical and theoretical approaches to Jewish education. Sponsors programs and projects. *Bikurim; Crisis Curricula; Mekasher; CAJE Jewish Education News.*

COUNCIL FOR JEWISH EDUCATION (1926). 114 Fifth Ave., NYC 10011. (212)675-5656. Pres. Elliot Schwartz; Comptroller Jack M. Horden. Fellowship of Jewish education professionals, comprising administrators and supervisors of national and local Jewish educational institutions and agencies, and teachers in Hebrew high schools and Jewish teachers colleges, of all ideological groupings; conducts annual national and regional conferences in all areas of Jewish education; represents the Jewish education profession before the Jewish community; cosponsors, with the Jewish Education Service of North America, a personnel committee and other projects; cooperates with Jewish Agency Department of Education and Culture in promoting Hebrew culture and studies; conducts lectureship at Hebrew University. *Jewish Education; Sheviley Hahinuch.*

DROPSIE COLLEGE FOR HEBREW AND COGNATE LEARNING (1907). 250 N. Highland Ave., Merion, PA 19066. (215)667-1830. Pres. David M. Goldenberg. The only nonsectarian and nontheological graduate institution in America completely dedicated to Judaic and Near Eastern studies; offers graduate programs in these areas. Courses include the cultures and languages of Arabic, Aramaic, Ugaritic, Akkadian, and ancient Egyptian peoples; offers MA and PhD degrees. *Jewish Quarterly Review.*

——, ALUMNI ASSOCIATION OF (1925). 250 N. Highland Ave., Philadelphia, PA 19066. (215)667-1830. Pres. Ezra Shereshevsky. Promotes good relationship between the college and graduates.

FEDERATION OF JEWISH MEN'S CLUBS, INC. (1929). 475 Riverside Dr., Suite 244, NYC 10115. (212)749-8100. Pres. Jules Porter; Exec. Dir. Rabbi Charles Simon. Promotes principles and objectives of Conservative Judaism by organizing, sponsoring, and developing men's clubs or brotherhoods; supports OMETZ Center for Conservative Judaism on Campus; promotes Home Library of Conservative Judaism and the Art of Jewish Living series; sponsors Hebrew Literacy Adult Education Program; presents awards for service to American Jewry. *Torchlight.*

GRATZ COLLEGE (1895). 10 St. and Tabor Rd., Philadelphia, PA 19141. (215)329-3363. Bd. Chmn. Stephen Sussman; Pres. Gary S. Schiff. Offers a wide variety of bachelor's, master's, teacher-training, continuing-education, and high-school-level programs in Judaic, Hebraic, and Middle Eastern studies. Grants BA and MA in

Jewish studies, Bachelor and Master of Hebrew Literature, MA in Jewish education, MA in Jewish music, certificates in Judaica librarianship, Sephardic studies, Jewish chaplaincy, and other credentials. Joint bachelor's programs with Temple University and Beaver College. Gratz College's Division of Community Services serves as the central agency for Jewish education in Greater Philadelphia, providing consultation and resources to Jewish schools, organizations, and individuals. *Various newsletters, a yearbook, and scholarly publications.*

HEBREW COLLEGE (1921). 43 Hawes St., Brookline, MA 02146. (617)277-1551. Pres. Eli Grad; Bd. Chmn. Leon Brock. Provides intensive programs of study in all areas of Jewish culture from high school through college and graduate school levels, also at branch in Hartford; maintains ongoing programs with most major local universities; offers the degrees of Master of Jewish Studies, Bachelor and Master of Hebrew Literature, and Bachelor and Master of Jewish Education, with teaching certification; trains men and women to teach, conduct, and supervise Jewish schools; offers extensive Ulpan program; offers courses designed to deepen the community's awareness of the Jewish heritage. *Hebrew College Bulletin.*

HEBREW THEOLOGICAL COLLEGE (1922). 7135 N. Carpenter Rd., Skokie, IL 60077. (312)267-9800. Pres. Rabbi Don Well; Bd. Chmn. Aaron Regensberg. An institution of higher Jewish learning which includes a division of advanced Hebrew studies, a school of liberal arts and sciences, a rabbinical ordination program, a graduate school in Judaic studies and pastoral counseling; the Fasman Yeshiva High School; a high school summer program combining Torah studies and computer science courses; and a Jewish studies program. *Newsletter; Annual Journal.*

HEBREW UNION COLLEGE—JEWISH INSTITUTE OF RELIGION (1875). 3101 Clifton Ave., Cincinnati, OH 45220. (513)221-1875. Pres. Alfred Gottschalk; Exec. Dean Eugene Mihaly; Exec. V. Pres. Uri D. Herscher; Chmn. Bd. of Govs. Richard J. Scheuer. Academic centers: 3101 Clifton Ave., Cincinnati, OH 45220 (1875), Samuel Greengus, Dean; 1 W. 4 St., NYC 10012 (1922), Paul M. Steinberg, Dean; 3077 University Ave., Los Angeles, CA

90007 (1954), Uri D. Herscher, Chief Admin. Officer; 13 King David St., Jerusalem, Israel (1963), Michael Klein, Dean. Prepares students for Reform rabbinate, cantorate, religious-school teaching and administration, community service, academic careers; promotes Jewish studies; maintains libraries and a museum; offers bachelor's, master's, and doctoral degrees; engages in archaeological excavations; publishes scholarly works through Hebrew Union College Press. *American Jewish Archives; Bibliographica Judaica; HUC—JIR Catalogue; Hebrew Union College Annual; Studies in Bibliography and Booklore; The Chronicle.*

————, AMERICAN JEWISH ARCHIVES (1947). 3101 Clifton Ave., Cincinnati, OH 45220. (513)221-1875. Dir. Jacob R. Marcus; Admin. Dir. Abraham Peck. Promotes the study and preservation of the Western Hemisphere Jewish experience through research, publications, collection of important source materials, and a vigorous public-outreach program. *American Jewish Archives; monographs, publications, and pamphlets.*

————, AMERICAN JEWISH PERIODICAL CENTER (1957). 3101 Clifton Ave., Cincinnati, OH 45220. Dir. Jacob R. Marcus; Codir. Herbert C. Zafren. Maintains microfilms of all American Jewish periodicals 1823–1925, selected periodicals since 1925. *Jewish Periodicals and Newspapers on Microfilm (1957); First Supplement (1960); Augmented Edition (1984).*

————, EDGAR F. MAGNIN SCHOOL OF GRADUATE STUDIES (1956). 3077 University Ave., Los Angeles, CA 90007. (213)-749-3424. Dir. Stanley Chyet. Supervises programs leading to PhD (Education), DHS, DHL, and MA degrees; participates in cooperative PhD programs with the University of Southern California.

————, JEROME H. LOUCHHEIM SCHOOL OF JUDAIC STUDIES (1969). 3077 University Ave. Los Angeles, CA 90007. (213)749-3424. Dir. David Ellenson. Offers programs leading to MA, BS, BA, and AA degrees; offers courses as part of the undergraduate program of the University of Southern California.

————, NELSON GLUECK SCHOOL OF BIBLICAL ARCHAEOLOGY (1963). 13 King David St., Jerusalem, Israel. Dir. Avraham

Biran. Offers graduate-level programs in Bible, archaeology, and Judaica. Summer excavations are carried out by scholars and students. University credit may be earned by participants in excavations. Consortium of colleges, universities, and seminaries is affiliated with the school.

———, RHEA HIRSCH SCHOOL OF EDUCATION (1967). 3077 University Ave., Los Angeles, CA 90007. (213)749-3424. Dir. Sara S. Lee. Offers PhD and MA programs in Jewish and Hebrew education; conducts joint degree programs with University of Southern California; offers courses for Jewish teachers, librarians, and early educators on a nonmatriculating basis; conducts summer institutes for professional Jewish educators.

———, SCHOOL OF EDUCATION (1947). 1 W. 4 St., NYC 10012. (212)674-5300. V. Pres. and Dean Paul M. Steinberg; Dir. Kerry Olitzky. Trains and certifies teachers and principals for Reform religious schools; offers MA degree with specialization in religious education; offers extension programs in various suburban centers.

———, SCHOOL OF GRADUATE STUDIES (1949). 3101 Clifton Ave., Cincinnati, OH 45220. Dean Samuel Greengus. Offers programs leading to MA and PhD degrees; offers program leading to DHL degree for rabbinic graduates of the college.

———, SCHOOL OF JEWISH COMMUNAL SERVICE (1968). 3077 University Ave., Los Angeles, CA 90007. Dir. Gerald B. Bubis. Offers certificate and master's degree to those employed in Jewish communal services, or preparing for such work; offers joint MA in Jewish education and communal service with Rhea Hirsch School; offers MA and MSW in conjunction with the University of Southern California School of Social Work, with the George Warren Brown School of Social Work of Washington University, and with the University of Pittsburgh School of Social Work.

———, SCHOOL OF JEWISH STUDIES (1963). 13 King David St., Jerusalem, Israel. Dean Michael Klein. Offers program leading to ordination for Israeli students; offers an academic, work-study year for undergraduate students from American colleges and universities; offers a one-year program in cooperation with Hebrew University for advanced students, and a one-year program for all first-year rabbinic students of the college and for master's degree candidates of the Rhea Hirsch School of Education.

———, SCHOOL OF SACRED MUSIC (1947). 1 W. 4 St., NYC 10012. (212)674-5300. V. Pres. and Dean Paul M. Steinberg; Dir. Lawrence A. Hoffman. Trains cantors and music personnel for congregations; offers MA degree. *Sacred Music Press.*

———, SKIRBALL MUSEUM (1913; 1972 in Calif.). 3077 University Ave., Los Angeles, CA 90007. Dir. Nancy Berman; Curator Grace Grossman. Collects, preserves, researches, and exhibits art and artifacts made by or for Jews, or otherwise associated with Jews and Judaism. Provides opportunity to faculty and students to do research in the field of Jewish art. *Catalogues of exhibits and collections.*

HERZLIAH-JEWISH TEACHERS SEMINARY (1967). Division of Touro College. 30 W. 44 St., NYC 10036. (212)575-0190. Pres. Bernard Lander; Dir. Jacob Katzman.

———, GRADUATE SCHOOL OF JEWISH STUDIES. Offers programs leading to MA in Jewish studies, including Hebrew language and literature, Jewish education, history, philosophy, and sociology. Admits men and women who have bachelor's degrees and backgrounds in Hebrew, Yiddish, and Jewish studies.

———, JEWISH PEOPLE'S UNIVERSITY OF THE AIR. (212)575-1819. Dir. Jacob Katzman; Coord. Marie Alderman. The educational outreach arm of Touro College, it produces and disseminates Jewish educational and cultural programming for radio broadcast and audio-cassettes.

———, MUSIC DIVISION (1964). Performing Arts Div. Dir. Cantor Marvin Antosofsky. Offers studies in traditional and contemporary music—religious, Yiddish, secular, and Hebraic; offers certificate and degree programs in Jewish music education and cantorial art, and artist diploma.

INSTITUTE FOR COMPUTERS IN JEWISH LIFE (1978). 845 N. Michigan Ave., Suite 843, Chicago, IL 60611. (312)787-7856. Pres. Thomas Klutznick; Exec. V. Pres. Irving J. Rosenbaum. Explores, develops, and disseminates applications of computer technology to appropriate areas of Jewish life, with special emphasis on Jewish education; provides access to the Bar-Ilan University Responsa Project; creates educational software for use in Jewish schools; provides consulting service and assistance for national Jewish organizations, seminaries, and synagogues. *Monitor.*

JEWISH CHAUTAUQUA SOCIETY, INC. (sponsored by NATIONAL FEDERATION OF TEMPLE BROTHERHOODS) (1893). 838 Fifth Ave., NYC 10021. (212)570-0707. Pres. Marshall Blair; Exec. Dir. Av Bondarin. Disseminates authoritative information on Jews and Judaism; assigns rabbis to lecture at colleges; endows courses in Judaism for college credit at universities; donates Jewish reference books to college libraries; sends rabbis to serve as counselor-teachers at Christian church summer camps and as chaplains at Boy Scout camps; sponsors institutes on Judaism for Christian clergy; produces motion pictures for public-service television and group showings. *Brotherhood.*

JEWISH EDUCATION IN MEDIA, INC. (1978). P.O. Box 180, Riverdale Station, NYC 10471. (212)362-7633. Exec. Dir. Rabbi Mark S. Golub. Seeks to promote Jewish identity and commitment through the creation of innovative and entertaining media materials, including radio and television programming, film, and audio and video cassettes for synagogue and institutional use.

JEWISH EDUCATION SERVICE OF NORTH AMERICA, INC. (JESNA) (1981). 730 Broadway, NYC 10003. (212)529-2000. Pres. Mark Schlussel; Acting Exec. V. Pres. David Resnick. Coordinates, promotes, and services Jewish education in federated communities of North America. Coordinating center for Jewish education bureaus; offers curricular advisement and maintains a National Educational Resource Center; runs regional pedagogic conferences; conducts evaluative surveys on Jewish education; engages in statistical and other educational research; provides community consultations; sponsors the National Board of License; administers Fellowships in Jewish Educational Leadership training program (FIJEL); provides placement of upper-level bureau and communal school personnel and educators. *Pedagogic Reporter; TRENDS; Information Research Bulletins; Jewish Education Directory; Annual Report.*

JEWISH MINISTERS CANTORS ASSOCIATION OF AMERICA, INC. (1896). 3 W. 16 St., NYC 10011. (212)675-6601. Pres. Henry Butensky. Furthers and propagates traditional liturgy; places cantors in synagogues throughout the U.S. and Canada; develops the cantors of the future. *Kol Lakol.*

JEWISH RECONSTRUCTIONIST FOUNDATION (1940). 270 W. 89 St., NYC 10024. (212)-496-2960. Bd. Chmn. Samuel Blumenthal; Exec. Dir. David A. Teutsch. Dedicated to the advancement of Judaism as the evolving religious civilization of the Jewish people. Coordinates the Federation of Reconstructionist Congregations and Havurot, Reconstructionist Rabbinical Association, and Reconstructionist Rabbinical College.

——, FEDERATION OF RECONSTRUCTIONIST CONGREGATIONS AND HAVUROT (1954). 270 W. 89 St., NYC 10024. (212)-496-2960. Pres. Lillian Kaplan; Exec. Dir. David A. Teutsch. Services affiliated congregations and havurot educationally and administratively; fosters the establishment of new Reconstructionist congregations and fellowship groups. Runs the Reconstructionist Press and provides programmatic materials. *Newsletter; Reconstructionist.*

——, RECONSTRUCTIONIST RABBINICAL ASSOCIATION (1975). Greenwood Ave. and Church Rd., Wyncote, PA 19095. (215)576-0800. Pres. Rabbi Ira J. Schiffer; Exec. Dir. Rabbi Richard Hirsh. Professional organization for graduates of the Reconstructionist Rabbinical College and other rabbis who identify with Reconstructionist Judaism; cooperates with Federation of Reconstructionist Congregations and Havurot in furthering Reconstructionism in N. America. *Raayanot.*

JEWISH TEACHERS ASSOCIATION—MORIM (1931). 45 E. 33 St., NYC 10016. (212)-684-0556. Pres. Phyllis L. Pullman; V. Pres. Eli Nieman. Promotes the religious, social, and moral welfare of children; provides a program of professional, cultural, and social activities for its members; cooperates with other organizations for the promotion of goodwill and understanding. *JTA Newsletter—Morim.*

JEWISH THEOLOGICAL SEMINARY OF AMERICA (1886; reorg. 1902). 3080 Broadway, NYC 10027. (212)678-8000. Chancellor Gerson D. Cohen; Chmn. Exec.

Com. Stephen M. Peck; Bd. Chmn. Howard M. Holtzmann. Operates undergraduate and graduate programs in Judaica, departments for training rabbis and cantors, a pastoral psychiatry center, Melton Center for Jewish Education, the Jewish Museum, and such youth programs as the Ramah Camps and the OMETZ-Center for Conservative Judaism on Campus. *Conservative Judaism; Seminary Progress.*

————, AMERICAN STUDENT CENTER IN JERUSALEM (1962). P.O. Box 196, Jerusalem, Israel. Dean Reuven Hammer; Dir. Midreshet Yerushalayim, Baruch Feldstern. Offers year-in-Israel programs for graduate students, including rabbinical and cantorial students, and a program of intensive Jewish studies for undergraduates.

————, CANTORS INSTITUTE AND SEMINARY COLLEGE OF JEWISH MUSIC (1952). 3080 Broadway, NYC 10027. (212)678-8038. Dean Morton M. Leifman. Trains cantors, music teachers, and choral directors for congregations. Offers programs in sacred music leading to degrees of BSM, MSM, and DSM, and diploma of *Hazzan.*

————, DEPARTMENT OF RADIO AND TELEVISION (1944). 3080 Broadway, NYC 10027. (212)678-8020. Exec. Prod. Milton E. Krents. Produces radio and TV programs expressing the Jewish tradition in its broadest sense, with emphasis on the universal human situation: "Eternal Light," a weekly radio program; 7 "Eternal Light" TV programs, produced in cooperation with NBC; and telecasts with ABC. Distributes program scripts and related reading lists.

————, INSTITUTE FOR ADVANCED STUDY IN THE HUMANITIES (1968). 3080 Broadway, NYC 10027. (212)678-8024. Dean Mayer Rabinowitz. Graduate program leading to MA degrees in all aspects of Jewish studies and PhD in Bible, Jewish education, history, literature, philosophy, or rabbinics; offers dual degree in social work.

————, INSTITUTE FOR RELIGIOUS AND SOCIAL STUDIES (1938). 3080 Broadway, NYC 10027. (212)678-8815. Dir. Gordon Tucker. A scholarly and scientific fellowship of clergymen and other religious teachers who desire authoritative information regarding some of the basic issues now confronting spiritually minded individuals.

————, MELTON RESEARCH CENTER (1960). 3080 Broadway, NYC 10027. (212)678-8031. Dirs. Eduardo Rauch, Barry W. Holtz. Devises new curricula and materials for Jewish education; has intensive program for training curriculum writers; recruits, trains, and retrains educators through seminars and in-service programs; maintains consultant and supervisory relationships with a limited number of pilot schools. *Melton Journal.*

————, SCHOCKEN INSTITUTE FOR JEWISH RESEARCH (1961). 6 Balfour St., Jerusalem, Israel. Librarian Yaakov Katzenstein. Incorporates Schocken library and its related research institutes in medieval Hebrew poetry and Jewish mysticism. *Schocken Institute Yearbook (P'raqim).*

————, SEMINARY COLLEGE OF JEWISH STUDIES-TEACHERS INSTITUTE (1909). 3080 Broadway, NYC 10027. (212)678-8826. Dean Paula Hyman. Offers complete college program in Judaica leading to BA degree; conducts joint programs with Columbia University and Barnard enabling students to receive two BA degrees after four years.

————, UNIVERSITY OF JUDAISM (1947). 15600 Mulholland Dr., Los Angeles, CA 90024. (213)476-9777. Pres. David L. Lieber; V. Pres. Max Vorspan, Alexander Graubart, Marshall T. Meyer. West Coast school of JTS. Serves as center of undergraduate and graduate study of Judaica; offers preprofessional and professional programs in Jewish education and allied fields, including a prerabbinic program and joint program enabling students to receive BA from UCLA and BHL from U. of J. after four years, and an experimental undergraduate program in the humanities, Lee College, as well as a broad range of adult education and Jewish activities.

MACHNE ISRAEL, INC. (1940). 770 Eastern Pkwy., Brooklyn, NY 11213. (718)493-9250. Pres. Menachem M. Schneerson (Lubavitcher Rebbe); Dir., Treas. M.A. Hodakov; Sec. Nissan Mindel. The Lubavitcher movement's organ dedicated to the social, spiritual, and material welfare of Jews throughout the world.

MERKOS L'INYONEI CHINUCH, INC. (THE CENTRAL ORGANIZATION FOR JEWISH

EDUCATION) (1940). 770 Eastern Parkway, Brooklyn, NY 11213. (718)493-9250. Pres. Menachem M. Schneerson (Lubavitcher Rebbe); Dir., Treas. M.A. Hodakov; Sec. Nissan Mindel. The educational arm of the Lubavitcher movement. Seeks to promote Jewish education among Jews, regardless of their background, in the spirit of Torah-true Judaism; to establish contact with alienated Jewish youth; to stimulate concern and active interest in Jewish education on all levels; and to promote religious observance as a daily experience among all Jews; maintains worldwide network of regional offices, schools, summer camps, and Chabad-Lubavitch Houses; publishes Jewish educational literature in numerous languages and monthly journal in five languages: *Conversaciones con la juventud; Conversations avec les jeunes; Schmuessen mit kinder un yugent; Sihot la No-ar; Talks and Tales.*

MESIVTA YESHIVA RABBI CHAIM BERLIN RABBINICAL ACADEMY (1905). 1593 Coney Island Ave., Brooklyn, NY 11230. (718)377-0777. Pres. Sol Eiger; Admin. Yerachmiel Stuppler. Maintains fully accredited elementary and high schools; collegiate and postgraduate school for advanced Jewish studies, both in America and Israel; Camp Morris, a summer study retreat; Prof. Nathan Isaacs Memorial Library; Gur Aryeh Publications.

MIRRER YESHIVA CENTRAL INSTITUTE (in Poland 1817; in U.S. 1947). 1791–5 Ocean Parkway, Brooklyn, NY 11223. Pres. and Dean Rabbi Shrage Moshe Klamanowitz; Exec. Dir. and Sec. Manfred Handelsman. Maintains rabbinical college, postgraduate school for Talmudic research, accredited high school, and Kollel and Sephardic divisions; dedicated to the dissemination of Torah scholarship in the community and abroad; engages in rescue and rehabilitation of scholars overseas.

NATIONAL COMMITTEE FOR FURTHERANCE OF JEWISH EDUCATION (1941). 824 Eastern Parkway, Brooklyn, NY 11213. (718)735-0200. Pres. J. James Plessen; Bd. Chmn. Martin Domansky; Sec. Milton Kramer; Exec. V. Pres. Jacob J. Hecht. Seeks to disseminate the ideals of Torah-true education among the youth of America; aids poor, sick, and needy in U.S. and Israel; provides aid to hundreds of Iranian Jewish youth through the Iranian Children's Fund; maintains camp for underprivileged children; sponsors Hadar

HaTorah and Machon Chana, seeking to win back college youth and others to the fold of Judaism; maintains schools and dormitory facilities. *Panorama; Passover Handbook; Seder Guide; Spiritual Suicide; Focus.*

NATIONAL COUNCIL OF BETH JACOB SCHOOLS, INC. (1945). 1415 E. 7 St., Brooklyn, NY 11230. (718)979-7400. Bd. Chmn. Shimon Newhouse; Sec. David Rosenberg. Operates Orthodox all-day schools from kindergarten through high school for girls, a residence high school in Ferndale, NY, a national institute for master instructors, and a summer camp for girls. *Baís Yaakov Digest; Pnimia Call.*

NATIONAL COUNCIL OF YOUNG ISRAEL (1912). 3 W. 16 St., NYC 10011. (212)-929-1525. Pres. Harold M. Jacobs; Exec. V. Pres. Rabbi Ephraim H. Sturm. Maintains a program of spiritual, cultural, social, and communal activity aimed at the advancement and perpetuation of traditional, Torah-true Judaism; seeks to instill in American youth an understanding and appreciation of the ethical and spiritual values of Judaism. Sponsors kosher dining clubs and fraternity houses and an Israel program. *Viewpoint; Hashkofa series; Masorah newspaper.*

——, AMERICAN FRIENDS OF YOUNG ISRAEL SYNAGOGUES IN ISRAEL (1926). 3 W. 16 St., NYC 10011. (212)929-1525. Chmn. Jack Levy; Exec. V. Pres. Rabbi Ephraim H. Sturm. Promotes Young Israel synagogues and youth work in synagogues in Israel.

——, ARMED FORCES BUREAU (1912). 3 W. 16 St., NYC 10011. (212)929-1525. Advises and guides the inductees into the armed forces with regard to Sabbath observance, *kashrut,* and Orthodox behavior. *Guide for the Orthodox Serviceman.*

——, EMPLOYMENT BUREAU (1912). 3 W. 16 St., NYC 10011. (212)929-1525. Exec. V. Pres. Rabbi Ephraim H. Sturm; Employment Dir. Dorothy Stein. Operates an on-the-job training program under federal contract; helps secure employment, particularly for Sabbath observers and Russian immigrants; offers vocational guidance. *Viewpoint.*

——, INSTITUTE FOR JEWISH STUDIES (1947). 3 W. 16 St., NYC 10011. (212)-929-1525. Pres. Harold M. Jacobs; Exec.

V. Pres. Rabbi Ephraim H. Sturm. Introduces students to Jewish learning and knowledge; helps form adult branch schools; aids Young Israel synagogues in their adult education programs. *Bulletin.*

———, YOUNG ISRAEL COLLEGIATES AND YOUNG ADULTS (formerly INTERCOLLEGIATE COUNCIL AND YOUNG SINGLE ADULTS) (1951; reorg. 1982). 3 W. 16 St., NYC 10011. (212)929-1525. Chmn. Kenneth Block; Dir. Richard Stareshefsky. Organizes and operates kosher dining clubs on college and university campuses; provides information and counseling on *kashrut* observance at college; gives college-age youth understanding and appreciation of Judaism and information on issues important to Jewish community; arranges seminars and meetings; publishes pamphlets and monographs. *Hashkafa.*

———, YOUNG ISRAEL YOUTH (formerly YISRAEL HATZAIR) (reorg. 1968). 3 W. 16 St., NYC 10011. (212)929-1525. Chmn. Eugene Wilk; Dir. Richard Stareshefsky. Fosters a program of spiritual, cultural, social, and communal activities for the advancement and perpetuation of traditional Torah-true Judaism; strives to instill an understanding and appreciation of the high ethical and spiritual values and to demonstrate compatibility of ancient faith of Israel with good Americanism. Operates Achva Summer Mission study program in Israel. *Monthly newsletter.*

NATIONAL JEWISH HOSPITALITY COMMITTEE (1973). 201 S. 18 St., Rm. 1519, Philadelphia, PA 19103. (215)546-8293. Pres. Allen S. Maller; Exec. Dir. Steven S. Jacobs. Assists converts and prospective converts to Judaism, persons involved in intermarriages, and the parents of Jewish youth under the influence of cults and missionaries, as well as the youths themselves. *Our Choice.*

NATIONAL JEWISH INFORMATION SERVICE FOR THE PROPAGATION OF JUDAISM, INC. (1960). 5174 W. 8 St., Los Angeles, CA 90036. (213)936-6033. Pres. Rabbi Moshe M. Maggal; V. Pres. Lawrence J. Epstein; Sec. Rachel Maggal. Seeks to convert non-Jews to Judaism and revert Jews to Judaism; maintains College for Jewish Ambassadors for the training of Jewish missionaries and the Correspondence Academy of Judaism for instruction on Judaism through the mail. *Voice of Judaism.*

NATIONAL JEWISH RESOURCE CENTER (1974). 421 Seventh Ave., NYC 10001. (212)714-9500. Chmn. Herschel Blumberg; Pres. Irving Greenberg; Exec. V. Pres. Paul Jeser. Devoted to leadership education and policy guidance for the American Jewish community. Conducts weekend retreats and community gatherings, as well as conferences on various topics. *Perspectives.*

NER ISRAEL RABBINICAL COLLEGE (1933). 400 Mt. Wilson Lane, Baltimore, MD 21208. (301)484-7200. Pres. Rabbi Jacob I. Ruderman; V. Pres. Rabbi Herman N. Neuberger. Trains rabbis and educators for Jewish communities in America and worldwide. Offers bachelor's master's and doctoral degrees in Talmudic law, as well as teacher's diploma. College has four divisions: Mechina High School, Rabbinical College, Teachers Training Institute, Graduate School. Maintains an active community-service division. Operates special program for Iranian Jewish students. *Ner Israel Bulletin; Alumni Bulletin; Ohr Hanair Talmudic Journal; Iranian B'nei Torah Bulletin.*

OZAR HATORAH, INC. (1946). 411 Fifth Ave., NYC 10016. (212)684-4733. Pres. Joseph Shalom; Int. Pres. S.D. Sassoon; Exec. Dir. Rabbi H. Augenbaum. Establishes, maintains, and expands schools for Jewish youth, providing religious and secular studies, worldwide.

P'EYLIM—AMERICAN YESHIVA STUDENT UNION (1951). 3 W. 16 St., NYC 10011. (212)989-2500. Pres. Jacob Y. Weisberg; Dir. Avraham Hirsch. Aids and sponsors pioneer work by American graduate teachers and rabbis in new villages and towns in Israel; does religious, organizational, and educational work and counseling among new immigrant youth; maintains summer camps for poor immigrant youth in Israel; belongs to worldwide P'eylim movement which has groups in Argentina, Brazil, Canada, England, Belgium, the Netherlands, Switzerland, France, and Israel; engages in relief and educational work among North African immigrants in France and Canada, assisting them to relocate and reestablish a strong Jewish community life. *P'eylim Reporter; News from P'eylim.*

RABBINICAL ALLIANCE OF AMERICA (IGUD HARABONIM) (1944). 156 Fifth Ave., Suite 807, NYC 10010. (212)242-6420. Pres.

Rabbi Abraham B. Hecht; Menahel Rabbinical Court Rabbi Herschel Kurzrock. Seeks to promulgate the cause of Torah-true Judaism through an organized rabbinate that is consistently Orthodox; seeks to elevate the position of Orthodox rabbis nationally, and to defend the welfare of Jews the world over. Also has Beth Din Rabbinical Court and marriage and family counseling. *Perspective; Nahalim.*

RABBINICAL ASSEMBLY (1900). 3080 Broadway, NYC 10027. (212)678-8060. Pres. Rabbi Alexander M. Shapiro; Exec. V. Pres. Rabbi Wolfe Kelman. Seeks to promote Conservative Judaism, and to foster the spirit of fellowship and cooperation among rabbis and other Jewish scholars; cooperates with the Jewish Theological Seminary of America and the United Synagogue of America. *Conservative Judaism; Proceedings of the Rabbinical Assembly.*

RABBINICAL COLLEGE OF TELSHE, INC. (1941). 28400 Euclid Ave., Wickliffe, OH 44092. (216)943-5300. Pres. Rabbi Mordecai Gifter; V. Pres. Rabbi Abba Zalka Gewirtz. College for higher Jewish learning specializing in Talmudic studies and rabbinics; maintains a preparatory academy including a secular high school, postgraduate department, teacher-training school, and teachers' seminary for women. *Pri Etz Chaim; Peer Mordechai; Alumni Bulletin.*

RABBINICAL COUNCIL OF AMERICA, INC. (1923; reorg. 1936). 275 Seventh Ave., NYC 10001. (212)807-7888. Pres. Rabbi Louis Bernstein; Exec. V. Pres. Rabbi Binyamin Walfish. Promotes Orthodox Judaism in the community; supports institutions for study of Torah; stimulates creation of new traditional agencies. *Hadorom; Record; Sermon Manual; Tradition.*

RECONSTRUCTIONIST RABBINICAL COLLEGE (1968). Church Rd. and Greenwood Ave., Wyncote, PA 19095. (215)576-0800. Bd. Chmn. Benjamin Wm. Mehlman; Pres. Ira Silverman; Dean Arthur Green. Coeducational. Trains rabbis for all areas of Jewish communal life: synagogues, academic and educational positions, Hillel centers, Federation agencies; requires students to pursue outside graduate studies in religion and related subjects; confers title of rabbi and grants degrees of Master and Doctor of Hebrew Letters. *RRC Report.*

RESEARCH INSTITUTE OF RELIGIOUS JEWRY, INC. (1941; reorg. 1954). 471 W. End Ave., NYC 10024. (212)874-7979. Chmn. Isaac Strahl; Sec. Marcus Levine. Engages in research and publishes studies concerning the situation of religious Jewry and its problems all over the world.

SHOLEM ALEICHEM FOLK INSTITUTE, INC. (1918). 3301 Bainbridge Ave., Bronx, NY 10467. Pres. Burt Levey; Sec. Noah Zingman. Aims to imbue children with Jewish values through teaching Yiddish language and literature, Hebrew and the Bible, Jewish history, the significance of Jewish holidays, folk and choral singing, and facts about Jewish life in America and Israel. *Kinder Journal* (Yiddish).

SOCIETY FOR HUMANISTIC JUDAISM (1969). 28611 W. Twelve Mile Rd., Farmington Hills, MI 48018. (313)478-7610. Founder Rabbi Sherwin Wine; Exec. Dir. Miriam Jerris; Pres. Leonard Cherlin. Established to promote an alternative in Jewish life. Publishes educational and ceremonial materials; trains humanistic Jewish leaders; organizes humanistic congregations and groups; provides a public voice for humanistic Jews. *Humanistic Judaism.*

SOCIETY OF FRIENDS OF THE TOURO SYNAGOGUE, NATIONAL HISTORIC SHRINE, INC. (1948). 85 Touro St., Newport, RI 02840. (401)847-4794. Pres. Aaron Slom; Exec. Sec. Theodore Lewis. Assists in the maintenance of the Touro Synagogue as a national historic site. *History of Touro Synagogue.*

SPERTUS COLLEGE OF JUDAICA (1925). 618 S. Michigan Ave., Chicago, IL 60605. (312)922-9012. Pres. Howard A. Sulkin; Bd. Chmn. Fred Bernheim; V. Pres. for Academic Affairs Byron L. Sherwin. Provides Chicago-area colleges and universities with specialized undergraduate and graduate programs in Judaica and serves as a department of Judaic studies to these colleges and universities; serves as Midwest Jewish information center, through its Asher Library, Maurice Spertus Museum of Judaica, Katzin Memorial Rare Book Room, and Chicago Jewish Archives. Grants degrees of MA in Jewish education, Jewish studies, and Jewish communal service; BA and Bachelor of Judaic Studies. Has community outreach/extension studies program for adults.

SYNAGOGUE COUNCIL OF AMERICA (1926). 327 Lexington Ave., NYC 10016. (212)-686-8670. Pres. Rabbi Mordecai Waxman; Exec. V. Pres. Rabbi Henry D. Michelman. Serves as spokesman for, and coordinates policies of, national rabbinical and lay synagogal organizations of Conservative, Orthodox, and Reform branches of American Judaism. Sponsors Institute for Jewish Policy Planning and Research. *SCA Report; Analysis.*

———, INSTITUTE FOR JEWISH POLICY PLANNING AND RESEARCH OF (1972). 327 Lexington Ave., NYC 10016. (212)686-8670. Pres. Rabbi Mordecai Waxman; Exec. V. Pres. Rabbi Henry D. Michelman. Seeks to strengthen American Jewry by conducting and promoting systematic study of major issues confronting its future vitality, for which it enlists informed academic and lay people, sponsors research and analysis on the subject, and disseminates findings to synagogues and other Jewish organizations. *Analysis of Jewish Policy Issues.*

TORAH SCHOOLS FOR ISRAEL—CHINUCH ATZMAI (1953). 167 Madison Ave., NYC 10016. (212)889-0606. Pres. Moshe Feinstein; Exec. Dir. Henach Cohen. Conducts information programs for the American Jewish community on activities of the independent Torah schools educational network in Israel; coordinates role of American members of international board of governors; funds special programs of Mercaz Hachinuch Ha-Atzmai B'Eretz Yisroel. *Israel Education Reporter.*

TORAH UMESORAH—NATIONAL SOCIETY FOR HEBREW DAY SCHOOLS (1944). 160 Broadway, NYC 10038. (212)406-4190. Pres. Sheldon Beren; Chmn. Exec. Com. David Singer; Exec. V. Pres. Joshua Fishman. Establishes Hebrew day schools throughout U.S. and Canada and services them in all areas, including placement and curriculum guidance; conducts teacher-training institutes on campuses of major yeshivahs and seminars and workshops for in-service training of teachers; publishes textbooks and supplementary reading material; conducts research in ethics and character education; supervises federal aid programs for Hebrew day schools throughout the U.S. *Olomeinu—Our World; Tempo; Torah Umesorah Report; Machberet Hamenahel.*

———, INSTITUTE FOR PROFESSIONAL ENRICHMENT (1973). 22 E. 28 St., NYC 10016. (212)683-3216. Dir. Bernard Dov Milians. Provides enriched training and upgraded credentials for administrative, guidance, and classroom personnel of Hebrew day schools and for Torah-community leaders; offers graduate and undergraduate programs, in affiliation with accredited universities which award full degrees: MA in early childhood and elementary education; MS in family counseling; MBA in management; MS in special education, reading; BS in education; BA in human relations, social sciences, education, gerontology. *Professional Enrichment News (PEN).*

———, NATIONAL ASSOCIATION OF HEBREW DAY SCHOOL ADMINISTRATORS (1960). 1114 Ave. J, Brooklyn, NY 11230. Pres. David H. Schwartz. Coordinates the work of the fiscal directors of Hebrew day schools throughout the country. *NAHDSA Review.*

———, NATIONAL ASSOCIATION OF HEBREW DAY SCHOOL PARENT-TEACHER ASSOCIATIONS (1948). 160 Broadway, NYC 10038. (212)406-4190. Pres. Mrs. Henry C. Rhein; Exec. Sec. Mrs. Samuel Brand; Bd. Chmn. Mrs. Clarence Horwitz. Acts as a clearinghouse and service agency to PTAs of Hebrew day schools; organizes parent-education courses and sets up programs for individual PTAs. *National Program Notes; PTA Bulletin; Fundraising with a Flair; PTA with a Purpose for the Hebrew Day School.*

———, NATIONAL CONFERENCE OF YESHIVA PRINCIPALS (1956). 160 Broadway, NYC 10038. (212)406-4190. Pres. Rabbi Kalman Rosenbaum; Bd. Chmn. Rabbi Yitzchock Merkin; Exec. V. Pres. Rabbi A. Moshe Possick. A professional organization of primary and secondary yeshivah day-school principals which seeks to make yeshivah day-school education more effective. *Machberet Hamenahel.*

———, NATIONAL YESHIVA TEACHERS BOARD OF LICENSE (1953). 160 Broadway, NYC 10038. (212)406-4190. Bd. Chmn. Rabbi Elias Schwartz; Exec. Consult. Rabbi Zvi H. Shurin. Issues licenses to qualified instructors for all grades of the Hebrew day school and the general field of Torah education.

TOURO COLLEGE (1970). 30 W. 44 St., NYC 10036. (212)575-0190. Pres. Bernard Lander; Bd. Chmn. Max Karl. Chartered by NY State Board of Regents as a nonprofit four-year college with liberal arts programs leading to BA, BS, and MA degrees, emphasizing relevance of Jewish heritage to general culture of Western civilization. Offers JD degree and a biomedical program leading to the MD from Technion-Israel Institute of Technology, Haifa.

————COLLEGE OF LIBERAL ARTS AND SCIENCES. 30 W. 44 St., NYC 10036. Dean Stanley Boylan. Offers comprehensive Jewish studies along with studies in the arts, sciences, humanities, and preprofessional studies in health sciences, law, accounting, business, computer science, and finance. Coordinate and extension programs at Women's Division (221 W. 51 St., NYC), Flatbush Center in Brooklyn, and Yeshiva Ohr Hachayim in Queens.

————DIVISION OF HEALTH SCIENCES. 30 W. 44 St., NYC 10036, and the Long Island campus in Huntington. Offers three programs: (1) Five-year program leading to MD degree from the Faculty of Medicine of Technion-Israel Institute of Technology, Haifa; includes one year of advanced clinical rotations in Israel; (2) Physician Assistant program; (3) Physical Therapist program.

————FLATBUSH PROGRAM. 1277 E. 14 St., Brooklyn, NY 11230. Offers evening classes to students attending a yeshiva or seminary during the day; nine majors include accounting, business management, education, and computer science.

————GRADUATE PROGRAM IN JEWISH STUDIES. 30 W. 44 St., NYC 10036. Offered in conjunction with Herzliah-Jewish Teachers Seminary Division.

————INSTITUTE OF JEWISH LAW. Based at Touro School of Law, serves as a center and clearinghouse for study and teaching of Jewish law.

————JEWISH PEOPLE'S UNIVERSITY OF THE AIR. Presents Sunday radio courses on New York stations WEVD and WNYC, carried by satellite to NPR's 320 affiliated stations nationwide; covers all aspects of Jewish culture and offers course outlines and cassettes.

————SCHOOL OF CAREER AND URBAN STUDIES. 240 E. 123 St., NYC 10021.

Dean Jacquelyn L. Petersen. Offers educational opportunities to minority groups and older people; courses in the arts, sciences, humanities, and special programs of career studies.

————SCHOOL OF LAW. Long Island Campus, 300 Nassau Rd., Huntington, NY 11743. Dean John Bainbridge. Offers studies leading to JD degree.

————YESHIVA OHR HACHAYIM. 141–61 71 Ave., Kew Garden Hills, NY 11367. A higher academy of Jewish learning, offers classes in Talmud, Bible, Jewish philosophy, education, and community services.

UNION OF AMERICAN HEBREW CONGREGATIONS (1873). 838 Fifth Ave., NYC 10021. (212)249-0100. Pres. Rabbi Alexander M. Schindler; Bd. Chmn. Charles J. Rothschild, Jr. Serves as the central congregational body of Reform Judaism in the Western Hemisphere; serves its approximately 850 affiliated temples and membership with religious, educational, cultural, and administrative programs. *Keeping Posted; Reform Judaism.*

————, AMERICAN CONFERENCE OF CANTORS (1956). 838 Fifth Ave., NYC 10021. (212)249-0100. Pres. Murray E. Simon; Exec. Dir. Raymond Smolover. Members receive investiture and commissioning as cantors at ordination-investiture ceremonies at Hebrew Union College—Jewish Institute of Religion, Sacred School of Music. Through Joint Placement Commission, serves congregations seeking cantors and music directors. Dedicated to creative Judaism, preserving the best of the past, and encouraging new and vital approaches to religious ritual, music and ceremonies.

————, COMMISSION ON SOCIAL ACTION OF REFORM JUDAISM (*see* p. 368)

————, NATIONAL ASSOCIATION OF TEMPLE ADMINISTRATORS OF (1941). 838 Fifth Ave., NYC 10021. (212)249-0100. Pres. Shirley Chernela; Admin. Sec. Norman Fogel. Fosters Reform Judaism; prepares and disseminates administrative information and procedures to member synagogues of UAHC; provides and encourages proper and adequate training of professional synagogue executives; formulates and establishes professional ideals and standards for the synagogue executive; provides placement services. *NATA Journal.*

——, NATIONAL ASSOCIATION OF TEMPLE EDUCATORS (1955). 838 Fifth Ave., NYC 10021. (212)249-0100. Pres. Kenneth A. Midlo. Represents the temple educator within the general body of Reform Judaism; fosters the full-time profession of the temple educator; encourages the growth and development of Jewish religious education consistent with the aims of Reform Judaism; stimulates communal interest in and responsibility for Jewish religious education. *NATE News; Compass* magazine.

——, NATIONAL FEDERATION OF TEMPLE BROTHERHOODS (1923). 838 Fifth Ave., NYC 10021. (212)570-0707. Pres. Herbert Panoff; Exec. Dir. Av Bondarin. Promotes Jewish education among its members, along with participation in temple, brotherhood, and interfaith activities; sponsors the Jewish Chautauqua Society. *Brotherhood.*

——, NATIONAL FEDERATION OF TEMPLE SISTERHOODS (1913). 838 Fifth Ave., NYC 10021. (212)249-0100. Pres. Constance Kreshtool; Exec. Dir. Eleanor R. Schwartz. Serves more than 640 sisterhoods of Reform Judaism; promotes interreligious understanding and social justice; awards scholarships and grants to rabbinic students; provides braille and large-type Judaic materials for Jewish blind; supports projects for Israel, Soviet Jewry, and the aging; is an affiliate of UAHC and is the women's agency of Reform Judaism; works on behalf of the Hebrew Union College—Jewish Institute of Religion; cooperates with World Union for Progressive Judaism. *Notes for Now.*

——, NORTH AMERICAN FEDERATION OF TEMPLE YOUTH (NFTY; formerly NATIONAL FEDERATION OF TEMPLE YOUTH) (1939). 838 Fifth Ave., NYC 10021. (212)249-0100. Dir. Ramie Arian; Asst. Dirs. Terry Goldstein, Carol Siegel; Pres. Mitchell Warren. Seeks to train Reform Jewish youth in the values of the synagogue and their application to daily life through service to the community and congregation; runs department of summer camps and national leadership training institute; arranges overseas academic tours, work programs, international student exchange programs, and college student programs in the U.S. and Israel, including accredited study programs in Israel. *Ani V'Atah; The Jewish Connection.*

——, AND CENTRAL CONFERENCE OF AMERICAN RABBIS: COMMISSION ON JEWISH EDUCATION (1923). 838 Fifth Ave., NYC 10021. (212)249-0100. Chmn. Murray Blackman; Dir. Rabbi Daniel B. Syme. Develops curricula and teachers' manuals; conducts pilot projects and offers educational guidance and consultation at all age levels to member congregations and affiliates and associate bodies. *What's Happening; Compass; E*[3].

——, AND CENTRAL CONFERENCE OF AMERICAN RABBIS: JOINT COMMISSION ON SYNAGOGUE ADMINISTRATION (1962). 838 Fifth Ave., NYC 10021. (212)-249-0100. Chmn. Harold J. Tragash; Dir. Myron E. Schoen. Assists congregations in management, finance, building maintenance, design, construction, and art aspects of synagogues; maintains the Synagogue Architectural Library, consisting of photos, slides, and plans of contemporary and older synagogue buildings. *Synagogue Service.*

UNION OF ORTHODOX JEWISH CONGREGATIONS OF AMERICA (1898). 45 W. 36 St., NYC 10018. (212)563-4000. Pres. Julius Berman; Exec. V. Pres. Pinchas Stolper. Serves as the national central body of Orthodox synagogues; sponsors National Conference of Synagogue Youth, Our Way program for the Jewish deaf, Yachad program for developmentally disabled youth, Israel Center in Jerusalem, *aliyah* department, national OU Kashruth supervision and certification service; provides educational, religious, and organizational guidance to synagogues and groups; represents the Orthodox Jewish community in relation to governmental and civic bodies and the general Jewish community. Publishes synagogue programming publications and books of Jewish interest. *Jewish Action; OU Kosher Directory; OU Passover Directory; OU News Reporter; Synagogue Spotlight; Our Way magazine; Yachad magazine.*

——, NATIONAL CONFERENCE OF SYNAGOGUE YOUTH (1954). 45 W. 36 St., NYC 10018. (212)563-4000. Pres. Howie Siegel; Dir. Natl. Affairs Yitzchok Rosenberg; Dir. Natl. Programs Raphael Butler. Serves as central body for youth groups of Orthodox congregations; provides such national activities and services as educational guidance, Torah study groups, community service, programs consultation, Torah library, Torah fund scholarships, Ben

Zakkai Honor Society, Friends of NCSY; conducts national and regional events including week-long seminars, summer Torah tours in over 200 communities, Israel summer seminar for teens and collegiates, cross-country tours, and Camp NCSY East. Divisions include Senior NCSY in 18 regions and 465 chapters, Junior NCSY for preteens, "Our Way" for the Jewish deaf, Yachad for the developmentally disabled, and NCSY in Israel. *Keeping Posted with NCSY; Face the Nation—President's Newsletter; Oreich Yomeinu—Education Newsletter.*

——, WOMEN'S BRANCH (1923). 84 Fifth Ave., NYC 10011. (212)929-8857. Pres. Nancy I. Klein; Admin. Rita Siff. Seeks to spread the understanding and practice of Orthodox Judaism, and to unite all Orthodox women and their synagogal organizations; services affiliates with educational and programming materials, leadership and organizational guidance, and has an NGO representative at the UN. *Hachodesh; Hakol.*

UNION OF ORTHODOX RABBIS OF THE UNITED STATES AND CANADA (1900). 235 E. Broadway, NYC 10002. (212)964-6337. Pres. Rabbi Moshe Feinstein; Dir. Rabbi Hersh M. Ginsberg. Seeks to foster and promote Torah-true Judaism in the U.S. and Canada; assists in the establishment and maintenance of *yeshivot* in the U.S.; maintains committee on marriage and divorce and aids individuals with marital difficulties; disseminates knowledge of traditional Jewish rites and practices and publishes regulations on synagogal structure; maintains rabbinical court for resolving individual and communal conflicts. *Hapardes.*

UNION OF SEPHARDIC CONGREGATIONS, INC. (1929). 8 W. 70 St., NYC 10023. (212)873-0300. Pres. The Haham Solomon Gaon; Sec. Joseph Tarica; Bd. Chmn. Victor Tarry. Promotes the religious interests of Sephardic Jews; prepares and distributes Sephardic prayerbooks; provides religious leaders for Sephardic congregations.

UNITED LUBAVITCHER YESHIVOTH (1940). 841-853 Ocean Parkway, Brooklyn, NY 11230. (718)859-7600. Pres. Eli N. Sklar; Chmn. Exec. Com. Rabbi S. Gourary. Supports and organizes Jewish day schools and rabbinical seminaries in the U.S. and abroad.

UNITED SYNAGOGUE OF AMERICA (1913). 155 Fifth Ave., NYC 10010. (212)533-7800. Pres. Franklin D. Kreutzer; Exec. V. Pres. Benjamin Z. Kreitman. National organization of Conservative Jewish congregations. Maintains 12 departments and 20 regional offices to assist its affiliated congregations with religious, educational, youth, community, and administrative programming and guidance; aims to enhance the cause of Conservative Judaism, further religious observance, encourage establishment of Jewish religious schools; embraces all elements essentially loyal to traditional Judaism. *Program Suggestions; United Synagogue Review; Yearbook Directory and Buyers' Guide; President's Newsletter.*

——, COMMISSION ON JEWISH EDUCATION (1930). 155 Fifth Ave., NYC 10010. (212)260-8450. Chmn. Rabbi Joel H. Zaiman; Dir. Morton K. Siegel. Promotes higher educational standards in Conservative congregational schools and Solomon Schechter Day Schools and publishes material for the advancement of their educational programs. Provides guidance and information on resources, courses, and other projects in adult Jewish education; prepares and publishes pamphlets, study guides, tracts, and texts for use in adult-education programs; publishes the *Jewish Tract* series and distributes El-Am edition of Talmud. Distributes black-and-white and color films of "Eternal Light" TV programs on Jewish subjects, produced by Jewish Theological Seminary in cooperation with NBC. *Briefs; Impact; In Your Hands; Your Child.*

——, JEWISH EDUCATORS ASSEMBLY OF (1951). 15 East 26 St., NYC 10010. (212)-532-4949. Pres. Michael Korman; Exec. Dir. Jacob S. Rosen. Promotes, extends, and strengthens the program of Jewish education on all levels in the community in consonance with the philosophy of the Conservative movement. *Yearbook; Newsletters; Tamtzit.*

——, JOINT COMMISSION ON SOCIAL ACTION (1958). 155 Fifth Ave., NYC 10010. (212)533-7800. Cochmn. Rabbi Zachary I. Heller, Ella Berman; Dir. Ruth M. Perry. Consists of representatives of United Synagogue of America, Women's League for Conservative Judaism, Rabbinical Assembly, and Federation of Jewish Men's Clubs; reviews public issues and cooperates with civic and Jewish community organizations to achieve social-action goals. *Today: Hayom.*

——, KADIMA OF (formerly PRE-USY; reorg. 1968). 155 Fifth Ave., NYC 10010. (212)533-7800. Dir. Enid L. Miller. Involves Jewish preteens in a meaningful religious, educational, and social environment; fosters a sense of identity and commitment to the Jewish community and Conservative movement; conducts synagogue-based chapter programs and regional Kadima days and weekends. *Mitzvah of the Month; Kadima Kesher; Advisors Aid series; Chagim; Games; quarterly Kadima magazine.*

——, NATIONAL ASSOCIATION OF SYNAGOGUE ADMINISTRATORS OF (1948). 155 Fifth Ave., NYC 10010. (212)533-7800. Pres. Harvey L. Brown. Aids congregations affiliated with the United Synagogue of America to further aims of Conservative Judaism through more effective administration (PALS Program); advances professional standards and promotes new methods in administration; cooperates in United Synagogue placement services and administrative surveys. *NASA Newsletter; NASA Journal.*

——, UNITED SYNAGOGUE YOUTH OF (1951). 155 Fifth Ave., NYC 10010. (212)-533-7800. Pres. David Stern; Exec. Dir. Paul Freedman. Seeks to strengthen identification with Conservative Judaism, based on the personality development, needs, and interests of the adolescent, in a Mitzvah framework. *Achshav; Tikun Olam; A.J. Heschel Honor Society Newsletter; USY Alumni Assn. Newsletter; USY Program Bank.*

VAAD MISHMERETH STAM (1976). 4902 16 Ave., Brooklyn, NY 11204. (718)438-4963. Exec. Dir. Rabbi Yakov Basch. A nonprofit consumer-protection agency dedicated to preserving and protecting the halachic integrity of Torah scrolls, phylacteries, and *mezuzot.* Makes presentations and conducts examination campaigns in schools and synagogues. *A Guide to Mezuzah; The Halachic Encyclopedia of the Sacred Alphabet; Yalkut Tzurat Haotiyot.*

WEST COAST TALMUDICAL SEMINARY (Yeshiva Ohr Elchonon Chabad) (1953). 7215 Warring St., Los Angeles, CA 90046. (213)937-3763. Pres. Abraham Linderman; V. Pres. Rabbi Shlomo Cunin, Rabbi Levi Bukiet. Provides facilities for intensive Torah education as well as Orthodox rabbinical training on the West Coast; conducts an accredited college preparatory high school combined with a full program of Torah-Talmudic training and a graduate Talmudical division on the college level. *Torah Quiz.*

WOMEN'S LEAGUE FOR CONSERVATIVE JUDAISM (1918). 48 E. 74 St., NYC 10021. (212)628-1600. Pres. Selma Weintraub; Exec. Bernice Balter. Constitutes parent body of Conservative women's groups in U.S., Canada, Puerto Rico, Mexico, and Israel; provides them with programs in religion, education, social action, Israel affairs, leadership training, services to the disabled, and community affairs; publishes books of Jewish interest; contributes to support of Jewish Theological Seminary and its residence halls. *Women's League Outlook; Ba'Olam.*

WORLD COUNCIL OF SYNAGOGUES (1957). 155 Fifth Ave., NYC 10010 (212)533-7693. Pres. Marshall Wolke; Exec. Dir. Zipporah Liben. International representative of Conservative organizations and congregations; promotes the growth and development of the Conservative movement in Israel and throughout the world; supports educational institutions overseas; holds biennial international conventions; represents the world Conservative movement on the Executive of the World Zionist Organization. *Jerusalem Newsletter; Spectrum.*

WORLD UNION FOR PROGRESSIVE JUDAISM, LTD. (1926). 838 Fifth Ave., NYC 10021. (212)249-0100. Pres. Gerard Daniel; Exec. Dir. Richard G. Hirsch; N. Amer. Dir. Benjamin A. Kamin. Promotes and coordinates efforts of Reform, Liberal, and Progressive congregations throughout the world; supports new congregations; assigns and employs rabbis overseas; sponsors seminaries and schools; organizes international conferences of Liberal Jews. *International Conference Reports; News and Views; Shalhevet* (Israel); *Teshuva* (Argentina); *Ammi.*

YAVNE HEBREW THEOLOGICAL SEMINARY (1924). P.O. Box 185, Brooklyn, NY 11218. (718)436-5610. Pres. Nathan Shapiro; Exec. Dir. Rabbi Solomon K. Shapiro. School for higher Jewish learning; maintains Machon Maharshal branch in

Jerusalem for higher Jewish education and for an exchange student program. *Yavne Newsletter.*

YESHIVA UNIVERSITY (1886). 500 W. 185 St., NYC 10033. (212)960-5400. Pres. Norman Lamm; Chmn. Bd. of Trustees, Herbert Tenzer. The nation's oldest and largest independent university founded under Jewish auspices, celebrating its 100th anniversary in 1986, with a broad range of undergraduate, graduate, and professional schools, a network of affiliates, publications, a widespread program of research and community outreach, and a museum. Curricula lead to bachelor's, master's, doctoral, and professional degrees. Undergraduate schools provide general studies curricula supplemented by courses in Jewish learning; graduate schools prepare for careers in medicine, law, social work, Jewish education, psychology, Semitic languages, literatures, and cultures, and other fields. It has five undergraduate schools, seven graduate and professional schools, and three affiliates, with its four main centers located in Manhattan and the Bronx. *Alumni Review/Inside Yeshiva University; Yeshiva University Report.*

Undergraduate schools for men at Main Center: Yeshiva College (Dean Norman Rosenfeld) provides liberal arts and sciences curricula; grants BA and BS degrees. Isaac Breuer College of Hebraic Studies (Dean Rabbi Jacob M. Rabinowitz) awards Hebraic Studies and Hebrew teacher's diploma, AA, BA, and BS. James Striar School of General Jewish Studies (Dir. Rabbi Benjamin Yudin) grants AA degree. Yeshiva Program/Mazer School of Talmudic Studies (Dir. Rabbi Zevulun Charlop) offers advanced course of study in Talmudic texts and commentaries.

Undergraduate school for women at Midtown Center, 245 Lexington Ave., NYC 10016: Stern College for Women (Dean Karen Bacon) includes Teachers Institute for Women; offers liberal arts and sciences curricula supplemented by Jewish studies courses; awards BA, BS, BS in education, AA, Jewish Studies certificate, Hebrew teacher's diploma.

Sponsors one high school for boys and one for girls (Manhattan).

Universitywide services include Center for Continuing Education, Holocaust Studies Program, Interdisciplinary Educational Conference on Bereavement and Grief, Yeshiva University Research Institute.

———, ALBERT EINSTEIN COLLEGE OF MEDICINE (1955). Eastchester Rd. and Morris Pk. Ave., Bronx, NY 10461. (212)-430-2000. Pres. Norman Lamm; Chmn. Bd. of Overseers Burton P. Resnick; Dean Dr. Dominick P. Purpura. Prepares physicians, conducts research in the health sciences, and provides patient care; awards MD degree; includes Sue Golding Graduate Division of Medical Sciences (Dir. Dr. Susan Henry), which grants PhD degree. Einstein College's clinical facilities and affiliates encompass Jack D. Weiler Hospital of Albert Einstein College of Medicine, Bronx Municipal Hospital Center, Montefiore Hospital and Medical Center, and the Rose F. Kennedy Center for Research in Mental Retardation and Human Development. *AECOM News; AECOM Today; Einstein Quarterly Journal of Biology and Medicine.*

———, ALUMNI OFFICE, 500 W. 185 Street, NYC 10033. Dir. E. Yechiel Simon. Seeks to foster a close allegiance of alumni to their alma mater by maintaining ties with all alumni and servicing the following associations: Yeshiva College Alumni (Pres. Aaron Weitz); Stern College Alumnae (Pres. Paula G. From and Rachel E. Oppenheim); Albert Einstein College of Medicine Alumni (Pres. Dr. Marvin Kirschner); Ferkauf Graduate School Alumni (Pres. Alvin I. Schiff); Wurzweiler School of Social Work Alumni (Pres. Linda Poskanzer); Bernard Revel Graduate School—Harry Fischel School Alumni (Pres. Bernard Rosensweig); Rabbinic Alumni (Pres. Rabbi Alvin Marcus); Benjamin N. Cardozo School of Law Alumni (Pres. Rosemary C. Byrne). Alumni Council (Chmn. Abraham S. Guterman) offers guidance to Pres. and Bd. of Trustees on university's academic development and service activities. *Alumni Review/Inside Yeshiva University; AECOM Alumni News; Jewish Social Work Forum; Alumnews.*

———, BELFER INSTITUTE FOR ADVANCED BIOMEDICAL STUDIES (1978). Eastchester Rd. and Morris Pk. Ave., Bronx, NY 10461. Dir. Dr. Ernest R. Jaffé. Integrates and coordinates the Medical College's postdoctoral research and training programs in the biomedical sciences; awards certificate at term's completion.

———, BENJAMIN N. CARDOZO SCHOOL OF LAW (1976). 55 Fifth Ave., NYC 10003. Pres. Norman Lamm; Bd. Chmn. Charles Ballon; Dean Monroe E. Price. Provides innovative courses of study within a traditional legal framework; program includes judicial internships; grants Doctor of Law (JD) degree. Center for Professional Development assists students in obtaining employment. Leonard and Bea Diener Institute of Jewish Law explores American and Jewish jurisprudence. *Cardozo Law Review; Arts and Entertainment Law Journal; Women's Annotated Legal Bibliography; Cardozo Law Forum.*

———, BERNARD REVEL GRADUATE SCHOOL (1937). 500 W. 185 St., NYC 10033. Dean Leo Landman. Offers graduate work in Judaic studies and Semitic languages, literatures, and cultures; confers MS, MA, and PhD degrees.

———, DAVID J. AZRIELI GRADUATE INSTITUTE OF JEWISH EDUCATION AND ADMINISTRATION (1945). 245 Lexington Ave., NYC 10016. Dir. Yitzchak Handel. Offers MS degree in Jewish elementary and secondary education; Specialist's Certificate and EdD programs in administration and supervision of Jewish education. Block Education Program, under a grant from the Jewish Agency's L.A. Pincus Fund for the Diaspora, prepares administrators in Jewish education for positions throughout the U.S.; grants EdD degree.

———, FERKAUF GRADUATE SCHOOL OF PSYCHOLOGY (1957). 1165 Morris Pk. Ave., NYC 10461. Dean Morton Berger. Offers MA in general psychology; PsyD in clinical and school psychology; and PhD in clinical, developmental-experimental psychology, and in school, social, health, and bilingual educational-developmental psychology. Center for Psychological and Psychoeducational Services offers counseling, diagnostic evaluation, and psychotherapy.

———, HARRY FISCHEL SCHOOL FOR HIGHER JEWISH STUDIES (1945). 500 W. 185 St., NYC 10033. Dean Leo Landman. Offers summer graduate programs in Judaic studies and Semitic languages, literatures, and cultures; confers MS, MA, and PhD degrees.

———, (affiliate) RABBI ISAAC ELCHANAN THEOLOGICAL SEMINARY (1896). 2540 Amsterdam Ave., NYC 10033. Chmn. Bd.

of Trustees Charles H. Bendheim; Dir. Rabbi Zevulun Charlop. Offers comprehensive program for preparing Orthodox rabbis; grants *semikhah* (ordination) and the degrees of Master of Religious Education, Master of Hebrew Literature, Doctor of Religious Education, and Doctor of Hebrew Literature. Includes Rabbi Joseph B. Soloveitchik Center of Rabbinic Studies, Marcos and Adina Katz Kollel (Institute for Advanced Research in Rabbinics, Dir. Rabbi Hershel Schachter), Kollel L'Horaah (Yadin Yadin, Dir. Rabbi Nison Alpert), Caroline and Joseph S. Gruss Kollel Elyon (Dir. Rabbi Aharon Kahn), Chaver Program (Dir. Rabbi J. David Bleich), Caroline and Joseph S. Gruss Institute in Jerusalem (Dir. Rabbi Aharon Lichtenstein). Brookdale Chaplaincy Internship Program trains prospective rabbis to work effectively with the elderly. Maybaum Sephardic Fellowship Program trains rabbis for service in Sephardic communities here and abroad, offering courses in Sephardic Halakhah, Spanish or Arabic, and other pertinent areas. Morris and Nellie L. Kawaler Rabbinic Training Program emphasizes professional aspects of the rabbinate: chaplaincy, homiletics, pastoral counseling, practical *halakhah*, and the role of the rabbi in the community. Philip and Sarah Belz School of Jewish Music (Dir. Cantor Bernard Beer) provides professional training of cantors and other musical personnel for the Jewish community; awards Associate Cantor's certificate and cantorial diploma. Jacob E. Safra Institute of Sephardic Studies (Dir. Rabbi Solomon Gaon) serves Sephardic communities, offering courses, lectures, and scholarly conferences about the Sephardic heritage; *The American Sephardi.* Max Stern Division of Communal Services (Dean Rabbi Robert Hirt) provides personal and professional service to the rabbinate and related fields, as well as educational, consultative, organizational, and placement services to congregations, schools, and communal organizations throughout North America and abroad. Joseph and Rachel Ades Sephardic Community Outreach Program provides educational, religious, and cultural programs and personnel to Sephardic communities. Stone-Sapirstein Center for Jewish Education identifies and trains future educators through programs of learning, service, and internship; works with schools in the community and across the country offering consultation and assistance; sponsors academic programs, lectures, and special projects throughout the university. National Commission on Torah Education and Educators Council of America formulate uniform educational standards, provide guidance to professional staffs, rabbis, and lay leaders with regard to curriculum, and promote Jewish education. Camp Morasha (Dir. Zvi Reich) offers Jewish studies program.

————, WOMEN'S ORGANIZATION (1928). 500 W. 185 St., NYC 10033. Pres. Ann Arbesfeld; Dir. Deborah Steinhorn. Supports Yeshiva University's national scholarship program for students training in education, community service, law, medicine, and other professions, and its development program. *YUWO News Briefs.*

————, WURZWEILER SCHOOL OF SOCIAL WORK (1957). 500 W. 185 St., NYC 10033. Pres. Norman Lamm.; Chmn. Bd. of Governors Herbert H. Schiff; Dean Lloyd Setleis. Offers graduate programs in social casework, social group work, community social work; grants MSW and DSW degrees; two-year, full-time Concurrent Plan combines classroom study and supervised field instruction; the Extended Plan permits a period of up to five years to complete requirements for some master's degree candidates. Block Education Plan (Dir. Samuel M. Goldstein) provides field instruction in Jewish communities in the U.S., Canada, Europe, and Israel. Clergy Plan (Dir. Irving N. Levitz) provides training in counseling for clergymen of all denominations. Plan for Employed Persons (Dir. Harriet Katz) is specifically designed for people working in social agencies.

————, YESHIVA UNIVERSITY GERONTOLOGICAL INSTITUTE, Brookdale Institute for the Study of Gerontology (1976). 500 W. 185 St., NYC 10033. Dir. Celia B. Weisman. Offers an interdisciplinary program for professionals holding master's degrees in such fields as social work, psychology, counseling, or nursing, or having ordination; fosters and coordinates Universitywide research, study, and activities related to the process and problems of aging; grants post-master's certificate.

————, (affiliate) YESHIVA UNIVERSITY OF LOS ANGELES (1977). 9760 W. Pico Blvd., Los Angeles, CA 90035. (213)553-4478.

Dean Rabbi Marvin Hier; Bd. Chmn. Samuel Belzberg; Dir. Academic Programs Rabbi Sholom Tendler. Grants BA degree in Jewish studies. Has university program and graduate studies department. Also provides Jewish studies program for beginners. Affiliates are Yeshiva University of Los Angeles High School and the Jewish Studies Institute.

————, SIMON WIESENTHAL CENTER (1977). 9760 W. Pico Blvd., Los Angeles, CA 90035. (213)553-9036. On campus of Yeshiva University of Los Angeles. Dean Rabbi Marvin Hier; Assoc. Dean Rabbi Abraham Cooper; Dir. Dr. Gerald Margolis. Branch Offices: 5715 N. Lincoln Ave., Suite #16, Chicago, IL 60659. (312)989-0022; 342 Madison Ave., Suite #437, NYC, 10017. (212)370-0320. Legal Counsel Martin Mendelsohn, Washington, DC. Programs include: Wiesenthal Holocaust Museum; library; archives; "Testimony to the Truth" Oral History Program; photo archive; educational outreach; Scholars' Forum; International Social Action Agenda. *Simon Wiesenthal Center Annual,; Response magazine; Social Action Update; Page One,* a syndicated weekly radio news magazine presenting contemporary Jewish issues.

YESHIVATH TORAH VODAATH AND MESIVTA RABBINICAL SEMINARY (1918). 425 E. 9 St., Brooklyn, NY 11218. (718)941-8000. Pres. Henry Hirsch; Bd. Chmn. Fred F. Weiss; Sec. Earl H. Spero. Offers Hebrew and secular education from elementary level through rabbinical ordination and postgraduate work; maintains a teachers institute and community-service bureau; maintains a dormitory and a nonprofit camp program for boys. *Chronicle; Mesivta Vanguard; Thought of the Week; Torah Vodaath News.*

————, ALUMNI ASSOCIATION (1941). 425 E. 9 St., Brooklyn, NY 11218. (718)941-8000. Pres. Marcus Saffer; Bd. Chmn. Seymour Pluchenik. Promotes social and cultural ties between the alumni and the schools through fund raising; offers vocational guidance to students; operates Camp Torah Vodaath; sponsors research fellowship program for boys. *Annual Journal; Hamesivta Torah periodical.*

SOCIAL, MUTUAL BENEFIT

AMERICAN FEDERATION OF JEWS FROM CENTRAL EUROPE, INC. (1942). 570

Seventh Ave., NYC 10018. (212)921-3871. Pres. Curt C. Silberman; Exec. V. Pres. Herbert A. Strauss; Exec. Asst. Katherine Rosenthal. Seeks to safeguard the rights and interests of American Jews of Central European descent, especially in reference to restitution and indemnification; through its Research Foundation for Jewish Immigration, sponsors research and publications on the history of Central European Jewry and the history of its immigration and acculturation in the U.S.; sponsors a social program for needy Nazi victims in the U.S. in cooperation with United Help, Inc. and other specialized social agencies; undertakes cultural activities, annual conferences, publications, and lecture programs; member, Council of Jews from Germany.

AMERICAN SEPHARDI FEDERATION (1972). 8 W. 40 St., Suite 1601, NYC 10018. (212)-730-1210. Pres. Leon Levy; Exec. V. Pres. Joseph Tarica. Seeks to preserve the Sephardi heritage in the U.S., Israel, and throughout the world by fostering and supporting religious and cultural activities of Sephardi congregations, organizations, and communities, and uniting them in one overall organization; supports Jewish institutions of higher learning and those that train Sephardi lay and religious leaders to serve their communities everywhere; assists Sephardi charitable, cultural, religious, and educational institutions everywhere; disseminates information by the publication, or assistance in the publication, of books and other literature dealing with Sephardi culture and tradition in the U.S., organizes youth and young-adult activities throughout the U.S.; supports efforts of the World Sephardi Federation to alleviate social disparities in Israel. *Sephardi World; Sephardic Connection.*

AMERICAN VETERANS OF ISRAEL (1949). c/o Samuel E. Alexander, 548 E. Walnut St., Long Beach, NY 11561. (516)431-8316. Pres. Larry Hoffman; Sec. Samuel E. Alexander. Maintains contact with American and Canadian volunteers who served in Aliyah Bet and/or Israel's War of Independence; promotes Israel's welfare; holds memorial services at grave of Col. David Marcus; is affiliated with World Mahal. *Newsletter.*

ASSOCIATION OF YUGOSLAV JEWS IN THE UNITED STATES, INC. (1940). 247 W. 99 St., NYC 10025. (212)865-2211. Pres. Sal

Musafia; Sec. Mile Weiss. Assists members and Jews and Jewish organizations in Yugoslavia; cooperates with organization of former Yugoslav Jews in Israel and elsewhere. *Bulletin.*

BNAI ZION—THE AMERICAN FRATERNAL ZIONIST ORGANIZATION (1908). 136 E. 39 St., NYC 10016. (212)725-1211. Pres. Ernest Zelig; Exec. V. Pres. Mel Parness. Fosters principles of Americanism, fraternalism, and Zionism; offers life insurance, Blue Cross and Blue Shield and other benefits to its members. Sponsors various projects in Israel: settlements, youth centers, medical clinics, Beit Halochem Rehabilitation Center for Israeli Disabled War Veterans, Bnai Zion Home for Retardates in Rosh Ha'ayin, and the Herman Z. Quittman Center in Hakfar Hashwedi in Jerusalem. Has Young Leadership Division—TAMID. *TAMID Outlet; Beit Halochem Newsletter; Bnai Zion Voice.*

BRITH ABRAHAM (1887). 136 E. 39 St., NYC 10016. (212)725-1211. Grand Master Robert Freeman. Protects Jewish rights and combats antisemitism; supports Soviet and Ethiopian emigration and the safety and dignity of Jews worldwide; furnishes regular financial assistance to Beit Halochem for the Israeli war disabled, Haifa Medical Center, Rosh Ha'ayin Home for Retarded Children, Kupat Cholim diagnostic centers, libraries, educational facilities, and other institutions to relieve the social burdens on the Israeli economy; aids and supports various programs and projects in the U.S., Hebrew Excellence Program—Gold Medal Presentation in high schools and colleges; Camp Loyaltown; Brith Abraham and Bnai Zion Foundations. *Voice.*

BRITH SHOLOM (1905). 3939 Conshohocken Ave., Philadelphia, PA 19131. (215)878-5696. Pres. Sidney Waldman; Exec. Dir. Mervin L. Krimins. Fraternal organization devoted to community welfare, protection of rights of Jewish people, and activities which foster Jewish identity and provide support for Israel; sponsors Brith Sholom House for senior citizens in Philadelphia and Brith Sholom Beit Halochem in Haifa, a rehabilitation center for Israel's permanently war-wounded. *Brith Sholom Presents; Monthly News Bulletin.*

CENTRAL SEPHARDIC JEWISH COMMUNITY OF AMERICA (1940). 8 W. 70 St., NYC

10023. (212)787-2850. Pres. Emilie Levy; Sec. Isaac Molho. Seeks to foster Sephardic culture, education, and communal institutions. Sponsors wide range of activities; raises funds for Sephardic causes in U.S. and Israel.

FREE SONS OF ISRAEL (1849). 932 Broadway, NYC 10010. (212)260-4222. Grand Master Hyman H. Robinson; Grand Sec. Murray Birnback. Promotes fraternalism; supports State of Israel, UJA, Soviet Jewry, Israel Bonds, and other Jewish charities; fights antisemitism; awards scholarships. Local lodges have own publications. *National Reporter; Digest.*

JEWISH LABOR BUND (Directed by WORLD COORDINATING COMMITTEE OF THE BUND) (1897; reorg. 1947). 25 E. 21 St., NYC 10010. (212)475-0059. Exec. Sec. Jacob S. Hertz. Coordinates activities of Bund organizations throughout the world and represents them in the Socialist International; spreads the ideas of socialism as formulated by the Jewish Labor Bund; publishes books and periodicals on world problems, Jewish life, socialist theory and policy, and on the history, activities, and ideology of the Jewish Labor Bund. *Unser Tsait* (U.S.); *Lebns-Fragn* (Israel); *Unser Gedank* (Australia); *Unser Shtimme* (France).

JEWISH SOCIALIST VERBAND OF AMERICA (1921). 45 E. 33 St., NYC 10016. (212)-686-1536. Pres. Meyer Miller; Natl. Sec. Herman Yonish. Promotes ideals of democratic socialism and Yiddish culture; affiliated with Social Democrats, USA. *Der Wecker.*

ROUMANIAN JEWISH FEDERATION OF AMERICA, INC. (1956). 135 W. 106 St., #2M, NYC 10025. (212)866-0692. Pres. Charles H. Kremer; Treas. Albert Sigal. Interested in protecting the welfare, preserving the culture, and easing the plight of Jews of Rumanian descent throughout the world. Works to influence the Rumanian government to grant freedom of worship to Jews and permission for their emigration to Israel.

SEPHARDIC JEWISH BROTHERHOOD OF AMERICA, INC. (1915). 97-29 64 Rd., Rego Park, NY 11374. (718)459-1600. Pres. Nick Levi; Sec. Jack Ezratty. Promotes the industrial, social, educational, and religious welfare of its members; offers funeral

and burial benefits, scholarships, and aid to the needy. *Sephardic Brother.*

UNITED ORDER TRUE SISTERS, INC. (1846). 212 Fifth Ave., NYC 10010. (212)679-6790. Pres. Anita Sporn; Exec. Officer Dorothy Giuriceo. Philanthropic, community service; Natl. Project Cancer Service. *Echo.*

WORKMEN'S CIRCLE (1900). 45 E. 33 St., NYC 10016. (212)889-6800. Pres. Barnett Zumoff; Exec. Dir. Jack Noskowitz. Provides fraternal benefits and activities, Jewish educational programs, secularist Yiddish schools for children, community activities, both in Jewish life and on the American scene, cooperation with the labor movement. *The Call; Kinder Zeitung; Kultur un Lebn.*

———, DIVISION OF JEWISH LABOR COMMITTEE (*see* p. 369)

SOCIAL WELFARE

AMC CANCER RESEARCH CENTER (formerly JEWISH CONSUMPTIVES' RELIEF SOCIETY, 1904; incorporated as AMERICAN MEDICAL CENTER AT DENVER, 1954). 6401 W. Colfax Ave., Lakewood, CO 80214. (303)233-6501. Pres. Manfred L. Minzer, Jr.; Chmn. Bd. of Trustees, Randolph B. Heller. A national cancer hospital that provides the finest specialized treatment available to patients, regardless of ability to pay; as a progressive science research center, pursues promising leads in the prevention, detection, and control of cancer. *Clinical Cancer Newsletter.*

———, NATIONAL COUNCIL OF AUXILIARIES (1904; reorg. 1936). 6401 W. Colfax Ave., Lakewood, CO 80214. (303)233-6501. Pres. Lillian Solomon. Provides support for the AMC Cancer Research Center through fund raising, information dissemination, and acting as admissions officers for patients from chapter cities throughout the country. *Bulletin.*

AMERICAN JEWISH CORRECTIONAL CHAPLAINS ASSOCIATION, INC. (formerly NATIONAL COUNCIL OF JEWISH PRISON CHAPLAINS) (1937). 10 E. 73 St., NYC 10021. (212)879-8415. (Cooperates with the New York Board of Rabbis and Jewish Family Service). Pres. Irving Koslowe; Exec. Dir. Paul L. Hait; Assoc. Dir. Moses A. Birnbaum. Provides religious services and guidance to Jewish men and women in penal and correctional institutions; serves as a liaison between inmates and their families; upgrades the quality of correctional ministrations through conferences, professional workshops, and conventions. *Bulletin.*

AMERICAN JEWISH SOCIETY FOR SERVICE, INC. (1949). 15 E. 26 St., Rm. 1304, NYC 10010. (212)683-6178. Pres. E. Kenneth Marx; Exec. Dir. Elly Saltzman. Conducts two voluntary work-service camps each summer to enable young people to live their faith by serving other people. *Newsletter.*

ASSOCIATION OF JEWISH COMMUNITY OR-GANIZATION PERSONNEL (1969). 1175 College Ave., Columbus, OH 43209. (614)-237-7686. Pres. Darrell Friedman; Exec. Dir. Ben Mandelkorn. An organization of professionals engaged in areas of fund raising, endowments, budgeting, social planning, financing, administration and coordination of services. Objectives are to develop and enhance professional practices in Jewish communal work; to maintain and improve standards, practices, scope and public understanding of the field of community organization, as practiced through local federations and national agencies.

ASSOCIATION OF JEWISH FAMILY AND CHILDREN'S AGENCIES (1972). 40 Worth St., Rm. 800, NYC 10013-2904. (212)608-6660. Pres. Cynthia B. Kane; Exec. Dir. Martin Greenberg. The national service organization for Jewish family and children's agencies in Canada and the U.S. Reinforces member agencies in their efforts to sustain and enhance the quality of Jewish family and communal life. *In-Box; Bimonthly Bulletin; Directory.*

BARON DE HIRSCH FUND (1891). 130 E. 59 St., NYC 10022. (212)980-1000, ext. 184. Pres. Ezra Pascal Mager; Mng. Dir. Robert B. Goldmann. Aids Jewish immigrants and their children in the U.S. and Israel by giving grants to agencies active in educational and vocational fields; has limited program for study tours in U.S. by Israeli agriculturists.

B'NAI B'RITH INTERNATIONAL (1843). 1640 Rhode Island Ave. NW, Washington, DC 20036. (202)857-6600. Pres. Gerald Kraft; Exec. V. Pres. Daniel Thursz. International Jewish organization with affiliates in 48 countries. Programs include communal service, social action, and public affairs, with emphasis on preserving Judaism through projects in and for Israel and for Soviet Jewry; teen and college-age movements; adult Jewish education. *The International Jewish Monthly; Shofar.*

————, ANTI-DEFAMATION LEAGUE OF (*see* p. 368)

————, CAREER AND COUNSELING SER-VICES (1938). 1640 Rhode Island Ave. NW, Washington, DC 20036. (202)857-6532. Chmn. Burton M. Wanetik; Natl. Dir. Max F. Baer. Offers educational and career counseling to Jewish youth and adults on a group and individual basis through professionally staffed centers in New York, North Jersey, and Philadelphia.

————, HILLEL FOUNDATIONS, INC. (*see* p. 379)

————, KLUTZNICK MUSEUM (*see* p. 372)

————, YOUTH ORGANIZATION (*see* p. 379)

B'NAI B'RITH WOMEN (1897). 1640 Rhode Island Ave. NW, Washington, DC 20036. (202)857-6628. Pres. Beverly Davis; Exec. Dir. Elaine Binder. Provides programs and services that affect and concern Jewish women through youth and adult education and public affairs programs, human rights endeavors and community-service activities; supports a variety of services to Israel, including a home for emotionally disturbed boys. *Women's World, Leadership Letter, Public Affairs Update, Direct Line.*

CITY OF HOPE NATIONAL MEDICAL CEN-TER AND BECKMAN RESEARCH INSTI-TUTE (1913). 208 W. 8 St., Los Angeles, CA 90014. (213)626-4611. Pres. Abraham S. Bolsky; Exec. Dir. Ben Horowitz. Provides free quality care to patients from all over U.S. suffering from cancer, heart and respiratory ailments, genetic and metabolic disorders. Consultation service available to hospitals. As a pilot medical center, seeks improvements in quality, economy, and efficiency of health care. *Pilot; President's Newsletter; City of Hope Quarterly.*

CONFERENCE OF JEWISH COMMUNAL SER-VICE (1899). 111 Prospect St., E. Orange, NJ 07017. (201)676-6070. Pres. Ferne Katleman; Exec. Dir. Joel Ollander. Serves as forum for all professional philosophies in community service, for testing new experiences, proposing new ideas, and questioning or reaffirming old concepts; umbrella organization for eight major Jewish communal service groups. Concerned with advancement of professional personnel practices and standards. *Concurrents; Journal of Jewish Communal Service.*

COUNCIL OF JEWISH FEDERATIONS, INC. (1932). 730 Broadway, NYC 10003. (212)-475-5000. Pres. Shoshana S. Cardin; Exec. V. Pres. Carmi Schwartz. Provides national and regional services to 200 associated federations embracing 800 communities in the U.S. and Canada, aiding in fund raising, community organization, health and welfare planning, personnel recruitment, and public relations. *Directory of Jewish Federations, Welfare Funds and Community Councils; Directory of Jewish Health and Welfare Agencies* (triennial); *Jewish Communal Services: Programs and Finances (1977); Yearbook of Jewish Social Services; Annual Report.*

HOPE CENTER FOR THE RETARDED (1965). 3601 Martin L. King Blvd., Denver, CO 80205. (303)388-4801. Pres. Lester Goldstein; Exec. Dir. George E. Brantley; Sec. Helen Fonda. Provides services to developmentally disabled of community: preschool training, day training and work activities center, speech and language pathology, occupational arts and crafts, recreational therapy, and social services.

INTERNATIONAL COUNCIL ON JEWISH SOCIAL AND WELFARE SERVICES (1961). 60 E. 42 St., NYC 10165. (NY liaison office with UN headquarters.) (212)687-6200. Chmn. Kenneth Rubin; Exec. Sec. Theodore D. Feder. Provides for exchange of views and information among member agencies on problems of Jewish social and welfare services, including medical care, old age, welfare, child care, rehabilitation, technical assistance, vocational training, agricultural and other resettlement, economic assistance, refugees, migration, integration and related problems, representation of views to governments and international organizations. Members: six national and international organizations.

JWB (1917). 15 E. 26 St., NYC 10010. (212)-532-4949. Pres. Esther Leah Ritz; Exec. V. Pres. Arthur Rotman. Major service agency for Jewish community centers and camps serving more than a million Jews in the U.S. and Canada; U.S.-government-accredited agency for providing services and programs to Jewish military families and hospitalized veterans; promotes Jewish culture through its Book and Music Councils, JWB Lecture Bureau, Jewish Media Service, and Jewish educational, cultural, and Israel-related projects. *JWB Circle; Zarkor; JWB Personnel Reporter.*

——, COMMISSION ON JEWISH CHAPLAINCY (1940). 15 E. 26 St., NYC 10010. Chmn. Rabbi Barry H. Greene; Dir. Rabbi E. David Lapp. Recruits, endorses, and serves Jewish military and Veterans Administration chaplains on behalf of the American Jewish community and the three major rabbinic bodies; trains and assists Jewish lay leaders where there are no chaplains, for service to Jewish military personnel, their families, and hospitalized veterans.

——, JEWISH BOOK COUNCIL (*see* p. 373)

——, JEWISH MUSIC COUNCIL (*see* p. 373)

JEWISH BRAILLE INSTITUTE OF AMERICA, INC. (1931). 110 E. 30 St., NYC 10016. (212)889-2525. Pres. Jane Evans; Exec. V. Pres. Gerald M. Kass. Serves the religious, cultural, and educational needs of the Jewish blind and visually impaired by producing books of Judaica, including prayerbooks in Hebrew and English braille, large print, and audio cassettes. Maintains free lending library of Hebrew, English, and Yiddish cassettes for the Jewish blind and visually impaired in 40 countries. *Jewish Braille Review; JBI Voice; Or Chadash.*

JEWISH CONCILIATION BOARD OF AMERICA, INC. (1930). 235 Park Ave. S., NYC 10003. (212)777-9034. Pres. Milton J. Schubin; Exec. Dir. Beatrice Lampert. Offers dispute-resolution services to families, individuals, and organizations. Social-work, rabbinic, and legal expertise are available for family and divorce mediation and arbitration. Fee—sliding scale.

JEWISH FUND FOR JUSTICE (1984). 1334 G St. NW, Washington, DC 20005. (202)-638-0550. Pres. Si Kahn; Exec. Dir. Lois Roisman. A national grant-making institution supporting efforts to combat poverty in the U.S. Acts as a catalyst to increase Jewish communal and individual involvement in social-justice issues; participates in grant-making coalitions with other religious and ethnic groups.

LEVI ARTHRITIS HOSPITAL (sponsored by B'nai B'rith) (1914). 300 Prospect Ave., Hot Springs, AR 71901. (501)624-1281. Pres. Harry Levitch; Admin. D. E. Wagoner. Maintains a nonprofit, nonsectarian hospital for treatment of sufferers from arthritis and related diseases. *Levi Letter.*

NATIONAL ASSOCIATION OF JEWISH FAMILY, CHILDREN'S AND HEALTH PROFESSIONALS (1965). 1115 E. 65 St., Kansas City, MO 64131. (816)333-1172. Pres. Lee M. Kalik; V. Pres. Arnold Marks, Melvin Cohen. Brings together Jewish caseworkers and related professionals in Jewish family, children's, and health services. Seeks to improve personnel standards, further Jewish continuity and identity, and strengthen Jewish family life; provides forums for professional discussion at national conference of Jewish communal service and regional meetings; takes action on social-policy issues. *Newsletter.*

NATIONAL ASSOCIATION OF JEWISH VOCATIONAL SERVICES (formerly JEWISH OCCUPATIONAL COUNCIL) (1940). 386 Park Ave. S., NYC 10016. (212)685-8355. Pres. Harold Friedman; Exec. Dir. Harvey P. Goldman. Acts as coordinating body for all Jewish agencies in U.S., Canada, and Israel, having programs in educational-vocational guidance, job placement, vocational rehabilitation, skills-training, sheltered workshops, and occupational research. *Newsletter; NAJVS Reports.*

NATIONAL CONGRESS OF JEWISH DEAF (1956; inc. 1961). 9102 Edmonston Court, Greenbelt, MD 20770. TTY (301)345-8612. Exec. Dir. Alexander Fleischman; Pres. Kenneth Rothschild. Congress of Jewish congregations, service organizations, and associations located throughout the U.S. and Canada, advocating religious and cultural ideals and fellowship for the Jewish deaf. *Quarterly.*

NATIONAL COUNCIL OF JEWISH PRISON CHAPLAINS, INC. (*see* American Jewish Correctional Chaplains Association, Inc.)

NATIONAL COUNCIL OF JEWISH WOMEN (1893). 15 E. 26 St., NYC 10010. (212)-532-1740. Pres. Barbara A. Mandel; Exec. Dir. Dadie Perlov. Operates programs in education, social and legislative action, and community service for children and youth, the aging, the disadvantaged in Jewish and general communities; concerns include juvenile justice system as basis for legislative reform and community projects; deeply involved in women's issues; promotes education in Israel through NCJW Research Institute for Innovation in Education at Hebrew University, Jerusalem. *NCJW Journal; From the Desk of the President; Washington Newsletter; NACS Newsletter.*

NATIONAL JEWISH CENTER FOR IMMUNOLOGY AND RESPIRATORY MEDICINE (formerly NATIONAL JEWISH HOSPITAL/NATIONAL ASTHMA CENTER) (1899). 1400 Jackson St., Denver, CO 80206. (303)388-4461; 1-800-222-5864; Pres. Michael K. Schonbrun; V. Pres. Public Affairs, Jerry L. Colness. Leading medical center for study and treatment of respiratory diseases, allergies, and immune system disorders. Clinical emphasis on asthma, emphysema, tuberculosis, chronic bronchitis, and interstitial lung diseases; immune system disorders such as juvenile rheumatoid arthritis and immune deficiency disorders. *New Directions; Update; Annual Report.*

NATIONAL JEWISH COMMITTEE ON SCOUTING (Boy Scouts of America) (1926). 1325 Walnut Hill La., Irving, TX 75038-3096. (214)659-2059. Chmn. Murray L. Cole; Exec. Dir. Fred Tichauer. Seeks to bring Jewish youth closer to Judaism through Scouting programs. Works through local Jewish committees on Scouting to organize Cub Scout packs, Boy Scout troops, and Explorer posts in synagogues, Jewish community centers, and other Jewish organizations wishing to draw Jewish youth. *Ner Tamid for Boy Scouts and Explorers; Scouting in Synagogues and Centers.*

NATIONAL JEWISH GIRL SCOUT COMMITTEE (1972). Synagogue Council of America, 327 Lexington Ave., NYC 10016. (212)686-8670. Chmn. Rabbi Herbert W. Bomzer; Field Chmn. Shirley W. Parker. Under the auspices of the Synagogue Council of America, serves to further Jewish education by promoting Jewish award programs, encouraging religious services, promoting cultural exchanges with Israeli Boy & Girl Scout Federation, and extending membership in the Jewish community by assisting councils in organizing Girl Scout troops and local Jewish Girl Scout committees. *Newsletter.*

NORTH AMERICAN ASSOCIATION OF JEW-ISH HOMES AND HOUSING FOR THE AGING (1960). 2525 Centerville Rd., Dallas, TX 75228. (214)327-4503. Pres. Ira C. Robbins; Exec. V. Pres. Herbert Shore. Serves as a national representative of voluntary Jewish homes and housing for the aged; conducts annual meetings, conferences, workshops and institutes; provides for sharing information, studies and clearinghouse functions. *Directory; Perspectives.*

WORLD CONFEDERATION OF JEWISH COMMUNITY CENTERS (1947). 15 E. 26 St., NYC 10010. (212)532-4949. Pres. Esther Leah Ritz; Exec. Dir. Haim Zipori. Serves as a council of national and continental federations of Jewish community centers; fosters development of the JCC movement worldwide; provides a forum for exchange of information among centers. *Newsletter.*

ZIONIST AND PRO-ISRAEL

ALYN—AMERICAN SOCIETY FOR HANDICAPPED CHILDREN IN ISRAEL (1954). 19 W. 44 St., NYC 10036. (212)869-8085. Chmn. Simone P. Blum; Exec. Dir. Nathan N. Schorr. Supports the work of ALYN Orthopaedic Hospital and Rehabilitation Center for Physically Handicapped Children, located in Jerusalem, which encompasses a 100-bed hospital and outpatient clinics, and houses the Helena Rubinstein Foundation Research Institute for research in neuromuscular diseases. *ALYN News.*

AMERICA-ISRAEL CULTURAL FOUNDATION, INC. (1939). 485 Madison Ave., NYC 10022. (212)751-2700. Bd. Chmn. Isaac Stern; Pres. Carl Glick. Membership organization supporting Israeli cultural institutions, such as Israel Philharmonic and Israel Chamber Orchestra, Tel Aviv Museum, Rubin Academies, Bat Sheva Dance Co., Omanut La'am, and Tzlil Am; sponsors cultural exchange between U.S. and Israel; awards scholarships in all arts to young Israelis for study in Israel and abroad. *Hadashot.*

AMERICA-ISRAEL FRIENDSHIP LEAGUE, INC. (1971). 134 E. 39 St., NYC 10016. (212)213-8630. Pres. Herbert Tenzer; Exec. Dir. Ilana Artman. Seeks to create broad-based support for Israel among the American public and expand the scope of the relationship between the two nations through educational and cultural exchange programs. *Newsletter.*

AMERICAN ASSOCIATES, BEN-GURION UNIVERSITY OF THE NEGEV (1973). 342 Madison Ave., Suite 1924, NYC 10173. (212)-687-7721. Pres. Jack J. Spitzer, Bd. Chmn. Irwin H. Goldenberg; Exec. Dir. Donald L. Gartner. Serves as the university's publicity and fund-raising link to the U.S. The Associates are committed to publicizing university activities and curricula, securing student scholarships, transferring contributions, and encouraging American interest in the university. *AABGU Reporter; BGU Bulletin; Negev.*

AMERICAN COMMITTEE FOR SHAARE ZEDEK HOSPITAL IN JERUSALEM, INC. (1949). 49 W. 45 St., NYC 10036. (212)-354-8801. Pres. Charles Bendheim; Bd. Chmn. Ludwig Jesselson; Sr. Exec. V. Pres. Morris Talansky. Raises funds for the various needs of the Shaare Zedek Medical Center, Jerusalem, such as equipment and medical supplies, nurse training, and research; supports exchange program between Shaare Zedek Medical Center and Albert Einstein College of Medicine, NY. *Heartbeat magazine.*

AMERICAN COMMITTEE FOR THE WEIZMANN INSTITUTE OF SCIENCE, INC. (1944). 515 Park Ave., NYC 10022. (212)-752-1300. Pres. Maurice M. Weiss; Bd. Chmn. Norman D. Cohen; Exec. V. Pres. Stephen L. Stulman. Secures support for basic and applied scientific research. *Interface; Rehovot; Research.*

AMERICAN FRIENDS OF HAIFA UNIVERSITY (1969). 206 Fifth Ave., 4th fl., NYC 10010. (212)696-4022. Exec. Dir. Dalia Katz; Pres. Sigmund Strochlitz. Supports the development and maintenance of the various programs of the University of Haifa, among them the Center for Holocaust Studies, Arab Jewish Center, Yiddish Department, Bridging the Gap project, Department of Management, School of Education, and Fine Arts Department; arranges overseas academic programs for American and Canadian students. *Newsletter.*

AMERICAN FRIENDS OF THE HAIFA MARITIME MUSEUM, INC. (1977). 18 E. 74 St., P.O. Box 616, NYC 10021. (212)776-4509. Pres. Edward Neufeld; Treas. Bernard Weissman. Supports National Maritime Museum in Haifa. Promotes interest in maritime life among American Jews. *Quarterly Bulletin.*

AMERICAN FRIENDS OF THE HEBREW UNIVERSITY (1925; inc. 1931). 11 E. 69 St., NYC 10021. (212)472-9800. Pres. Fred S. Lafer; Exec. V. Pres. Robert A. Pearlman; Bd. Chmn. Harvey L. Silbert. Fosters the growth, development, and maintenance of the Hebrew University of Jerusalem; collects funds and conducts programs of information throughout the U.S., interpreting the work of the university and its significance; administers American student programs and arranges exchange professorships in the U.S. and Israel. *News from the Hebrew University of Jerusalem; Scopus magazine.*

AMERICAN FRIENDS OF THE ISRAEL MUSEUM (1968). 10 E. 40 St., Rm. 1208, NYC 10016. (212)683-5190. Pres. Romie Shapiro; Exec. Dir. Michele Cohn Tocci. Raises funds for special projects of the Israel Museum in Jerusalem; solicits contributions of works of art for exhibition and educational purposes. *Newsletter.*

AMERICAN FRIENDS OF THE JERUSALEM MENTAL HEALTH CENTER—EZRATH NASHIM, INC. (1895). 10 E. 40 St., NYC 10016. (212)725-8175. Pres. Anita Blum; Exec. Dir. Sylvia Hilton. Supports research, education, and patient care at the Jerusalem Mental Health Center, which includes a 250-bed hospital, comprehensive outpatient clinic, drug abuse clinic, geriatric center, and the Jacob Herzog Psychiatric Research Center; Israel's only nonprofit, voluntary psychiatric hospital; is used as a teaching facility by Israel's major medical schools. *Friend to Friend; To Open the Gates of Healing.*

AMERICAN FRIENDS OF THE TEL AVIV MUSEUM (1974). c/o M.J. Schubin, 425 Park Ave., NYC 10022. (212)407-8287. Pres. Roy V. Titus; Chmn. Leon L. Gildesgame. Solicits contributions of works of art to enrich the Tel Aviv Museum collection; raises funds to support development, maintenance, and expansion of the educational work of the museum.

AMERICAN FRIENDS OF THE TEL AVIV UNIVERSITY, INC. (1955). 342 Madison Ave., NYC 10017. (212)687-5651. Bd. Chmn. Ivan J. Novick; Pres. Herbert A. Friedman. Promotes, encourages, aids, and advances higher education at Tel Aviv University and elsewhere. Among the many projects in the more than 50 research institutes are: the Moshe Dayan Center for Middle Eastern & African Studies, the Jaffe Center for Strategic Studies; 25 institutes in different fields of medicine; and the Institute for Cereal Crops Improvement. *Tel Aviv University Report; AFTAU Newsletter.*

AMERICAN ISRAEL PUBLIC AFFAIRS COMMITTEE (AIPAC) (1954). 444 North Capitol St., NW, Suite 412, Washington, DC 20001. (202)638-2256. Pres. Robert Asher; Exec. Dir. Thomas A. Dine. Registered to lobby on behalf of legislation affecting Israel, Soviet Jewry, and arms sales to Middle East; represents Americans who believe support for a secure Israel is in U.S. interest. Works for a strong U.S.-Israel relationship.

AMERICAN-ISRAELI LIGHTHOUSE, INC. (1928; reorg. 1955). 30 E. 60 St., NYC 10022. (212)838-5322. Pres. Mrs. Leonard F. Dank; Sec. Frances Lentz. Provides education and rehabilitation for the blind and physically handicapped in Israel to effect their social and vocational integration into the seeing community; built and maintains Rehabilitation Center for the Blind (Migdal Or) in Haifa. *Tower.*

AMERICAN JEWISH LEAGUE FOR ISRAEL (1957). 30 E. 60 St., NYC 10022. (212)-371-1583. Pres. Rabbi Reuben M. Katz; Bd. Chmn. Rabbi Aaron Decter. Seeks to unite all those who, notwithstanding differing philosophies of Jewish life, are committed to the historical ideals of Zionism; works, independently of class or party, for the welfare of Israel as a whole. Not identified with any political parties in Israel. *Bulletin of the American Jewish League for Israel.*

AMERICAN PHYSICIANS FELLOWSHIP, INC. FOR MEDICINE IN ISRAEL (1950). 2001 Beacon St., Brookline, MA 02146. (617)-232-5382. Pres. Dr. Mortimer B. Lipsett; Sec. Manuel M. Glazier. Helps Israel become a major world medical center; secures fellowships for selected Israeli physicians and arranges lectureships in Israel by prominent American physicians; supports Jerusalem Academy of Medicine; coordinates U.S. and Canadian medical and paramedical emergency volunteers to Israel; maintains Israel Institute of the History of Medicine; contributes medical books, periodicals, instruments, and drugs. *APF News.*

AMERICAN RED MAGEN DAVID FOR IS-RAEL, INC. (1941). 888 Seventh Ave., NYC 10106. (212)757-1627. Natl. Chmn. Joseph Handelman; Pres. Louis Rosenberg; Exec. V. Pres. Benjamin Saxe. An authorized tax-exempt organization; the sole support arm in the U.S. of Magen David Adom in Israel with a national membership and chapter program; educates and involves its members in activities of Magen David Adom, Israel's Red Cross Service; raises funds for MDA's emergency medical services, including collection and distribution of blood and blood products for Israel's military and civilian population; supplies ambulances, bloodmobiles, and mobile cardiac rescue units serving all hospitals and communities throughout Israel; supports MDA's 73 emergency medical clinics and helps provide training and equipment for volunteer emergency paramedical corps. *Lifeline.*

AMERICAN SOCIETY FOR TECHNION–ISRAEL INSTITUTE OF TECHNOLOGY (1940). 271 Madison Ave., NYC 10016. (212)889-2050. Pres. Martin Kellner; Exec. V. Pres. Melvyn H. Bloom. Supports the work of the Technion–Israel Institute of Technology, Haifa, which trains nearly 10,000 students in 20 departments and a medical school, and conducts research across a broad spectrum of science and technology. *ATS Newsletter; ATS Women's Division Newsletter; Technion magazine.*

AMERICAN ZIONIST FEDERATION (1939; reorg. 1949 and 1970). 515 Park Ave., NYC 10022. (212)371-7750. Pres. Benjamin Cohen; Exec. Dir. Karen Rubinstein. Coordinates the work of the Zionist constituency in the areas of education, *aliyah,* youth and young leadership and public and communal affairs. Seeks to involve the Zionist and broader Jewish community in programs and events focused on Israel and Zionism (e.g., Zionist Shabbat, Scholars-in-Residence, Yom Yerushalayim) and through these programs to develop a greater appreciation for the Zionist idea among American Jewry. Composed of 16 national Zionist organizations, 10 Zionist youth movements, and affiliated organizations. Offices in Boston, Chicago, Los Angeles, New York. Groups in Baltimore, Detroit, Philadelphia, Pittsburgh, Rochester, Washington, DC. *Issue Analysis, Spectrum.*

AMERICAN ZIONIST YOUTH FOUNDATION, INC. (1963). 515 Park Ave., NYC 10022. (212)751-6070. Bd. Chmn. Eli Zborowski; Exec. Dir. Donald Adelman. Sponsors educational programs and services for American Jewish youth, including tours to Israel, programs of volunteer service or study in leading institutions of science, scholarship, and the arts; sponsors field workers who promote Jewish and Zionist programming on campus; prepares and provides specialists who present and interpret the Israeli experience for community centers and federations throughout the country. *Activist Newsletter; Guide to Education and Programming Material; Programs in Israel.*

———, AMERICAN ZIONIST YOUTH COUNCIL (1951). 515 Park Ave., NYC 10022. (212)751-6070. Chmn. Marc Sussman. Acts as spokesman and representative of Zionist youth in interpreting Israel to the youth of America; represents, coordinates, and implements activities of the Zionist youth movements in the U.S.

AMERICANS FOR A SAFE ISRAEL (1971). 147 E. 76 St., NYC 10021. (212)988-2121. Chmn. Herbert Zweibon; Dir. Peter Goldman; Assoc. Dir. Stephen Karetzky. Seeks to educate the public to the necessity of a militarily strong Israel within defensible borders, viz., those which include Judea, Samaria, Gaza, and the Golan. Holds that a strong Israel is essential for the security of America and the rest of the free world. Produces pamphlets, magazines, video tapes, and radio shows and provides speakers.

AMERICANS FOR PROGRESSIVE ISRAEL (1949). 150 Fifth Ave., Suite 911, NYC 10011. (212)255-8760. Pres. Harry Mouchine. A socialist Zionist group that calls for a just and durable peace between Israel and its Arab neighbors; works for the liberation of all Jews; seeks the democratization of Jewish communal and organizational life; promotes dignity of labor, social justice, brotherhood of nations, and a deepening understanding of Jewish heritage. Affiliate of American Zionist Federation, World Union of Mapam, Hashomer Hatzair, and Kibbutz Artzi Fed. of Israel. *Israel Horizons; Progressive Israel; API Newsletter.*

AMIT WOMEN (formerly AMERICAN MIZRACHI WOMEN) (1925). 817 Broadway,

NYC 10003. (212)477-4720. Pres. Frieda C. Kufeld; Exec. Dir. Marvin Leff. Conducts social service, child care, Youth Aliyah villages, and vocational-educational programs in Israel in an environment of traditional Judaism; promotes cultural activities for the purpose of disseminating Zionist ideals and strengthening traditional Judaism in America. *AMIT Woman.*

AMPAL—AMERICAN ISRAEL CORPORATION (1942). 10 Rockefeller Plaza, NYC 10020. (212)586-3232. Pres. Michael Jaffe; Bd. Chmn. Ephraim Reiner. Finances and invests in Israeli economic enterprises; mobilizes finance and investment capital in the U.S. through sale of own debenture issues and utilization of bank credit lines. *Annual Report; Prospectuses.*

ARZA—ASSOCIATION OF REFORM ZIONISTS OF AMERICA (1977). 838 Fifth Ave., NYC 10021. (212)249-0100. Pres. Rabbi Charles Kroloff; Exec. Dir. Rabbi Eric Yoffie. Individual Zionist membership organization devoted to achieving Jewish pluralism in Israel and strengthening the Israeli Reform movement. Chapter activities in the U.S. concentrate on these issues, and on strengthening American public support for Israel. *ARZA Newsletter.*

BAR-ILAN UNIVERSITY IN ISRAEL (1955). 853 Seventh Ave., NYC 10019. (212)751-6366. Pres. Emanuel Rackman; Chmn. Bd. of Trustees Ludwig Jesselson; Pres. Amer. Bd. of Overseers Mrs. Jerome L. Stern. A liberal arts and sciences institution, located in Ramat-Gan, Israel and chartered by Board of Regents of State of New York. *Update; Bar-Ilan News; Academic Research; Philosophia.*

BETAR ZIONIST YOUTH MOVEMENT, INC. (1935). 41 E. 42 St., Suite 617, NYC 10017. (212)687-4502. Pres. Mitch Chupak. Teaches Jewish youth love of the Jewish people and prepares them for *aliyah;* emphasizes learning Hebrew; keeps its members ready for mobilization in times of crisis; stresses Jewish pride and self-respect; seeks to aid and protect Jewish communities everywhere. *Herut; Etgar.*

COUNCIL FOR A BEAUTIFUL ISRAEL ENVIRONMENTAL EDUCATION FOUNDATION (1973). 350 Fifth Ave., 19th fl., NYC 10118. (212)947-5709. Pres. Zita Rosenthal; Exec. Dir. Carol Perlberger. A support group for the Israeli body, whose activities include education, town planning, lobbying for legislation to protect and enhance the environment, preservation of historical sites, and the improvement and beautification of industrial and commercial areas. *Quarterly Newsletter.*

DROR—YOUNG KIBBUTZ MOVEMENT—HABONIM (1948). 27 W. 20 St., NYC 10011. (212)675-1168. Pres. Shlomo Ravid. Provides an opportunity for individuals who have spent time in Israel, on a kibbutz program, to continue their contact with the kibbutz movement through regional and national activities and seminars; sponsors two *garinim* to kibbutz each year and a teenage summer program. *New Horizons.*

——, CHAVURAT HAGALIL (1978). Pres. Shlomo Ravid. Aids those aged 27–35 in making *aliyah* to an Israeli kibbutz. Affiliated with TAKAM.

——, GARIN YARDEN, THE YOUNG KIBBUTZ MOVEMENT (1976). Pres. Shlomo Ravid. Aids those aged 19–26 interested in making *aliyah* to an Israeli kibbutz; affiliated with TAKAM.

EMUNAH WOMEN OF AMERICA (formerly HAPOEL HAMIZRACHI WOMEN'S ORGANIZATION) (1948). 370 Seventh Ave., NYC 10001. (212)564-9045. Pres. Beverly Segal; Exec. Dir. Shirley Singer. Maintains and supports 200 educational and social welfare institutions in Israel within a religious framework, including nurseries, day-care centers, vocational and teacher-training schools for the underprivileged. Also involved in absorption of Ethiopian immigrants. *The Emunah Woman; Lest We Forget; Emunah Connection.*

FEDERATED COUNCIL OF ISRAEL INSTITUTIONS—FCII (1940). 1475 47 St., Brooklyn, NY 11219. (718)853-6920. Bd. Chmn. Z. Shapiro; Exec. V. Pres. Rabbi Julius Novack. Central fund-raising organization for over 100 affiliated institutions; handles and executes estates, wills, and bequests for the traditional institutions in Israel; clearinghouse for information on budget, size, functions, etc. of traditional educational, welfare, and philanthropic institutions in Israel, working cooperatively with the Israeli government and the overseas department of the Council of Jewish Federations. *Annual Financial Reports.*

FUND FOR HIGHER EDUCATION (1970). 1500 Broadway, NYC 10036. (212)354-4660. Pres. William C. Spencer; V. Pres. Sondra G. Kolker. Supports, on a project-by-project basis, institutions of higher learning in the U.S. and Israel. *In Response II; Annual Report.*

GIVAT HAVIVA EDUCATIONAL FOUNDATION, INC. (1966). 150 Fifth Ave., Suite 911, NYC 10011. (212)255-2992. Chmn. Sydney A. Luria. Supports programs in Israel to further Jewish-Arab rapprochement, narrow economic and educational gaps within Israeli society, and improve educational opportunities for various disadvantaged youth. Affiliated with the Givat Haviva Center of the Kibbutz Artzi Federation, the Menachem Bader Fund, and other projects. In the U.S., GHEF, Inc. sponsors educational seminars, public lectures and parlor meetings with Israeli speakers, as well as individual and group trips to Israel. *News from Givat Haviva; Special Reports.*

HABONIM-DROR LABOR ZIONIST YOUTH (1934). 27 W. 20 St., 9th fl., NYC 10011. (212)255-1796. Sec.-Gen. Marc Sussman; Chief Exec. Officer Paul Parter; Editor Ian Schwartz. Fosters identification with pioneering in Israel; stimulates study of Jewish life, history, and culture; sponsors community-action projects, seven summer camps in North America, programs in Israel, and *garinei aliyah* to Kibbutz Grofit and Kibbutz Gezer. *Progressive Zionist Bulletin; Haboneh; Hamaapil; Iggeret L'Chaverim; Batnua.*

HADASSAH, THE WOMEN'S ZIONIST ORGANIZATION OF AMERICA, INC. (1912). 50 W. 58 St., NYC 10019. (212)355-7900. Pres. Ruth Popkin; Exec. Dir. Judith Manelis. In America helps interpret Israel to the American people; provides basic Jewish education as a background for intelligent and creative Jewish living; sponsors Hashachar, largest Zionist youth movement in U.S., which has four divisions: Young Judaea, Intermediate Judaea, Senior Judaea, and Hamagshimim; operates six Zionist youth camps in this country; supports summer and all-year courses in Israel. Maintains in Israel Hadassah–Hebrew University Medical Center for healing, teaching, and research; Hadassah Community College; Seligsberg/Brandeis Comprehensive High School; and Hadassah Vocational Guidance Institute. Is largest organizational contributor to Youth Aliyah and to Jewish National Fund for land purchase and reclamation. *Update; Headlines; Hadassah Magazine.*

————, HASHACHAR (formerly YOUNG JUDAEA and JUNIOR HADASSAH) (1909 reorg. 1967). 50 W. 58 St., NYC 10019. (212)355-7900. Pres. of Senior Judaea (high school level) Ben Dworkin; Coordinator of Hamagshimim (college level) Julie Baretz; Dir. Paul Goldberg. Seeks to educate Jewish youth from the ages of 9–27 toward Jewish and Zionist values, active commitment to and participation in the American and Israeli Jewish communities; maintains summer camps and year programs in Israel. *Hamagshimim Journal; Kol Hat'nua; The Young Judaean.*

HASHOMER HATZAIR, SOCIALIST ZIONIST YOUTH MOVEMENT (1923). 150 Fifth Ave., Suite 911, NYC 10011. (212)929-4955. Sec. Jeremy Peters; Central Rep. Avraham Israeli. Seeks to educate Jewish youth to an understanding of Zionism as the national liberation movement of the Jewish people. Promotes *aliyah* to kibbutzim. Affiliated with AZYC and Kibbutz Artzi Federation. Espouses socialist ideals of peace, justice, democracy, and brotherhood. *Young Guard.*

HEBREW UNIVERSITY—TECHNION JOINT MAINTENANCE APPEAL (1954). 11 E. 69 St., NYC 10021. (212)517-3376. Dir. Clifford B. Surloff. Conducts maintenance campaigns formerly conducted by the American Friends of the Hebrew University and the American Technion Society; participates in community campaigns throughout the U.S., excluding New York City.

HERUT-U.S.A., INC. (UNITED ZIONIST-REVISIONISTS OF AMERICA) (1925). 41 E. 42 St., NYC 10017. (212)687-4502. Chmn. Eryk Spektor; Exec. Dir. Rabbi Dov Aharoni-Fisch. Supports Jabotinskean Herut policy in Israel for peace with security; seeks Jewish unity for Israel's defense; preaches Zionist commitment, *aliyah,* Jewish education, and mobilization of Jewish resources; advocates historic right to Eretz Israel and to Jewish residency throughout the land. Affiliated groups: Betar Youth Organization; Tagar Zionist Collegiate Activists; Herut New Leadership Division; Tel Hai Fund, Inc. *Shalom; Zionism Today.*

JEWISH NATIONAL FUND OF AMERICA (1901). 42 E. 69 St., NYC 10021. (212)-879-9300. Pres. Charlotte Jacobson; Exec. V. Pres. Samuel I. Cohen. Exclusive fundraising agency of the world Zionist movement for the afforestation, reclamation, and development of the land of Israel, including construction of roads, parks, and recreational areas, preparation of land for new communities and industrial facilities; helps emphasize the importance of Israel in schools and synagogues throughout the U.S. *JNF Almanac; Land and Life.*

KEREN OR, INC. (1956). 1133 Broadway, NYC 10010. (212)255-1180. Bd. Chmn. Edward Steinberg; Pres. N. Arnold Levin; Exec. V. Pres. Jacob Igra. Funds the Keren-Or Center for Multihandicapped Blind Children in Jerusalem, providing long-term basic training, therapy, rehabilitative, and early childhood education to the optimum level of the individual; conducts, with major hospitals, outpatient clinics in Haifa and Be'er Sheva; involved in research into causes of multihandicapped blind birth; campaign under way for new multipurpose building on government land-grant in Ramot.

LABOR ZIONIST ALLIANCE (formerly FARBAND LABOR ZIONIST ORDER; now uniting membership and branches of POALE ZION—UNITED LABOR ZIONIST ORGANIZATION OF AMERICA and AMERICAN HABONIM ASSOCIATION) (1913). 275 Seventh Ave., NYC 10001. (212)989-0300. Pres. Ezra Spicehandler; Exec. Dir. Menahem Jacobi. Seeks to enhance Jewish life, culture, and education in U.S. and Canada; aids in building State of Israel as a cooperative commonwealth, and its Labor movement organized in the Histadrut; supports efforts toward a more democratic society throughout the world; furthers the democratization of the Jewish community in America and the welfare of Jews everywhere; works with labor and liberal forces in America. *Jewish Frontier; Yiddisher Kempfer.*

LEAGUE FOR LABOR ISRAEL (1938; reorg. 1961). 275 Seventh Ave., NYC 10001. (212)989-0300. Pres. Ezra Spicehandler; Exec. Dir. Menahem Jacobi. Conducts Labor Zionist educational and cultural activities, for youth and adults, in the American Jewish community. Promotes educational travel to Israel.

NATIONAL COMMITTEE FOR LABOR ISRAEL —ISRAEL HISTADRUT CAMPAIGN (1923). 33 E. 67 St., NYC 10021. (212)628-1000. Pres. Aaron L. Solomon; Exec. V. Pres. Eliezer Rafaeli. Maintains relationship between labor Israel and American trade union movement and the American Jewish community in support of the health, education, and social-welfare institutions of the Histadrut in Israel. *Backdrop-Histadrut.*

———, AMERICAN TRADE UNION COUNCIL FOR HISTADRUT (1947). 33 E. 67 St., NYC 10021. (212)628-1000. Chmn. Matthew Schoenwald; Dir. Herbert A. Levine. Carries on educational activities among American and Canadian trade unions for health, educational, and welfare activities of the Histadrut in Israel. *Shalom.*

PEC ISRAEL ECONOMIC CORPORATION (formerly PALESTINE ECONOMIC CORPORATION) (1926). 511 Fifth Ave., NYC 10017. (212)687-2400. Pres. Joseph Ciechanover; Exec. V. Pres. Frank J. Klein; Sec.-Asst. Treas. William Gold. Primarily engaged in the business of organizing, financing, and administering business enterprises located in or affiliated with enterprises in the State of Israel, through holdings of equity securities and loans. *Annual Report.*

PEF ISRAEL ENDOWMENT FUNDS, INC. (1922). 342 Madison Ave., NYC 10173. (212)599-1260. Chmn. Sidney Musher; Sec. Burt Allen Solomon. Uses funds for Israeli educational and philanthropic institutions and for constructive relief, modern education, and scientific research in Israel. *Annual Report.*

PIONEER WOMEN/NA'AMAT, THE WOMEN'S LABOR ZIONIST ORGANIZATION OF AMERICA, INC. (1925). 200 Madison Ave., NYC 10016. (212)725-8010. Pres. Phyllis Sutker; Exec. Dir. Shoshonna Ebstein. Supports 1,000 child-care and vocational-training installations, legal aid, university scholarships, and social services for women, teenagers, and children throughout Israel. In the U.S., Pioneer Women/Na'amat advocates progressive legislation for women's rights and child welfare; supports Jewish education and Habonim-Dror, the Labor Zionist youth movement. *Pioneer Woman.*

POALE AGUDATH ISRAEL OF AMERICA, INC. (1948). 3190 Bedford Ave., Brooklyn, NY 11210. (718)377-4111. Pres. Rabbi

Fabian Schonfeld; Exec. V. Pres. Rabbi Moshe Malinowitz. Aims to educate American Jews to the values of Orthodoxy and *aliyah;* supports kibbutzim, trade schools, *yeshivot,* moshavim, kollelim, research centers, and children's homes in Israel. *PAI Views; PAI Bulletin.*

———, WOMEN'S DIVISION OF (1948). Pres. Aliza Widawsky; Presidium: Sarah Ivanisky, Miriam Lubling, Bertl Rittenberg. Assists Poale Agudath Israel to build and support children's homes, kindergartens, and trade schools in Israel. *Yediot PAI.*

RELIGIOUS ZIONISTS OF AMERICA. 25 W. 26 St., NYC 10010. (212)889-5260.

———, BNEI AKIVA OF NORTH AMERICA (1934). 25 W. 26 St., NYC 10010. (212)-889-5260. Exec. Pres. Danny Mayerfield; V. Pres. Alan Silverman; Sec. Yitzchak Fuchs. Seeks to interest youth in *aliyah* to Israel and social justice through pioneering *(halutziut)* as an integral part of their religious observance; sponsors five summer camps, a leadership training camp for eleventh graders, a work-study program on a religious kibbutz for high school graduates, summer tours to Israel; establishes nuclei of college students for kibbutz or other settlement. *Akivon; Hamvaser; Pinkas Lamadrich; Daf Rayonot; Ma'Ohalai Torah; Zraim.*

———, MIZRACHI-HAPOEL HAMIZRACHI (1909; merged 1957). 25 W. 26 St., NYC 10010. (212)689-1414. Pres. Hermann Merkin; Exec. V. Pres. Israel Friedman. Dedicated to building the Jewish state based on principles of Torah; conducts cultural work, educational program, public relations; sponsors NOAM and Bnei Akiva; raises funds for religious educational institutions in Israel. *Horizon; Kolenu; Mizrachi News Bulletin.*

———, MIZRACHI PALESTINE FUND (1928). 25 W. 26 St., NYC 10010. Chmn. Joseph Wilon; Sec. Israel Friedman. Fundraising arm of Mizrachi movement.

———, NATIONAL COUNCIL FOR TORAH EDUCATION OF MIZRACHI-HAPOEL HAMIZRACHI (1939). 25 W. 26 St., NYC 10010. Pres. Israel Shorr; Dir. Meyer Golombek. Organizes and supervises *yeshivot* and Talmud Torahs; prepares and trains teachers; publishes textbooks and educational materials; conducts a placement agency for Hebrew schools; organizes summer seminars for Hebrew educators in cooperation with Torah Department of Jewish Agency; conducts *ulpan.*

———. NOAM-HAMISHMERET HATZEIRA (1970). 25 W. 26 St., NYC 10010. (212)-684-6091. Chmn. Stuart Apfel; Exec. Dir. Cary Katz. Sponsors five core groups to settle in Israel; conducts summer and year volunteer and study programs to Israel; organizes educational programs for young adults in the U.S., through weekly meetings, *shabbatonim,* leadership seminars, etc. *Bechol Zot; B'Darche Noam.*

SOCIETY OF ISRAEL PHILATELISTS (1948). 1125 E. Carson St., #2, Long Beach, CA 90807. (213)595-9224. Pres. Jerome L. Byers; Exec. Sec. Irvin Girer. Promotes interest in, and knowledge of, all phases of Israel philately through sponsorship of chapters and research groups, maintenance of a philatelic library, and support of public and private exhibitions. *Israel Philatelist.*

STATE OF ISRAEL BONDS (1951). 730 Broadway, NYC 10003. (212)677-9650. Intl. Chmn. Sam Rothberg; Pres. Yehudah Halevy; Exec. V. Pres. Morris Sipser. Seeks to provide large-scale investment funds for the economic development of the State of Israel through the sale of State of Israel bonds in the U.S., Canada, Western Europe, and other parts of the free world.

THEODOR HERZL FOUNDATION (1954). 515 Park Ave., NYC 10022. (212)752-0600. Chmn. Kalman Sultanik; Sec. Isadore Hamlin. Cultural activities, lectures, conferences, courses in modern Hebrew and Jewish subjects, Israel, Zionism, and Jewish history. *Midstream.*

———, HERZL PRESS. Chmn. Kalman Sultanik; Editor Mordecai S. Chertoff. Publishes books and pamphlets on Israel, Zionism, and general Jewish subjects.

———, THEODOR HERZL INSTITUTE. Chmn. Jacques Torczyner; Dir. Sidney Rosenfeld. Program geared to review of contemporary problems on Jewish scene here and abroad, presentation of Jewish heritage values in light of Zionist experience of the ages, study of modern Israel, and Jewish social research with particular consideration of history and impact of Zionism. Lectures, forums, Encounter with Creativity; musicales, recitals, concerts; holiday celebrations; visual art programs, Nouveau Artist Introductions. *Annual Program Preview, Herzl Institute Bulletin.*

UNITED CHARITY INSTITUTIONS OF JERUSALEM, INC. (1903). 1141 Broadway, NYC 10001. (212)683-3221. Pres. Zevulun Charlop; Sec. Sam Gabel. Raises funds for the maintenance of schools, kitchens, clinics, and dispensaries in Israel; free loan foundations in Israel.

UNITED ISRAEL APPEAL, INC. (1925). 515 Park Ave., NYC 10022. (212)688-0800. Chmn. Irwin S. Field; Exec. V. Chmn. Irving Kessler. As principal beneficiary of the United Jewish Appeal, serves as link between American Jewish community and Jewish Agency for Israel, its operating agent; assists in resettlement and absorption of refugees in Israel, and supervises flow of funds and expenditures for this purpose. *Briefings.*

UNITED STATES COMMITTEE SPORTS FOR ISRAEL, INC. (1948). 275 S. 19 St., Philadelphia, PA 19103. (215)546-4700. Pres. Robert E. Spivak; Exec. Dir. Barbara G. Lissy. Sponsors U.S. participation in, and fields and selects U.S. team for, World Maccabiah Games in Israel every four years; promotes education and sports programs in Israel; provides funds and technical and material assistance to Wingate Institute for Physical Education and Sport in Israel; sponsors coaching programs in Israel. *USCSFI Newsletter; Commemorative Maccabiah Games Journal.*

WOMEN'S LEAGUE FOR ISRAEL, INC. (1928). 515 Park Ave., NYC 10022. (212)838-1997. Pres. Marilyn Schwartzman; Sr. V. Pres. Trudy Miner; Exec. Dir. Bernice Backon. Promotes the welfare of young people in Israel; built and maintains homes in Jerusalem, Haifa, Tel Aviv, and Natanya; in cooperation with Ministry of Labor and Social Affairs, operates live-in vocational training center for girls, including handicapped, in Natanya, and weaving workshop for the blind. *Bulletin; In League.*

WORLD CONFEDERATION OF UNITED ZIONISTS (1946; reorg. 1958). 30 E. 60 St., NYC 10022. (212)371-1452. Copres. Bernice S. Tannenbaum, Kalman Sultanik, Melech Topiol. The largest Diaspora-centered Zionist grouping in the world, distinguished from all other groups in the Zionist movement in that it has no association or affiliation with any political party in Israel, but derives its inspiration and strength from the whole spectrum of Zionist, Jewish, and Israeli life; supports projects identified with Israel; sponsors nonparty *halutzic* youth movements in the Diaspora; promotes Zionist education and strives for an Israel-oriented creative Jewish survival in the Diaspora. *Zionist Information Views.*

WORLD ZIONIST ORGANIZATION—AMERICAN SECTION (1971). 515 Park Ave., NYC 10022. (212)752-0600. Chmn. Bernice S. Tannenbaum; Exec. V. Chmn. Isadore Hamlin. As the American section of the overall Zionist body throughout the world, it operates primarily in the field of *aliyah* from the free countries, education in the Diaspora, youth and *hechalutz*, organization and information, cultural institutions, publications; conducts a worldwide Hebrew cultural program including special seminars and pedagogical manuals; disperses information and assists in research projects concerning Israel; promotes, publishes, and distributes books, periodicals, and pamphlets concerning developments in Israel, Zionism, and Jewish history. *Israel Scene; Five Fifteen.*

——, DEPARTMENT OF EDUCATION AND CULTURE (1948). 515 Park Ave., NYC 10022. (212)752-0600. Exec. Counselor Arthur Levine; Exec. Dir. Yoel Rappel. Seeks to foster a wider and deeper knowledge of the Hebrew language and literature and a better understanding and fuller appreciation of the role of Israel in the destiny of Jewry and Judaism, to introduce the study of Israel as an integral part of the Jewish school curriculum, and to initiate and sponsor educational projects designed to implement these objectives.

——, NORTH AMERICAN ALIYAH MOVEMENT (1968). 515 Park Ave., NYC 10022. (212)752-0600. Pres. Maurice Friedlander; Exec. Dir. Marsha Kirshblum. Promotes and facilitates *aliyah* and *klitah* from the U.S. and Canada to Israel; serves as a social framework for North American immigrants to Israel. *Aliyon.*

——, ZIONIST ARCHIVES AND LIBRARY OF THE (1939). 515 Park Ave., NYC 10022. (212)752-0600. Acting Librarian Esther Togman. Serves as an archives and information service for material on Israel,

Palestine, the Middle East, Zionism, and all aspects of Jewish life.

ZIONIST ORGANIZATION OF AMERICA (1897). ZOA House, 4 E. 34 St., NYC 10016. (212)481-1500. Pres. Alleck A. Resnick; Exec. V. Pres. Paul Flacks. Public affairs programming to foster the unity of the Jewish people through General Zionism; parent organization of four institutes which promote the understanding of Zionism within the Jewish and non-Jewish world; sponsors of Masada Youth summer programs in Israel, ZOA House in Tel Aviv, and international high school programs at Kfar Silver, Ashkelon.

PROFESSIONAL ASSOCIATIONS*

AMERICAN CONFERENCE OF CANTORS, UNION OF AMERICAN HEBREW CONGREGATIONS (Religious, Educational)

AMERICAN JEWISH CORRECTIONAL CHAPLAINS ASSOCIATION, INC. (Social Welfare)

AMERICAN JEWISH PRESS ASSOCIATION (Cultural)

AMERICAN JEWISH PUBLIC RELATIONS SOCIETY (1957). 234 Fifth Ave., NYC 10001. (212)697-5895. Pres. Martin J. Warmbrand; Treas. Hyman Brickman. Advances professional status of workers in the public-relations field in Jewish communal service; upholds a professional code of ethics and standards; serves as a clearinghouse for employment opportunities; exchanges professional information and ideas; presents awards for excellence in professional attainments, including the "Maggid Award" for outstanding literary or artistic achievement which enhances Jewish life. *The Handout.*

ASSOCIATION OF HILLEL/JEWISH CAMPUS PROFESSIONALS (Religious, Educational)

ASSOCIATION OF JEWISH CENTER WORKERS (Community Relations)

ASSOCIATION OF JEWISH CHAPLAINS OF THE ARMED FORCES (Religious, Educational)

ASSOCIATION OF JEWISH COMMUNITY ORGANIZATION PERSONNEL (Social Welfare)

ASSOCIATION OF JEWISH COMMUNITY RELATIONS WORKERS (Community Relations)

CANTORS ASSEMBLY OF AMERICA (Religious, Educational)

CENTRAL CONFERENCE OF AMERICAN RABBIS (Religious, Educational)

CONFERENCE OF JEWISH COMMUNAL SERVICE (Social Welfare)

COUNCIL OF JEWISH ORGANIZATIONS IN CIVIL SERVICE (Community Relations)

JWB COMMISSION ON JEWISH CHAPLAINCY (Social Welfare)

JEWISH EDUCATORS ASSEMBLY OF THE UNITED SYNAGOGUE OF AMERICA (Religious, Educational)

JEWISH MINISTERS CANTORS ASSOCIATION OF AMERICA, INC. (Religious, Educational)

JEWISH TEACHERS ASSOCIATION—MORIM (Religious, Educational)

NATIONAL ASSOCIATION OF HEBREW DAY SCHOOL ADMINISTRATORS, TORAH UMESORAH (Religious, Educational)

NATIONAL ASSOCIATION OF SYNAGOGUE ADMINISTRATORS, UNITED SYNAGOGUE OF AMERICA (Religious, Educational)

NATIONAL ASSOCIATION OF TEMPLE ADMINISTRATORS, UNION OF AMERICAN HEBREW CONGREGATIONS (Religious, Educational)

NATIONAL ASSOCIATION OF TEMPLE EDUCATORS, UNION OF AMERICAN HEBREW CONGREGATIONS (Religious, Educational)

NATIONAL CONFERENCE OF YESHIVA PRINCIPALS OF TORAH UMESORAH (Religious, Educational)

RABBINICAL ASSEMBLY (Religious, Educational)

RABBINICAL COUNCIL OF AMERICA (Religious, Educational)

RECONSTRUCTIONIST RABBINICAL ASSOCIATION, JEWISH RECONSTRUCTIONIST FOUNDATION (Religious, Educational)

UNION OF ORTHODOX RABBIS OF THE U.S. AND CANADA (Religious, Educational)

WORLD CONFERENCE OF JEWISH COMMUNAL SERVICE (Community Relations)

---

*For fuller listing see under categories in parentheses.

WOMEN'S ORGANIZATIONS*

AMIT WOMEN (Zionist and Pro-Israel)

B'NAI B'RITH WOMEN (Social Welfare)

BRANDEIS UNIVERSITY NATIONAL WOMEN'S COMMITTEE (1948). 415 South St., Waltham, MA 02254. (617)647-2194. Pres. Barbara J. Ehrlich; Exec. Dir. Carol S. Rabinovitz. Responsible for support and maintenance of Brandeis University libraries; sponsors University on Wheels and, through its chapters, study-group programs based on faculty-prepared syllabi, volunteer work in educational services, and a program of New Books for Old sales; constitutes largest "Friends of a Library" group in U.S. *Imprint.*

HADASSAH, THE WOMEN'S ZIONIST ORGANIZATION OF AMERICA, INC. (Zionist and Pro-Israel)

NATIONAL COUNCIL OF JEWISH WOMEN (Social Welfare)

NATIONAL FEDERATION OF TEMPLE SISTERHOODS, UNION OF AMERICAN HEBREW CONGREGATIONS (Religious, Educational)

PIONEER WOMEN/NA'AMAT, THE WOMEN'S LABOR ZIONIST ORGANIZATION OF AMERICA (Zionist and Pro-Israel)

UNITED ORDER TRUE SISTERS (Social, Mutual Benefit)

WOMEN'S AMERICAN ORT FEDERATION, AMERICAN ORT FEDERATION, INC. (Overseas Aid)

WOMEN'S BRANCH OF THE UNION OF ORTHODOX JEWISH CONGREGATIONS OF AMERICA (Religious, Educational)

WOMEN'S DIVISION OF POALE AGUDATH ISRAEL OF AMERICA (Zionist and Pro-Israel)

WOMEN'S DIVISION OF THE JEWISH LABOR COMMITTEE (Community Relations)

WOMEN'S DIVISION OF THE UNITED JEWISH APPEAL (Overseas Aid)

WOMEN'S LEAGUE FOR CONSERVATIVE JUDAISM (Religious, Educational)

WOMEN'S LEAGUE FOR ISRAEL, INC. (Zionist and Pro-Israel)

YESHIVA UNIVERSITY WOMEN'S ORGANIZATION (Religious, Educational)

YOUTH AND STUDENT ORGANIZATIONS*

AMERICAN ZIONIST YOUTH FOUNDATION, INC. (Zionist and Pro-Israel)

———, AMERICAN ZIONIST YOUTH COUNCIL

B'NAI B'RITH HILLEL FOUNDATIONS, INC. (Religious, Educational)

B'NAI B'RITH YOUTH ORGANIZATION (Religious, Educational)

BNEI AKIVA OF NORTH AMERICA, RELIGIOUS ZIONISTS OF AMERICA (Zionist and Pro-Israel)

BNOS AGUDATH ISRAEL, AGUDATH ISRAEL OF AMERICA, GIRLS' DIVISION (Religious, Educational)

DROR—YOUNG KIBBUTZ MOVEMENT— HABONIM (Zionist and Pro-Israel)

HABONIM-DROR LABOR ZIONIST YOUTH (Zionist and Pro-Israel)

HASHACHAR, HADASSAH (Zionist and Pro-Israel)

HASHOMER HATZAIR, SOCIALIST ZIONIST YOUTH MOVEMENT (Zionist and Pro-Israel)

JEWISH STUDENT PRESS-SERVICE (1970)— JEWISH STUDENT EDITORIAL PROJECTS, JEWISH PRESS FEATURES. 15 East 26 St., Suite 1350, NYC 10010. (212)679-1411. Dir. Joyce Fine. Serves all Jewish student and young adult publications, as well as many Anglo-Jewish newspapers, in North America, through monthly feature packets of articles and graphics. Holds annual national and local editors' conference for member publications. Provides technical and editorial assistance; keeps complete file of member publications since 1970; maintains Israel Bureau. *Jewish Press Features.*

KADIMA, UNITED SYNAGOGUE OF AMERICA (Religious, Educational)

NATIONAL CONFERENCE OF SYNAGOGUE YOUTH, UNION OF ORTHODOX JEWISH CONGREGATIONS OF AMERICA (Religious, Educational)

---

*For fuller listing see under categories in parentheses.

NOAM-HAMISHMERET HATZEIRA, RELI-GIOUS ZIONISTS OF AMERICA (Zionist and Pro-Israel)

NORTH AMERICAN FEDERATION OF TEM-PLE YOUTH, UNION OF AMERICAN HE-BREW CONGREGATIONS (Religious, Educational)

NORTH AMERICAN JEWISH STUDENTS AP-PEAL (1971). 15 E. 26 St., NYC, 10010. (212)679-2293. Pres. Adam Whiteman; Exec. Dir. Roberta Shiffman. Serves as central fund-raising mechanism for four national, independent, Jewish student organizations; insures accountability of public Jewish communal funds used by these agencies; assists Jewish students undertaking projects of concern to Jewish communities; advises and assists Jewish organizations in determining student project feasibility and impact; fosters development of Jewish student leadership in the Jewish community. Beneficiaries include local and regional Jewish student projects on campuses throughout North America; current constituents include Jewish Student Press Service, Student Struggle for Soviet Jewry, *Response*, and Yugntruf; beneficiaries include Tulane University Soviet Jewry Lobby (New Orleans); Israel Education Day (Los Angeles); Brandeis' *Focus* (Waltham, MA); and a northeastern Women Rabbinical Students' Conference held in New York.

NORTH AMERICAN JEWISH STUDENTS' NETWORK (1969). 1 Park Ave., #418, NYC 10016. (212)689-0790. Pres. Moshe Ronen; U.S. Chmn. Philip Machlin; Exec. Dir. Daniel J. Duman. Coordinates information and programs among all Jewish student organizations in North America; promotes development of student-controlled Jewish student organizations; maintains contacts and coordinates programs with Jewish students throughout the world through the World Union of Jewish Students; runs the Jewish Student Speakers Bureau; sponsors regional, national, and North American conferences. *Network Spectrum*.

NORTH AMERICAN JEWISH YOUTH COUN-CIL (Community Relations)

STUDENT STRUGGLE FOR SOVIET JEWRY, INC. (Community Relations)

UNITED SYNAGOGUE YOUTH, UNITED SYN-AGOGUE OF AMERICA (Religious, Educational)

YOUNG ISRAEL COLLEGIATES AND YOUNG ADULTS, NATIONAL COUNCIL OF YOUNG ISRAEL (Religious, Educational)

YUGNTRUF YOUTH FOR YIDDISH (1964). 3328 Bainbridge Ave., Bronx, NY 10467. (212)654-8540. Chmn. Itzek Gottesman; Editor Paul Glasser. A worldwide, non-political organization for high school and college students with a knowledge of, or interest in, Yiddish. Spreads the love and use of the Yiddish language, especially among young adults, but activities also reach out to other age groups. Organizes artistic and social activities. Offers services of full-time field worker to assist in forming Yiddish courses and clubs throughout the U.S. *Yugntruf.*

ZEIREI AGUDATH ISRAEL, AGUDATH IS-RAEL OF AMERICA, YOUTH DIVISION (Religious, Educational)

CANADA

CANADA-ISRAEL SECURITIES, LTD., STATE OF ISRAEL BONDS (1953). 1255 University St., Montreal, PQ H3B 3B2. (514)878-1871. Pres. Thomas O. Hecht; Exec. V. Pres. Julius Briskin. Sale of State of Israel Bonds in Canada.

CANADIAN ASSOCIATION FOR LABOR IS-RAEL (HISTADRUT) (1944). 4770 Kent Ave., Suite 301, Montreal, PQ H3W 1H2. Pres. Nathan Kaporovsky; Exec. Dir. Flora Naglie. Raises funds for Histadrut medical, cultural, and educational programs for the workers and families of Israel. Public relations work with trade unions to inform and educate them about the State of Israel.

CANADIAN B'NAI B'RITH (1964). 15 Hove St., Suite 200, Downsview, ONT M3H 4Y8. (416)633-6224. Pres. Alan Borden; Exec. V. Pres. Frank Dimant. Canadian Jewry's largest service organization; makes representations to all levels of government on matters of Jewish concern; promotes humanitarian causes and educational programs, community volunteer projects, adult Jewish education and leadership development; dedicated to human rights; sponsors youth programs of B'nai B'rith Youth Org. and Hillel. *Covenant; Communiqué.*

——, LEAGUE FOR HUMAN RIGHTS (1970). Chmn. David Matas. Dedicated to monitoring human rights, combating racism and racial discrimination, and preventing bigotry and antisemitism, through education and community relations. Sponsors Holocaust Education Programs, the R. Lou Ronson Research Institute on Anti-Semitism; distributor of Anti-Defamation League materials in Canada. *The Reporter; Christians & Jews Today.*

CANADIAN FOUNDATION FOR JEWISH CULTURE (1965). 4600 Bathurst St., Willowdale, ONT M2R 3V2. (416)635-2883. Pres. Mira Koschitzky; Exec. Sec. Edmond Y. Lipsitz. Promotes Jewish studies at university level and encourages original research and scholarship in Jewish subjects; awards annual scholarships and grants-in-aid to scholars in Canada.

CANADIAN FRIENDS OF THE ALLIANCE ISRAÉLITE UNIVERSELLE (1958). P.O. Box 578 Victoria Station, Montreal, PQ H3Z 2Y6. (514)481-3552. Pres. Joseph Nuss. Supports the educational work of the Alliance.

CANADIAN FRIENDS OF THE HEBREW UNIVERSITY (1944). 208-1 Yorkdale Rd., Toronto, ONT M6A 3A1. (416)789-2633. Pres. Ralph Halbert; Exec. Dir. Joel Alpert. Represents and publicizes the Hebrew University in Canada; serves as fundraising arm for the university in Canada; processes Canadians for study at the university. *Scopus; Ha-Universita.*

CANADIAN JEWISH CONGRESS (1919; reorg. 1934). 1590 Ave. Docteur Penfield, Montreal, PQ H3G 1C5. (514)931-7531. Pres. Milton Harris; Exec. V. Pres. Alan Rose. The official voice of Canadian Jewish communities at home and abroad; acts on all matters affecting the status, rights, concerns and welfare of Canadian Jewry; internationally active on behalf of Soviet Jewry, Jews in Arab lands, Holocaust remembrance and restitution; largest Jewish archives in Canada. *National Small Communities Newsletter; Community Relations Newsletter; Intercom; National Archives Newsletter; Bulletin du Cercle Juif.*

CANADIAN ORT ORGANIZATION (Organization of Rehabilitation Through Training) (1942). 5165 Sherbrooke St. W., Suite 208, Montreal, PQ H4A 1T6. (514)481-2787. Pres. J.A. Lyone Heppner; Exec. Dir. Mac Silver. Carries on fund-raising projects in support of the worldwide vocational-training school network of ORT. *Canadian ORT Reporter.*

———, WOMEN'S CANADIAN ORT (1948). 3101 Bathurst St., Suite 404, Toronto, ONT M6A 2A6. (416)787-0339. Pres. Harriet Morton; Exec. Dir. Diane Uslaner. *Focus.*

CANADIAN SEPHARDI FEDERATION (1973). 4735 Cote Ste. Catherine St., Montreal, PQ H3W 1M1. (514)731-3334. Pres. Joseph Benarrosh; Exec. Dir. Marcel Elbaz. Preserves and promotes Sephardic identity, particularly among youth; works for the unity of the Jewish people; emphasizes relations between Sephardi communities all over the world; seeks better situation for Sephardim in Israel; supports Israel by all means. Participates in *La Voix Sépharade, Le Monde Sépharade,* and *Sephardi World.*

CANADIAN YOUNG JUDAEA (1917). 788 Marlee Ave., Toronto, ONT M6B 3K1. (416)787-5350. Pres. Michael Goldbach; Exec. Dir. Risa Epstein. Strives to attract Jewish youth to Zionism, with goal of *aliyah;* operates six summer camps in Canada and one in Israel; is sponsored by Canadian Hadassah—WIZO and Zionist Federation of Canada, and affiliated with Hanoar Hatzioni in Israel. *Judaean; The Young Judaean.*

CANADIAN ZIONIST FEDERATION (1967). 1310 Greene Ave., Westmount, Montreal, PQ H3Z 2B2. (514)934-0804. Pres. Neri J. Bloomfield; Exec. V. Pres. Leon Kronitz. Umbrella organization of all Zionist and Israel-related groups in Canada; carries on major activities in all areas of Jewish life through its departments of education and culture, *aliyah,* youth and students, public affairs, and fund raising for the purpose of strengthening the State of Israel and the Canadian Jewish community. *Canadian Zionist Magazine.*

———, BUREAU OF EDUCATION AND CULTURE (1972). Pres. Neri J. Bloomfield; Exec. V. Pres. Leon Kronitz. Provides counseling by pedagogic experts, in-service teacher-training courses and seminars in Canada and Israel; national pedagogic council and research center; distributes educational material and teaching aids; conducts annual Bible contest and Hebrew-language courses for adults. *Al Mitzpe Hachinuch.*

FRIENDS OF PIONEERING ISRAEL (1950's). 1111 Finch Ave. W., Suite 154, Downsview, ONT M35 2E5 (416)736-0977. Exec. Dir. Yigal Gilboa. Acts as a progressive voice within the Jewish community on

Israeli and Canadian issues; expresses socialist and Zionist viewpoints; serves as a focal point for work of the progressive Zionist elements in Canada; acts as Canadian representative of Mapam and as the Canadian distributor of *New Outlook— Mideast Monthly.* Activities include lectures on political and Jewish topics open to the public; Jewish holiday celebrations.

HADASSAH—WIZO ORGANIZATION OF CANADA (1916). 1310 Greene Ave., 9th fl., Montreal, PQ H3Z 2B8. (514)937-9431. Pres. Cecily Peters; Exec. V. Pres. Lily Frank. Assists needy Israelis by sponsoring health, education, and social welfare services; seeks to strengthen and perpetuate Jewish identity; encourages Jewish and Hebrew culture in promoting Canadian ideals of democracy and pursuit of peace. *Orah.*

JEWISH IMMIGRANT AID SERVICES OF CANADA (JIAS) (1919). 5151 Cote Ste. Catherine Rd., Montreal, PQ H3W 1M6. (514)-342-9351. Pres. Daniel Morris; Exec. V. Pres. Herb Abrams. Serves as a national agency for immigration and immigrant welfare. *JIAS Bulletin.*

JEWISH NATIONAL FUND OF CANADA (KEREN KAYEMETH LE'ISRAEL, INC.) (1902). 1980 Sherbrooke St. W., Suite 300, Montreal, PQ H3H 2M7. Pres. Alexander (Bobby) Mayers; Exec. V. Pres. Michael Goldstein. Fund-raising organization affiliated with the World Zionist Organization; involved in afforestation, soil reclamation, and development of the land of Israel, including the construction of roads and preparation of sites for new settlements; helps to bring the message of "Keep Israel Green" to Jewish schools across Canada.

LABOR ZIONIST MOVEMENT OF CANADA (1939). 4770 Kent Ave., Montreal, PQ H3W 1H2. (514)342-9710. Chmn. Natl. Exec. Abraham Shurem. Disseminates information and publications on Israel and Jewish life; arranges special events, lectures, and seminars; coordinates communal and political activities of its constituent bodies (Pioneer Women/Na'amat, Labor Zionist Alliance, Poale Zion party, Habonim-Dror Youth, Israel Histadrut, affiliated Hebrew elementary and high schools in Montreal and Toronto).

MIZRACHI-HAPOEL HAMIZRACHI ORGANIZATION OF CANADA (1941). 159 Almore Ave., Downsview, ONT M3H 2H9. (416)-630-7575. Pres. Kurt Rothschild; Exec. Dir. Rabbi Menachem Gopin. Promotes religious Zionism, aimed at making Israel a state based on Torah; maintains Bnei Akiva, a summer camp, adult education program, and touring department; supports Mizrachi-Hapoel Hamizrachi and other religious Zionist institutions in Israel which strengthen traditional Judaism. *Mizrachi Newsletter; Or Hamizrach Torah Quarterly.*

NATIONAL COUNCIL OF JEWISH WOMEN OF CANADA (1947). 1111 Finch Ave. W., Suite 401, Willowdale, ONT M3J 2E5. (416)665-8251. Pres. Sheila Freeman; Exec. Dir. Eleanor Appleby. Dedicated to furthering human welfare in Jewish and non-Jewish communities, locally, nationally, and internationally; provides essential services, and stimulates and educates the individual and the community through an integrated program of education, service, and social action. *New Edition.*

NATIONAL JOINT COMMUNITY RELATIONS COMMITTEE OF CANADIAN JEWISH CONGRESS (1936). 4600 Bathurst St., Willowdale, ONT M2R 3V2 (416)635-2883. Chmn. David Satok; Exec. Dir. Manuel Prutschi. Seeks to safeguard the status, rights, and welfare of Jews in Canada; to combat antisemitism and promote understanding and goodwill among all ethnic and religious groups.

UNITED JEWISH TEACHERS' SEMINARY (1946). 5237 Clanranald Ave., Montreal, PQ H3X 2S5. (514)489-4401. Dir. A. Aisenbach. Trains teachers for Yiddish and Hebrew schools under auspices of Canadian Jewish Congress. *Yitonenu.*

ZIONIST ORGANIZATION OF CANADA (1892; reorg. 1919). 788 Marlee Ave., Toronto, ONT M6B 3K1. (416)781-3571. Pres. Max Goody; Exec. V. Pres. George Liban. Furthers general Zionist aims by operating six youth camps in Canada and one in Israel; maintains Zionist book club; arranges programs, lectures; sponsors Young Judaea, Youth Centre Project in Jerusalem Forest, Israel.

Jewish Federations, Welfare Funds, Community Councils[1]

UNITED STATES

ALABAMA

BIRMINGHAM

BIRMINGHAM JEWISH FEDERATION (1935; reorg. 1971); PO Box 9157 (35213); (205)-879-0416. Pres. Phyllis Weinstein; Exec. Dir. Richard Friedman.

MOBILE

MOBILE JEWISH WELFARE FUND, INC. (Inc. 1966); 1 Office Park, 404 C (36609); (205)-343-7197. Pres. Mrs. Paul Brown; V. Pres. Dr. Joel Grossman.

MONTGOMERY

JEWISH FEDERATION OF MONTGOMERY, INC. (1930); PO Box 1150 (36101); (205)-263-7674. Pres. Paul Handmacher; Exec. Sec. Ellen Loeb.

ARIZONA

PHOENIX

JEWISH FEDERATION OF GREATER PHOENIX (incl. surrounding communities) (1940); 1718 W. Maryland Ave. (85015); (602)249-1845. Pres. Jerry Gross; Exec. Dir. Lawrence M. Cohen.

TUCSON

JEWISH FEDERATION OF SOUTHERN ARIZONA (1942); 102 N. Plumer (85719); (602)-884-8921. Pres. Saul Syde; Exec. V. Pres. Charles Plotkin.

ARKANSAS

LITTLE ROCK

JEWISH FEDERATION OF LITTLE ROCK (1911); 221 Donaghey Bldg. (72201); (501)-372-3571. Pres. Philip E. Kaplan, Jr.; Exec. Dir. Nanci Goldman.

CALIFORNIA

FRESNO

JEWISH FEDERATION OF FRESNO; 5094 N. West Ave. (93711); (209)432-2162. Pres. Robert Boro; Exec. Dir. Lisa M. Goldman.

LONG BEACH

JEWISH COMMUNITY FEDERATION OF GREATER LONG BEACH AND WEST ORANGE COUNTY (1937); (sponsors UNITED JEWISH WELFARE FUND); 3801 E. Willow St. (90815); (213)426-7601. Pres. Robert Blakely; Exec. Dir. Oliver Winkler.

LOS ANGELES

JEWISH FEDERATION COUNCIL OF GREATER LOS ANGELES (1912; reorg. 1959); (sponsors UNITED JEWISH FUND); 6505 Wilshire Blvd. (90048); (213)852-1234. Pres. Bruce Hochman; Exec. V. Pres. Ted Kanner.

OAKLAND

JEWISH FEDERATION OF THE GREATER EAST BAY (1918); 3245 Sheffield Ave.

---

[1]This directory is based on information supplied by the Council of Jewish Federations. An asterisk (*) preceding a listing indicates an organization *not* affiliated with CJF.

(94602); (415)533-7462. Pres. Herbert Friedman; Exec. V. Pres. Melvin Mogulof.

ORANGE COUNTY

JEWISH FEDERATION OF ORANGE COUNTY (1964; Inc. 1965); (sponsors UNITED JEWISH WELFARE FUND); 12181 Buaro, Garden Grove (92640); (714)530-6636. Pres. Eleanor Burg; Exec. Dir. Gerald Lasensky.

PALM SPRINGS

JEWISH FEDERATION OF PALM SPRINGS-DESERT AREA (1971); 611 S. Palm Canyon Dr. (92264); (619)325-7281. Pres. Harry Tarler; Exec. Dir. Nat Bent.

SACRAMENTO

JEWISH FEDERATION OF SACRAMENTO (1948); PO Box 254589 (95865); (916)486-0906. Pres. Arlene Pearl; Exec. Dir. Arnold Feder.

SAN DIEGO

UNITED JEWISH FEDERATION OF SAN DIEGO COUNTY (1935); 4797 Mercury St. (92111); (619)571-3444. Pres. Dr. Gerald Kobernick; Exec. Dir. Steven M. Abramson.

SAN FRANCISCO

JEWISH COMMUNITY FEDERATION OF SAN FRANCISCO, THE PENINSULA, MARIN, AND SONOMA COUNTIES (1910; reorg. 1955); 121 Steuart St. (94105); (415)777-0411. Pres. Ron Kaufman; Exec. Dir. Rabbi Brian Lurie.

SAN JOSE

JEWISH FEDERATION OF GREATER SAN JOSE (incl. Santa Clara County except Palo Alto and Los Altos) (1930; reorg. 1950); 14855 Oka Rd., Los Gatos (95030); (408)-267-2770. Pres. Masha Dryan; Exec. Dir. Michael Papo.

SANTA BARBARA

*SANTA BARBARA JEWISH FEDERATION; PO Box 6782 (93111); (805)962-0770. Pres. M. Howard Goldman.

STOCKTON

*STOCKTON JEWISH WELFARE FUND (1972); 5105 N. El Dorado St. (95207); (209)-477-9306. Pres. Sandy Senderov.

VENTURA

*VENTURA COUNTY JEWISH COUNCIL— TEMPLE BETH TORAH (1938); 7620 Foothill Rd. (93004); (805)647-4181. Pres. Joyce Wittenberg.

COLORADO

DENVER

ALLIED JEWISH FEDERATION OF DENVER (1936); (sponsors ALLIED JEWISH CAMPAIGN); 300 S. Dahlia St. (80222); (303)321-3399. Pres. Steven Farber; Exec. Dir. Sheldon Steinhauser.

CONNECTICUT

BRIDGEPORT

JEWISH FEDERATION OF GREATER BRIDGEPORT, INC. (1936; reorg. 1981); (sponsors UNITED JEWISH CAMPAIGN); 4200 Park Ave. (06604); (203)372-6504. Pres. Joel Lichtenstein; Exec. Dir. Gerald A. Kleinman.

DANBURY

JEWISH FEDERATION OF GREATER DANBURY (1945); 54 Main St., Suite E (06810); (203)792-6353. Pres. Robert Soloff; Exec. Dir. Norman Mogul.

EASTERN CONNECTICUT

JEWISH FEDERATION OF EASTERN CONNECTICUT, INC. (1950; Inc. 1970); 302 State St., New London (06320); (203)442-8062. Pres. Harold Weiner; Exec. Dir. Jerome Fisher.

GREENWICH

GREENWICH JEWISH FEDERATION; 22 W. Putnam Ave., Suite 18 (06830); (203)622-1434. Pres. Robert Mann, Joan Mann; Acting Exec. Dir. Michele Seligman.

HARTFORD

GREATER HARTFORD JEWISH FEDERATION (1945); 333 Bloomfield Ave., W. Hartford (06117); (203)232-4483. Pres. Philip D. Feltman; Exec. Dir. Don Cooper.

NEW HAVEN

NEW HAVEN JEWISH FEDERATION (1928); (sponsors COMBINED JEWISH APPEAL); 1162 Chapel St. (06511); (203)562-2137. Pres. Dr. Milton Wallack; Exec. Dir. Susan Shimelman.

NORWALK

JEWISH FEDERATION OF GREATER NORWALK, INC. (1946; reorg. 1964); Shorehaven Rd., E. Norwalk (06855); (203)853-3440. Pres. Nancy Oberst; Exec. Dir. Joshua Gruber.

STAMFORD

UNITED JEWISH FEDERATION (Inc. 1973); 1035 Newfield Ave., PO Box 3038 (06905); (203)322-6935. Pres. Stephen Epstein; Exec. V. Pres. Steve Schreier.

WATERBURY

JEWISH FEDERATION OF WATERBURY, INC. (1938); 1020 Country Club Rd. (06708); (203)758-2441. Pres. Dr. Jerome Sugar; Exec. Dir. Eli J. Skora.

DELAWARE

WILMINGTON

JEWISH FEDERATION OF DELAWARE, INC. (1934); 101 Garden of Eden Rd. (19803); (302)478-6200. Pres. Martin Mand; Exec. Dir. Robert Kerbel.

DISTRICT OF COLUMBIA

WASHINGTON

UNITED JEWISH APPEAL—FEDERATION OF GREATER WASHINGTON, INC. (1935); 7900 Wisconsin Ave., Bethesda, MD (20814-3698); (301)652-6480. Pres. Paul S. Berger; Exec. V. Pres. Ted Farber.

FLORIDA

BREVARD COUNTY

*BREVARD JEWISH COMMUNITY COUNCIL; PO Box 1816, Merritt Island (32952); (305)-453-4695. Pres. Dr. Robert Mandel; Exec. Sec. Frances Singer.

DAYTONA BEACH

JEWISH FEDERATION OF VOLUSIA & FLAGLER COUNTIES, INC.; 637 N. Grandview Ave. (32018); (904)255-6260. Pres. Dr. Leonard Indianer; Exec. Sec. Iris Gardner.

FT. LAUDERDALE

JEWISH FEDERATION OF GREATER FT. LAUDERDALE (1967); 8358 W. Oakland Pk. Blvd. (33321); (305)748-8400. Pres. Brian Sherr; Exec. Dir. Joel Telles.

JACKSONVILLE

JACKSONVILLE JEWISH FEDERATION (1935); 10829-1 Old St. Augustine Rd. (32223); (904)262-2800. Pres. Aaron M. Scharf; Exec. V. Pres. Louis B. Solomon.

LEE COUNTY

JEWISH FEDERATION OF LEE COUNTY (1974); PO Box JJJ, Cape Coral (33910); (813)772-1777. Pres. Sheila Laboda.

MIAMI

GREATER MIAMI JEWISH FEDERATION, INC. (1938); 4200 Biscayne Blvd. (33137); (305)576-4000. Pres. Samuel I. Adler; Exec. V. Pres. Myron J. Brodie.

ORLANDO

JEWISH FEDERATION OF GREATER ORLANDO (1949); 851 N. Maitland Ave., PO Box 1508, Maitland (32751); (305)645-5933. Pres. Mark Cooper; Exec. Dir. Michael Meyer.

PALM BEACH COUNTY

JEWISH FEDERATION OF PALM BEACH COUNTY, INC. (1938); 501 S. Flagler Dr., Suite 305, W. Palm Beach (33401); (305)-832-2120. Pres. Erwin Blonder; Exec. Dir. Norman J. Schimelman.

PENSACOLA

*PENSACOLA FEDERATED JEWISH CHARITIES (1942); 1320 E. Lee St. (32503); (904)-438-1464. Pres. Joe Rosenbaum; Sec. Mrs. Harry Saffer.

PINELLAS COUNTY (incl. Clearwater and St. Petersburg)

JEWISH FEDERATION OF PINELLAS COUNTY, INC. (1950; reincorp. 1974); 302 S. Jupiter Ave., Clearwater (33515); (813)446-1033. Pres. Stanley Newwark; Exec. Dir. Paul Levine.

SARASOTA

SARASOTA-MANATEE JEWISH FEDERATION (1959); 2197 Ringling Blvd. (33577); (813)-365-4410. Pres. Adolph Shapiro; Exec. Dir. Jack Weintraub.

SOUTH BROWARD

JEWISH FEDERATION OF SOUTH BROWARD, INC. (1943); 2719 Hollywood Blvd., Hollywood (33020); (305)921-8810. Pres. Dr. Saul Singer; Exec. Dir. Sumner G. Kaye.

SOUTH COUNTY

SOUTH COUNTY JEWISH FEDERATION; 336 NW Spanish River Blvd., Boca Raton (33431); (305)368-2737. Pres. Marianne Bobick; Exec. Dir. Rabbi Bruce S. Warshal.

TAMPA

TAMPA JEWISH FEDERATION (1941); 2808 Horatio (33609); (813)875-1618. Pres. Judith Rosenkranz; Exec. Dir. Gary S. Alter.

GEORGIA

ATLANTA

ATLANTA JEWISH FEDERATION, INC. (1905; reorg. 1967); 1753 Peachtree Rd. NE (30309); (404)873-1661. Pres. Gerald Cohen; Exec. Dir. David I. Sarnat.

AUGUSTA

AUGUSTA JEWISH FEDERATION (1937); PO Box 3251, Sibley Rd. (30904); (404)736-1818. Pres. Joseph Goldberg; Exec. Dir. Louis Goldman.

COLUMBUS

JEWISH WELFARE FEDERATION OF COLUMBUS, INC. (1941); PO Box 6313 (31907); (404)563-4766. Pres. Dr. Robert Garnett; Sec. Irene Rainbow.

SAVANNAH

SAVANNAH JEWISH COUNCIL (1943); (sponsors UJA-FEDERATION CAMPAIGN); PO Box 6546, 5111 Abercorn St. (31405); (912)-355-8111. Pres. Millie Melaver; Exec. Dir. Stan Ramati.

HAWAII

HONOLULU

*JEWISH FEDERATION OF HAWAII (1956); 817 Cooke St. (96813); (808)531-4634. Pres. Robert Goldman; Exec. Dir. Barry Shain.

ILLINOIS

CHAMPAIGN-URBANA

CHAMPAIGN-URBANA JEWISH FEDERATION (member Central Illinois Jewish Federation) (1929); 503 E. John St., Champaign (61820); (217)367-9872. Pres. Daniel Bloomfield.

CHICAGO

JEWISH FEDERATION OF METROPOLITAN CHICAGO (1900); 1 S. Franklin St. (60606); (312)346-6700. Pres. Richard L. Wexler; Exec. Dir. Steven B. Nasatir.

JEWISH UNITED FUND OF METROPOLITAN CHICAGO (1968); 1 S. Franklin St. (60606); (312)346-6700. Pres. Richard L. Wexler; Exec. Dir. Steven B. Nasatir.

DECATUR

DECATUR JEWISH FEDERATION (member Central Illinois Jewish Federation) (1942); c/o Temple B'nai Abraham, 1326 W. Eldorado (62522); (217)429-5740. Pres. Marvin Tick; Treas. Charlotte Goldstein.

ELGIN

ELGIN AREA JEWISH WELFARE CHEST (1938); 330 Division St. (60120); (312)741-5656. Pres. Charles Zimmerman; Treas. Alvin Hass.

JOLIET

*JOLIET JEWISH WELFARE CHEST (1938); 250 N. Midland Ave. (60435); (815)741-4600. Pres. Sydney H. Scholar; Sec. Rabbi Morris M. Hershman.

PEORIA

JEWISH FEDERATION OF PEORIA (1933; Inc. 1947); 3100 N. Knoxville, Suite 17 (61603);

(309)686-0611. Pres. Dr. Charles Enda; Acting Exec. Dir. Marilyn Weigensberg.

QUAD CITIES

JEWISH FEDERATION OF THE QUAD CITIES (incl. Rock Island, Moline, Davenport, Bettendorf) (1938; comb. 1973); 224 18 St., Suite 511, Rock Island (61201); (309)793-1300. Pres. Lawrence Satin; Exec. Dir. Joseph Bluestein.

ROCKFORD

ROCKFORD JEWISH COMMUNITY COUNCIL (1937); 1500 Parkview Ave. (61107); (815)-399-5497. Pres. Ted Liebovich; Exec. Dir. Tony Toback.

SOUTHERN ILLINOIS

JEWISH FEDERATION OF SOUTHERN ILLINOIS (incl. SE Mo. and NW Ky.) (1941); 6464 W. Main, Suite 7A, Belleville (62223); (618)398-6100. Pres. Malcolm Zwick; Exec. Dir. Jordan Harburger.

SPRINGFIELD

SPRINGFIELD JEWISH FEDERATION (1941); 730 E. Vine St. (62703); (217)528-3446. Pres. Dorothy Friedman; Exec. Dir. Lenore Loeb.

INDIANA

EVANSVILLE

EVANSVILLE JEWISH COMMUNITY COUNCIL, INC. (1936; Inc. 1964); PO Box 5026 (47715); (812)477-7050. Pres. Alan Newman; Exec. Sec. Maxine P. Fink.

FORT WAYNE

FORT WAYNE JEWISH FEDERATION (1921); 227 E. Washington Blvd. (46802); (219)422-8566. Pres. Stanley Levine; Exec. Dir. Michael Pousman.

INDIANAPOLIS

JEWISH WELFARE FEDERATION, INC. (1905); 615 N. Alabama St., Suite 412 (46204); (317)637-2473. Pres. Dr. Edward Gabovitch; Exec. V. Pres. Harry Nadler.

LAFAYETTE

FEDERATED JEWISH CHARITIES (1924); PO Box 708 (47902); (317)742-9081. Pres. Arnold Cohen; Fin. Sec. Louis Pearlman, Jr.

MICHIGAN CITY

MICHIGAN CITY UNITED JEWISH WELFARE FUND; 2800 Franklin St. (46360); (219)874-4477. Pres. Nate Winski; Treas. Harold Leinwand.

NORTHWEST INDIANA

THE JEWISH FEDERATION, INC. (1941; reorg. 1959); 2939 Jewett St., Highland (46322); (219)972-2251. Pres. Warren Yalowitz; Exec. Dir. Barnett Labowitz.

SOUTH BEND

JEWISH FEDERATION OF ST. JOSEPH VALLEY (1946); 804 Sherland Bldg. (46601); (219)233-1164. Pres. Frederick Baer; Exec. V. Pres. Bernard Natkow.

IOWA

DES MOINES

JEWISH FEDERATION OF GREATER DES MOINES (1914); 910 Polk Blvd. (50312); (515)277-6321. Pres. Dorothy Bucksbaum; Acting Exec. Dir. Elaine Steinger.

SIOUX CITY

JEWISH FEDERATION (1921); 525 14 St. (51105); (712)258-0618. Pres. Jack Bernstein; Exec. Dir. Doris E. Rosenthal.

KANSAS

TOPEKA

*TOPEKA-LAWRENCE JEWISH FEDERATION (1939); 3237-SW Westover Rd. (66604); (913)357-4244. Pres. Dr. Mark Greenberg.

WICHITA

MID-KANSAS JEWISH FEDERATION, INC. (1935); 400 N. Woodlawn, Suite 8 (67208); (316)686-4741. Pres. Howard Marcus; Adm. Nancy Matassarin.

KENTUCKY

LEXINGTON

CENTRAL KENTUCKY JEWISH ASSOCIATION; 333 Waller, Suite 5 (40504); (606)252-7622. Pres. Jack Miller; Adm. Judy Saxe.

LOUISVILLE

JEWISH COMMUNITY FEDERATION OF LOUISVILLE, INC. (1934); (sponsors UNITED JEWISH CAMPAIGN); PO Box 33035, 3630 Dutchman's Lane (40232); (502)451-8840. Pres. Allan B. Solomon; Exec. Dir. Frank Fogelson.

LOUISIANA

ALEXANDRIA

THE JEWISH WELFARE FEDERATION AND COMMUNITY COUNCIL OF CENTRAL LOUISIANA (1938); 1262 Heyman Lane (71301); (318)442-1264. Pres. Harold Katz; Sec.-Treas. Mrs. George Kuplesky.

BATON ROUGE

JEWISH FEDERATION OF GREATER BATON ROUGE (1971); PO Box 80827 (70898); (504)769-0561, 769-0504. Pres. Bill Emmich; Exec. Dir. Michael Yuspeh.

MONROE

*UNITED JEWISH CHARITIES OF NORTHEAST LOUISIANA (1938); 2400 Orrel Pl. (71201); (318)387-0730. Pres. Morris Mintz; Sec.-Treas. Herman Dubin.

NEW ORLEANS

JEWISH FEDERATION OF GREATER NEW ORLEANS (1913; reorg. 1977); 1539 Jackson Ave. (70130); (504)525-0673. Pres. Donald Mintz; Exec. Dir. Jane Buchsbaum.

SHREVEPORT

SHREVEPORT JEWISH FEDERATION (1941; Inc. 1967); 2030 Line Ave. (71104); (318)-221-4129. Pres. Carl Arnold; Exec. Dir. Monty Pomm.

MAINE

LEWISTON-AUBURN

LEWISTON-AUBURN JEWISH FEDERATION (1947); (sponsors UNITED JEWISH APPEAL); 74 Bradman St., Auburn (04210); (207)786-4201. Pres. Robert Laskoff; Adm. Elliot Gruber.

PORTLAND

JEWISH FEDERATION COMMUNITY COUNCIL OF SOUTHERN MAINE (1942); (sponsors UNITED JEWISH APPEAL); 57 Ashmont St. (04103); (207)773-7254. Pres. Harvey Berman; Adm. Cecelia Levine.

MARYLAND

BALTIMORE

ASSOCIATED JEWISH CHARITIES & WELFARE FUND, INC. (a merger of the Associated Jewish Charities & Jewish Welfare Fund) (1920; reorg. 1969); 101 W. Mt. Royal Ave. (21201); (301)727-4828. Bd. Chmn. Jonathan Kolker; Pres. Stephen D. Solender.

MASSACHUSETTS

BERKSHIRES

JEWISH FEDERATION OF THE BERKSHIRES (1940); 235 East St., Pittsfield (01201); (413)-442-4360. Pres. Dr. Stuart Masters; Exec. Dir. Rhoda Kaminstein.

BOSTON

COMBINED JEWISH PHILANTHROPIES OF GREATER BOSTON, INC. (1895; reorg. 1961);

72 Franklin St. (02110); (617)542-8080. Pres. Sherman H. Starr; Exec. V. Pres. David H. Rosen.

FRAMINGHAM

GREATER FRAMINGHAM JEWISH FEDERATION (1968; Inc. 1969); 76 Salem End Rd., Framingham Centre (01701); (617)879-3301. Pres. Beverly Nesson; Exec. Dir. Lawrence Lowenthal.

HAVERHILL

*HAVERHILL UNITED JEWISH APPEAL, INC.; 514 Main St. (01830); (617)372-4481. Pres. Manuel M. Epstein.

LAWRENCE

*JEWISH COMMUNITY COUNCIL OF GREATER LAWRENCE (1906); 580 Haverhill St. (01841); (617)686-4157. Pres. Sidney Swartz; Exec. Dir. Irving Linn.

LEOMINSTER

LEOMINSTER JEWISH COMMUNITY COUNCIL, INC. (1939); 268 Washington St. (01453); (617)534-6121. Pres. Martin Shaeval; Sec.-Treas. Howard J. Rome.

NEW BEDFORD

JEWISH FEDERATION OF GREATER NEW BEDFORD, INC. (1938; Inc. 1954); 467 Hawthorn St., N. Dartmouth (02747); (617)997-7471. Pres. Nathan Barry; Exec. Dir. Larry Katz.

NORTH SHORE

JEWISH FEDERATION OF THE NORTH SHORE, INC. (1938); 4 Community Rd., Marblehead (01945); (617)598-1810. Pres. Howard Rich; Exec. Dir. Gerald S. Ferman.

SPRINGFIELD

SPRINGFIELD JEWISH FEDERATION, INC. (1938); (sponsors UNITED JEWISH WELFARE FUND SJF/UJA CAMPAIGN); 1160 Dickinson (01108); (413)737-4313. Pres. Jay Loevy; Exec. Dir. Joel Weiss.

WORCESTER

WORCESTER JEWISH FEDERATION, INC. (1947; Inc. 1957); (sponsors JEWISH WELFARE FUND); 633 Salisbury St. (01609); (617)756-1543. Pres. Nancy Leavitt; Exec. Dir. Joseph Huber.

MICHIGAN

DETROIT

JEWISH WELFARE FEDERATION OF DETROIT (1899); (sponsors ALLIED JEWISH CAMPAIGN); Fred M. Butzel Memorial Bldg., 163 Madison (48226); (313)965-3939. Pres. Joel Tauber; Exec. V. Pres. Wayne Feinstein.

FLINT

FLINT JEWISH FEDERATION (1936); 120 W. Kearsley St. (48502); (313)767-5922; Pres. Natalie Pelavin; Exec. Dir. David Nussbaum.

GRAND RAPIDS

JEWISH COMMUNITY FUND OF GRAND RAPIDS (1930); 1410 Pontiac SE (49506); (616)452-6619. Pres. Joseph N. Schwartz; Exec. Sec. Barbara Kravitz.

KALAMAZOO

*KALAMAZOO JEWISH FEDERATION (1949); c/o Congregation of Moses, 2501 Stadium Dr. (49008); (616)349-8396. Pres. Allyson Gall.

LANSING

GREATER LANSING JEWISH WELFARE FEDERATION (1939); PO Box 975, E. Lansing (48823); (517)351-3197. Pres. Dr. Murray Vinnik; Exec. Sec. Harold S. Kramer.

SAGINAW

*SAGINAW JEWISH WELFARE FEDERATION (1939); 1424 S. Washington Ave. (48601); (517)753-5230. Pres. Norman Rotenberg; Fin. Sec. Sandi Feldman.

MINNESOTA

DULUTH

JEWISH FEDERATION & COMMUNITY COUNCIL (1937); 1602 E. 2 St. (55812); (218)724-8857. Pres. Manley Goldfine; Sec. Adm. Sharon K. Eckholm.

MINNEAPOLIS

MINNEAPOLIS FEDERATION FOR JEWISH SERVICES (1929; Inc. 1930); 811 La Salle Ave. (55402); (612)339-7491. Pres. Stephen Lieberman; Exec. Dir. Herman Markowitz.

ST. PAUL

UNITED JEWISH FUND AND COUNCIL (1935); 790 S. Cleveland, Suite 201 (55116); (612)690-1707. Pres. Gerald Hirschhorn; Exec. Dir. Kimball Marsh.

MISSISSIPPI

JACKSON

JACKSON JEWISH WELFARE FUND, INC. (1945); PO Box 12329 (39211); (601)944-0607. Pres. Irving Feldman; V. Pres. Janis Goldstein.

MISSOURI

KANSAS CITY

JEWISH FEDERATION OF GREATER KANSAS CITY (1933); 25 E. 12 St. (64106); (816)421-5808. Pres. Arthur Brand; Exec. Dir. Sol Koenigsberg.

ST. JOSEPH

UNITED JEWISH FUND OF ST. JOSEPH (1915); 509 Woodcrest Dr. (64506); (816)-279-7154. Pres. Sidney I. Naidorf; Exec. Sec. Martha Rothstein.

ST. LOUIS

JEWISH FEDERATION OF ST. LOUIS (incl. St. Louis County) (1901); 12 Millstone Campus Dr. (63146); (314)432-0020. Pres. Israel Goldberg.

NEBRASKA

LINCOLN

LINCOLN JEWISH WELFARE FEDERATION, INC. (1931; Inc. 1961); PO Box 80014 (68501); (402)464-0602. Pres. Harry Allen; Exec. Dir. Gary Hill.

OMAHA

JEWISH FEDERATION OF OMAHA (1903); 333 S. 132 St. (68154); (402)334-8200. Pres. Howard Kaslow.

NEVADA

LAS VEGAS

JEWISH FEDERATION OF LAS VEGAS (1973); 1030 E. Twain Ave. (89109); (702)732-0556. Pres. Hal Ober; Exec. V. Pres. Jerome Countess.

NEW HAMPSHIRE

MANCHESTER

JEWISH FEDERATION OF GREATER MANCHESTER (1913; reorg. 1974); 698 Beech St. (03104); (603)627-7679. Pres. Frances Winneg; Exec. Dir. Earnest Siegel.

NEW JERSEY

ATLANTIC COUNTY

FEDERATION OF JEWISH AGENCIES OF ATLANTIC COUNTY (1924); 5321 Atlantic Ave., Ventnor City (08406); (609)822-7122. Pres. Irwin Yeagle; Exec. Dir. Bernard Cohen.

BAYONNE

*BAYONNE JEWISH COMMUNITY COUNCIL; 1050 Kennedy Blvd. (07002); (201)436-6900. Pres. Alan Apfelbaum; Exec. Dir. Alan J. Coren.

BERGEN COUNTY

UNITED JEWISH COMMUNITY OF BERGEN COUNTY (Inc. 1978); 111 Kinderkamack Rd., PO Box 4176, N. Hackensack Station, River Edge (07661); (201)488-6800. Pres. Andrew Sklover; Exec. V. Pres. James Young.

CENTRAL NEW JERSEY

JEWISH FEDERATION OF CENTRAL NEW JERSEY (sponsors UNITED JEWISH CAMPAIGN); (1940; merged 1973); Green Lane, Union (07083); (201)351-5060. Pres. Richard Goldberger; Exec. V. Pres. Burton Lazarow.

CLIFTON-PASSAIC

JEWISH FEDERATION OF GREATER CLIFTON-PASSAIC (1933); (sponsors UNITED JEWISH CAMPAIGN); 199 Scoles Ave., Clifton (07012). (201)777-7031. Pres. Elliott Taradash; Exec. Dir. Yosef Muskin.

CUMBERLAND COUNTY

JEWISH FEDERATION OF CUMBERLAND COUNTY (incl. the Jewish Community Council) (Inc. 1971) (sponsors ALLIED JEWISH APPEAL); 629 Wood St., Suite 204, Vineland (08360); (609)696-4445. Pres. Adele Greenblatt; Exec. Dir. Gail Milgram Beitman.

DELAWARE VALLEY

JEWISH FEDERATION OF THE DELAWARE VALLEY (1929; reorg. 1982); (includes lower Bucks County, PA and Mercer County, NJ); 20-28 N. Pennsylvania Ave., Morrisville, PA (19067); (215)736-8022. Pres. Fred Edelman; Exec. Dir. Charles P. Epstein. (Also see listing under Pennsylvania.)

ENGLEWOOD

(Merged with Bergen County)

GREATER MIDDLESEX COUNTY

JEWISH FEDERATION OF GREATER MIDDLESEX COUNTY (formerly Northern Middlesex County and Raritan Valley) (organized 1975); (sponsors UNITED JEWISH APPEAL); 100 Metroplex Dr., Suite 101, Edison (08817); (201)985-1234. Pres. Alvin Rockoff; Exec. Dir. Michael Shapiro.

JERSEY CITY

UNITED JEWISH APPEAL (1939); 71 Bentley Ave. (07304); (201)332-6644. Chmn. Mel Blum; Exec. Sec. Madeline Mazer.

METROWEST NEW JERSEY

UNITED JEWISH FEDERATION OF METROWEST (1923); (sponsors UNITED JEWISH APPEAL); 60 Glenwood Ave., E. Orange (07017); (201)673-6800; (212)943-0570. Pres.

James Schwarz; Exec. V. Pres. Howard Charish.

MONMOUTH COUNTY

JEWISH FEDERATION OF GREATER MONMOUTH COUNTY (formerly Shore Area) (1971); 100 Grant Ave., PO Box 210, Deal Park (07723); (201)531-6200. Pres. Dr. Lawrence Karasic; Exec. Dir. Marvin Relkin.

MORRIS-SUSSEX COUNTY

(Merged with MetroWest NJ)

NORTH JERSEY

JEWISH FEDERATION OF NORTH JERSEY (formerly Jewish Community Council) (1933); (sponsors UNITED JEWISH APPEAL DRIVE); 1 Pike Dr., Wayne (07470); (201)-595-0555. Pres. Philip E. Sarna; Exec. Dir. Barry Rosenberg.

NORTHERN MIDDLESEX COUNTY

(See Greater Middlesex County)

OCEAN COUNTY

OCEAN COUNTY JEWISH FEDERATION; 301 Madison Ave., Lakewood (08701); (201)363-0530. Pres. Marlene Perlmutter; Exec. Dir. Michael Ruvel.

RARITAN VALLEY

(See Greater Middlesex County)

SOMERSET COUNTY

JEWISH FEDERATION OF SOMERSET COUNTY (1960); 120 Finderne Ave., Bridgewater (08807); (201)725-6994. Pres. Dr. Daniel Frimmer; Adm. Mgr. Elaine Auerbach.

SOUTHERN NEW JERSEY

JEWISH FEDERATION OF SOUTHERN NEW JERSEY (incl. Camden and Burlington Counties) (1922); (sponsors ALLIED JEWISH APPEAL); 2393 W. Marlton Pike, Cherry Hill (08002); (609)665-6100. Pres. Michael Varbalow; Exec. V. Pres. Stuart Alperin.

NEW MEXICO

ALBUQUERQUE

JEWISH COMMUNITY COUNCIL OF ALBUQUERQUE, INC. (1938); 12800 Lomas NE, Suite F (87112); (505)292-1061. Pres. Harold Albert; Exec. Dir. Elisa M. Simon.

NEW YORK

ALBANY

GREATER ALBANY JEWISH FEDERATION (1938); (sponsors JEWISH WELFARE FUND); 350 Whitehall Rd. (12208); (518)459-8000.

Pres. Herman Ungerman; Exec. Dir. Dan Flax.

BROOME COUNTY

JEWISH FEDERATION OF BROOME COUNTY (1937; Inc. 1958); 500 Clubhouse Rd., Binghamton (13903); (607)724-2332. Pres. Dr. Gerald A. Hubal; Exec. Dir. Jackie Jacobs.

BUFFALO

JEWISH FEDERATION OF GREATER BUFFALO, INC. (1903); (sponsors UNITED JEWISH FUND CAMPAIGN); 787 Delaware Ave. (14209); (716)886-7750. Pres. Ann H. Cohn; Exec. Dir. Harry Kosansky.

DUTCHESS COUNTY

*JEWISH WELFARE FUND—UJA (1941); 110 Grand Ave., Poughkeepsie (12603); (914)471-9811. Pres. Milton Klein.

ELMIRA

ELMIRA JEWISH WELFARE FUND, INC. (1942); PO Box 3087, Grandview Rd. Ext. (14905); (607)734-8122. Pres. Dr. Edward J. Grandt; Exec. Dir. Mark Steiner.

GLENS FALLS

*GREATER GLENS FALLS JEWISH WELFARE FUND (1939); PO Box 177 (12801); (518)792-6438. Chmn. Walter Stern.

KINGSTON

JEWISH FEDERATION OF GREATER KINGSTON, INC. (1951); 159 Green St. (12401); (914)338-8131. Pres. Judith Golub.

NEW YORK CITY

FEDERATION OF JEWISH PHILANTHROPIES OF NEW YORK (incl. Greater New York, Nassau, Suffolk, and Westchester Counties) (1917); 130 E. 59 St. (10022); (212)980-1000. Pres. Daniel Shapiro; Exec. V. Pres. William Kahn.

UNITED JEWISH APPEAL—FEDERATION OF JEWISH PHILANTHROPIES CAMPAIGN, INC. (1974); 130 E. 59 St. (10022); (212)980-1000. Pres. Robert Arnow; Bd. Chmn. Stephen M. Peck; Exec. V. Pres./Campaign Dir. Ernest W. Michel; Exec. V. Pres. William Kahn.

UNITED JEWISH APPEAL OF GREATER NEW YORK, INC. (incl. Greater New York, Nassau, Suffolk, and Westchester Counties) (1939); 130 E. 59 St. (10022); (212)980-1000. Pres. Morton Kornreich; Exec. V. Pres. Ernest W. Michel.

NIAGARA FALLS

JEWISH FEDERATION OF NIAGARA FALLS, NY, INC. (1935); Temple Beth Israel, Bldg.

#5, College & Madison Ave. (14305); (716)-284-4575. Pres. Howard Kushner; Exec. Dir. Linda Boxer.

ORANGE COUNTY
JEWISH FEDERATION OF GREATER ORANGE COUNTY (1977); 360 Powell Ave., Newburgh (12550); (914)562-7860. Pres. Norman Hecht; Exec. Dir. Marilyn Chandler.

ROCHESTER
JEWISH COMMUNITY FEDERATION OF ROCHESTER, NY, INC. (1937); 441 East Ave. (14607); (716)461-0490. Pres. Elliott Landsman; Exec. Dir. Avrom Fox.

ROCKLAND COUNTY
UNITED JEWISH COMMUNITY OF ROCKLAND COUNTY, NEW YORK; 300 N. Main St., Spring Valley (10977); (914)352-7100. Pres. Dr. William Schwartz; Exec. Dir. Robert Posner.

SCHENECTADY
JEWISH FEDERATION OF GREATER SCHENECTADY (1938); (sponsors SCHENECTADY UJA AND FEDERATED WELFARE FUND); 2565 Balltown Rd. (12309); (518)393-1136. Pres. Stanley Kivort; Exec. Dir. Haim Morag.

SYRACUSE
SYRACUSE JEWISH FEDERATION, INC. (1918); 2223 E. Genesee St., PO Box 510 DeWitt; (13214); (315)422-4104. Pres. Gerald Meyer; Exec. V. Pres. Barry Silverberg.

TROY
TROY JEWISH COMMUNITY COUNCIL, INC. (1936); 2430 21 St. (12180); (518)274-0700. Pres. Richard Hanft.

UTICA
JEWISH FEDERATION OF UTICA, NY, INC. (1933; Inc. 1950); (sponsors UNITED JEWISH APPEAL OF UTICA); 2310 Oneida St. (13501); (315)733-2343. Pres. Robert Sossen; Exec. Dir. Meyer L. Bodoff.

NORTH CAROLINA

ASHEVILLE
FEDERATED JEWISH CHARITIES OF ASHEVILLE, INC.; 236 Charlotte St. (28801); (704)-253-0701. Pres. Stephen Lurey; Exec. Dir. Geoffrey Brown.

CHARLOTTE
CHARLOTTE JEWISH FEDERATION (1940); PO Box 13369 (28211); (704)372-4688. Pres.

Stanley Greenspon; Exec. Dir. Marvin Bienstock.

DURHAM-CHAPEL HILL
DURHAM-CHAPEL HILL JEWISH FEDERATION & COMMUNITY COUNCIL; 1509 Crestwood Lane; Chapel Hill (27514); (919)933-6810. Pres. Ernest Elial.

GREENSBORO
GREENSBORO JEWISH FEDERATION (1940); 713A N. Greene St. (27401); (919)272-3189. Pres. Michael Berkelhammer; Exec. Dir. Sherman Harris.

WINSTON-SALEM
*WINSTON-SALEM JEWISH COMMUNITY COUNCIL; 471 Archer Rd. (27106); (919)773-2532. Pres. Arnold Sidman.

OHIO

AKRON
AKRON JEWISH COMMUNITY FEDERATION (1935); 750 White Pond Dr. (44320); (216)-867-7850. Pres. David Sokol.

CANTON
CANTON JEWISH COMMUNITY FEDERATION (1935; reorg. 1955); 2631 Harvard Ave., NW (44709); (216)452-6444. Pres. Stanley Greenwald; Exec. Dir. Jay Rubin.

CINCINNATI
JEWISH FEDERATION OF CINCINNATI (merger of the Associated Jewish Agencies and Jewish Welfare Fund) (1896; reorg. 1967; 1811 Losantiville, Suite 320 (45237); (513)351-3800. Pres. Robert M. Blatt, Exec. Dir. Aubrey Herman.

CLEVELAND
JEWISH COMMUNITY FEDERATION OF CLEVELAND (1903); 1750 Euclid Ave. (44115); (216)566-9200. Pres. Henry Goodman; Exec. Dir. Stephen H. Hoffman.

COLUMBUS
COLUMBUS JEWISH FEDERATION (1926); 1175 College Ave. (43209); (614)237-7686. Pres. Miriam Yenkin; Exec. Dir. Alan Gill.

DAYTON
JEWISH FEDERATION OF GREATER DAYTON (1943); 4501 Denlinger Rd. (45426); (513)854-4150. Pres. Charles Abramovitz; Exec. V. Pres. Peter Wells.

STEUBENVILLE
JEWISH COMMUNITY COUNCIL (1938); PO Box 472 (43952); (614)282-9031. Pres.

Morris Denmark; Exec. Sec. Mrs. Joseph Freedman.

TOLEDO

JEWISH WELFARE FEDERATION OF GREATER TOLEDO (1907; reorg. 1960); 6505 Sylvania Ave., PO Box 587, Sylvania (43560); (419)885-4461. Pres. Robert Gersten; Exec. Dir. Steven J. Edelstein.

YOUNGSTOWN

YOUNGSTOWN AREA JEWISH FEDERATION (1935); PO Box 449, 505 Gypsy Lane (44501); (216)746-3251. Pres. Nathan Monus.

OKLAHOMA

OKLAHOMA CITY

JEWISH FEDERATION OF GREATER OKLAHOMA CITY (1941); 3022 NW Expressway #116 (73112); (405)949-0111. Pres. Dianne Schonwald; Exec. Dir. Garth Potts.

TULSA

JEWISH FEDERATION OF TULSA (1938); (sponsors TULSA UNITED JEWISH CAMPAIGN); 2021 E. 71 St. (74136); (918)495-1100. Pres. Susan Fenster; Exec. Dir. David Bernstein.

OREGON

PORTLAND

JEWISH FEDERATION OF PORTLAND (incl. state of Oregon and adjacent Washington communities) (1920; reorg. 1956); 6651 SW Capitol Highway (97219); (503)245-6219. Pres. Harold Pollin; Exec. Dir. Murray Schneier.

PENNSYLVANIA

ALTOONA

FEDERATION OF JEWISH PHILANTHROPIES (1920; reorg. 1940); 1308 17 St. (16601); (814)944-4072. Pres. Morley Cohn.

DELAWARE VALLEY

JEWISH FEDERATION OF DELAWARE VALLEY (incl. Lower Bucks County, PA and Mercer County, NJ); (1929; reorg. 1982); 20–28 N. Pennsylvania Ave., Morrisville, PA (19067); (215)736-8022. Pres. Fred Edelman; Exec. Dir. Charles Epstein. (Also see listing under New Jersey.)

ERIE

JEWISH COMMUNITY COUNCIL OF ERIE (1946); 701 G. Daniel Baldwin Bldg., 1001 State St. (16501); (814)455-4474. Pres. Richard Lechtner.

HARRISBURG

UNITED JEWISH FEDERATION OF GREATER HARRISBURG (1941); 100 Vaughn St. (17110); (717)236-9555. Pres. Dr. Harris Freedman; Exec. Dir. Elliot Gershenson.

HAZELTON

*JEWISH COMMUNITY COUNCIL (1960); Laurel & Hemlock Sts. (18201); (717)454-3528. Pres. Anthony Coffina.

JOHNSTOWN

UNITED JEWISH FEDERATION OF JOHNSTOWN (1938); 1334 Luzerne St. Ext. (15905); (814)255-1447. Pres. Isadore Glosser.

LANCASTER

*LANCASTER JEWISH FEDERATION (1928); 2120 Oregon Pike (17601); (717)569-7352. Pres. Clifford Firestone; Exec. Dir. Paul L. Spiegal.

NORRISTOWN

*TIFERES ISRAEL JEWISH CENTER (serving Central Montgomery County) (1936); 1541 Powell St. (19401); (215)275-8797. Pres. Alvin Schwartz; Rabbi: David Maharam.

PHILADELPHIA

FEDERATION OF JEWISH AGENCIES OF GREATER PHILADELPHIA (1901; reorg. 1956); 226 S. 16 St. (19102); (215)893-5600. Pres. Bennett Aaron; Exec. V. Pres. Robert Forman.

PITTSBURGH

UNITED JEWISH FEDERATION OF GREATER PITTSBURGH (1912; reorg. 1955); 234 McKee Pl. (15213); (412)681-8000. Pres. Leon L. Netzer; Exec. V. Pres. Howard Rieger.

READING

JEWISH FEDERATION OF READING, PA., INC. (1935); (sponsors UNITED JEWISH CAMPAIGN); 1700 City Line St. (19604); (215)921-2766. Pres. George Viener; Exec. Dir. Daniel Tannenbaum.

SCRANTON

SCRANTON-LACKAWANNA JEWISH FEDERATION (incl. Lackawanna County) (1945); 601 Jefferson Ave. (18510); (717)961-2300. Pres. Leonard Krieger; Exec. Dir. Seymour Brotman.

WILKES-BARRE

JEWISH FEDERATION OF GREATER WILKES-BARRE (1935); (sponsors UNITED JEWISH

APPEAL); 60 S. River St. (18702); (717)822-4146. Pres. Dr. David Greenwald; Exec. Dir. Allan Greene.

YORK

*YORK COUNCIL OF JEWISH CHARITIES, INC.; 120 E. Market St. (17401); (717)843-0918. Pres. Tim Grumbacher; Exec. Dir. Alan Dameshek.

RHODE ISLAND

PROVIDENCE

JEWISH FEDERATION OF RHODE ISLAND (1945); 130 Sessions St. (02906); (401)421-4111. Pres. Charles Samdperil; Exec. V. Pres. Elliot Cohan.

SOUTH CAROLINA

CHARLESTON

CHARLESTON JEWISH FEDERATION (1949); 1645 Raoul Wallenberg Blvd., PO Box 31298; (29407); (803)571-6565. Pres. Herb Rosner; Exec. Dir. Steven Wendell.

COLUMBIA

COLUMBIA UNITED JEWISH WELFARE FEDERATION (1960); 4540 Trenholm Rd., PO Box 6968 (29206); (803)787-2023. Pres. Samuel Jay Tenenbaum; Exec. Dir. Alex Grossberg.

SOUTH DAKOTA

SIOUX FALLS

JEWISH WELFARE FUND (1938); National Reserve Bldg. (57102); (605)336-2880. Pres. Laurence Bierman; Exec. Sec. Louis R. Hurwitz.

TENNESSEE

CHATTANOOGA

CHATTANOOGA JEWISH FEDERATION (1931); PO Box 8947, 5326 Lynnland Terrace (37411); (615)894-1317. Pres. Robert Siskin; Exec. Dir. Morris Rombro.

KNOXVILLE

KNOXVILLE JEWISH FEDERATION (1939); 6800 Deane Hill Dr., PO Box 10882 (37919); (615)693-5837. Chmn. Harold Leibowitz; Adm. Barbara Bogartz.

MEMPHIS

MEMPHIS JEWISH FEDERATION (incl. Shelby County) (1935); 6560 Poplar Ave., PO Box 38268 (38138); (901)767-7100. Pres. Arthur Malkin, Jr.; Exec. Dir. Leslie Gottlieb.

NASHVILLE

JEWISH FEDERATION OF NASHVILLE & MIDDLE TENNESSEE (1936); 801 Perry Warner Blvd. (37205); (615)356-3242. Pres. Sandy Averbuch; Exec. Dir. Jay M. Pilzer.

TEXAS

AUSTIN

JEWISH COMMUNITY COUNCIL OF AUSTIN (1939; reorg. 1956); 11713 Jollyville Rd. (78759); (512)331-1144. Pres. Scott Blech; Exec. Dir. Marilyn Stahl.

BEAUMONT

*BEAUMONT JEWISH FEDERATION OF TEXAS, INC. (1967); PO Box 1981 (77704); (713)833-5427.

CORPUS CHRISTI

CORPUS CHRISTI JEWISH COMMUNITY COUNCIL (1953); 750 Everhart Rd. (78411); (512)855-6239. Pres. David Feltoon; Exec. Dir. Andrew Lipman.

COMBINED JEWISH APPEAL OF CORPUS CHRISTI (1962); 750 Everhart Rd. (78411); (512)855-6239. Pres. Jerry Kane; Exec. Dir. Andrew Lipman.

DALLAS

JEWISH FEDERATION OF GREATER DALLAS (1911); 7800 Northaven Rd., Suite A (75230); (214)369-3313. Pres. Harold Kleinman; Exec. Dir. Morris A. Stein.

EL PASO

JEWISH FEDERATION OF EL PASO, INC. (incl. surrounding communities) (1937); 405 Mardi Gras, PO Box 12097 (79913-0097); (915)584-4437. Pres. Samuel Ellowitz.

FORT WORTH

JEWISH FEDERATION OF FORT WORTH AND TARRANT COUNTY (1936); 6801 Dan Danciger Rd. (76133); (817)292-3081. Pres. Bernie Appel; Exec. Dir. Harvey Freiman.

GALVESTON

GALVESTON COUNTY JEWISH WELFARE ASSOCIATION (1936); PO Box 146 (77553); (409)744-8295. Pres. Harold Levine; Treas. Harry Schreiber.

HOUSTON

JEWISH FEDERATION OF GREATER HOUSTON (1937); 5603 S. Braeswood Blvd. (77096); (713)729-7000. Pres. Noel Graubart; Exec. Dir. Hans Mayer.

SAN ANTONIO

JEWISH FEDERATION OF SAN ANTONIO (incl. Bexar County) (1922); 8434 Ahern Dr. (78216); (512)341-8234. Pres. Susan Jacobson; Exec. Dir. Alan Bayer.

WACO

JEWISH WELFARE COUNCIL OF WACO (1949); PO Box 8031 (76710); (817)776-3740. Pres. Sam Harelik; Exec. Sec. Mrs. Maurice Labens.

UTAH

SALT LAKE CITY

UNITED JEWISH COUNCIL AND SALT LAKE JEWISH WELFARE FUND (1936); 2416 E. 1700 S. (84108); (801)581-0098. Pres. Sandy Dolowitz; Exec. Dir. Bernard Solomon.

VIRGINIA

NEWPORT NEWS—HAMPTON—WILLIAMSBURG

UNITED JEWISH COMMUNITY OF THE VIRGINIA PENINSULA, INC. (1942); 2700 Spring Rd., Newport News (23606); (804)595-5544. Pres. Rhoda Mazur; Exec. Dir. Norman Olshansky.

RICHMOND

JEWISH COMMUNITY FEDERATION OF RICHMOND (1935); PO Box 8237, 5403 Monument Ave. (23226); (804)288-0045. Pres. Alan Wurtzel; Exec. Dir. Robert Hyman.

ROANOKE

JEWISH COMMUNITY COUNCIL; PO Box 1074 (24005); (703)774-2828. Chmn. Arthur Levin.

TIDEWATER

UNITED JEWISH FEDERATION OF TIDEWATER (incl. Norfolk, Portsmouth, and Virginia Beach) (1937); 7300 Newport Ave., PO Box 9776, Norfolk (23505); (804)489-8040. Pres. Dr. Sanford Lefcoe; Exec. Dir. A. Robert Gast.

WASHINGTON

SEATTLE

JEWISH FEDERATION OF GREATER SEATTLE (incl. King County, Everett, and Bremerton) (1926); 510 Securities Bldg., 1904

Third Ave. (98101); (206)622-8211. Pres. Raymond Galante; Exec. Dir. Rabbi Melvin Libman.

SPOKANE

*JEWISH COMMUNITY COUNCIL OF SPOKANE (incl. Spokane County) (1927); (sponsors UNITED JEWISH FUND); 521 Parkade Plaza (99201); (509)838-4261. Pres. C. Eugene Huppin.

WEST VIRGINIA

CHARLESTON

FEDERATED JEWISH CHARITIES OF CHARLESTON, INC. (1937); PO Box 1613 (25326); (304)346-7500. Pres. Alvin Preiser; Exec. Sec. William H. Thalheimer.

HUNTINGTON

*FEDERATED JEWISH CHARITIES (1939); PO Box 947 (25713); (304)523-9326. Pres. William H. Glick; Sec. Andrew Katz.

WISCONSIN

GREEN BAY

*GREEN BAY JEWISH WELFARE FUND; PO Box 335 (54305); (414)432-9347. Treas. Betty Frankenthal.

KENOSHA

KENOSHA JEWISH WELFARE FUND (1938); 6537 Seventh Ave. (53140); (414)658-8635. Pres. Edward Chulew; Sec.-Treas. Mrs. S. M. Lapp.

MADISON

MADISON JEWISH COMMUNITY COUNCIL, INC. (1940); 310 N. Midvale Blvd., Suite 325 (53705); (608)231-3426. Pres. Mark Laufman; Exec. Dir. Steven Morrison.

MILWAUKEE

MILWAUKEE JEWISH FEDERATION, INC. (1902); 1360 N. Prospect Ave. (53202); (414)-271-8338. Pres. Martin Stein; Exec. Dir. Robert Aronson.

RACINE

RACINE JEWISH WELFARE COUNCIL (1946); 944 S. Main St. (53403); (414)633-7093. Cochmn. Robert Goodman, Arthur Schaefer; Exec. Sec. Mary Ann Waisman.

CANADA

ALBERTA

CALGARY

CALGARY JEWISH COMMUNITY COUNCIL (1962); 1607 90th Ave. SW (T2V 4V7); (403)-253-8600. Pres. Bruce R. Liban; Exec. Dir. Drew Staffenberg.

EDMONTON

JEWISH FEDERATION OF EDMONTON (1954; reorg. 1982); 7200 156 St. (T5R 1X3); (403)-487-5120. Pres. Judith Goldsand; Exec. Dir. Howard Bloom.

BRITISH COLUMBIA

VANCOUVER

*JEWISH COMMUNITY FUND & COUNCIL OF VANCOUVER (1932); 950 W. 41 Ave. (V5Z 2N7); (604)266-8371. Pres. Ronald Coleman; Exec. Dir. Isaac Moss.

MANITOBA

WINNIPEG

WINNIPEG JEWISH COMMUNITY COUNCIL (1938; reorg. 1973); (sponsors COMBINED JEWISH APPEAL OF WINNIPEG); 370 Hargrave St. (R3B 2K1); (204)943-0406. Pres. Mendle M. Meltzer; Exec. V. Pres. Izzy Peltz.

ONTARIO

HAMILTON

HAMILTON JEWISH FEDERATION (1934; merged 1971); (sponsors UNITED JEWISH WELFARE FUND); 57 Delaware Ave. (L8M 1T6); (416)528-8570. Pres. Leslie J. Pasis; Exec. Dir. Sid Brail.

LONDON

LONDON JEWISH COMMUNITY COUNCIL (1932); 536 Huron St. (24) (N5Y 4J5); (519)-673-3310. Pres. Allan Richman; Exec. Dir. Howard Borer.

OTTAWA

JEWISH COMMUNITY COUNCIL OF OTTAWA (1934); 151 Chapel St. (K1N 7Y2); (613)-232-7306. Pres. Gerald Berger; Exec. Dir. Gittel Tatz.

TORONTO

TORONTO JEWISH CONGRESS (1937); 4600 Bathurst St.; Willowdale (M2R 3V2); (416)-635-2883. Pres. Ronald Appleby; Exec. Dir. Steven Ain.

WINDSOR

JEWISH COMMUNITY COUNCIL (1938); 1641 Ouellette Ave. (N8X 1K9); (519)254-7558. Pres. Harold M. Taub; Exec. Dir. Joseph Eisenberg.

QUEBEC

MONTREAL

ALLIED JEWISH COMMUNITY SERVICES (1965); 5151 Cote St. Catherine Rd. (H3W 1M6); (514)735-3541. Pres. Carl Laxer; Exec. V. Pres. John Fishel.

Jewish Periodicals[1]

UNITED STATES

ARIZONA

ARIZONA POST (1946). 102 N. Plumer Ave., Tucson, 85719. (602)791-9962. Sandra R. Heiman. Fortnightly. Jewish Federation of S. Arizona.

GREATER PHOENIX JEWISH NEWS (1947). PO Box 26590. Phoenix, 85068. (602)870-9470. Flo Eckstein. Weekly.

CALIFORNIA

B'NAI B'RITH MESSENGER (1897). 2510 W. 7 St., Los Angeles, 90057. (213)380-5000. Rabbi Yale Butler. Weekly.

HERITAGE-SOUTHWEST JEWISH PRESS (1914). 2130 S. Vermont Ave., Los Angeles, 90007. Dan Brin. Weekly. (Also SAN DIEGO JEWISH PRESS-HERITAGE, San Diego [weekly]; CENTRAL CALIFORNIA JEWISH HERITAGE, Sacramento and Fresno area [monthly]; ORANGE COUNTY JEWISH HERITAGE, Orange County area [weekly].)

ISRAEL TODAY (1973). 16661 Ventura Blvd., Encino, 91436. (818)786-4000. Phil Blazer. Daily.

ISRAEL TODAY SAN DIEGO (1979). 500 Fesler St., Suite 103, El Cajon, 92020. (619)440-5890. Carol Rosenberg. Biweekly.

JEWISH NEWSPAPER (1985). 15445 Ventura Blvd, Suite 10-223, Sherman Oaks, 91413. (818)909-7034. Yehuda Lev. Fortnightly.

JEWISH SPECTATOR (1935). PO Box 2016, Santa Monica, 90406. (213)829-2484. Trude Weiss-Rosmarin. Quarterly.

JEWISH STAR (1956). 693 Mission St., #302, San Francisco, 94105. (415)421-4874. Nevon Stuckey. Bimonthly.

LOS ANGELES JEWISH COMMUNITY BULLETIN (1958). 6505 Wilshire Blvd., Los Angeles, 90048. (213)852-7707. Manuel Chait. Weekly. Jewish Federation Council of Greater Los Angeles.

NORTHERN CALIFORNIA JEWISH BULLETIN (1946). 121 Steuart St., Suite 302, San Francisco, 94105. (415)957-9340. Marc Klein. Weekly. San Francisco Jewish Community Publications.

WESTERN STATES JEWISH HISTORY (1968). 2429 23 St., Santa Monica, 90405. (213)-450-2946. Norton B. Stern. Quarterly. Western States Jewish History Association.

COLORADO

INTERMOUNTAIN JEWISH NEWS (1913). 1275 Sherman St., Suite 215–217, Denver, 80203. (303)861-2234. Miriam H. Goldberg. Weekly.

CONNECTICUT

CONNECTICUT JEWISH LEDGER (1929). PO Box 1688, Hartford, 06101. (203)233-2148. Berthold Gaster. Weekly.

CONTEMPORARY JEWRY (1974 under the name JEWISH SOCIOLOGY AND SOCIAL RESEARCH). Center for Judaic Studies and Contemporary Jewish Life, University of Connecticut, U-145J, Storrs, 06268. (203)-486-2271, 486-4423. Arnold Dashefsky, J. Alan Winter. Annually.

---

[1]The information in this directory is based on replies to questionnaires circulated by the editors. For organization bulletins, see the directory of Jewish organizations.

JEWISH DIGEST (1955). 1363 Fairfield Ave., Bridgeport, 06605. (203)384-2284. Jonathan D. Levine. Nine times a year.

DISTRICT OF COLUMBIA

ALERT (1970). 1411 K St. NW, Suite 402. Washington, 20005. (202)393-4117. Nurit Erger. Monthly. Union of Councils for Soviet Jews.

B'NAI B'RITH INTERNATIONAL JEWISH MONTHLY (1886 under the name MENORAH). 1640 Rhode Island Ave. NW, Washington, 20036. (202)857-6645. Marc Silver. Ten times a year. B'nai B'rith.

JEWISH VETERAN (1896). 1811 R St. NW, Washington, 20009. (202)265-6280. Pearl Laufer. Irregularly. Jewish War Veterans of the U.S.A.

NEAR EAST REPORT (1957). 500 N. Capitol St. NW, Suite 307, Washington, 20001. (202)638-1225. M. J. Rosenberg. Weekly. Near East Research, Inc.

WASHINGTON JEWISH WEEK (1965). 1317 F St. NW, Washington, 20004. (202)783-7200. Charles Fenyvesi. Weekly.

FLORIDA

JEWISH FLORIDIAN GROUP (1927). PO Box 012973, Miami, 33101. (305)373-4605. Fred K. Shochet. Weekly.

JEWISH JOURNAL (1977). PO Box 23909, Ft. Lauderdale, 33307. (305)563-3200. Dorothy P. Rubin. Weekly.

PALM BEACH JEWISH WORLD (1982). 2405 Mercer Ave., W. Palm Beach, 33401. (305)833-8331. Tina Hersh. Weekly.

SOUTHERN JEWISH WEEKLY (1924). PO Box 3297, Jacksonville, 32206. (904)355-3459. Isadore Moscovitz. Weekly.

GEORGIA

JEWISH CIVIC PRESS (1965). 3179 Maple Dr. NE, Atlanta, 30305. (404)262-6786. Abner Tritt. Monthly.

SOUTHERN ISRAELITE (1925). PO Box 77388, 188 15 St. NW, Atlanta, 30357. (404)876-8248. Vida Goldgar. Weekly.

ILLINOIS

CHICAGO JUF NEWS (1972). 1 S. Franklin St., Chicago, 60606. (312)444-2853. Joseph Aaron. Monthly. Jewish Federation of Metropolitan Chicago.

JEWISH CHICAGO (1982). 1234 Sherman, Evanston, 60202. (312)864-8084. Avy Meyers. Monthly.

JEWISH COMMUNITY NEWS (1945). 6464 W. Main, Suite 7A, Belleville, 62223. (618)-398-6100. Jordan Harburger. Bimonthly. Jewish Federation of Southern Illinois.

SENTINEL (1911). 323 S. Franklin St., Chicago, 60606. (312)663-1101. J. I. Fishbein. Weekly.

INDIANA

ILLIANA NEWS (1975). 2939 Jewett St., Highland, 46322. (219)972-2250. Barnett Labowitz. Ten times a year. Jewish Federation, Inc. of Northwest Indiana.

INDIANA JEWISH POST AND OPINION (1935). PO Box 449097, Indianapolis, 46202. (317)927-7800. Greg Birnbaum. Weekly.

JEWISH POST AND OPINION. PO Box 449097, Indianapolis, 46202. (317)927-7800. Greg Birnbaum. Weekly.

KENTUCKY

KENTUCKY JEWISH POST AND OPINION (1931). 1551 Bardstown Rd., Louisville, 40205. (502)459-1914. Gabriel Cohen. Weekly.

LOUISIANA

JEWISH CIVIC PRESS (1965). PO Box 15500, 924 Valmont St., New Orleans, 70115. (504)895-8784. Abner Tritt. Monthly.

JEWISH TIMES (1974). 1539 Jackson Ave., New Orleans, 70130. (504)524-3147. Joan D. Jacob. Biweekly.

MARYLAND

AMERICAN JEWISH JOURNAL (1944). 1220 Blair Mill Rd., Silver Spring, 20910. (301)-585-1756. David Mondzac. Quarterly.

BALTIMORE JEWISH TIMES (1919). 2104 N. Charles St., Baltimore, 21218. (301)752-3504. Gary Rosenblatt. Weekly.

MASSACHUSETTS

AMERICAN JEWISH HISTORY (1893). 2 Thornton Rd., Waltham, 02154. (617)891-8110. Marc Lee Raphael. Quarterly. American Jewish Historical Society.

BOSTON JEWISH TIMES (1945). Box 18427, Boston, 02118. (617)357-8635. Sten Lukin. Weekly.

JEWISH ADVOCATE (1902). 251 Causeway St., Boston, 02114. (617)227-5130. Bernard M. Hyatt. Weekly.

JEWISH REPORTER (1970). 76 Salem End Rd., Framingham, 01701. (617)879-3300. Harvey S. Stone. Monthly. Greater Framingham Jewish Federation.

JEWISH WEEKLY NEWS (1945). PO Box 1569, Springfield, 01101. (413)739-4771. Leslie B. Kahn. Weekly.

JOURNAL OF THE NORTH SHORE JEWISH COMMUNITY. 564 Loring Ave., Salem, 01970. (617)741-1558. Barbara Wolf. Biweekly. North Shore Jewish Press Ltd.

MOMENT (1975). 462 Boylston St., Boston, 02116. (617)536-6252. Leonard Fein. Monthly (except Jan.-Feb. and July-Aug.). Jewish Educational Ventures.

MICHIGAN

DETROIT JEWISH NEWS (1942). 20300 Civic Center Dr., Suite 240, Southfield, 48076. (313)354-6060. Gary Rosenblatt. Weekly.

HUMANISTIC JUDAISM. 28611 W. Twelve Mile Rd., Farmington Hills, 48018. (313)-478-7610. M. Bonnie Cousens, Ruth D. Feldman. Quarterly. Society for Humanistic Judaism.

MICHIGAN JEWISH HISTORY (1960). 24680 Rensselaer, Oak Park, 48237. (313)548-9176. Phillip Applebaum. Semiannually. Jewish Historical Society of Michigan.

MINNESOTA

AMERICAN JEWISH WORLD (1912). 4509 Minnetonka Blvd., Minneapolis, 55416. (612)920-7000. Stacey R. Bush. Semiweekly.

MISSOURI

KANSAS CITY JEWISH CHRONICLE (1920). 7373 W. 107 St., Suite 250, Overland Park, 66212. (913)648-4620. Stan Rose. Weekly.

MISSOURI JEWISH POST AND OPINION (1948). 8235 Olive St., St. Louis, 63132. (314)993-2842. Kathie Sutin. Weekly.

ST. LOUIS JEWISH LIGHT (1947). 12 Millstone Campus Dr., St. Louis, 63146. (314)-432-3353. Robert A. Cohn. Weekly. Jewish Federation of St. Louis.

NEBRASKA

JEWISH PRESS (1921). 333 S. 132 St., Omaha, 68154. (402)334-8200. Morris Maline. Weekly. Jewish Federation of Omaha.

NEVADA

JEWISH REPORTER (1976). 1030 E. Twain Ave., Las Vegas, 89109. (702)732-0556. Jerry Countess. Monthly. Jewish Federation of Las Vegas.

LAS VEGAS ISRAELITE (1965). PO Box 14096, Las Vegas, 89114. (702)876-1255. Michael Tell. Biweekly.

NEW JERSEY

JEWISH COMMUNITY VOICE (1941). 2393 W. Marlton Pike, Cherry Hill, 08002. (609)-665-6100. Fredda Sacharow. Biweekly. Jewish Federation of Southern NJ.

JEWISH HORIZON (1981). Green Lane, Union, 07083. (201)351-1473. Fran Gold. Weekly. Jewish Federation of Central NJ.

JEWISH JOURNAL/JEWISH VOICE (merged 1985). PO Box 1359, Highland Park, 08816. (201)246-1905. Rhea Basroon. Bimonthly. Jewish Federation of Greater Middlesex County.

JEWISH NEWS (1947). 60 Glenwood Ave., E. Orange, 07017. (201)678-3900. Charles Baumohl. Weekly. Jewish Federation of MetroWest.

JEWISH RECORD (1939). 1537 Atlantic Ave., Atlantic City, 08401. (609)344-5119. Martin Korik. Weekly.

JEWISH STANDARD (1931). 57 Cedar Lane, Teaneck, 07666. (201)837-3313. Morris J. Janoff. Weekly.

JOURNAL OF JEWISH COMMUNAL SERVICE (1899). 111 Prospect St., E. Orange, 07017. (201)676-6070. Sanford N. Sherman. Quarterly. Conference of Jewish Communal Service.

NEW YORK

AFN SHVEL (1941). 200 W. 72 St., Suite 40, NYC, 10023. (212)787-6675. Mordkhe Schaechter. Quarterly. Yiddish. League for Yiddish, Inc.

ALBANY JEWISH WORLD (1965). 1104 Central Ave., Albany, 12205. (518)459-8455. Sam S. Clevenson. Weekly.

ALGEMEINER JOURNAL (1972). 404 Park Ave. S., NYC, 10016. (212)689-3390. Gershon Jacobson. Weekly. Yiddish.

AMERICAN JEWISH YEAR BOOK (1899). 165 E. 56 St., NYC, 10022. (212)751-4000. Milton Himmelfarb, David Singer. Annually. American Jewish Committee and Jewish Publication Society.

AMERICAN ZIONIST (1910). 4 E. 34 St., NYC, 10016. (212)481-1500. Carol Binen. Quarterly. Zionist Organization of America.

AMIT WOMAN (1925). 817 Broadway, NYC, 10003. (212)477-4720. Micheline Ratzersdorfer. Six times a year. AMIT Women.

AUFBAU (1934). 2121 Broadway, NYC, 10023. (212)873-7400. Gert Niers, Henry Marx. Fortnightly. German. New World Club, Inc.

BITZARON (1939). PO Box 623, Cooper Station, NYC, 10003. (212)598-3958. Hayim Leaf. Bimonthly. Hebrew. Hebrew Literary Foundation.

BUFFALO JEWISH REVIEW (1918). 15 E. Mohawk St., Buffalo, 14203. (716)854-2192. Harlan C. Abbey. Weekly. Kahaal Nahalot Israel.

COMMENTARY (1945). 165 E. 56 St., NYC, 10022. (212)751-4000. Norman Podhoretz. Monthly. American Jewish Committee.

CONGRESS MONTHLY (1933). 15 E. 84 St., NYC, 10028. (212)879-4500. Maier Deshell. Seven times a year. American Jewish Congress.

CONSERVATIVE JUDAISM (1945). 3080 Broadway, NYC, 10027. (212)678-8060. Rabbi David Silverman. Quarterly. Rabbinical Assembly.

ECONOMIC HORIZONS (1953). 500 Fifth Ave., NYC, 10110. (212)354-6510. Laurie Tarlowe. Quarterly. American-Israel Chamber of Commerce and Industry, Inc.

HADAROM (1957). 275 Seventh Ave. NYC, 10001. (212)807-7888. Rabbi Gedalia Schwartz. Annually. Hebrew. Rabbinical Council of America.

HADASSAH MAGAZINE (1921). 50 W. 58 St., NYC, 10019. (212)355-7900. Alan M. Tigay. Monthly (except for combined issues of June–July and Aug.–Sept.).

Hadassah, Women's Zionist Organization of America.

HADOAR (1921). 1841 Broadway, NYC, 10023. (212)581-5151. Shlomo Shamir, Yael Feldman. Weekly. Hebrew. Histadruth Ivrith of America.

ISRAEL HORIZONS (1952). 150 Fifth Ave., Suite 911, NYC, 10011. (212)255-8760. Richard Yaffe. Bimonthly. Americans for Progressive Israel.

ISRAEL QUALITY (1976). 500 Fifth Ave., NYC, 10110. (212)354-6510. Beth Belkin, Laurie Tarlowe. Quarterly. American-Israel Chamber of Commerce and Industry, Inc. and Government of Israel Trade Center.

JWB CIRCLE (1946). 15 E. 26 St., NYC, 10010. (212)532-4949. Lionel Koppman. Bimonthly. JWB.

JEWISH ACTION (1950). 45 W. 36 St., NYC, 10018. (212)563-4000. Heidi Tenzer. Quarterly. Union of Orthodox Jewish Congregations of America.

JEWISH AMERICAN RECORD (1973). GPO Box 317, NYC, 10116. Alex Novitsky. Monthly.

JEWISH BOOK ANNUAL (1942). 15 E. 26 St., NYC, 10010. (212)532-4949. Jacob Kabakoff. Annually. English-Hebrew-Yiddish. JWB Jewish Book Council.

JEWISH BOOK WORLD (1945). 15 E. 26 St., NYC, 10010. (212)532-4949. William Wollheim. Quarterly. JWB Jewish Book Council.

JEWISH BRAILLE INSTITUTE VOICE (1978). 110 E. 30 St., NYC, 10016. (212)889-2525. Jacob Freid. Ten times a year (sound cassettes). Jewish Braille Institute of America, Inc.

JEWISH BRAILLE REVIEW (1931). 110 E. 30 St., NYC, 10016. (212)889-2525. Jacob Freid. Ten times a year. English-Braille. Jewish Braille Institute of America, Inc.

JEWISH CURRENT EVENTS (1959). 430 Keller Ave., Elmont, 11003. Samuel Deutsch. Biweekly.

JEWISH CURRENTS (1946). 22 E. 17 St., Suite 601, NYC, 10003. (212)924-5740. Morris U. Schappes. Monthly. Association for Promotion of Jewish Secularism, Inc.

JEWISH EDUCATION (1929). 426 W. 58 St., NYC, 10019. (212)245-8200. Alvin I. Schiff. Quarterly. Council for Jewish Education.

JEWISH FORWARD (1897). 45 E. 33 St., NYC, 10016. (212)889-8200. Simon Weber. Weekly. Yiddish. Forward Association, Inc.

JEWISH FRONTIER (1934). 15 E. 26 St., 13th fl., NYC, 10010. (212)683-3530. Jonathan Goldberg. Monthly. Labor Zionist Letters, Inc.

JEWISH GUARDIAN (1974). GPO Box 2143, Brooklyn, 11202. (718)384-4661. Pinchus David. Irregularly. English-Hebrew. Neturei Karta of U.S.A.

JEWISH JOURNAL (1969). 1841 Broadway, NYC, 10023. (212)265-3274. Daniel Santacruz. Weekly.

JEWISH LEDGER (1924). 148 S. Fitzhugh St., Rochester, 14608. (716)232-1802. Donald Wolin. Weekly.

JEWISH MUSIC NOTES (1945). 15 E. 26 St., NYC, 10010. (212)532-4949. Laura Leon-Cohen. Semiannually. JWB Jewish Music Council.

JEWISH OBSERVER (1963). 5 Beekman St., NYC, 10038. (212)791-1800. Nisson Wolpin. Monthly (except July and Aug.). Agudath Israel of America.

JEWISH OBSERVER OF SYRACUSE (1977). PO Box 5004, Syracuse, 13250. (315)422-4104. Sherry Chayat. Biweekly.

JEWISH POST AND RENAISSANCE (1977). 57 E. 11 St., NYC, 10003. (212)420-0042. Charles Roth. Monthly.

JEWISH PRESS (1950). 338 Third Ave., Brooklyn, 11215. (718)858-3300. Sholom Klass. Weekly.

JEWISH SOCIAL STUDIES (1939). 2112 Broadway, Room 206, NYC, 10023. (212)-724-5336. Tobey B. Gitelle. Quarterly. Conference on Jewish Social Studies, Inc.

JEWISH TELEGRAPHIC AGENCY COMMUNITY NEWS REPORTER (1962). 165 W. 46 St., Suite 511, NYC, 10036. (212)575-9370. Murray Zuckoff. Weekly.

JEWISH TELEGRAPHIC AGENCY DAILY NEWS BULLETIN (1917). 165 W. 46 St., Suite 511, NYC, 10036. (212)575-9370. Murray Zuckoff. Daily.

JEWISH TELEGRAPHIC AGENCY WEEKLY NEWS DIGEST (1933). 165 W. 46 St., Suite 511, NYC, 10036. (212)575-9370. Murray Zuckoff. Weekly.

JEWISH WEEK (1876; reorg. 1970). 1 Park Ave., NYC, 10016. (212)686-2320. Phillip Ritzenberg. Weekly.

JOURNAL OF REFORM JUDAISM (1953). 21 E. 40 St., NYC, 10016. (212)684-4990. Samuel Stahl. Quarterly. Central Conference of American Rabbis.

JUDAISM (1952). 15 E. 84 St., NYC, 10028. (212)879-4500. Robert Gordis. Quarterly. American Jewish Congress.

KIBBUTZ JOURNAL (1984). 27 W. 20 St., 9th fl., NYC, 10011. (212)255-1338. Theodora Saal. Three times a year. Kibbutz Aliya Desk.

KOL HAT'NUAH (1943). 50 W. 58 St., NYC, 10019. (212)355-7900. Jennifer Sylvor. Monthly (Nov.-June). Hashachar.

KOSHER DIRECTORY (1925). 45 W. 36 St., NYC, 10018. (212)563-4000. Chaim Plotzker. Annually. Union of Orthodox Jewish Congregations of America.

KOSHER DIRECTORY, PASSOVER EDITION (1923). 45 W. 36 St., NYC, 10018. (212)-563-4000. Chaim Plotzker. Annually. Union of Orthodox Jewish Congregations of America.

KULTUR UN LEBN—CULTURE AND LIFE (1967). 45 E. 33 St., NYC, 10016. (212)-889-6800. Joseph Mlotek. Quarterly. Yiddish. Workmen's Circle.

LAMISHPAHAH. 1841 Broadway, NYC, 10023. (212)581-5151. Moshe Pelli. Ten times a year. Hebrew. Histadruth Ivrith of America.

LILITH—THE JEWISH WOMEN'S MAGAZINE (1976). 250 W. 57 St., NYC, 10019. (212)-757-0818. Susan Weidman Schneider. Quarterly.

LONG ISLAND JEWISH WORLD (1971). 115 Middle Neck Rd., Great Neck, 11021. (516)829-4000. Jerome W. Lippman. Weekly.

MIDSTREAM (1954). 515 Park Ave., NYC, 10022. (212)752-0600. Joel Carmichael. Monthly (bimonthly June–Sept.). Theodor Herzl Foundation, Inc.

MODERN JEWISH STUDIES ANNUAL (1977). Queens College, Kiely 802, 65-30 Kissena Blvd., Flushing, 11367. (718)520-7067. Joseph C. Landis. Annually. American Association of Professors of Yiddish.

MORNING FREIHEIT (1922). 43 W. 24 St., NYC, 10010. (212)255-7661. Paul Novick. Weekly. Yiddish-English.

OLOMEINU—OUR WORLD (1945). 160 Broadway, NYC, 10038. (212)227-1000. Rabbi Yaakov Fruchter, Nosson Scherman. Monthly. English-Hebrew. Torah Umesorah-National Society for Hebrew Day Schools.

OR CHADASH (1981). 110 E. 30 St., NYC, 10016. (212)889-2525. Gerald M. Kass. Two to four times a year (sound cassettes). Hebrew. Jewish Braille Institute of America, Inc.

PEDAGOGIC REPORTER (1949). 730 Broadway NYC, 10003. (212)675-5656. Mordecai H. Lewittes. Quarterly. Jewish Education Service of North America, Inc.

PIONEER WOMAN (1926). 200 Madison Ave., NYC, 10016. (212)725-8010. Judith A. Sokoloff. Five times a year. English-Yiddish-Hebrew. Pioneer Women/Na'amat, the Women's Labor Zionist Organization of America.

PRESENT TENSE (1973). 165 E. 56 St., NYC, 10022. (212)751-4000. Murray Polner. Quarterly. American Jewish Committee.

PROCEEDINGS OF THE AMERICAN ACADEMY FOR JEWISH RESEARCH (1920). 3080 Broadway, NYC, 10027. (212)678-8864. Isaac E. Barzilay. Annually. Hebrew-Arabic-English. American Academy for Jewish Research.

RABBINICAL COUNCIL RECORD (1953). 275 Seventh Ave. NYC, 10001. (212)807-7888. Rabbi Louis Bernstein. Quarterly. Rabbinical Council of America.

RECONSTRUCTIONIST (1935). 270 W. 89 St., NYC, 10024. (212)496-2960. Jacob J. Staub. Eight times a year. Federation of Reconstructionist Congregations and Havurot.

REFORM JUDAISM (1972; formerly DIMENSIONS IN AMERICAN JUDAISM). 838 Fifth Ave., NYC, 10021. (212)249-0100. Aron Hirt-Manheimer. Quarterly. Union of American Hebrew Congregations.

REPORTER. 500 Clubhouse Rd., Binghamton, 13903. (607)724-2360. Marc Goldberg. Weekly. Jewish Federation of Broome County.

RESPONSE (1967). 15 E. 26 St., Suite 1350, NYC, 10010. (212)679-1412. Nancy Sinkoff. Quarterly. Jewish Educational Ventures, Inc.

SEVEN ARTS FEATURE SYNDICATE (see News Syndicates, p. 434)

SHEVILEY HA-HINNUKH (1939). 114 Fifth Ave., NYC, 10011. (212)675-5656. Mathew Mosenkis. Quarterly. Hebrew. Council for Jewish Education.

SH'MA (1970). Box 567, Port Washington, 11050. (516)944-9791. Eugene B. Borowitz. Biweekly (except June, July, Aug.).

SHMUESSEN MIT KINDER UN YUGENT (1942). 770 Eastern Pkwy., Brooklyn, 11213. (718)493-9250. Nissan Mindel. Monthly. Yiddish. Merkos L'Inyonei Chinuch, Inc.

SPECTRUM (1982). 515 Park Ave., NYC, 10022. (212)371-7750. Karen Rubinstein. Quarterly. American Zionist Federation.

SYNAGOGUE LIGHT (1933). 47 Beekman St., NYC, 10038. (212)227-7800. Meyer Hager. Quarterly. Union of Chassidic Rabbis.

SYRACUSE JEWISH OBSERVER (1978). 2223 E. Genesee St., Syracuse, 13214-0510. (315)422-4104. Judith Rubenstein. Fortnightly. Syracuse Jewish Federation.

TALKS AND TALES (1942). 770 Eastern Pkwy., Brooklyn, 11213. (718)493-9250. Nissan Mindel. Monthly (also Hebrew, French, and Spanish editions). Merkos L'Inyonei Chinuch, Inc.

TRADITION (1958). 275 Seventh Ave., NYC, 10001. (212)807-7888. Walter Wurzburger. Quarterly. Rabbinical Council of America.

TRENDS (1982). 730 Broadway, NYC, 10003. (212)260-0006. Quarterly. Jewish Education Service of North America, Inc.

UNITED SYNAGOGUE REVIEW (1943). 155 Fifth Ave., NYC, 10010. (212)533-7800. Marvin S. Wiener. Quarterly. United Synagogue of America.

UNSER TSAIT (1941). 25 E. 21 St., NYC, 10010. (212)475-0059. Jacob S. Hertz. Monthly. Yiddish. Jewish Labor Bund.

DER WECKER (1921). 45 E. 33 St., NYC, 10016. (212)686-1538. Elias Schulman. Bimonthly. Yiddish. Jewish Socialist Verband of America.

WOMEN'S AMERICAN ORT REPORTER (1966). 315 Park Ave. S., NYC, 10010. (212)505-7700. Elie Faust-Levy. Quarterly. Women's American ORT, Inc.

WOMEN'S LEAGUE OUTLOOK (1930). 48 E. 74 St., NYC, 10021. (212)628-1600. Yvette Rosenberg. Quarterly. Women's League for Conservative Judaism.

WORKMEN'S CIRCLE CALL (1934). 45 E. 33 St., NYC, 10016. (212)889-6800. Walter L. Kirschenbaum. Bimonthly. Workmen's Circle.

YEARBOOK OF THE CENTRAL CONFERENCE OF AMERICAN RABBIS (1890). 21 E. 40 St., NYC, 10016. (212)684-4990. Elliot L. Stevens. Annually. Central Conference of American Rabbis.

YIDDISH (1973). Queens College, Kiely 802, 65-30 Kissena Blvd., Flushing, 11367. (718)520-7067. Joseph C. Landis. Quarterly. Queens College Press.

YIDDISHE HEIM (1958). 770 Eastern Pkwy., Brooklyn, 11213. (718)493-9250. Rachel Altein, Tema Guarary. Quarterly. English-Yiddish. Agudas Nshei Ub'nos Chabad.

YIDDISHE KULTUR (1938). 1123 Broadway, Room 203, NYC, 10010. (212)691-0708. Itche Goldberg. Monthly (except June–July, Aug.–Sept.). Yiddish. Yiddishe Kultur Farband, Inc.—YKUF.

YIDDISHE VORT (1953). 5 Beekman St., NYC, 10038. (212)791-1800. Joseph Friedenson. Monthly. Yiddish. Agudath Israel of America.

YIDDISHER KEMFER (1906). 275 Seventh Ave., NYC, 10001. (212)675-7808. Mordechai Strigler. Weekly. Yiddish. Labor Zionist Letters, Inc.

YIDISHE SHPRAKH (1941). 1048 Fifth Ave., NYC, 10028. (212)231-7905. Mordkhe Schaechter. Irregularly. Yiddish. Yivo Institute for Jewish Research, Inc.

YIVO ANNUAL OF JEWISH SOCIAL SCIENCE (1946). 1048 Fifth Ave., NYC, 10028. (212)535-6700. David Roskies. Biannually. Yivo Institute for Jewish Research, Inc.

YIVO BLETER (1931). 1048 Fifth Ave., NYC, 10028. (212)535-6700. Editorial board. Irregularly. Yiddish. Yivo Institute for Jewish Research, Inc.

YOUNG ISRAEL VIEWPOINT (1952). 3 W. 16 St., NYC, 10011. (212)929-1525. Yaakov Kornreich. Monthly (except July, Aug.). National Council of Young Israel.

YOUNG JUDAEAN (1912). 50 W. 58 St., NYC, 10019. (212)355-7900. Mordecai Newman. Seven times a year. Hadassah Zionist Youth Commission.

YOUTH AND NATION (1933). 150 Fifth Ave., NYC, 10011. (212)929-4955. Shlomit Segal. Quarterly. Hashomer Hatzair Zionist Youth Movement.

YUGNTRUF (1964). 3328 Bainbridge Ave., Bronx, 10467. (212)654-8540. Hershl Glasser. Quarterly. Yiddish. Yugntruf Youth for Yiddish.

NORTH CAROLINA

AMERICAN JEWISH TIMES—OUTLOOK (1934; reorg. 1950). PO Box 33218, Charlotte, 28233. (704)372-3296. Rick Rierson. Monthly.

OHIO

THE AMERICAN ISRAELITE (1854). 906 Main St., Room 505, Cincinnati, 45237. (513)621-3145. Phyllis R. Singer. Weekly.

AMERICAN JEWISH ARCHIVES (1947). 3101 Clifton Ave., Cincinnati, 45220. (513)221-1875. Jacob R. Marcus, Abraham J. Peck. Semiannually. American Jewish Archives of Hebrew Union College—Jewish Institute of Religion.

CLEVELAND JEWISH NEWS (1964). 13910 Cedar Rd., Cleveland, 44118. (216)371-0800. Cynthia Dettelbach. Weekly. Cleveland Jewish Publication Co.

DAYTON JEWISH CHRONICLE (1961). 118 Salem Ave., Dayton, 45406. (513)222-0783. Anne M. Hammerman. Weekly.

INDEX TO JEWISH PERIODICALS (1963). PO Box 18570, Cleveland Hts., 44118. (216)-321-7296. Miriam Leikind, Bess Rosenfeld, Jean H. Foxman. Semiannually.

OHIO JEWISH CHRONICLE (1921). 2831 E. Main St., Columbus, 43209. (614)237-4296. Judith Franklin, Steve Pinsky, Diane Levi. Weekly.

STARK JEWISH NEWS (1920). 2631 Harvard Ave. NW, 44709. (216)452-6444. Adele Gelb. Monthly. Canton Jewish Community Federation.

STUDIES IN BIBLIOGRAPHY AND BOOKLORE (1953). 3101 Clifton Ave., Cincinnati, 45220. (513)221-1875. Herbert C. Zafren. Irregularly. English-Hebrew-German. Library of Hebrew Union College—Jewish Institute of Religion.

YOUNGSTOWN JEWISH TIMES (1935). PO Box 777, Youngstown, 44501. (216)746-6192. Harry Alter. Fortnightly.

OKLAHOMA

SOUTHWEST JEWISH CHRONICLE (1929). 314-B N. Robinson St., Oklahoma City, 73102. (405)236-4226. E. F. Friedman. Quarterly.

TULSA JEWISH REVIEW (1930). 2205 E. 51 St., Tulsa, 74105. (918)749-7751. Dianna Aaronson. Monthly. Tulsa Section, National Council of Jewish Women.

PENNSYLVANIA

JEWISH CHRONICLE (1962). 315 S. Bellefield Ave., Pittsburgh, 15213. (412)687-1000. Joel Roteman. Weekly. Pittsburgh Jewish Publication and Education Foundation.

JEWISH EXPONENT (1887). 226 S. 16 St., Philadelphia, 19102. (215)893-5740. Albert Erlick. Weekly. Federation of Jewish Agencies of Greater Philadelphia.

JEWISH QUARTERLY REVIEW (1910). 250 Highland Ave., Merion, 19066. (215)667-1830. Leon Nemoy and faculty. Quarterly. Dropsie College.

JEWISH TIMES OF THE GREATER NORTH-EAST (1925). 2417 Welsh Rd., Philadelphia, 19114. (215)464-3900. Leon E. Brown. Weekly. Federation of Jewish Agencies of Greater Philadelphia.

NEW MENORAH (1979). 6723 Emlen St., Philadelphia, 19119. (215)849-5385. Arthur Waskow, Shana Margolin. Bimonthly. B'nai Or Religious Fellowship.

RHODE ISLAND

RHODE ISLAND JEWISH HISTORICAL NOTES (1954). 130 Sessions St., Providence, 02906. (401)331-1360. Annually. Rhode Island Jewish Historical Association.

TENNESSEE

HEBREW WATCHMAN (1925). 277 Jefferson Ave., Memphis, 38103. (901)526-2215. Herman I. Goldberger. Weekly.

TEXAS

JEWISH CIVIC PRESS (1965). PO Box 35656, Houston, 77235. (713)491-1512. Abner Tritt. Monthly.

JEWISH HERALD-VOICE (1908). PO Box 153, Houston, 77001. (713)630-0391. Joseph W. and Jeanne F. Samuels. Weekly.

JEWISH JOURNAL OF SAN ANTONIO (1973). 8434 Ahern, San Antonio, 78216. (512)-341-8234. Norma Grubman. Monthly. Jewish Federation of San Antonio.

TEXAS JEWISH POST (1947). PO Box 742, Fort Worth, 76101. (817)927-2831. 11333 N. Central Expressway, Dallas, 75243. (214)692-7283. Jimmy Wisch. Weekly.

VIRGINIA

UJF NEWS (1959). 7300 Newport Ave., Norfolk, 23462. (804)489-8040. Reba Karp. Weekly. United Jewish Federation of Tidewater.

WASHINGTON

JEWISH TRANSCRIPT (1924). Securities Building, Room 510, Seattle, 98101. (206)-624-0136. Philip R. Scheier. Bimonthly. Jewish Federation of Greater Seattle.

M'GODOLIM: THE JEWISH QUARTERLY (1979). 2921 E. Madison St., #7, Seattle, 98112-4237. (206)322-1431. Keith S. Gormezano. Quarterly. Hebrew-English.

WISCONSIN

WISCONSIN JEWISH CHRONICLE (1921). 1360 N. Prospect Ave., Milwaukee, 53202. (414)271-2992. Andy Muchin. Weekly. Milwaukee Jewish Federation.

NEWS SYNDICATES

JEWISH PRESS FEATURES (1970). 15 E. 26 St., Suite 1350, NYC, 10010. (212)679-1411. Joyce Fine. Monthly. Jewish Student Press Service.

JEWISH TELEGRAPHIC AGENCY, INC. (1917). 165 W. 46 St., Suite 511, NYC., 10036. (212)575-9370. Murray Zuckoff. Daily.

SEVEN ARTS FEATURE SYNDICATE and WORLDWIDE NEWS SERVICE (WNS) (1923). 165 W. 46 St., Suite 511, NYC, 10036. (212)575-9370. John Kayston. Semiweekly.

CANADA

BULLETIN DU CERCLE JUIF DE LANGUE FRANÇAISE DU CONGRES JUIF CANADIEN (1952). 1590 Avenue Docteur Penfield, Montreal, PQ, H3G 1C5. (514)931-7531. M. Mayer Levy. Quarterly. French. Canadian Jewish Congress.

CANADIAN JEWISH HERALD (1977). 17 Anselme Layigne Blvd., Dollard des Ormeaux, PQ, H9A 1N3. (514)684-7667. Dan Nimrod. Irregularly.

CANADIAN JEWISH NEWS (1960). 562 Eglinton Ave. E., Suite 401, Toronto, ONT M4P 1P1. (416)483-9331. Maurice Lucow. Weekly.

CANADIAN JEWISH OUTLOOK (1963). 6184 Ash St., #3, Vancouver, BC V5Z 3G9. (604)324-5101. Ben Chud, Henry Rosenthal. Monthly.

CANADIAN ZIONIST (1934). 1310 Greene Ave., Suite 800, Montreal, PQ H3Z 2B2. (514)934-0804. Suite 800, Leon Kronitz. Five times a year. Canadian Zionist Federation.

JEWISH POST (1925). 117 Hutchings St., Winnipeg, MAN R2W 3R6. (204)694-3332. Matt Bellan. Weekly.

JEWISH STANDARD (1929). 67 Mowat Ave., Suite 319, Toronto, ONT M6K 3E3. (416)537-2696. Julius Hayman. Semimonthly.

JEWISH WESTERN BULLETIN (1930). 3268 Heather St., Vancouver, BC V5Z 3K5. (604)879-6575. Samuel Kaplan. Weekly.

JOURNAL OF PSYCHOLOGY AND JUDAISM (1976). 1747 Featherston Dr., Ottawa, ONT K1H 6P4. (613)731-9119. Reuven P. Bulka. Semiannually. Center for the Study of Psychology and Judaism.

KANADER ADLER-JEWISH EAGLE (1907). 4180 De Courtrai, Suite 218, Montreal, PQ H3S 1C3. (514)735-6577. Mordechai Husid. Weekly. Yiddish. Combined Jewish Organizations of Montreal.

OTTAWA JEWISH BULLETIN & REVIEW (1954). 151 Chapel St., Ottawa, ONT K1H 7Y2. (613)232-7306. Cynthia Engel. Biweekly. Jewish Community Council of Ottawa.

UNDZER VEG (1932). 272 Codsell Ave., Downsview, ONT M3H 3X2. 636-4024. Joseph Kligman. Quarterly. Yiddish-English. Achdut HaAvoda-Poale Zion of Canada.

WESTERN JEWISH NEWS (1926). PO Box 87, 400–259 Portage Ave., Winnipeg, MAN R3C 2G6. 942-6361. Pauline Essers. Weekly. Yiddish-Hebrew.

WINDSOR JEWISH COMMUNITY BULLETIN (1938). 1641 Ouellette Ave., Windsor, ONT N8X 1K9. (519)973-1772. Joseph Eisenberg. Irregularly. Windsor Jewish Community Council.

Necrology: United States[1]

ADAMS, THEODORE L., rabbi, communal worker; b. Bangor, Maine, Feb. 23, 1915; d. NYC, Sept. 4, 1984; educ.: Yeshiva U. (ordination, PhD), Columbia U.; rabbi: Cong. Mt. Sinai, Jersey City, NJ, 1938–1953; Cong. Ohab Zedek, NYC, 1953–1974; asst. to pres. and asst. prof., Touro Coll., since 1974; mem.: OPA (WWII), Jersey City Planning Comm., Civil Rights Comm., Stryker's Bay (Manhattan) Community Council; consultant, NJ Youth Conf.; delegate, Mid-Century White House Conf. on Children and Youth; pres. and hon. pres.: Synagogue Council of Amer., Rabbinical Council of Amer.; v. chmn., Natl. Hapoel Hamizrachi; bd. mem.: Jewish Welfare Board, Jewish Material Claims Conf.; recipient: Mordecai Ben David Award, Yeshiva U.

AGUS, IRVING A., professor; b. Swislocz, Poland, Feb. 20, 1910; d. NYC, July 18, 1984; in U.S. since 1927; educ.: NYU, Dropsie (PhD); educational dir., Baron Hirsch Cong., Memphis, Tenn., 1939–1945; prin., Hebrew Acad. of Long Island, 1945–1947; dean, Fischel Inst. for Research in Talmud, Jerusalem, 1947–1949; prin., Akiba Acad., Philadelphia, 1949–1951; prof. of Jewish history, Yeshiva U., 1951–1977; recognized authority on Jewish life in the Middle Ages and on German Jewish history; editorial bd. mem. and managing editor, *Jewish Quarterly Review;* author: *Rabbi Meir of Rothenburg* (1947); *Responsa of the Tosaphists* (1954); *Dibrei*

Yemei Yisrael, 2 vols. (1957–1967); *Urban Civilization in Pre-Crusade Europe* (1965); *The Heroic Age of Franco-German Jewry* (1969); recipient: La Med Found. Prize for *Rabbi Meir of Rothenburg.*

BAKER, LEONARD S., writer; b. Pittsburgh, Pa., Jan. 24, 1931; d. Washington, DC, Nov. 23, 1984; educ.: U. of Pittsburgh, Columbia U. School of Journalism; U.S. army, 1952–1954; reporter, *St. Louis Globe-Democrat,* 1955–1956; Washington reporter, *Newsday,* 1956–1965; free-lance writer, editor, lecturer since 1965; bd. mem., treas., Temple Micah; author: *The Johnson Eclipse: A President's Vice-Presidency* (1966); *Back to Back: The Duel Between FDR and the Supreme Court* (1967), *The Guaranteed Society* (1968), *Roosevelt and Pearl Harbor* (1970), *Brahmin in Revolt* (1972), *John Marshall: A Life in Law* (1974), *Days of Sorrow and Pain: Leo Baeck and the Berlin Jews* (1978), *Brandeis and Frankfurter: A Dual Biography* (1984); recipient: Pulitzer Prize, 1979, for Leo Baeck biography.

BAMBERGER, FRITZ, scholar, administrator; b. Frankfurt-am-Main, Germany, Jan. 7, 1902; d. NYC, Sept. 22, 1984; in U.S. since 1939; educ: U. of Berlin (PhD); research prof., Acad. for Jewish Research, Berlin, 1926–1933; prof., Coll. of Jewish Studies, Berlin, 1933–1934; mem., bd. of ed. for Jews, Berlin, and pres., Jewish Teachers Coll. of Prussia, 1934–1938; mem. faculty, Coll. of Jewish Studies,

---

[1] Including Jewish residents of the United States who died between January 1 and December 31, 1984.

Chicago, 1939–1944; research dir., *Coronet* and *Esquire* magazines, 1942–1948; editorial dir., *Coronet,* 1948–1952, and editor, 1952–1956; exec. dir. *Esquire* and *Coronet,* 1956–1961; prof. of intellectual history and asst. to pres., Hebrew Union Coll.–Jewish Inst. of Religion, NYC, 1962–1979; emer. prof. since 1979; v. pres., Leo Baeck Inst.; v. chmn., N. Amer. bd., World Union of Progressive Judaism; v. pres., Selfhelp Community Services; author: *Enstehung des Wertproblems* (1924), *Moses Mendelssohn* (1929), *Das System des Maimonides* (1935), *Das neunte Schuljahr* (1937), *Zunz's Conception of History* (1941), *Leo Baeck—The Man and the Idea* (1958), *The Philosophy of Julius Guttmann* (1960), *Books Are the Best Things* (1962); articles in many publications; recipient; hon. DHL, HUC-JIR, 1982.

BEN-AMI, YITSHAQ, businessman, communal worker; b. Tel Aviv, Palestine, June 11, 1913; d. NYC, Dec. 31, 1984; in U.S. since 1939; educ.: Hebrew U. of Jerusalem; exec., Philipp Brothers division of Englehard Minerals and Chemicals Corp., 1958–1975; joined Irgun Zeva'i Le'ummi, 1932; Irgun coord. of illegal immigration from Europe, 1937–1939; cofounder, Amer. Friends for a Jewish Palestine, 1939, and subsequently of the Com. for a Jewish Army and the Emergency Com. to save the Jewish People of Europe; served U.S. army, 1943–1945; exec. dir., Amer. League for a Free Palestine, 1946–1948; participated in attempt to bring arms to Palestine aboard the SS *Altalena,* June 1948; bd. mem., Herut Zionists of Amer.; lecturer, radio, and TV commentator; author: *Years of Wrath, Days of Glory: Memoirs from the Irgun.*

BOKSER, BEN ZION, rabbi, scholar; b. Luboml, Poland, July 4, 1907; d. NYC, Jan. 31, 1984; in U.S. since 1920; educ.: CCNY, Columbia U. (PhD), Jewish Theological Seminary of Amer.; rabbi, Forest Hills Jewish Center, NYC, since 1935; adj. prof., Queens College, CUNY; cofounder and dir., Center for the Study of Ethics and Public Policy, Queens College; visiting and adj. prof. of homiletics, JTS, 1950–1973; editor, for 30 years, "Eternal Light" radio programs; chmn. for two terms, Rabbinical Assembly Com. on Jewish Law and Standards; author: many works, including: *Pharisaic Judaism in Transition* (1935, 1973), *From the World of the Cabbalah:*

The Philosophy of Rabbi Judah Loew of Prague (1957), *The Prayer Book (Weekday, Sabbath and Festival)* (1957 and rev. eds. thereafter), *The High Holyday Prayer Book* (1959), *The Legacy of Maimonides* (1962), *Judaism: Profile of a Faith* (1963), *Judaism and the Christian Predicament* (1967), *Jews, Judaism, and the State of Israel* (1973), *The Gifts of Life and Love: A Treasury of Inspirations* (1975), *Abraham Isaac Kook* (1978), *The Jewish Mystical Tradition* (1981); recipient; hon. DD, JTS; JWB Jewish Book Council Award for Best Book on Jewish Thought, for *Judaism: Profile of a Faith,* and many other honors.

BONUS, BEN, theater personality; b. Horodenko, Poland, Nov. 9, 1920; d. Miami, Fla., Apr. 6, 1984; in U.S. since 1939; a prominent figure in the American Yiddish theater, founded the Yiddish Mobile Theater in 1946 and later the Farband Players, which toured the U.S. and Canada; produced and performed in over 100 musicals and plays, including three Broadway revues: *Let's Sing Yiddish* (1966); *Sing Israel Sing* (1967), and *Light, Lively and Yiddish* (1970); last appeared on the stage in Nov. 1983, with wife, actress Mina Bern, in *Let There Be Joy;* mem.: Jewish Theatrical Alliance, Hebrew Actors' Union, Workmen's Circle.

BROIDO, THEODORE K., communal worker; b. NYC, (?), 1928; d. NYC, Aug. 12, 1984; joined administrative staff, Union of Amer. Hebrew Congs. in 1949, serving successively as dir. regional activities, dir. administration, dir. NY and NJ regions, assoc. dir. NY Fed. of Reform Synagogues, and admin. sec. of the Union; a founder of ARZA (Assn. of Reform Zionists of Amer.); mem: Zionist General Council, Jewish Agency Assembly; bd. mem., Amer. Zionist Fed.

CAHN, JUDAH, rabbi, communal worker; b. NYC, Dec. 19, 1912; d. Sarasota, Fla., March 24, 1984; educ.: NYU, Columbia U., Hebrew Union Coll.–Jewish Inst. of Religion; rabbi, Temple Sinai, Springfield, Mass., 1936–1942; natl. administrator, B'nai B'rith Hillel Founds., 1942–1946; rabbi, Temple Israel, Lawrence, NY, 1946–1959; founding rabbi, Metropolitan Synagogue, NYC, since 1959; faculty mem.: Springfield Coll. (Mass.), U. of Mass., New School for Social Research, HUC-JIR; one of three members of NY State Education Dept. Adv. Com. on

Human Relations and Community Tensions, set up to ease racial imbalance in schools, 1959–1974; bd. mem., NAACP, 1947–1964, and v. pres. 1954–1964; pres., NY Bd. of Rabbis; chmn., UJA-Fed. Rabbinical Adv. Council; bd. mem. and hon. v. pres., Amer. ORT Fed.; chmn., Anti-Defamation League's Middle Eastern Affairs com. and mem. NY regional adv. cabinet of ADL; bd. mem., Jewish Telegraphic Agency.

CHILEWICH, NIUSIA, communal worker; b. Grodno, Russia, Sept. 12, 1913; d. St. Thomas, V.I., Apr. 2, 1984; in U.S. since 1965; volunteer worker and contributor to many causes; founder, bd. chmn., and pres., Council for a Beautiful Israel; founder, E.L.E.M.-Youth in Distress; treas., Netzer Found.; bd. mem., Gotham Division UJA-Fed. Women's Campaign.

CHOMSKI, ISAAC, physician, communal worker; b. Warsaw, Poland, Nov. 21, 1903; d. NYC, July 3, 1984; in U.S. since 1941; educ.: Universities of Paris and Montpellier; physician in private practice since 1944; official doctor to Consulate of Israel in NY, Israel UN Mission, and Jewish Agency; in 1941, with wife, Masha, accompanied 111 refugee children on three-week journey from France to U.S., the first group granted visas through the U.S. Com. for the care of European Children, headed by Eleanor Roosevelt and Marshall Field 3rd; mem., Amer. Medical Assn., Medical Soc. of NY; fellow, Amer. Geriatrics Soc.; mem., Amer. Physicians Fellowship for Medicine in Israel; recipient: Israel Defense Ministry decoration "for service to the State."

CUTLER, MAX, physician, medical researcher; b. Zhitomir, Russia, May 9, 1899; d. Camarillo, Calif., July 6, 1984; in U.S. since 1907; educ.: U. of Georgia, Johns Hopkins U. Medical School, Curie Inst. (Paris), Radiumhemet (Stockholm); Rockefeller fellow in cancer research, Memorial Hosp., NYC, 1926–1930; dir., tumor clinic, Michael Reese Hosp., Chicago, 1931–1937; founder and dir., Chicago Tumor Inst., 1938–1952, where he introduced and developed important radiation techniques; in private practice and consultant on breast cancer at UCLA, 1952–1979; med. dir., Beverly Hills Cancer Research Found., 1966–1980; author: three books on cancer and over 100 articles.

ECKSTEIN, OTTO, economist; b. Ulm, Germany, Aug. 1, 1927; d. Boston, Mass., Mar. 22, 1984; in U.S. since 1939; educ.: Princeton U., Harvard U. (PhD); U.S. army, 1946–47; mem. faculty, Harvard U., beginning 1952, prof. since 1963; co-founder., Data Resources, Inc., leading computer-based econ. forecasting firm, 1968; tech. dir., U.S. Cong. Joint Econ. Com. study on employment, growth, and price levels, 1959–1960; mem., Council of Economic Advisers to Pres. Lyndon Johnson, in which position helped develop Great Society programs, 1964–1966; served on various presidential commissions and as consultant to govt. agencies and corps.; v. pres., Amer. Econ. Assn., 1981; pres., Eastern Econ. Assn., 1984; trustee, Radcliffe Coll., dir., Paine Webber, Inc.; trustee, Combined Jewish Philanthropies of Greater Boston; author: various works, including *Public Finance* (1964), *The Great Recession* (1978), *Core Inflation* (1981), *The DRI Model of the U.S. Economy* (1983), and *DRI Report on U.S. Manufacturing Industries* (1984).

FEUER, LEON, I., rabbi, communal worker; b. Hazelton, Pa., May 23, 1903; d. Toledo, Ohio, Sept. (?), 1984; educ.: U. of Cincinnati, Hebrew Union Coll.-Jewish Inst. of Religion; asst. rabbi, The Temple, Cleveland, Ohio, 1927–1935; sr. rabbi, Temple Shomer Emunim, Toledo, Ohio, 1935–1975; adj. prof., U. of Toledo; dir., Washington bureau, Amer. Zionist Emergency Council, 1943–1944; natl. v. pres., Zionist Org. of Amer., 1945–1948; pres: Toledo UN Assn., 1946–1949; Central Conf. Amer. Rabbis, 1963–1965; mem. exec., Jewish Agency for Israel, 1966–1971; author: *Jewish Literature Since the Bible, The Jew and His Religion, Why a Jewish State;* recipient: hon. degrees, HUC-JIR, Bowling Green State U.

FRISCH, LEO H., editor, publisher; b. Suvalk, Poland, 1890; d. Minneapolis, Minn., June 29, 1984; in U.S. since 1901; educ.: U. of Minn.; editor-publisher, *The American Jewish World,* a weekly, 1912–1972; mem., Minn. Newspaper Assn., Minn. Press Club; bd. mem., Jewish Telegraphic Agency 1940s and 1950s; v. pres., Amer. Jewish Press Assn.; life bd. mem., Talmud Torah of Minneapolis; mem. exec. bd., Minneapolis Fed. for Jewish Service; recipient: B'nai B'rith award for 70 years of service (1982).

GAMORAN, MAMIE G., author, communal worker; b. NYC, Jan. 17, 1900; d. NYC, July 26, 1984; author of books for children and other works, including: *Voice of the Prophets* (1929), *Hillel's Happy Holidays* (1939), *The New Jewish History*, 3 vols. (1953, 1955, 1957), *Talks to Jewish Teachers* (with Dr. Emanuel Gamoran, 1966), *The Jewish Times* (1975), *The Hebrew Spirit in America* (1975); natl. bd. mem., Hadassah, since 1950; bd. mem.: Hebrew Arts School for Music and Dance; *Hadoar*; v. pres., Histadruth Ivrith of Amer.

GEBINER, RAYMOND, communal worker; b. Rovno, Russia, May 13, 1903; d. San Juan, P.R., Feb. 9, 1984; in U.S. since 1922; educ.: Columbia U., Cooper Union, the Rand School; teacher, Workmen's Circle schools, 1928–1945; educational dir., Local 60, ILGWU; dir., Children's Colony at Camp Eden (Jewish Socialist Farband); HIAS staff member since 1950, first as Yiddish public relations writer, later exec. sec. of HIAS Council of Orgs.; columnist, *Jewish Daily Forward;* weekly radio show host, "The Voice of HIAS," station WEVD; mem. exec. bd.: Workmen's Circle, Yiddish Writers' Union, Jewish Labor Com.

GOLDSTEIN, RUBY, sports personality; b. NYC, Oct. 7, 1907; d. Miami Beach, Fla., Apr. 22, 1984; a professional lightweight and welterweight boxer, 1925–1937, with a record of 50–5, was known as "the Jewel of the Ghetto"; served in U.S. army in WWII as physical ed. instr.; granted a referee's license in 1943, went on to become one of the most celebrated ring officials in modern times, working in 39 championship fights during a 21-year career.

GRAUBART, DAVID, rabbi, author; b. Staszow, Poland, Apr. 6, 1906; d. Chicago, Ill., Apr. 27, 1984; in U.S. since 1922 (?); educ.: Ill. Inst. of Technology, Hebrew Theol. Coll., Jewish Theological Seminary of Amer., U. of Indiana (PhD); prof. of Talmud, Spertus Coll. of Judaica; mem., Com. on Jewish Law and Standards, Rabbinical Assembly of Amer., presiding judge, RA Beth Din, Chicago region; pres., RA Chicago region; mem.: Zionist Org. of Amer., Labor Zionist Org. of Amer., Chicago Bd. of Rabbis, Mercaz; author: *Beyond This Present* (1940); *Attitude of Judaism to Non-Jews* (1949); numerous articles in English, Yiddish, and Hebrew on Jewish biomedical ethics and other subjects; editor: *Responsa Chavalim Ba-Neimin* by Rabbi J.L.

Graubart; coeditor, *Shkolnick Aphorisms* (1976); *Jewish Family Bible;* Yiddish editor, *Britannica World Language Dictionary;* contributing editor, *Jewish Daily Forward* and *The Forward.*

GRUNWALD, JOSEF, rabbi; b.(?), Hungary, 1902; d. Valhalla, NY, Aug. 11, 1984; in U.S. since end of WWII, in which his wife and ten children perished; founder and head of Pupa Hasidic movement (Kehilath Yakov), with some 10,000 members worldwide; established congregations and schools in Brooklyn (Williamsburg and Borough Park) and Monsey, NY, Montreal, and Jerusalem, and was building Kiryas Pupa near Mt. Kisco in Westchester County, NY.

GUILDEN, IRA, businessman, philanthropist; b. NYC,(?), 1896; d. NYC, Nov. 11, 1984; chmn. and chief exec. officer, Baldwin Securities Corp.; chmn., John B. Stetson Co.; dir.: Hilton Internatl., Atlas Genl. Corp., Metro-Goldwyn-Mayer, First Women's Financial Corp.; a founder, pres., and since 1973 bd. chmn., Israel Bond Org.; a founder, pres., and major benefactor, Boys Town Jerusalem; chmn.; Keren-Or, Inc.; Internatl. Affairs Comm., Amer. Jewish Congress; active also in behalf of Jewish Natl. Fund., Brookdale Hosp. Medical Center (Brooklyn), Albert Einstein Coll. of Medicine, and Belfer Graduate School of Science (Yeshiva U.).

HABER, SAMUEL L., internatl. relief administrator, communal worker; b. Harlau, Rumania, Oct. 12, 1903; d. Akron, Ohio, Nov. 3, 1984; in U.S. since 1911; educ.: U. of Wisconsin; U.S. govt. economist and statistician (WPA), 1925–1943; served in U.S. army, 1943–1946, attached to military govt. in Württemberg-Baden and Bavaria, Germany; joined staff of Amer. Jewish Joint Distribution Com. in 1947, serving successively as dir. for Germany in charge of developing programs for the rescue, rehabilitation, and emigration of over 200,000 displaced persons, 1947–1954; dir., Morocco, 1954–1957; asst. dir. gen., Geneva, 1958–1964; asst. exec. v. chmn., NY, 1964–1967; exec. v. chmn., 1967–1976; hon. exec. v. pres. since 1976; various positions in behalf of Hebrew U. of Jerusalem: mem. bd. of govs., chmn. exec. com., Inst. of Contemporary Jewry; bd. mem. and natl. chmn., Associates Div., Amer. Friends of the Hebrew U.; a founder and bd. mem., Interfaith Hunger Appeal; v.

pres., Internatl. Council on Jewish Social and Welfare Services; v. pres., Israel Education Fund; v. chmn., Amer. Council of Voluntary Agencies; recipient: Ben Mordecai Award, Yeshiva U.; ALEH Award, State of Israel; hon. DHL, Hebrew Union Coll.-Jewish Inst. of Religion.

HELD, MOSHE, professor; b. Warsaw, Poland, (?), 1924; d. Beersheba, Israel, June 9, 1984; educ.: Hebrew U. of Jerusalem; prof. of Semitic languages and cultures, Columbia U.; adj. prof., Jewish Theological Seminary of Amer.

HELLMAN, LILLIAN, playwright; b. New Orleans, La., June 20, 1905(?); d. Martha's Vineyard, Mass., June 30, 1984; educ.: NYU, Columbia U.; major American playwright whose works included *The Children's Hour* (1934), *The Little Foxes* (1939), *Watch on the Rhine* (1941), and other works for stage and screen; one of three books of memoirs, *Pentimento* (1974), inspired 1977 film *Julia;* was a controversial figure on the political and social scene throughout her life.

HOLLENDER, SAMUEL S., businessman, communal worker; b. Chicago, Ill., Dec. 8, 1900; d. Chicago, Ill., Oct. 17, 1984; genl. partner, S.S. Hollender, Ltd., optical co.; mem. bd. govs., Chicago Opera Co.; a founder, Roosevelt U.; natl. bd. dirs., Chicago Medical School; life mem., Chicago Art Inst.; mem.: Masons (32nd), Shriners; bd. mem.: Cong. Emanuel (life); Jewish Fed. of Chicago; Union of Amer. Hebrew Congs.; World Union for Progressive Judaism; Amer. Jewish Joint Distribution Com.; Amer. Jewish Com.; mem., bd. govs., Hebrew Union Coll.; natl. chmn., combined appeal, UAHC-HUC-JIR (1948–1954); genl. chmn. and pres., Combined Jewish Appeal, Chicago; mem.: B'nai B'rith, Zeta Beta Tau; recipient: hon. DHL, HUC-JIR, and numerous awards, including Man of Valor, UAHC; Julius Rosenwald Memorial Award, Jewish Fed. of Chicago; Award of Merit, Cong. Emanuel.

KAPLAN, HENRY S., physician, medical researcher; b. Chicago, Ill., Apr. 24, 1918; d. Stanford, Calif., Feb. 4, 1984; educ.: U. of Chicago, Rush Medical Coll.; prof. of radiology, Stanford U. School of Medicine, since 1948; dir., Louis B. Mayer Cancer Biology Laboratory; coinventor of the medical linear accelerator, the cornerstone

of present radiation therapy for cancer; codeveloper of a treatment for Hodgkin's disease that has made it more than 80-percent curable; also credited with important findings in cancer biology; recipient: numerous awards and honors, including the Atoms for Peace Prize, the first Charles F. Kettering Prize (General Motors Cancer Research Found.); Order of Merit from Italy; Chevalier of the French Legion of Honor; first radiologist to be elected to the Natl. Acad. of Sciences (1972).

KIEVAL, HOWARD, communal worker; b. NYC, Apr. 4, 1918; d. NYC, Sept. 20, 1984; educ.; CCNY, Case Western Reserve U.; dir., Jewish Fed. of Raritan Valley, NJ; exec. sec., Alumni Assn. of CCNY; exec. dir., Big Brothers, Inc; dir., NY region, Amer. Soc. for Technion–Israel Inst. of Technology; school bd. chmn., Park Ave. Synagogue, NYC.

KLEIN, JULIUS, military officer, public relations counsel; b. Chicago, Ill., Sept. 5, 1901; d. Chicago, Ill., April 6, 1984; educ.: Sophien Coll., Berlin; U. of Virginia School of Military Govt.; U.S. soldier and war correspondent, WWI; editor, Hearst newspapers, 1926–1933; exec., RKO Universal Pictures, 1934–1939; chmn., Julius Klein Public Relations, since 1947; joined army reserves 1933; in WWII served in Pacific and Philippines; promoted to colonel, 1944; achieved postwar rank of major general, U.S. army reserves; retired 1966; commander, Jewish War Veterans, 1947–1948; active publicist for creation of Israel; focus of controversy for alleged influence peddling on behalf of W. German clients in 1966 Senate investigation of Sen. Thomas J. Dodd; Republican candidate for U.S. Senate, 1954; pres., Natl. Shrine to Jewish War Dead; hon. dir., Hebrew Theol. Coll.; mem.: Ill. Armory Bd., Public Relations Soc. of Amer., Chicago Foreign Relations Council, B'nai B'rith, Masons, Amer. Legion, Amvets, Jewish War Veterans. Recipient: Legion of Merit (2 clusters), Soldier's Medal for Heroism, Bronze Star, and other military honors; Govt. of Israel War of Independence and Remembrance medals; VA Distinguished Service Award.

KOHS, SAMUEL C., psychologist, communal worker; b. NYC, June 2, 1890; d. San Francisco, Calif., Jan. 23, 1984; educ.: CCNY, Clark U., Stanford U. (PhD); asst. prof. of psychology, Reed Coll., 1918–1923; lect., extension div., U. of Oregon,

1919–1923; psychologist, Portland, Ore. court of domestic relations, 1919–1923; exec. dir.: Oakland, Calif. Jewish Welfare Fed., 1924–1926; Eureka Benevolent Soc., 1926–1928; Fed. of Jewish Charities, Brooklyn, NY, 1928–1933; prof., Graduate School for Jewish Social Work, NYC, 1931–1939; dir.: Natl. Refugee Service Resettlement Div., 1938–1940; Jewish Welfare Bd. Bureau of War Records, 1942–1945; field sec., JWB Western States Div. and organizer of its youth council, 1945–1956; author: *Intelligence Measurement* (1923), *The Roots of Social Work* (1966), other books and articles, including "Jewish War Records of World War II," AJYB, Vol. 47.

LEVIN, SOLOMON I., rabbi, communal worker; b. Koleliszki, Poland, Oct. 26, 1886; d. Minneapolis, Minn., July 11, 1984; in U.S. since 1910; rabbi, Cong. Sharei Zedek and Sharei Chesed and dean of Minneapolis Orthodox Jewish community for over 63 years; founder and pres., Rabbinical Kashrut Council; bd. mem.: Minneapolis Fed., Jewish Children's Home, Jewish Social Service Bureau, Minneapolis Talmud Torah, Torah Acad.; pres., Mizrachi chapter; sponsored state *kashrut* laws that have served as models for other states; active proponent of child-welfare and animal-protection legislation; author: *Minchat Shlomo, responsa* on use of modern inventions in the home, and many articles on Jewish law; coauthor, *The Kosher Code.*

LIEBERMAN, GEORGE B., rabbi; b. Wysoke-Litovsk, Poland, Feb. 19, 1910; d. Southampton, NY, July 23, 1984; in U.S. since 1925; educ.: Western Reserve U., Hebrew Union Coll., W. Va. Wesleyan U. (LittD); rabbi: Eoff St. Temple, Wheeling, W. Va., 1936–1944; Temple Israel, Canton, Ohio, 1945–1953; Central Synagogue, Rockville Centre, NY, 1954–1979; faculty mem.: W. Liberty Coll. (W. Va.), 1941–1945; Molloy Coll., 1970–1984; HUC-JIR, 1975–1983; visiting scholar-sr. assoc., St. Antony's Coll., Oxford U., 1969–1970; pres., Assn. of Reform Rabbis of NY; mem., N. Amer. bd., World Union of Progressive Judaism; bd. mem., NY Fed. of Reform Synagogues' Counselling Center; first chmn., Central Conf. of Amer. Rabbis' Com. on Soviet Jewry; mem., rabbinic missions to USSR, 1956, 1966; in 1967 broadcast first Passover message to Soviet Jews, over Voice of Amer.; recipient: hon. doctorates, Molloy

Coll., HUC-JIR; honored by establishment of named chair at HUC-JIR (1975).

MAGNIN, EDGAR F., rabbi; b. San Francisco, Calif., July 1, 1890; d. Beverly Hills, Calif., July 17, 1984; educ.: U. of Cincinnati; Hebrew Union Coll. (ordination, DD); rabbi, Wilshire Blvd. Temple, Los Angeles, since 1915; lect., U. of S. Calif., 1934–1955; founding pres., Coll. of Jewish Studies (now Rhea Hirsch School of Educ., HUC-JIR); delivered inaugural prayer for Pres. Richard Nixon, 1969; a founder of Natl. Council on Alcoholism; active in a wide range of civic, social, cultural, and educational as well as Jewish causes and organizations; author: *How to Live a Richer and Fuller Life,* journal articles, and newspaper columns; recipient: Amer. Red Cross 50-Year Service Award, City of Los Angeles Award, Outstanding Mason of the Year Award, hon. degrees and numerous other honors.

MANSON, HAROLD P., publicist, communal worker; b. NYC, Oct. 23, 1918; d. NYC, Dec. 16, 1984; educ.: Yeshiva U.; dir. of information, Amer. Zionist Emergency Council, 1944–1948, in which post frequently served as U.S. spokesman for the Yishuv in Palestine; Middle East correspondent, Overseas News Agency, 1948; dir. public relations, Jewish Agency, 1949; mem. exec. staff, Zionist Org. of Amer., 1950–1959; dir. public relations, Amer. Friends of Hebrew U., 1959–1966 and dir. of its office of academic affairs since 1966; recipient: Rothberg Prize for Jewish Education, Hebrew U. of Jerusalem.

METZKER, ISAAC, writer; b. Galicia, Poland, July 27, 1901; d. Bridgeport, Conn., Oct. 6, 1984; in U.S. since 1924; teacher, Workmen's Circle schools, 1933–1942; U.S. army, 1942–1943; mem., editorial staff, *Jewish Daily Forward,* since 1945; pres., Yiddish Writers Union; mem., PEN Internatl.; author: short stories and novels published in the *Forward* and in several collections, among them *Toly un Toby* (1936) and *Oifn Zeiden's Felder* (1953); editor of the English-language work *A Bintel Brief: Sixty Years of Letters from the Lower East Side to the Jewish Daily Forward* (1971) and Vol. II of that work, *Letters to the Jewish Daily Forward 1950–1980* (1981); recipient: Bimko Award, La Med Found. Prize, Jacob Gladstein Award for achievement in Yiddish; Workmen's Circle citation.

MINSKOFF, HENRY H., businessman, philanthropist; b. NYC, May 27, 1911; d. NYC, Aug. 13, 1984; educ.: Lehigh U., Columbia U.; pres. since 1950, Sam Minskoff & Sons, investment builders and general contractors; dir., Sterling Natl. Bank and Trust Co.; dir. and v. chmn., Gemco Natl.; mem., adv. council, NYU Real Estate Inst.; dir.: Citizens Tax Council, Lexington School for the Deaf; benefactor, St. Mary's Hosp., Palm Beach, Fla.; trustee, Park East Synagogue, NYC; hon. trustee, Temple Israel Center, White Plains, NY; dir., JCC, Harrison, NY; pres. and chmn., United Home for Aged Hebrews, New Rochelle; a founder, Albert Einstein Coll. of Medicine; a founder, benefactor, and pres., Sam and Esther Minskoff Cultural Center and Park East Day School, NYC.

OLAN, LEVI A., rabbi, scholar; b. (?), Russia, Mar. 22, 1903; d. Dallas, Tex., Oct. 17, 1984; in U.S. since 1906; rabbi: Temple Emanuel, Worcester, Mass., 1929–1948; Temple Emanu-El, Dallas, Tex., since 1949; pres., Central Conf. of Amer. Rabbis, 1967–1969; visiting prof.: U. of Tex., Austin; Emory U.; U. of Tex., Arlington; Inst. of Religion and Human Development, Houston; MLA Program, Southern Methodist U.; Leo Baeck Coll., London; author: *Prophetic Faith and the Secular Age* (1982), *Maturity in an Immature World* (1984), and a number of monographs, including *Rethinking the Liberal Religion* and *Judaism and Modern Theology*; recipient: hon. doctorates from Hebrew Union Coll., Austin Coll., Southern Methodist U.; a festschrift, *A Rational Faith: Essays in Honor of Levi A. Olan*, was published in 1977.

PEERCE, JAN (Jacob Pincus Perelmuth), operatic tenor; b. NYC, June 3, 1904; d. NYC, Dec. 15, 1984; after brief career as a violinist with dance bands, decided to become a singer; began as vocal soloist at Radio City Music Hall and on radio, 1932–1940; operatic debut, Philadelphia, 1938; Metropolitan Opera debut, 1941; soloist, Metropolitan Opera, 1941–1968; first American to sing with the Bolshoi Opera, Moscow, following WWII, in 1956; Broadway debut (as Tevye in *Fiddler on the Roof*), 1971; golden anniversary recital, Carnegie Hall, 1980; made early operatic broadcasts and recordings with Toscanini and the NBC Symphony; extensive international concert tours and recordings of Yiddish and

liturgical music as well as opera brought critical acclaim and worldwide popularity; generous performer in aid of many Jewish causes; a founder, Albert Einstein Coll. of Medicine; Hon Father-in-Israel (Amit Women); author (with Alan Levy): *Bluebird of Happiness,* a book of memoirs (1976); recipient: Tarbut Medal, Mt. Scopus Award, Handel Medallion of the City of NY.

SAMUELS, HOWARD, businessman, politician; b. Rochester, NY, Dec. 3, 1919; d. NYC, Oct. 26, 1984; educ.: MIT; served U.S. army, WWII; early developer, with brother Richard, of plastic clothesline and plastic packaging; founder, Kordite Co., which was sold to Mobile Corp. in 1958; under sec. of Commerce and dir., Small Business Admin., in Johnson and Carter admins.; first pres., NYC Offtrack Betting Corp.; pres. and chief exec. officer, N. Amer. Soccer League, since 1982; mem. adv. bd., Save the Theatres, Inc.; a founder, Fund for New Priorities; sr. v. pres., Amer. Jewish Cong.; chmn., Israel Bond Org.'s Greater NY campaign; bd. mem., Friends of David Yellin Teachers Coll.; mem., Anti-Defamation League's civil rights and discrimination coms.; fellow, Brandeis U.; mem., Cong. Rodeph Sholom, NYC.

SCHIFF, JACK, professor, business consultant; b. NYC, Feb. 26, 1918; d. NYC, Jan. 24, 1984; prof. and provost, Pace U.; author: *Salesmanship Fundamentals* (1964, 1970, 1976); coauthor: *Strategic Management of the Sales Territory* (1980); contributing editor: *Handbook of Business Administration, Handbook of Modern Marketing;* bd. mem., Beth El Synagogue, New Rochelle, NY, for 25 years; recipient: Distinguished Service Award, Phi Delta Kappa, Pace U.; Torch and Scroll Award, CUNY.

SEGAL, BERNARD, rabbi, communal worker; b. Lipno, Poland, Nov. 15, 1907; d. Jerusalem, Israel, June 3, 1984; in U.S. since 1922; educ.: Columbia U., Jewish Theological Seminary of Amer. (ordination, DHL); rabbi: Patchogue, NY Jewish Center, 1933–1934; Queens Jewish Center, NYC, 1935–1940; chaplain, U.S. army, 1940–1946, attaining rank of lieutenant colonel and, subsequently, in the reserves, of colonel; exec. v. pres., Rabbinical Assembly of Amer., 1945–1949; exec. v. pres., JTS, 1950–1953; exec. dir., United Synagogue of Amer., 1953–1970, and its exec. v. pres., 1970–1976; a founder and pres.,

Assn. of Jewish Chaplains; a founder, World Council of Synagogues; mem.: Mayor's Comm. on Middle Income Housing, NYC; Com. on Religion in Amer. Life; dir., Natl. Ramah Comm.; recipient: hon. DD, JTS.

SHAPIRO, LEON, professor, writer; b. Kiev, Russia, July 14, 1905; d. NYC, Dec. 25, 1984; in U.S. since 1941; educ.: Kiev U., U. of Toulouse, France; imprisoned in Russia in 1923 for anti-Bolshevik activities, then exiled to Palestine; a student in France at the start of WWII, worked for Amer. Jewish Joint Distribution Com. in rescue activity until emigration to U.S. in 1941; researcher-editor, JDC in NY, 1941–1950; asst. dir., Conf. on Jewish Material Claims Against Germany, 1954–1966; asst. exec. dir., Memorial Found. for Jewish Culture, 1964–1972; prof. of Russian Jewish hist., Rutgers U., mid-1960s to 1978; for 35 years a regular contributor to the AJYB of articles on Jews in the USSR and Eastern Europe and of world Jewish population estimates; bd. mem., American ORT Fed.; author: *The History of ORT* (1980), an updated version, with biographical essay, of Simon Dubnow's *History of the Jews in Russia and Poland* (1975); the essay "Jews After Stalin" in *Russian Jewry 1917–1967* (1969); *Jewish Children in Liberated Europe*, a JDC Research Dept. publication (1946), and numerous articles and reviews in encyclopedias and periodicals.

SHAW, IRWIN, writer; b. NYC, Feb. 27, 1913; d. Davos, Switzerland, May 16, 1984; educ.: Brooklyn Coll.; internationally acclaimed novelist, short story writer, playwright, screenwriter, essayist, journalist; published works include the novels *The Young Lions* (1948) and *Rich Man, Poor Man* (1970) and (with photographer Robert Capa) *The Face of Israel* (1950), a journalist's report on the new state.

SHEINKOPF, MOSES DAN, rabbi; b. Lomza, Poland, June 15, 1900; d. Springfield, Mass., Apr. 1, 1984; in U.S. since 1922; educ.: Slobodka Yeshiva, Lithuania; dean, Torah Vadaath Yeshiva, Brooklyn, mid-1920s; rabbi: Beth Israel Synagogue, Waterbury, Conn., 1928–1940; United Orthodox Congregations, Springfield, Mass., 1941–1977; v. pres. and chmn. exec. com., Union of Orthodox Rabbis of the U.S. and Canada, for many years; its hon. pres. since 1964; chief rabbi, Springfield Vaad Ha-Kashruth; bd. mem.: Springfield Jewish

Fed., JCC, Mikvah Assn., Family Service, Heritage Acad. Day School, Jewish Nursing Home of Western Mass.; author: *Sefer Gilyonot*, a collection of articles on Jewish law.

SILBERMAN, MORTON, businessman, communal worker; b. Brooklyn, NY, (?), 1924; d. Washington, DC, Feb. 28, 1984; educ.: U. of Pennsylvania; pres., East Coast Supply Corp.; v. pres. and pres., Greater Miami Jewish Fed.; founding pres., Jewish Fed. of Palm Beach; bd. mem., Council of Jewish Feds.; chmn., UJA, Florida region; v. pres. and pres. (since 1982), American Israel Public Affairs Com. (AIPAC); recipient: Human Relations Award, American Jewish Com.

SILVER, CHARLES H., businessman, civic leader; b. (?), Rumania, (?), 1886; d. NYC, Aug. 24, 1984; in U.S. since 1889; joined Amer. Woolens Co. at age 15 as office boy, retired in 1954 as v. pres. and dir.; pres., NYC bd. of educ., 1955–1961; adviser, U.S. delegation at UN Human Rights Comm., Geneva; v. pres., Alfred E. Smith Memorial Found. and chmn. of its annual dinner; trustee, Beth Israel Medical Center beginning 1928, and pres. since 1947; trustee, Yeshiva U.; a founder, Albert Einstein Coll. of Medicine; bd. mem., Fed. of Jewish Philanthropies; overseer, Jewish Theological Seminary of Amer.; pres. and patron, Internatl. Synagogue at Kennedy airport; pres., Temple B'nai Jeshurun; recipient: first Man of the Twentieth Century Award, Natl. Conf. of Christians and Jews; Victory Medal, State of Israel; hon. degrees, Yeshiva U., St. John's U., Fordham U.

SPIEGEL, SHALOM, professor; b. Bukovina, Rumania, Jan. 26, 1899; d. NYC, May 24, 1984; in U.S. since 1928; educ.: U. of Vienna (PhD); instr., Reali School, Haifa, Palestine, 1922–1928; lect., Haifa Technion, 1925–1928; prof. of biblical and post-biblical lit., and librarian, Jewish Inst. of Religion, NYC, 1929–1943; William Prager prof. of medieval Hebrew lit., Jewish Theological Seminary of Amer., 1943–1973; trustee, Israel Matz Found.; chmn., educational advisory com., Hadassah; sec., Alexander Kohut Memorial Found,; author: *Hebrew Reborn* (1930), *Ezekiel or Pseudo-Ezekiel* (1931), *Noah, Daniel and Job* (1945), *Me-Agadot ha-Akedah* (1950), *Amos Versus Amaziah* (1958), *The Last Trial* (1967); fellow: Amer. Acad. of Arts and Sciences (1983); Amer. Acad. of Jewish Research; hon. mem., Israel Acad. of the Hebrew Language; recipient: La Med. Found. Prize, 1950; hon. DHL, JTS, 1973.

TRAGER, FRANK N., professor, internatl. affairs consultant; b. NYC, Oct. 19, 1905; d. Carmel, Calif., Aug. 26, 1984; educ.: NYU (PhD); instr., Johns Hopkins U., 1928–1934; with Resettlement Admin., 1935–1936; sec., treas., NY State Socialist party, mid-1930s; natl. labor sec., Socialist party of U.S., 1936–1937; program dir., Amer. Jewish Com., 1938–1943; U.S. army, 1943–1945; program dir., Anti-Defamation League, 1946–1951; dir., AID mission, Burma, 1951–1953; prof., NYU, 1953–1981; dir., Natl. Security Educ. Program, NYU; dir. of studies, Natl. Strategy Information Center since 1966; consultant on Southeast Asia and natl. defense: Rand Corp., Stanford Research Inst., Hudson Inst., Depts. of State and Defense; fellow: Hudson Inst., Council on Foreign Relations; mem., Foreign Policy Research Inst.; editorial bd. mem., *Orbis;* chmn., Amer.-Asian Educational Exchange; chmn. exec. com., Chinese Cultural Center (Republic of China), NYC; active defender of U.S. govt. policy during Vietnam war and supporter of U.S. ties to Nationalist China; author: numerous articles, monographs, and books, including: *Building a Welfare State in Burma* (1958), *Marxism in Southeast Asia: A Study of Four Countries* (1959), *Burma: From Kingdom to Republic* (1966), and *Why Vietnam?* (1966).

VILE, HY, businessman, communal worker; b. (?), Poland, Sept. 10, 1902; d. Kansas City, Mo., Oct. 22, 1984; in U.S. since 1905; cofounder, Kansas City Printing Co.; chmn., Vile Goller Fine Arts & Lithographing Co.; pres., Printing Industry Trade Assn. of Kansas City; bd. mem., St. Mary's Hospital, St. Mary's Coll.; sec., Harry S. Truman Good Neighbor Award Found., Eddie Jacobson Memorial Found.; chmn., Mayor's Prayer Breakfast; pres. and bd. mem., Men's Club pres. and Sunday school teacher (26 years), Beth Shalom Synagogue; lifetime hon. trustee, Hyman Brand Hebrew Acad.; bd. mem. and past pres., Jewish Geriatric and Convalescent Center, Shalom Plaza; bd. mem., Jewish Fed., JCC; newspaper columnist, *Kansas City Jewish Chronicle;* recipient: Man of the Year Award, Jewish Theological Seminary of Amer.; Heritage Award, Yeshiva

U.; IMA/ABBA Award, Hadassah; awards and citations from B'nai B'rith, Israel Bonds, Catholic Community Services, and other organizations.

WEINBERG, JULIUS, professor, communal worker; b. Cleveland, Ohio, May 9, 1922; d. Cleveland, Ohio, Feb. 8, 1984; educ.: Mirrer Yeshiva (NYC), Case Western Reserve U., U. of Michigan (PhD); exec. staff, Jewish Community Council, Detroit, Mich., 1945–1953; rabbi and educational dir., Beth Israel Cong., Ann Arbor, Mich., 1953–1962; prof. of Amer. hist., Cleveland State U., since 1965; bd. mem.: Jewish Fed., Cleveland Hebrew Schools, Bureau of Jewish Ed., Coll. of Jewish Studies, and other institutions; coeditor: *Social Control, Words That Made American History,* and *The Social Fabric;* author: *An Introduction to the History of Soviet Jewry* as well as essays and articles on American Jews and Jewish life in various publications.

WEISBERG, JOSEPH, lawyer, newspaper editor; b. Boston, Mass., June 10, 1911; d. Boston, Mass., Apr. 9, 1984; educ.: Harvard Coll., Harvard Law School; reporter for *Boston Post* during college years; in private law practice, 1936–1946; editor and publisher, *The Jewish Advocate,* since 1946; mem., Mass. Bd. of Educ., 1965–1973; founder and pres., Amer. Jewish Press Assn.; bd. mem., Jewish Telegraphic Agency; past pres. and hon. trustee, Temple Israel, Boston; trustee: Combined Jewish Philanthropies of Greater Boston, Brandeis U., Beth Israel Hosp., New England Sinai Hosp.; exec. council mem., Amer. Jewish Historical Soc.; mem., New England and Overseas Press Clubs, Assn. of World Jewish Journalists; recipient: awards and citations from many civic, professional, and Jewish groups, including the Union of Amer. Hebrew Congs., Zionist Org. of Amer., and the Mass. legislature.

WOHLBERG, HARRY I., rabbi, professor; b. (?), Czechoslovakia, Sept. 4, 1904; d. NYC, Feb. 4, 1984; in U.S. since 1923; rabbi, Cong. Shomrei Emunah, Brooklyn, for 37 years; prof. of Bible and homiletic lit., Yeshiva U., 1947–1973; pres., alumni assn., Rabbi Isaac Elchanan Theological Seminary; v. pres., Religious Zionists of Amer. and chmn., its natl. education com.; mem. exec. com., Rabbinical Council of Amer.; trustee, Bar-Ilan U.; recipient: hon. DHL, Yeshiva U.; communal leadership award, Religious Zionists of Amer.

YOUNIN, WOLF, writer, educator; b. Irkutsk, Siberia, Feb. 29, 1908; d. NYC, May 31, 1984; in U.S. since 1930; long-time editor, reporter, and folklore columnist *("Shprakhvinkln")* for Yiddish dailies *Der Tog, Tog-Morgn Zhurnal* (until 1971), and *Jewish Daily Forward;* Yiddish teacher: 92nd St. Y, Berlitz School, first Yiddish course at Rutgers U. (1972–1977), Columbia U. summer sessions; coauthor, with Sylvia Younin, of radio course, "Let's Learn Yiddish," broadcast on WEVD and WNYC in early 1970s and later issued as teaching cassettes by Workmen's Circle; coeditor: *Yiddisher Folklore,* journal published by YIVO, 1954–1961; author: a dictionary of Hebrew elements in Yiddish, published in installments in the *Forward;* numerous plays and musicals (including three produced on Broadway by Ben Bonus); a volume of poetry, *Lieder* (1936);

a verse novel, *Der Draytsnter Sheyvet* (1956), as well as short stories, oratorios, and art songs.

ZWEIG, PAUL, poet, critic; b. NYC, July 14, 1935; d. Paris, France, Aug. 30, 1984; chmn., dept. of comparative lit., Queens Coll., CUNY; author: several works of literary criticism, including the highly acclaimed *Walt Whitman: The Making of a Poet* (1984); three volumes of poetry, including, posthumously, *Eternity's Woods* (1985); an autobiography, *Three Journeys* (1976); numerous essays and book reviews in the *New York Times, New Republic, Harper's, Partisan Review, Saturday Review, American Poetry Review,* and other leading publications; recipient: Guggenheim and Natl. Endowment of the Arts fellowships and other prestigious grants and honors.

Calendars

SUMMARY JEWISH CALENDAR, 5746–5750 (Sept. 1985–Aug. 1990)

HOLIDAY	5746 (1985)			5747 (1986)			5748 (1987)			5749 (1988)			5750 (1989)		
Rosh Ha-shanah, 1st day	M	Sept.	16	Sa	Oct.	4	Th	Sept.	24	M	Sept.	12	Sa	Sept.	30
Rosh Ha-shanah, 2nd day	T	Sept.	17	S	Oct.	5	F	Sept.	25	T	Sept.	13	S	Oct.	1
Fast of Gedaliah	W	Sept.	18	M	Oct.	6	S	Sept.	27	W	Sept.	14	M	Oct.	2
Yom Kippur	W	Sept.	25	M	Oct.	13	Sa	Oct.	3	W	Sept.	21	M	Oct.	9
Sukkot, 1st day	M	Sept.	30	Sa	Oct.	18	Th	Oct.	8	M	Sept.	26	Sa	Oct.	14
Sukkot, 2nd day	T	Oct.	1	S	Oct.	19	F	Oct.	9	T	Sept.	27	S	Oct.	15
Hosha'na' Rabbah	S	Oct.	6	F	Oct.	24	W	Oct.	14	S	Oct.	2	F	Oct.	20
Shemini 'Azeret	M	Oct.	7	Sa	Oct.	25	Th	Oct.	15	M	Oct.	3	Sa	Oct.	21
Simhat Torah	T	Oct.	8	S	Oct.	26	F	Oct.	16	T	Oct.	4	S	Oct.	22
New Moon, Heshwan, 1st day	T	Oct.	15	S	Nov.	2	F	Oct.	23	T	Oct.	11	S	Oct.	29
New Moon, Heshwan, 2nd day	W	Oct.	16	M	Nov.	3	Sa	Oct.	24	W	Oct.	12	M	Oct.	30
New Moon, Kislew, 1st day	Th	Nov.	14	T	Dec.	2	S	Nov.	22	Th	Nov.	10	T	Nov.	28
New Moon, Kislew, 2nd day				W	Dec.	3							W	Nov.	29
Hanukkah, 1st day	S	Dec.	8	Sa	Dec.	27	W	Dec.	16	S	Dec.	4	Sa	Dec.	23
New Moon, Tevet, 1st day	F	Dec.	13	Th	Jan. 1987	1	M	Dec.	21	F	Dec.	9	Th	Dec.	28
New Moon, Tevet, 2nd day				F	Jan.	2	T	Dec.	22				F	Dec.	29
Fast of 10th of Tevet	S	Dec.	22	S	Jan.	11	Th	Dec.	31	S	Dec.	18	S	Jan. 1990	7

	1986			1987			1988			1989			1990		
New Moon, Shevat	Sa	Jan.	11	Sa	Jan.	31	W	Jan.	20	Sa	Jan.	7	Sa	Jan.	27
Hamishshah-'asar bi-Shevaṭ	Sa	Jan.	25	Sa	Feb.	14	W	Feb.	3	Sa	Jan.	21	Sa	Feb.	10
New Moon, Adar I, 1st day	S	Feb.	9	S	Mar.	1	Th	Feb.	18	S	Feb.	5	S	Feb.	25
New Moon, Adar I, 2nd day	M	Feb.	10	M	Mar.	2	F	Feb.	19	M	Feb.	6	M	Feb.	26
New Moon, Adar II, 1st day	T	Mar.	11							T	Mar.	7			
New Moon, Adar II, 2nd day	W	Mar.	12							W	Mar.	8			
Fast of Esther	M	Mar.	24	Th	Mar.	12	W	Mar.	2	M	Mar.	20	Th	Mar.	8
Purim	T	Mar.	25	S	Mar.	15	Th	Mar.	3	T	Mar.	21	S	Mar.	11
Shushan Purim	W	Mar.	26	M	Mar.	16	F	Mar.	4	W	Mar.	22	M	Mar.	12
New Moon, Nisan	Th	Apr.	10	T	Mar.	31	Sa	Mar.	19	Th	Apr.	6	T	Mar.	27
Passover, 1st day	Th	Apr.	24	T	Apr.	14	Sa	Apr.	2	Th	Apr.	20	T	Apr.	10
Passover, 2nd day	F	Apr.	25	W	Apr.	15	S	Apr.	3	F	Apr.	21	W	Apr.	11
Passover, 7th day	W	Apr.	30	M	Apr.	20	F	Apr.	8	W	Apr.	26	M	Apr.	16
Passover, 8th day	Th	May	1	T	Apr.	21	Sa	Apr.	9	Th	Apr.	27	T	Apr.	17
Holocaust Memorial Day	T	May	6	S	Apr.	26	Th	Apr.	14	T	May	2	S	Apr.	22
New Moon, Iyar, 1st day	F	May	9	W	Apr.	29	S	Apr.	17	F	May	5	W	Apr.	25
New Moon, Iyar, 2nd day	Sa	May	10	Th	Apr.	30	M	Apr.	18	Sa	May	6	Th	Apr.	26
Israel Independence Day	W	May	14	M	May	4	F	Apr.	22	W	May	10	M	Apr.	30
Lag Ba'omer	T	May	27	S	May	17	Th	May	5	T	May	23	S	May	13
Jerusalem Day	F	June	6	W	May	27	S	May	15	F	June	2	W	May	23
New Moon, Siwan	S	June	8	F	May	29	T	May	17	S	June	4	F	May	25
Shavu'ot, 1st day	F	June	13	W	June	3	S	May	22	F	June	9	W	May	30
Shavu'ot, 2nd day	Sa	June	14	Th	June	4	M	May	23	Sa	June	10	Th	May	31
New Moon, Tammuz, 1st day	M	July	7	Sa	June	27	W	June	15	M	July	3	Sa	June	23
New Moon, Tammuz, 2nd day	T	July	8	S	June	28	Th	June	16	T	July	4	S	June	24
Fast of 17th of Tammuz	Th	July	24	T	July	14	S	July	3	Th	July	20	T	July	10
New Moon, Av	W	Aug.	6	M	July	27	F	July	15	W	Aug.	2	M	July	23
Fast of 9th of Av	Th	Aug.	14	T	Aug.	4	S	July	24	Th	Aug.	10	T	July	31
New Moon, Elul, 1st day	Th	Sept.	4	T	Aug.	25	Sa	Aug.	13	Th	Aug.	31	T	Aug.	21
New Moon, Elul, 2nd day	F	Sept.	5	W	Aug.	26	S	Aug.	14	F	Sept.	1	W	Aug.	22

CONDENSED MONTHLY CALENDAR
(1985–1987)

1984, Dec. 25–Jan. 22, 1985] ṬEVET (29 DAYS) [5745

Civil Date	Day of the Week	Jewish Date	SABBATHS, FESTIVALS, FASTS	PENTATEUCHAL READING	PROPHETICAL READING
Dec. 25	T	Ṭevet 1	New Moon, second day; Ḥanukkah, seventh day	Num. 28:1–15 Num. 7:48–53	
26	W	2	Ḥanukkah, eighth day	Num. 7:54–8:4	
29	Sa	5	Wa-yiggash	Gen. 44:18–47:27	Ezekiel 37:15–28
Jan. 3	Th	10	Fast of 10th of Ṭevet	Exod. 32:11–14 34:1–10	Isaiah 55:6–56:8 (afternoon only)
5	Sa	12	Wa-yeḥi	Gen. 47:28–50:26	I Kings 2:1–12
12	Sa	19	Shemot	Exod. 1:1–6:1	Isaiah 27:6–28:13 29:22–23 *Jeremiah 1:1–2:3*
19	Sa	26	Wa-'era'	Exod. 6:2–9:35	Ezekiel 28:25–29:21

*Italics are for
Sephardi Minhag.*

1985, Jan. 23–Feb. 21] SHEVAṬ (30 DAYS) [5745

Civil Date	Day of the Week	Jewish Date	SABBATHS, FESTIVALS, FASTS	PENTATEUCHAL READING	PROPHETICAL READING
Jan. 23	W	Shevaṭ 1	New Moon	Num. 28:1–15	
26	Sa	4	Bo'	Exod. 10:1–13:16	Jeremiah 46:13–28
Feb. 2	Sa	11	Be-shallaḥ (Shabbat Shirah)	Exod. 13:17–17:16	Judges 4:4–5:31 *Judges 5:1–31*
6	W	15	Hamishshah–'asar bi-Shevaṭ		
9	Sa	18	Yitro	Exod. 18:1–20:23	Isaiah 6:1–7:6 9:5–6 *Isaiah 6:1–13*
16	Sa	25	Mishpaṭim (Shabbat Sheḳalim)	Exod. 21:1–24:18 Exod. 30:11–16	II Kings 12:1–17 *II Kings 11:17–12:17*
21	Th	30	New Moon, first day	Num. 28:1–15	

Italics are for Sephardi Minhag.

1985, Feb. 22–Mar. 22]   ADAR (29 DAYS)   [5745

Civil Date	Day of the Week	Jewish Date	SABBATHS, FESTIVALS, FASTS	PENTATEUCHAL READING	PROPHETICAL READING
Feb. 22	F	Adar 1	New Moon, second day	Num. 28:1–15	
23	Sa	2	Terumah	Exod. 25:1–27:19	I Kings 5:26–6:13
Mar. 2	Sa	9	Tezawweh (Shabbat Zakhor)	Exod. 27:20–30:10	I Samuel 15:2–34 *I Samuel 15:1–34*
6	W	13	Fast of Esther	Exod. 32:11–14 34:1–10	Isaiah 55:6–56:8 (afternoon only)
7	Th	14	Purim	Exod. 17:8–16	Book of Esther (night before and in the morning)
8	F	15	Shushan Purim		
9	Sa	16	Ki tissa'	Exod. 30:11–34:35	I Kings 18:1–39 *I Kings 18:20–39*
16	Sa	23	Wa-yakhel, Pekude (Shabbat Parah)	Exod. 35:1–40:38 Num. 19:1–22	Ezekiel 36:16–38 *Ezekiel 36:16–36*

Italics are for Sephardi Minhag.

1985, Mar. 23–Apr. 21] NISAN (30 DAYS) [5745

Civil Date	Day of the Week	Jewish Date	SABBATHS, FESTIVALS, FASTS	PENTATEUCHAL READING	PROPHETICAL READING
Mar. 23	Sa	Nisan 1	Wa-yiḳra' (Shabbat Ha-ḥodesh) New Moon	Levit. 1:1–5:26 Exod. 12:1–20 Num. 28:9–15	Ezekiel 45:16–46:18 *Ezekiel 45:18–46:15*
30	Sa	8	Ẓaw (Shabbat Ha-gadol)	Levit. 6:1–8:36	Malachi 3:4–24
Apr. 5	F	14	Fast of Firstborn		
6	Sa	15	Passover, first day	Exod. 12:21–51 Num. 28:16–25	Joshua 5:2–6:1, 27
7	S	16	Passover, second day	Levit. 22:26–23:44 Num. 28:16–25	II Kings 23:1–9, 21–25
8	M	17	Ḥol Ha-moʻed, first day	Exod. 13:1–16 Num. 28:19–25	
9	T	18	Ḥol Ha-moʻed, second day	Exod. 22:24–23:19 Num. 28:19–25	
10	W	19	Ḥol Ha-moʻed, third day	Exod. 34:1–26 Num. 28:19–25	
11	Th	20	Ḥol Ha-moʻed, fourth day	Num. 9:1–14 Num. 28:19–25	
12	F	21	Passover, seventh day	Exod. 13:17–15:26 Num. 28:19–25	II Samuel 22:1–51
13	Sa	22	Passover, eighth day	Deut. 15:19–16:17 Num. 28:19–25	Isaiah 10:32–12:6
18	Th	27	Holocaust Memorial Day		
20	Sa	29	Shemini	Levit. 9:1–11:47	I Samuel 20:18–42
21	S	30	New Moon, first day	Num. 28:1–15	

Italics are for Sephardi Minhag.

1985, Apr. 22–May 20]   IYAR (29 DAYS)   [5745

Civil Date	Day of the Week	Jewish Date	SABBATHS, FESTIVALS, FASTS	PENTATEUCHAL READING	PROPHETICAL READING
Apr. 22	M	Iyar 1	New Moon, second day	Num. 28:1–15	
26	F	5	Israel Independence Day		
27	Sa	6	Tazria', Meẓora'	Levit. 12:1–15:33	II Kings 7:3–20
May 4	Sa	13	Aḥare mot, Ḳedoshim	Levit. 16:1–20:27	Amos 9:7–15 *Ezekiel 20:2–20*
9	Th	18	Lag Ba-'omer		
11	Sa	20	Emor	Levit. 21:1–24:23	Ezekiel 44:15–31
18	Sa	27	Be-har, Be-ḥukkotai	Levit. 25:1–27:34	Jeremiah 16:19–17:14
19	S	28	Jerusalem Day		

1985, May 21–June 19]   SIWAN (30 DAYS)   [5745

Civil Date	Day of the Week	Jewish Date	SABBATHS, FESTIVALS, FASTS	PENTATEUCHAL READING	PROPHETICAL READING
May 21	T	Siwan 1	New Moon	Num. 28:1–15	
25	Sa	5	Be-midbar	Num. 1:1–4:20	Hosea 2:1–22
26	S	6	Shavu'ot, first day	Exod. 19:1–20:23 Num. 28:26–31	Ezekiel 1:1–28 3:12
27	M	7	Shavu'ot, second day	Deut. 15:19–16:17 Num. 28:26–31	Habbakuk 3:1–19 *Habbakuk 2:20–3:19*
June 1	Sa	12	Naso'	Num. 4:21–7:89	Judges 13:2–25
8	Sa	19	Be-ha'alotekha	Num. 8:1–12:16	Zechariah 2:14–4:7
15	Sa	26	Shelaḥ lekha	Num. 13:1–15:41	Joshua 2:1–24
19	W	30	New Moon, first day	Num. 28:1–15	

Italics are for Sephardi Minhag.

1985, June 20–July 18]   TAMMUZ (29 DAYS)   [5745

Civil Date	Day of the Week	Jewish Date	SABBATHS, FESTIVALS, FASTS	PENTATEUCHAL READING	PROPHETICAL READING
June 20	Th	Tammuz 1	New Moon, second day	Num. 28:1–15	
22	Sa	3	Korah	Num. 16:1–18:32	I Samuel 11:14–12:22
29	Sa	10	Hukkat	Num. 19:1–22:1	Judges 11:1–33
July 6	Sa	17	Balak	Num. 22:2–25:9	Micah 5:6–6:8
7	S	18	Fast of 17th of Tammuz	Exod. 32:11–14 34:1–10	Isaiah 55:6–56:8 (afternoon only)
13	Sa	24	Pinehas	Num. 25:10–30:1	Jeremiah 1:1–2:3

1985, July 19–Aug. 17]   AV (30 DAYS)   [5745

Civil Date	Day of the Week	Jewish Date	SABBATHS, FESTIVALS, FASTS	PENTATEUCHAL READING	PROPHETICAL READING
July 19	F	Av 1	New Moon	Num. 28:1–15	
20	Sa	2	Mattot, Mas'e	Num. 30:2–36:13	Jeremiah 2:4–28 3:4 *Jeremiah 2:4–28 4:1–2*
27	Sa	9	Devarim (Shabbat Ḥazon)	Deut. 1:1–3:22	Isaiah 1:1–27
28	S	10	Fast of 9th of Av	Morning: Deut. 4:25–40 Afternoon: Exod. 32:11–14 34:1–10	(Lamentations is read the night before.) Jeremiah 8:13–9:23 Isaiah 55:6–56:8
Aug. 3	Sa	16	Wa-etḥannan (Shabbat Naḥamu)	Deut. 3:23–7:11	Isaiah 40:1–26
10	Sa	23	'Eḳev	Deut. 7:12–11:25	Isaiah 49:14–51:3
17	Sa	30	Re'eh New Moon, first day	Deut. 11:26–16:17 Num. 28:9–15	Isaiah 66:1–23 *Isaiah 66:1–23 I Samuel 20:18–42*

1985, Aug. 18–Sept. 15]   ELUL (29 DAYS)   [5745

Civil Date	Day of the Week	Jewish Date	SABBATHS, FESTIVALS, FASTS	PENTATEUCHAL READING	PROPHETICAL READING
Aug. 18	S	Elul 1	New Moon, second day	Num. 28:1–15	
24	Sa	7	Shofeṭim	Deut. 16:18–21:9	Isaiah 51:12–52:12
31	Sa	14	Ki teze'	Deut. 21:10–25:19	Isaiah 54:1–55:5
Sept. 7	Sa	21	Ki tavo'	Deut. 26:1–29:8	Isaiah 60:1–22
14	Sa	28	Niẓẓavim	Deut. 29:9–30:20	Isaiah 61:10–63:9

*Italics are for
Sephardi Minhag.*

1985, Sept. 16–Oct. 15]   TISHRI (30 DAYS)   [5746

Civil Date	Day of the Week	Jewish Date	SABBATHS, FESTIVALS, FASTS	PENTATEUCHAL READING	PROPHETICAL READING
Sept. 16	M	Tishri 1	Rosh Ha-shanah, first day	Gen. 21:1–34 Num. 29:1–6	I Samuel 1:1–2:10
17	T	2	Rosh Ha-shanah, second day	Gen. 22:1–24 Num. 29:1–6	Jeremiah 31:2–20
18	W	3	Fast of Gedaliah	Exod. 32:11–14 34:1–10	Isaiah 55:6–56:8 (afternoon only)
21	Sa	6	Wa-yelekh (Shabbat Shuvah)	Deut. 31:1–30	Hosea 14:2–10 Micah 7:18–20 Joel 2:15–27 *Hosea 14:2–10* *Micah 7:18–20*
25	W	10	Yom Kippur	Morning: Levit. 16:1–34 Num. 29:7–11 Afternoon: Levit. 18:1–30	Isaiah 57:14–58:14 Jonah 1:1–4:11 Micah 7:18–20
28	Sa	13	Ha'azinu	Deut. 32:1–52	II Samuel 22:1–51
30	M	15	Sukkot, first day	Levit. 22:26–23:44 Num. 29:12–16	Zechariah 14:1–21
Oct. 1	T	16	Sukkot, second day	Levit. 22:26–23:44 Num. 29:12–16	I Kings 8:2–21
2–4	W–F	17–19	Ḥol Ha-mo'ed	W Num. 29:17–25 Th Num. 29:20–28 F Num. 29:23–31	
5	Sa	20	Ḥol Ha-mo'ed	Exod. 33:12–34:26 Num. 29:26–31	Ezekiel 38:18–39:16
6	S	21	Hosha'na' Rabbah	Num. 29:26–34	
7	M	22	Shemini 'Azeret	Deut. 14:22–16:17 Num. 29:35–30:1	I Kings 8:54–66
8	T	23	Simḥat Torah	Deut. 33:1–34:12 Gen. 1:1–2:3 Num. 29:35–30:1	Joshua 1:1–18 *Joshua 1:1–9*
12	Sa	27	Be-re'shit	Gen. 1:1–6:8	Isaiah 42:5–43:10 *Isaiah 42:5–21*
15	T	30	New Moon, first day	Num. 28:1–15	

Italics are for
Sephardi Minhag.

1985, Oct. 16–Nov. 13]   ḤESHWAN (30 DAYS)   [5746

Civil Date	Day of the Week	Jewish Date	SABBATHS, FESTIVALS, FASTS	PENTATEUCHAL READING	PROPHETICAL READING
Oct. 16	W	Ḥeshwan 1	New Moon, second day	Num. 28:1–15	
19	Sa	4	Noaḥ	Gen. 6:9–11:32	Isaiah 54:1–55:5 *Isaiah 54:1–10*
26	Sa	11	Lekh lekha	Gen. 12:1–17:27	Isaiah 40:27–41:16
Nov. 2	Sa	18	Wa-yera'	Gen. 18:1–22:24	II Kings 4:1–37 *II Kings 4:1–23*
9	Sa	25	Ḥayye Sarah	Gen. 23:1–25:18	I Kings 1:1–31

1985, Nov. 14–Dec. 12]   KISLEW (29 DAYS)   [5746

Civil Date	Day of the Week	Jewish Date	SABBATHS, FESTIVALS, FASTS	PENTATEUCHAL READING	PROPHETICAL READING
Nov. 14	Th	Kislew 1	New Moon	Num. 28:1–15	
16	Sa	3	Toledot	Gen. 25:19–28:9	Malachi 1:1–2:7
23	Sa	10	Wa-yeẓe'	Gen. 28:10–32:3	Hosea 12:13–14:10 *Hosea 11:7–12:12*
30	Sa	17	Wa-yishlaḥ	Gen. 32:4–36:43	Hosea 11:7–12:12 *Obadiah 1:1–21*
Dec. 7	Sa	24	Wa-yeshev	Gen. 37:1–40:23	Amos 2:6–3:8
8–12	S-Th	25–29	Hanukkah, first to fifth days	S Num. 7:1–17 M Num. 7:18–29 T Num. 7:24–35 W Num. 7:30–41 Th Num. 7:36–47	

Italics are for Sephardi Minhag.

1985, Dec. 13–Jan. 10, 1986] ṬEVET (29 DAYS) [5746

Civil Date	Day of the Week	Jewish Date	SABBATHS, FESTIVALS, FASTS	PENTATEUCHAL READING	PROPHETICAL READING
Dec. 13	F	Tevet 1	New Moon Hanukkah, sixth day	Num. 28:1–15 Num. 7:42–47	
14	Sa	2	Mi-keẓ Hanukkah, seventh day	Gen. 41:1–44:17 Num. 7:48–53	Zechariah 2:14–4:7
15	S	3	Hanukkah, eighth day	Num. 7:54–8:4	
21	Sa	9	Wa-yiggash	Gen. 44:18–47:27	Ezekiel 37:15–28
22	S	10	Fast of 10th of Ṭevet	Exod. 32:11–14 34:1–10	Isaiah 55:6–56:8 (afternoon only)
28	Sa	16	Wa-yeḥi	Gen. 47:28–50:26	I Kings 2:1–12
Jan. 4	Sa	23	Shemot	Exod. 1:1–6:1	Isaiah 27:6–28:13 29:22–23 *Jeremiah 1:1–2:3*

1986, Jan. 11–Feb. 9] SHEVAṬ (30 DAYS) [5746

Civil Date	Day of the Week	Jewish Date	SABBATHS, FESTIVALS, FASTS	PENTATEUCHAL READING	PROPHETICAL READING
Jan. 11	Sa	Shevat 1	Wa-’era’ New Moon	Exod. 6:2–9:35 Num. 28:9–15	Isaiah 66:1–24
18	Sa	8	Bo’	Exod. 10:1–13:16	Jeremiah 46:13–28
25	Sa	15	Be-shallaḥ (Shabbat Shirah) Hamishshah-‘asar bi-Shevaṭ	Exod. 13:17–17:16	Judges 4:4–5:31 *Judges 5:1–31*
Feb. 1	Sa	22	Yitro	Exod. 18:1–20:23	Isaiah 6:1–7:6 9:5–6 *Isaiah 6:1–13*
8	Sa	29	Mishpaṭim	Exod. 21:1–24:18	I Samuel 20:18–42
9	S	30	New Moon, first day	Num. 28:1–15	

Italics are for Sephardi Minhag.

1986, Feb. 10–Mar. 11]   ADAR I (30 DAYS)   [5746

Civil Date	Day of the Week	Jewish Date	SABBATHS, FESTIVALS, FASTS	PENTATEUCHAL READING	PROPHETICAL READING
Feb. 10	M	Adar 1	New Moon, second day	Num. 28:1–15	
15	Sa	6	Terumah	Exod. 25:1–27:19	I Kings 5:26–6:13
22	Sa	13	Teẓawweh	Exod. 27:20–30:10	Ezekiel 43:10–27
Mar. 1	Sa	20	Ki tissa'	Exod. 30:11–34:35	I Kings 18:1–39 *I Kings 18:20–39*
8	Sa	27	Wa-yakhel (Shabbat Sheḳalim)	Exod. 35:1–38:20 Exod. 30:11–16	II Kings 12:1–17 *II Kings 11:17–12:17*
11	T	30	New Moon, first day	Num. 28:1–15	

1986, Mar. 12–Apr. 9]   ADAR II (29 DAYS)   [5746

Civil Date	Day of the Week	Jewish Date	SABBATHS, FESTIVALS, FASTS	PENTATEUCHAL READING	PROPHETICAL READING
Mar. 12	W	Adar II 1	New Moon, second day	Num. 28:1–15	
15	Sa	4	Peḳude	Exod. 38:21–40:38	I Kings 7:40–50
22	Sa	11	Wa-yikra (Shabbat Zakhor)	Levit. 1:1–5:26 Deut. 25:17–19	I Samuel 15:2–34 *I Samuel 15:1–34*
24	M	13	Fast of Esther	Exod. 32:11–14 34:1–10	Isaiah 55:6–56:8 (Afternoon only)
25	T	14	Purim	Exod. 17:8–16	Book of Esther (night before and in the morning)
26	W	15	Shushan Purim		
29	Sa	18	Ẓaw (Shabbat Parah)	Levit. 6:1–8:36 Num. 19:1–22	Ezekiel 36:16–38 *Ezekiel 36:16–36*
Apr. 5	Sa	25	Shemini (Shabbat Ha-ḥodesh)	Levit. 9:1–11:47 Exod. 12:1–20	Ezekiel 45:16–46:18 *Ezekiel 45:18–46:15*

Italics are for Sephardi Minhag.

1986, Apr. 10–May 9] NISAN (30 DAYS) [5746

Civil Date	Day of the Week	Jewish Date	SABBATHS, FESTIVALS, FASTS	PENTATEUCHAL READING	PROPHETICAL READING
Apr. 10	Th	Nisan 1	New Moon	Num. 28:1–15	
12	Sa	3	Tazria'	Levit. 12:1–13:59	II Kings 4:42–5:19
19	Sa	10	Meẓora' (Shabbat Ha-gadol)	Levit. 14:1–15:33	Malachi 3:4–24
23	W	14	Fast of Firstborn		
24	Th	15	Passover, first day	Exod. 12:21–51 Num. 28:16–25	Joshua 5:2–6:1, 27
25	F	16	Passover, second day	Levit. 22:26–23:44 Num. 28:16–25	II Kings 23:1–19, 21–25
26	Sa	17	Ḥol Ha-mo'ed, first day	Exod. 33:12–34:26 Num. 28:19–25	Ezekiel 37:1–14
27	S	18	Ḥol Ha-mo'ed, second day	Exod. 13:1–16 Num. 28:19–25	
28	M	19	Ḥol Ha-mo'ed, third day	Exod. 22:24–23:19 Num. 28:19–25	
29	T	20	Ḥol Ha-mo'ed, fourth day	Num. 9:1–14 Num. 28:19–25	
30	W	21	Passover, seventh day	Exod. 13:17–15:26 Num. 28:19–25	II Samuel 22:1–51
May 1	Th	22	Passover, eighth day	Deut. 15:19–16:17 Num. 28:19–25	Isaiah 10:32–12:6
3	Sa	24	Aḥare mot	Levit. 16:1–18:30	Ezekiel 22:1–16
6	T	27	Holocaust Memorial Day		
9	F	30	New Moon, first day	Num. 28:1–15	

Italics are for Sephardi Minhag.

1986, May 10–June 7]   IYAR (29 DAYS)   [5746

Civil Date	Day of the Week	Jewish Date	SABBATHS, FESTIVALS, FASTS	PENTATEUCHAL READING	PROPHETICAL READING
May 10	Sa	Iyar 1	Kedoshim New Moon, second day	Levit. 19:1–20:27 Num. 28:9–15	Isaiah 66:1–24
14	W	5	Israel Independence Day		
17	Sa	8	Emor	Levit. 21:1–24:23	Ezekiel 44:15–31
24	Sa	15	Be-har	Levit. 25:1–26:2	Jeremiah 32:6–27
27	T	18	Lag Ba'omer		
31	Sa	22	Be-ḥukkotai	Levit. 26:3–27:34	Jeremiah 16:19–17:14
June 6	F	28	Jerusalem Day		
7	Sa	29	Be-midbar	Num. 1:1-4:20	I Samuel 20:18–42

1986, June 8–July 7]   SIWAN (30 DAYS)   [5746

Civil Date	Day of the Week	Jewish Date	SABBATHS, FESTIVALS, FASTS	PENTATEUCHAL READING	PROPHETICAL READING
June 8	S	Siwan 1	New Moon	Num. 28:1–15	
13	F	6	Shavu'ot, first day	Exod. 19:1–20:23 Num. 28:26–31	Ezekiel 1:1–28 3:12
14	Sa	7	Shavu'ot, second day	Deut. 15:19–16:17 Num. 28:26–31	Habbakuk 3:1–19 *Habbakuk 2:20–3:19*
21	Sa	14	Naso'	Num. 4:21–7:89	Judges 13:2–25
28	Sa	21	Be-ha'alotekha	Num. 8:1–12:16	Zechariah 2:14–4:7
July 5	Sa	28	Shelaḥ lekha	Num. 13:1–15:41	Joshua 2:1–24
7	M	30	New Moon, first day	Num. 28:1–15	

Italics are for Sephardi Minhag.

1986, July 8–Aug. 5]   TAMMUZ (29 DAYS)   [5746

Civil Date	Day of the Week	Jewish Date	SABBATHS, FESTIVALS, FASTS	PENTATEUCHAL READING	PROPHETICAL READING
July 8	T	Tammuz 1	New Moon, second day	Num. 28:1–15	
12	Sa	5	Koraḥ	Num. 16:1–18:32	I Samuel 11:14–12:22
19	Sa	12	Huḳḳat, Balaḳ	Num. 19:1–25:9	Micah 5:6–6:8
24	Th	17	Fast of 17th of Tammuz	Exod. 32:11–14 34:1–10	Isaiah 55:6–56:8 (afternoon only)
26	Sa	19	Pineḥas	Num. 25:10–30:1	Jeremiah 1:1–2:3
Aug. 2	Sa	26	Maṭṭot, Mas'e	Num. 30:2–36:13	Jeremiah 2:4–28 3:4 *Jeremiah 2:4–28 4:1–2*

Italics are for
Sephardi Minhag.

1986, Aug. 6–Sept. 4]   AV (30 DAYS)   [5746

Civil Date	Day of the Week	Jewish Date	SABBATHS, FESTIVALS, FASTS	PENTATEUCHAL READING	PROPHETICAL READING
Aug. 6	W	Av 1	New Moon	Num. 28:1–15	
9	Sa	4	Devarim (Shabbat Ḥazon)	Deut. 1:1–3:22	Isaiah 1:1–27
14	Th	9	Fast of 9th of Av	Morning: Deut. 4:25–40 Afternoon: Exod. 32:11–14 34:1–10	(Lamentations is read the night before.) Jeremiah 8:13–9:23 Isaiah 55:6–56:8
16	Sa	11	Wa-ethannan (Shabbat Naḥamu)	Deut. 3:23–7:11	Isaiah 40:1–26
23	Sa	18	'Ekev	Deut. 7:12–11:25	Isaiah 49:14–51:3
30	Sa	25	Re'eh	Deut. 11:26–16:17	Isaiah 54:11–55:5
Sept. 4	Th	30	New Moon, first day	Num. 28:1–15	

1986, Sept. 5–Oct. 3]   ELUL (29 DAYS)   [5746

Civil Date	Day of the Week	Jewish Date	SABBATHS, FESTIVALS, FASTS	PENTATEUCHAL READING	PROPHETICAL READING
Sept. 5	F	Elul 1	New Moon, second day	Num. 28:1–15	
6	Sa	2	Shofeṭim	Deut. 16:18–21:9	Isaiah 51:12–52:12
13	Sa	9	Ki teẓe'	Deut. 21:10–25:19	Isaiah 54:1–10
20	Sa	16	Ki tavo'	Deut. 26:1–29:8	Isaiah 60:1–22
27	Sa	23	Niẓẓavim, Wa-yelekh	Deut. 29:9–31:30	Isaiah 61:10–63:9

1986, Oct. 4–Nov. 2] **TISHRI (30 DAYS)** [5747

Civil Date	Day of the Week	Jewish Date	SABBATHS, FESTIVALS, FASTS	PENTATEUCHAL READING	PROPHETICAL READING
Oct. 4	Sa	Tishri 1	Rosh Ha-shanah, first day	Gen. 21:1–34 Num. 29:1–6	I Samuel 1:1–2:10
5	S	2	Rosh Ha-shanah, second day	Gen. 22:1–24 Num. 29:1–6	Jeremiah 31:2–20
6	M	3	Fast of Gedaliah	Exod. 32:11–14 34:1–10	Isaiah 55:6–56:8 (afternoon only)
11	Sa	8	Ha'azinu (Shabbat Shuvah)	Deut. 32:1–52	Hosea 14:2–10 Micah 7:18–20 Joel 2:15–27 *Hosea 14:2–10* *Micah 7:18–20*
13	M	10	Yom Kippur	Morning: Levit. 16:1–34 Num. 29:7–11 Afternoon: Levit. 18:1–30	Isaiah 57:14–58:14 Jonah 1:1–4:11 Micah 7:18–20
18	Sa	15	Sukkot, first day	Levit. 22:26–23:44 Num. 29:12–16	Zechariah 14:1–21
19	S	16	Sukkot, second day	Levit. 22:26–23:44 Num. 29:12–16	I Kings 8:2–21
20–23	M-Th	17–20	Ḥol Ha-mo'ed	M Num. 29:17–25 T Num. 29:20–28 W Num. 29:23–31 Th Num. 29:26–34	
24	F	21	Hosha'na' Rabbah	Num. 29:26–34	
25	Sa	22	Shemini 'Azeret	Deut. 14:22–16:17 Num. 29:35–30:1	I Kings 8:54–66
26	S	23	Simḥat Torah	Deut. 33:1–34:12 Gen. 1:1–2:3 Num. 29:35–30:1	Joshua 1:1–18 *Joshua 1:1–9*
Nov. 1	Sa	29	Be-re'shit	Gen. 1:1–6:8	I Samuel 20:18–42
2	S	30	New Moon, first day	Num. 28:1–15	

Italics are for
Sephardi Minhag.

1986, Nov. 3–Dec. 2]   ḤESHWAN (30 DAYS)   [5747

Civil Date	Day of the Week	Jewish Date	SABBATHS, FESTIVALS, FASTS	PENTATEUCHAL READING	PROPHETICAL READING
Nov. 3	M	Heshwan 1	New Moon, second day	Num. 28:1–15	
8	Sa	6	Noaḥ	Gen. 6:9–11:32	Isaiah 54:1–55:5 *Isaiah 54:1–10*
15	Sa	13	Lekh lekha	Gen. 12:1–17:27	Isaiah 40:27–41:16
22	Sa	20	Wa-yera'	Gen. 18:1–22:24	II Kings 4:1–37 *II Kings 4:1–23*
29	Sa	27	Ḥayye Sarah	Gen. 23:1–25:18	I Kings 1:1–31
Dec. 2	T	30	New Moon, first day	Num. 28:1–15	

1986, Dec. 3–Jan. 1, 1987]   KISLEW (30 DAYS)   [5747

Civil Date	Day of the Week	Jewish Date	SABBATHS, FESTIVALS, FASTS	PENTATEUCHAL READING	PROPHETICAL READING
Dec. 3	W	Kislew 1	New Moon, second day	Num. 28:1–15	
6	Sa	4	Toledot	Gen. 25:19–28:9	Malachi 1:1–2:7
13	Sa	11	Wa-yeẓe'	Gen. 28:10–32:3	Hosea 12:13–14:10 *Hosea 11:7–12:12*
20	Sa	18	Wa-yishlaḥ	Gen. 32:4–36:43	Hosea 11:7–12:12 *Obadiah 1:1–21*
27	Sa	25	Wa-yeshev Ḥanukkah, first day	Gen. 37:1–40:23 Num. 7:1–17	Zechariah 2:14–4:7
Dec. 28–31	S-W	26–29	Ḥanukkah, second to fifth days	S Num. 7:18–29 M Num. 7:24–35 T Num. 7:30–41 W Num. 7:36–47	
Jan. 1	Th	30	New Moon, first day; Ḥanukkah, sixth day	Num. 28:1–15 Num. 7:42–47	

Italics are for Sephardi Minhag.

1987, Jan. 2–Jan. 30] TEVET (29 DAYS) [5747

Civil Date	Day of the Week	Jewish Date	SABBATHS, FESTIVALS, FASTS	PENTATEUCHAL READING	PROPHETICAL READING
Jan. 2	F	Tevet 1	New Moon, second day; Hanukkah, seventh day	Num. 28:1–15 Num. 7:48–53	
3	Sa	2	Mi-kez Hanukkah, eighth day	Gen. 41:1–44:17 Num. 7:54–8:4	Zechariah 2:14–4:7
10	Sa	9	Wa-yiggash	Gen. 44:18–47:27	Ezekiel 37:15–28
11	S	10	Fast of 10th of Tevet	Exod. 32:11–14 34:1–10	Isaiah 55:6–56:8 (afternoon only)
17	Sa	16	Wa-yehi	Gen. 47:28–50:26	I Kings 2:1–12
24	Sa	23	Shemot	Exod. 1:1–6:1	Isaiah 27:6–28:13 29:22–23 *Jeremiah 1:1–2:3*

*Italics are for
Sephardi Minhag.*

1987, Jan. 31–Mar. 1]　　　SHEVAṬ (30 DAYS)　　　[5747

Civil Date	Day of the Week	Jewish Date	SABBATHS, FESTIVALS, FASTS	PENTATEUCHAL READING	PROPHETICAL READING
Jan. 31	Sa	Shevaṭ 1	Wa-'era' New Moon	Exod. 6:2–9:35 Num. 28:1–15	Isaiah 66:1–24
Feb. 7	Sa	8	Bo'	Exod. 10:1–13:16	Jeremiah 46:13–28
14	Sa	15	Be-shallaḥ (Shabbat Shirah) Ḥamishshah-'asar bi-Shevaṭ	Exod. 13:17–17:16	Judges 4:4–5:31 *Judges 5:1–31*
21	Sa	22	Yitro	Exod. 18:1–20:23	Isaiah 6:1–7:6 9:5–6 *Isaiah 6:1–13*
28	Sa	29	Mishpaṭim (Shabbat Sheḳalim)	Exod. 21:1–24:18 Exod. 30:11–16	II Kings 12:1–17 *II Kings 11:17–12:17* *I Samuel 20:18–42*
Mar. 1	S	30	New Moon, first day	Num. 28:1–15	

Italics are for Sephardi Minhag.

1987, Mar. 2–Mar. 30]   ADAR (29 DAYS)   [5747

Civil Date	Day of the Week	Jewish Date	SABBATHS, FESTIVALS, FASTS	PENTATEUCHAL READING	PROPHETICAL READING
Mar. 2	M	Adar 1	New Moon, second day	Num. 28:1–15	
7	Sa	6	Terumah	Exod. 25:1–27:19	I Kings 5:26–6:13
12	Th	11	Fast of Esther	Exod. 32:11–14 34:1–10	Isaiah 55:6–56:8 (afternoon only)
14	Sa	13	Teẓawweh (Shabbat Zakhor)	Exod. 27:20–30:10 Deut. 25:17–19	I Samuel 15:2–34 *I Samuel 15:1–34*
15	S	14	Purim	Exod. 17:8–16	Book of Esther (night before and in the morning)
16	M	15	Shushan Purim		
21	Sa	20	Ki tissa' (Shabbat Parah)	Exod. 30:11–34:35 Num. 19:1–22	Ezekiel 36:16–38 *Ezekiel 36:16–36*
28	Sa	27	Wa-yakhel, Peḳude (Shabbat Ha-hodesh)	Exod. 35:1–40:38 Exod. 12:1–20	Ezekiel 45:16–46:18 *Ezekiel 45:18–46:15*

Italics are for Sephardi Minhag.

Civil Date	Day of the Week	Jewish Date	SABBATHS, FESTIVALS, FASTS	PENTATEUCHAL READING	PROPHETICAL READING
Mar. 31	T	Nisan 1	New Moon	Num. 28:1–15	
Apr. 4	Sa	5	Wa-yikra'	Levit. 1:1–5:26	Isaiah 43:21–44:24
11	Sa	12	Zaw (Shabbat Ha-gadol)	Levit. 6:1–8:36	Malachi 3:4–24
13	M	14	Fast of Firstborn		
14	T	15	Passover, first day	Exod. 12:21–51 Num. 28:16–25	Joshua 5:2–6:1, 27
15	W	16	Passover, second day	Levit. 22:26–23:44 Num. 28:16–25	II Kings 23:1–9, 21–25
16	Th	17	Hol Ha-mo'ed, first day	Exod. 13:1–16 Num. 28:19–25	
17	F	18	Hol Ha-mo'ed, second day	Exod. 22:24–23:19 Num. 28:19–25	
18	Sa	19	Hol Ha-mo'ed, third day	Exod. 33:12–34:26 Num. 28:19–25	Ezekiel 37:1–14
19	S	20	Hol Ha-mo'ed, fourth day	Num. 9:1–14; Num. 28:19–25	
20	M	21	Passover, seventh day	Exod. 13:17–15:26 Num. 28:19–25	II Samuel 22:1–51
21	T	22	Passover, eighth day	Deut. 15:19–16:17 Num. 28:19–25	Isaiah 10:32–12:6
25	Sa	26	Shemini	Levit. 9:1–11:47	II Samuel 6:1–7:17
26	S	27	Holocaust Memorial Day		
29	W	30	New Moon, first day	Num. 28:1–15	

Italics are for Sephardi Minhag.

1987, Apr. 30–May 28]   IYAR (29 DAYS)   [5747

Civil Date	Day of the Week	Jewish Date	SABBATHS, FESTIVALS, FASTS	PENTATEUCHAL READING	PROPHETICAL READING
Apr. 30	Th	Iyar 1	New Moon, second day	Num. 28:1–15	
May 2	Sa	3	Tazria', Mezora'	Levit. 12:1–15:33	II Kings 7:3–20
4	M	5	Israel Independence Day		
9	Sa	10	Aḥare mot, Kedoshim	Levit. 16:1–20:27	Amos 9:7–15 *Ezekiel 20:2–20*
16	Sa	17	Emor	Levit. 21:1–24:23	Ezekiel 44:15–31
17	S	18	Lag Ba-'omer		
23	Sa	24	Be-har, Be-ḥukkotai	Levit. 25:1–27:34	Jeremiah 16:19–17:14
27	W	28	Jerusalem Day		

1987, May 29–June 27]   SIWAN (30 DAYS)   [5747

Civil Date	Day of the Week	Jewish Date	SABBATHS, FESTIVALS, FASTS	PENTATEUCHAL READING	PROPHETICAL READING
May 29	F	Siwan 1	New Moon	Num. 28:1–15	
30	Sa	2	Be-midbar	Num. 1:1–4:20	Hosea 2:1–22
June 3	W	6	Shavu'ot, first day	Exod. 19:1–20:23 Num. 28:26–31	Ezekiel 1:1–28 3:12
4	Th	7	Shavu'ot, second day	Deut. 15:19–16:17 Num. 28:26–31	Habbakuk 3:1–19 *Habbakuk 2:20–3:19*
6	Sa	9	Naso'	Num. 4:21–7:89	Judges 13:2–25
13	Sa	16	Be-ha'alotekha	Num. 8:1–12:16	Zechariah 2:14–4:7
20	Sa	23	Shelaḥ lekha	Num. 13:1–15:41	Joshua 2:1–24
27	Sa	30	Koraḥ New Moon, first day	Num. 16:1–18:32 Num. 28:9–15	Isaiah 66:1–24 *Isaiah 66:1–24* *I Samuel 20:18–42*

Italics are for
Sephardi Minhag.

1987, June 28–July 26]   TAMMUZ (29 DAYS)   [5747

Civil Date	Day of the Week	Jewish Date	SABBATHS, FESTIVALS, FASTS	PENTATEUCHAL READING	PROPHETICAL READING
June 28	S	Tammuz 1	New Moon, second day	Num. 28:1–15	
July 4	Sa	7	Ḥukkat	Num. 19:1–22:1	Judges 11:1–33
11	Sa	14	Balak	Num. 22:2–25:9	Micah 5:6–6:8
14	T	17	Fast of 17th of Tammuz	Exod. 32:11–14 34:1–10	Isaiah 55:6–56:8 (afternoon only)
18	Sa	21	Pineḥas	Num. 25:10–30:1	Jeremiah 1:1–2:3
25	Sa	28	Maṭṭot, Mas'e	Num. 30:2–36:13	Jeremiah 2:4–28 3:4 *Jeremiah 2:4–28 4:1–2*

Italics are for
Sephardi Minhag.

1987, July 27–Aug. 25] AV (30 DAYS) [5747

Civil Date	Day of the Week	Jewish Date	SABBATHS, FESTIVALS, FASTS	PENTATEUCHAL READING	PROPHETICAL READING
July 27	M	Av 1	New Moon	Num. 28:1–15	
Aug. 1	Sa	6	Devarim (Shabbat Ḥazon)	Deut. 1:1–3:22	Isaiah 1:1–27
4	T	9	Fast of 9th of Av	Morning: Deut. 4:25–40 Afternoon: Exod. 32:11–14 34:1–10	(Lamentations is read the night before.) Jeremiah 8:13–9:23 Isaiah 55:6–56:8
8	Sa	13	Wa-ethannan (Shabbat Naḥamu)	Deut. 3:23–7:11	Isaiah 40:1–26
15	Sa	20	'Eḳev	Deut. 7:12–11:25	Isaiah 49:14–51:3
22	Sa	27	Re'eh	Deut. 11:26–16:17	Isaiah 54:11–55:5
25	T	30	New Moon, first day	Num. 28:1–15	

1987, Aug. 26–Sept. 23] ELUL (29 DAYS) [5747

Civil Date	Day of the Week	Jewish Date	SABBATHS, FESTIVALS, FASTS	PENTATEUCHAL READING	PROPHETICAL READING
Aug. 26	W	Elul 1	New Moon, second day	Num. 28:1–15	
29	Sa	4	Shofeṭim	Deut. 16:18–21:9	Isaiah 51:12–52:12
Sept. 5	Sa	11	Ki teze'	Deut. 21:10–25:19	Isaiah 54:1–10
12	Sa	18	Ki tavo'	Deut. 26:1–29:8	Isaiah 60:1–22
19	Sa	25	Niẓẓavim, Wa-yelekh	Deut. 29:9–31:30	Isaiah 61:10–63:9

Italics are for Sephardi Minhag.

Civil Date	Day of the Week	Jewish Date	SABBATHS, FESTIVALS, FASTS	PENTATEUCHAL READING	PROPHETICAL READING
Sept. 24	Th	Tishri 1	Rosh Ha-shanah, first day	Gen. 21:1–34 Num. 29:1–6	I Samuel 1:1–2:10
25	F	2	Rosh Ha-shanah, second day	Gen. 22:1–24 Num. 29:1–6	Jeremiah 31:2–20
26	Sa	3	Ha'azinu (Shabbat Shuvah)	Deut. 32:1–52	Hosea 14:2–10 Micah 7:18–20 Joel 2:15–27 *Hosea 14:2–10* *Micah 7:18–20*
27	S	4	Fast of Gedaliah	Exod. 32:11–14; 34:1–10	Isaiah 55:6–56:8 (afternoon only)
Oct. 3	Sa	10	Yom Kippur	Morning: Levit. 16:1–34 Num. 29:7–11 Afternoon: Levit. 18:1–30	Isaiah 57:14–58:14 Jonah 1:1–4:11 Micah 7:18–20
8	Th	15	Sukkot, first day	Levit. 22:26–23:44 Num. 29:12–16	Zechariah 14:1–21
9	F	16	Sukkot, second day	Levit. 22:26–23:44 Num. 29:12–16	I Kings 8:2–21
10	Sa	17	Ḥol Ha-mo'ed	Exod. 33:12–34:26 Num. 29:17–22	Ezekiel 38:18–39:16
11-13	S-T	18-20	Ḥol Ha-mo'ed	S Num. 29:20–28 M Num. 29:23–31 T Num. 29:26–34	
14	W	21	Hosha'na' Rabbah	Num. 29:26–34	
15	Th	22	Shemini 'Azeret	Deut. 14:22–16:17 Num. 29:35–30:1	I Kings 8:54–66
16	F	23	Simḥat Torah	Deut. 33:1–34:12 Gen. 1:1–2:3 Num. 29:35–30:1	Joshua 1:1–18 *Joshua 1:1–9*
17	Sa	24	Be-re'shit	Gen. 1:1–6:8	Isaiah 42:5–43:10 *Isaiah 42:5–21*
23	F	30	New Moon, first day	Num. 28:1–15	

Italics are for Sephardi Minhag.

1987, Oct. 24–Nov. 21]   ḤESHWAN (29 DAYS)   [5748

Civil Date	Day of the Week	Jewish Date	SABBATHS, FESTIVALS, FASTS	PENTATEUCHAL READING	PROPHETICAL READING
Oct. 24	Sa	Heshwan 1	Noaḥ New Moon, second day	Gen. 6:9–11:32 Num. 28:9–15	Isaiah 66:1–24
31	Sa	8	Lekh lekha	Gen. 12:1–17:27	Isaiah 40:27–41:16
Nov. 7	Sa	15	Wa-yera'	Gen. 18:1–22:24	II Kings 4:1–37 *II Kings 4:1–23*
14	Sa	22	Ḥayye Sarah	Gen. 23:1–25:18	I Kings 1:1–31
21	Sa	29	Toledot	Gen. 25:19–28:9	I Samuel 20:18–42

1987, Nov. 22–Dec. 21]   KISLEW (30 DAYS)   [5748

Civil Date	Day of the Week	Jewish Date	SABBATHS, FESTIVALS, FASTS	PENTATEUCHAL READING	PROPHETICAL READING
Nov. 22	S	Kislew 1	New Moon	Num. 28:1–15	
28	Sa	7	Wa-yeze'	Gen. 28:10–32:3	Hosea 12:13–14:10 *Hosea 11:7–12:12*
Dec. 5	Sa	14	Wa-yishlaḥ	Gen. 32:4–36:43	Hosea 11:7–12:12 *Obadiah 1:1–21*
12	Sa	21	Wa-yeshev	Gen. 37:1–40:23	Amos 2:6–3:8
16-18	W-F	25-27	Hanukkah, first to third days	W Num. 7:1–17 Th Num. 7:18–29 F Num. 7:24–35	
19	Sa	28	Mi-kez Hanukkah, fourth day	Gen. 41:1–44:17 Num. 7:30–35	Zechariah 2:14–4:7
20	S	29	Hanukkah, fifth day	Num. 7:36–47	
21	M	30	New Moon, first day; Hanukkah, sixth day	Num. 28:1–15 Num. 7:42–47	

Italics are for Sephardi Minhag.

1987, Dec. 22–Jan. 19, 1988] ṬEVET (29 DAYS) [5748

Civil Date	Day of the Week	Jewish Date	SABBATHS, FESTIVALS, FASTS	PENTATEUCHAL READING	PROPHETICAL READING
Dec. 22	T	Ṭevet 1	New Moon, second day; Ḥanukkah, seventh day	Num. 28:1–15; Num. 7:48–53	
23	W	2	Ḥanukkah, eighth day	Num. 7:54–8:4	
26	Sa	5	Wa-yiggash	Gen. 44:18–47:27	Ezekiel 37:15–28
31	Th	10	Fast of 10th of Ṭevet	Exod. 32:11–14; 34:1–10	Isaiah 55:6–56:8 (afternoon only)
Jan. 2	Sa	12	Wa-yeḥi	Gen. 47:28–50:26	I Kings 2:1–12
9	Sa	19	Shemot	Exod. 1:1–6:1	Isaiah 27:6–28:13 29:22–23 *Jeremiah 1:1–2:3*
16	Sa	26	Wa-'era'	Exod. 6:2–9:35	Ezekiel 28:25–29:21

Italics are for Sephardi Minhag.

The Jewish Publication Society of America

REPORT OF NINETY-SEVENTH YEAR

OFFICERS
(Elected June 16, 1985)

President
CHARLES R. WEINER

Chairman of the Board
MURIEL M. BERMAN

Vice-Presidents
ROBERT P. ABRAMS
IRWIN T. HOLTZMAN
JAY I. KISLAK
MARTIN MEYERSON
MARVIN WACHMAN

Treasurer
LEON J. PERELMAN

Secretary
NORMA F. FURST

Honorary Presidents
EDWIN WOLF 2nd
JOSEPH M. FIRST
WILLIAM S. FISHMAN
JEROME J. SHESTACK
A. LEO LEVIN
EDWARD B. SHILS
MURIEL M. BERMAN

Executive Vice-President
NATHAN BARNETT

Executive Director Emeritus
LESSER ZUSSMAN

Chairman Publication Committee
CHAIM POTOK

*ARTHUR A. COHEN, New York
*GERSON D. COHEN, New York
STEPHEN P. COHEN, New York
MARTIN D. COHN, Hazleton
PAUL COWAN, New York
*MOSHE DAVIS, Jerusalem
*SAMUEL DININ, Los Angeles
*AZRIEL EISENBERG, New York
DANIEL J. ELAZAR, Philadelphia
MARCIA FALK, Los Angeles
RAYMOND FEDERMAN, Buffalo
*LOUIS FINKELSTEIN, New York
*JOSEPH M. FIRST, Philadelphia
MICHAEL FISHBANE, Waltham
MARVIN FOX, Waltham
*H. LOUIS GINSBERG, New York
*ELI GINZBERG, New York
*NAHUM N. GLATZER, Watertown
LEONARD GOLD, New York
JUDAH GOLDIN, Swarthmore
*ROBERT GORDIS, New York
*ALFRED GOTTSCHALK, Cincinnati
BLU GREENBERG, Riverdale
MOSHE GREENBERG, Jerusalem
JONAS C. GREENFIELD, Jerusalem
EDWARD GREENSTEIN, New York
LEO GUZIK, New York
*ABRAHAM HALKIN, Jerusalem
SUSAN HANDELMAN, Maryland
GEOFFREY HARTMAN, New Haven
JUDITH HAUPTMAN, New York
MAX HAUSEN, Wynnewood
ESTHER HAUTZIG, New York
KATHRYN HELLERSTEIN, Boston
MARK HELPRIN, New York
*LOUIS HENKIN, New York
*ARTHUR HERTZBERG, Englewood
MILTON HINDUS, Waltham
BARRY HOLTZ, New York
JOHANNA HURWITZ, Great Neck
DAVID JACOBSON, Philadelphia
*OSCAR I. JANOWSKY, Jamesburg
JOHANNA KAPLAN, New York
*LOUIS L. KAPLAN, Baltimore
ABRAHAM J. KARP, Rochester
*ABRAHAM KATSH, New York
FRANCINE KLAGSBRUN, New York

*MILTON R. KONVITZ, Ithaca
JAMES KUGEL, Boston
SAMUEL T. LACHS, Bryn Mawr
*NORMAN LAMM, New York
*ARTHUR J. LELYVELD, Cleveland
*JACOB R. MARCUS, Cincinnati
MILTON MELTZER, New York
DEBORAH MENASHE, New York
ALAN MINTZ, New York
MARK MIRSKY, New York
STEPHEN MITCHELL, Berkeley
RELA GEFFEN MONSON, Philadelphia
*HARRY M. ORLINSKY, New York
CYNTHIA OZICK, New Rochelle
CHAIM POTOK, Philadelphia *Chairman*
BERNARD PUCKER, Boston
THEODORE K. RABB, Princeton
*ELLIS RIVKIN, Cincinnati
MARK ROSENTHAL, Philadelphia
DAVID ROSKIES, New York
HOWARD M. SACHAR, Washington
NORBERT SAMUELSON, Philadelphia
JONATHAN D. SARNA, Cincinnati
RAYMOND SCHEINDLIN, New York
HAROLD SCHIMMEL, Jerusalem
GRACE SCHULMAN, New York
DAVID SHAPIRO, New York
JEROME J. SHESTACK, Philadelphia
*DAVID SIDORSKY, New York
*SEYMOUR SIEGEL, New York
ALAIN SILVERA, Philadelphia
DAVID W. SILVERMAN, Philadelphia
*HAYM SOLOVEITCHIK, New York
*HARRY STARR, New York
DAVID STERN, Philadelphia
MAX TICKTIN, Washington
JEFFREY H. TIGAY, Philadelphia
*ISADORE TWERSKY, Cambridge
MAXWELL WHITEMAN, Philadelphia
ELIE WIESEL, New York
LEON WIESELTIER, Washington
RUTH WISSE, Montreal
EDWIN WOLF 2nd, Philadelphia
*GERALD I. WOLPE, Philadelphia

*emeritus

REPORT OF THE 97th JPS ANNUAL MEETING

The 97th annual meeting of the Jewish Publication Society was held on June 16, 1985, at the Bellevue Stratford Hotel in Philadelphia. The honorable Charles R. Weiner presided.

Robert P. Frankel, chairman of the nominating committee, presented the new slate of officers and trustees. Charles R. Weiner was reelected president of the Society, and the following vice-presidents were reelected: Robert P. Abrams, Jay I. Kislak, Martin Meyerson, and Marvin Wachman. Irwin T. Holtzman was newly elected a vice-president. Leon J. Perelman was reelected treasurer and Norma F. Furst, secretary.

Reelected as trustees were Bernard Frank, Allentown; James O. Freedman, Iowa City; Maxwell E. Greenberg, Los Angeles; Richard Maass, White Plains; Rela G. Monson, Philadelphia; Jerry Wagner, Bloomfield; and Sonia B. Woldow, Philadelphia.

Newly elected trustees were Edward J. Bloustein, since 1971 president of Rutgers, the State University of New Jersey, and author of numerous works on law; Herschel Blumberg, president of Prince George Center, Inc., Hyattsville, MD, chairman, National Jewish Center for Learning and Leadership, former national chairman, United Jewish Appeal, and member, board of governors, the Jewish Agency; Edward E. Elson, president of Atlanta News Agency, Atlanta, GA, and treasurer, the American Jewish Committee; Walter L. Field, Birmingham, MI, author of several books, including *A People's Epic, Symphony of Threes, The Tale of the Horse,* and *Gleanings from the Bible;* Jack E. Goldman, Norwalk, CT, chairman of the board, Cauzin Systems, Inc., recently retired senior vice-president and chief scientist, Xerox Corporation, chairman of the board and past president, American Technion Society; Alvin P. Gutman, president of Pressman-Gutman Company, board member, Heart Fund Council of New York and Hood Museum of Dartmouth College, current chairman, the Philadelphia Museum of Judaica, trustee, Rodeph Shalom Synagogue and Albert Einstein Medical Center; Roberta K. Levy, Minneapolis, MN, judge in Hennepin County municipality and president, the Talmud Torah of Minneapolis; Mitchell E. Panzer, Philadelphia, attorney, member, board of directors, Philadelphia Jewish Archives Center, National Foundation for Jewish Culture, and Jewish Education Service of North America, Inc.; David V. Wachs, Bensalem, PA, chairman of the board and secretary, Charming Shoppes, Inc., member, Republican Jewish Coalition, Israel Center for Social and Economic Programs, and the State of Israel Presidents' Club.

Judge Weiner presented an engraved silver plate to retiring executive vice-president Bernard I. Levinson and expressed appreciation for his ten years of service. This was followed by the introduction of Nathan Barnett, the newly appointed executive vice-president. Judge Weiner reported that Mr. Barnett had served many years in Jewish communal service, first as executive director of the Delaware Jewish Federation, followed by a position as senior vice-president of the Albert Einstein Medical Center in Philadelphia. Mr. Barnett delivered brief remarks expressing his pleasure upon assuming his new position.

David Rosenberg, editor of JPS, reported on the books that had recently been published. He noted that JPS was continuing its high standard of publishing and that the new directions he had outlined in last year's report had resulted in several notable authors being published by JPS. He reiterated the Society's intention to blend the scholarly books, which are its hallmark, with belles lettres and contemporary Judaica and to introduce new authors.

Muriel M. Berman, chairman of the board, reported on the JPS centennial program contemplated for 1988. Pointing out how rare it is for an organization to continue functioning for 100 years, she asserted that JPS had served the Jewish community well over this long period of time. The board of trustees of JPS and its editors make up a "Who's Who" of American Jewry in every period, she said, and one could almost write the history of the American Jewish community through the history of JPS leadership. A crown to the centennial program will be the publication of the five volumes of the JPS Torah Commentary, a project that was initiated by the Society 25 years ago.

Following the business proceedings of the meeting, Dr. Berman introduced Allan A. Ryan, Jr., who discussed his recent book *Quiet Neighbors: Prosecuting Nazi War Criminals in America.* Mr. Ryan was appointed director of the U.S. Justice Department's Office of Special Investigations in 1980, and in 1983 the attorney general assigned him to conduct the U.S. government's investigation of Nazi war criminal Klaus Barbie.

From the Annual Report of JPS President Charles R. Weiner

This has been an extraordinary year for me as president of the Jewish Publication Society. During this period there have been a number of structural changes that are meaningful to the future of the Society. First, there is David Rosenberg, our new editor, who now has been aboard for 15 months. Then, there is our new executive vice-president, Nathan Barnett, who has been here only three and one-half months. I am also very pleased to announce the appointment of Nahum M. Sarna as academic consultant on Judaica. Obviously, we will have a period of adjustment, but because of the new staffing, we plan not only to begin to expand our membership but also to enlarge the number of books published each year.

I am very enthused about our upcoming birthday: in 1988 we will be 100 years young. I really mean "young," with pride and enthusiasm. With our centennial celebration under the leadership and direction of Muriel M. Berman, it promises to be a banner year!

The Jewish Publication Society—with its limited resources but with tremendous effort—has accomplished much, and we should be proud of our achievements. But the time has come for us to enlarge our scope. Therefore, we are embarking on a Century Fund Campaign, which we expect to culminate in 1988 with the raising of three million dollars.

I mentioned accomplishments—let me enumerate: I am pleased to report that the long-awaited one-volume translation of the *Tanakh*, the complete Jewish Bible, will be published in October. This work is the culmination of the historic new translation project that was undertaken by JPS three decades ago and has already become the standard for our time.

Also, I recently attended the Jewish Book Council's awards ceremonies. Of the 11 awards given, 4 were won by the Jewish Publication Society: History—*Encounter with Emancipation: The German Jews in the United States 1830–1914* by Naomi W. Cohen; Jewish Thought—*Halakhic Man* by Joseph B. Soloveitchik, translated by Lawrence Kaplan; Scholarship—*The Wars of the Lord, Book One: Immortality of the Soul* by Levi ben Gershom (known as Gersonides), translated by Seymour Feldman; Illustrated Children's Books—*Mrs. Moskowitz and the Sabbath Candlesticks,* written and illustrated by Amy Schwartz.

This year, in a joint publishing endeavor with the Jewish Theological Seminary, the Society published a limited edition of *The Selected Letters of Cyrus Adler.* Cyrus Adler was a great leader in American Jewish history —and a pious Jew. He was born in Van Buren, Arkansas, in 1863, and died in 1940, a year after being appointed by Franklin Roosevelt as the Jewish representative on a commission of world religious leaders to consult on world peace. He was the Jewish Theological Seminary's third president, serving from 1915. He was also chairman of the editorial board of the Jewish Publication Society for the new translation of the Bible, the 1917 translation, that is. Dr. Adler had a vision for the Society. He, too, wanted to broaden its horizons and enlarge its scope. Here, in a letter to Simon Wolf dated December 16, 1908, he expresses his desire that the Society publish books for sale to nonmembers:

You made a remark at our meeting on Sunday last, with which I heartily sympathized, namely, that The Jewish Publication Society ought to be publisher of a number of the series which are now issued by independent Societies. I have been of this opinion for a long time, and a number of years ago, was instrumental in having the Board of Trustees recommend to the Society an amendment to the Constitution, which does not require the distribution to all the members, of all the publications of the Society. This amendment was defeated at the time, largely through the instrumentality of Mr. Philip Cowen, who saw in it a threat to publish either a newspaper or a magazine. I revived the matter several years ago, but the Board did not deem it feasible at the time. I am absolutely convinced that the expansion of the Publication Society in any considerable way beyond its present scope, requires the adoption of such an amendment. It could then become the publisher for any Society upon some definite commercial basis, and gradually widen its sphere into that of a general Jewish publishing and book concern. Important as increased capital is, I consider this alteration in the Constitution as an essential preliminary for the enlargement of the work. If anything is to be done in the matter this year it ought to be taken up at our January meeting of the Board of Trustees.

Sound familiar? In 1910, Dr. Adler was very optimistic about the Society. Here is what he had to say in a letter he wrote to Solomon Schechter:

The Bible Translation Board had a meeting at Atlantic City lasting ten days, and we worked on the sixth chapter of Jeremiah. We shall have a meeting in New York at the end of November and the beginning of December lasting for about eight days. I think the work has made reasonable progress and if we hold three or four meetings here, another two years will see the work finished. The Jewish Publication Society, in general, is looking up. It seems to have lived through its worst days. It has gained nearly one thousand members since last May and also doubled the sale of books, and we may probably come into our own after twenty-two years of hard work.

Today, it's 97 years of hard work. Have we "come into our own"? I concur with Cyrus Adler's optimistic outlook: "The Jewish Publication Society is looking up!"

JPS Treasurer's Report for 1984

While JPS continues to be in sound financial condition, we did not sell as many books in 1984 as we did in 1983. Income from the sale of books, memberships, and contributions amounted to $1,200,913., a drop of 3½ percent.

On the other hand, our Endowment Fund has continued to increase under the guidance of our Investment Committee.

JPS Publications

In 1984 JPS published the following new volumes:

Title and Author	Printed
CLARA'S STORY by Clara Isaacman and Joan Grossman	4,000
ENCOUNTER WITH EMANCIPATION: The German Jews in the United States 1830–1914 by Naomi W. Cohen	3,300
HALAKHIC MAN by Rabbi Joseph Soloveitchik	5,000
THE HANUKKAH OF GREAT-UNCLE OTTO by Myron Levoy	5,000
A JEWISH BESTIARY by Mark Podwal	5,000
THE JEWS OF CZECHOSLOVAKIA—VOLUME III Edited by Avigdor Dagan, with Gertrude Hirschler and Lewis Weiner	3,000
MRS. MOSKOWITZ AND THE SABBATH CANDLESTICKS by Amy Schwartz	5,000
THE SEVEN GOOD YEARS AND OTHER STORIES by I.L. PERETZ (Retold by Esther Hautzig)	5,000
THE WARS OF THE LORD by Levi ben Gershom (Gersonides)	3,000
THE WORLD IS A ROOM AND OTHER STORIES by Yehuda Amichai	5,000
AMERICAN JEWISH YEAR BOOK—Volume 84 Edited by Milton Himmelfarb and David Singer (copublished with the American Jewish Committee)	2,000
BACK TO THE SOURCES Edited by Barry W. Holtz (copublished with Summit Books)	1,500
JEWISH EXPERIENCE IN THE ART OF THE TWENTIETH CENTURY by Avram Kampf (copublished with Bergin & Garvey)	1,000
THE JEWISH HERITAGE IN AMERICAN FOLK ART The Jewish Museum and Museum of American Folk Art (copublished with Universe Books)	1,500
THE NIGHTMARE OF REASON: A Life of Franz Kafka by Ernst Pawel (copublished with Farrar, Straus & Giroux)	1,000

1984 Reprints

During 1984 JPS reprinted the following books:

THE BEST OF K'TONTON by Sadie Rose Weilerstein (3,000); THE HOLY SCRIPTURES (20,000); BLESSED IS THE MATCH by Marie Syrkin (2,000);

COMMUNITY AND POLITY by Daniel J. Elazar (1,500); THE DEVIL AND THE JEWS by Joshua Trachtenberg (5,000); THE FIVE MEGILLOTH AND THE BOOK OF JONAH (3,000); A HISTORY OF THE JEWS by Solomon Grayzel (4,000); THE FIRST JEWISH CATALOG edited by Richard Siegel, Sharon and Michael Strassfeld (15,000); THE SECOND JEWISH CATALOG edited by Sharon and Michael Strassfeld (10,000); THE THIRD JEWISH CATALOG edited by Sharon and Michael Strassfeld (10,000); THE JEWISH KIDS CATALOG by Chaya M. Burstein (10,000); THE JEWS IN THE RENAISSANCE by Cecil Roth (2,000); LEGENDS OF THE BIBLE by Louis Ginzberg (3,000); LEGENDS OF THE JEWS, Vol. I, by Louis Ginzberg (1,500); LETTERS TO AN AMERICAN JEWISH FRIEND by Hillel Halkin (2,000); MANDARINS, JEWS AND MISSIONARIES by Michael Pollak (3,000); MEKILTA DE-RABBI ISHMAEL (3-volume set) edited by Jacob C. Lauterbach (2,000); PATHWAYS THROUGH THE BIBLE by Mortimer J. Cohen (3,000); SABBATH: THE DAY OF DELIGHT edited by Abraham E. Millgram (2,000); THE TORAH (20,000); THE WRITINGS (5,000); JEWISH COOKING AROUND THE WORLD by Hanna Goodman (2,000).

SPECIAL ARTICLES IN VOLUMES 51–85
OF THE AMERICAN JEWISH YEAR BOOK

OBITUARIES

Leo Baeck	By Max Gruenewald 59:478–82
Jacob Blaustein	By John Slawson 72:547–57
Martin Buber	By Seymour Siegel 67:37–43
Abraham Cahan	By Mendel Osherowitch 53:527–29
Albert Einstein	By Jacob Bronowski 58:480–85
Felix Frankfurter	By Paul A. Freund 67:31–36
Louis Ginzberg	By Louis Finkelstein 56:573–79
Jacob Glatstein	By Shmuel Lapin 73:611–17
Sidney Goldmann	By Milton R. Konvitz 85:401–03
Hayim Greenberg	By Marie Syrkin 56:589–94
Abraham Joshua Heschel	By Fritz A. Rothschild 74:533–44
Horace Meyer Kallen	By Milton R. Konvitz 75:55–80
Mordecai Kaplan	By Ludwig Nadelmann 85:404–11
Herbert H. Lehman	By Louis Finkelstein 66:3–20
Judah L. Magnes	By James Marshall 51:512–15
Alexander Marx	By Abraham S. Halkin 56:580–88
Reinhold Niebuhr	By Seymour Siegel 73:605–10
Joseph Proskauer	By David Sher 73:618–28
Maurice Samuel	By Milton H. Hindus 74:545–53
Leo Strauss	By Ralph Lerner 76:91–97
Max Weinreich	By Lucy S. Dawidowicz 70:59–68
Chaim Weizmann	By Harry Sacher 55:462–69
Stephen S. Wise	By Philip S. Bernstein 51:515–18
Harry Austryn Wolfson	By Isadore Twersky 76:99–111

Index